HISTORY OF THE OTTOMAN EMPIRE
AND MODERN TURKEY

Volume II: Reform, Revolution, and Republic: The Rise of Modern Turkey, 1808–1975

HISTORY OF THE OTTOMAN EMPIRE AND MODERN TURKEY

Volume II: Reform, Revolution, and Republic:
The Rise of Modern Turkey, 1808–1975

STANFORD J. SHAW

Professor of History
University of California, Los Angeles

EZEL KURAL SHAW

Associate Research Historian
G.E. von Grunebaum Center for Near Eastern Studies,
University of California, Los Angeles

CAMBRIDGE UNIVERSITY PRESS

Cambridge
London   New York   Melbourne

Published by the Syndics of the Cambridge University Press
The Pitt Building, Trumpington Street, Cambridge CB2 1RP
Bentley House, 200 Euston Road, London NW1 2DB
32 East 57th Street, New York, NY 10022, USA
296 Beaconsfield Parade, Middle Park, Melbourne 3206, Australia

First published 1977

Printed in the United States of America
Typeset, printed, and bound by Vail-Ballou Press, Inc., Binghamton, New York

Library of Congress Cataloging in Publication Data
Shaw, Stanford Jay.
History of the Ottoman Empire and Modern Turkey.
Vol. 2 by S. J. Shaw and E. K. Shaw.
Bibliography: p.
Includes index.
CONTENTS: v. 1. Empire of the Gazis: the rise and decline of the Ottoman Empire,
1280–1808, v. 2. Reform, revolution, and republic: the rise of modern Turkey, 1808–1975.
1. Turkey – History – Ottoman Empire, 1288–1918.
2. Turkey – History – 1918–1960.
3. Turkey – History – 1960–   I. Shaw Ezel Kural.   II. Title.
DR440.S5   949.61   76-9179
ISBN 0 521 214491 hard covers
ISBN 0 521 29166 6 paperback

CONTENTS

TABLES

PREFACE

During the nineteenth century the Ottoman Empire witnessed a sustained effort of reform that saw the long-preserved and honored institutions of the classical Ottoman state replaced by new ones, inspired by an increasing knowledge of European thought, society, and government and modified to satisfy Ottoman needs and conditions. In the process the scope of government was extended far beyond the limits imposed by the traditional Ottoman way into every aspect of life, overwhelming the autonomous religious, economic, and social groups that had survived for so long as the substrata of Ottoman society. A new, modern, westernized ruling bureaucracy replaced the old Ruling Class, extended its power throughout the empire, and created a highly complex system of government that ruled with an autocracy unmatched in traditional times.

The era of modern Ottoman reforms began in the last decade of the reign of Sultan Mahmut II (1808–1839), who laid the foundations for what followed. His work was extended and at least partially completed during the Tanzimat reform period, which encompassed the reigns of his sons Abdulmecit I (1839–1861) and Abdulaziz (1861–1876), and it was carried out by the reformist bureaucracy of the Men of the Tanzimat, led by able statesmen such as Mustafa Reşit Paşa, Âli Paşa, and Fuat Paşa.

Reform in the Ottoman Empire was a complex process; each solution created new problems. The application of new laws and practices was slowed for a number of reasons. First of all, the empire remained very large, with a heterogeneous society and relatively poor communications. Second, the inexperience of the reformers and the greed of the imperial powers of Europe for profits at the expense of the relatively undeveloped empire and its people perpetuated and deepened a series of economic problems inherited from the past. Third, demands for social and political reforms, themselves consequences of the Tanzimat, conflicted with the desire of its leaders to modernize as rapidly and efficiently as possible, without the delays and compromises inherent in any democratic system. Fourth, nationalistic elements among the subject minorities, nourished and sustained by Russia and, to a lesser extent, the other Western powers, demanded autonomy or independence from the empire and dramatized their ambitions with sporadic terrorism within the Ottoman dominions and with anti-Muslim propaganda in Europe and America. Finally, the great powers, though held back from breaking up and partitioning the empire by their concern to preserve the European balance of power, intervened in internal Ottoman affairs to secure political and economic advantages for themselves. While the Ottoman reformers adjusted themselves and their programs as much as possible to meet these and other challenges, they lacked the knowledge, experience, and strength needed to solve them within the relatively short time left by their enemies.

Though the Tanzimat reforms were accompanied by an extension of the principle of representative government, ironically they culminated in the sovereign autocracy of Abdulhamit II (1876–1909), who brought them to full realization. After a brief period of democracy following his deposition, there was a return to autocracy led not by his successors but rather by the leaders of the Young Turk regime (1908–1918), who continued the reforms in many areas while dragging an unprepared empire into the quagmire of World War I, where devastation and defeat led to its ultimate dissolution. Well meant but not always well executed, frustrated by many problems not of its own making as well as many that were, the Ottoman reform brought the empire closer to contemporary European society and institutions but failed to preserve it. The foundations had been laid, however, for the Republic of Turkey, which rose on the ruins of the empire under the leadership of Mustafa Kemal Atatürk (1923–1938) and his successors.

The story of modern Ottoman and Turkish history has been told many times, but usually on the basis of European source materials and in the context of European ambitions and prejudices. It has only been in recent years that a beginning has been made in telling the story on the basis of Turkish sources. It is the object of this work to bring together the Western and Turkish sources, adding the results of the authors' research in the Ottoman archives and libraries and presenting the story in its own context.

We would like to pay tribute to the small band of pioneering scholars who have begun this work since the end of World War II: Ömer Lütfi Barkan, of the University of Istanbul, Cavit Baysun, of the University of Ankara, Niyazi Berkes, of McGill University, Roderic Davison, of George Washington University, Halil Inalcık, of the University of Chicago, Kemal Karpat, of the University of Wisconsin, Enver Ziya Karal, of the University of Ankara, Ercüment Kuran, of Hacettepe University, Ankara, Barnard Lewis, of Princeton University, Şerif Mardin, of the Bosporus University, Istanbul, Lewis V. Thomas, of Princeton University, and Ismail Hakkı Uzunçarşılı, of Istanbul. We also would like to express our particular gratitude to Midhat Sertoğlu, Turgut Işıksal, and Rauf Tuncay, of the Başbakanlık Archives, Istanbul; and to the directors and staffs of the Topkapı Palace Archives and Library, the Istanbul University Library, the Istanbul Municipal Library, the Istanbul Archaeological Museum Library, the Hakkı Tarık Us Library, the Süleymaniye Library, and the Bayezit General Library, Istanbul; the Turkish National Library and the Library of the Turkish Historical Society in Ankara; the British Museum, Public Record Office, and Commonwealth Relations Office, London; the Bodleian Library, Oxford; the Cambridge University Library; the Quai d'Orsay Archives, Archives Nationales, Archives of the Ministry of War, Chateau de Vincennes and Bibliothèque Nationale, Paris; the Haus-, Hof- und Staatsarchiv and National Library, Vienna; the Harry Elkins Widener Library, Harvard University; the Firestone Library, Princeton University; and the University Research Library, University of California, Los Angeles, without whose help the research for this work could never have been completed. We would like to pay particular tribute to two scholars of European diplomatic history whose lack of prejudice and search for truth regarding the Turks have stimulated our own work: William L. Langer, of Harvard University, and Leften Stavrianos, of Northwestern University. Finally, we are grateful to the very competent and cooperative staff of the Cambridge University Press American office in New York, and in particular to Colin Jones, Rhona Johnson, Claire Komnick, and Richard Hollick, who have assisted us with great patience and dedication in producing this work.

The study of Ottoman history involves unusually complicated problems regarding transliteration and place names. Ottoman Turkish was written in the Arabic script, and its transliteration into Western characters has varied widely according to the language of the transliterators. Thus the sound rendered "j" in English has been presented as "dj" in French and "c" in modern Turkish. The names given individual cities and even entire provinces have also varied by language; thus Istanbul, Izmir, and Edirne in Turkish have remained Constantinople, Smyrna, and Adrianople in most Western languages. For purposes of consistency and accuracy, in this work the modern Turkish spellings and place names have been used, with only a few modifications when they have become particularly accepted in English, or are renderings of Arabic or Persian phrases. Ottoman dates are rendered into their European equivalents for book citations only when the original calendar in use is given or can be deduced from internal evidence. The Arabic article al- is transliterated according to the most common modern Turkish usage for each word but here, as in other respects, modern Turkish orthography is not consistent and has changed over time.

STANFORD J. SHAW
EZEL KURAL SHAW

Los Angeles, California
January 1977

ABBREVIATIONS

Ahmad

Ahmet Midhat

Allen and Muratoff

Arapyan

Aristarchi

Asım

Ata

Atatürk Söylev

Atatürk TTB

Atasağun

Bayar

Bayur, *Kâmil Paşa*

Bayur, *Türk Inkilâbı Tarihi*

Berkes

Bıyıklıoğlu, *Atatürk Anadoluda*

BVA

Feroz Ahmad, *The Young Turks: The Committee of Union and Progress in Turkish Politics, 1908–1914,* Oxford, 1969.
Ahmet Midhat, *Zübdet el-hakayik,* Istanbul, 1295/1878.
W. E. D. Allen and Paul Muratoff, *Caucasian Battlefields: A History of the Wars on the Turco-Caucasian Border, 1828–1921,* Cambridge, 1953.
Kalost Arapyan, *Rusçuk âyânı Mustafa Paşa'nın hayatı ve kahramanlıkları,* tr. Esat Uras, Ankara, 1943.
G. Aristarchi Bey, *Législation ottomane, ou recueil des lois, règlements, ordonnances, traités, capitulations, et autres documents officiels de l'Empire Ottoman,* 7 vols., Constantinople, 1873–1888
Ahmet Asım Efendi, *Tarih-i Asım,* 2 vols., Istanbul, n.d.
Tayyarzade Ahmet Ata, *Tarih-i Ata,* 5 vols., Istanbul, 1292–3/1875–6.
Mustafa Kemal Atatürk, *Atatürk'ün Söylev ve Demeçleri,* 4 vols., Ankara, 1945–1964.
Mustafa Kemal Atatürk, *Atatürk'ün Tamim, Telgraf ve Beyannameleri,* Ankara, 1964 (vol. IV of the preceding entry).
Y. S. Atasağun, *Türkiye Cumhuriyeti Ziraat Bankası, 1888–1939,* Istanbul, 1939.
Celal Bayar, *Ben De Yazdım,* 8 vols., Istanbul, 1965–1972.
Hilmi Kâmil Bayur, *Sadrazam Kâmil Paşa – Siyasi Hayatı,* Ankara, 1954.
Yusuf Hikmet Bayur, *Türk Inkilâbı Tarihi,* 3 vols., in 10 parts, Ankara, 1940–1967.
Niyazi Berkes, *The Development of Secularism in Turkey,* Montreal, 1964.
Tevfik Bıyıklıoğlu, *Atatürk Anadolu'da (1919–1921),* I, Ankara, 1959.
Başvekâlet Arşivi. Prime Minister's Archives, Istanbul. For more information see S. J. Shaw,

"Ottoman Archival Materials for the Nineteenth and Early Twentieth Centuries: The Archives of Istanbul," IJMES, 6 (1975), 94–114. Collections consulted and cited: Bab-ı Âli Evrak Odası; Buyuruldu; Cevdet Askeri; Cevdet Dahiliye; Cevdet Maliye; Irade, Meclis-i Mahsus; Irade, Meclis-i Vâlâ; Irade, Dahiliye; Kanun-u Kalemiye; Maliyeden Müdevvere; Meclis-i Tanzimat; Mesail-i Mühimme; Teşkilat-ı Devair; and Yıldız.

Cebesoy, *Hâtıralar*
Ali Fuat Cebesoy, *Millî Mücadele hâtıraları*, I, Istanbul, 1953.

Cebesoy, *Siyasi hâtıraları*
Ali Fuat Cebesoy, *Gnrl. Ali Fuat Cebesoy'un siyasi hâtıraları*, 2 vols., Istanbul, 1957–1960.

Cemal Paşa, *Hâtırat*
Cemal Paşa, *Hâtırat, 1913–1922*, Istanbul, 1922 (published also as Djemal Pasha, *Memoires of a Turkish Statesman, 1913–1919*, New York, 1922, and as Cemal Paşa, *Hatıralar*, Istanbul, 1959).

Cevat
Ahmet Cevat, *Tarih-i Askeri-i Osmani, I – Yeniçeriler*, Istanbul, 1297/1880; Fr. tr. by G. Macridès, *Etat Militaire Ottoman depuis la Fondation de l'empire jusqu'a nos jours; Tome I Livre I: Le Corps des Janissaires*, Constantinople, 1882. Vol. II, books 2 and 3, on Selim III's military reforms, are in manuscript TY 4178 of the Istanbul University Library; vol. II, book 4, on Mahmut II's military reforms, and vol. III, book 5, on those from Abdulmecit to Abdulhamit II, are in manuscript TY 6127 in the same library.

Cevdet[1]
Ahmet Cevdet, *Tarih-i Cevdet*, 1st ed., 12 vols., Istanbul, 1270–1301/1854–1883.

Cevdet[2]
Ahmet Cevdet, *Tarih-i Cevdet: Tertib-i Cedit*, 2nd rev. ed., 12 vols., Istanbul, 1302–1309/1884–1891.

Cevdet Askeri
Collection of documents on military affairs in the BVA.

Cevdet Dahiliye
Collection of documents on internal affairs in BVA.

Cevdet Maliye
Collection of documents on financial affairs in BVA.

Cevdet, "Maruzat"
Ahmet Cevdet, "Cevdet Paşa'nın maruzatı," TTEM, 14, no. 1 (78), 1 Kânunusani 1340/1924, pp. 52–57, no. 2 (79), 1 Mart 1340/1924, pp. 109–120, no. 3 (80), 1 Mayıs 1340/1924, pp. 186–192, no. 5 (82), 1 Eylül 1340/1924, pp. 300–306, 15, no. 7 (84), 1 Kânunusani 1341/1925, pp. 55–72, no. 10 (87), 1 Temmuz 1341/1925, pp. 269–292, no. 11 (88), Eylül 1341/1925, pp. 336–56, no. 12 (89), 1 Teşrinisani 1341/1925, pp. 402–414, 16, no. 14 (91), 1 Mart 1926, pp. 117–132, no. 15

	(92), 1 Mayıs, 1926, pp. 165–190, no. 16 (93), 1 Temmuz 1926, pp. 220–233.
Cevdet, *Tezakir*	Ahmet Cevdet, *Tezakir,* ed. Cavid Baysun, 4 vols., Ankara, 1953–1967.
D	*Defter.* Collection of registers in archives of the Topkapı Palace Museum, Istanbul.
Danişmend	Ismail Hami Danişmend, *Izahlı Osmanlı Tarihi Kronolojisi,* 4 vols., Istanbul, 1947–1961; repr. in 5 vols., Istanbul, 1971–1972.
Davison	Roderic Davison, *Reform in the Ottoman Empire, 1856–1876,* Princeton, 1963.
Der Saadet Nüfus	Bab-ı Âli, Nezaret-i Umur-u Dahiliye, Sicil-i Nüfus Idare-i Umumiyesi, *Ba-Irade-i Senniye-i Cenab-ı Padişahi icra olunan tahrir-i sabık yoklaması mucibince der saadet ve bilad-ı selesede mevcut nüfusun istatistik cetvelidir,* Istanbul, 1302/1886–7.
Devereux	R. Devereux, *The First Ottoman Constitutional Period: A Study of the Midhat Constitution and Parliament,* Baltimore, 1963.
Dodd	C. H. Dodd, *Politics and Government in Turkey,* Manchester, England, 1969.
Düstur[1]	*Düstur,* vol. I, Istanbul, 1863, repr. 1865, 1872; vol. II, Istanbul 1873; vol. III, Istanbul, 1876; vol. IV, Istanbul, 1879. *Düstur Zeyil,* 4 vols., Istanbul, 1879–1884, *Düstur Birinci Tertib,* vols. IV–VIII, Ankara, 1937–1943. (Ottoman laws, 1883–1908).
Düstur[2]	*Düstur: Tertib-i Sani,* 11 vols., Istanbul, 1329/ 1911–28 (Ottoman laws, 1908–1922).
Düstur[3]	*Düstur: Tertib-i Salis,* 41 vols., Ankara, 1921– 1971 (Laws of the First Turkish Republic, 1920– 1970).
Düstur[4]	*Düstur: Dördüncü Tertib,* 3 vols. Ankara, 1961 (Laws issued by the National Unity Committee in 1960 and 1961).
Düstur[5]	*Düstur: Beşinci Tertib,* Laws issued by the Second Turkish Republic, Ankara, 1961 to date.
Du Velay	A. Du Velay, *Essai sur l'Histoire Financière de la Turquie,* Paris, 1903.
E	*Evrak.* Document collections of the Topkapı Palace Museum, Istanbul.
Edib, *Memoirs*	Halide Edib, *The Memoirs of Halide Edib,* London, 1926.
Edib, *Turkish Ordeal*	Halide Edib, *The Turkish Ordeal,* London, 1928.
Edib, *Turkey Faces West*	Halide Edib, *Turkey Faces West,* London, 1936.
EI[1]	*The Encyclopaedia of Islam,* Leiden, 1913– 1938.
EI[2]	*The Encyclopaedia of Islam: New Edition,* Leiden, 1954 to date.

Ergin, *Belediye* Osman Ergin, *Mecelle-i Umur-u Belediye,* 5 vols., Istanbul, 1914–1922.

Ergin, *Maarif* Osman Ergin, *Türkiye Maarif Tarihi,* 5 vols., Istanbul, 1939–1943.

Esat, *Tarih* Mehmet Esat Efendi, *Tarih-i Esat Efendi,* 2 vols., manuscript in Istanbul University Library, TY6002, TY6003, TY6004 and TY6005; vol. I also in Süleymaniye Library, Istanbul, Esat Efendi collection Y2084. References in this work for vol. I are to the Süleymaniye Library copy; and for vol. II are to the Istanbul University Library copy.

Esat, *Zafer* Mehmet Esat Efendi, *Üss-ü Zafer,* Istanbul, 1243/ 1827, 2nd ed., 1293/1876; Fr. tr. by Caussin de Perceval, *Précis historique de la destruction du corps des janissaires par le Sultan Mahmoud en 1826,* Paris, 1833.

Farhi David Farhi, "The Şeriat as a Political Slogan – or the 'Incident of the 31st Mart,'" *Middle Eastern Studies,* 7 (1971), 275–316.

Fatma Aliye, *Ahmet Cevdet* Fatma Aliye, *Cevdet Paşa ve Zamanı,* Istanbul, 1332/1914.

FO Foreign Office Archives, Public Record Office, London.

Gologlu, *Erzurum Kongresi* Mahmut Gologlu, *Erzurum Kongresi,* Ankara, 1968.

Gologlu, *Sivas Kongresi* Mahmut Gologlu, *Sivas Kongresi,* Ankara, 1969.

Gologlu, *Üçüncü Meşrutiyet* Mahmut Gologlu, *Üçüncü Meşrutiyet, 1920,* Ankara, 1970.

Gologlu, *Cumhuriyete doğru* Mahmut Gologlu, *Cumhuriyete Doğru, 1921–1922,* Ankara, 1971.

Gologlu, *Cumhuriyet* Mahmut Gologlu, *Türkiye Cumhuriyeti, 1923,* Ankara, 1971.

Gologlu, *Devrimler* Mahmut Gologlu, *Devrimler ve Tepkileri, 1924–1930,* Ankara, 1972.

Gologlu, *Tek Partili* Mahmut Gologlu, *Tek Partili Cumhuriyet, 1931–1938,* Ankara, 1974.

Gökbilgin M. Tayyip Gökbilgin, *Rumeli'de Yörükler, Tatarlar ve Evlad-ı Fatihan.* Istanbul, 1957.

Griffeths M. A. Griffeths, "The Reorganization of the Ottoman Army Under Abdülhamid II, 1880–1897," unpublished Ph.D. dissertation, University of California, Los Angeles, 1966.

Hershlag[1] Z. Y. Hershlag, *Turkey: An Economy in Transition,* The Hague, 1968.

Hershlag[2] Z. Y. Hershlag, *Introduction to the Modern Economic History of the Middle East,* Leiden, 1964.

Hershlag, *Challenge* Z. Y. Hershlag, *Turkey: The Challenge of Growth,* Leiden, 1968.

Uriel Heyd, *Foundations of Turkish Nationalism: The Life and Teachings of Ziya Gökalp*, London, 1950.
Uriel Heyd, *Revival of Islam in Modern Turkey*, Jerusalem, 1968.
Uriel Heyd, "The Ottoman Ulema and Westernization in the Time of Selim III and Mahmud II," *Scripta Hierosalymitana*, IX (Jerusalem, 1961), 63–96.
Richard G. Hovannisian, *The Republic of Armenia*, vol. I., *The First Year, 1918–1919*, Berkeley and Los Angeles, 1971.
Richard G. Hovannisian, *Armenia on the Road to Independence, 1918*, Berkeley and Los Angeles, 1967.
T. C. Genelkurmay Başkanlığı Harp Tarihi Dairesi, *Harp Tarihi Vesikaları Dergisi*, Ankara, 18 vols., 68 issues, 1510 documents, 1951–1969.
J. C. Hurewitz, *Diplomacy in the Near and Middle East: A Documentary Record*, 2 vols., Princeton, N.J., 1956.
J. C. Hurewitz, *The Middle East and North Africa in World Politics: A Documentary Record. Second Edition, Revised and Enlarged.* Volume I, *European Expansion, 1535–1914*, New Haven, Conn., 1975.
T. C. Maarif Vekâleti, *Islam Ansiklopedisi*, Istanbul and Ankara, 1940 to date.
Devlet-i Aliye-i Osmaniye, Maliye Nezareti, *Ihsaiyat-ı Maliye. Varidat ve Masarif-i Umumiyeyi Muhtevidir*, 3 vols., Istanbul, 1327–30/1911–4.
International Journal of Middle East Studies, vol. I (1970) to date.
Ibnulemin Mahmut Kemal Inal, *Osmanlı Devrinde Son Sadrıazamlar*, 6 vols. in 14 parts, Istanbul, 1940–1953.
Halil Inalcık, "Sened-i Ittifak ve Gülhane Hatt-ı Hümâyûnu," *Belleten*, 28 (1964), 603–622.
Halil Inalcık, "Tanzimat'ın uygulanması ve sosyal tepkileri," *Belleten*, 28 (1964), 623–690.
Halil Inalcık, *Tanzimat ve Bulgar Meselesi*, Ankara, 1943.
Devlet-i Osmaniye, Nezaret i Umur-u Ticaret ve Nafia, İstatistik-i Umumi İdaresi, *Devlet-i Âliye-i Osmaniyenin Bin Üçyüz Onüç Senesine Mahsus İstatistik-i Umumisidir*, Istanbul, 1316/1898.
T. C. Devlet Istatistik Enstitüsü, *Türkiye İstatistik Yıllığı*.
A. Juchereau de St. Denys, *Histoire de l'Empire*

	Ottoman depuis 1792 jusqu'en 1844, 4 vols., Paris, 1844.
Juchereau, *Révolutions*	A. Juchereau de St. Denys, *Les Révolutions de Constantinople en 1807–1808,* 2 vols., Paris, 1819.
Kâmil Paşa	Kâmil Paşa, *Tarih-i siyasi. Devlet-i Âliye-i Osmaniye,* 3 vols., Istanbul, 1325–7/1907–9.
Kansu	Mazhar Müfit Kansu, *Erzurum'dan ölümüne kadar Atatürk'le beraber,* I, Ankara, 1966.
Karabekir	Kâzım Karabekir, *Istiklâl Harbimiz,* I, Istanbul, 1960.
Karabekir, *Enver Paşa*	Kâzım Karabekir, *Istiklâl Harbimizde Enver Paşa ve Ittihat ve Terakki Erkânı,* Istanbul, 1967.
Karabekir, *Esaslar*	Kâzım Karabekir, *Istiklâl Harbimizin esasları,* Istanbul, 1951.
Karal, OT	Enver Ziya Karal, *Osmanlı Tarihi,* vols. V–VIII, Ankara, 1952–1962.
Karpat, *Social Change*	Kemal Karpat, *Social Change and Politics in Turkey: A Structural-Historical Analysis,* Leiden, 1973.
Karpat, "Social Themes"	Kemal Karpat, "Social Themes in Contemporary Turkish Literature," *Middle East Journal,* 14 (1960), 29–44, 153–168.
Karpat, *Social Thought*	Kemal Karpat, *Political and Social Thought in the Contemporary Middle East,* London, 1968.
Karpat, "Society"	Kemal Karpat, "Society, Economics and Politics in Contemporary Turkey," *World Politics,* 17 (1964), 50–74.
Karpat, *Turkey's Politics*	Kemal Karpat, *Turkey's Politics: The Transition to a Multi-Party System,* Princeton, N.J., 1959.
Kaynar	Reşat Kaynar, *Mustafa Reşit Paşa ve Tanzimat,* Ankara, 1954.
Kili, *Constitutional Developments*	Suna Kili, *Turkish Constitutional Developments and Assembly Debates on the Constitutions of 1924 and 1961,* Istanbul, 1971.
Kili, *Kemalism*	Suna Kili, *Kemalism,* Istanbul, 1969.
Kılıç Ali, *Istiklâl Mahkemesi*	Kılıç Ali, *Istiklâl Mahkemesi hatıraları,* Istanbul, 1955.
Landau	Jacob M. Landau, *Radical Politics in Modern Turkey,* Leiden, 1974.
Langer, *Diplomacy of Imperialism*	William L. Langer, *The Diplomacy of Imperialism,* New York, 1956.
Levy	Avigdor Levy, "The Military Policy of Sultan Mahmud II, 1808–1839," unpublished Ph.D. dissertation, Harvard University, 1968.
Lewis	Bernard Lewis, *The Emergence of Modern Turkey,* London and New York, 1961, 2nd ed., 1968.
Lewis, "Baladiyya"	Bernard Lewis, "Baladiyya," EI², I, 972–975.
Lütfi	Ahmet Lütfi, *Tarih-i Lütfi,* vols. I–VIII, Istanbul, 1290–1328/1873–1910; vols. IX–XIII, covering the years 1846–1876, are found only in manuscript

	form at the Turkish Historical Society, Ankara, MS 531/1–7, 5032–4, and 4812, and at the Istanbul Archaeological Museum, MS 1340–1345, 1349.
Mahmut Celâleddin, *Mirat-ı Hakikat*	Mahmut Celâleddin, *Mirat-ı Hakikat. Tarih-i Mahmut Celâleddin Paşa,* 3 vols. Istanbul, 1326–7/1908.
Mears	E. G. Mears, *Modern Turkey: A Politico-Economic Interpretation with Selected Chapters by Representative Authorities,* New York, 1924.
MEJ	*Middle East Journal,* Washington, D.C., 1, (1947) to date.
Midhat, *Mirat-ı hayret*	Midhat Paşa, *Mirat-ı Hayret. Sultan Abdülaziz Han merhumunun esbabı hal'i,* ed. Ali Haydar Midhat, Istanbul, 1325/1909 (vol. II of Midhat Paşa's Memoirs).
Midhat, *Tabsira-i ibret*	Midhat Paşa, *Tabsira-i ibret. Midhat Paşa. hayatı siyasiyesi, hidematı, menfa hayatı,* ed. Ali Haydar Paşa, Istanbul, 1325/1909 (vol. I of Midhat Paşa's Memoirs).
Miller	William Miller, *The Ottoman Empire and Its Successors, 1801–1927,* London, repr. 1966.
Mondros Mütarekesi	Tevfik Bıyıklıoğlu, *Türk Istiklâl Harbi, Cilt I. Mondros Mütarekesi ve tatbikatı,* Ankara, 1962.
Muahedat Mecmuası	*Muahedat Mecmuası,* 5 vols., Istanbul, 1294–98/1877–81.
Mufassal Osmanlı Tarihi	[Midhat Sertoğlu], *Resimli-Haritalı Mufassal Osmanlı Tarihi,* vol. V, Istanbul, 1962, and vol. VI, Istanbul, 1963.
Mühlmann	C. Mühlmann, *Deutschland und die Türkei, 1913–1914,* Berlin, 1929.
Muhtar, *Rusya Seferi*	Ahmet Muhtar Paşa, *1244 (1828) Türkiye Rusya Seferi ve Edirne Muahedesi,* 2 vols., Ankara, 1928.
Niyazi	Ahmet Niyazi, *Hatırat-ı Niyazi yahut tarihçe-i Inkilâb-ı kebir-i Osmaniyeden bir sahife,* Istanbul, 1326/1910.
Noradounghian	Gabriel Noradounghian, *Recueil d'actes internationaux de l'empire ottoman,* 4 vols., Paris, 1897–1903.
NUC	National Union Committee (for text discussion, refer to Index).
Nutuk	Mustafa Kemal Atatürk, *Nutuk,* 3 vols., Ankara, 1960–1961.
Orhonlu, "Kaldırımcılık"	Cengiz Orhonlu, "Mesleki bir teşekkül olarak kaldırımcılık ve Osmanlı şehir yolları hakkında bazı düşünceler," *Güney-Doğu Avrupa Araştırmaları Dergisi,* 1, (1972), 93–138.
Orhonlu, "Kayıkçılık"	Cengiz Orhonlu, "Osmanlı Türkleri devrinde Istanbulda kayıkçılık ve kayık işletmeciliği," *Tarih Dergisi,* 16 (1966), 109–134.

Orhonlu, "Mimarlar"	Cengiz Orhonlu, "Osmanlı teşkilatında hassa mimarlar," *Tarih Araştırmaları Dergisi,* 1 (1963), 157–202.
Özalp	Kâzım Özalp, *Milli Mücadele, 1919–1922,* 2 vols., Ankara, 1971–1972.
Pakalın, *Son Sadrâzamlar*	Mehmet Zeki Pakalın, *Son Sadrâzamlar ve Başvekiller,* 5 vols., Istanbul, 1940–1948.
Pakalın, *Tanzimat Maliye*	Mehmet Zeki Pakalın, *Tanzimat Maliye Nazırları,* 2 vols., Istanbul, 1939–1940.
Pakalın, *Tarih Deyimleri*	Mehmet Zeki Pakalın, *Osmanlı tarih deyimleri ve terimleri sözlüğü,* 3 vols., Istanbul, 1946–1955.
Quataert	Donald Quataert, "Ottoman Reform and Agriculture in Anatolia, 1876–1908," unpublished Ph.D. dissertation, University of California, Los Angeles, 1973.
Reed	Howard A. Reed, "The Destruction of the Janissaries by Mahmud II in June 1826," unpublished Ph.D. dissertation, Princeton University, 1951.
RG	*Resmi Gazete.* Official newspaper of the Turkish Republic, Ankara, 1920 to date.
Robinson, *Developments*	Richard N. Robinson, *Developments Respecting Turkey,* 4 vols., New York, 1954–1957 (chronology of Turkish affairs, 1954–1957).
Robinson, *Investment*	(Richard N. Robinson), *Investment in Turkey: Basic Information for United States Businessmen,* Washington, D.C. 1956.
Robinson, *Republic*	Richard N. Robinson, *The First Turkish Republic,* Cambridge, Mass., 1963.
RPP	Republican People's Party (for text discussion, refer to Index).
Sait Paşa, *Hâtırat*	Sait Paşa, *Sait Paşanın Hâtıratı,* Istanbul, 1328/ 1912.
Salname	*Salname-i Devlet-i Âliye-i Osmaniye,* Official Ottoman yearbooks.
Schlechta-Wssehrd	Ottokar von Schlechta-Wssehrd, *Die Revolutionen in Constantinopel in den Jahren 1807 und 1808,* Vienna, 1882.
Selek	Sabahettin Selek, *Milli Mücadele, Anadolu İhtilâli,* 2 vols., Ankara, 1963–1965.
Shaw, "Archival Materials"	Stanford J. Shaw, "Ottoman Archival Materials for the Nineteenth and Early Twentieth Centuries: The Archives of Istanbul," IJMES, 6 (1975), 94–114.
Shaw, *Between Old and New*	S. J. Shaw, *Between Old and New: The Ottoman Empire Under Sultan Selim III, 1789–1807,* Cambridge, Mass., 1971.
Shaw, *Empire of the Gazis*	S. J. Shaw, *Empire of the Gazis: The Rise and Decline of the Ottoman Empire, 1280–1808,* New York and London, 1976.
Shaw, "Established	S. J. Shaw, "The Established Ottoman Military

Corps"

Shaw, "Origins"

Shaw, "Origins of
Representative Government"

Shaw, "Ottoman Legislative
Councils"

Shaw, "Ottoman Tax Reforms"

Shaw, "Promise of Reform"

Shaw, "Yıldız"

Shaw (E.K.), "Midhat Paşa"

Skendi

Söylemezoğlu

Speech

Stavrianos

Şanizade

Şimşir

Tanzimat

Tar. Ves.

TBMM, *Zabıt Ceridesi*

Testa

Corps Under Sultan Selim III," *Der Islam,* 40 (1965), 142–184.

S. J. Shaw, "The Origins of Ottoman Military Reform: The Nizam-ı Cedid Army of Sultan Selim III," *Journal of Modern History,* 37 (1965), 291–306.

S. J. Shaw, "The Origins of Representative Government in the Ottoman Empire: An Introduction to the Provincial Councils, 1839–1876," *Near Eastern Round Table, 1967–1968,* ed. R. B. Winder, New York, 1969, pp. 53–142.

S. J. Shaw, "The Central Legislative Councils in the Nineteenth Century Ottoman Reform Movement before 1876," IJMES, 1 (1970), 51–84.

S. J. Shaw, "The Nineteenth Century Ottoman Tax Reforms and Revenue System," IJMES, 6 (1975), 421–459.

S. J. Shaw, "A Promise of Reform: Two Complimentary Documents," IJMES, 4 (1973), 359–365.

S. J. Shaw, "The Yıldız Palace Archives of Abdulhamit II," *Archivum Ottomanicum, 3* (1971), 211–237.

Ezel Kural Shaw, "Midhat Paşa, Reformer or Revolutionary?" unpublished Ph.D. dissertation, Harvard University, 1975.

Stavro Skendi, *The Albanian National Awakening, 1878–1912,* Princeton, 1967.

Kemali Söylemezoğlu, *Başımıza gelenler,* Istanbul, 1939.

Mustafa Kemal, *A Speech Delivered by Ghazi Mustapha Kemal, President of the Turkish Republic, October 1927,* Leipzig, 1929.

Leften Stavrianos, *The Balkans Since 1453,* New York, 1958, 2nd ed., 1963.

Mehmet Ataullah Şanizade, *Tarih-i Şanizade,* 4 vols., Istanbul, 1290–1/1873–4.

Bilâl N. Şimşir, *İngiliz Belgelerinde Atatürk (1919–1938),* Cilt I. Nisan 1919–Mart 1920. Atatürk in British Documents (1919–1938), vol. I, April 1919–March 1920, Ankara, 1973.

T. C. Maarif Vekâleti, *Tanzimat,* I (only volume published), Istanbul, 1940.

Tarih Vesikaları, nos. 1–18, Ankara, 1943–1961.

T. C. Türkiye Büyük Millet Meclisi, *Zabıt Ceridesi,* Ankara, 1921 to date.

Baron Ignatz de Testa, et al., *Recueil des traités de la Porte ottoman avec les puissances étrangeres depuis 1536 . . . ,* 11 vols., Paris, 1864–1911.

Tevetoğlu, *Atatürkle Samsuna Çıkanlar*	Fethi Tevetoğlu, *Atatürk'le Samsuna Çıkanlar,* Ankara, 1971.
Tevetoğlu, *Türkiyede Sosyalist*	Fethi Tevetoğlu, *Türkiye'de sosyalist ve komünist faaliyetleri,* Ankara, 1967.
TKS	Topkapı Sarayı (Topkapı Palace) Archives and Library, Istanbul.
TOEM	*Tarih-i Osmani Encümeni Mecmuası, 77* numbers, Istanbul, 1326–38/1908–19.
Trumpener	Ulrich Trumpener, *Germany and the Ottoman Empire, 1914–1918,* Princeton, N.J., 1968.
TTEM	*Türk Tarih Encümeni Mecmuası* (continuation of TOEM), nos. 78–101, Istanbul and Ankara, 1921–1930.
Tunaya	Tarık Z. Tunaya, *Türkiyede Siyasi Partiler, 1859–1952,* Istanbul, 1952.
Türk İstiklâl Harbi	Genelkurmay Başkanlığı Harp Tarihi Dairesi, *Türk İstiklâl Harbi,* 6 vols., Ankara, 1962–1968.
TV	*Takvim-i Vekâyi,* nos. 1–2119 (1831–1878), 1–283 (1890–1), 1–4608 (1908–1923).
Uzunçarşılı, *Alemdar*	Ismail Hakkı Uzunçarşılı, *Meşhur Rumeli Âyanlarından Tirsinikli Ismail, Yılık oğlu, Süleyman Ağalar ve Alemdar Mustafa Paşa,* Istanbul, 1942.
Uzunçarşılı, *Kapukulu*	Ismail Hakkı Uzunçarşılı, *Osmanlı Devleti Teşkilâtından Kapukulu Ocakları,* 2 vols., Ankara, 1943–1944.
Uzunçarşılı, *Merkez*	Ismail Hakkı Uzunçarşılı, *Osmanlı Devletinin Merkez ve Bahriye Teşkilâtı,* Ankara, 1948.
Uzunçarşılı, *Saray*	Ismail Hakkı Uzunçarşılı, *Osmanlı Devletinin Saray Teşkilâtı,* Ankara, 1945.
Uzunçarşılı, *Yıldız*	Ismail Hakkı Uzunçarşılı, *Midhat Paşa ve Yıldız Mahkemesi,* Ankara, 1967.
Vakayi-i Enderun	Hızır Ilyas Efendi, *Vakâyi-i Letâif-i Enderun,* Istanbul, 1276/1859.
Von Moltke, *Bulgaria*	Helmuth von Moltke, *The Russians in Bulgaria and Rumelia in 1828 and 1829,* London, 1854.
Von Moltke, *Zustände*	Helmuth von Moltke, *Briefe über Zustände und Begebenheiten in der Türkei aus den Jahren 1835 bis 1839,* Berlin, 1841.
Walsh, *Residence*	Robert Walsh, *A Residence at Constantinople . . . ,* 2 vols., London, 1836.
Weber	F. G. Weber, *Eagles on the Crescent: Germany, Austria and the Diplomacy of the Turkish Alliance, 1914–1918,* Ithaca, N.Y., 1970.
Webster	D. E. Webster, *The Turkey of Atatürk: Social Process in The Turkish Reformation,* Philadelphia, Pa., 1939.
Weiker, *Political Tutelage*	Walter Weiker, *Political Tutelage and Democracy in Turkey: The Free Party and Its Aftermath,* Leiden, 1973.

Weiker, *Revolution*	Walter Weiker, *The Turkish Revolution, 1960–1961. Aspects of Military Politics,* Washington, D.C., 1963.
Yalman, *Turkey*	Ahmet Emin Yalman, *Turkey in My Time,* Norman, Okla., 1956.
Yalman, *World War*	Ahmet Emin (Yalman), *Turkey in the World War,* New Haven and London, 1930.
Yalman, *Yakın Tarihte*	Ahmet Emin Yalman, *Yakın Tarihte Gördüklerim ve Geçirdiklerim,* 4 vols., Istanbul, n.d.
Young	George Young, *Corps de droit ottoman; recueil des codes, lois, règlements, ordonnances et actes les plus importants du droit interieur et d'études sur le droit coutumier de l'Empire ottoman,* 7 vols., Oxford, 1905–1906.
Zabıt Ceridesi	Hakkı Tarık Us, *Meclis-i Mebusan, 1293/1877 Zabıt Ceridesi,* 2 vols., Istanbul, 1940–1954.

NOTE ON PRONUNCIATION

The modern standard Turkish spelling system has been employed in this book with only a few exceptions. The Latin letters used in this system are pronounced about the same as their English equivalents, with the following exceptions:

Letter	English pronunciation
c	j
ç	ch
ğ	lengthens preceding vowel; thus *ağa* is pronounced a–a
ı	like the *a* in *serial* or *io* in *cushion*
j	zh
ö	like the German ö
ş	sh
ü	like the German ü
v	lighter than English v

The modern Turkish tendency to change the final Ottoman letters d and b into t and p has been followed, thus Murat, Mahmut, and *kitap,* but these letters return to d and b when followed by vowels, as Mahmudu and *kitabı.* Arabic terms used in Ottoman Turkish have been given their Turkish pronunciations and spellings, thus *mültezim* and *mütevelli* rather than *multazim* and *mutawalli.*

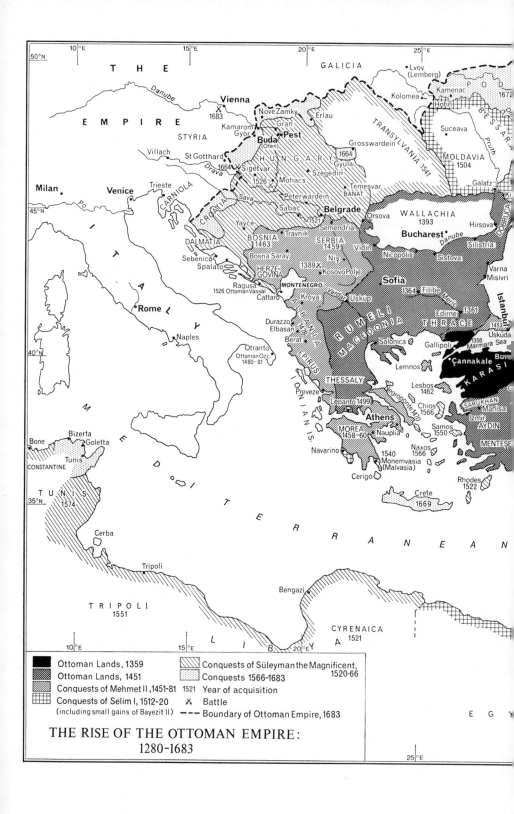

THE RISE OF THE OTTOMAN EMPIRE:
1280-1683

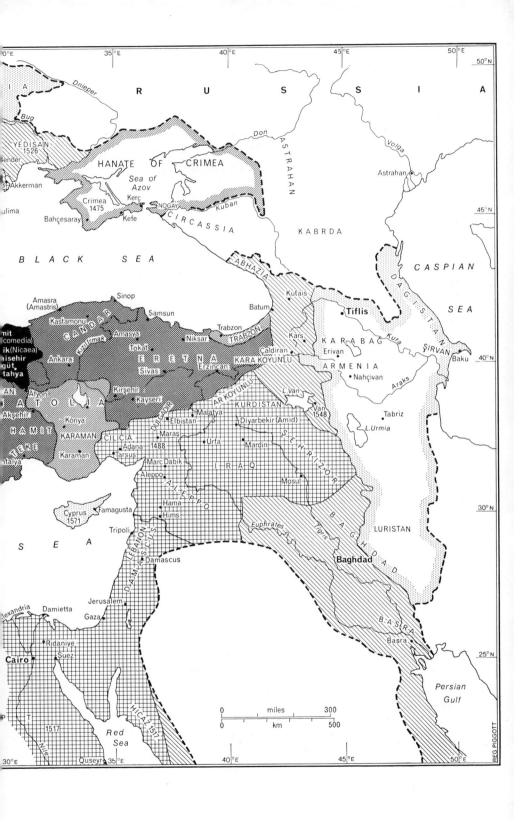

Map labels

50°N · 10°E · 15°E · 20°E · 25°E

Danube

Boundary 1683

Vienna
1683✕
AUSTRIA

Budapest

HUNGARY
to Austria 1699

Grosswardein

TRANSYLVANIA
to Austria 1699

Vinnits
PODOLI
to
Poland
1699

Dniester
Chernovtsy

BUKOVINA

Jassy
MOLDAVIA
1829

BESSARABIA

Milan

Venice
Trieste

Agram

Drava

.Mohacs

Temesvar
BANAT
to Austria
1718

45°N

ITALY

Po

Sava

CROATIA

Carlowitz

Belgrade
Passarowitz
SERBIA
to Austria
1718–39

to Austria
1718–39
1829

Craiova

RUMANIA
Created 1859
1878

Bucharest

Galati.
Ibrail
Ismai

DOBRUCA

BOSNIA
to Austria–Hungary
1878

Sarajevo
1817
1878

**HERZE-
GOVINA**

DALMATIA
to Venice 1699–1797
to Austria 1797 & 1816
to Italy 1805–9
to France 1809–16

1718 Ragusa

Cattaro
1878

Scutari
(Shkodra)

Niš

Vidin

Plevna
Sistova

Silistria
Küçük
Kaynarca

Constan

BULGARIA
1878 1908

Varna
Burgas

Sofia

EAST RUMELIA
1878 Filibe (Plovdiv)

to Bulgaria 1885

to Bulgaria
1913

ALBANIA
1913

to
Serbia
1913

Üsküp
(Skopje)

Vardar

MACEDONIA
1913
to Greece

Janina

EPIRUS

Corfu

Larisa

THESSALY
to Greece 1881

Ionian Is.
to Venice until 1797
France 1797-9 & 1807-9
Br. Prot. 1815-63
to Greece 1863

GREECE
1830

Missolonghi

MOREA
to Venice
1685-99
1715-18

Athens

Argos

Navarino

Salonica Thasos
Kavala

Edirne
to Greece
1920-22

Maritsa

to Bulgaria
1913

Bosporu

Istanbu

Üsküdar (Scutari)
Marmara Sea

Gallipoli

Lemnos

Dardanelles

Mudanya

to Greece
1920-22

Negroponte
(Euboea)

Mytilene

Chios

İzmir

Samos

Menderes

Dodecanese
to Italy 1912

Muğla.

Cerigo

Rhodes

Candia Spinalonga
Canea **CRETE** Turkey 1718
Turkey 1718 to Greece 1908

MEDITERRANEAN

Tunis

TUNIS
Nominally Subject
until 1881

Tripoli

TRIPOLI
Ottoman Vassal until 1835
Ottoman Province 1835–1912
to Italy 1912

Bengazi

CYRENAICA
Ottoman Vassal until 1835
Ottoman Province 1835–1912

L · I · B · Y · A

E · G · Y
1811

Br. Occupation 1882
Br. Protectorate 1914

1922

35°N

40°N

Rome

Legend

◼ Losses 1683-99 (*Treaty of Karlowitz*)	▦ Turkey in 1923
◼ Losses 1700 -18 (*Treaty of Passarowitz*)	1878 Date or period of autonomy
▥ Losses 1719 -74 *Treaty of Küçük Kaynarca*	1830 Date of independence
⟋ Losses 1775 -1812 *Treaty of Bucharest*	–·– Boundaries of spheres of influence in Anatolia after the 1914-18 War
⊠ Losses 1813-29/30 *Treaty of Edirne*	······ Boundary after Treaty of Sèvres 1920
▤ Losses 1830-78 *Treaty of Berlin*	—— Boundary after Treaty of Lausanne 1923
⟍ Losses 1879-1915 *Treaties of London & Bucharest*	
⣿ Losses 1916-23 *Treaty of Lausanne*	

0 miles 300
0 km 500

DECLINE OF THE
OTTOMAN EMPIRE
AND RISE OF THE TURKISH REPUBLIC
1683-1975

1

The Beginnings of Modern Ottoman Reform:
The Era of Mahmut II, 1808–1839

On May 29, 1807, Sultan Selim III was deposed, the reformed *Nizam-ı Cedit* army disbanded, and his effort to modernize the Ottoman Empire momentarily blocked. Reaction again prevailed within the Ottoman Ruling Class. During the short reign of his successor Mustafa IV (1807–1808), the Janissaries and their allies attempted to eliminate all those who had dared oppose the old order. Yet this did not happen. The supporters of Selim, those who had managed to survive, joined under the leadership of the Danubian notable Bayraktar Mustafa Paşa to rescue Selim and restore his reforms. Bayraktar brought his army to Istanbul, but before it could break into the palace, Selim was assassinated. To realize their goal Bayraktar Mustafa and his supporters placed on the throne Selim's cousin Mahmut II (1808–1839), who had shared Selim's palace imprisonment and was known to hold many of the same reforming ideas (July 28, 1808).[1]

Mahmut in time emerged as a far stronger and much more successful reformer than Selim. But his was a very long reign, and it was only much later, in 1826, that he was able to destroy the Janissary corps, thus depriving the conservatives of their military arm and setting Ottoman reform on a new course of destroying old institutions and replacing them with new ones mainly imported from the West.

What made Mahmut II different from Selim III? They had been raised together. They had received the same traditional palace education spiced with occasional information about the outside world and had had little opportunity to gain the practical experience needed to transform their ideas into reality. But Mahmut witnessed the results of Selim's weakness and indecision. He also saw how successful even the limited reforms instituted in the *Nizam-ı Cedit* program had been. Early in his reign Mahmut seems to have realized that: (1) reforms, to be successful, had to encompass the entire scope of Ottoman institutions and society, not only a few elements of the military; (2) the only way that reformed institutions could operate was through the destruction of the ones they were replacing, so that the latter could not hinder their operation; and (3) the reforms had to be carefully planned and support assured before they were attempted. These considerations emerge as the backbone of Mahmut's reform policy in subsequent years.

Bayraktar Mustafa Paşa as Grand Vezir, July 28–November 15, 1808

Mahmut II started his reign under the domination of the man who had brought him to power, Bayraktar Mustafa Paşa, the first provincial notable ever to achieve the pinnacle of power in the Ottoman state. Bayraktar Mustafa himself was a product of the traditional Ottoman system, and his concept of reform was very much in the same mold. Although he had risen as a provincial notable, once in

1

power he appears to have felt an identity of interests with the central government, at least to the extent of realizing that his own power in Bulgaria and that of his fellows could continue only if the empire itself survived in the face of Russian expansion. His first step was to eliminate the opponents of Selim's reforms. With Bayraktar Mustafa's army giving the reformers a kind of power that Selim never had, the rebellious soldiers were driven out and killed or sent into exile. Conservatives were removed from the institutions of the Ruling Class and replaced with men willing to accept the new leadership and reforms.

The Document of Agreement

Bayraktar's rise demonstrated that the power of the provincial notables could not be ignored. Their opposition had contributed to the destruction of the *Nizam-ı Cedit,* and they might well have undermined reform again. Thus Bayraktar Mustafa attempted to use his prestige among them to get them to agree to reforms. He invited all the important notables to come to Istanbul for a general deliberation on the problems of the empire. Perhaps no other leader at the time could have gotten the highly independent and fractious notables to come, but he was able to do so. From Anatolia came the leaders of powerful dynasties such as the Karaosmanoğlu and Çapanoğlu as well as Kadi Abdurrahman Paşa, governor of Karaman and the strongest notable supporter of Selim, who brought some 3000 soldiers trained in the new way, perhaps as an example as well as a warning to all those assembled. Most of the important notables of Rumeli also came. But there were exceptions. Ali Paşa of Janina, who held much of Albania and northern Greece, sent only a small contingent of soldiers led by a representative. The smaller notables of Bulgaria, who were Bayraktar Mustafa's rivals in that province, avoided a move that they feared might strengthen him at their expense. So also did Muhammad Ali, who was soon to make Egypt into the most powerful province of the empire and later to attack Mahmut II on two occasions. The notables and governors of the more distant Arab and Anatolian provinces were unable to travel the long distance to Istanbul in time, but they did in fact support any effort that would lessen the power of the provincial Janissary garrisons over them.[2] After being received by the sultan at his summer residence in Kâğıthane (September 29, 1808), the notables held a series of meetings to discuss Bayraktar Mustafa's proposed reforms, resulting finally in a Document of Agreement (*Sened-i Ittifak*) signed by all present on October 7, 1808.

The notables and provincial governors signing the document confirmed their loyalty to the sultan and promised to recognize the grand vezir as his absolute representative (articles 1 and 4). The Ottoman tax system was to be applied in full throughout the empire, in all their provinces, without any diversion of revenues rightfully belonging to the sultan (article 3), and in return the sultan promised to levy taxes justly and fairly (article 7). Because the empire's survival depended on the strength of the army, the notables promised to cooperate in the recruitment of men in their provinces. The new army was to be organized "in accordance with the system presented during the discussion" (article 2), of which no exact details were indicated. The notables were to rule justly in their own territories (article 5). They promised to respect each other's territory and autonomy, to act separately and collectively as guarantors for each other's fulfillment of the promises, and to support the central government against any opposition to its reforms, marching to Istanbul whenever they heard of any uprising, without even wasting time to secure the sultan's permission (article 6). The agreement thus included no specific program of military reform, but the entire drift of the discussion and the provisions indicated that Selim's *Nizam-ı Cedit* would be restored with the full support of those present. Some sources indicate that Bayraktar Mustafa also proposed reforms for the older military corps, including an end to irregularities in appointments, requirements for unmarried members to live in the barracks and for all members to accept discipline and training in order to receive their salaries, and even the use of European-style weapons, but such plans did not appear in the document itself.[3]

Some writers refer to the document as the "Magna Carta of the Ottomans," an agreement between the ruler and his notables that could serve as a written constitution. The attempts to delimit the powers of the sultan with respect to taxes and to establish a reciprocity of responsibilities and obligations as well as to make a distinction between the government and the sultan were, indeed, steps toward constitutionalism. But the sultan, not wishing to limit his own sovereign power, avoided signing it, resenting in particular its confirmation of the rights and privileges of the provincial notables and promises that he would govern justly. And in the end only four of the notables signed. The remainder returned to their homes during the conference once they saw that they would have to limit their own independence by promising to help the government, to rule justly, and to keep each other in line. Also, unlike the Magna Carta, the Document of Agreement was not subsequently used to further the cause of constitutionalism in the Ottoman Empire.[4] Thus it had only a limited effect and significance.

The Segban-ı Cedit Army

Whether because he now felt assured of support from the notables, or perhaps because he feared they might soon act against him, immediately after the Document of Agreement Bayraktar Mustafa tried to restore the *Nizam-ı Cedit*, though in a cautious and concealed manner so as not to alarm its opponents. The nucleus for the new force was the 3000-man rapid-fire rifle force brought to the conference by Kadi Abdurrahman Paşa, to which he added other *Nizam-ı Cedit* survivors and soldiers brought by the Karaosmanoğlu and Çapanoğlu leaders. The old *Nizam-ı Cedit* barracks at Levent Çiftliği and Üsküdar were repaired and turned over to the new corps (October 3, 1808), about 5,000 volunteers were enrolled, and orders were issued for recruitment around the empire as soon as possible. To avoid resistance from the Janissaries the new force was not called *Nizam-ı Cedit*, but rather was made part of the old order, attached to the *kapıkulu* army, after the extinct *Segban* (keepers of the hounds) corps, an affiliate of the Janissaries, becoming the New *Segban*s (*Segban-ı Cedit*).[5] As its commander the grand vezir appointed a former *Nizam-ı Cedit* officer, Süleyman Ağa, and Kadi Abdurrahman Paşa served as actual military leader. While it was not given a separate treasury, a new Ministry for Affairs of the Holy War (*Umur-u Cihadiye Nezareti*), a name with particular appeal to the ulema, was established to secure the necessary revenues. A force of some 160,000 men divided into 100 regiments (*bölük*) and 3 divisions was envisaged, but for the moment the corps had about 10,000 men and officers in all.

Other Military Reforms

The navy was reorganized under the command of Bayraktar Mustafa's tutor and close adviser, Abdullah Ramiz Efendi, who dismissed incompetents, retired old ships, and began to build new ones. The barracks at Galata, which had become centers for riots and sedition, were closed and the sailors were required to live at the dockyard or on their ships.[6] Bayraktar Mustafa also tried to reform the Janissary corps. He issued orders that prohibited the sale of positions, restored the old system of promotion by seniority, and required all members to accept training and discipline. He proposed that Janissary pay tickets held for income and not service be abolished, in the process saving money that could be used for the reformed army and navy. But Mahmut II, ever the politician, feared that cutting off the incomes of thousands of persons so suddenly would stimulate a revolt. Thus he ordered that such holdings be canceled in return for bulk payments equal to half their value, while only those not surrendering them voluntarily would be subject to confiscation without compensation.[7]

The Conservative Reaction

These measures stimulated the rise of conservative opposition to the sultan and his chief minister. Those called to serve in the new corps or to surrender their sinecure memberships in the old corps were indignant at the loss of their privileges. The old corps and the mass of the people were not deceived by the names attached to the new army, and they resented its presence. And Bayraktar Mustafa and his men, unaccustomed to the power of office as well as to life in a great metropolis, soon began to act in such an arrogant and destructive manner as to alienate the sultan and those who had originally supported them. Bayraktar acted as though he were the real ruler, issued orders without going through the formality of discussion and assent, and reacted to Mahmut's protests by contemplating his replacement with Selim Giray, claimant to the Crimean Hanate and then resident in Istanbul.[8] Bayraktar and his associates stimulated general hostility by using their positions to amass wealth for themselves, confiscating many timars and the properties of religious foundations whose administrators could not produce deeds attesting to their rights. The mass of the people of Istanbul became incensed by the swaggering attitude of the grand vezir's soldiers who roamed through the streets, inflicting themselves on the hapless shop- and homeowners. Finally, Bayraktar Mustafa seems to have alienated everyone by his boorishness and bluntness and his apparent delight in frightening and insulting all who came near him.[9]

The Overthrow of Bayraktar Mustafa and the Triumph of Reaction

Bayraktar's army and personal guard and the *Segban* army – part of which was still in the process of mobilization and training – made him all powerful in Istanbul. His enemies therefore incited the notables of Bulgaria against him, securing an attack on Rusçuk in mid-October. Bayraktar was forced to send most of his soldiers back to defend his position there and to replace them with unemployed mountaineers hired from Rumeli. The grand vezir's new forces wandered in the streets of Istanbul, sharing its delights and ravaging even more than had their predecessors, but failed to provide adequate protection to their master.[10] Finally, the first public appearance of the *Segban-ı Cedit* men at the evening meal breaking the fast of the last day of Ramazan, the most sacred night of the Muslim year (November 14, 1808), precipitated a revolt against Bayraktar. The Janissaries present were so outraged by this open flaunting of their enemies that they ran to their barracks and raised the entire corps in rebellion, helped by the spread of the (false) news that the grand vezir intended to abolish their corps altogether. Early the next morning the rebels broke into the Porte, where the gates were open because of the holiday, forcing Bayraktar and his personal guard to take refuge in a small stone powder magazine nearby. Finally, when the Janissaries were about to break in through the roof, the powder barrels blew up, either accidentally or by the hand of Bayraktar Mustafa, who was killed along with his men and several hundred Janissaries outside.[11]

Again Istanbul fell to the scourge of victorious military rebels, who demanded that the sultan give them a new *ağa* as well as a grand vezir more acceptable to them. Mahmut thus was in a situation similar to that of Selim a short time before. But he had learned his lesson well. He knew that concessions would only encourage the rebels to demand more and more until his throne would certainly have been lost to the deposed Mustafa, who had many partisans in and out of the palace. Instead of giving in, then, he temporized while ordering Ramiz Paşa and Kadi Abdurrahman to bring their troops to the palace (November 15). He then rejected the rebel demands, and when the Janissaries attacked, they were beaten back by its reinforced garrison. Mahmut further secured his position by ordering the execution of Prince Mustafa, thus depriving the rebels of the alternative candidate to the throne.[12]

A full-scale conflict followed. The Janissaries obtained the support of the artisans and the city mob and mounted a general assault on the palace from the direction of Aya Sofya, and cut off its water supply (November 16, 1808). The new *Segbans* responded with sorties outside the walls, but they were not yet fully organized and trained, and against the numerical superiority of the attackers they could not break out of the circle. The navy ships in the Golden Horn began bombarding the Janissary barracks as well as their lines around the palace, but this started huge fires that destroyed large sections of the Sultan Ahmet, Aya Sofya, and Divan Yolu quarters, with thousands of innocent civilians being killed. The Janissary leaders then decided that they could not win and that compromise was best, signing a Document of Obedience (*Sened-i Itaat*) to the sultan in return for an amnesty. But the settlement was upset by the lower-ranking Janissaries, who still opposed continuation of the *Segbans*, as well as by others who were shocked by Mustafa's execution and demanded that Mahmut be deposed. Mahmut continued to hold the palace with the support of the *Segbans*, however. The ulema finally got the rebellious soldiers to agree to new negotiations as the only alternative to eliminating the house of Osman altogether. The fate of the *Segban* corps was the most difficult issue to solve. Finally, after long discussions, on November 17 an agreement was reached by which the *Segbans* would be disbanded, but their members would be allowed to leave Istanbul without harm, and the sultan would not be required to surrender any of his supporters who had taken refuge in the palace. Under the circumstances it was the best possible compromise to end the stalemate.[13] But the agreement was not kept by the rebels. As the *Segbans* left the palace in accordance with the compromise, disarmed and without their uniforms, they were set upon by those waiting outside, while other mobs attacked and destroyed their barracks, killing those inside. A number of notables who had supported the reforms were killed, including Ramiz Paşa and Kadi Abdurrahman. It seemed, indeed, that reaction had won out again. But Mahmut remained on the throne, firmly committed to reform, and now convinced that new corps could not be effectively built unless the old ones whose interests were being threatened were destroyed, that in fact reform could not be limited only to the military but had to span the whole spectrum of Ottoman institutions and society. The lessons were, indeed, to be applied during the years that followed.[14]

The Years of Preparation, 1808–1826

The results of the momentous events of November 1808 were not as decisive as those of the revolution that had overthrown Selim III the previous year. Warfare had come to an end not through unconditional surrender but as the result of compromise. Mahmut II, therefore, emerged in not quite as weak a position in relation to the rebel leaders as had Mustafa IV. But the basic elements of power certainly were not in his hands. The provinces were under the domination of notables who, for all practical purposes, had repudiated their obligations to him. The new *Segban* corps, established as an instrument of personal power as well as a first step toward modernizing the army, was gone, and the sole military force was composed of the same corps that had opposed reform all along. But Mahmut II had demonstrated great determination and perseverance during the crisis. He had demonstrated his willingness to fight, and fight well, for policies that he believed in, in stark contrast to Selim's vacillation and essential weakness. This reputation was to serve him in good stead as he spent the next 18 years working to rebuild a cadre of devoted soldiers and statesmen and waiting for the day when events would enable him to act once again in accordance with the lessons he had learned.

Restoration of the Military Establishment

With the loss of the *Segban*s, Mahmut's first step had to be to restore the traditional corps so that he would have some force strong enough to defend the empire against its enemies, particularly Russia, with whom a war was still being waged. Once again, decrees were issued requiring the Janissaries and *Sipahi*s to live up to their traditional regulations, to appoint and promote officers according to ability rather than bribery and politics, and to remove all those failing to train and serve with the corps. But of course after the disbanding of the *Segban*s, these decrees could not be enforced effectively. The Janissaries remained at best an undisciplined, ill-trained, and poorly armed mob, far better able to act in defense of the old order than to compete with the new armies of Europe. The feudal *Sipahi*s now dissolved into a rural aristocracy, with most of the timars falling into the hands of owners of large estates, who in many cases were the autonomous provincial notables and their allies. The sultan was, however, more successful in reviving the other older corps that had already been the recipients of reforms and that were much more willing to accept discipline and reinforcement now, particularly the Cannon and allied Cannon-Wagon corps (numbering 4,910 and 2,129 men respectively), which had been built into effective fighting forces by the end of Selim's reign.[15] Mahmut soon was able to appoint his own protégés to command them. He raised their salaries, provided them with new equipment and better barracks, and quietly doubled their strength, so that by 1826 they numbered close to 10,000 cannoneers and 4,400 cannon-wagon men in all, forming a loyal and effective counterweight to the Janissaries.[16] Mahmut also built a new force of mounted artillerymen of some 1,000 men, trained and organized in the Western style, and though it was routed and largely destroyed by the Russians in 1812, it subsequently was rebuilt and provided the sultan with a well-trained, well-paid, and loyal force as his personal guard against the machinations of his opponents.[17]

External threats to the empire necessitated continued emphasis on the military system. Mahmut worked to rebuild and modernize the fleet, mostly under the direction of Grand Admiral Mehmet Husrev Paşa (last governor of Egypt before Muhammad Ali), who served 12 years in the post in two terms of duty (December 22, 1811–March 2, 1818; December 9, 1822–February 9, 1827). New warships were built, particularly as part of the Porte's response to the Greek insurrection. To replace the Greek sailors from the Aegean Islands, Muslim sailors were recruited and given high salaries and favorable conditions of employment to get the men to accept the severe training and discipline required.[18] After the Russian war was ended, the Danube flotilla also was modernized along with its bases at Ibrail, Silistria, Rusçuk, and Vidin.[19] From the earliest years of Mahmut's reign the forts along the empire's boundaries were repaired and a new corps of frontier garrisons able and willing to resist the enemy was created.[20] The artillery and naval arsenals and the gunpowder factory established by Selim at Azadlı were reorganized and modernized with help from foreign technicians. Mahmut's men made certain that the officers and men manning them were loyal and discreet.[21] Finally, new cannons, muskets, and smaller arms were purchased in Europe and stored in the palace and elsewhere to prepare for the day when they might openly be used in the service of the sultan.[22]

As the sultan's personal guard gave him increased confidence, he moved to do what he could to reform the Janissaries and get his men into key positions of command over them as well. Officers and men who openly defied his authority or protested his other military measures were punished, sent into exile, and sometimes secretly executed. Senior corps officers were gradually replaced by juniors who were more open to palace influence and thus more trustworthy insofar as the sultan was concerned.[23] It was in this manner that Mahmut secured the assistance of Hüseyin Ağa, who rose to be *ağa* of the entire corps (February 26, 1823). Rising through the patronage of Silahtar Ali Paşa, Hüseyin took advantage of the latter's service as grand vezir (March 10–December 13, 1823) to remove dissidents in the corps by dismissal, forced retirement, and banishment, to such an extent that the sultan awarded him with the rank of vezir and title of *paşa,* after which he came to be known as Ağa Hüseyin Paşa or simply Ağa Paşa, becoming one of the leading military figures during the remainder of the reign.[24] When these harsh policies stirred opposition within the corps, Mahmut later removed Ağa Paşa as commander (October 1823) and sent him to serve as governor of Bursa and Izmit as well as commander of the Bosporus forts to protect him from his enemies until more propitious times, all the while ensuring that these important forces near the capital were commanded by a trustworthy and able officer.[25]

Ağa Hüseyin's departure from the Janissary corps did not mean an end to Mahmut's efforts to gain the support of its officers. It even helped him by providing another vacancy at the top and new opportunities to promote trusted men to key positions throughout the corps. Among those who rose in this way was Celaleddin Mehmet Ağa, who, in September 1825, became the last commander of the corps and used that position to help the sultan to undermine and finally destroy it.[26] There was also Pabuççu Ahmet, an officer at the Naval Arsenal who organized a force of boatmen and porters there and in the Golden Horn, put them at the sultan's disposal, and in return secured various naval appointments culminating in that of grand admiral soon after the Janissaries were destroyed (October 24, 1828–January 13, 1830).[27] These were, however, mainly political efforts, and they were not transformed into policies to reform or discipline the corps. So it remained as incompetent as it had been earlier, failing again and again against the Greek rebels and causing street disturbances in Istanbul at the least provocation, while its units stationed in the provinces continued to cause more trouble for the local officials and the populace than for the enemy.[28]

The Struggle for Political Power

Mahmut II was slow to extend his power and to introduce reforms because he was far from being master in his own house. Real power in the Ruling Class remained in the hands of the leaders of the established institutions, who would have been most happy to dethrone the sultan had there been any other member of the Ottoman line available to replace him.

There were several foci of political strength in the Ottoman establishment during the first two decades of Mahmut's regime, with the *şeyhulislam* representing and controlling the ulema, the *ağa*s of the Janissary and other corps and the regimental commanders leading the military factions, and the *reis ul-küttap* representing the ever more powerful scribes in the endemic struggles for power. The sultan played the game as best he could, shifting appointments between one faction and another, never leaving any of his opponents in power long enough to build bases of support, and gradually creating sufficient power of his own to undermine their overall strength and establish his own supporters in positions of importance.

Most influential and long-lived among the conservative leaders of the time was Mehmet Sait Halet Efendi (1761–1823), a member of the ulema and closely attached to the Galip Dede *mevlevi* dervish lodge of Galata. Halet had served as Ottoman ambassador to Paris as a result of court favor during Selim's reign, but his long service (1802–1806) there had only strengthened his opposition to Western-style innovations in the Ottoman Empire. Following his return to Istanbul he participated in the conservative coalition that secured Selim's overthrow, but due to his pro-British attitudes he was in exile in Kütahya during the overthrow of Mustafa IV and brief dominance of Bayraktar Mustafa. Hence he was in a position to serve Mahmut II in his early years. His role in ending the long reign of the Baghdad Mamluk leader Süleyman Ağa and establishing direct Ottoman rule in Iraq (1810) gained him the particular favor of the sultan, and his appointment as steward of the sultan's court (*kethüda-ı rikab-ı hümayun*) and then as *nişancı* of the Imperial Council (September 10, 1815), made him Mahmut's close political and military adviser. Though Halet supported and helped organize Mahmut's military campaigns against the notables as well as various foreign enemies, he opposed all efforts at modernization, particularly reform of the Janissary corps, and built a political coalition of conservative leaders. It appears that even his support of Mahmut's desire to weaken the provincial notables was in fact an attempt to strengthen his friends among the Janissaries and the ulema by eliminating their main rivals for power in the provinces.[29]

Halet's main opposition came from Grand Admiral Mehmet Husrev Paşa, from *Reis ul-küttap* Canip Mehmet Besim Efendi (1817–1821), who combined the best elements of Western and Islamic cultures, and from Mehmet Sait Galip Paşa (1763–1829), perhaps the greatest liberal of his time. Born in Istanbul, the young Galip had risen as a career official in the scribal corporation, gaining distinction as Selim's special ambassador to Paris for the negotiations that culminated in the Peace of Amiens (1802). Galip produced a report to the sultan that had a major influence on Selim's reform efforts,[30] and then he became the most influential leader of the scribal corporation during the next decade, serving as *reis* three times (mid-October 1806–July 25, 1807; April 16, 1808–July 1811; and January 22–mid-July 1814). He was an active member of the Rusçuk Committee that put Mahmut on the throne. He strongly supported Bayraktar Mustafa's reform efforts and was saved from execution by the rebels due only to his reputation for honesty and, perhaps, also to a disinclination on the part of the rebels to alienate the scribes.[31] Galip finally used Halet's expedition against Ali Paşa of Janina (1820), leading to the death of the latter and also to the beginnings of the Greek Revolution (March 1821), as a pretext to secure his dismissal and exile (November 1822) and have him strangled there shortly afterward.[32]

Halet's removal gave Mahmut much more freedom to manipulate political groups and individuals. Halet was replaced as grand vezir by a rival, Deli Abdullah Paşa (November 10, 1822–March 10, 1823), who was given the task of rooting Halet's favorites out of government, after which he too was dismissed, ostensibly because of his failure to control the Janissary corps.[33] Abdullah was replaced by the sultan's former sword bearer, Silahtar Ali Paşa (March 10–December 13, 1823), whose principal contribution was to further the placement of loyal men into key positions of the Janissary corps while keeping the *şeyhulislam* from reacting too strongly to the sultan's moves.[34] His replacement was Galip Paşa, who was brought to power in the hope that his experience in foreign affairs would enable him to resolve the problems posed by the Greek Revolution and that he would help the sultan in developing plans to destroy the Janissary corps (December 13, 1823–September 14, 1824).[35] Galip devoted himself to both tasks, securing the intervention of Muhammad Ali's army to stifle the Greeks and using the defeat inflicted previously on the Janissaries by the latter to further discredit them, convincing most Ottomans and the mass of the people that this institution was by now too decrepit to save the empire. Galip also placed the sultan's men into the other *kapıkulu* corps, thus preparing for the day when the Janissaries would finally be eliminated. Interminable court intrigues – and the consideration that as a scribe he would not be able to lead the army when the time came to settle the score with the Janissaries – led to Galip's replacement by the able soldier Benderli Selim Mehmet Paşa (September 14, 1824–1828), who had gained military experience fighting against the Russians as well as in Syria and Tripoli and who had previously served for a short time as grand vezir (March 28–April 30, 1821).[36] Thus this parade of leaders gradually reflected the sultan's increasing domination of the political processes and his determination to establish his own control as soon as the time was opportune.

The Reforms of Muhammad Ali in Egypt

Almost everything Mahmut II was hoping to do in Istanbul was already being carried out by a seemingly far more successful reform activity taking place in the province of Egypt, setting a precedent that served both as a model and an incentive for much of what the sultan undertook after 1826. Leading these reforms was the most famous modernizer in nineteenth-century Middle Eastern history, Mehmet Ali, or, as he is called in Arabic, Muhammad Ali, Ottoman governor of Egypt from 1805 to 1848 and founder of the dynasty that was to rule the country for over a century. The problems facing Muhammad Ali were very similar to those of Mahmut II. Having shared the basic institutions of the Ottoman Empire for three centuries, the problems they experienced were interrelated; and hence the solutions attempted were similar. Yet while Mahmut II had to proceed cautiously, Muhammad

Ali was able to carry out reforms far more rapidly and completely because the French expedition to Egypt (1798–1801), and the subsequent restoration of Ottoman rule there, had effectively removed the old Ruling Class and with it the opposition from vested interests that so frustrated Selim and Mahmut. The presence of Mamluk, Ottoman, and British forces in Egypt following the French withdrawal enabled Muhammad Ali, who entered the country as leader of the Albanian and Bosnian contingent in the Ottoman army, to pose as defender of the interests of the people and the rights of the sultan against the various occupiers. He was proclaimed governor by popular acclaim (May 14, 1805) and then confirmed by the sultan's emissary when he reached the country and saw the extent of his support.

Once Muhammad Ali became governor, his main problem was to establish his predominance in a political spectrum where he was only one of a number of competing elements. His immediate solution was to rely on the support of the native ulema and artisan and merchant guild leaders as well as the sultan and Ottoman garrison against his Mamluk opponents, who were led by Muhammad Elfi Bey, a Mamluk protégé of the British. The new governor fulfilled his financial obligations to Istanbul and at the same time applied judicious bribery in the sultan's court to frustrate the maneuvers of the British ambassador to have him transferred to Salonica (1806). Muhammad Ali then solidified his position by defeating the Mamluks and scattering their armies in the name of both the sultan and the people of Egypt. At the renewal of the Ottoman war with Russia (1806–1808) Britain attempted to occupy Egypt once again, but Muhammad Ali united the country in general opposition to the foreign threat. Later, most of the remaining Mamluks were wiped out by massacre in the Citadel (March 1, 1811). His Albanian and Bosnian soldiers, who had sought to use his victory for their own advantage, were used to fulfill the sultan's request for help against the Wahhabis in Arabia (1811–1812), and their success against the latter earned Muhammad Ali additional prestige in both Istanbul and Cairo. He conciliated the Egyptian ulema by restoring all their properties taken by the Mamluks and also by continuing the advisory councils introduced by the French to give them some voice in governmental policy. Large bribes caused them to overlook his gradual consolidation of authority in his own hands until it was too late. Meanwhile, he continued to recognize Ottoman suzerainty and pay the regular tribute. He gave military support when needed, again in Arabia against the Wahhabis (1818–1820) and against the Greek rebels.

But even as Muhammad Ali built his power by conciliating or removing the main political elements in Egypt, he developed his own independent bases of strength, mainly by introducing the reforms that were to be pursued during the remaining years of his long tenure in office. These involved building a modern army and centralized administration dependent on him alone, developing the economic wealth of the country to finance his reforms, promoting a quasi-dynastic idea, and developing his family and followers into a new and permanent nobility to support him and his descendants.

His first step had to be the creation of an army to use against his military rivals in the country. He attempted to do this by modernizing the Ottoman corps under his command, putting a force of French deserters in command of a unit of black slaves, using Mamluk and Greek officers to direct the operation, and bringing in French advisers to train the force in the use of European weapons and tactics (August 1815).[37] But the reluctance of the Ottoman soldiers to accept the new ways undermined this effort. Its failure left Muhammad Ali convinced that the only real means of gaining the strength and independence he wanted was to create an entirely new army. If his sole aim in creating it was to maintain his rule in Egypt, it would have been quite enough to organize and develop it according to his own Ottoman experience. But it appears that he had larger ambitions, perhaps the conquest of the entire Ottoman Empire and its revival under his leadership.

He chose, therefore, to build his new army on the model of the British and French forces he had witnessed in his early years in Egypt as well as of the *Nizam-ı Cedit,* calling it also the *Nizamiye,* or "ordered" army. To man the *Nizamiye* he first tried to use white slaves from the Caucasus and blacks from the Sudan and Central Africa, thus essentially reviving the old Mamluk system. But these soon proved unsuitable for the modern kind of army he had in mind. Starting in 1823, then, he turned to a source previously ignored by the Ottomans and Mamluks, the peasants of Egypt, sending out press gangs and instituting a system of forced conscription. This freed him from outside control of the slave systems and gave him a substantial reserve of men, but it was accomplished at the cost of a harsh system of procurement that ultimately disrupted Egyptian agriculture and led to a series of uprisings. To command the new army he imported hundreds of officers and technical experts from Europe and established military and technical schools to train Egyptians, some of whom were sent to Europe for advanced training. Factories were opened to make military equipment according to European standards. Within a short time Muhammad Ali had a large and efficient infantry force whose abilities were soon demonstrated in Greece, Arabia, Syria, and Anatolia as well as in Egypt itself. The success of the infantry led him to develop a modern artillery and sapper corps (1824–1828) and to open an engineering school with a faculty of Europeans as well as some Ottomans trained earlier in Istanbul during the reign of Selim III. A regiment was established to care for fortification, transportation, road building, and mining. A modern fleet was built in both the Mediterranean and the Red Sea, and cavalry units on European lines were established in the early 1830s.

To finance the new army Muhammad Ali needed a far more productive state than that which he had taken over. To achieve efficient exploitation of resources the scope of the state was enlarged beyond that traditionally accepted by the Ottomans. Foreign agricultural experts were brought to improve methods of cultivation and irrigation. New crops were introduced, such as cotton, sugar, rice, and indigo, to sell abroad and provide the foreign exchange needed to import experts and weapons. Since the peasants lacked the capital and know-how to produce these new crops, the state became the capitalist in many cases, taking over large areas, providing the land and seed, and transforming many peasants into little more than hired laborers. On the other hand, living conditions for many peasants improved somewhat because Muhammad Ali built hospitals and clinics, introduced a quarantine system to end the scourge of plague, and provided a system of medical schools to train native doctors, mainly under the direction of a French doctor named Clot Bey. He also created a new and modern tax system and built roads to give the collectors more direct access to the taxpayers than had been possible in the past, carrying out a new cadastral survey to make certain that every source of wealth and its tax obligation were recorded.

Muhammad Ali developed new sources of revenue by building Egyptian industry and trade and establishing state factories when necessary. European merchants and industrialists were invited to come and settle to provide the necessary capital and know-how for private enterprise, thus establishing the powerful colony of foreign residents that, in conjunction with the new dynasty and aristocracy, monopolized much of the political and economic life of the country until the revolution of 1952. He also built a merchant marine and entered into direct diplomatic and commercial contact with the nations of Europe despite his ostensible subservience to the sultan.

This economic success was achieved at a price, however. The Western orientation of Egypt's economy greatly increased its dependence on world markets and made it vulnerable to European economic fluctuations. Foreigners controlled and manipulated the Egyptian economy. The independence and the initiative of large segments of the Subject Class were destroyed in both town and country, with native participation excluded except at the most menial levels.

To carry out these programs and to ensure that the new wealth was efficiently diverted to the treasuries of the state as well as those of the ruler and his family, Muhammad Ali built a modern administrative system. His aim was efficient, autocratic, and centralized government, mainly on French lines. To this end he replaced the partially autonomous tax farmers with salaried officials paid by the treasury and, thus, under its direct control (1806–1814). To secure efficient farm management he encouraged the creation of large estates by members of his own family and other members of the Ruling Class, forming a Turko-Circassian aristocracy that remained a powerful support of the dynasty and shared control of the country with the foreign merchants and bankers. To train men for the new salaried bureaucracy Muhammad Ali built a substantial system of secular schools and imported European teachers. He also issued a system of law codes to build up the power of the bureaucracy, which, under his direct control, extended its authority throughout the country.

In all these efforts he went ahead with a disregard for tradition and with a severity far in excess of other Ottoman reformers. Those who dared to oppose his reforms were suppressed without mercy. The peasants and urban workers soon found that an efficient government was able to force them to pay far more in taxes than they had paid under the old inefficient systems. And when they resisted taxes, conscription, and government controls, they were rapidly dealt with by the new army. When the ulema and guild leaders finally awoke to their loss of power, they also were put in their places, from which they had emerged only briefly during and after the French expedition. Direct governmental control over the institutions of Islam were imposed in the guise of reforms introduced into the Azhar University (1820–1830). The result was a relatively efficient state and army, but at a terrible cost that was to sap the strength of the country during the last half of the nineteenth century.

Conclusion of the War with Russia and England

Mahmut II certainly was impressed by the spectacular successes of his Egyptian governor, but he was restricted not only by his internal political difficulties but also by the urgent need to act against foreign enemies as well as the provincial notables who had gained control of much of the empire. One of the most remarkable aspects of early nineteenth-century Ottoman history was his successful resolution of these foreign and domestic problems before any of the major reforms were introduced or carried out.

Following the Franco-Russian agreement at Tilsit (June 14, 1807) to settle the problems of Europe at least partially by dividing the Ottoman Empire, England, and later France, became convinced that Russia could not be allowed to gain control of Istanbul and the Straits if Europe's balance of power was to be preserved. Bonaparte felt so strongly about this that he abandoned his plan to strike overland against the British in India so as to devote full attention to Europe. Early in October 1808 he imposed his views on Czar Alexander at Erfurt. He stipulated that he would live up to his Tilsit Treaty obligations to support Russia in its war with the Ottoman Empire, which had been going on since 1806, only if the Ottomans were supported by Austria or some other European power, and that if Russia gained control of the Principalities, then both powers would guarantee the integrity of the remaining parts of the empire, including Istanbul and the Straits. Relations between the allies deteriorated after that, leading eventually to Bonaparte's famous Russian campaign beginning late in 1812. England's reaction to Tilsit and its aftermath was to bring its own war with the Ottomans to a rapid conclusion, forcing Mahmut to accept peace by blockading both the Dardanelles and Izmir. In the Peace of Kala-i Sultaniye (the Dardanelles) (January 5, 1809), Britain promised to evacuate all occupied Ottoman territories, including Egypt, in return for peace, and the sultan restored the old British Capitulatory privileges in his empire. Britain agreed to the Ottoman stipulation that the Straits be closed to all foreign warships in time of peace, making this part of international law for the first time. In many ways even more important were the secret agreements that provided that if there was a French attack on the Ottoman Empire, the British fleet would give the sultan all necessary assistance to defend the coasts of the Aegean and Adriatic as well as his frontiers against Austria and Russia. Britain also agreed that if it made peace with Russia, it would work to obtain an Ottoman-Russian peace that would guarantee the continued integrity of the sultan's territories.[38] Thus rivalries among the European powers neutralized Mahmut's enemies and put him at an advantage.

Britain's direct intrusion into the diplomatic affairs of the Middle East was resented by both France and Russia, especially since it was followed by British occupation of the Ionian Islands, previously held by France, and also by efforts to secure an Anglo-Austrian-Ottoman alliance against Russia. Meanwhile, the Russo-Turkish war dragged on. The Russians avoided fulfillment of their previous promise to leave the Principalities and tried to get French help in return for promises to attack Austria if it showed any hostility to Bonaparte. In negotiations with the Ottomans at Jassy, the czar's agents also demanded Bessarabia and major forts in the Caucasus. The sultan ended the negotiations, and the strain between Russia and France increased. Despite Ottoman resistance, the Russians were able to take the remaining Danubian forts of Ismail (December 1809) and Ibrail (January 1810), push through Bulgaria, take Rusçuk, Nicopolis, and Giurgevo (August–September), and cross the Balkan Mountains. Russian assistance encouraged the Serbian nationalists, led by Kara George, to rebuff Ottoman offers to provide autonomy, thus transforming what had started as a revolt against Janissary tyranny in Belgrade into a war for independence from Ottoman rule, even though both the Russians and the French subsequently withheld major assistance in fear of endangering their future position in other parts of the Ottoman Empire.

Ottoman-Russian negotiations and hostilities dragged on, with the Russians hoping for peace to face the threat of a French attack. But the Ottomans refused peace because of the Czar's insistence on retaining all territories taken south of the Dniester. The campaign of 1811 took a turn for the worse insofar as the Ottomans were concerned when the able but aged Grand Vezir Yusuf Ziya was replaced by Laz Ahmet Ağa (April 15, 1811), while Marshal Kutuzoff took command of the czar's forces. The latter soon was able to outflank and rout the main Ottoman army near Rusçuk, forcing the grand vezir to accept a truce and to enter into negotiations at Bucharest (January 1812). It was just at this time, however, that Bonaparte began his famous invasion of Russia (June 1812), forcing the czar to make peace with the Ottomans on Ottoman terms despite the sultan's military weakness. Alexander authorized signature of the Treaty of Bucharest (May 28, 1812), which returned both Moldavia and Wallachia to the sultan along with Little Wallachia, leaving only Bessarabia to Russia. The czar also had to return all his gains north of the Black Sea and in the Caucasus, although he did get the Ottomans to agree to respect Serbian autonomy and to refrain from punishing the Serbs for their role during the war. The Russians did at least regain their commercial position and the right to protect Christians and to station consuls in the sultan's dominions, thus enabling them to instigate revolts and undermine the sultan's rule from within.[39]

Suppression of the Balkan Notables

The Peace of Bucharest and Bonaparte's invasion of Russia gave Mahmut a respite that he used to good advantage to reassert the government's authority in the provinces. When at all possible, the notables were reduced by peaceful means. When a notable holding an official position died, it was not assigned to his heirs, but rather to new officials from Istanbul, who compensated his relatives and followers with appointments elsewhere in the empire. Only when such measures failed was the mainly unreformed Ottoman army used, usually with unexpected and surprising effect. By such methods Thrace, Macedonia, the Danubian shores, and much of Wallachia were taken from the notables and put under direct Ottoman control once again between 1814 and 1820.

The Serbian Revolt

Suppression of the notables in Serbia and Greece was much more difficult, however, since they were involved in incipient stages of national revolutions and therefore had much more popular support. The end of the Russian war enabled Hurşit Ahmet to divert the main Ottoman army from the Principalities to Serbia, where Kara George's centralization policy had alienated the notables and bandits who had at first supported him to gain independence from the Porte. When the Ottomans invaded Serbia from Niş, Vidin, and Bosnia, therefore, they were able to rout his army easily (October 7, 1813) and occupy most of the country, while Kara George fled to refuge in Habsburg territory. The Serbian notables who accepted the restoration of Ottoman rule were appointed *knezes* (princes) of their districts. One of them, a rival of Kara George, Miloş Obrenoviç, led the effort to secure local compliance and was rewarded in return with the appointment as grand *knez* of the central Serbian district of the Shumadia. But many of his countrymen continued to resist, claiming that Kara George was still their leader and inaugurating the feud between the two families that was to continue to modern times. As these Serbs attacked the newly restored Janissary garrisons, the latter replied with the same kind of misrule that had stimulated the Serbian revolt in the first place, causing Miloş himself to take the lead in what now became a second Serbian Revolution starting on Palm Sunday, 1815. Even this, however, was not a true independence movement, for Miloş still considered himself a vassal of the sultan and worked to unite all Serbia under his control in general subservience to the Ottomans. He was helped by events in Europe, where Bonaparte's defeat at Waterloo freed Russia for possible new actions against the Ottomans, forcing Mahmut to make a settlement that made Miloş supreme *knez* of all Serbia and allowed the Serbs to have their own national assembly and army. The Ottomans continued to be represented by the governor of Belgrade as well as by garrisons and feudal *Sipahis* settled on their timars (January 1816). Miloş then used continued Ottoman fear of a new Russian intervention to expand his powers gradually, starting a slow evolution toward complete autonomy under Ottoman suzerainty, which was to be formalized in the Treaty of Edirne (September 29, 1829). The sultan recognized Miloş as hereditary prince of Serbia and agreed to remove all Ottoman garrisons and feudal soldiers from the country, leaving them only in certain forts along the frontier. The Serbs were to pay their taxes in the form of an annual bulk tribute rather than through direct collection by Ottoman officials.

Suppression of the Anatolian Notables

In the meantime, Hurşit Ahmet Paşa suppressed the Anatolian notables by the same combination of trickery and force that had worked so well in the Balkans. The governor of Trabzon eliminated the principal notables along the Black Sea coast during the summers of 1812 and 1813. With the death of Çapanoğlu Süleyman Bey (1814) the local governors were able to exploit divisions in his family to occupy his districts in northeastern and eastern Anatolia during the next two years. The death of Karaosmanoğlu Hüseyin Ağa early in 1816 had the same result around Saruhan and Aydın, though with much more bloodshed than had been the case in Çapanoğlu territories. By the end of 1817, therefore, almost all of Anatolia was once again under direct central control.

Suppression of the Arab Notables

Restoration of direct Ottoman rule in the more distant Arab provinces was far more difficult and less successful. The Saudi/Wahhabi revolt in Arabia was suppressed only with the help of a large Egyptian army brought by Muhammad Ali's son Ibrahim Paşa, who forced Abdullah Ibn Saud to surrender in September 1818, ending the early Saudi state. The Egyptians occupied most of Necd and the Hicaz, and only the most distant provinces remained outside their control (1818–1820). This was not direct Ottoman rule, but it did bring to an end the raids of the Saudis and their supporters into southern Iraq, and the sultan was satisfied. Egyptian presence in the peninsula disintegrated following Ibrahim Paşa's return to Egypt (1822), with the Saudis subsequently rebuilding their state and army in Necd under the leadership of Turki ibn Abdullah ibn Muhammad ibn Saud (1823–1834).[40] In Syria the governor of Aleppo replaced the fractious Janissary garrison and then undertook a series of campaigns that reduced most of the notables in northern Syria and Elbistan (1815–1820), but this was partly negated by Başir II, who extended his Lebanese dominion into a sizable Syrian principality, supplanting most of the notables in the south and ruling unopposed until the arrival of the Egyptians a decade later (1831). In Iraq, Halet Efendi used disputes among the Mamluks to secure the assassination of Süleyman Paşa the Great (1810). But the Mamluks here were too strong for the Ottomans to rule directly, and after a series of weak successors had eliminated each other, rule fell to Davut Paşa (1813–1828), who managed to restore Mamluk domination for another two decades. After his death, tribal groups dominated the country until direct Ottoman rule was restored with the appointment of the famous reformer Midhat Paşa as governor (1869–1872). In addition to the Mamluks in Baghdad, Ottoman rule in Iraq also was threatened during the nineteenth century by Kurdish tribal groups from the north, by the Muntafik and other bedouins again invading from Arabia, and by intervention by the Kacar rulers of Iran, leading finally to a new war in the east.

War with Iran

The war with Iran was the result not so much of Iranian strength and aggression, as had been the case in the eighteenth century, but rather of Iranian weakness in the face of Russian attacks and Iran's desire to compensate with gains against its neighbor to the west. By this time Iran had fallen under the rule of the Kacar dynasty (1794–1925), whose current representative was Fath Ali Şah (1797–1834). Britain, Russia, and France had been competing for his favor. Bonaparte considered Iran an alternative base to Egypt for an attack on the British in India, and Britain in turn sought not only to keep the French out but also to keep the Russians from outflanking the Ottomans in the east and reaching the open sea via the Persian Gulf. Then in 1798 the British gained their first foothold in Iran by encouraging the Kacars to regain control of Afghanistan. In 1800 the Russians conquered Georgia, leading the British to send Sir John Malcolm on a series of missions to Iran and to conclude a political and commercial agreement that promised British arms and money in case of war with either France or Russia. A competing French mission in 1806 offered to support Iranian efforts to reconquer the Caucasus as well as India, leading to the Treaty of Finkenstein with France (May 1807), after which a French military mission trained the Iranian army. Bonaparte, however, lost interest in Iran after Tilsit, leading Fath Ali to replace the French with British advisers, establishing British primacy in the country, which was to last to modern times. But with most of the Iranian army still tribal, the British were able to do little. The Iranians were routed on the Araxes by a new Russian invasion that took the remainder of the Caucasus (October 12, 1815), thus starting the conflict of Russia and Britain for ascendancy that was to dominate Iranian political life for the next century.

While the British worked to rebuild Fath Ali's army, the Russians tried to gain favor by encouraging him to take advantage of Mahmut's domestic and foreign diversions and to compensate for his losses to Russia by retaking some territories from the Ottomans. Persian raids into the areas of Baghdad and Şehrizor followed. A progression of border incidents finally led Mahmut to declare war on Iran (October 1820) and to assign the governor of Erzurum, his old favorite Husrev Paşa, to lead the campaign in the north while the Mamluks of Baghdad were in charge of operations in the south. But it was the Iranians who were successful. One army captured Bayezit (September 1821) and advanced on Erzurum while a second took Bitlis and went toward Diyarbekir with the help of the refugee notables. Eventually, however, cholera devastated the invaders and forced them to seek peace. By the agreement of Erzurum (July 28, 1823) the previous peace terms were restored. Iranian merchants and pilgrims were allowed to enter the sultan's territory once again, and Iranian claims to a few border areas were accepted to secure the peace that was urgently needed to fight the Greek rebels. Further Iranian adventures against the Ottomans were prevented by a new Russian invasion that captured Erivan and even Tabriz (1827) and forced the şah to accept a new boundary along the Aras River and to pay a heavy war indemnity to the victors (1828).

Ali Paşa of Janina and the Greek Revolution

Greek ethnic feeling, long preserved in the Orthodox *millet,* also had found expression through the successes of the wealthy Phanariote Greeks of Istanbul, who had attained significant political and financial power in the empire. The Treaty of Karlowitz (1699) also had made possible a renewal of Ottoman trade relations with Austria and the rest of the Habsburg Empire, with Greece becoming a prosperous middleman for much of the trade of the Mediterranean with Central Europe. The Ottoman treaties with Russia in 1774 and 1794 not only opened the Straits to the commercial ships of Russia and Austria but also specified that the sultan's Greek subjects would be allowed to sail their own ships under the protection of the Russian flag. The diversion of the French and British fleets during the wars of the French Revolution enabled enterprising Greek merchants to develop their own fleets and, in fact, to gain a stranglehold over much of the Ottoman sea trade with Europe – all of which stimulated industry and agriculture in Greece. The prosperity of the Greek merchant class and the growth of Greek mercantile colonies abroad made some Greeks far more aware of European ways and thoughts than were most Ottomans and stimulated the rise of intellectuals, and political leaders who spread the ideas of nationalism as well as revolution and independence.

Most Greeks seem to have been satisfied with their situation in the Ottoman Empire as it was, particularly with the new prosperity. But the conflict between Ali Paşa of Janina and the sultan seems to have prepared the background for revolution and facilitated the activities of the *Philiki Hetairia* (Society of Friends), which began as a small secret society organized originally among Greek merchants living in the Crimea (1814). The organization secured partisans throughout the Ottoman Empire under the leadership of Alexander Ipsilanti, member of a leading Phanariote family, who had gone to Russia to study and had remained to serve in the Russian army. Russia was not actively supporting the movement at this time, and most Greeks still remembered Russian betrayals in their previous attempts at uprisings. But Ipsilanti's membership in the Russian army and the fact that another Phanariote scion, John Capodistrias, was a close adviser of the czar, enabled the society to gain the support of some *millet* and other leaders with the promise of Russian intervention.

Ipsilanti first attempted to raise the people of Wallachia and Moldavia against the sultan to divert the Ottomans from the revolution he was preparing in Greece. Leading a force of Greeks from Russia, he crossed the Pruth into Moldavia (March 6, 1821) and began to march toward Jassy. But what misrule existed in the Principalities had been inflicted by his own Phanariote relatives rather than by the Ottomans, and there was little local inclination to join him, even on the part of Tudor Vladimirescu, a Wallachian peasant then beginning his own peasant revolt against the nobles. Alexander I was so angry when he heard the news that he dismissed Ipsilanti from the army, refused to send any help, and even allowed the sultan to send troops into Moldavia to meet the attack. Ipsilanti's force was routed (June 7, 1812), and he had to flee to Hungary while his followers scattered. The abortive move had no effect in Greece, but it did stimulate a national movement in the Principalities that was to lead ultimately to an end of Phanariote domination and the establishment of Rumanian union and independence.

In the meantime, the *Philiki Hetairia* had been organizing cells in Greece with much more success and with some help from the Orthodox *millet* leaders, who hoped to use it as a lever against the Phanariotes. Prior to 1820 their main obstacle had been Ali Paşa of Janina, the old notable who had been extending his power in

Albania southward into mainland Greece and even the Morea. Halet Efendi still was influential in Istanbul, and, perhaps at the instigation of the Phanariotes, he got the sultan to ignore the *Hetairia* and instead to concentrate on ending Ali's power. Thus began the series of events that was to destroy the last power in the western Balkans capable of putting down the nationalists. Ali Paşa and his sons were dismissed from their official positions, and land and sea expeditions were prepared against them (April 1820). Ali's friends in Istanbul attempted to secure forgiveness for him, but wisely anticipating Halet's eventual triumph he also prepared his defenses at home, attempting to obtain the cooperation of the Greek nationalists in his struggle with Istanbul (May 23, 1820). Ali's friendship was just what the latter needed to gain thousands more adherents around the province. The Porte declared Ali a rebel, Ottoman forces occupied his territories, and he was put under siege in Janina (August 1820), holding out for over a year before shortages finally forced him to surrender on the assumption that he would be granted an imperial pardon. Halet Efendi refused to accept the arrangement, however, and the local commander at Janina, Hurşit Ahmet, had Ali killed (January 24, 1822), thus ending his long rule.[41]

With Ali gone and the Ottoman army then returning to Istanbul, there was no power left in Greece strong enough to suppress the *Hetairia* and its followers. Even while the Ottomans were besieging Ali in Janina, the nationalists began a revolt in the Morea in late March 1821. Within a month many of the Aegean Islands had joined, and the movement spread north of the Gulf on Corinth, although for the most part it consisted of local revolts without central direction or coordination. The Morea, Athens, Thebes, and Missolonghi fell quickly (summer 1822). The Ottomans were able to march in from the north, suppress the outbreaks in Macedonia and Thessaly, and recapture Athens and Corinth, but they could not move south into the Morea in the face of popular opposition. The stalemate then continued for three years. The Ottomans reacted with a general suppression of Greeks elsewhere in the empire, dismissing many from government positions and hanging the patriarch because of his support of the revolt. It was from this point forward that European religious bigotry was to rear its ugly head, with every massacre inflicted on innocent Muslim villagers ignored, while Muslim measures of self-defense were emblazoned throughout Europe as examples of Muslim "brutality."

In the Morea two national assemblies were held (January and December 1822); they proclaimed Greek independence and a new constitution, with Alexander Mavrocordatos, another Phanariote, being elected first president of what was to that point the Greek Republic. Real power, however, remained in the hands of the rebels, including groups of organized land magnates, merchants, and shipowners, who looked for greater profits in a state entirely free from Ottoman control. By 1823 there was a civil war among them, but the Ottomans still were unable to break into the Morea, contributing further to general public dissatisfaction in Istanbul with the Janissaries and the rest of the old army. It was at this point that Mahmut called on the assistance of his still loyal governor of Egypt, who had just won prestige in Istanbul from his son's successful campaigns against the Wahhabis.

Muhammad Ali was receptive to the idea of intervening in Greece not only because of his desire to act as a loyal vassal but also because of his own origins in Albania, his interest in establishing his rule in Greece, and the disruption that the revolt had caused in Egypt's trade with the Aegean. He accepted the sultan's call in return for promises that he would be appointed governor of both the Morea and Crete. Ibrahim Paşa brought an expeditionary force of some 17,000 men to Crete and then to the Morea (February 1825). He overwhelmed the rebels and devastated the countryside as he advanced, while the Ottomans renewed their attacks in the north, pushing the rebel remnants back to Missolonghi, which finally was taken after a long siege (April 30, 1825–April 23, 1826). For all practical purposes, then, the Greek revolution was at an end, and with Ali Paşa of Janina gone and the Serbs cowed, Mahmut II had succeeded in reestablishing centralized control throughout most of his empire.

Background to the Auspicious Event

The sultan had been preparing the way to eliminate the Janissary corps for some time, as we have seen, by appointing his own men to key positions in the corps. He also worked to get the support of the ulema, whose cooperation with the Janissaries had sealed the doom of so many reform measures in the past. Ulema loyal to the sultan were promoted to high positions, while those who opposed him were dismissed or exiled. He also followed a careful policy of observing religious traditions and rituals to win over most ulema. He built new mosques and established religious foundations, required all Muslims to keep their children in the religious schools until a later age, and gave the local imams authority to enforce these regulations. When *Şeyhulislam* Mekkizâde Mustafa Asım Efendi seemed reluctant to go along with the sultan's plans, he was replaced by the much more loyal and energetic Kadizâde Mehmet Tahir Efendi (November 26, 1825–May 6, 1828).[42]

In order to gain the support of the mass of the people, Mahmut worked not only through their natural leaders among the ulema but also through a concentrated propaganda campaign unequaled in Ottoman history. He emphasized his own firmness, resolution, and enlightenment while pointing out the decrepit state of the Janissaries, their inability to defend the empire against its enemies, as shown in the campaigns against the Greeks and Persians, and the contrast between them and the modern and efficient Egyptian army. If Muhammad Ali's ambitions against the Porte were to be given some credence, the situation required immediate attention.[43]

All through the winter and spring of 1826 the sultan met with his close advisers to formulate strategy and make final plans for reforms when the time was ripe. While some proposed establishing modern military units within the Janissary corps itself, Ağa Hüseyin countered this with the argument that it would be impossible to get the cooperation of the lesser corps officers and most of the men and that suppression of the corps was the only solution. The *ağa* of the corps and his chief assistants were persuaded to go along by a combination of argument and bribery.[44]

Formation of the Eşkinciyan Corps

Once the cooperation of the major Janissary officers was assured, Mahmut assembled the chief officials of the Ruling Class and got them to sign a declaration supporting military modernization to save the empire.[45] The grand vezir's secretary then read a regulation that marked a fundamental change in the nature of Ottoman reform. Instead of organizing a new and separate military force, the sultan now declared that reform would take place within the Janissary corps in a select group of active Janissaries (*Eşkinciyan*) composed of 150 of the ablest men in each of the 51 Janissary corps stationed permanently in Istanbul.[46] They would live in the Janissary barracks and train with their fellows during the week, but also would have one day additional practice in the use of rifles and European tactics and organization far from the city, at Kâğıthane and Davut Paşa. They would, however, be subject to the traditional Janissary organization, in a single chain of rank, with command and promotion arranged entirely according to seniority within the chain. The group would be paid by the Imperial Treasury rather than a separate treasury such as the *Irad-ı Cedit*, but its men would get higher salaries to attract the ablest soldiers to its ranks.[47] The extra funds needed for its operation would be secured by modernizing the existing tax system and eventually abolishing the tax farm system so that all revenues would come to the treasury, thus anticipating by some 30 years a policy that would find favor in the period of the Tanzimat.

Enrollment of men for the new force began at once. On June 12 representatives of each of its companies assembled at the Et Meydanı in Istanbul in the presence of a large number of dignitaries to receive their weapons, uniforms, and officers, the latter including two surviving members of the *Nizam-ı Cedit*. Muskets were distributed, and training exercises were begun.[48]

The Janissary Revolt and the Auspicious Event

The Janissaries, however, were yet to be heard from. In fact, a number of the officers who earlier had agreed to support the sultan began to work secretly to organize an uprising to destroy the new force before it could get started. Mahmut tried to counter the fears of the thousands of artisans holding corps pay tickets for revenue by assuring them they could keep them for the remainder of their lives – but this did little to calm the opposition. Mahmut therefore alerted the older corps, which had been somewhat modernized and were loyal to him, in particular the Artillery corps and the garrisons protecting the Bosporus. His fears were well founded. On the night of June 14, only two days after the new force had begun to drill, the Janissaries overturned their soup cauldrons and began to revolt. The next day they were joined by thousands of artisans and others fearing the loss of salaries or simply offended by the sultan's attempt to innovate one of the most traditional institutions of all. Groups of rebels scattered throughout the city, sacking the Porte as well as the homes of supporters of the *Eşkinciyan*. In response the grand vezir summoned the loyal troops and asked leading members of the government and ulema to gather at the Topkapı Palace in support of the sultan, who, in contrast to Selim, rushed in from his summer quarters at Beşiktaş and summarily rejected rebel demands that the new corps be abolished. The standard of the Prophet was unfurled and agents sent throughout the city to urge the faithful to join the attack on the Janissaries who had revolted. The sultan, indeed, had done his work well. With the general populace accepting him as a moderate reformer, acting on the basis of religion and tradition against the corrupt Janissaries, the latter had little chance. The rebels were forced to withdraw to their own barracks at Et Meydanı, where they were quickly put under siege. The artillery finally broke down the barracks' gates and enabled the troops to move in. The rebels found in the drill yard were slaughtered and the buildings set aflame, with all inside perishing (June 15, 1826). Strong measures followed to hunt out the remaining Janissaries in Istanbul and around the empire. The corps itself was abolished the next day, although to assuage popular feeling all those holding payroll tickets who had not been active or involved in the corps' misdeeds were allowed to continue collecting their revenues for the remainder of their lives, as had been promised earlier by the sultan. In most cases the provincial Janissaries were taken by surprise and forced to dissolve without resistance. Where resistance was attempted – at Izmit,

Vidin, and Edirne – force, executions, and banishments were applied, but for the most part corps members were simply absorbed into the general population.

The destruction of the Janissary corps was carried out so smoothly and with such little opposition that the sultan and his advisers were emboldened to go on to end the other institutions connected with it. First to go was the *Bektaşi* order of dervishes, which had provided it with spiritual sustenance and popular support since early times. In Istanbul some of its leaders were executed and its buildings destroyed (July 10, 1826). Throughout the empire its followers were scattered and its properties confiscated and turned over to the ulema for use as mosques, schools, caravansarais, hospitals, and the like. The order, however, continued to survive illegally. It revived after Mahmut's death and continued to flourish until dissolved along with the other dervish orders by the Turkish Republic, after which it has continued to survive surreptitiously to the present day. The *Bektaşis* were followed by the *yamak* auxiliaries and other smaller units allied with the Janissaries, who represented a potential for disorder even though they had not participated as units in the Janissary revolt. The Artillery corps took over the *yamaks'* function of guarding the Bosporus forts, while the *acemi oğlans*, long maintained to train and supply young Janissaries, soon followed the demise of their main object of existence.

Finally, to maintain the support of the principal groups of the Ruling Class, both for the destruction of the Janissaries and the measures that were to follow, Mahmut made various gestures of a practical nature, freely bestowing gifts and promotions, abolishing the old tradition of confiscating the estates of deceased members of the Ruling Class for the benefit of the treasury, and turning the old residence of the Janissary *ağa* over to the *şeyhulislam* as his first official residence. With official and popular support, then, the sultan's actions met with very little reaction, let alone protest, even though there were, of course, individuals who grumbled for one reason or another.[49]

Mahmut II's destruction of the Janissaries and their allies, called the Auspicious Event (*vakayi hayriye*) by the Turks from that time forward, was an event of major importance in Ottoman history. For the first time reform had been undertaken by destroying an old institution, making it possible for the new institutions to function without being hindered by obsolete practices. The other branches of the old Ruling Class also had been deprived of their principal military weapon so that in subsequent years, as Mahmut's example was applied far outside the military sphere, those with vested interests in the old order could resist only with words but not with the kind of violence and force that had disrupted all previous Ottoman reform initiatives.

The New Reformers

In the years preceding the destruction of the Janissaries, Mahmut II had gradually, almost stealthily, filled the high bureaucracies of the Ruling Class with young Ottomans who were energetic, ambitious, loyal to him, and determined to carry out his reform desires. In the remaining 13 years of Mahmut's reign, many of these emerged as leading figures, reforming when they could, often competing among themselves for power, but always remaining the instruments of a sultan who was determined to do what he could to modernize the empire and who himself became the dominant figure in Ottoman politics while pursuing this end.

Many of the early reformers rose in the Scribal Institution but had their careers cut short because of internal intrigues. Most prominent among them was Mehmet Sait Pertev Paşa (1785–1837), a protégé of Galip Efendi, who become leader of the scribes as *reis ul-küttap* (1827–1830) and then lieutenant (*kethüda*) of the grand vezir (1831–1836), holding that office when it was transformed into that of minister of the interior (*umur-u mülkiye nazırı*) in March 1836. Pertev was ousted and soon after put to death (late November 1837) as a result of the intrigues of his rival, Akif Paşa (1787–1845). Akif followed Pertev through the major offices of the Scribal Institution, serving also as *reis* (1832–1835) and as the first minister of foreign affairs (*hariciye nazırı*) in 1835 until ousted by Pertev's intrigues. After Pertev's death, Akif replaced him as minister of the interior in 1837 before himself falling to the plots of Pertev's partisans. Eventually replacing both Pertev and Akif as administrative leader of reform during Mahmut II's later years was a protégé of both of them, Mustafa Reşit Paşa (1800–1858). With their help he first rose in the Scribal Institution, joining Pertev in negotiations with the Russians and Egyptians and so gaining the sultan's favor in the process that he became *âmedi* in 1832, then ambassador to Paris (1834–1835, 1835–1836) and London (1836–1837), and finally foreign minister as well (1837–1839). Mustafa Reşit became the real leader of the Ottoman reform movement even while representing the empire in the difficult negotiations then under way with the great powers of Europe. He trained a substantial group of protégés and entered them into principal offices throughout the scribal and administrative system, so extensively that they remained in command through much of the remainder of the century, long after their master had passed on.

While Reşit led the ministers and scribes, leadership in the military was assumed by the old warrior Husrev Paşa (1756–1855), who had risen as a lieutenant of Ağa Hüseyin during the campaign that drove the French out of Egypt and was the last Ottoman governor of Egypt before Muhammad Ali. During Mahmut's early years, Husrev served in many roles, fighting the notables in Anatolia and the Greek rebels in the Morea and modernizing the fleet as grand admiral (1811–1818), though ultimately being dismissed due to rivalry with Halet Efendi. Following the destruction of the Janissary corps, he was the second commander of the new reformed army and, like Reşit, built his political power by training his own corps of military slaves and entering them into the army and government in the old Ottoman manner.

Finally, in the *Ilmiye* institution, which encompassed the Muslim cultural and religious leaders in the empire, Mahmut worked mainly through Yasincizâde Seyyit Abd ul-Wahhab Efendi, who served as *şeyhulislam* in 1821 and 1822 and rose again to the post after Halet's fall, serving from 1828 to 1833. He was succeeded by another of Halet's opponents, Mekkizâde Mustafa Asım, who had been *şeyhulislam* also in 1818–1819 and 1823–1825, each time falling to conservative pressure. He now held the post well into the reign of Mahmut's successor, Abdulmecit, until his death in 1846, all the while keeping most of the ulema from actively opposing the sultan's reforms.

The New Army

Destruction of the Janissary corps required the creation of an entirely new army, since even the *Eşkinciyan,* being a part of the former, were destroyed with it. The same decree (June 16, 1826) that abolished the already destroyed corps also created the basic organization of the new army that was to replace it, the *Muallem Asakir-i*

Mansure-i Muhammadiye (The Trained Victorious Soldiers of Muhammad), and appointed its first commander (now called *serasker,* or head soldier), Ağa Hüseyin Paşa. He was given control of the Bosporus forts as well as the Nine Towers of Istanbul (the seven towers of Yedi Kule plus the Galata tower and the former tower of the Janissaries, the main observation posts over old Istanbul) and of the police of Istanbul to give him and his army the strength needed to suppress opposition. Recruitment proceeded rapidly in Istanbul. Within three days one regiment was manned by about 1500 men, and training proceeded in the courtyard in front of the Süleymaniye mosque. Soon after, the new army was transferred to the old imperial palace at Bayezit, long a residence for lesser members of the sultan's family, which became the *Bab-ı Serasker* (Headquarters of the Commander in Chief) until the end of the empire, while barracks also were constructed at the same locations as those of Selim III's army, at Davut Paşa, Levent, and Üsküdar.[50] A week later the official regulation for the new army was issued, modeled after the *Nizam-ı Cedit* except in minor details. It was to be composed initially of 12,000 men, all stationed in Istanbul, organized into 8 regiments (*tertips*), each commanded by a colonel (*binbaşı*). Each regiment would have 12 cannons and 12 musket companies. Promotion was to be by seniority, although ability could be considered in exceptional cases. The old salary tickets, so often sold to others in the past, were replaced by a modern salary roll, with members having to be present to receive their pay. Recruits had to be aged between 15 and 30 years. Terms of service were set at 12 years, after which the men could resign if they wished, but without pensions. Retirement with pension could be allowed only because of age or infirmity suffered in the course of duty. Each company was given a religious school led by an imam, who was to train the men in religious principles and lead them in prayer.[51]

The new force was called an army (*ordu*), and, as we have seen, its commander was the head soldier (*serasker*), indicating the sultan's intention for it eventually to incorporate all the fighting forces of the empire. But for the moment it did no more than replace the Janissaries in the military hierarchy, with the other corps remaining as independent as they had been before. Because of the *serasker*'s extra responsibilities in charge of the Bosporus forts and the Istanbul police, however, his office did also assume political power and later developed into a real Ministry of War. As the regulation also established a superintendent (*nazır*) to control administrative and supply matters, at first the *serasker*'s authority was not clear even within the *Mansure* army. But after clashes occurred over finances, Ağa Hüseyin managed to have the post occupied by officials of low rank, leaving the *serasker* supreme.[52]

By the summer of the same year, the army was doing well enough in Istanbul for the sultan to order several governors to raise provincial regiments. Each was organized exactly the same as the original regiments, with trained officers sent from Istanbul. The colonels were directly subordinate to the *serasker* in military matters and to the provincial governors in matters of administration and local policy, while all arms, supplies, and salaries came from Istanbul.[53] The Army Engineering School, continued from the eighteenth century, was expanded to provide needed engineering officers for each regiment, and an engineering department was established at the *Bab-ı Serasker* to organize, assign, and supervise the army engineers. As time went on, corps salaries were raised enormously to get capable men. Additional transport divisions were organized. Regimental bands were introduced on western lines, at first under the direction of Giuseppe Donizetti, brother of the famed composer, who remained in Istanbul for many years and stimulated the rise of Western-style music in the empire (1828–1856).

There were, of course, many problems involved in the creation of a new army, and Ağa Hüseyin, though a brave and able soldier, was basically a man of the old school, not fully sympathetic with the new ways. So Mahmut soon turned to Mehmet Husrev Paşa, who had advocated modernization as early as 1801 after seeing both the British and French forces in Egypt and had modernized the fleet while serving as grand admiral. On May 8, 1827, Husrev replaced Ağa Hüseyin as *serasker*, with additional appointments as governor of Anadolu and *sancak* bey of a number of smaller districts to give him the financial and political power to fight the battles of the new army in and out of the councils of state.[54] Under Mehmet Husrev's energetic leadership the *Mansure* army was modernized along the lines introduced in France since the time of the revolution. The battalion (*tabur*) now was made the basic unit, with internal division into eight musket companies (*bölük*). Regiments (*alays*), consisting of three battalions, were each put under a colonel (*miralay*) and a lieutenant (*kaymakam*).[55] Within a short time there were 10 new battalions in Istanbul and 21 in the provinces, with some 27,000 men. Most of the principal officers came from Husrev's slave group. In general, the regulations of the new army were disguised as much as possible to avoid upsetting the ulema, but the latter knew what was going on and finally secured the right to appoint a preacher to each barracks in addition to the imams to counter the influence of "infidel" innovations.[56]

Reform of the Old Kapıkulu Corps

The surviving corps of the old army were also touched by reform. Mahmut wanted to create an elite imperial guard on the model of those attached to the great ruling houses of Europe, so he simply took the old *Bostancı* corps, long in charge of guarding the imperial palaces and their environs, supplied it with new officers and men, and reorganized it as the "Trained Imperial Gardeners" (*Muallem Bostanıyan-ı Hassa,* usually known simply as the *Hassa*).[57] It was given barracks and training grounds in the Topkapı Palace and soon regained its old job of guarding its gates as well as those of the newer palaces then rising at Dolmabahçe and Beşiktaş along the Bosporus and patrolling the quays of Istanbul. Imams were also assigned to this corps, but they were appointed by and responsible to the director of the imperial library rather than the *şeyhulislam,* thus removing the direct influence of the ulema from this corps at least. Service in the *Hassa* corps was distinguished both by very high salaries and also the possibility of promotion to high positions in the palace or government.[58]

The sultan wanted to parallel the *Mansure* army with a new and Western-style cavalry corps, but he decided not to establish it in Istanbul to avoid high costs and possible opposition to another innovation. So the new Imperial Cavalry Regiment was based at Silistria, on the Danube, where there were many excellent horses as well as horsemen among the nomadic Tatar inhabitants of the Dobruca. It was made part of the *Mansure* army and formed into three groups composed, respectively, of Tatar and Turkish horsemen from the Dobruca and Christian Cossacks who had been pushed across the Danube by the Russian advances into the Ukraine earlier in the century. Each ethnic group was charged with filling vacancies in its own ranks, with individual villages having to furnish a certain number of horses and men according to their size and wealth in return for tax exemptions. Although the Ottomans had employed the Christian troops of vassals as auxiliaries in campaigns and Greek sailors had served in the fleet, this was the first time that Christians were armed and made regular parts of the Ottoman land forces, a matter of some note though it did not attract much attention then, perhaps because of its seclusion at Silistria.

Soon after, Mahmut also established a regular cavalry regiment in Istanbul because of the need for horsemen in official ceremonies and also because of Husrev Paşa's desire to have cavalrymen training with the *Mansure* infantry in simulated battle conditions. The new regiment was included in the *Mansure* army like its Silistrian version, but it was organized exactly like the *Mansure* infantry units and had artillery forces attached to it (February 1, 1827), with 1582 men in all.[59] By the summer of 1827 the corps was sufficiently organized and trained for half its men to be sent to fight in Greece. During late 1827, both cavalry regiments were put under the training command of an Italian captain named Calosso, who introduced French organization and drill, including the new battalion reform. Both regiments served well in the war against Russia. Though some of the Cossacks deserted, causing the sultan to send the rest to Anatolia for the remainder of the war, they were returned to Silistria afterward and continued to serve.

The traditional Ottoman artillery forces were divided among the Cannon corps (*Topçu*) and its auxiliary, the Cannon-Wagon corps (*Arabacı*), as well as the forces charged with caring for the specialized tasks of mining and sapping (*Lağımcıyan*) and mortar bombing (*Humbaracıyan*), all of which had been modernized considerably during the eighteenth century. Selim III had reorganized and partially joined the Cannon and Cannon-Wagon corps (1793), drilling them along Prussian lines, with their financial and supply services united under a single superintendent while their *ağa*s retained separate military authority. Mahmut II worked to increase their numbers and efficiency, but he retained Selim's organization until 1827, adding only a new regiment of mounted artillery and building the force up to about 14,000 cannoneers and 4,414 cannon-wagon men in all, half stationed in Istanbul and along the Bosporus and half in the provinces. Since the artillerymen had made an important contribution to the Auspicious Event, Mahmut left them alone, attaching them to the *Mansure* for military purposes and also using them to police Istanbul while the *Mansure* army was being organized.[60] The superintendent of the Cannon and Cannon-Wagon corps was now made the main military as well as administrative officer of both corps as well as of the foundries and factories attached to them. He shared only matters of discipline and military procedure with the corps' *ağa*s, who thus remained commanders in name alone. The mounted artillery and cannon transport corps now emerged as the most modern and efficient artillery forces in the sultan's service, remaining together in Istanbul rather than being scattered around the empire with the older corps and following the more modern battalion organization under officers responsible directly to the grand vezir.[61]

Among the most important changes introduced in 1827 were requirements that all artillerymen, mounted and unmounted, train regularly with the *Mansure* battalions to foster a spirit of cooperation and to prepare for joint actions against the enemy. Civilian experts were provided for technical matters, while the corps' secretariats were reduced to save on costs. It was very difficult, however, to change the corps in practice, so that the Miners and Bombardiers remained as undisciplined as they had been and the Ottoman artillery overall remained below the standards of the empire's major European enemies both in equipment and manpower.[62]

The remaining *kapıkulu* corps were almost completely reorganized in Mahmut's early years. The Armorers (*Cebeciyan*) corps – previously charged with transporting the Janissaries' weapons and ammunition – was disbanded, and a new Armory corps (*Cebehane Ocağı*) was created to provide and transport military equipment to all the fighting forces of the army.[63] The chief armorer acted as both administrative and technical chief, helped by technical assistants and independent artisans working at the armory or at their own shops under government contracts. The corps was organized so that detachments could be added to the *Mansure* infantry as needed to care for its weapons and ammunition. Similar regulations reorganized the old Tent corps into the *Mehterhane* corps, which was given the job of transporting equipment to the army's camps during campaigns (October 17, 1826). But the division of the task of supplying the various needs of the army among the *Mehterhane*, the Armorers, and the supply services of the individual corps caused inefficiency and duplication of effort. The state factories did become somewhat more efficient, but as time went on, the private artisans supplied a great deal of the equipment and the army became more and more dependent on expensive imports to fill its need, another problem that lasted into the Tanzimat period and beyond.[64]

Reorganization of the Feudal and Irregular Groups

Mahmut hoped to do away with the feudal and irregular groups as soon as possible, but as the danger of a new war with Europe increased, he saw that it would be necessary to use as many of them as could be reactivated and supplied, at least until the *Mansure* army was fully organized. Husrev Paşa persuaded the sultan to order the reorganization of the feudal cavalry as a branch of the *Mansure* army, with feudal holders retaining their revenues but those serving actively being required to accept modern military organization and procedures (February 24, 1828).[65] As in the *Mansure*, the basic unit was the battalion, composed of 889 men and officers and commanded by a major for military matters. The entire task of assigning and administering the fiefs was handled by the battalion's secretariat, which was charged with making certain that the fief income of each man was appropriate to his rank and duties. When feudal officers rose to ranks requiring salaries above the sums provided by their fiefs, they were compensated by the treasury. However, no fief holder was allowed to collect more than 3500 kuruş annually from his fief, and anything over this amount had to be sent to the treasury to compensate for its expenditures for the feudal system. All fief holders were inspected, and those unable to join the active battalions when called were subjected to confiscation of their fiefs. In peacetime, fief holders had to perform active service in rotation, but all had to serve in wartime. As time went on, fief holders unable or unwilling to serve when called were allowed to pay the treasury to hire a replacement, known as a retainer (*cebeli*).[66] In practice, however, it was extremely difficult to get the feudatories to accept the new regulations and to perform active military service or provide compensation. Thus by the end of 1828 only two battalions were up to strength and two more were in the process of organization, indicating that only a very small number of the reputed 30,000 feudatories in existence at the time were willing or able to serve. Soon, therefore, Mahmut saw dissolution of the corps as the only solution.[67]

Services not delivered by the feudatories could be secured from the Turkish nomadic tribesmen (generally called *yörüks*) settled in Rumeli, and long organized under the name *Evlad-ı Fatihân* (Sons of the Conquerors), mainly in Macedonia.

The nomad men had been divided into groups of six, each of which had to send one of its number for active service, in return for which their communities were exempted from all state taxes. The system had provided about 1000 men to the army at a given time, but it had broken down by the nineteenth century, with the communities involved paying special taxes in lieu of service. Mahmut now restored and modernized the corps (March 11, 1828). The villages in question were required to provide enough men to maintain four battalions in the corps, each with 814 men, and to pay the army treasury 1.2 million kuruş annually for their support. Though this substantially increased their obligation in both men and money, fortunately the non-Muslim villages in the areas inhabited by the *Fatihân* now also were required to contribute, thus lessening the obligation of each village. The corps was required to police the village areas in addition to helping the army, all under the authority of the *serasker,* since it now was considered to be part of the *Mansure* army. Village men subject to service went in rotation as before, but they had to train regularly while at home, and all had to come in wartime. They received salaries from the treasury but at lower rates than those for *Mansure* men, since they served only on a part-time basis. The four battalions were actually organized and manned, and two were sent to the Russian front in 1828, but we have no information on the extent of their actual contribution to the war effort.[68]

Reform of the Navy

Selim III had made progress in modernizing the Ottoman navy, but it was neglected during the first half of Mahmut's reign, with the sole exception of Husrev Paşa's short term as grand admiral. Corruption and nepotism again were common, construction and repair came to a halt, and the remaining ships of the fleet wasted away, leaving it with no more than 15,000 officers and men and ten ships of the line compared with over twice those numbers in Selim's later years. Soon after Mehmet Husrev took over the *Mansure* army, however, Mahmut appointed as Grand Admiral Topal Izzet Mehmet Paşa (1827–8), one of Husrev's protégés, who introduced a major reorganization to revive the navy (September 22, 1827).[69] As before, political appointees were at the top, as the grand admiral and *emin* of the Imperial Dockyard (*Tersane*), who administered matters of supply and finance. But under them a permanent professional staff was created led by the scribe of the navy (*kalyonlar kâtibi*), who was charged with advising them on technical matters and translating and applying their orders to meet the real needs of the fleet. The basic naval hierarchy created by Selim III was retained, but salaries were raised to attract qualified men. Only graduates of the Naval School thereafter could be appointed as captains. Incompetents were weeded out, and the remaining force of 8000 men was organized into three divisions, 4200 sailors (*reis*), 3000 cannoneers (*topçu*), and 800 marines (*tüfenkçi*). Clear lines of authority were provided for officers of different ranks aboard ship and on shore, and Naval School graduates were to receive practical training before they were given commands. The Naval Engineering School was enlarged and its curriculum modernized to provide trained officers. The Naval Arsenal similarly was modernized, and strict security was established to prevent theft. A regular supply of timber from southwestern Anatolia was provided so that at least two ships of the line as well as many smaller ships could be built each year. Calls were sent out to the coasts of the Black Sea and Syria for Muslim sailors to replace the Greeks who had formerly performed most of the empire's naval service. But it took time for such drastic changes to be effected, and it still was basically an unreformed fleet that was to sail to disaster at Navarino in 1829.

Internal Problems

As early as the winter of 1826, the development of the army began to slacken and opposition arose as the result of various problems. A severe plague spread through Istanbul, extending also to the *Mansure* barracks, with heavy loss of life. Several fires of unknown origin devastated the old part of the city, destroying even the buildings of the Sublime Porte itself (August 31, 1826). To secure additional funds for recruitment and reform the government took over all the Imperial Foundations, formerly administered by high officials for religious and pious purposes, and administered them through a new Ministry of Religious Foundations (*Nezaret-i Evkaf*), which was supposed to turn all surplus funds over to the treasury for general purposes. This not only gave the treasury large new financial resources but also threatened hundreds of ulema with the loss of their pensions and undermined the financial power of the ulema, who were left with control only of the foundations established to support the Holy Cities of Mecca and Medina.[70] Those benefiting from tax farms were similarly threatened late the same year by an order that required that the larger ones be taken over and administered directly by a new military treasury (called the *Mukata'at Hazinesi*) created to support the *Mansure* army. A similar treasury was established to support the fleet (*Tersane Hazinesi*).[71] A new market excise tax, the "Holy War Taxes" (*Rüsumat-ı Cihadiye*), was imposed on shops and markets for the benefit of the military treasury.[72] And finally, though the sultan had promised to pay lifetime pensions to surviving Janissary corps members, so many of those who applied were imprisoned and executed that the remainder chose to forgo their claims, while many others were wrongfully caught up in the process to eliminate active Janissaries, creating a climate of fear around the empire.[73] In consequence, it is not surprising that opposition to the sultan and his reforms began to spring up everywhere, not only among former Janissaries and conservatives but also among the ulema, artisans, merchants, and even former partisans of reform who were affected in some way or other by the sultan's financial and military policies.

There were, indeed, problems in building the new army. It was difficult to secure sufficient trained officers. Muhammad Ali had not formed his new force in Egypt until after Colonel Sève had trained 500 officers for it previously (1816–1819). But the Ottomans went ahead and modernized the army without such a pool, so that many incompetents rose to command and gained promotions through the same conditions of nepotism and favoritism that had ruined the old army.[74] The sultan tried to solve the problem first by establishing an elite corps of youths trained in his own palace service, the *Enderun-u Hümayun Ağavatı Ocağı* (Corps of *Ağa*s of the Imperial Palace Service), to provide officers for the *Mansure* army, basically thus restoring the old *gulâm* system that had produced so many Janissaries and ministers in the past. He enrolled some 250 slaves from his own household as well as sons of Ruling Class dignitaries who were already training as palace pages. They were organized on the model of the *Mansure* and trained under the direction of former *Nizam-ı Cedit* officers as well as the cavalry expert Captain Calosso (who took the name Rüstem Bey) and Donizetti.[75] The corps soon expanded to about 400 youths. Its graduates entered the army as vacancies occurred, rising very rapidly and soon almost monopolizing the officer corps. They did provide a certain uniformity and discipline, but the favoritism thus shown to the graduates of the sultan's court school caused discontent among the other officers in the *Mansure* army. Many members of the palace corps also became more interested in palace life than in military training. Their discipline and expertise declined accordingly, and they began to be a cause of disorder rather than order in the army, so that the corps finally was abolished altogether in May 1830.[76] Mahmut found it almost impossible to hire foreign officers, since the European powers now were preparing to intervene on behalf of the Greek rebels while Muhammad Ali was not at all anxious to strengthen the army of the sultan he soon was to attack.[77]

The only solution was a new system of military technical education to train Muslim Ottomans as officers. For youths below the minimum enrollment age for the *Mansure* army a special training center (*Talimhane*) was organized in the former barracks of the old *Acemi oğlan* corps. Students were trained in infantry drill as well as religion and crafts, and when they reached the age of 15, they entered the army as regular soldiers or as corporals or clerks if they were qualified.[78] A similar school was provided in the palace for the slaves and upper-class boys enrolled in the sultan's new *Hassa* corps.[79] As noted, the Naval Engineering School and Army Engineering School were enlarged and reinvigorated, and in March 1827 an Army Medical School (*Tıbhane*) was opened.[80] But in all of these enrollment was limited, students were not prepared, and instruction was poor. Progress was made, but it was very slow, and the results were hardly adequate to rescue the army from the incompetents who continued to lead it long after the destruction of the Janissary corps. Hence by the end of 1828 the Ottoman army had about 50 active battalions in all, with an effective strength of between 30,000 and 35,000 officers and men, mainly in the *Mansure* and *Hassa* forces, with an additional 20,000 men in the feudal cavalry and the artillery and the innumerable irregulars subject to the sultan's call – but their organization, discipline, leadership, and training still were very questionable.[81]

The Greek Revolution

In addition to the internal problems, Mahmut II's foreign enemies left him with little repose during the years following the destruction of the Janissaries. The death of Czar Alexander and the accession of Nicholas I late in 1825 placed Russia in the hands of a monarch willing to use force to gain his ends, particularly in the Morea and Crete, where he feared the rise of Muhammad Ali as an obstacle to his own ambitions. Britain was leaning away from open support of the Porte and toward an effort to mediate a settlement in Greece, in conjunction with the Russians, to avoid a new Russo-Ottoman war that might prove disastrous for the latter. On March 17, 1826, Russia sent an ultimatum to the sultan demanding full restoration of the privileges of the Principalities and the autonomy of Serbia, as provided in the Treaty of Bucharest (1812). Under British pressure, Mahmut gave in to the Russian demands and signed the Convention of Akkerman (October 7, 1826), adding recognition of Russian domination of the Caucasus and allowing Russian merchant ships the right of free access to all Ottoman waters, including the Straits.[82] Russia, however, continued to pressure the Ottomans to give in to the Greek rebels, and it proposed joint intervention with Britain to accomplish this end. The latter attempted to avoid a situation that would require it to help Russia in the Middle East, instead joining Metternich in pressuring Mahmut to accept allied mediation to avoid giving Russia a pretext for intervention on its own.

In Istanbul, Akif Paşa led a strong group that supported the sultan's reforms but deeply resented the foreign intervention and advised Mahmut to make war on the Russians in order to regain lost territory and prestige. Mehmet Husrev, Galip Paşa, Grand Vezir Selim Paşa, and others, on the other hand, insisted that the empire still lacked the men and resources to fight the Russians successfully and advised acceptance of the mediation offers.[83] Mahmut leaned toward the former group's advice. He informed the powers that he was the legal ruler of Greece and that the rebels had to be crushed; he sent the allied Ottoman and Egyptian forces in Greece ahead, enabling them to continue their advance and to capture Athens in June 1827. In response, Britain was pushed into signing a new treaty at London with France and Russia (July 6, 1827) providing for joint intervention if either party refused mediation. When Mahmut continued to resist, the allied fleets moved into the eastern Mediterranean and blockaded the Dardanelles as well as the Morea to cut off new supplies to the Ottoman forces, although they were instructed not to engage in actual warfare with either the Ottomans or the Egyptians, a very fine point indeed (early September 1827). In response, the Egyptian ships that had brought Ibrahim Paşa and his men to the Morea joined the main Ottoman fleet at anchor at Navarino, which was put under close blockade in early October by the allied squadrons. The allies first withdrew toward Zanta hoping to lure the Ottomans into battle in the open sea, but the latter remained at anchor. Finally, on October 20, the allies began to enter the harbor, publicly declaring their hope of convincing Ibrahim Paşa to return to Egypt but in fact intending to open battle. When met with an Ottoman fire ship sailing toward them, the allied ships replied with an intense artillery barrage that completely destroyed some 57 Ottoman and Egyptian ships and killed 8000 soldiers and sailors within three hours. With the kind of attitude that was to characterize European relations with the Porte during the remainder of the century, the allies blamed the Ottomans for the battle because of their attempt to resist the move into the harbor!

The Battle of Navarino was of immense importance to all parties. It completely destroyed the new Ottoman fleet, cut Ibrahim Paşa off from reinforcements and supplies from home, and assured the Greek rebels of ultimate victory. In a sense also it provided the pattern for a series of European interventions in Ottoman affairs that was to reduce the empire to what appeared at times later in the century to be a puppet dancing at the end of an imperialistic string. But it did not mean the end of the war. Although Britain and France hoped that Navarino would force the Ottomans to accept mediation, it had the opposite effect: Akif and Pertev joined in pressuring the sultan to resist any settlement, despite the Akkerman agreement, getting him to call all Muslims to arms to resist the Russians and Greeks (December 18) and to close the Straits to all foreign ships (February 5, 1828). The czar, just freed from a nagging war with Iran (1827), did not really want mediation now, but instead used the situation to fulfill his ambition to break up the Ottoman Empire by force. In response to Mahmut's determination, Nicholas declared war (April 28, 1828). Within a week his troops were marching once again into Moldavia as well as through the Caucasus and into eastern Anatolia, while his Mediterranean fleet began to supply large amounts of arms and ammunitions to the Greek rebels. At this point the death of George Canning (August 8, 1827) and his replacement with the less decisive Duke of Wellington left Britain unable to act, with the duke not wishing to do anything that might upset cooperation with the Russians even though he too feared their advances into the Middle East.

War with Russia

With the Janissary corps and the navy gone and the *Mansure* army still in the process of training, it was difficult for the sultan to organize successful resistance. His armies in the Balkans, now commanded by Ağa Hüseyin Paşa, consisted mainly of the Tatar and feudal irregulars. Mahmut tried to get ships from his Algerian vassals, but they were being blockaded by the French as the first step of a campaign to occupy that part of the empire. Muhammad Ali responded to the sultan's appeals for help with an offer of some money, adding a subsequent offer of troops only if he were given a governorship in Anatolia in return.[84] A supply system was set up to support the troops along the frontiers, but what could be sent was often delayed or lost due to poor roads and corrupt local officials. On the other hand, the Russians had some 100,000 men ready to attack, and they made rapid advances into the Principalities in three columns, the first taking Ibrail (June 16) and flooding into the Dobruca, the second attacking Silistria, and the third acting defensively to keep the Ottoman garrisons busy along the Danube from Rusçuk to Vidin (October 11, 1828).[85] In central Bulgaria the Ottomans were relatively successful, with Husrev Paşa making Silistria and Şumla the bases for his entire defense and holding on to them against fierce attacks. To the east the Russians did quite well, advancing along the eastern coast of the Black Sea, taking Anapa and Ahıska, and then moving into eastern Anatolia to take Kars (July 1828) with the assistance of the local Armenian populace. Thus did the so-called Armenian Question have its beginning. In the meantime, the allies got Muhammad Ali to withdraw his troops from the Morea (October 1828) and to turn key positions over to the new Greek government led by John Capodistrias. A new tripartite agreement signed in London provided for a relatively small but autonomous Greek state, including territory from Volo on the Aegean to Arta in the west as well as Crete and a number of Greek islands, ruled by a hereditary prince invested by the sultan and paying him an annual tribute. British fears of Russian supremacy in the new state prevented it from being given any more land or independence.

Husrev Paşa had been able to organize staunch resistance in many places in 1828, but the following year's campaign was disastrous. Many of the new recruits were young and completely untrained, and the spread of plague as well as food shortages caused by the continued Allied naval blockade contributed to a high mortality rate. By the summer of 1829 Ottoman resistance had collapsed. The Russians moved through the passes of the Balkan Mountains, bypassing Şumla and taking Edirne after a siege of only three days (August 19–22).[86] In Anatolia the Russians took Erzurum (July 8, 1829) and moved toward Trabzon, with their mounted forces reaching even farther west.[87] The game was up, and the terrified sultan asked the powers to mediate a settlement.

The Treaty of Edirne

Russia now was in a position to occupy the rest of the Ottoman Empire, but it did not do so because this would have been opposed by its European friends as well as enemies. Instead, the czar resolved to make a peace that would leave the Ottoman

Empire intact but too weak to prevent the spread of Russian influence or to frustrate Russian advances in the future. In the peace treaty of Edirne (September 14, 1829) the territorial provisions were harsh, but not as bad as they might have been. Russian troops were to evacuate all their conquests south of the Pruth, including the Principalities, Dobruca, and Bulgaria. But the czar was to retain control of the mouths of the Danube and have the right of free trade along its course, while the Ottomans had to agree to establish no fortifications along it or the Pruth, thus leaving the Russians easy access to Ottoman territory in case of a new war. In the east the Russian gains were much more extensive. The sultan accepted Russian acquisitions in the Caucasus, including Georgia and the areas of Nahcivan and Erivan recently taken from Iran, and the czar returned only the east Anatolian cities of Erzurum, Kars, and Bayezit. The Russians also subsequently interpreted the treaty to signify consent to their control of Circassia, though this had never been part of the Ottoman Empire and was not actually mentioned. Even more important were provisions establishing the autonomy of Serbia, Greece, and the Principalities under Russian protection and granting to Russia the same Capitulatory rights in the Ottoman Empire enjoyed by the subjects of other European states. The Ottoman Empire was required to pay Russia a war indemnity of 400 million kuruş over a period of ten years, a terrible burden on a state whose annual budget at the time was no more than half that amount, even though the sum subsequently was reduced in return for additional territorial concessions to Greece.[88]

The First Egyptian War, 1831–1833

The end of the war with Russia and settlement of the Greek Question did not end Mahmut's military involvements or territorial losses. In 1830 the powers forced him to accept full Greek independence and, two years later, to establish Samos and the Cyclade Islands as an autonomous principality under Greek rule. On July 5, 1830, after a blockade of three years, the French conquered Algiers and began spreading through the countryside, thus taking the sultan's most important North African possession. Soon afterward (August 29), he was forced to widen the privileges granted the autonomous Serbian state, recognizing the hereditary rule of Miloş Obrenoviç and giving him six additional districts from the provinces of Vidin and Bosnia. And, worst of all, he soon was engaged in a disastrous war with his Egyptian governor. Muhammad Ali had emerged from his involvement in the Greek Revolution with considerable prestige but little compensation for the expenditures that he had made to help the sultan. Greek independence had deprived him of the territories that he had expected to rule as a reward. He had asked for Syria, only to be offered Crete, which he rejected, since it had been in a constant state of revolt since the start of the Greek Revolution and promised to cost him far more than he could secure from it in taxes and other revenues. When urged by the allies to withdraw his forces from Greece, he had complied without consulting the sultan. During the subsequent war with Russia, as we have seen, he reneged on earlier promises to send troops, and he also urged his friends in northern Albania to revolt against the sultan. This led Mahmut to order the governor of Syria to prepare for an Egyptian attack. When the letter fell into Muhammad Ali's hands, he saw that his request for Syria was being rejected and decided to attack in order to obtain what he considered to be just compensation. His pretexts were minor: The Ottomans had failed to return some 6000 *fellahin* who had fled into

Syria during the war; and the governor of Acre had neglected to pay him money owed as his contribution to the war effort. Soon afterward, Ibrahim Paşa led a combined land-sea expeditionary force into Syria. Within a short time he took Gaza, Jaffa, Jerusalem, and Haifa, then Acre after a siege (November 16, 1831–May 27, 1832). With the help of the emir of Lebanon, Başir II al-Şihabi, the rest of Syria, Sidon, Beirut, Tripoli, and finally Damascus (June 18, 1832) also passed into Ibrahim's hands.

The Ottoman reaction was very slow in coming. In March 1832 Mahmut officially declared Muhammad Ali and his son rebels, dismissed them from their positions, and appointed Ağa Hüseyin, now governor of Edirne, to lead the campaign against them. By this time Ibrahim had established his defenses and made promises of Arab self-rule to gain local support. Thus when the Ottoman troops finally entered Syria, it was they rather than the Egyptians who were treated as foreign invaders. The modern Egyptian army easily prevailed over the Ottomans in two battles in early July, at Homs and Belen, between Alexandretta and Antioch. Muhammad Ali then stopped his son's advance, hoping to secure all of Syria by negotiations with the sultan or through mediation of the powers without further bloodshed. But Mahmut was adamant, especially since Britain, while refusing his pleas for help, was not pressing him to settle. Despite the efforts of Stratford de Redcliffe to secure an Anglo-Ottoman alliance and those of Palmerston to do something to prevent the Ottomans from turning to Russia, Britain remained preoccupied with elections at home and problems in Belgium and Portugal. Austria was committed to supporting its Russian ally, which in turn was only waiting for events that would enable it to increase its influence in the Ottoman Empire.

Mahmut, therefore, went ahead preparing a new army against Muhammad Ali, this time commanded by Grand Vezir Reşit Mehmet Paşa, Husrev's protégé and ally. In the meantime, once diplomatic efforts had proved unsuccessful, Ibrahim Paşa led his army through Cilicia onto the Anatolian plateau, where he gained support from those who opposed the sultan for one reason or another and occupied Konya on November 21. Reşit Mehmet tried to cut off the Egyptians from their supplies in Syria, but Ibrahim led his forces out of Konya and routed the Ottomans nearby (December 21), thus in a single blow opening the way for a complete conquest of Anatolia, although Muhammad Ali was still posing as the sultan's loyal subject acting only to secure what was due him in Syria.

The Ottoman disaster at Konya stimulated Czar Nicholas to do something to prevent the establishment of a powerful new Middle Eastern state that could and would resist Russian penetration far better than the Ottomans had been able to do. As the British and French offered no concrete assistance, Mahmut turned to the czar, resulting in the arrival in Istanbul on December 25 of a Russian military mission to prepare for the arrival of Russian troops. In reaction to this the French and British emissaries in Cairo got Muhammad Ali to agree to accept mediation for a settlement that would assure his rule in Syria. But Ibrahim Paşa advanced again, occupying Kütahya (February 2, 1833), and asked the sultan's permission to spend the winter in Bursa, only 50 miles from the capital. Mahmut was now thoroughly frightened, and in reaction he granted permission for a Russian fleet to come through the Black Sea to help defend Istanbul and for a Russian army to march through the Principalities. The former arrived in the Bosporus on February 20, and Russian soldiers settled into their tents across the Bosporus, at Hünkâr Iskelesi, shortly thereafter. This alarmed the French and British even more, and their ambassadors in Istanbul got the sultan to agree to get the Russian troops out and to give Syria to Muhammad Ali (but without Cilicia) as the basis for a settlement; at the same time they threatened the latter with a blockade of his coasts and the withdrawal of French military assistance if he refused to cooperate (February 21, 1833). Despite this pressure, however, Ibrahim's advances emboldened Muhammad Ali to demand more, including Cilicia, and to threaten a march on Istanbul if the sultan did not agree (March 9, 1833). When the Russians admitted that they would be unable to send troops in time to defend Istanbul from the Egyptians, Mahmut caved in and granted all the Egyptian demands if only Ibrahim's troops were withdrawn. At the same time, he invited the Russians to land their troops at Büyükdere, on the European side of the Bosporus, to put them in a position to help defend Istanbul in case Ibrahim made a surprise attack. Their landing (April 5) created consternation in Istanbul, particularly among the ulema and the populace, who opposed the use of infidels against Muslims however threatening the latter might be. But the Russian presence convinced Ibrahim that it would no longer be practical for him to entertain wider ambitions. Thus new negotiations were opened in Kütahya, with the sultan represented by a young âmedi, Mustafa Reşit Efendi (later Paşa). The result was an agreement (March 29, 1833) granting Ibrahim the governorships of Damascus and Aleppo and also the post of muhassıl of Adana. The latter concession so angered the sultan that he ordered Mustafa Reşit's execution but was dissuaded by the latter's political allies. Muhammad Ali was confirmed as governor of Egypt and Crete, and Ibrahim also was made governor of Cidde, thus establishing their position in control of much of the Arab world. Ibrahim soon evacuated Anatolia, and the crisis seemed to be over.

The Treaty of Hünkâr Iskelesi

Czar Nicholas, however, was not satisfied with a direct Ottoman-Egyptian settlement. He wanted to perpetuate Russian domination and the diminution of the traditional French and British influence in Istanbul. Thus in response to Mahmut's previous request for a defensive alliance against the possibility of Egyptian attack, he sent the able diplomat A. F. Orlov, whose negotiating skill produced the famous Ottoman-Russian treaty signed at the Russian camp at Hünkâr Iskelesi, which incorporated most of the czar's ambitions (July 8, 1833). The Treaty of Edirne was confirmed. Each party agreed to help the other if its territories were attacked during the next eight years, with the nature and cost of such help to be determined by subsequent negotiation. The Russians secretly repudiated the need for Ottoman help, with the sole exception of a promise by the sultan to close the Straits to foreign ships of war in wartime, thus assuring Russia that its Black Sea coast would be free from naval attack from Britain, France, or any other enemy.[89]

The treaty in fact went no further than several other alliances previously signed by the Porte with Britain and France as well as Russia, and its references to the Straits did no more than incorporate the generally accepted provisions of international law concerning international waterways in wartime. But Palmerston and his colleagues in Paris and Berlin interpreted the agreement through the czar's eyes and in the light of the czar's intentions, fearing that it really gave Russia a special position in Istanbul as well as the right to intervene in case of future crises. That these fears later proved to be false – with the Ottoman Empire continuing to seek out and accept the advice and help of all its European "friends" – did not prevent France and England from falling into such a state of Russophobia that thereafter they were determined to defend Ottoman survival in order to keep the Russians out, opposing subsequent efforts of Muhammad Ali and others to upset the situation and create a power vacuum that the czar might use to his benefit.

New Unrest at Home

Settlement of the major foreign crises freed Mahmut II to concentrate on internal reforms for the first time since the destruction of the Janissaries, but the severe defeats inflicted by the Egyptians as well as by powers purporting to be friends led to increased internal opposition during the rest of his reign, particularly in the light of the economic and financial rigors that were the result of both the reform efforts and the wars. Revolts followed in Anatolia, Bosnia, Macedonia, and Iraq, and with the relative weakness of the army, they were only partially put down. In addition many ulema, especially those on the lower levels, who had at least remained neutral to his reforms, now turned against him, attributing the defeats to the reforms and complaining about what they considered to be the sultan's infidel ways as well as the presence of foreigners in the capital. Mahmut's use of the *Mansure* army to suppress the unrest only added to the discontent.[90]

New Awareness and Beginnings of the Ottoman Press

Despite all these difficulties, Mahmut emerged from the wars an even more dedicated advocate of reform than before, now extending its scope to include all aspects of Ottoman life, not only the military. He began to develop a program that, though only partly carried out during the remaining six years of his reign, provided the backbone and model for the Tanzimat reform era that followed.

Mahmut cultivated an interest in what went on outside the palace. He began to go out to see what the actual problems of the empire were, how his regulations were working, and what in the life style of the Europeans gave rise to the ulema's objections. He also worked to broaden horizons by developing an Ottoman press, not only for the publication of books but also to provide regular Ottoman newspapers in the empire. French newspapers had been published in Istanbul as early as 1796 and in Izmir since 1824, but these were available only to the small foreign communities and did not reach the mass of his subjects, let alone members of the Ruling Class. Mahmut wanted to enlighten his subjects, not only about his reform efforts in reaction to the complaints of his opponents, but also to give them regular information about what was happening in and out of the Empire, to make them participants in contemporary European civilization. Muhammad Ali's *Vekayi-i Mısriyye* (Events of Egypt) had begun publication in 1829. Two years later, on July 25, 1831, Mahmut followed suit with the first Ottoman-language newspaper, the *Takvim-i Vekayi* (Calendar of Events), issued by the government on a more or less weekly basis to provide copies of the laws and decrees then being issued as well as news of events in and out of the empire. The French version, the *Moniteur Ottoman,* was issued periodically to provide news of interest to Europeans resident in the empire.[91] Even though no more than 5000 copies of the former and 300 of the latter were printed and their circulation was limited to high officials and foreign embassies, their readership and impact were much wider and the way was opened for the development of a substantial Ottoman press in subsequent years.

The Reformers

Mahmut still worked through the cadre of reform officials that had helped shape his earlier plans, Pertev Paşa in interior affairs; Akif in foreign affairs; Husrev and his protégés, and later rivals Halil Rifat and Sait Mehmet in the military; and, finally, Mustafa Reşit Paşa, who during his first term as foreign minister (1837–1838) prepared reform programs in many areas and convinced the sultan to carry through many of them. Grand Vezirs Reşit Mehmet Paşa (1829–1833) and Mehmet Emin Rauf Paşa (1833–1839) acted mainly as political mediators, attempting to balance conflicting interests while participating in the factional activities and disputes endemic in Ottoman governmental life. Mahmut and his successors followed Selim's old policy of appointing political rivals to positions where they could watch and check each other, keeping them relatively balanced so that the sultan could control and use all of them, but in the process further exacerbating the divisions among the reformers.

The Central Government

Mahmut's desire to achieve increased centralization necessitated changes first of all in the structure of the central government in Istanbul, generally involving denigration of the traditional power of the military and religious classes in favor of an ever-expanding bureaucracy of administrators and scribes centered in the palace and the Sublime Porte. Selim III's reform policies had left the old Imperial Council, once the center of Ottoman governmental life, mainly supplanted by the Sublime Porte (*Bab-ı Âli*). The latter was directed by the grand vezir and *reis ul-küttap* through subordinate sections devoted respectively to domestic and foreign affairs, though the Imperial Council also survived, with no clear delineation of authority or function between its powers and those of the Porte. In response to the need for specialized knowledge and efficiency in administration, Mahmut began the process by which the central government was divided by function into departments and ministries and, eventually, by which the executive and legislative functions were separated, though in the process he left a struggle for power between palace and Porte that was to continue right into the twentieth century.

The executive came first. The offices of the *serasker* (commander in chief) and the grand admiral had been functioning as equivalents of ministries for some time. Now they were given real ministerial organization so that they could accomplish their tasks with some efficiency. In addition, the office of the lieutenant of the grand vezir (*sadaret kethüdası*) was transformed into the Ministry of the Interior (called first Ministry of Civil Administration Affairs, or *Umur-u Mülkiye Nezareti*, in 1836, and then, after Pertev was ousted, simply Ministry of the Interior, or *Nezaret-i Dahiliye*), retaining this title even after it was joined to the grand vezirate in 1838 to give the occupant of that office sufficient administrative authority to establish his primacy among the ministers.[92] On March 11, 1836, the office of *reis ul-küttap* was transformed into the Ministry of Foreign Affairs (*Nezaret-i Hariciye*), and the first minister, Pertev Efendi, included domestic reform matters within its purview, establishing a practice that was retained during the rest of the century. Within the Porte the *Âmedi* department, whose scribes had handled both domestic and foreign affairs in support of the grand vezir and the *reis*, was now simply divided between the two ministries.[93] The *Çavuşbaşı* and *Tezkereci* departments of the Porte were organized into the Ministry of Judicial Pleas

(*Nezaret-i Deavi*), later called the Ministry of Justice (*Nezaret-i Adliye*). The Army Treasury (*Mansure Hazinesi* or *Mukata'at Hazinesi*), which by now collected most state revenues to provide for the rapidly increasing expenditures of the armed forces, was transformed into the Ministry of Finance (*Nezaret-i Umur-u Maliye*), assuming the financial duties of the former Imperial Treasury (*Hazine-i Amire*), as well as those of the Treasury of the Mint (*Darphane Hazinesi*), and leaving only the Treasury of the Sultan (*Ceb-i Hümayun*) as an independent financial organ, although it had to depend on the new ministry for at least part of its revenues.[94] Finally, outside the Porte itself, the *şeyhulislam* was given the former headquarters of the Janissary *ağa*, near the Süleymaniye mosque, as a center for his own department, which came to include not only his traditional functions as leader of the *Ilmiye* class and grand mufti but also those of directing the operation of the entire system of courts formerly directed by the *kazaskers* of Anatolia and Rumeli, who now were his subordinates. The resulting *Bab-ı Meşihat* (Abode of the *Şeyhulislam*) thus became the center for an administrative organization and hierarchy of ulema very similar to and parallel with those being developed in the other ministries of government.[95] The Ministry of Religious Foundations established just before the Egyptian war to handle all the Imperial Foundations except those of the Holy Cities was joined to the Imperial Mint (*Darphane-i Amire*), which already administered the latter, thus uniting the finances of all the foundations in a single department and making it the second most important treasury in the governmental system.[96]

Economics was not considered important enough for a full-fledged ministry, particularly since foreign trade was assigned to the Ministry of Foreign Affairs. But in 1838 a Council of Agriculture and Trade (*Meclis-i Ziraat ve Ticaret*), soon afterward transformed into the Council of Public Works (*Meclis-i Nafia*), was created to discuss and propose programs to improve agriculture, industry, domestic trade, and public works, although it was put under the direction of the Foreign Ministry so as not to threaten the latter's overall power.[97] It was only a year later, after its functions were carefully defined to emphasize internal economic development, that it was established as a regular Ministry of Trade (*Nezaret-i Ticaret*), with separate councils within its structure to handle matters of agriculture, public works, and trade.[98]

Finally, with the grand vezir now being less the absolute lieutenant of the sultan that he had been in earlier times and more a coordinator of the activities of the ministers, his title was changed officially (though usually not in usage) to prime minister (*baş vekil*). Theirs were changed from supervisor (*nazır* or *vezir*) to minister (*vekil*), even though they were individually appointed by and responsible to the sultan rather than to the prime minister. Within these limitations, a cabinet – variously called *Meclis-i Hass-ı Vükelâ* (the Sultan's Council of Ministers), *Meclis-i Hass* (the Sultan's Council), or *Meclis-i Vükelâ* (Council of Ministers) – was created under the chairmanship of the prime minister to coordinate the executive activities of the ministries and, thus, form the policy of "the government" and also, and in the Ottoman context much more important, to pass on legislative proposals and submit them to the sultan.[99] The center of these activities, the Sublime Porte, whose wooden buildings already had been destroyed several times by fire and were to suffer the same fate several times more in the later years of the century, was rebuilt so that it could house not only the offices of the grand vezir and the Imperial Council but also those of the more important ministries.

What of legislation itself? The old system, wherein all laws were considered by the Imperial Council before being issued in the sultan's name as *fermans*, or in important matters bearing his signature as imperial rescripts (*hatt-ı hümayun*), was inadequate for handling extensive and complex legislation. Neither the new cabinet nor the ministers themselves had the time and expertise to consider every proposal in detail. To fill this need, at the recommendation of Mustafa Reşit, the sultan created a series of advisory councils early in 1838, each composed of distinguished current and former officials, both to review legislative proposals and to originate new ones. The Supreme Council of Judicial Ordinances (*Meclis-i Vâlâ-yı Ahkâm-ı Adliye*) was to meet in the palace itself with the purpose of creating an "ordered and established" state by means of "beneficent reorderings" (*tanzimat-ı hayriye*) of state and society. The name of the reform movement that was to result from its work, Tanzimat, was thus derived from the decree establishing this council. The Deliberative Council of the Sublime Porte (*Dar-ı Şurayı Bab-ı Âli*) was to meet at the Porte to consider other legislation, except that concerning the military, which was left to a third council, the Deliberative Council of the Army (*Dar-ı Şurayı Askeri*) which met at the *Bab-ı Serasker* (March 24, 1838). The councils began meeting weekly, with the sultan sometimes in attendance, particularly at the Supreme Council. Though members at first were supposed to serve part time while continuing their regular official duties, within a short time they were allowed to devote their entire service to these councils. They then began to discuss not only matters submitted to them but also, in the absence of contrary instructions, other matters that they deemed important, thus in fact intervening directly in matters officially considered within the scope of the ministers and functional departments. Their findings and recommendations were incorporated into protocols (*mazbata*) presented for the approval of the Council of Ministers, which also added its opinions and recommendations for changes when desired. Still at the top of the new legislative process was the sultan. But with the grand vezir now clearly devoted to the affairs of the Porte, the sultan's private secretary (*baş kâtib-i şehriyari*) became the official in charge of checking and communicating the facts of each case and the opinions of the relevant ministries and councils to the sultan. He also communicated the latter's decision in writing at the base of the document conveying the grand vezir's recommendation, an inscription whose name, the *irade* ("will" of the sultan) thereafter was applied to all such imperial orders in place of *ferman*, with *hatt-ı hümayun* being used only for those documents to which, as before, the sultan's personal signature was affixed.

In 1835 the entire bureaucracy of the Ruling Class was reorganized into three divisions, with the old Imperial and Scribal classes being brought together in the Scribal Class/*Kalemiye*, while the Military/*Seyfiye* and Religious and Cultural/ *Ilmiye* classes remained more or less the same. In addition, the different levels and ranks of each group were recast to provide equivalents, thus giving the *serasker* a rank equal to that of the grand vezir and the *şeyhulislam* and ranking their subordinates accordingly, as shown in Table 1.1. All were now paid only by salary according to rank, and the structure of a complex bureaucratic hierarchy on modern lines was established.[100] It is interesting to note, incidentally, that the rank of *hacegân*, once at the top of the Scribal Class, had been so inflated by appointments early in the nineteenth century that it now represented the lowest rather than the highest class of administrators. Since educational reforms eliminated the entry of apprentices into the ranks of the bureaucracy before the age of 18, the educational apparatus previously maintained by the departments was abandoned with the exception of new foreign-language schools established in each of the major

Table 1.1. *The Tanzimat structure of titles and ranks*

Serasker	Şeyhulislam	Grand vezir
Müşir (field marshal) and vezir	*Sadr-ı Rumeli* (*kazasker of Rumeli*)	*Rütbe-i evvel* (rank 1)
Ferik (divisional general)	*Sadr-ı Anadolu* (*kazasker* of Anatolia)	*Rütbe-i sani, sınıf-ı evvel* (rank 2, class 1)
Mirimiran (brigadier general)	*Istanbul payesi* (rank of the kadi of Istanbul)	*Rütbe-i sani, sınıf-ı sani* (rank 2, class 2)
Miriliva (major general)	*Harameyn mollası payesi* (rank of the kadi of the Holy Cities)	*Rütbe-i salis, sınıf-ı evvel* (rank 3, class 1)
Miralay (colonel)	*Bilad-ı Erbaa mollası payesi* (rank of the mollas of the "Four Cities" of Edirne, Bursa, Damascus, and Cairo)	*Rütbe-i salis, sınıf-ı sani* (rank 3, class 2)
Kaymakam (lieutenant), or *alay emini* (regimental commander)	*Mahreç mollası payesi* (molla with the rank of *mahreç*)	*Rütbe-i rabi* (rank 4)
Binbaşı (major)	*Istanbul müderrislik payesi* (rank of an Istanbul *medrese* teacher)	*Divan-ı Hümayun hacegânı* (rank of *hace/hoca of* the Imperial Council)

departments (usually called *Tercüme Odası*, or Translation Office) to handle the duties of translation and to train young Ottomans to replace the Greeks who had traditionally performed this function but who had been driven from official life following the Greek Revolution. The first and most famous of these translation offices was established in the Foreign Ministry in 1833, and it became a major source not only of diplomats and educated bureaucrats but also of the new intelligentsia that emerged during the remaining years of the empire.[101]

Mahmut went on to reorganize the bureaucracy that staffed these offices of government. In 1834 he modified, and later eliminated entirely, the traditional system by which the higher administrative and scribal officials had to be reappointed each year, since this had subjected them to tremendous political and social pressures. He went on to establish a regular salary system in place of the traditional fees (*bahşiş*), which previously had provided the bulk of official revenues. This would not only reduce the officials' opportunity to take bribes but also subject them to far more regular central control than was possible when they had possessed at least semiautonomous sources of revenue of their own. Of course, the officials in question were far more willing to accept the new salaries than they were to forgo the old fees, so that it was at this time that the term *bahşiş* began to acquire its more modern connotation of "bribe."[102] Finally Mahmut issued penal codes (*ceza kanunnamesi*) especially for officials and judges in which the old system of arbitrary confiscation of property and punishment of officials by nonjudicial means was abolished and replaced by a regular system of penalties and punishments for specific crimes regardless of the rank and position of the officials in question. On one hand the new bureaucrats were rescued from the highly insecure and precarious positions in which their predecessors had found themselves as slaves of an absolute master. Thus was founded the highly autocratic tradition of Ottoman bureaucracy which was to survive well into the period of the Republic. On the other hand the code defined the limits of bureaucratic power, excluding recognized practices such as profiting from authority to make official purchases, appointing relatives and favorites to official positions, and, of course, accepting bribes.[103] We shall examine later Mahmut's role in developing a new secular system of schools intended to provide the state with the educated and dedicated bureaucrats needed to operate the new system (see pp. 47–48).[104]

Provincial Administration

Mahmut's aim in provincial administration was to establish a just system of rule and taxation, first of all by resuming the old practice of making regular cadastral surveys of population and property and by assessing taxes according to individual ability to pay rather than by the customary (*örfi*) and excise (*ihtisap*) taxes inherited from the past. A census of the entire empire, except for Egypt and Arabia, was carried out between 1831 and 1838. Although still based on the old principle of counting only male heads of households, primarily for tax and military purposes, the census did include movable and fixed property and the values of shops and factories so that taxes could be set and adjusted fairly in both town and country.[105]

According to new regulations issued soon afterward, tax farmers were to be replaced by salaried agents of the central government called *muhassıl*s (collectors). The governors and other provincial officials were to end their exactions and rule justly according to law, and relatively independent financial and military officials sent by and responsible to the relevant Istanbul ministries were to supervise to prevent the absolute and unlimited misrule that had been inflicted on the subjects in the past. The provincial military garrisons, now also responsible to Istanbul rather than to the governors, were to enforce obedience to the law on the part of subject and official while restoring security and ending the depredations of bandits, notables, bedouins, and the like.[106]

The new practices were introduced first in the province of Hüdavendigâr (Bursa) and the *sancak* of Gallipoli, which were to be experimental models for the new system.[107] To facilitate the transmission of orders and the supervision of officials as well as the collection of taxes, Mahmut also established the first regular Ottoman postal system, building special postal roads when necessary, repairing the old ones when possible, and establishing regular stopping points (*menzil*) along the road for the postal messengers, first from Istanbul to Izmit, then Istanbul to Edirne, and finally, as time went on, to other parts of the empire.[108] In addition, to control the population and prevent the kind of mass movements that had so upset financial and social stability in the eighteenth century and earlier, a system of passports was introduced, not merely for subjects wishing to travel outside the empire, but also for subjects and foreigners wishing to travel from one place to another within the sultan's dominions. Such persons were required to secure a travel permit (*mürur tezkeresi*) from their local police officer, issued by the Ministry of the Interior, and to display it when required along the way, with severe punishments being applied to those failing to carry them. This was the first step toward a system developed later in the century by which the entire population was registered and given identity cards as part of an all-encompassing census procedure.

Even though some of these reforms were limited first to the areas of Bursa and Gallipoli, the difficulty of finding enough bureaucrats able and willing to collect taxes and administer the laws fairly in return for salaries alone made it impossible for the government to replace the tax farmers and recalcitrant bureaucrats as rapidly as had been anticipated. Thus reform came slowly. Mahmut's measures did, however, provide the nucleus for provincial reforms in the empire in the years that followed.[109]

The Military

Mahmut was shocked by his army's defeat at Konya and was determined to modernize his army so that it could never again be subjected to such humiliation. He participated directly in the planning and execution of most of his military projects, himself visiting barracks, training grounds, forts, schools, and factories, inspecting troops, sometimes even tasting their food.[110] He also was the first sultan in centuries to travel outside the capital for purposes other than conquest or relaxation in Edirne, going to Silivri early in 1829 to look into the shipment of supplies and men to the front,[111] and personally going to visit Gallipoli and the Dardanelles in June 1831 to inspect frontier fortifications,[112] and also going on a month-long trip through eastern and northern Bulgaria in April 1837, visiting Şumla as well as the Danubian ports of Varna, Silistria, and Rusçuk.

Mahmut sought military reform first and foremost by elaborating on and extending the centralized organization begun soon after the Janissaries were destoyed. To increase the powers of the *serasker,* the office of the superintendent (*nazır*) was eliminated and replaced with a mere scribe who acted as no more than an executive assistant in financial and supply matters, while the *nazır*'s financial powers went to the Ministry of Finance.[113] Husrev Paşa already had begun the process of extending the *serasker*'s powers over the other corps, appointing the best of his former slaves to command them and using his prestige as commander of the *Mansure* to act more or less as minister of war during the Russian war. After the war, his title was changed to Commander in Chief of the Victorious Troops of Muhammad and Protector of Istanbul (*Asâkir-i Mansure-yi Muhammadiye Seraskeri ve Dersaadet Muhafızı*) to distinguish him from the other *serasker*s appointed to command campaign armies on the eastern or western front. As such he was recognized as supreme supervisor of all the army corps as well as commander of the *Mansure* army.[114] The last step was taken in March 1838 when all the fighting corps were incorporated into the *Mansure* army while the other still independent corps, factories, and warehouses were grouped into three departments under his control:

1. The Imperial Guards (*Hassa*), who included not only the guards but also the sultan's personal bodyguards (*Hademe-i Rikâb-ı Hümayun*), the Imperial Band (*Mehter-i Hümayun*), the Army Medical School (*Tıbhane-i Âmire*), and the School of the General Staff (*Mekteb-i Harbiye*)

2. The Ordinance Department (*Tophane*), including the Artillery, Cannon-Wagon, Bombardier, and Sapper and Miner corps and also the garrisons, armaments, and fortifications of the empire as well as the Army Engineering School (*Mühendishane-i Berri-i Hümayun*)

3. The Department of War Supplies (*Mühimmat-ı Harbiye*), which included all

the corps charged with providing the army with food, housing, tents, small arms, and gunpowder

The *serasker* thus was now commander in chief in fact as well as name, and with the change of the army's name from *Mansure* to *Asakir-i Muntazama* (the Ordered Troops), the process of military centralization was complete. The Seraskerate also was now considered to be one of the ministries, and the *serasker* as commander in chief was equal in rank to the grand vezir and the *şeyhülislam*, as we have seen.[115]

The navy continued as a separate organization, still under the grand admiral. The formerly independent superintendent of dockyards (*tersane emini*) was supplanted by subordinate directors for supply and military matters, and the admiral himself was helped in administrative and political matters by a civilian official appointed as his undersecretary (*müsteşar*), who increasingly assumed actual power in operating the ministry, while the former was left with primarily military functions.[116]

Between the establishment of the *Mukata'at* (later renamed *Mansure*) Treasury in 1826 and of the Ministry of Finance a decade later, efforts were made to regularize the army's financial system. This military treasury was given substantial revenues right from the start, not only the *mukata'as* formerly controlled by the Imperial Treasury and Mint, but also the Holy War Taxes, the confiscated properties of the Janissaries and their supporters, and all timars that could be seized. However it was no more than a collector of funds, with expenditures being in the hands of the *serasker,* causing inefficiency and waste. Mahmut first tried to control this problem by setting up a new Department of the Superintendent of Military Expenditures (*Masarifat Nezareti*) to control military expenditures (mid-June 1830), but it was not too effective until the superintendent and his subordinates were made directly responsible for salaries and the purchase of food, supplies, uniforms, and the like, leaving only the more technical military functions to the *serasker*'s departments. The navy remained outside the control of the *serasker,* but its construction and supply departments also had to cooperate closely with the superintendence, resulting in savings in all military purchases as time went on.

The *Mansure* Treasury was by far the largest state treasury then in operation, that of the mint being a distant second, while the Imperial Treasury existed almost only in name. But since the army continued to spend more and more money and also perhaps because its reorganized financial system was more effective than those of the civilian treasuries, Mahmut kept transferring more and more revenues to it, including the poll tax and sheep tax. Finally, the superintendent was given the additional title of treasurer (*defterdar*), the Imperial Treasury was abolished, and its remaining revenues were turned over to the Mint Treasury (*Darphane Hazinesi*), whose supervisor was given the same rank as that of the *Mansure* Treasury, thus leaving state finances under two treasuries, for military and civilian affairs (November 1834). The process of transferring state revenues to the former continued, however, so that finally in February 1838 it was transformed into the new Ministry of Finance, and the mint was limited to its original activities of making and distributing coins. The Army Treasury thus emerged as the state's central financial organ, evidencing the tremendous burden the new military force placed on the total resources of the empire. Soon afterward the final step was taken when the Superintendency of Expenditures was abolished and its functions were assumed by subordinate departments of the Ministry of Finance (April 1839).

It should be noted, thus, that the Ministry of Finance, though based on the *Mansure* Army Treasury, included the state treasury. It once again had to meet all state expenses, not merely those of the army, and to curb the latter accordingly even though it continued to absorb as much as 70 percent of the total finances of the state during Mahmut's later years.[117]

Beneath the new organizations at the top, the different military services were restructured and modernized. The infantry regiments (*alay*), each including about 3,500 men and officers, became the main administrative units of the new army, whose total complement was raised to about 65,000 men, of whom 11,000 were *Hassa* guards.[118] The cavalry forces attached to both were enlarged and strengthened, though much more slowly than the infantry and artillery due to their decreasing military value. Many feudal timars were confiscated, and those remaining were modernized to support the provincial cavalry, with new arrangements being made for agents to collect the feudatories' revenues so that they could remain in training and under discipline at the provincial centers at all times. The use of *cebeli* substitutes was discouraged, with the fiefs being confiscated if the holders refused to serve personally. Efforts also were made to develop the provincial regiments under local command, appealing to a kind of provincial pride that had not yet developed in the regular army. By the end of Mahmut's reign the provincial cavalry had some 6,000 officers and men, but for the most part they remained irregular and poorly led and trained.

In the artillery corps the independent corps were abolished and all the positions that previously had been compensated with fiefs were given salaries as in the bureaucracy. The unified corps was regrouped into six regiments, according to current French patterns, with the core unit being the battery, possessing its own artillery and transport. The arrival of Prussian advisers in 1833 caused the artillery to shift toward the Prussian system, with more mobile forces built around light howitzers instead of cannon and a general standard applied of three artillery pieces for every thousand infantry men. However, the Ottomans were not really able to keep pace with the rapid developments then taking place in the science of artillery in Europe, and many corps continued to resist even the limited reform efforts that were attempted.[119]

Another advance made in the military during Mahmut's reign was the establishment of a real reserve militia (*redif*) in the years after 1833. Here the sultan made a sustained effort to gain general approval, explaining it as an organization that would enable the population to care for their own security while providing a pool of trained men who could be brought to war more rapidly and effectively than had been the case in the past. The militia system would screen and train men in advance so that only those who were fit and ready to serve would be sent to the front, and then only in accordance with the needs and capacity of each village.[120] General consent was obtained in a series of meetings convoked in Istanbul and the main provincial centers, and the *redif* militia law then was proclaimed on July 8, 1834.[121] *Redif* battalions were established in every province, though in some areas where the Muslim population was small several *sancaks* were joined together in individual battalions so that there would be 40 in all with some 57,000 men. The members were aged between 23 and 32. They were allowed to marry, and they were commanded by local notables, selected by the governors and submitted to approval by the Porte. The units came together in the provincial capitals twice a year, in April and September, for organized drill, all under the general supervision of the provincial governors and, ultimately, the *serasker*. Salaries were only one quarter of those of the regular troops except when the *redif* forces went on active duty, when they were the same.[122]

Organization of the *redif* proceeded rapidly. By 1836 there were 32 *redif* battalions in operation, though there was some local opposition because of the fear of many notables that the central government would use these forces to restrict their autonomy. Mahmut, however, feared the reverse, that this organization would strengthen the notables and provincial officials against the centralizing tendencies of his administrative reforms. In September 1836, then, he reorganized the system to enlarge the *redif* and also attach it more directly to central control.[123] The organization now was modeled directly on that of the regular army, with the battalions reduced to 800 men and officers each. Every province now had to supply 3 battalions instead of 1 battalion, and the total force therefore came to about 100,000 men in 120 battalions, considerably larger than before. The power of the provincial notables was reduced by grouping the provincial battalions into regional regiments headed by Ottoman officials given the rank of *müşir* and based at Edirne, Niş, and Şumla, in Europe, and at Bursa, Konya, Ankara, Aydın, Erzurum, and Sivas, in Anatolia. In addition, *redif* cavalry units were organized in both Anatolia and Rumelia[124] and brought to Istanbul once a year for more advanced training than could be provided in the provinces.

There were serious problems, however. The notables resented the new regulations and ended their cooperation. Enrollment lagged considerably. Desertion was frequent, and since the *redif* forces received only what muskets and cannon were left over from the regular army, they remained poorly armed and trained. Nevertheless, the *redif* was a major advance. The structure was laid for the provincial armies established later during the Tanzimat. The local security forces were greatly augmented. A beginning was made in checking the powers of the notables and provincial officials, and for the first time the empire was provided with a reserve of at least partly trained men who could and did help the active army.

To what extent were the old problems of supply and armament solved under the new organization? Food and other necessities now were provided directly by a military commissariat within the Seraskerate. Rations were purchased centrally and then distributed to the commissary officers (*vekiliharç*) for each of the Istanbul barracks, while the stores for the provincial troops were bought locally by the governors with funds from the *Bab-ı Serasker*. There certainly continued to be illegal skimming of funds on all levels, but under the new system the men were far better fed and supplied than before. Also the various needs of the new army stimulated the development of the first modern factories in the empire. A Sewing Factory (*Dikimhane-i Amire*) was opened in 1827 to make uniforms, footwear, canteens, and the like. Some textile factories were built in Izmit and Üsküdar to provide needed cloth. A fez factory (*fezhane*) was established in Izmir with the help of the governor of Tunis (1835) to provide headgear. The Artillery foundry (*Tophane*) now emerged as the principal establishment for the manufacture and repair of cannons, mortars, wagons, mines, and projectiles in place of a number of old foundries, and it applied the latest techniques of metal alloy, and the like, to produce far better equipment than the Ottomans had in the past. There also was a modern Gun Factory (*Tüfenkhane*) built at Dolmabahçe, on the Bosporus, which manufactured muskets, carbines, pistols, lances, bayonets, axes and other tools, while new Imperial Gunpowder Mills (*Baruthane-i Amire*) built at Bakırköy (1830) and Yeşilköy (San Stefano) (1838), produced far more stable compounds than those of the past. Considerable progress was made, but general inefficiency and a lack of high standards left the Porte still largely dependent on imports from Europe for the rest of the reign.[125]

Foreign Advisers

Defeat at the hands of Russia did not shake the sultan and his advisers too much because by this time they were conditioned to accept the superiority of the military establishments of Europe. But defeat at the hands of a Muslim leader like Muhammad Ali was another matter, particularly since he was nominally subordinate to the sultan. It was in reaction to this that the sultan was finally forced to accept the need for the same kind of foreign advice, which had been used so successfully in Egypt. France was not called on because of its help to the Egyptian governor, while Britain was not yet sufficiently trusted because of its long association with Russia. Mahmut also feared falling under the exclusive control of one or another power when accepting such help. Once the principle had been accepted, then, the sources of help were diversified both to prevent overreliance on one state and also to follow the old Ottoman ploy of using the rivalries of various powers for the empire's advantage.

Many of the foreign advisers came because of the personal leanings of individual Ottoman officers. Russian officers were brought back by Ahmet Fevzi Paşa, commander of the *Hassa* guards, when he returned from a special mission to St. Petersburg (1834), and by his rival, *Serasker* Husrev Paşa, who placed a Russian, Lieutenant Cavaloff, in charge of training the *Mansure* infantry in Istanbul (1834). As the sultan had hoped, the other powers, for fear of being left out, responded with their own offers of help. In 1835 Britain began to supply industrial and military equipment, including blast furnaces and steam drills, and British engineers and workers came to help establish and maintain them. British officers arrived in 1836 to redesign and rebuild Ottoman fortifications, though Mahmut's suspicions limited their contributions. He still was seeking help from a state having no previous interests in the Middle East and, finally, settled on Prussia, a rising European power with a military reputation. From 1833 to 1839 several Prussian missions advised the Ottomans, providing them with far superior officers and receiving therefore much more respect and attention than had ever been the case with the missions of the other powers. By far the most skillful of the Prussians helping the Porte at this time was a young lieutenant, Helmuth von Moltke, who later in his career was to become one of the most prominent military men in Europe. Most of the missions undertaken by von Moltke and others were technical, such as mapping frontier areas and recommending improvements in fortifications, modernizing factories, establishing model battalions and squadrons in the infantry and cavalry, and training Ottoman soldiers and officers in the use of the latest weapons and tactics. But even the Prussians had only limited success, not so much because of their relatively small numbers but as a result of continued Ottoman reluctance to accept the advice of infidels, even those who were admired and respected. In addition, the Prussians generally shared the European attitude of scorn for Muslims, associating largely with Westerners and members of the minorities in the empire, joining them in making fun of their hosts, and in the process bringing on themselves much of the hostility and lack of understanding that prevailed.[126]

Municipal Organization

Mahmut II began the process by which real municipal government was created in the Ottoman Empire. Under the traditional Ottoman system, the scope of governmental function and control in the cities was very limited. Urban officials regulated city affairs only insofar as they involved the performance of other official duties for the government. In cooperation with the guilds, which were the real regulators and controllers of municipal economic life, in Istanbul and the other major cities the *muhtesip* regulated market prices and weights because of his official duty of imposing and collecting the market taxes due the treasury. The *şehir emini* (city commissioner) enforced building and street regulations and organized water and food supplies as part of his duty of building, maintaining, and supplying government buildings. In Istanbul, police and firefighting duties were carried out by the military corps in the areas around their barracks. In the smaller towns and villages, the police were in the hands of the local *subaşı*, appointed by the governor to help the kadis in enforcing the rulings of the Muslim religious courts. Beyond this, most duties akin to what modern society includes in urban government were performed by the guilds and *millets*, the latter through their own courts, schools, hospitals, homes for the aged and infirm, and the like, and also by private police guards hired for the residential quarters. The only coordination between the activities of the government officials and these private organizations came from the lieutenants of the *millet* chiefs, called *kethüdas* in the Muslim villages or quarters of the larger cities and *kocabaşıs* in the non-Muslim areas, but their authority and functions were very limited.

The transformation of this traditional structure of urban rule into real municipal government began during Mahmut II's reign, not so much as part of a specific plan, but rather in reaction to a number of problems, many created by his reforms, that led to the appointment of officials and groups with specifically urban duties. So it was that with the destruction of the corps that had traditionally cared for Istanbul's police, particularly the Janissaries and *Bostancıs*, and the transfer of that duty to the new *Mansure* army, the capital developed a special police structure of its own. It was manned by 150 professional policemen (*kavas*) and 500 irregulars (*seymen*) stationed at headquarters (*tomruk*) in the main quarters of the city, which served not only to house the men and officers but also the police courts, where violators of the law were judged and fined by sergeants (1826).[127] This organization became the basis for the first separate police force ever established in the Ottoman Empire. While the *Mansure* army also cared for the Janissaries' old duty of firefighting in Istanbul as well, in 1828 the central government built a series of fire stations (*harik tulumbaları*) at key points throughout the capital, manning them with a new corps of civilian firefighters (*tulumbacılar*) recruited especially for this purpose.[128] The new Holy War excise taxes imposed on shops and markets to finance the cost of the new army as well as the war against Russia also led to the transformation of the *muhtesip* into a real urban official with powers wider than mere market regulation, although the old name was preserved in only slightly altered form as *ihtisap ağası* (September 3, 1826).[129] With power to regulate not only the guilds but also persons from outside the city without regular homes or employment, the *ihtisap ağası* was given means to extend the scope of a single office over the entire population of the city, though the continued control of the police by the *serasker*, as commander of the *Mansure* army, severely limited his power. Soon afterward, as part of the new census structure that Mahmut was building up for tax and conscription purposes, local mayors (*muhtar*) or lieutenants (*kâhya*) were appointed in every Muslim or non-Muslim quarter of every city of the empire, under the authority of the *ihtisap ağası* in Istanbul, at first to count the people and later to enforce the clothing regulations. As the first regular representatives of the central government in the local quarters they provided means by which the state could and did supplement and then supplant the power of the guilds and the *millets*.[130] They soon built their authority through their functions of retaining the census records of their quarters, entering all changes, issuing statements to identify local residents so that they could secure the passports now required for travel, and keeping the records of property and wealth that formed the basis of the new tax system. Soon they were reinforced and assisted by councils of elders representing the major religious, economic, and social interests of their localities, which thus brought a really popular element into the process of centralized government.[131] In Istanbul the *şehir emini* as such was abolished, with those of his duties that had a bearing on the construction of government buildings and regulation of private buildings being turned over to the sultan's chief architect (*mimar başı*), who was given the new title director of imperial buildings (*ebniye-i hassa müdürü*), thus leaving the *ihtisap ağası* and his assistants in the quarters as the principal city-wide municipal officials of government in Istanbul and the other main cities of the empire.[132] This structure formed the basis for the real municipalities created during the Tanzimat era, after 1839.

Education

In the end, reforms in the army and administration had to rely on the development of an educational system able to give young Ottomans the knowledge needed for them to perform their duties. The basic problem was the traditional system of education, controlled by the *millets*, with the religious schools of the ulema monopolizing Muslim education and the latter guarding this prerogative in particular because of its importance in maintaining their influence over subjects and rulers alike. Even in the traditional context most Muslim schools were no longer giving a good education because of the same conditions of neglect that had sapped the strength of the other traditional institutions of the empire. Elementary instruction in arithmetic, science, and foreign languages had to be provided to young Muslims if they were to study in higher technical schools. Mahmut could not openly supplant the traditional Muslim school system with a modern secular one, since this would have been too much for the ulema to accept. His solution, therefore, was to leave the Muslim schools as they were while building up beside them a new secular system of education. Mahmut thus inaugurated a bifurcation in Ottoman education, the existence of two separate systems that followed different philosophies and curriculums, a situation that was to divide Ottoman society for a century until the religious schools finally were ended by the Turkish Republic.

But where to begin the secular system? To avoid ulema opposition, instead of starting at the elementary level with the *mekteps*, Mahmut began with those graduates of the *mekteps* who did not choose to go on with an *Ilmiye* career. He established for them (usually young men between ages of 12 and 16) special schools to provide the instruction needed for them to go on to the technical schools. Two *Rüşdiye* (adolescence) schools for young Muslim males were opened at the Süleymaniye and Sultan Ahmet mosques in Istanbul, providing elements of grammar, history, and mathematics for those wishing to go on to the military technical schools. For those wishing to enter the bureaus of government, the *Mekteb-i Maarif-i Adliye* (School of Education of "the just one," that is, the sultan) and the *Mekteb-i Maarif-i Edebiye* (School of Literary Education) were established, providing lessons in Arabic, French, geography, history, political science, and mathematics. A *Mekteb-i Irfaniye* (School of Knowledge) also was opened at the Porte for those scribes already in government services wishing to advance their ranks and positions by acquiring modern, secular knowledge.[133] Thus were laid the bases for the secular system of education that was to spread to all levels after 1839.

Mahmut also revived and expanded the higher technical schools. The Naval Engineering School (*Mühendishane-i Bahri-i Hümayun*) and Army Engineering School (*Mühendishane-i Berri-i Hümayun*) survived into the nineteenth century in little more than name, with the faculty and students of the latter mainly dispersed and the building of the former in Kasımpaşa being destroyed by fire in 1821 without being replaced, though it did continue to have a small student body and faculty. As a first step, Mahmut began to send students to Europe to provide instructors for the schools as well as officers for his army, again following the example of Muhammad Ali (1827). In addition to a new medical school (*Tıbhane-i Amire*), with sections on medicine, surgery, anatomy, and the medical sciences, the sultan also established a separate School of Surgery (*Cerrahhane*) in 1832, and an Imperial School of Medicine (*Mekteb-i Şahane-i Tıbbiye*) in the old palace school at Galatasaray in 1839, but shortages of equipment and textbooks and the longstanding Muslim reluctance to dissect the human body made progress slow and difficult. In 1828 the sultan revived the Army Engineering School under the direction of Hoca Ishak Efendi, a Jewish convert, who revised the curriculum and raised the standards of instruction, building the student body to about 200 men by the end of Mahmut's reign. The Naval Engineering School also was enlarged and moved to new quarters at Heybeli Ada, an island in the Sea of Marmara. An Imperial School of Music (*Müzika-i Hümayun Mektebi*) was established in 1836 to provide the new army with regimental bands. Finally, in consequence of the continued shortage of trained officers in the army, Mahmut established a new School for Military Sciences (*Mekteb-i Ulûm-u Harbiye*). Since this was done as a result of the urgings of the director of the imperial guards, Namık Paşa, and against the advice of Husrev Paşa, it was placed under the control and supervision of the *Hassa* command to keep it out of the *serasker*'s way. Classes began in the Maçka section of Istanbul in 1836, and within three years there were about 200 students enrolled.[134]

Thus there were several advanced technical schools in operation by the end of Mahmut's reign, with about 1000 students enrolled at any one time. There were, however, problems that limited their effectiveness. Invariably the quarters were small and inadequate, and the schools had to move from one building to another, as even these often were taken over by institutions having more political influence. Equipment and books were almost nonexistent. Some of the instructors were devoted and able, but most were not. Politics often subverted what progress was made. The few foreign instructors who were in the country were needed more in the army, so that few could spend very much time at the schools. And, since few of the students had sufficient preparation, the schools still had to devote time to teaching the basic elements of arithmetic, history, geography, and the like, despite the elaborate programs of study developed for them and published in the *Takvim-i Vekayi* and elsewhere. Mahmut's reign thus provided Ottoman secular education only with a hesitant start. Its extension and success really had to await the more sustained efforts of the Tanzimat reformers.

The Awakening of Ottoman Society

Mahmut II's reign brought not merely a new awareness of and admiration for the West but also a feeling that the traditional Ottoman ways had to be abandoned for the empire to survive and hold its own against a technologically advanced Europe. The Ottomans could no longer afford to look down on the West, and gradually change permeated different areas of their lives, from wearing apparel to language, thought, and even entertainment.

Mahmut himself took the lead, transferring his abode in 1815 from the ancient Topkapı Palace on the heights of old Istanbul to a more modern palace built along the Bosporus at Dolmabahçe. It now became the official residence of the ruler, remaining such until Abdulaziz transferred to the newer palace built on the hills above at Yıldız late in the century. Into the Dolmabahçe Palace went Western sofas, tables, and chairs, replacing the pillows and divans of the old palace. Mahmut began to dress like a European monarch, shortening his beard and wearing his own version of contemporary Western hats, frock coats, and trousers. In place of the splendid isolation of his predecessors (even Selim III crept around the streets of Istanbul incognito), he began to appear in public, often riding in European-style carriages (*fayton*). Sometimes he went into the provinces to investigate conditions. He was the first sultan to attend public receptions, concerts, operas, and ballet performances given in some of the Western embassies, and with Donizetti's help he imported Western musicians and developed the *Hassa* musicians into a Western-style military band so that he could offer concerts to his European guests.

Once again the sultan participated in the meetings of his chief officials, regularly attending the Council of Ministers and giving his judgments on the spot, in the process providing a model of dress and behavior that the ministers emulated. Soon ministers, bureaucrats, and military officers also began to appear in frock coats or Western-style uniforms and trousers, with the fez, earlier established as the official headgear of the *Mansure* army, being accepted as the most prominent mark of the modern man, obliterating the differences of religion, rank, and class that the turban had symbolized and manifested in traditional Ottoman society. In 1829, after it had been in fact accepted by most ranks of society, modern clothing was made compulsory by law for male civilians as well as soldiers and bureaucrats, with turbans and robes being allowed only for religious officials of the different *millets*. The sultan began to learn French, and it was not long before the translation offices in the departments and schools offering foreign-language training were thronged by youths wishing to prepare themselves to rise in the new elite. Contact between Ottomans and foreigners increased greatly, with beneficial results on all sides. Of course, all these were outward manifestations of a will to change that was difficult to extend especially to areas where the ulema had a vested interest and expressed their opposition. The religious institution itself remained basically unreformed and the major bastion of conservatism in Ottoman society. But still, as in other areas, a beginning had been made in undermining its position.[135]

The Second Egyptian Crisis

Disastrous new defeats inflicted by Muhammad Ali on Mahmut just before the latter's death brought the reign to a cataclysmic end. The new conflict was not entirely the fault of the Egyptian governor. Mahmut himself was deceived by the initial military reforms to feel that he was ready to force Muhammad Ali back into his place and particularly to reclaim Syria. He was discouraged only by British Prime Minister Palmerston, who while opposing Muhammad Ali because of his attachment to France, correctly discerned that it would be disastrous to attack before the reforms in Istanbul had been given time to develop some real substance in the army. Nor was Russia anxious for a new conflict, knowing it would never be able to retain its current dominance in the empire if a new war made either Mahmut II or Muhammad Ali stronger. There were, however, serious sources of dispute, heightened by Mahmut's resentment and Muhammad Ali's ambition. In 1834 the latter's attempt to reduce his annual tribute to the Porte strained relations soon after peace had been achieved. In addition, while Egyptian rule in Syria had been welcomed locally at the start, Ibrahim Paşa's modern conscription and tax systems as well as his use of forced labor, efforts to give equal rights to Christians, and imposition of state monopolies over the main products of the province led to a series of revolts that encouraged Mahmut to intervene.

As early as May 22, 1834, an Ottoman army prepared to enter Syria, and only strong British and Russian pressure preserved the peace. On May 25, 1838, things boiled up again when Muhammad Ali, growing anxious to assure his dynasty as he became older, declared his intention to establish himself as an independent monarch. Mahmut again mobilized his army, but this time even the French were opposed to changing the status quo, and Muhammad Ali backed down. Britain in the end gained most from this particular situation. Palmerston and Mustafa Reşit used it to agree on the commercial treaty of Balta Limanı (August 1838), by which the old British Capitulatory privileges in the Ottoman Empire were confirmed and expanded. Renewed British commercial interest in the Middle East marked the end of Mahmut's distrust of British policy and inaugurated a closer relationship that, in the long run, was to provide the empire with the support it needed in its greatest hours of crisis.[136]

Despite the continued endeavours of the powers to calm both the Ottomans and the Egyptians, both sides prepared for war. Ibrahim Paşa built up a force of 50,000 soldiers at Aleppo and fortified the Cilician gates from Syria onto the Anatolian plateau. Mahmut also amassed a sizable force in eastern Anatolia north of the Euphrates and sent a contingent of Prussian advisers, including von Moltke, to help its operations. This force was, however, composed primarily not of the trained *Mansure* forces but of local Kurdish and Turkish tribesmen, whose mere presence, it was hoped, would stimulate a general uprising against Ibrahim in Syria, thus making possible a restoration of Ottoman rule without the confrontation against which the powers had been warning. But when the Ottoman army crossed the Euphrates and began advancing toward Aleppo (April 21, 1839), there was no uprising, since the Syrians were far too effectively cowed by the Egyptian bureaucrats and troops. In the meantime, Ibrahim grouped his forces on the heights overlooking the valley between Nezib and Birecik, guarding the approaches to Aleppo. When the Ottomans made a frontal assault, then, mainly at the instigation of the ulema present and in disregard of von Moltke's advice, they were routed, with most of the men killed and only a few able to flee back into Anatolia (June 24, 1839). On June 30, 1839, Mahmut II, whose health had been weakening for several months, succumbed to tuberculosis, apparently before receiving the news of the disaster and therefore not, as has often been reported, in direct reaction to it. To all those who had supported his reforms, however, the defeat was a blow despite the fact that it involved the old army and not the new. What would now happen to the beginnings of modernization that Mahmut had made? Would there be a new period of reaction like that which had followed Selim III's reign? The answer came with the proclamation of the Tanzimat reforms at the beginning of the next reign, assuring continuity with Mahmut II's policies.

Notes to Chapter 1

1 Shaw, *Empire of the Gazis*, pp. 273–277.

2 Cevdet[1], IX, 3–5; Juchereau, *Révolutions*, II, 199–209; Uzunçarşılı, *Alemdar*, pp. 138–143.

3 Şanizade, I, 66–72; Cevdet[1], IX, 332–338; Juchereau, *Révolutions*, II, 343–346; Karal, OT, V, 96.

4 Berkes, pp. 90–91; Lewis, pp. 74–75; Inalcık, "Sened".

5 Cevdet[1], IX, 9, 12; Şanizade, I, 97–98; Uzunçarşılı, *Alemdar*, pp. 144–145; Karal, OT, V, 97.

6 Asım, II, 237–240; Şanizade, I, 99–100; Cevdet[1], IX, 16 Uzunçarşılı, *Alemdar*, p. 147.

7 Uzunçarşılı, *Alemdar*, pp. 145–146; Asım, II, 237–238; Şanizade, I, 78–79; Cevdet[1], IX, 10–11; Karal, OT, V, 97; Schlechta-Wssehrd, pp. 191–192.

8 Uzunçarşılı, *Alemdar*, p. 212; Juchereau, *Histoire*, II, 250–251.

9 Şanizade, I, 98; Asım, II, 240; Cevdet[1], IX, 15–18.

10 Uzunçarşılı, *Alemdar*, pp. 213–214, I, 105; Cevdet[1], IX, 20; Schlechta-Wssehrd, p. 198.

11 Asım, II, 243; Şanizade, I, 107–109; Cevdet[1], IX, 26, 30–31, 33–35; Juchereau, *Révolutions*, II, 233.

12 Uzunçarşılı, *Alemdar*, p. 165.

13 Asım, II, 258–259; Şanizade, I, 141; Cevdet[1], IX, 47.

14 Levy, pp. 60–86; Asım, II, 237–260; Şanizade, I, 91, 100–105, 107–112, 116–148; Cevdet[1], IX, 12–55; Juchereau, *Histoire*, II, 250–271, and *Révolutions*, II, 217–239; Schlechta-Wssehrd, pp. 199–228; Şanizade, I, 105–144; Arapyan, pp. 16–26; Uzunçarşılı, *Alemdar*, pp. 154–183.

15 Shaw, *Between Old and New*, pp. 122–123.

16 BVA, Kanunname-i Askeri, II, 1a–b; Uzunçarşılı, *Kapukulu*, II, 108.

17 BVA, Kepeci, nos. 3258, 3259; Kanunname-i Askeri, II, 1a–7b; Cevdet Askeri, no. 449; Şanizade, II, 156; Cevdet[1], XII, 167; Levy, pp. 101–103.

18 Esat, *Tarih*, I, 258a–b, 296b–297a; Cevdet[1], XII, 122; Levy, pp. 103–105.

19 Şanizade, III, 22–25.

20 Cevdet[2], X, 218–219; Şanizade, IV, 98, 104–106, 128–129; Levy, p. 106; BVA, Kepeci, nos. 4825–6, 4829–35, 4985.

21 Lütfi, V, 145–146.

22 BVA, HH 48523, 48958; BVA, Kepeci, 6699, 6702, 6706; Levy, p. 106.

23 Reed, pp. 51–70; Levy, p. 107; Esat, *Tarih*, I, 8a, 41a, 94a–b, 139a–141a, 155b, 248a–b, 290b, 316b; Şanizade, I, 185, 201–202, II, 11–13, 76–78, 234–237, 291–292, III, 89–90; *Vakayi-i Enderun*, pp. 206–207, 223, 238–239, 288–289; Cevdet[1], IX, 208, 210, 228, 273, 293, XII, 61, 79–80, 123–151; BVA, HH 17884, 17328; Uzunçarşılı, *Kapukulu*, I, 522.

24 Howard Reed, "Agha Hüseyin Pasha," EI[2], III, 628–629; Levy, pp. 108–109; Esat, *Tarih*, I, 162a–b; *Vakayi-i Enderun*, p. 271.

25 Cevdet[1], XII, 82–84, 96–97; Levy, pp. 108–109; Walsh, *Residence*, II, 502–518.

26 Cevdet[1], XII, 123, 151.

27 Cevat, I, 369; Walsh, *Residence*, II, 518–520; Levy, p. 109.

28 Şanizade, I, 349–353, IV, 103–104, III, 50–53, 87–88; Cevdet[1], IX, 208–210, XI, 71–73.

29 Cevdet[1], XI, 5–7, 93–94; Şanizade, III, 50–54.

30 Shaw, *Between Old and New*, p. 450, n. 26.

31 Cevdet[1], IX, 40; Şanizade, I, 139.
32 Levy p. 97; Cevdet[1], XII, 64–65; Tekindağ, "Halet Efendi," IA, V, 123–125.
33 Cevdet[1], XII, 64–66, 81–82; Esat, Tarih, I, 137a–b.
34 Cevdet[1], XII, 82, 96; Esat, Tarih, I, 194a.
35 Cevdet[1], XII, 84.
36 Levy, pp. 97–101; Orhan Köprülü, "Galib Paşa," IA, IV, 710–714.
37 Cevdet[1], IV, 286; Farhi, pp. 154–155.
38 Muahedat Mecmuası, I, 266–270.
39 Muahedat Mecmuası, IV, 49.
40 R. B. Winder, Saudi Arabia in the Nineteenth Century, New York, 1965, pp. 16–95.
41 Dennis N. Skiotis, "The Lion and the Phoenix: Ali Pasha and the Greek Revolution, 1819–1822," unpublished Ph.D. dissertation (Harvard University, 1971).
42 Heyd, "Ulema," pp. 77–79; Esat, Tarih, I, 268b–272a; Cevdet[1], XII, 159, 165.
43 Levy, pp. 117–120.
44 Cevdet[1], XII, 169–170; Lütfi, I, 126–128; Esat, Zafer, pp. 11–14; Reed, pp. 113–117; Levy, pp. 123–126.
45 Esat, Zafer, pp. 14–22; Cevdet[1], XII, 170–173; Levy, pp. 126–130; Reed, pp. 116–129.
46 Esat, Zafer, pp. 36–40; Cevdet[1], XII, 307–309; Levy, pp. 129–130.
47 BVA, HH48112; Esat, Zafer, pp. 22–32; Esat, Tarih, II, 110a–118b; Cevdet[1], XII, 297–306; Lütfi, I, 350–356; Reed, pp. 130–146; Levy, pp. 131–143.
48 Esat, Zafer, pp. 64–65; Cevdet[1], XII, 174–175; Levy, p. 145; Uzunçarşılı, Kapukulu, I, 545–546; Lütfi, I, 132–133.
49 Reed, pp. 190–287; Levy, pp. 146–170; Esat, Zafer, pp. 71–97, summarized in his Tarih, II, 137b–142b; Cevdet[1], XII, 177–196; Lütfi, I, 136–147 describe the Auspicious Event. The ferman abolishing the Janissaries is in BVA, Cevdet Askeri 25109 and TKS E5528; it was reproduced in Esat, Zafer, pp. 111–112; Cevdet[1], XII, 311–315; Lütfi, I, 357–361; Uzunçarşılı, Kapukulu, I, 666–672; Reed, pp. 242–249; and the Times (London), August 24 and 25, 1826.
50 Esat, Zafer, pp. 107–108, 191–193; Levy, pp. 177–181; Ata, III, 108–109.
51 Levy, pp. 183–196; BVA, HH48112, 17708; TKS, E4286; Esat, Tarih, II, 180b–188b; Lütfi, I, 191–193; Cevdet[1], XII, 215–216, 316–322.
52 Istanbul University Library, anonymous manuscript TY5824, fol. 121b–125a; Levy, pp. 201–208.
53 Lütfi, I, 199–200; BVA, Cevdet Askeri 54811; BVA, Kanunname-i Askeri, I, 15–22, 41; Levy, pp. 208–212.
54 Lütfi, I, 235–237; BVA, HH23325; Levy, p. 232.
55 July 25, 1827/1 Muharrem 1243; BVA, Cevdet Askeri 449, Kanunname-i Askeri, II, 1a–b.
56 Levy, pp. 232–238; BVA, Kanunname-i Askeri, II, 29a–30a.
57 August 31, 1826; BVA, HH48115; Lütfi, I, 91–101, VI, 41a–48a; Istanbul University Library, TY5824, fol. 63a–79a; Esat, Zafer, pp. 253–254; Levy, pp. 243–248.
58 Levy, pp. 243–249; Lütfi, I, 201; BVA, Cevdet Askeri 216.
59 BVA, Kanunname-i Askeri, I, 45–52; Istanbul University Library, TY5824, fol. 59a–62a.
60 BVA, Kanunname-i Askeri, II, 1a–b; Uzunçarşılı, Kapukulu, II, 108; Levy, pp. 269–271; Cevdet[2], XII, 176.
61 Lütfi, I, 253.
62 Levy, pp. 273–297; TV, no. 1, 25 Cemazi I 1247, no. 2, 7 Cemazi II 1247; von Moltke, Bulgaria, pp. 18–19.
63 Levy, p. 299; Esat, Zafer, pp. 250–252; Cevdet[1], XII, 215–216; BVA, HH17655.
64 Levy, pp. 309–322; Lütfi, I, 257–258.
65 Lütfi, I, 258–259; BVA, Kanunname-i Askeri, II, 95a–96b.
66 Levy, pp. 326–332; BVA, Kanunname-i Askeri, II, 97a, 98a.

67 Levy, pp. 334–335; BVA, Kanunname-i Askeri, II, 97b, 99a, 102b.
68 Gökbilgin, pp. 255–256, 336–339; Levy, pp. 341–342; BVA, Cevdet Askeri 6295.
69 Levy, pp. 347–349; BVA Kanunname-i Askeri, II, 64a–72a.
70 Lütfi, I, 198–199, 205–206.
71 Lütfi, I, 230–231.
72 Lütfi, I, 240.
73 BVA, HH17379.
74 BVA, Cevdet Askeri 877.
75 Ata, III, 109–113; Levy, pp. 379–380; *Vakayi-i Enderun*, pp. 375–377, 387–389, 394–396, 406–408.
76 Ata, III, 114–118; *Vakayi-i Enderun*, pp. 491–496.
77 Levy, pp. 386–391; Lütfi, I, 196–198.
78 Lütfi, I, 201–203; Cevdet[1], XII, 200; BVA, Kanunname-i Askeri, I, 13–14, VI, 9b–11a.
79 BVA, Kanunname-i Askeri, I, 109–111.
80 Rıza Tahsin, *Mirat-ı Mektep-i Tıbbiye*, Istanbul, 2 vols., 1328–1330/1912–1914, I, 4–10.
81 Levy, pp. 405–406; Lütfi, I, 295; BVA, Cevdet Askeri 629, 686.
82 *Muahedat Mecmuası*, IV, 65, 69; Noradounghian, II, 121, 125.
83 Lütfi, I, 291–293, 391–420; Ata, III, 255–275.
84 Lütfi, II, 58–60.
85 Muhtar, *Rusya Seferi*, I, 91–100, 126–189; Lütfi, II, 45–50.
86 Lütfi, II, 82–85, 97–100; Muhtar, *Rusya Seferi*, II, 31–34; von Moltke, *Bulgaria*, pp. 364–415.
87 Lütfi, I, 394, II, 74–79; Allen and Muratoff, pp. 23–45.
88 *Mufassal Osmanlı Tarihi*, IV, 2912–2916; *Muahedat Mecmuası*, IV, 70, 83; Noradounghian, II, 166, 174.
89 *Muahedat Mecmuası*, IV, 90; Noradounghian, II, 229.
90 Lütfi, II, 94, 144–146, 164, 168–169, III, 146–147; Heyd, "Ulema," pp. 71–74.
91 Lütfi, II, 172. No complete set of the latter has yet been found.
92 TV 155 (9 Recep 1253); Lütfi, V, 147; FO 78/330, March 21, 1838.
93 Lütfi, V, 108.
94 Late April 1838; Lütfi, V, 104–105.
95 Lütfi, V, 66; Berkes, p. 98.
96 Lütfi, V, 124.
97 Lütfi, V, 128; TV 167 (14 Rebi II 1254), 170 (13 Cemazi II 1254).
98 Lütfi, VI, 28–29; TV 180 (6 Rebi II 1255), 192 (26 Zilkade 1255); BVA Mesail-i Mühimme 10.
99 Lütfi, V, 113–114.
100 BVA, HH24031; Lütfi, V, 26, 126–127, 132; TV 121 (end of Ramazan 1251).
101 Lütfi, IV, 176, V, 45; Lewis, p. 38.
102 Shaw, "Ottoman Tax Reforms," p. 74.
103 Kaynar, pp. 295–301.
104 The development of the Ottoman bureaucracy in the nineteenth century has been described in a series of studies by Carter V. Findley in "The Legacy of Tradition to Reform: Origins of the Ottoman Foreign Ministry," IJMES, 1 (1970), 335–338, "The Foundation of the Ottoman Foreign Ministry: The Beginnings of Bureaucratic Reform Under Selim III and Mahmud II," IJMES, 3 (1972), 388–416, and an as yet unpublished paper, "The Metamorphosis of the Ottoman Ruling Class in the Period of Reform."
105 Enver Ziya Karal, *Osmanlı İmparatorluğunda ilk nüfus sayımı*, Ankara, 1943; Lütfi, II, 175, III, 142–146. Earlier, right after the Janissaries were destroyed, a census of men of military age in Istanbul alone showed some 45,000 Muslims, 30,000 Armenians, and 20,000 Greeks, excluding Catholics, who were counted separately. Lütfi, I, 280–281, II, 175.
106 Lütfi, V, 122–123.

107 Lütfi, III, 143; TV no. 169, August 9, 1838.
108 Lütfi, IV, 165.
109 TV 174 (14 Ramazan 1254/December 3, 1838).
110 BVA, HH48364; TV 1 (25 Cemazi I 1247), 9 (26 Recep 1247), and 33 (24 Safar 1248); Levy, pp. 457–458.
111 Lütfi, II, 61–62.
112 Moniteur Ottoman, November 5, 1831.
113 BVA, Maliyeden Müdevvere 9002, pp. 199–201, 219–220; Kanunname-i Askeri, II, 33b–38a.
114 TV 18 (14 Şevval 1247), 52 (4 Şevval 1248).
115 Lütfi, V, 28–29, 117; Levy, pp. 460–471.
116 Lütfi, V, 91, III, 148; BVA, HH48394, 48403.
117 Levy, pp. 490–506; Lütfi, V, 104–105.
118 Levy, pp. 539–545; TKS, E 119/41–78.
119 Levy, pp. 537–564.
120 Lütfi, IV, 140–141.
121 BVA, Maliyeden Müdevvere 9002, fol. 206–210.
122 Levy, pp. 573–580.
123 Lütfi, V, 74, 164–170; Levy, pp. 582–587; BVA, HH17983, 17702.
124 BVA, Cevdet Askeri 15667; Maliyeden Müdevvere 9002, fol. 110–111, 168–170.
125 Levy, pp. 508–536.
126 Levy, pp. 608–617; Helmut von Moltke, Briefe über Zustände und Begebenheiten in der Türkei aus den Jahren 1835 bis 1839, 5th ed., Berlin, 1891.
127 Lütfi, II, 171; Moniteur Ottoman, III/78 (January 22, 1834).
128 Lütfi, I, 251; BVA, HH27922r.
129 September 3, 1826; Lütfi, I, 241; BVA, HH24051; Buyruldu, II, 1–18, 30; Ergin, Belediye, I, 338–354.
130 1829; Lütfi, II, 173, 269–273, V, 35–37.
131 Lütfi, II, 173; Lewis, pp. 388–389.
132 Lütfi, III, 165.
133 Lütfi, V, 137; Berkes, pp. 99–121; Lewis, pp. 63–86; Ihsan Sungu, "Mekteb-i Maarif-i Adliyenin Tesisi," Tar. Ves., I/3 (1941), 212–225.
134 Levy, pp. 635–641; Lütfi, IV, 168–169; Rıza Tahsin, Mirat-ı Mekteb-i Tıbbiye, Istanbul, 1328–1330/1912–1914.
135 Lewis, pp. 97–101; Berkes, pp. 122–128; Lütfi, I, 191–193, 255–256, II, 148, 171–172, 269, IV, 100, V, 43, 50, 55, 63–64, VIII, 69–70.
136 Cavit Baysun, "Mustafa Reşid Paşa ve Londra elçilikleri esnasında siyasi yazılar," Tar. Ves., I/1, 31–40, II/9, 208–219, II/12, 452–461; Muahedat Mecmuası, I, 272–277; F. E. Bailey, British Policy and the Turkish Reform Movement, Cambridge, Mass., 1942.

2

The Era of Modern Reform: The Tanzimat, 1839–1876

The *Tanzimat-ı Hayriye,* or "Auspicious Reorderings," was a period of sustained legislation and reform that modernized Ottoman state and society, contributed to the further centralization of administration, and brought increased state participation in Ottoman society between 1839 and 1876. Its antecedents lay in the passion for "ordering" (*nizam*) that had guided the efforts of Gazi Hasan Paşa and Halil Hamit Paşa during the reign of Abdulhamit I (1774–1789) as well as those of Selim III and Mahmut II. It was the latter who made the Tanzimat possible by extending the scope of Ottoman government far beyond its traditional bounds to include the right and even the duty to regulate all aspects of life and changing the concept of Ottoman reform from the traditional one of attempting to preserve and restore the old institutions to a modern one of replacing them with new ones, some imported from the West. The successes as well as the failures of the Tanzimat movement in many ways directly determined the course reform was to take subsequently in the Turkish Republic to the present day. Leading the Tanzimat were Mahmut's sons, Abdulmecit I (1839–1861) and Abdulaziz (1861–1876), whose reigns encompassed the entire period and who provided the context in which the Tanzimat bureaucrats could and did proceed at their work.

The Accession of Abdulmecit I

The beginnings of the new reign were hardly auspicious. The old warrior Mehmet Husrev Paşa, who had fallen out of favor in Mahmut's later years, used his position as head of the Supreme Council (*Meclis-i Vâlâ*) to gain influence over his young and inexperienced heir-apparent, Abdulmecit, and planned to use the new regime to regain power. Even as Mahmut was being laid to rest, Husrev literally seized the seals of authority from Grand Vezir Mehmet Emin Rauf Paşa, getting the new ruler to appoint him grand vezir (July 2, 1839) and naming his former slaves and protégés to the chief positions of government as well as the palace. Mustafa Reşit, leader of the more liberal elements of the Ruling Class, was in Europe, helpless to do anything about this situation. In the end, however, Mehmet Husrev's usurpation of power proved a blessing in disguise for the reformers, for the blame for the military consequences of Mahmut's rash advance fell on the conservatives, while the reformers were able to absolve themselves of all responsibility for the defeat and gain the gratitude of the sultan and the masses for the diplomatic efforts used by Mustafa Reşit to save the empire.

Resolution of the Eastern Crisis

At the beginning of the reign the new sultan and the grand vezir faced a series of disasters. Grand Admiral Ahmet Fevzi Paşa, a rival of Mehmet Husrev, sailed the entire Ottoman fleet across the Mediterranean to Alexandria and surrendered it to the Egyptians in the fear that Husrev, himself an opponent of Muhammad Ali, might use his new power to turn the fleet over to the Russians in preparation for a joint attack.[1] Istanbul fell into a new panic. Abdulmecit immediately offered Muhammad Ali hereditary possession of the governorship of Egypt, but the latter demanded also hereditary rule of Syria and Adana as well as the dismissal of Husrev (June 20, 1839). Britain, France, Austria, and Prussia formed a new entente to resolve the crisis before it gave the Russians an opportunity for intervention. Russia joined also, realizing that preservation of the status quo was needed if it were to retain as much power as it had gained in 1829. Representing the Porte in London at this critical time was the foreign minister and now also ambassador, Mustafa Reşit, who negotiated with Palmerston and others not merely to resolve the crisis to the advantage of the Porte but also to gain foreign support for the reforms that would have to follow to strengthen the Ottoman government. Within a short time an agreement was reached among the five powers on a settlement that would leave Muhammad Ali in control only of Egypt, though as hereditary governor, while Syria and Cilicia would be returned to the sultan. Husrev Paşa and the cabinet in the meantime had resolved to accept all of Muhammad Ali's demands, thus leaving a truncated empire that most certainly would have fallen under Russian influence. But Mustafa Reşit returned in time to convince the sultan that the powers would be able to secure a better settlement and also bring to an end the Russian advantages granted at Hünkâr Iskelesi. The Russian dominance at the Porte established in 1833 thus was replaced by that of the powers who went on to rescue the empire at the price of direct intervention in Ottoman internal affairs during the remainder of the century.

Such intervention, then, replaced warfare with diplomacy during the next year. Now it was Muhammad Ali who wanted to use the victory of Nezib to send Ibrahim Paşa's army into Anatolia, but this time it was the latter who demurred, recognizing all too well what effect direct allied intervention might have. The negotiations that followed were in order to resolve the conflicting interests of the powers rather than of the parties themselves. The French hoped to assure their influence in the Levant by extending Muhammad Ali's power into Syria under their domination. Palmerston, on the other hand, insisted that the Egyptian leader leave Syria, hoping to strengthen the Ottomans and weaken the Egyptians and thus the French. Nicholas I stayed out of the crisis mainly because his own political and financial problems would have made it very difficult to provide the help promised to the Ottomans in the earlier agreements let alone take any active measures to occupy the western portions of the empire. He cooperated with the other allies, asking in return British support for a proposal to close the Straits permanently to warships in peace or war, thus to protect his southern shores and possibly break the cooperation between Britain and France, which had cramped his influence in Europe in the 1830s. Palmerston was agreeable, but British public opinion was inflamed by the idea of any cooperation with the Russians; hence it was dropped.

Back in Istanbul, Mustafa Reşit was given full credit for gaining the support of the powers. Abdulmecit moved to reward him and also further nurture Britain's determination to save the empire by promising a new reform program in an

Imperial Rescript proclaimed at Gülhane (November 3, 1839) (see pp. 59–61), declaring his intentions to widen and extend the reforms begun by his predecessor and thus to do his part to strengthen the empire. Soon, however, the sultan resumed the old political game, rapidly appointing and dismissing grand vezirs, ministers, and other officials, playing on the rivalries and factions so that he could control all of them. Thus even though Mustafa Reşit, as foreign minister, dominated also in domestic policy, his rival, Mehmet Husrev, remained grand vezir until June 1840. Then he was replaced, not by Mustafa Reşit, but rather by Mahmut's last grand vezir, Mehmet Emin Rauf Paşa (1840–1841, 1842–1846), who was relatively neutral in the political conflicts.

While Husrev Paşa remained in office the Porte insisted on full Egyptian withdrawal from Syria. Muhammad Ali refused, and the negotiations deadlocked. Once he was out, however, both sides became much more willing to bargain. The Egyptians then offered to return the Ottoman fleet intact if only their other demands were met. But Britain was not willing to allow so much to France's ally; on July 12, 1840, it signed the London agreement with the Ottomans, Russians, Austrians, and Prussians, promising to support the sultan against Egypt in return for his agreement to close the Straits to warships in war and peace. Muhammad Ali then was warned that if he accepted the offer and submitted to the sultan within ten days of notification, he would be allowed to keep hereditary rule of Egypt and life rule of southern Syria. If he accepted after ten days, only Egypt would be his. But if he waited any longer, even this would be lost – he would be no more than an Ottoman governor, with no hereditary rights. All Ottoman laws would apply in his domain. His armed forces would be under the sultan's command; and he still would have to surrender the Ottoman fleet. The French initially advised Muhammad Ali to resist but were unable to provide him with needed assistance. An Ottoman fleet joined British and Austrian ships near Cyprus in mid-September 1840. Beirut was bombarded, and forces of the three allies landed. British agents in the Lebanon stimulated a revolt that forced Başir to restore his loyalty to the sultan (October 5, 1840). The British force then defeated Ibrahim (October 10) and captured the major coastal cities, forcing him to abandon Damascus as well and retire to Egypt (February 1841). In the meantime, Muhammad Ali lost his last hope for French support when Emperor Louis-Philippe, angered by the diplomatic isolation that French policy in Egypt had created, appointed a new cabinet more willing to cooperate with general European policy (October 21, 1840). When a British fleet commanded by Admiral Napier began to blockade Alexandria and threatened to land troops, Muhammad Ali realized the game was up and agreed to withdraw all his remaining forces from Syria, give up his claims to it as well as Crete and the Arabian peninsula, and to accept the sultan as suzerain once again. The Ottoman fleet was allowed to sail back to Istanbul; and soon afterward (February 13, 1841), a decree was issued establishing Muhammad Ali as governor of Egypt, with the position to remain thereafter in the hands of his family.

The Eastern Crisis was not quite ended, however. The sultan's decree also limited the size of the Egyptian armed forces, specified the applicability of all Ottoman laws in Egypt, set the annual tribute at one-fourth of Egypt's revenues, and allowed the sultan to decide which of Muhammad Ali's heirs should succeed. But Muhammad Ali demanded modifications of the latter two points. With the support of the powers, which by now were anxious to settle the affair at whatever price, he was able to obtain the sultan's agreement to provisions allowing succession to the eldest son of the ruling governor and fixing the tribute at only 40 million kuruş annually, a far smaller sum. Mustafa Reşit resisted these changes, demanding also the permanent stationing of an Ottoman financial expert in Egypt to supervise its finances. But allied pressure and the liberal distribution of Egyptian largess at the highest levels in Istanbul finally secured his dismissal as foreign minister and the sultan's acceptance of the new arrangement.

Only the question of the Straits remained to be settled. As in other matters, Palmerston again prevailed in his desire to close these waterways to all warships, and the sultan was convinced on the grounds that it was traditional Ottoman policy to keep all foreign ships out of the Black Sea (The Straits Convention, July 13, 1841). The settlement, of course, not only protected Russia from the threat of foreign warships on its southern flanks, but also protected the other powers from Russian warships in the Straits and the Mediterranean. Russian ascendancy at the Porte had finally been replaced with that of all the powers, as exercised by their ambassadors, marking a far more real foreign presence than had been the case in the past. But the threats to the empire that had seemed so dangerous during the previous decade were gone, and a close and friendly relationship between the Ottoman and Egyptian courts followed, especially after Muhammad Ali's death in 1848. The Eastern Crisis fell into the background, and the Ottomans were free to put their house in order.

Father of the Tanzimat: Mustafa Reşit Paşa

The reforms that followed often imitated many of Mahmut II's programs and plans, but they were carried through mainly under the leadership of Mustafa Reşit Paşa, epitome of the Men of the Tanzimat (tanzimatçılar), a group he created to assist and succeed him eventually in the effort to transform Ottoman state and society. Who was Mustafa Reşit? Born in Istanbul in 1800, he was the son of the administrator of one of the religious foundations of Sultan Bayezit II. He started out as a student and apprentice in the Ilmiye institution. But his father's death in 1810 forced him to abandon the life of study that had been planned for him and instead to enter the service of an uncle, Ispartalı Seyyit Ali Paşa, accompanying him on an expedition to the Morea (1821), where he witnessed both the rout that the old Ottoman army suffered at the hands of the Greek rebels and the successes of Muhammad Ali's modern forces. It was the direct experience of the superiority of the new military institutions and ways that alerted Mustafa Reşit early in his career to the need for learning from Europe.

The experience in the Morea also seems to have convinced the young Mustafa that life in the Ilmiye was not for him; hence he joined the many young Muslims who were then aspiring to enter the newly revised scribal service of the Porte. He failed on several occasions due to the intense competition. But he finally gained an apprenticeship through the influence of his uncle's friend and former colleague, Beylikçi Akif Efendi, whose protégé he now became, rising rapidly in rank and position. During the war with Russia that followed the destruction of the Janissaries (1826–1828), Mustafa Reşit became seal bearer (mühürdar) to Grand Vezir Selim Paşa through Akif's recommendation, going to the front at Şumla. His reports on the battles and events in Rumeli so impressed the sultan that he transferred Mustafa Reşit to the more important Âmedi office, then the central bureau for both domestic and foreign affairs, placing him under the patronage of its chief, Pertev Efendi. Mustafa Reşit became his right-hand man, staying with him when he became reis ul-küttap (1827–1830) and then foreign minister and going with him to Cairo (June 22–July 1, 1830) to carry out the negotiations that led to Muhammad Ali's intervention in Crete. He so won the latter's esteem that he was offered a high position if he remained in Egypt, and he rejected the offer only after being persuaded by Pertev. This marked the beginning of Mustafa Reşit's rapid rise. In 1832 he was the Ottoman representative in the negotiations held with Muhammad Ali and Ibrahim Paşa, first in Cairo and then at Kütahya after Ibrahim advanced there (March 1833). Mustafa Reşit became *âmedci* late in 1832 and retained the post while serving as ambassador to Paris (1834–1836). There he was introduced to Europe and its statesmen for the first time, negotiating at the Quai d'Orsay over the questions of the French occupation of Algiers, as well as the Egyptian menace, and stopping in Vienna to speak with Metternich. Only now did he begin to learn French and English, thus much later in life than his protégés, who were well prepared before they went to Europe, giving them a considerable advantage.

After almost two years in Paris, Mustafa Reşit was transferred to the ambassadorship to the Court of St. James in London, using the occasion to converse with Palmerston and other leading English statesmen of the day about what should be done to reform the empire. With Mehmet Husrev leading the opposition to reform late in Mahmut's reign, the sultan sought to strengthen the reformers by bringing Mustafa Reşit back as foreign minister (July 13, 1837), now with the rank of vezir and title *paşa,* and by removing Husrev from the Seraskerate. During this his first term as foreign minister (July 1837–August 1838), Mustafa Reşit elaborated his plans for reform and worked to remove Mahmut's old suspicion of the British. He soon got the sultan to begin the Tanzimat by issuing decrees that attempted to end bribery and the confiscation of property, and to resume census surveys in Bursa and Gallipoli as a step toward administrative and financial reforms in the provinces. A committee of experts in agriculture, industry, and trade was formed to develop plans for the economic revitalization of the empire. Mustafa Reşit urged the sultan to achieve more equality among his subjects of different religions, getting him to state at one point: "I distinguish my Muslim subjects in the mosque, my Christian subjects in the church, and my Jewish subjects in the synagogue, but there is no other difference among them. My love and justice for all of them is very strong and they are all my true children."[2]

In pursuit of his desires for a general reform program Reşit persuaded the sultan to establish advisory councils at the palace and the Porte. But to balance and control his favorites, Mahmut appointed Husrev to chair the former, even though he basically opposed the reforms that Mustafa Reşit had in mind. Reşit sent himself as ambassador to London to get British support in the second Egyptian crisis, signing the trade convention of Balta Limanı (1838) and then returning home to get the sultan to proclaim the reform decree of Gülhane in order to assure the new relationship. When it finally came, therefore, the decree was issued at a time of increased foreign involvement in Ottoman affairs, but it was written by Mustafa Reşit to continue and expand the reforms already undertaken, in response to Ottoman problems and needs, and not merely as a concession to European or English pressure.[3]

The Imperial Rescript of Gülhane

The Ottoman reform program, as developed by Mustafa Reşit Paşa out of the reforms of Mahmut II, modified and developed by his own experience and observations in consideration of the empire's current needs, was officially proclaimed on Sunday, November 3, 1839, in a decree signed by the sultan (called *Hatt-ı Hümayun,* or Imperial Rescript) and read by Mustafa Reşit to an assemblage of dignitaries representing the principal institutions, classes, and groups of Ottoman society as well as various foreign missions. All were gathered at the square of Gülhane, beneath the walls of the Topkapı Palace, looking out at the Sea of Marmara at the northern end of the park that today bears the same name.[4] The document[5] consisted of two parts, the protocol (*mazbata*), or text itself, prepared under Mustafa Reşit's guidance at the Porte by its consultative council, and the sultan's statement of authorization, the *irade,* including his assent to the creation of new institutions that would (1) guarantee his subjects' security of life, honor, and property, (2) establish a regular system to assess and levy taxes, and (3) develop new methods to assure a fair system of conscripting, training, and maintaining the soldiers of his armed forces:

> The question of assessment of taxes also (is important), since a state, for the protection of its territory, most certainly needs money to provide for soldiers and other required expenditures. Since money can be secured by taxes imposed on the subjects, it is very important that this be dealt with in a proper way. Although, thank God, the people of our well-protected dominions already have been delivered from the scourge of monopolies, which previously were thought to be (suitable) revenues, the harmful system of tax farms, which never has produced useful fruit and is highly injurious, still is in use. This means handing over the political and financial affairs of a state to the will of a man and perhaps to the grip of compulsion and subjugation, for if he is not a good man, he will care only for his own benefit, and all his actions will be oppressive. Hereafter, therefore, it is necessary that everyone of the people [*ehali*] shall be assigned a suitable tax according to his possessions and ability, and nothing more shall be taken by anyone, and that the necessary expenditures for our land and sea forces as well as for other matters also shall be limited and set by the appropriate laws.

> The military also is one of the most important matters. While it is a sacred duty of the people to provide soldiers for the defense of the motherland [*vatan*], the system in force until now has not taken into account the actual population of each locality; some localities have been burdened beyond their capacity, and others have provided fewer soldiers than they could, causing disorder as well as damage to agriculture and trade, with their lifetime terms causing a lack of energy in service as well as lessening of the population. Therefore it is necessary to establish suitable procedures for taking soldiers from the localities when needed and to take them in rotation for terms of four or five years. . . .

The decree then went on to emphasize the duty of the state to protect the subjects and their rights:

> If security of property lacks, and people are not free from anxiety, no one cares for his state or his *millet* or works for the building of prosperity. On the other hand, if the situation is the opposite, that is, if property is fully secure, then the individual will care for his own affairs and his zeal for state and *millet* and love of motherland will increase daily. . . .

> In sum, until these laws and regulations have been introduced, it will not be possible to gain strength, prosperity, tranquillity, and repose. . . . Therefore hereafter until the pleas of the criminal are examined and adjudged publicly, in

accordance with the laws of the *Şeriat,* no one shall be executed, secretly or publicly; and no one may attack the reputation and honor of another; everyone shall be free to possess and use his properties completely and fully, without interference from anyone; and if a person commits a crime, and his heirs are free of complicity in that crime, the latter shall not be deprived of their rights of inheritance. All the subjects of our illustrious Sultanate, both Muslims and the members of the other *millets,* shall benefit from these concessions without exception. . . .

Finally, to decree and execute the laws needed to carry out the sultan's promises the Council of Judicial Ordinances (*Meclis-ı Ahkâm-ı Adliye*), established at the Porte since 1838, was made the sole consultative and legislative body, supplanting the Council of the Porte, with such new members as were needed to carry on its work.

The decree of Gülhane was not, thus, in any way an Ottoman constitution that limited the powers of the sultan, because he issued it and could abrogate it at will. But he did promise to limit his authority by accepting any law produced by the legislative machinery that he was creating, the first step toward such a limitation. And the decree did formalize the new interpretation of the scope and responsibility of the state to include the protection of security of life, honor, and property and the provision of equal justice for all subjects, regardless of religion. Though presented in the context of the Ottoman experience and expressing particular goals rather than abstract principles, the decree of Gülhane thus encompassed many of the ideals contained in the French Declaration of the Rights of Man and the Citizen of 1789.

The Men of the Tanzimat

The promises of Gülhane were brought to reality during the next 40 years by a group of ministers and bureaucrats collectively referred to as the Men of the Tanzimat, comprising Mustafa Reşit Paşa and his protégés, men whom he had trained and brought to power in the traditional Ottoman way to support his endeavors.

Through the first two decades leadership was provided by Mustafa Reşit, who served six times as grand vezir and three times as foreign minister, always driving the reforms onward while firmly basing the empire's survival on the friendship with England that he had established in 1838. He remained as foreign minister until 1841, falling from office when he refused to give in to Muhammad Ali's demands. He then served as ambassador to Paris (1840–1845) while the sultan tried to guide the reforms forward himself, returning later to become foreign minister (1845–1846) and grand vezir several times, with the sultan's resentment over his power leading to his dismissals, but being reappointed over and over again to further the reforms (see Table 2.1). As foreign minister (1853–1854) and then grand vezir (1854–1855) during the troubled years of the Crimean War and afterward, he fought the Russian demands regarding the Holy Places and secured British support. Mustafa Reşit was grand vezir at the time of his death on January 7, 1858, but his prime was past, and by then real power lay in the hands of his protégés, Âli and Fuat.

Mehmet Emin Âli Paşa (1815–1871), son of an Istanbul shopkeeper, like his master started as a *medrese* student and then transferred into the newly developed scribal service of the Porte (September 1, 1830). He learned French in the Translation Office and rose in its service, going as a junior clerk on missions to Vienna

Table 2.1. Offices held by the principal men of the Tanzimat, 1839–1876

Year	Mustafa Reşit Paşa	Âli Paşa	Fuat Paşa
1839	Foreign minister, 1837–1841		
1840	Ambassador to Paris, 1840–1845		First translator of the Porte, 1838–1852
1841		Ambassador to London,	
1842		1841–1844	
1843			
1844		Member of Supreme Council,	
1845		1844–1846	
1846	Grand vezir, 1846–1848	Foreign minister, 1846–1848	
1847			
1848		Foreign minister, 1848–1852	
1849			
1850			
1851			
1852	Grand vezir, 1852	Grand vezir, 1852	Foreign minister, 1852
1853	Foreign minister, 1853–1854		Member, Council of the
1854	Grand vezir, 1854–1855	Foreign minister, 1854–1855	Tanzimat, 1852–1855
1855		Grand vezir, 1855–1856	Foreign minister, 1855–1856
1856	Grand vezir, 1856–1857	Foreign minister, 1856–1858	Chairman, Council of the
1857	Grand vezir, 1857–1858		Tanzimat, 1856–1858
1858	Died, 1858	Grand vezir, 1858–1859	Foreign minister,
1859		Chairman, Council of the	1858–1860
1860		Tanzimat, 1859–1861	
1861			Grand vezir, 1861–1863
1862			
1863			Grand vezir, 1863–1866
1864			
1865			
1866			
1867		Grand vezir, 1867–1871	Foreign minister,
1868			1867–1869
1869			Died, 1869
1870			
1871		Died, 1871	
1872			
1873			
1874			
1875			
1876			

(1835–1836) and St. Petersburg (1837) and thus gaining a much wider and deeper knowledge of Europe and its ways than that of Mustafa Reşit. Âli's real rise to power came as a result of his service as Reşit's personal scribe and translator during the latter's embassy to London. He then rose in the Foreign Ministry, became ambassador to London (1841–1844) while Reşit was out of office, and, when Reşit was restored to power, he returned to Istanbul as a member of the principal legislative body of the time, the Supreme Council of Judicial Ordinances (*Meclis-i Vâlâ-yı Ahkâm-ı Adliye*), thus gaining a knowledge of domestic problems. He became foreign minister during Mustafa Reşit's next two terms as grand vezir (1846–1848, 1848–1852), with both winning fame in Europe for their role in receiving refugees from the 1848 revolutions in Austria and Russia and resisting the demands of these powers for their imprisonment and return.

At this point the careers of Mustafa Reşit and Âli became intertwined with that of another of Reşit's protégés, Keçecizade Mehmet Fuat Paşa (1815–1869), who was the same age as Âli but somewhat slower in rising to high position. From an ulema family in Istanbul, Fuat began a *medrese* education but had to leave when his father was dismissed from his position and banished to the provinces. Without family support the young Fuat studied in the medical school (*Tıbhane-i Amire*) for a time. Using the knowledge of French that he gained, he became scribe to Tahir Paşa, governor of Tunis, spending almost four years there (1832–1836) before his master's death forced him to seek a new patron. Whereas Âli had been Mustafa Reşit's protégé for some time, Fuat entered his service only in 1837. He rose to become first translator of the Porte while Reşit and Âli were in London, and he became a friend of Âli's and, as a result, protégé of Reşit only after their return, while they were in power the first two years after Gülhane (1839–1841), and again between 1846 and 1852. It was only in 1848 that he achieved equality in rank and influence with Âli and Reşit as a result of his brilliant negotiations with the Russians in Bucharest and then St. Petersburg regarding the refugees from the 1848 revolutions then flooding into the empire, and also those with Muhammad Ali's successor in Egypt, Prince 'Abbas (1852).

In 1852 Mustafa Reşit was removed as prime minister, ostensibly because of disputes with the director of the arsenal, but in fact due to the sultan's desire to regain some control of state affairs. That this was not a move against reform as such was shown when the sultan replaced him with Âli in his first term as grand vezir (1852–1853) and accepted his recommendation that Fuat succeed him as foreign minister (1852–1853). Reform continued under their leadership, but there rose a division between Reşit and his protégés that was to last until his death. Partly it was due simply to the pique of the master now suddenly supplanted by men who owed everything to him. Reşit was a strong supporter of Britain and was in close contact with Palmerston and the famous British ambassador to the Porte, Stratford de Redcliffe. Âli and Fuat, on the other hand, were much friendlier to France. Âli and Fuat were in power in 1852 when their support of the French position in the disputes over the Holy Places preceding the Crimean War led to their fall. Both stayed out of the limelight for some time, with Âli later becoming chairman and Fuat a member of the new reform legislature then established as the Council of the Tanzimat. With the outbreak of the war there was no need to conciliate the Russians any further by keeping them out of office; thus Mustafa Reşit became foreign minister (1853–1854) and then grand vezir (1854–1855), bringing Âli back as foreign minister. The differences surfaced again over the terms of the Treaty of Paris, when Âli replaced him as grand vezir (1855–1856) and Fuat became foreign minister. Stratford de Redcliffe's intrigues finally secured Reşit's restoration to his fifth and sixth terms as grand vezir, while Âli held the post of foreign minister and Fuat returned to the Council of the Tanzimat as chairman.

During the final two decades of the Tanzimat, reform was in the hands of Mustafa Reşit's protégés. Âli served as grand vezir in 1858–1859, falling from that office when he tried to limit palace extravagances. He became chairman of the Council of the Tanzimat (1859–1861), while Fuat remained as foreign minister (1858–1860), going to Lebanon to settle the crisis that had led to foreign intervention there and developing a plan for autonomy that settled that question. Âli's service as grand vezir came to an end with the accession of the new sultan, Abdulaziz (1861–1876), who preferred the more decisive Fuat to the slower and more cautious Âli. Made grand vezir twice (1861–1863, 1863–1866), Fuat made a vain effort to secure the kind of autonomy that Abdulmecit had allowed Âli. Fuat resigned in 1866 in opposition to the sultan's plan to marry the daughter of the Egyptian governor Ismail Paşa to unite the empire once again, while Âli followed a year later due to disputes over the resolution of the revolt in Crete and the settlement of relations with the new Serbian state.

When the revolt in Crete had reached such a state of crisis that Russian intervention was imminent, the British and French managed to get the sultan to reappoint Âli to his final term as grand vezir (1867–1871), with Fuat again as foreign minister, accompanying Abdulaziz on his famous trip through Europe (summer 1867) and serving as acting grand vezir while Âli went to Crete in a final, successful effort to end the revolt with a grant of increased autonomy (1867–1868). But with the double burden, Fuat fell ill. After a trip to France to seek rest and medical help, he died in Nice (February 12, 1869), with Âli succumbing two years later at his *yalı* in Bebek on the shores of the Bosporus (September 7, 1871).

Mustafa Reşit, Âli, and Fuat were the best known of the nineteenth-century Ottoman reformers, but there were many other aspiring bureaucrats who were largely unknown to the world while remaining in the service of the vast bureaucracy that was created as the instrument of Ottoman modernization. Two who rose out of the crowd to make significant contributions to the work of reform were Ahmet Cevdet Paşa and Ahmet Şefik Midhat Paşa, the former a member of the ulema who performed major work in his own branch of the Ruling Class as well as an administrator, the latter a scribe and provincial reformer who rose as one of the leaders of the constitutional movement that ended the Tanzimat in 1876.

Ahmet Cevdet (1822–1895) is one of the most underrated men of the Tanzimat period. Born in Bulgaria of a local notable family, he went much further in the ulema studies than most of his colleagues, doing advanced work in Istanbul (1839–1845) with some of the leading teachers of his time. Even in these early years, however, he displayed not only brilliance but also impatience with the old methods and curriculum. Dissatisfied with the traditional arithmetic and algebra lessons taught in the *medreses*, he took lessons from teachers at the Army Engineering School. He also developed an early interest in the science of history, learning to treat it not merely as a chronicle of events but also as a study of the human experience by means of critical evaluation of the sources. He went on to supplement his interests with studies of Islamic, international, and French law – all before he had reached the age of 30.

Ahmet Cevdet actually graduated from the *medrese* and received a diploma (*icaze*) that qualified him to serve in an *Ilmiye* position. But at this point he made a contact that was to alter fundamentally the rest of his career. Mustafa Reşit was about to enter his first term as grand vezir and was anxious to find a member of the ulema to teach him enough about the Islamic religious law so that he could avoid open conflict with it when introducing reforms. He wanted a learned man but one who was open-minded and willing to discuss problems. Ahmet Cevdet was the obvious answer. Cevdet thereafter lived in Mustafa Reşit's house, tutored him and his children and also a number of his protégés, remaining there until the master's death in 1858. Cevdet now received what he later called his "second education" in the techniques of state administration and politics under the guidance of the old master, becoming the latter's personal scribe and adviser and at times working closely with Fuat and Âli.

Reşit soon appointed Cevdet to various educational positions as his agent in the same way that Âli and Fuat represented him in the administration. In 1850–1851 Cevdet served as director of a school established to train male teachers for the new secular school system, developing an interest in modern methods of teaching. He also became chief scribe to the Council on Education created by Reşit to prepare new laws and regulations for the secular schools. His career as a historian began in 1852 when the Society of Knowledge (*Encümen-i Daniş*), created by Reşit to advance Ottoman culture, assigned him to compile a history of the Ottoman Empire from the Treaty of Küçük Kaynarca to the destruction of the Janissary corps (1774–1826) on the basis of the state records placed at his disposal. He served also as state chronicler (*vakanüvis*) from 1855 to 1861, working both to complete his history as well as to record the events of his own time, the actual requirement of the position. He also then secured his first *Ilmiye* position, becoming kadi of Galata (1856) in addition to his other secular duties.

When Mustafa Reşit rose to his sixth term as grand vezir, he began to think of Ahmet Cevdet as more loyal and conservative than the now powerful and independent Âli and Fuat; thus he made Cevdet a member of the Council of the Tanzimat, where the latter played an active and important role in preparing laws in his own specialities, despite his relative youth, virtually writing the new regulations on landownership and cadastral surveys. As his history project progressed, he mainly abandoned the old annalistic approach for one emphasizing problems and topics, with an increasingly critical examination of the sources. He also was the principal author of the regulation that created the new Supreme Council of Judicial Ordinances in place of the Council of the Tanzimat (1861), himself becoming a member of the new body.

It was during the decade of the 1860s, while Âli and Fuat dominated the government, that Ahmet Cevdet finally had to take the step that he had long been avoiding: transferring from the *Ilmiye* to the Scribal Institution, exchanging his position among the ulema for that of vezir, and, at the same time, giving up his position as official chronicler. A number of important missions led to this step. In 1861 he went as special agent to Albania with wide powers to suppress revolts and develop a new administrative system. After this, when Fuat became grand vezir the second time, it was rumored that Cevdet would achieve his greatest ambition by becoming *şeyhulislam,* but this was denied him due to the strong opposition of many ulema who resented his enlightened and liberal interpretation of religious matters. He therefore became inspector general in Bosnia and Herzegovina (1863–1864), extending the Tanzimat reforms there despite the opposition of the Habsburgs, who wanted the area for themselves, as well as of the Slavic national groups. He now was identified as a leading provincial troubleshooter. His next effort was to settle the nomadic tribes and establish order in Kozan in southeastern Anatolia (1865). After his official transfer to the Scribal Institution (1866), he was able to accept regular administrative positions, becoming governor of the new province of Aleppo, which was formed to apply the Tanzimat provincial reforms recently introduced by Fuat.

It is ironic that Ahmet Cevdet's greatest contributions to the fields of law and justice were made after he left the *Ilmiye*. In 1868, when the Supreme Council was divided into separate legislative and judicial bodies, Cevdet was made chairman of the latter, subsequently becoming the first minister of justice and writing the major pieces of legislation that established the beginnings of a secular court system in the empire for the first time. He also led a number of ministers and members of the ulema who opposed Âli's desire to introduce an entirely secular, French-inspired corpus of civil law for these courts, instead convincing the sultan that the new civil law code should be based on principles derived from Islamic law, modernized to meet current realities. Cevdet served as chairman of the commission established to draw up the new law code, to which the simple name *Mecelle* (Law Collection) was given, a task that occupied him until the last volume was published in 1876.

Despite the many positions that he had held, Cevdet still was only 50 years of age in 1872. During the last two decades of his life, he served in many ministerial positions, mainly in education and justice, while slowly completing the two major works of his life, the Ottoman history and the *Mecelle*. In 1873 he became minister of pious foundations, then minister of education (1873–1874), undertaking major changes in the secular system of education that had been introduced, reforming the elementary and middle schools, established a new level of preparatory schools for students wishing to go on to the secondary and technical schools, and also expanding teacher-training schools. At this time efforts were made to depose Abdulaziz to secure a constitution. Cevdet – basically a conservative man with a strong reverence for tradition despite his openness to new ideas – opposed the idea and as a result was hated by the constitutionalists thereafter. As an administrator, however, he also opposed the corrupt government of Mahmut Nedim. Thus the grand vezir sent him out of Istanbul as inspector general to Rumeli and then as governor of Syria for a short time (1875–1876). He played no role in the events leading to Abdulaziz's deposition and death and the succession first of Murat V (1876) and then of Abdulhamit II (1876–1909), but his basic reverence for the traditional ways left him hostile to those who accomplished these deeds and imposed a constitution that limited the sovereignty of the sultan and the holy law of Islam. He was close to Abdulhamit, therefore, as the latter began to restore the autocracy of the palace, serving as minister of justice (1876–1877), of the interior (1877) and then of pious foundations (1878–9), commerce (1879) and justice (1879–1882). It was at this time that he was involved in the most difficult assignment of his life, acting as the sultan's main prosecutor and interrogator of Midhat Paşa when the latter was accused, tried, and convicted of the murder of the former sultan, Abdulaziz, a process that sultan and minister pushed through more because of Midhat's personality and the Constitution he had introduced than the actual facts of the case (1881).

Ahmet Cevdet retired from public office for a number of years after the trial (1882–1886). He now devoted his attention to giving a modern education to his daughters, completing his Ottoman history, and also bringing together all the records on current events that he had begun compiling while court historian. He turned over his *Tezakir* (Memoirs) covering the years from 1839 to 1890, to his successor as official historian, Ahmet Lütfi Efendi, and also wrote the *Maruzat*, a summary of expositions covering the years from 1839 to 1876 for the personal reference of Abdulhamit. Still only 64 years old, Cevdet's last official position was minister of justice (1886–1890); he resigned finally due to quarrels with Prime Minister Yusuf Kâmil Paşa and then served as minister without portfolio and acted as an elder statesman until his death on May 25, 1895.

Finally, there was Midhat Paşa, in some ways the most courageous and farsighted, in others the most foolhardy, and certainly the most tragic of all the Men of the Tanzimat. The start of his career was very similar to that of his contemporaries Âli and Fuat. Ahmet Şefik Midhat (1822–1884) was also born in Istanbul of an ulema father, spent his early years in religious schools, but then entered the offices of the Imperial Council (1833) as the protégé of Akif Paşa and subsequently transferred into the offices of the grand vezir (1840). It was at this point that Midhat's career diverged from that of his colleagues, leaving him forever marked as an outsider among the Men of the Tanzimat. Whereas they gained the patronage of Mustafa Reşit Paşa and rose rapidly as the result of his influence, Midhat found it necessary to leave the department in order to advance. He left Istanbul and spent five years in the service of several provincial governors, in the process acquiring a far more intimate knowledge of provincial affairs than Âli and Fuat. In 1846 he returned to the Porte, entering the department in charge of preparing the protocols of the *Meclis-i Vâlâ* and remaining there for over a decade, rising to the position of chief scribe in 1861. It was during this time that his previous provincial experience led his superiors to give him temporary assignments of investigating wrongdoing outside the capital, jobs that he performed so capably and honestly that he incurred the everlasting enmity of several malingering bureaucrats who subsequently were to cause him considerable trouble once they regained their places in the Ottoman hierarchy. Included among the malefactors was the governor of Syria, Kıbrıslı Mehmet Paşa, who managed to escape punishment due to his status as a protégé of the sultan and who later as grand vezir did all he could to secure vengeance from the unrepentant Midhat. At the time, though, since Mustafa Reşit Paşa was in power, Midhat was rewarded for his service by being made chief scribe of the Anatolian Department of the *Meclis-i Vâlâ* (1853). The conclusion of the Crimean War, however, changed the situation in Istanbul, when Reşit left the grand vezir's office and his successor Âli placed Kıbrıslı Mehmet in charge while he and Fuat went to Paris to attend the peace conference (1856). The acting grand vezir immediately tried to get Midhat imprisoned by accusing him of holding an illegal tax farm, violating a recent decree that forbade state employees from maintaining such holdings. But the accusation was disproved in open trial, leaving Midhat stronger than ever at the Porte. Following the Peace of Paris, when Reşit returned to his sixth term as grand vezir, he sent Midhat on an ·investigatory mission to Bulgaria, which resulted in accusations against several local governors, though again they were not punished due to the sultan's intervention. Midhat was so angry that he obtained Âli's permission to go to Europe for a rest (1858). This provided Midhat with an opportunity to observe European civilization and draw from the experience in subsequent years.

On his return Midhat was made chairman of the *Meclis-i Vâlâ,* and he did so well in expediting legislation and in directing the trial at Kuleli of those involved in a conservative plot against the throne that he finally gained palace favor. Kıbrıslı Mehmet, during his third term as grand vezir (1860–1861), appointed Midhat as governor of Niş to get him away from the sultan. But Midhat used his service there (1861–1864) to develop the techniques of provincial reform that were to become the basis for the new provincial reform law of 1864, and which he subsequently was to apply as governor of the Danube province formed out of much of Bulgaria (1864–1868). Midhat was recalled to Istanbul (1867–1868) to help the central government evaluate the provincial reforms and recommend modifications on the basis of experience. When Âli returned from settling the problems of Crete, he reorganized the *Meclis-i Vâlâ* into separate legislative (*Şurayı Devlet*) and judicial (*Divan-ı Ahkam-ı Adliye*) branches, with Midhat appointed chairman of the former (and Ahmet Cevdet of the latter), thus marking his emergence into a significantly high position in Istanbul. But Midhat still found it difficult to defer to his superiors. He was nobody's servant, and in attempting to apply his own ideas he clashed repeatedly with Âli, who had expected his protégé to accept his will. Midhat pushed through a number of important regulations, modifying the land tax system, developing a new regulation on mines, establishing banks to provide low-interest loans to cultivators, and encouraging the working class to open savings accounts by using interest earnings as an incentive. But his clashes with Âli led finally to his dismissal and exile (January 31, 1869) to the post of governor of Baghdad, thus depriving the Tanzimat of the energy and ability of a man it could ill afford to lose, especially now that Fuat was gone. In Baghdad, however, Midhat went ahead with his old energy to apply the Tanzimat provincial reforms, also successfully suppressing the tribes and ending Persian border incursions. New tax systems, land distribution to peasants, dams for irrigation and navigation, and improvements in cultivation methods also marked Midhat's term and made him, in truth, the founder of modern Iraq. Midhat's involvement in the momentous events that ended the Tanzimat and introduced a constitution into the Ottoman Empire, from 1871 until his death in 1884, will be discussed later.

These, then, were the most important Men of the Tanzimat. To what extent did they have a common approach? How did they differ as persons and as political leaders? Mustafa Reşit Paşa, of course, differed considerably from the others both in age and experience. He was born during the reign of Selim III. Though educated in the traditional institutions, he was able to see their shortcomings and adopt a new policy based on his observations in Europe. It was he who had made the Porte into an instrument of reform as well as political power. Âli and Fuat were his political children. They did not have to create the reform institutions in the Porte. That battle had been fought and won by Reşit. They only had to defend it and apply it to the problems of the time. They were much more skillful in politics, at times appointing members of opposing factions to important positions either to gain their support or to throw all the blame on them in crucial situations. They were far more willing to compromise to achieve ultimate objectives than was Reşit. But they also were somewhat different from one another.

Âli was short in stature, meticulous, cautious, and quiet; he emphasized etiquette and seniority. He tended to postpone decisions as long as possible before acting so as to consider all alternatives and consequences. He was alert, self-controlled, and a strong believer in following the proper lines of personal and administrative etiquette. He was the true politician of the two, playing off the foreign ambassadors, the palace, and the ulema to maintain the power of the Porte. He believed in gradual reform, putting everything in its place as needed. Fuat, on the other hand, was tall, handsome, friendly, and eloquent. He believed in pushing ahead rapidly. He was blunter in his relations with the sultan and opposing politicians and often alienated people and created enmities.[6] As for Ahmet Cevdet, he was the most brilliant of all the leading Men of the Tanzimat. His lifelong attachment to the ulema, however, left him anxious to restore and modernize the old institutions to meet the needs of the time and prevent them from being swept away. So it was that he developed the *Mecelle* legal code, opposing Abdulaziz's deposition and the Constitution, and finally supported Abdulhamit II against the constitutionalists, even while remaining open to new ways and applying major reforms in the areas of justice and education. Midhat Paşa, for his part, was the most Western and least diplomatic of all. He was not hesitant in telling others where they had failed and how they could correct their errors by accepting his judgment. He had tremendous energy and devotion and introduced modern reforms on both the provincial and central levels with an intensity and a determination to see them put into practice that was almost unique among the Men of the Tanzimat. He was very much like Mustafa Kemal Atatürk, founder of the Turkish Republic. He was the only Tanzimat leader with an interest in the problems of the mass of the people and a desire to improve their lot. But his unwillingness to bow to authority and tendency to speak his mind earned him enemies, frustrating many of his reform efforts and contributing to his downfall.

The Men of the Sultan: Ruling Class Politics in the Tanzimat Era

The shift in political power from palace to Porte, engineered by Mustafa Reşit and maintained by his successors, was hardly acceptable to the two sultans of the time despite their overall support for reform. Many other members of the Ruling Class also opposed the reforms either because of genuine feeling for the ways of the past or simply because of their fear of losing their places within the ruling circles of state. This opposition coalesced under the leadership of three major institutions, the Inner Service of the palace (*Mabeyin-i Hümayun*), led by the sultans, their mothers, relatives, and protégés, the *Bab-ı Meşihat,* led by the *şeyhulislam* and representing the ulema, and the *Bab-ı Serasker,* as representative of the army. Each group built its power very much as Mustafa Reşit had done, developing and training protégés and placing them in important positions. Of these groups, the least successful politically during the nineteenth century was the ulema. Their basic sources of power, the endowment revenues and the systems of Muslim education and justice, were undermined by the reforms, and their influence among the masses and power over the students of religion no longer had the kind of impact that they had when they were supplemented and enforced by the Janissaries. The few members of the ulema who did benefit from the secular education of the time, such as Ahmet Cevdet, entered the service of the Porte and were absorbed by it, thus basically becoming its agents in countering the ulema's influence rather than contributing to it.

It was, then, the *Bab-ı Serasker* and the palace that formed the most potent political alliance against the Porte during the years of the Tanzimat. The alliance was forged by the aged but still active founder of the new army, Mehmet Husrev Paşa, who died in 1855 at the age of 99 after having served as *serasker* between 1827 and 1836 and then again for a short time in 1846. His policies were not formed in consequence of opposition to reform as such; he had, in fact, built the new army, and even in his eighties he worked to eliminate corruption and install further modernization. He was grand vezir when the Gülhane proclamation was made, and he supported it. But he opposed Mustafa Reşit Paşa's concentration of power at the Porte, establishing a meeting of minds between the leaders of the army and the palace that filtered down to all ranks. His protégé and immediate successor as *serasker* (1836–1838, 1839–1840), Halil Rifat Paşa (d. 1856), who married into the imperial family (and so bore the title *damat,* son-in-law), subsequently served four times as grand admiral (1830–1832, 1843–1845, 1847–1848, 1854–1855) as well as chairman of the *Meclis-i Vâlâ* (1842–1845, 1848–1849), putting him in a good position to build and maintain the conservative group, usually in cooperation with Husrev. This cooperation was further developed by Damat Mehmet Ali Paşa (1813–1868), married in 1845 to Mahmut II's daughter Adile Sultan and subsequently grand admiral five times (1845–1847, 1848–1849, 1851–1852, 1855–1858, and 1858–1863), serving also as *serasker* (1849–1851, 1853–1854) and as grand vezir once (1852–1853). It was through Damat Mehmet in particular that the sultan chose, trained, and entered into state service a number of young protégés. The palace, however, was far less fortunate in its choices than was Mustafa Reşit Paşa. Perhaps the most prominent of these was Kıbrıslı Mehmet Emin Paşa (1813–1881), whose problems with Midhat Paşa have already been noted. His uncle, chief of Mahmut II's private treasury, entered him into the palace service at an early age, securing rapid advancement for him in the *Hassa* regiment (1832–1833) and then a couple of years study in France (1833–1835) at the sultan's expense to fit him to compete with Reşit's men. Through palace influence he rose rapidly in the army, serving in a series of provincial military posts, at Acre (1844–1845), Jerusalem (1845–1847), Tirnova (1847) and Belgrade (1847–1848).

Though his administrative mismanagement led to numerous complaints, none of these served to dislodge him due to palace support and the sultan's conviction that the accusations were due mainly to politics. In 1848 he was made vezir and ambassador to London because of "his wide knowledge of Europe and European languages" (1848–1850). He then served as governor of Aleppo (1850–1851), brutally suppressing bedouin revolts; but when he was appointed governor of the far more difficult island of Crete, he declined the honor (1851) and returned to Istanbul. In 1851 he became field marshal (*müşir*) in the Imperial army in the Arab provinces, based in Syria, and while he managed to stay in that position despite Midhat's findings of mismanagement and corruption, he finally was dismissed in 1853 because of his evident failure to organize the forces at his disposal for participation in the Crimean War. This failure was, however, rewarded with even higher positions. He served as grand admiral during the latter part of the war (1854–1855) and then as grand vezir three times when the Men of the Tanzimat were out of power, in 1854, 1859, and 1860–1861, gaining the reputation of being the most stupid and pompous of all the politicians of the era, with Âli at times appointing him to high positions to baffle and confuse his enemies.

The key balancing force in Tanzimat politics among palace, army, and Porte was Mütercim Mehmet Rüştü Paşa (1811–1882), an officer in the new army (1825–1843) and protégé of Husrev and Halil Rifat, who rose to be *serasker* (1852–1853, 1855–1856, and 1857–1859, 1861–1863, and 1867–1868) and grand vezir (1859–1860, 1866–1867, 1872–1873, 1876, and 1878), at times also serving on the Council of the Tanzimat and as director of the arsenal. While Rüştü originally rose as the candidate of the palace/army clique, he was by far the ablest of the lot, respected by friend and foe alike, and was often brought to power by the Men of the Tanzimat when they wanted a job handled ably by someone who could conciliate the opposition and get its cooperation and also who would work for the good of the empire rather than for personal benefit. Throughout his career Rüştü never let politics interfere with his desire to continue the reforms, thus representing also the sincere reform desires of the sultans whom he served over the years.

In this clash of policy and ambition, party and individual rivalries, the foreign embassies often played decisive rolls, intervening with money and political pressure, supporting one politician or another to secure their own aims in both Ottoman domestic and foreign policy. The British and, to a lesser extent, the French supported the Porte as the best hope for policies that would maintain the empire, and the Austrians and Russians supported the palace and army for opposite reasons. Influential also were the members of the Egyptian ruling family, who gradually increased their own independence, transforming their governorship into an autonomous khedivate and influencing Ottoman politics through liberal gifts to the politicians of Istanbul, in particular those of the palace. Finally, not to be overlooked but perhaps better left to a later discussion, there were new political forces rising among younger members of the Ruling Class as well as some subjects, men known generally as Young Ottomans, who opposed the autocratic behavior of the Men of the Tanzimat and the shift of power from the sultan to the Porte without a corresponding extension of the representative principle (see pp. 131–132).

Considering this complex political situation, it is not surprising that there was a high degree of political instability during the Tanzimat. From 1839 to 1876 there were 39 different terms as grand vezir, 33 as foreign minister, with each position often being held several times by the same person (see Appendix A). What is wondrous in all of this is not so much the political instability, but rather the general stability of the empire's institutional development through much of the period, with few relapses to reaction even when the conservatives were in power. This continuity of policy was provided mainly by the bureaucratic substratum of the new Ottoman system.

The New Ruling Class

The Tanzimat created a centralized government based on the new Ruling Class, the bureaucrats, now called *memurs*. This class constituted a modern generation of Ottomans that sustained the tempo of modernization mainly oblivious to, or even in spite of, the waves of political and military crisis that hit the empire during much of the century. Before examining the specific reforms, we must first examine the new system of government and the bureaucrats who made it work.

The Central Government

The Executive

Executive and administrative duties on the central level were distributed among functional ministries, some gathered under the wings of the grand vezir at the Sublime Porte and contributing to its power, others, particularly those involved with the military, religion, and justice, building their own centers of power in other parts of the capital. Each ministry developed originally as both an executive and a legislative body, assisted by internal advisory councils (*meclis*), which themselves sometimes rose to be ministries once their duties and developing staffs justified their separation. Since the leading Men of the Tanzimat themselves often served as grand vezir (*sadr-ı azam*)[7] and/or as minister of interior and foreign affairs, these departments of the Porte in particular tended to develop authority far beyond that indicated by their names alone.

Ministry of the Interior (Nezaret-i Dahiliye). The Ministry of the Interior was created in 1836 out of the office of the lieutenant of the grand vezir (*sadaret kethüdası*) to handle the domestic portions of his duties. It was taken back by the grand vezir two years later to give him the power he needed to dominate the other ministers. During much of the Tanzimat, it remained under the grand vezir, administered by his undersecretary (*sadaret müsteşarı*) but with its own autonomous bureaucratic structure and responsibilities, so that when, because of Fuat's illness and death in 1869, Âli found it too burdensome to act as both foreign minister and grand vezir, he was able to separate the Interior Ministry from the latter without too much difficulty, restoring its independent existence (February 18, 1869), which it retained until the end of the empire.

The Ministry of the Interior was responsible for the central administration of all internal matters in the empire. As did the other ministries, it was in charge of receiving proposals on regulations and laws within its area of competence and evaluating them before they were sent on to the legislative bodies and the sultan. It also was responsible for executing them if he gave his approval in the form of an *irade*. It controlled the organization and operations of the provincial and local administrations and police forces and, thus, the appointment, promotion, disciplining, inspection, direction, and regulation of all bureaucrats outside the central government, from the governors down to the police chiefs and municipal officials. It was charged also with recommending all laws, regulations, and administrative acts that might increase the comfort and wealth of all notables and subjects, for promoting industry and trade, regulating publications, and the like. Once independent, it was allowed to develop its own budget, unlike the other ministries, and to communicate directly with the responsible legislative bodies without the intervention or even the approval of the grand vezir, thus making its minister quite powerful.[8]

To carry out its functions the ministry was organized into departments, including that of the undersecretary (*müsteşar*) himself, which supervised provincial officials and determined their policies. There were three departments to deal with civil service affairs: one in charge of selection, another of keeping records of appointments, ranks, and promotions, and a third of administering the retirement fund. Separate departments also organized and administered the population censuses, supervised the empire's press and regulated and settled the refugees entering the empire. To regulate Istanbul and the other municipalities a corps of *kapı kethüda*s was established at the ministry to represent each provincial governor and to centralize the ministry's activities concerning his province; and three inspectors were maintained around the empire to supervise and inspect administration in each of its three major areas, Rumeli, Anatolia, and the Arab world. Special committees also were maintained at the ministry to organize and supervise health and sanitation and to regulate the affairs of the Holy Cities.

Ministry of Foreign Affairs (Nezaret-i Hariciye). Since this ministry was Mustafa Reşit Paşa's base of power in his early years, in addition to its nominal duties it handled a number of matters that normally would have been left to other ministries, including internal reform legislation, the status and regulation of foreign subjects and non-Muslims in the empire, and foreign commercial as well as political relations. Various matters of legislation and record-keeping – previously handled by the Imperial Council and then by the Porte under the authority of the *reis ul-küttap* in the name of the grand vezir – now were placed entirely under the jurisdiction of the Foreign Ministry. To handle these functions, the ministry was divided into two principal sections, each under an undersecretary (*müsteşar*) and divided into departments headed by chief scribes. The foreign affairs section had departments to deal with foreign affairs, foreign trade, receiving foreign representatives as well as making arrangements for the proper ranking of all Ottomans participating in official ceremonies, and supervising the foreign press. The second section, consisting mainly of the old Imperial Council departments handling internal affairs, had two departments: that of the Imperial Council itself (*Divan-ı Hümayun Kalemi*), headed by the scribe of imperial orders, which issued and recorded all imperial orders, letters of the sultan to foreign rulers and officials, and other communications and notes exchanged with foreign governments or their representatives at the Porte, treaties, and documents (*berat*) that assigned, appointed, and removed officials and sanctioned travel within and outside the empire. The Department of non-Muslim Religious Affairs (*Mezahib-i Gayr-i Müslim Dairesi*) was divided into sections for each *millet* and charged with issuing orders concerning them and their members originating not only in the ministry itself but also in all other departments and ministries of government. In addition, there were two lesser sections, the Translation Office (*Tercüme Odası*) and the ministry's Archives Department (*Hariciye Evrak Odası*), which later developed into the archives for all the departments of the Sublime Porte.[9]

Ministry of Finance (Nezaret-i Maliye *or* Bab-ı Defteri). The Ministry of Finance, which united all the principal treasuries and financial departments of state, was created by Mahmut II in early 1838; but it was dissolved into its constituent departments by Grand Vezir Mehmet Husrev Paşa during his brief period of dominance following the accession of Abdulmecit, in a last vain effort to regain full financial independence for the army (August 2, 1839). Soon after Mustafa Reşit's return to Istanbul and the issuance of the Gülhane proclamation, however, the *Mansure* and Imperial treasuries were united again and eventually the Ministry of Finance was restored (June 20, 1839).[10]

At first the various component sections were intended to be fairly autonomous under the minister and his undersecretary, with separate treasuries (*hazine*) and accounting departments (*muhasebe kalemi*) to deal with revenues and expenditures, while special departments handled the financial administration of Anatolia and Rumeli and issued general financial orders.[11] In July 1842 the position of undersecretary of the ministry was abolished and replaced by two treasurers (*defterdars*) for the *Mansure* and Imperial treasuries, whose primary job was to assist the minister with the difficult task of collecting taxes and other revenues.

This structure remained almost without change through the Crimean War when, as part of the financial reforms then introduced by Fuat Paşa (see page 98), a new Accounting Council (*Divan-ı Muhasebat*) was established within the ministry. It was given the job of checking the accounts of all ministries and departments as well as of individual bureaucrats of the central and provincial governments. It also was charged with drawing up a budget in advance of the financial year, a major innovation, receiving proposals from the departments, reconciling them with expected revenues, and then presenting the result to the minister, the legislative council, and the Council of Ministers for final sanction. Its agents were sent around the empire to make sure that all financial regulations were carried out, to settle disputes between state officials and taxpayers, and to recommend whatever changes were needed to make the system work better.[12] To carry out its work the Accounting Council was given a chairman and 7 financial experts as members, with a staff of 10 scribes. Due to the immensity of its job, the membership was raised to 10 and the staff to 21 during the next decade, but this was hardly enough for the complex Ottoman financial system, so that it never was as effective as its creators had hoped.[13]

During the last decade of the Tanzimat, the Accounting Council was divided into two. Half the members and staff were formed into the *Meclis-i Maliye* (Financial

Council), which prepared the annual budgets and dealt with taxes, tax farms, and collection matters; the other half remained as the *Meclis-i Muhasebe-i Maliye* (Financial Accounting Council), which continued to check the accounts of ministries, departments, and bureaucrats and dealt with matters such as census and property records, foundations, and state bonds. The ministry was again reorganized under a single undersecretary (*maliye müsteşarı*), who replaced the separate treasurers and treasuries with a single treasury called simply the *Maliye Hazinesi* (Financial Treasury).[14]

Economic and Social Councils and Ministries. Each of the major ministries had an advisory council (*meclis*) composed of retired experts, senior scribes, and bureaucrats between regular assignments, which served to advise the ministers on general policy and proposed legislation as well as improved methods of operation. Several councils that dealt with economic and social matters acquired such an importance over the years that they finally became ministries. The Council on Agriculture and Industry established by Mahmut II in 1838 was formed into the Ministry of Trade (*Nezaret-i Ticaret*) in 1839; that on Education organized in June 1846 was developed into the Ministry of Public Education (*Nezaret-i Maarif-i Umumi*) in 1856; a restored Council on Agriculture was made into the Ministry of Agriculture (*Nezaret-i Ziraat*) in 1846, only to be absorbed again into the Ministry of Trade, subsequently renamed the Ministry of Trade and Agriculture (*Nezaret-i Ticaret ve Ziraat*) in 1862; and its Council on Public Works, established originally in 1837 and though abolished and re-created several times subsequently, finally was made into a separate Ministry of Public Works (*Nezaret-i Nafia*) in February 1870.[15] The two latter ministries finally were united into a single Ministry of Public Works and Commerce (*Nezaret-i Nafia ve Ticaret*), with a commercial section dealing with industry and foreign-trade statistics (foreign trade as such remained under the Foreign Ministry) and a public works section encouraging, supervising and/or controlling railroads, bridges, roads, post and telegraph systems, and all other installations concerned with communications.

The Religious Institution (Bab-ı Meşihat). Located away from the Porte and under the authority of ministers who at least in two instances (the *serasker* and the *şeyhulislam*) were equal in rank with the grand vezir, and thus doubly removed from his control, were several ministries that survived with little change from the time of Mahmut II. The office of the *şeyhulislam,* located in the old quarters of the Janissary *ağa* near the Süleymaniye mosque, was now developed into a full administrative department in all but name, with the undersecretary handling staff and political problems, and separate departments headed by the *kazasker*s (also called simply *sadr*) appointing and supervising the kadis and courts in Anatolia and Rumeli except for those in Istanbul and Galata, which were under a separate department. A Supreme Religious Court (*Fetvahane-i Celile*) was organized at the ministry to carry out the *şeyhulislam*'s judicial and legal functions, both as supreme jurisconsult (grand mufti) and as the last resort of appeal from the lower religious courts. His lesson assistant (*ders vekili*) headed a department that supervised the training of ulema in the religious schools and assigned and supervised teachers in the primary *mektep*s and secondary *medrese*s. His *fetva emini* was in charge of issuing all his judicial and religious opinions, and there were other scribes who handled financial matters. In 1849 the Imperial Mint (*Darphane*), already located in the Topkapı Palace, was joined to the sultan's private treasury (renamed *Hazine-i Hassa*) as the Ministry of the Sultan's Treasury (*Hazine-i Hassa Nezareti*). It subsequently was turned over to the Ministry of Pious Foundations (*Nezaret-i Evkaf-ı Hümayun*), which was united with the administration of the foundations of the Holy Cities and restored as a separate department of government in 1837 with headquarters opposite the Aya Sofya mosque. Its minister and staff were put under the control of the *şeyhulislam*, since they all had to be ulema and most of their revenues were devoted to supporting the ulema and foundations.

The Military Departments. The *Bab-ı Serasker*, transformed formally into a Ministry of War only in 1900, developed its organization during the nineteenth century as the army itself was reorganized (see page 85), with the *serasker* being assisted by the Department of the General Staff (*Erkân-ı Harbiye*) and departments devoted to military transportation, engineering, infantry, cavalry, artillery, supplies, justice, retirement, fortifications and military buildings, communications, and statistics. Separate departments also were established to administer each of the provincial armies once they had been organized as well as the provincial gendarmerie, the firefighters assigned to the area adjacent to the Seraskerate in Istanbul, military construction, and the military schools. The Imperial Arsenal (*Tophane-i Amire*) was maintained as an autonomous department under a field marshal (*müşir*) appointed by the *serasker*, with an advisory council of experts appointed by the grand vezir. Six provincial armies, later increased to seven, were organized to coordinate and carry out all army activities in the provinces, including the reserves and cavalry, with commanders (*müşir*) appointed by and responsible to Istanbul, but with extensive autonomy to arrange military and supply matters according to local problems and conditions.

The grand admiral (or *kapudan-ı derya*) managed the fleet's affairs at the Imperial Dockyard (*Tersane-i Amire*) at Kasımpaşa, on the Golden Horn in Istanbul. Relatively little attention was paid it until the reign of Abdulmecit, who devoted a great deal of money to modernizing construction work here as well as at Izmit and Gemlik, and the old sailing vessels finally were completely replaced by steamships. It was only following several naval disasters suffered in 1866 during the revolt in Crete that a new Ministry of the Navy (*Nezaret-i Bahriye*) was created, still at Kasımpaşa, with the minister and his undersecretary caring for all duties of administration and finance while the grand admiral was limited only to commanding the fleet. An advisory council composed of retired naval officers was formed to help, and a British naval mission led by Admiral Hobart provided advice and technical assistance as a modern fleet was created within a fairly short time.[16]

Ministry of Justice. The Ministry of Judicial Pleas (*Nezaret-i Deavi*) created by Mahmut II was in charge of the expanding secular court system of the empire, becoming the Ministry of Justice (*Nezaret-i Adliye*) in 1870. Its organization was modified as the new system of secular justice was developed during the century and as it took over many of the judicial duties of the councils and ministries at the Porte. By the end of the century the Ministry of Justice included a Supreme Judicial Council (*Encümen-i Adliye*), a Court of Cassation (*Mahkeme-i Temyiz*), divided into civil, criminal, and administrative sections, and an Appeals Court (*Mahkeme-i Istinaf*), with sections for criminal, civil, correctional, and commercial justice. In Istanbul its jurisdiction included also the Court of the First Instance for Istanbul (*Der Saadet Bidayet Mahkemesi*), also divided into civil, criminal, and administrative sections, and the Tribunal of Commerce (*Mahkeme-i Ticaret*), or mixed courts, with judges representing the different foreign merchant communities then active in the empire and with separate civil and maritime branches. In addition to supervising and staffing the secular judicial system, the ministry also was charged with training judges and supervising the system of secular legal education.

The Grand Vezirate. Above all the executive departments of the Porte was the office of the Grand Vezir himself, variously called the Grand Vezirate (*Sadaret-i Uzma*), the prime ministry (*Baş Vekâlet*), and even by itself the Sublime Porte (*Bab-ı Âli*), though the latter term strictly speaking encompassed all the departments under his supervision and control, including but not limited to his own. In 1839 the department consisted of no more than that of *Âmedi-i Divan-ı Hümayun,* the domestic portion of the department that had contained the Foreign Ministry before Mustafa Reşit Paşa separated the two (see page 36). The *Âmedi* office included the correspondence office of the grand vezir and his archives (*Bab-ı Âli Evrak Odası,* or Document Room of the Porte). As the Men of the Tanzimat, led by the grand vezir, built up the power of the Porte, they transferred to it most of the remaining bureaus of the Imperial Council originally given to the Foreign Ministry, including the *Teşrifat Kalemi,* which was in charge of protocol, official rankings, and ceremonials. Also under the grand vezir's authority at the Porte were the various central legislative bodies, and it is to these that we must now turn.

The Legislative Organs

Less a separate branch of government than an integral part of the process by which the empire was administered, the new legislative bodies developed by the Tanzimat were as important as were the executive offices in providing a base of continuity in the governing of the empire and in supporting modernization despite political turmoil.[17] The process by which the old Imperial Council was supplanted in its legislative functions by new organs better able to meet the needs of the time had been begun by Mahmut II. The *Meclis-i Vâlâ-yı Ahkâm-ı Adliye* (Supreme Council of Judicial Ordinances), established in 1838 at the palace, and the *Dar-ı Şurayı Bab-ı Âli* (Advisory Council of the Porte), advisory bodies on reform for Mahmut and the grand vezir, were the nuclei for the legislative bodies that were to follow during the Tanzimat period.

The Meclis-ı Vâlâ-yı Ahkâm-ı Adliye/*Supreme Council of Judicial Ordinances*

There were several problems that hindered the councils during the last year of Mahmut's reign. First, since they were new governmental bodies imposed on an existing system and since their exact duties and relationship to other officials never were made clear, their advice often was not heeded. Second, since their original objective was to secure the advice of experts, members were appointed according to their qualifications regardless of rank. But while this was a meritorious and liberal idea, with the Ottoman mentality the result was that only the higher-ranked members were heeded. A third problem was the part-time nature of the appointments, with the members spending most of their time on their regular administrative duties. Finally, since the distinction between the two councils was never clarified nor the scope of their authority defined, whenever their recommendations touched the interests of individual ministers or departments, the latter's opinions had to prevail according to the old Ottoman doctrine of *had*.

By eliminating the Advisory Council of the Porte and specifying the Supreme Council of Judicial Ordinances as the principal source of reform legislation and discussion, the Imperial Rescript of Gülhane made the latter the sole body charged with discussing important matters requiring legislation, investigating each problem regardless of the *had*s of ministers or others involved, and then presenting proposals for legislation. These were recommended to the sultan for ratification, not only by the Council of Ministers, but also by a special council (*Meclis-i Hass-ı Umumi*) composed of senior ministers, retired officials, and all the members of the Supreme Council, thus ensuring for the latter a far more influential voice in the process of ratification than when this was handled by the Council of Ministers alone. Its scope was limited in the sense that it could consider only those measures referred to it by the Council of Ministers or the departments. But in fact this was stated vaguely enough in its regulation for it to go ahead and prepare legislation on whatever it wished, since almost anything could be considered relevant to the problems referred to it. It was given ten full-time members, chosen from senior officials from all four institutions of the Ruling Class.[18] A new headquarters for the council was built at the Porte, indicating that however much the Tanzimat was decreed by the sultan, it was executed by Mustafa Reşit Paşa and his associates rather than by the palace, beginning the shift of power to the former. After an official opening in the presence of the sultan (March 8, 1840), the council set to work with an intensity rarely seen in Ottoman governmental circles before that time. Discussions were regulated so that all members could be heard regardless of rank. Members could not leave the chamber during debates. No one could interrupt a speaker until he was finished, and the council soon began to call and interrogate officials of the ministries, at least those at the Porte, though the latter did not have to attend or answer questions if they did not wish to do so. Efforts were made to modify individual recommendations to secure consensus, but some were drawn up by majority vote, with the sultan being informed of the reasons for the dissent so that he could make his own judgment.

Despite the regulations, the Supreme Council soon developed its own set of problems. Some members kept their old positions and sent deputies to attend the council meetings. Since quorums often lacked as a result, decisions had to be postponed. The Council of Ministers began to meet at the same time as the Supreme Council, making it almost impossible for the latter to get anyone from the Porte to testify and provide needed information. Senior members also continued to prevail in discussions, with the experience and judgment of the junior members being ignored. To solve these problems the council secured passage of a new regulation (July 18, 1841), which provided equal rank (rank 1, class 2) for all members as well as penalties for those who violated any of the previous regulations. Members also were ordered to divide into small expert committees to consider proposals before they were decided on in the general meetings, thus providing the basis for the departmental type of organization that was to be developed under its successors. So that ministers and other important officials would be available, the Supreme Council was ordered to hold meetings requiring such interrogations on Saturdays, while the Council of Ministers was forbidden from meeting on that day. Finally, the Supreme Council was ordered not only to give its opinions about law proposals drawn up by other bodies but also to draw up its own draft laws and regulations (called *tezakir*), which were to be and did become the bases for all subsequent Tanzimat legislation.

The new regulation mainly achieved its purpose, and during the next 15 years the Supreme Council operated successfully as the main legislative organ. To be sure, the autocratic Men of the Tanzimat made very certain that it would be amenable to their wishes, saving the high-paying positions of chairman and lieutenant of the council for members who best reflected the wishes of the Porte and also varying the salaries of other members according to their tractability on important issues. Over 90 percent of the council's recommendations were promulgated by the sultan without change. The council also exercised a judicial function, acting as a special administrative court of first instance for trials of important administrative and political leaders accused of violating the law, and as' a final court of appeal for criminal cases originally decided by the provincial councils under the Tanzimat criminal code.[19]

The Council of the Tanzimat

The very success of the Supreme Council, however, assured its doom. So completely did it assume the burden of preparing legislation that it was overwhelmed by the immensity and bulk of its work and fell badly behind. This was a major factor in slowing the Tanzimat immediately before the Crimean War. In addition, the Tanzimat now was in the hands of the second generation of Men of the Tanzimat, led by Âli and Fuat, who wanted rapid progress, while the council was a bastion for the more conservative older Men of the Tanzimat, now led by Mustafa Reşit Paşa. So for both administrative and political reasons in 1854 the Supreme Council was left only with its judicial functions while an entirely new legislative body was created with the name High Council of the Tanzimat (*Meclis-i Âli-i Tanzimat*).[20]

The major objective of the new council was, simply, to complete and extend the Tanzimat reforms. To give it the power needed to push legislation through it was made separate from and equal to the Council of Ministers, above the ministries, and its chairman was given direct access to the sultan. Whereas the Supreme Council had been officially able to discuss only matters submitted to it, the new council could consider legislation on any subject it deemed suitable and it also could receive and consider proposals submitted directly to it by officials or subjects, thus admitting the latter to the process of legislation for the first time. It could summon officials for testimony, and it could send its agents to secure information from the records of the ministers and to investigate how the latter were carrying out the laws. This was the first time since the Ottoman legislative and executive functions were differentiated by the reformers that the former was given some power of supervision over the latter, thus beginning the long process toward responsible parliamentary government. No proposal could be made into law without the consent of the Council of the Tanzimat. Departments and ministries could propose new regulations for themselves, but even these could not be enforced until they went through the full legislative process.

The continued existence of the Supreme Council, however, soon produced confusion and conflicts of authority. While the old council was supposed to limit itself to judicial matters, in fact it also continued to draw up legislative codes of its own, with the Council of the Tanzimat limiting its attention primarily to regulations establishing the organization and operation of major governing bodies. The relationship of the two bodies seems to have been connected to the fluctuating politics of the time, with the Council of the Tanzimat dominating when Âli and Fuat were in power and the Supreme Council emerging when their enemies held the grand vezirate. Also as the need to organize and reorganize governmental bodies increased during the latter years of the Tanzimat, the burden on the Council of the Tanzimat was so huge that it had to transfer some of this work to the old council. The latter in turn was so busy with both legislative and judicial business that it had to divide itself into five specialized committees, dealing respectively with administration, finance, military affairs, foreign affairs, and justice. The tremendous increase in the work of both councils was due also to the subsequent creation of provincial legislative councils, which sent to Istanbul large numbers of proposed measures relating to their areas. Increasing the number of members on the two councils at the central level resulted in further complications and delay. Members found it easier to avoid any kind of expression of opinion, and debates came to be dominated by political and personal disputes. The resulting backlog of legislation at the top soon caused similar paralysis at the provincial level. By 1860, then, the Council of the Tanzimat to a certain extent fell into the same kind of confusion that had stimulated its creation.[21]

Supreme Council of Judicial Ordinances

A long investigation of the situation concluded that the difficulty was the old Ottoman tendency to create new institutions to deal with new problems without destroying the old or relating them one to another. In consequence, an order issued on September 9, 1861, made an effort to rationalize the legislative process by merging the two councils into a new Supreme Council of Judicial Ordinances (*Meclis-i Vâlâ-yı Ahkâm-ı Adliye*), which in turn was divided into three departments: (1) the Department of Laws and Regulations, which assumed the legislative functions of both old councils; (2) the Department of Administration and Finance, charged with administrative investigation; and (3) the Department of Judicial Cases, which assumed the *Meclis-i Vâlâ*'s judicial functions, acting as a court of appeals for cases decided by the provincial councils of justice, as a court of appeals for cases decided by the provincial councils of justice, and as a court of first instance in cases involving officials of the central government. The council as a whole and its individual departments could originate discussions and law proposals on their own. To expedite the flow of business it was allowed to arrange its order of business in terms of the importance of individual problems rather than simply according to the order in which they were received or brought up. Secret ballots were authorized for important problems, with the minority arguments now being given anonymously in separate protocols. Since members of the new council still were appointed by the Council of Ministers, its ability to supervise the latter was limited despite its right to investigate. But its power to question members of the executive and to try such officials for misdeeds led to increased effectiveness in the supervision of the government, and the efficient flow of legislation in the new council greatly contributed to the success of the Tanzimat when Âli and Fuat were in power during the 1860s.[22]

The Council of State (Şurayı Devlet) and the Council for Judicial Regulations (Divan-ı Ahkâm-ı Adliye)

Change in the legislative process, when it came once again, was less the result of new failures on the part of the Supreme Council than in consequence of criticism of the Tanzimat autocracy levied both by Europeans, who cloaked their basic belief in the supremacy of Christian institutions and ways in advocacy of representation for the non-Muslim subjects in the process of government, and by the Young Ottoman intellectuals, who were claiming that the achievements of the Tanzimat meant nothing unless the representative principle was adopted and extended. Though Fuat and Âli believed in reform from above, the success of the provincial representative councils and continued pressure from England finally convinced them that further changes should be introduced at the central level.

As a result, in 1867 the Supreme Council again was divided into separate legislative and judicial bodies, the former called the Council of State (Şurayı Devlet) and the latter the Council of Judicial Regulations (Divan-ı Ahkâm-ı Adliye), with Midhat Paşa and Ahmet Cevdet Paşa as their chairmen, respectively. The new Council of Judicial Regulations was to settle cases connected with the secular laws and regulations and to act as final court of appeal for the civil Nizamiye court system then being established, while the Council of State was made the central legislative body. The former was supposed to prepare all projects for laws and regulations, investigate matters of public administration, decide on disputes among and between executive and judicial bodies, give advice to the ministries on the enforcement of laws and regulations already in effect, and judge government officials accused of misconduct. It was divided into five departments with ten members each, for interior/war, finance/religious endowments, justice/law, public works/trade/agriculture, and public education. For the first time, membership was representative of the major interests in the empire, but under severe restrictions. All members were officially appointed by the sultan. Nominations for membership were asked for and received from the governors as well as many municipal officials, who in turn secured the nominations from their advisory councils and millet and guild leaders. Members were finally chosen by the Council of Ministers from lists of candidates representing each group in each province, with additional names being added only on rare occasions. Thus all the important classes and interests among non-Muslims as well as Muslims were represented, and these representatives provided some kind of popular input into the legislative process on the central level.

But in consequence of even this limited sort of representation, the Council of State's powers were severely restricted compared with those of its predecessors. It could deliberate only on matters submitted to it, and ministries and departments could bypass it and submit legislative proposals directly to the Council of Ministers. It could no longer examine the state budget or interrogate ministers, with these functions being transferred to a special annual assembly of ministers and notables (Meclis-i Umumi, or General Council), which for all practical purposes was under the control of the grand vezir. Despite the liberal pressures, therefore, Âli and Fuat made sure that the new Council of State would be subservient to the Porte and not disrupt the flow of essential legislation.[23] In practice, however, the Council of State's right to investigate execution of laws and regulations did give it a means of developing more power than was envisaged in its regulation. In addition, its representative nature, however limited, also encouraged its members to be more independent of the ministers than their predecessors had been.

As time passed, the organizations of the two bodies were modified. On May 6, 1869, the Council of State was given a number of judicial duties, and a new Department of Court Cases was appointed to handle them. The Council of Justice now became mainly an appellate court for cases from lower jurisdictions, and, thus, the origin for the more modern Court of Appeal (Mahkeme-i Temyiz), and the Council of State assumed jurisdiction over disputes between judicial and administrative officials and appeals against provincial decisions regarding administrative justice. Administrative justice in fact became such an important part of the council's work that late in the same year the new Department of Court Cases was divided into criminal and civil sections, while the Departments of Interior/War and Education were united into one, leaving the council with six departments as before.

During the remainder of the Tanzimat, the Council of State carried out most of its legislative and administrative work through its departments and rarely met as a whole, leading to unwarranted criticism by foreigners and some Ottomans that it was inactive and ineffective. In fact it continued to function effectively, facilitating a tremendously increased flow of legislation and also increasing the efficiency of the executive departments by subjecting them to close scrutiny. When Mahmut Nedim became grand vezir in 1871 he attempted to reorganize it into three departments, for reform legislation, interior affairs, and judicial affairs, using the reorganization as a tool to get rid of Midhat's supporters (February 10, 1872). Because this effort was only partly successful, however, he went on to abolish most of the council's remaining administrative and judicial functions (June 12, 1875) on the not entirely unwarranted grounds that they duplicated the work of the ministries and the courts, leaving it with only legislative duties, which soon were taken over by a new Reform Commission (*Islahat Komisyonu*), chaired by Ahmet Cevdet but staffed mainly by Mahmut Nedim's men and placed under his direct control. But when Midhat became grand vezir soon afterward, he abolished the latter and restored the Council of State to its former functions, with separate departments organized once again to handle public works, education, war, and provincial administration. We shall see later how the council continued to function as the empire's principal legislative body even during the period of the Parliament (1876–1878) as well as afterward.[24]

The Council of Ministers

Climaxing and culminating the executive and legislative organs of government on the central level was the Council of Ministers (*Meclis-i Vükelâ*, called sometimes *Meclis-i Hass*, or the Sultan's Council), which now became the principal executive and legislative coordination body while the Imperial Council was reduced to a kind of privy council, used to provide salaries to palace favorites and to ratify certain types of diplomatic and legislative acts. The exact composition of the Council of Ministers varied but in general included all the ministers, the *şeyhulislam*, the *serasker*, and the grand admiral or, more often, their undersecretaries, the directors (*müşir*) of the departments of police and the Arsenal (*Tophane*) of Istanbul – even though they were nominally subordinate to the minister of the interior and *serasker* respectively – the undersecretary of the grand vezir when he was in charge of the ministry of the Interior, the directors of the Departments of Excise Taxes (*Rüsumat Emini*) and Revenue Receipts (*Defter-i Hâkani*) when they were created late in the nineteenth century, and usually the lieutenant (*kethüda*) of the queen mother, who represented the palace. Since members were appointed by and responsible to the sultan for their departments, they were relatively independent of the grand vezir, in theory at least, lacking the unity and responsibility of the modern cabinet except, perhaps, during the strongest days of Reşit, Âli, and Fuat and in the later days of the Young Turks. At other times, with very little central control, individual and party politics predominated in its deliberations as they did in the legislative councils, making it very difficult to conduct business. The Council of Ministers did, however, perform a number of important political and legal functions. After 1850 it was this Council that swore fealty to new sultans in the official ceremony of enthronement, followed by the more general oath taken by all Ruling Class members present. It advised the grand vezir and sultan on important issues as well as legislative proposals, approved the state budget as part of the legislative process, and had the right to initiate legislation. Council decisions were communicated in the form of discussion protocols (*müzakerat zabıt varakası*) presented for each matter, which contained summaries of the issues as well as the arguments pro and con and the council's decisions. In addition, when legislative matters were involved these protocols were accompanied by separate statements (*mazbatas*) containing the final version of the law and regulation concerned and detailing the principal arguments. The council could and often did propose changes in the laws received from the legislative councils. It was up to the sultan to decide on the final form before affixing his *irade* along with explanations for his approval or disapproval of the matter in question.

The Sultanate

Remaining at least the symbolic centers of authority in Ottoman government and society, sultans Abdulmecit and Abdulaziz attempted to alter the organization and practices of the sultanate as much as they could to accord with the modernization of Ottoman life then in progress. Abandoning the Topkapı Palace to relatives and supernumeraries, they moved to the Dolmabahçe Palace, on the Bosporus. While Dolmabahçe continued to be used as the meeting place for official receptions, ceremonies, and council meetings, Abdulmecit spent most of his time at a new palace located slightly to the north, also on the Bosporus, at Çırağan, begun by Mahmut II in 1836 and actually finished only by Abdulaziz in 1872. Çırağan, with its European-style apartments for the sultan and his family and its beautiful gardens, soon became the favorite residence for as many members of the imperial family and their servants as could crowd in. The summers were spent at Kâğıthane, at the tip of the Golden Horn, the fabled center of Ahmet III's revelries during the Tulip Period, and more and more at a new palace built on the Anatolian shore of the Bosporus at Beylerbey. As the cares and duties of government were absorbed by the Porte, the sultan and his entourage had more time for frivolities. The Çırağan Palace proved too small for the ever-expanding imperial family, and it was gradually abandoned and left to fall into disrepair while the Dolmabahçe Palace was added to and modernized starting in 1865. In addition, a new pavilion was built on the heights overlooking Dolmabahçe, at Yıldız, to house the sultan and his personal entourage, while the official affairs of the sultanate as well as the apartments of the princes remained fixed at the older palace below.[25]

With at least four imperial residences constantly maintained in readiness to house the sultan, therefore, his family, his entourage, and his palace organization grew in complexity during the century. The Topkapı Palace organization remained mostly intact, with its positions being filled by supernumeraries and pensioners. New servants and staff were added for the new palaces, mostly at the expense of the Imperial Treasury, while that of the sultan paid only for food, clothing, and other personal needs of the ruler and his family. Mahmut II tried to manage this complex through his private treasury, the Privy Purse (*Ceb-i Hümayun*), whose chief was made supervisor of the entire Inner Palace Service (*Enderun-u Hümayun Nazırı*). But this did not suffice, since the treasury continued to be located at the Topkapı Palace, while the sultan and his family rarely went there. Hence in 1866 Abdulaziz created the new Treasury of the Sultan (*Hazine-i Hassa*) at the Çırağan Palace, incorporating the old Treasury which remained at the Topkapı Palace, while the new superintendent, the *hazine-i hassa nazırı*, was put in charge of the entire structure of administration and finance for all the imperial palaces. The staff was divided into scribes, headed by the chief scribe; chamberlains (*kurena*) for personal services headed by the chief chamberlain; and the staff of the *mâbeyin,* literally the area in between the mens' and ladies' quarters in the harem, who came to form the principal staff of servants and administrators in the new palaces. In 1866 the office of chief of the *mâbeyin* united with that of supervisor of the Treasury of the Sultan to form a new position, *mâbeyin müşiri* (marshal of the inbetween), with the same rank as that of the field marshals (*müşirs*) who commanded the provincial armies. Under this title the director of the sultan's personal affairs developed into one of the most influential officials of state, not only under Abdulaziz but even more under his successor, Abdulhamit II, when the palace came to direct state affairs. The other major change made during the last part of the century was the expansion of the military aides-de-camp (*yâverân-ı harp*) into two groups: (1) the *Yâverân-ı Ekrem,* distinguished former and current political and military leaders who formed the sultan's Privy Council, advising him, along with the Council of Ministers, on political and administrative policies, and (2) the *Fahri Yâverân-ı Ekrem,* which formed the sultan's actual guard of honor.

The habits and manners of the sultans also changed considerably during the nineteenth century. The old isolation broke down, at first because of the simple need to travel through the streets of the city from the new palaces to attend the Friday prayer in the traditional location, the Aya Sofya mosque outside the Topkapı Palace (even though private mosques were also built into the new palaces), and of course for the seasonal changes of residence. In addition, the sultans now were seen in public when they attended receptions in the European embassies or went to see theatrical performances. They began traveling regularly outside the capital to inspect conditions and see how the new laws were operating. In 1846 Abdulmecit went to Rumeli. In 1850 he sailed through the Dardanelles to Limnos, Crete, Samos, and Rhodes, where he met Abbas Paşa, governor of Egypt, before returning via Izmir. Abdulaziz traveled to Izmit and Bursa in 1862, to Alexandria and Cairo the next year, the first visit of a reigning sultan to Egypt since the conquest by Selim I, and finally in the summer of 1867 to Paris at the invitation of Emperor Napoleon III to attend the opening of the World Exhibition in that city, going on to London, where he sailed on the Thames with the king and visited Buckingham Palace before inspecting the British navy at Portsmouth.[26] This was a far cry, indeed, from the activities of the sultans of the past, whose very isolation created the aura of awe and splendor that was part of the tradition by which the subjects were taught to revere their ruler. Indeed the new accessibility, accompanied by the increased transfer of administrative responsibility to the Porte tended to diminish the sultan's effective power even further as the century went on.

Provincial Administration and Military Organization

Several approaches were tried to achieve a basic Tanzimat objective, the extension of central control into the provinces. At first, the powers of the provincial governors were weakened by giving most of their functions to officials sent by and responsible to Istanbul. Later, the state tried to operate through the governors, restoring their powers while extending control over them in other ways. The final solution was a combination of these, with the provincial government being a small-scale reflection of the central administrative structure, but with controls to assure the ultimate authority of Istanbul.

The first phase, developed by Mustafa Reşit Paşa himself before the Crimean War, was based on the premise that much of the misrule and inefficiency of provincial administration in the past had been due to the system that enabled most provincial officials, from the tax collectors up to the governors, to hold their positions autonomously, as tax farmers or fief holders, without real supervision or control by the central government as long as they performed the services or paid the taxes required in return. A series of measures was introduced following the Gülhane decree to remedy this situation.

On February 7, 1840, the old tax system was reorganized, with the different taxes formerly justified on the basis of religious law (*tekalif-i şeriye*) or collected as customary taxes (*tekalif-i örfiye*) being replaced by standardized cultivation taxes of 10 percent of the produce, still called by the traditional name *âşâr* (tithes), fixed head taxes on cattle and non-Muslims (the canonical *cizye*), and other service taxes (called *mürettebat*, or allocation taxes), all fixed according to the taxpayers' incomes and ability to pay. Collections now were made not by the governors or the tax farmers whom they appointed, but rather by civilian collectors (*muhassıl-ı emval*) sent from Istanbul to assess and collect the taxes of each district (*sancak/liva*) in return for regular salaries paid by the treasury. Loss of authority over tax collections made the governors much more subject to central authority and promised more revenues to the treasury and a fairer system to the subjects than had been the case in the past.[27]

The second step was reorganization of the administrative divisions in each province, using the traditional term *sancak,* but redrawing the boundaries to establish equal units of comparable population and wealth. Where the Tanzimat reforms were introduced, each *sancak* was headed by a *muhassıl,* and while waiting for the extension of the reforms in the districts still under the old system, *kaymakams* were named by the governors. The *sancaks* in turn were subdivided into counties, given the name that also applied to the conterminous judicial districts, *kaza,* and were headed by administrators (*müdürs*). These consisted of subdistricts (*nahiye*), each usually containing at least one important town or village. The latter were directed by mayors (*muhtars*), officials originally assigned by Mahmut II to represent the central government in the towns as well as in individual quarters of Istanbul and the other major cities. Provision of clear lines of authority among these officials was a major step forward in rationalizing the provincial system of the empire.[28]

The third step in reducing the autonomous powers of the governors was to provide them as well as the lesser provincial authorities with advisory councils composed of representatives of the Ruling Class as well as the principal subject groups in each area. There were two basic kinds of councils. In the provincial and district capitals there were created large councils (*büyük meclis*), each normally composed of 13 members, of whom 7 represented the government (the *muhassıl,* his subordinate, the local police chief, 2 scribes sent from Istanbul to assist him in tax matters, the local kadi, the Greek Orthodox priest of the district, and a representative of the next largest *millet*), and 6 represented the local notables and guilds.[29] The second category of advisory councils introduced in 1840 was that of small councils (*küçük meclis*) introduced into each *kaza* where the Tanzimat provincial reforms were being applied, with membership limited to five: the local representative of the *muhassıl,* the kadi, the police chief, and two local notables, one of whom had to be a non-Muslim and one a Muslim. Just as the *kaza* administrators were subordinate to the *muhassıls,* so also were their small councils subordinate to the larger ones, having to submit their decisions and recommendations to the latter for approval. The method by which popular representatives were chosen was extremely complicated. The notables of each village chose their own electors by lot. The electors from the different villages then came together in the *kaza* capital to choose candidates for its council, while the *kaza* council members in turn chose electors from among themselves to select representatives for the *sancak* and provincial councils established over them. Thus for the first time subjects were given the right to be represented in some way in the process of government, long before such representation was allowed in the central government, though in most cases those elected were members of the ruling establishments in each religious, economic, and social group and represented their interests and wishes rather than those of the mass of the people.[30]

The final step in Mustafa Reşit's effort to extend central control into the provinces involved a major reorganization of the army. In 1841 the army, now officially renamed *Asâkir-i Nizamiye-i Şahane* (The Ordered Soldiers of the Sultan), was for the first time divided into provincial commands, each led by a field marshal (*müşir*) appointed by and responsible to the *serasker* in Istanbul, thus completely ending the governors' control of the military forces within their domains. The Imperial Guard (*Hassa*) was transformed into the Imperial Army (*Hassa Ordusu*) and stationed across the Bosporus from Istanbul in Üsküdar, with responsibility for keeping order and security and enforcing the Tanzimat regulations in southwestern Anatolia. The *serasker*'s forces in Istanbul were organized as the Istanbul Army (*Istanbul Ordusu* or *Der Saadet Ordusu*), which was placed in charge of much of northwestern Anatolia and Thrace. The Third Army, of Rumeli, based originally in Monastir and later at Işkodra (Scutari of Albania), cared for the remainder of the European possessions of the empire. The Fourth Army, of Anatolia (*Anadolu Ordusu*), with its center at Sivas, guarded eastern Anatolia. The Fifth Army, called the Army of Arabia (*Arabistan Ordusu*), was based at Damascus and put in charge of Syria, Cilicia, Iraq, and the Arabian Peninsula until 1848, when a Sixth Army, based at Baghdad, was created for the latter two. New subarmies subsequently were established also in the Yemen, Crete, and Tripoli of Libya. The exact complement of each army and the division of its regiments among infantry, cavalry, artillery, and reserves depended on local conditions and varied considerably. Internal organization also varied, but in general each infantry regiment (*alay*) was divided into three battalions (*tabur*), each commanded by a *binbaşı;* these in turn were divided into squads (*bölük*) and messes (*manga*) of ten men, each of which was commanded by a corporal (*onbaşı*), groups of two by a sergeant (*çavuş*), four by a lieutenant (*mülâzim*), and eight by a captain (*yüzbaşı*), with the entire regiment commanded by a colonel (*miralay*). The cavalry regiments were divided into 6 squads and the artillery into 12 batteries, providing 72 cannon for each regiment, of which half were mobile and half fixed.

Soldiers completing their regular service were required to serve in the reserve (*redif*) forces for an additional seven years. These were organized into four major districts centered at the provincial army headquarters at Istanbul, Izmir, Monastir, and Sivas, with subordinate units stationed at the major garrison towns, all under the direct control of the appropriate *müşir*. Separate supply organizations and stores also were organized at the same places, thus providing the Ottoman army with a fully independent supply service around the empire for the first time. The provincial army forces and reserve units also became the bases for an army secular system of education, established at the elementary and intermediate levels, to train youths preparing to become soldiers and officers, thus constituting an alternative system of secular education in the empire. Assistance also was provided to the *müşirs* by irregular tribesmen, generally called *başı bozuks*, with some 65,000 warriors coming from Cossacks who had entered the empire in the Danube area as well as Tatars from the Dobruca and Turkoman and Kurdish warriors from eastern Anatolia.

Abdulaziz in particular was interested in modernizing both the army and navy to meet the Russian threat, and he increased their financial appropriations considerably, although, as we shall see, this caused additional financial difficulties. New rifles were purchased from Prussia, which also supplied officers to teach their use. Large-caliber cannons were acquired from the Krupp Works in Germany to reinforce the defenses of the Straits as well as the Danube and at Kars and Erzurum. Starting in 1869, major reforms were introduced into the army organization as a result of Prussian influence, mainly under the direction of the new *serasker*, Hüseyin Avni Paşa, who was himself one of the last protégés of Mustafa Reşit and Âli. At this time, the organization of the provincial armies was slightly revised, with the Imperial Guard being brought back to Istanbul as the First Army. A new Second Army of the Danube (*Tuna Ordusu*) was established at Şumla. The Third Army remained at Monastir. The Anatolian army transferred from Sivas to Erzurum. The Fifth and Sixth armies remained at Damascus and Baghdad, and the units already in the Yemen were organized as the new Seventh Army. Each army now was given an equal number of men, about 26,500 in all, with six infantry, four cavalry, one light-cannon, and one heavy-cannon regiment in addition to special units as needed to man the forts in its area.[31]

In the meantime, Mustafa Reşit Paşa's original provincial reforms had been undermined by a shortage of trained bureaucrats and inadequacies in tax collection resulting from the attempted replacement of the tax farmers with salaried tax collectors. The governors were unable to remedy the situation since their powers had been reduced by the 1840 reforms, while the advisory councils were unwilling to do so because they continued to represent their own and group interests rather than those of the government. Reşit's solution (March 1841) was to eliminate the *muhassıls* sent from Istanbul and to turn the provinces over to the provincial armies, with their commanders being appointed as governors and subordinate officers as *kaymakams* of the districts. They in turn chose local notables to act as *müdürs* of the *kazas* and administered financial affairs with the help of treasurers and scribes sent by the Ministry of Finance in Istanbul.[32] In the smaller *kazas* the advisory councils were abolished on the quite justified grounds that all they did was formalize the traditional consultations of local notables and provide them with salaries, at government expense, for doing what they would have done anyway to protect their own interests. In their place the *müdürs* were directed to assemble informal advisory councils to advise them on specific problems. In the larger *kazas* and at the *sancak* level the councils were retained, but elections were abolished and all members were appointed by the *kaymakams* to represent the major interests. Most important, the *müşirs* were ordered to establish provincial administrative councils (*eyalet idare meclisi*) with representatives chosen by the *sancak* councils with the sanction of the *kaymakams*, thus bringing subjects into provincial government, although still only in an advisory role. As time went on, the powers of the councils to participate in administrative decisions were extended by orders of the sultan. They were allowed to ask information from the governors on all matters, to send complaints about provincial administration to the grand vezir, and to testify to his representatives when they came as inspectors. They also were allowed to hear appeals from *Şeriat* court decisions involving large amounts of money, thus extending their powers into the judicial area. Finally, their scope was also enlarged so that they could discuss not only current problems but also measures that would "improve the state and benefit the security of the people," thus reflecting at the provincial level the extended scope of government that the Tanzimat had already introduced into the central government.

The changes improved the efficiency of provincial government. The *müşirs* maintained order and collected taxes, and the advisory councils initiated measures to improve local economic and living conditions and sent off requests for assistance from Istanbul for roads and other changes. In response to such proposals, a series of commissions of improvement were sent into Rumeli and Anatolia to interview the councils, notables, and subjects. They investigated conditions and prepared reports, most of which recommended the extension of the provincial reforms to include all the ideals of the Tanzimat, specifically the execution of new cadastral and population surveys to complete the work of reforming the tax system, and the construction of roads, bridges, and, where needed, irrigation systems, to improve the empire's economy and provide prosperity for its people. In response to these reports the Porte directed most funds available for public works to the provincial and district councils so that they could decide which local projects were most important and then give them the kind of direct supervision and control that could not be accomplished from Istanbul. The *livas* of Izmit and Gallipoli were chosen as models for the Tanzimat provincial reforms, with Izmir, Salonica, and Varna to be added as soon as feasible. Here the military governors were replaced by bureaucrats who were recent graduates of the new secular schools. Census and cadastral surveys were made, new tax registers drawn up, incompetent administrators and dishonest council members replaced, and roads, bridges, and irrigation systems built.

The new Tanzimat provincial system was spread to most provinces by the time of the Crimean War. But the financial difficulties caused by the war itself forced the government to abandon many of the public works programs and end all salaries for council members, leading most of them to resign and allowing the governors and other administrative officials to regain full power. The councils continued nominally, but often membership was limited to government officials and a few *millet* leaders. In Muslim areas the councils often were identical with the local *Şeriat* courts under the chairmanship of the kadis, who therefore again became important local officials. The new system was far more efficient and effective than the old, but it still was unable to provide sufficient funds to finance the expanding activities of the central government and army as well as the palace. Furthermore, the Reform Decree (*Islahat Fermanı*) issued in 1856 at the behest of the powers gave new impetus to certain types of provincial reform, particularly those involving popular participation in the process of government and the establishment of direct tax collection where the tax farms still survived.

Fuat Paşa was put in charge of solving both the financial and provincial problems, and after almost two years of study he secured the introduction of a new provincial law that concentrated power once again in the hands of the governors and aimed at extending the Tanzimat reforms to all parts of the empire. The Provincial Regulation of 1858 [33] retained the existing structure of provincial government, but the governor was made chief authority over all matters and the sole agent of the central government, with the army commanders and treasurers sent from Istanbul also responsible to him for their work in the provinces. Provincial officials and subjects were allowed to communicate directly to Istanbul only if they had evidence that the governor was violating the law; otherwise all such communications had to go through him. The administrative councils were revived on all levels, still advisory to the governors and *kaymakams*, but with the local *müdürs* being required to secure their approval before acting in financial and police matters or communicating with higher authorities. A Cadastral Department (*Tahrir-i Emlâk Nezareti*) was organized in the Ministry of Finance. It prepared surveys of people and property around the empire, working through provincial cadastral commissions organized by each governor, with members including both officials and local notables. They were organized into three-man cadastral committees, which, accompanied by scribes and engineers, set down all the lands, houses, plots of land, gardens, buildings, and the like, giving an estimated value for each. They also registered each male inhabitant, Muslim or non-Muslim, Ottoman or foreigner, and issued to each a population tax certificate (*vergi nüfus tezkeresi*), which stated his tax obligation and also served as an identity card.[34] As the cadastre was completed in each province, the Tanzimat administrative and tax reforms were fully applied to it, including newly established taxes on land and improvements, rental income, profits, and, ultimately, salaries, all on a progressive scale. In addition, completion of each provincial cadastre was followed by the introduction of a new conscription system for the army, with the number of men taken in each district being based on its population and agricultural needs and the terms of service limited initially to five years rather than life, but with each man being required to serve seven additional years in the reserves.[35]

In January 1860 efforts were made to accelerate the Tanzimat provincial reforms. To provide salaries high enough to allow the appointment of capable Tanzimat administrators to the more important provinces, the status of these governorships was charged to that of *mutasarrıflık*, a term once used on the district level, but now connotating positions of particularly high rank with higher salaries than those provided the regular governors. It was through this device that ranking Tanzimat figures like Midhat Paşa and Ahmet Cevdet Paşa were assigned to serve as provincial governors. The governors' power over provincial financial activities increased with the abolition of the independent treasurers and scribes sent from Istanbul and their replacement with accountants to assist the governors. In fact, however, there was little change, since the accountants still had to be members of the scribal corporation, giving its leaders and the Ministry of Finance more authority over them than was provided in the law.[36]

The new system worked reasonably well, but there were complaints about confusion in the highly structured provincial system, with duplication of effort and administrative tyranny leaving the subjects not much better off than they had been before the Crimean War, though the government was benefiting considerably. Fuat Paşa, author of the previous reform, again took the lead in investigating the difficulties, sending out a series of investigating commissions. Upon learning of Midhat Paşa's success in applying the Tanzimat system in Niş (1861–1864), Fuat invited him to Istanbul for consultation. The result was the promulgation of the Provincial

Reform Law of 1864, which began a new era in Ottoman provincial life, remaining the basis for government outside of Istanbul until the end of the empire.[37] The new regulation was mainly conceived as a means of extending orderly and efficient Tanzimat administration to the provinces. New large provincial units (vilayet) approximately equal in size replaced the older historic eyalets. The law defined the hierarchical composition and authority distribution within the new provinces. In contrast with the earlier Tanzimat trend of consolidating power in the hands of the central government, the scope of authority of the governor was increased, with supervision of the social, financial, security, and political affairs of the vilayet and execution of the laws being assigned to him. He controlled directly the actions of his immediate subordinates in the administrative hierarchy, the *mutasarrıf*s at the *sancak* level. He also was in charge of measures of public interest, such as education and improvement of communications. He fixed the time for the convocation of the local councils, received their recommendations, and carried out those that were within the range of his authority. He supervised the collection of taxes as well as the behavior of the tax collectors but could not use any of the revenues without authorization from the Porte.

Associated with the governor were administrative departments that paralleled the bureaucratic structure in Istanbul. Their functionaries, such as the provincial accountant, director of foreign affairs, public works supervisor, and inspector judge, were appointed by Istanbul and were responsible directly to their superiors in the capital.

The activities of the different departments were coordinated by the Administrative Assembly (*Idare Meclisi*), which consisted of the governor, department heads, and six representative members, three Muslims and three non-Muslims, elected from among the inhabitants. The maintenance of order and security was a prime responsibility of the governor. It was specifically stated that the assembly should not interfere with judicial affairs. Aside from carrying an echo of the principle of separation of powers, this provision soothed the ulema who were apprehensive of the impact of increased secularization.

The judicial affairs of the vilayet were put under three different courts: (1) the *Şeriat* court, with the kadi in charge; (2) the criminal court, composed of three Muslim and three non-Muslim members, presided over by the inspector judge; and (3) the commercial court, formed as indicated by the Commercial Code, with mixed membership. Over and above these was the Court of Appeals, composed of three Muslim and three non-Muslims, presided over by the inspector judge appointed by the *şeyhulislam* and advised by an official versed in law. Secondary courts at the *sancak* level, similarly organized, had to refer important cases to the relevant provincial court. The system of criminal and commercial courts, based on a secular conception of justice and law, subsequently developed into the *Nizamiye* (Regulation) courts.

The Provincial Law aimed at removing ambiguous administrative relationships by defining the relation of the parts to the whole. Each province (vilayet) was divided into *liva*s or *sancak*s (the terms being used interchangeably). Each *liva* had several *kaza*s, and each *kaza* was a collection of *nahiye*s, which in turn consisted of neighboring *karye*s, or villages. At each level councils were formed to introduce the elective-representative principle into the functioning of local government, a measure far more progressive than anything practiced in the capital. The Provincial General Assembly (*Meclis-i Umumi-i Vilayet*) was composed of two Muslims and two non-Muslims elected by each *sancak*. Convoked by the governor and meeting no more than 40 days a year, the assembly was charged with matters related to construction and the upkeep of roads and bridges, tax collection, improvement of agriculture and commerce, and discussion of requests from the *livas* and *kazas* on these and similar issues. The Porte and the sultan received the proposed laws from the Provincial General Assembly and could alter, reject, or promulgate them as they saw fit. The administrative councils at lower levels were small-scale models of this provincial organization.

At the lowest level, the Council of Elders (*Ihtiyar Meclisi*), one of the oldest representative organs in the Ottoman Empire, was retained. Each *millet* in the village elected its own Council of Elders and a headman or mayor (*muhtar*), the electors consisting of male Ottoman subjects over the age of 18 who paid a specified sum in direct taxes annually. The selection of *kaza* and *sancak* councils involved elaborate procedures: Three times the number of necessary appointees were nominated at the level these delegates were to hold office; the lower level was asked to eliminate a third; and the higher authority appointed half of the candidates from the reduced list, or a third of the original. Thus a compromise was achieved between the elective and appointive principles, securing a system of checks and balances that had a regulatory influence over an inexperienced and mostly illiterate electorate.

The new provincial system was in fact a means for a vast extension of the scope of government on all levels, with the object of fully carrying out the Tanzimat's ideals of protecting and promoting the lives and properties of the subjects. Education, public works, and military and tax reforms were basic parts of the new program. But all could not be introduced at the same time due to both insufficient funds and a lack of experience in administering the new law. Therefore, four model vilayets were chosen to provide laboratories for its application. Selected first for this role was the pilot project, the new Danube province (*Tuna vilayeti*), composed of the former eyalets of Silistria, Vidin, and Niş, including in its administrative scope the *sancak*s of Niş, Vidin, Sofia, Tolça, Varna, Rusçuk, and Tirnovo. This was followed by other consolidations of administrative organization, with much of northeastern Anatolia formed into Erzurum province; northern Syria was established as the province of Aleppo; and the historic boundaries of the province of Bosna were more or less retained. The administrative and judiciary officers of the new provinces received their salaries from Istanbul. Midhat Paşa and Cevdet Paşa were particularly successful in applying the new law in the Danube and Aleppo provinces respectively, with the new governmental bodies, elections, and courts being followed by cadastral surveys, new tax and conscription systems, schools, hospitals, roads, irrigation systems, and the like. The new Civil Service School (*Mekteb-i Mülkiye*) established in Istanbul (see page 109) began to produce graduates who were absorbed into the new provincial organization. By 1865 the four model provinces were fully organized and in operation. Damascus, Tripoli of Libya, and Edirne followed the next year. In 1867, 13 new vilayets were organized in the same way, including Bursa, Izmir, Trabzon, Salonica, Prizren, and Işkodra, with an autonomous Crete being organized as a vilayet by Âli Paşa in 1871. By the end of 1876 the new provincial system was in operation all over the empire, with the sole exception of the Arabian Peninsula and, of course, autonomous provinces like Egypt. The Council of State (*Şurayı Devlet*), which provided representation on the central level in 1868, thus was only a cap for the provincial system of representative councils and a direct means of conveying provincial opinions and problems into the central legislative process.

There is much that can be criticized in the new provincial system. In many cases the new levels of bureaucracy made the roles of government and subjects alike more difficult than before. Yet they did work. More money was collected for the treasury. Security improved, and the courts and administrators protected the subjects more effectively from misrule and oppression than had been the case in the past. The representative councils in particular were the first means provided for subjects to participate in the process of rule beyond the local level. While it appears on the surface that the councils represented only small oligarchies at the top – because they did provide functions for the leaders of the major social, religious, and economic groups – they were as representative as the empire's structure allowed at that time. Local initiative, opinions, and problems were incorporated into the functioning of government, and the Tanzimat's goals of improved education, agriculture, communications, and taxes were furthered through their support and participation.

Municipal Government

We have already seen the beginnings of Ottoman municipal organization in Istanbul during the reign of Mahmut II, when the imposition of excise taxes to support the new army led him to abolish the old *şehir emini* and extend the traditional function of the *muhtesip* (now called *ihtisap ağası*) of regulating and taxing the markets into a more comprehensive and central position. Acting for the central government, mayors (*muhtars*) were asked to register subjects in their quarters, replacing the kadis who had previously performed many municipal functions. But the *ihtisap ağası* did not really become the Istanbul mayor. His office was too completely dominated by the guild leaders, who long had cooperated with it to control the markets. Aside from the collection of the state's excise taxes, his activities were limited mainly to enforcing the market restrictions and price regulations desired by the guilds. His powers of regulation also were severely limited by the existence of other governmental agencies. Control of construction, streets, and water supply, formerly exercised by the *şehir emini*, first was turned over to the sultan's chief architect (*mimar başı*) and then to an autonomous Buildings Commission (*Meclis-i Ebniyâ*). The functions of police were carried out by the armed forces until 1845 and then by an urban police force placed under another council, called first the Police Council (*Polis Meclisi*) and then the Control Council (*Meclis-i Zabıta*), but still under strong military control.[38]

The city was becoming far too large, populated, and prosperous, however, for such a diffuse structure to meet its needs. During the years of the Crimean War, the number of Europeans resident in Galata and Beyoğlu (Pera) increased enormously, and as their financial power and commercial interests expanded, they built new houses, apartments, hotels, shops, and theaters that emulated contemporary European architectural styles. They also introduced the same kind of horse-drawn carriages that had previously been adapted for public transportation in the great cities of Europe. An Ottoman steamship company, the *Şirket-i Hayriye*, was founded in 1851, and it provided regular and rapid transportation from Istanbul to points along the Bosporus, replacing the oar-drawn *kayıks* that had monopolized this traffic since the eighteenth century when the shores of the Bosporus were first adorned by the dwellings of the wealthy.[39] In consequence of such developments, there was an increased demand for the same sort of municipal organization and services that major European cities had at the time, as well as for paved streets and sidewalks, sewers and fresh-water canals, and streetlighting and street cleaning. Neither the *ihtisap ağası* nor the Control Council could satisfy these demands, since they had no municipal income or employees. When the cadastral survey started by Mahmut II was completed in Istanbul in 1853, it was possible to establish a system of municipal property and income taxes, but even then the existing governmental structure could not or would not do so because of its close attachment to the traditional propertied classes.

In response to the situation, in 1854 the *ihtisap ağası* was replaced with a mayor of Istanbul, given the old name *şehir emini*. He was helped by a City Council (*Şehir Meclisi*), composed of 12 leading merchants and guild members, in performing tasks such as assessing the property and income taxes that were to replace the *ihtisap* excise taxes, keeping the streets and markets clean and in good order, regulating construction and repairs, arranging to supply the city with food and water, and enforcing the price and quality regulations previously established and maintained by the guilds and the *ihtisap ağası* – all under the general supervision and control of the central government. As it turned out, however, since the council was composed mainly of merchants and guild members, the latter duty came to occupy most of its attention, with the hopes for municipal services and the implementation of the new tax regulations rapidly being dashed. Moreover, the *şehir emini* had no more independent power than had his predecessor, since the Control Council still controlled the police; he was so required to coordinate his other activities with the relevant ministries of the central government that it was impossible for him to evolve any purely municipal functions or to respond to particular interests of the city itself.

An effective municipal organization for Istanbul was conceived only during the Crimean War period. The new Council of the Tanzimat (1854) appointed a City Ordering Commission (*Intizam-ı Şehir Heyeti*), composed of leading Ottoman and foreign residents, charged with the development of a new regulation to transform the existing structure into a municipal government. It soon submitted a series of reports recommending the establishment of a special municipal commission that would regulate and enforce urban laws and regulations and improve the city's physical make-up, with a separate municipal tax structure and tax-gathering organization to finance these activities.[40] The Council of the Tanzimat decided to apply these recommendations, but first only in those areas of the city that had led the demand for modernization and were occupied mainly by Europeans familiar with the new style of city government, namely, Galata and Beyoğlu; in anticipation of subsequent extension of the new system to other parts of the city they were given the name sixth district (*altıncı daire*), apparently in imitation of the part of Paris, the *sixième arrondissement,* where Mustafa Reşit and Âli had lived, which to them was the model of modern urban organization.[41] By an order of July 7, 1858, the new district was established under the control of the Municipal Council, composed of a chairman (*reis*) appointed for an indefinite term and 12 members appointed for terms of three years – all volunteers and unsalaried, with only their technical and scribal staffs being paid. The council was supposed to build and maintain streets, sidewalks, water conduits, gas lines and firefighting apparatus, to inspect and control food and food prices, weights and measures, and construction and building maintenance, and to supervise public places such as markets, hotels, theaters, restaurants, coffeehouses, and taverns. The cost of the new government was not to be borne by the treasury, but instead by the imposition of new income and property taxes of no more than 3 percent on the district's residents, with the

Municipal Council being authorized to conduct a cadastral survey of property and income within its jurisdiction so that the taxes could be levied regularly and fairly. It also was given the right to borrow money and to purchase or expropriate private property for public purposes. But its budgets and therefore its programs had to be approved by the Council of the Tanzimat, the Council of Ministers, and the sultan through the regular legislative channels before they could be put into effect, thus placing it firmly under the control of the central government.[42] Just as the Tanzimat had recognized the government's duty to care for the subjects in the provinces, the principle thus was extended to part of the capital. There was no hint of representative rule except insofar as the members of the City Ordering Commission came from the major groups of the district. Basically, it was the same sort of autonomous council as those that continued to operate Istanbul's police system and supervise its construction. What was particularly new, however, was its function of improving the physical layout of the city as well as the lives of its inhabitants.

With a population at least partly composed of Europeans and of Ottomans experienced in European city life, the work of the model city council progressed with a vitality that might not have been the case had it been established first in quarters more accustomed to the traditional Middle Eastern structure of city life. It quickly made a new survey of land and buildings and established a structure of taxes on these as well as on profits, thus setting up a model for similar systems established in other towns and cities throughout the empire just as soon as their surveys could be completed.[43]

The project was in fact so successful that in September 1864 the authority of the *şehir emini* was extended to the European and Asiatic shores of the Bosporus, including also Üsküdar and the Marmara islands.[44] In 1868 a new Municipal Regulation reorganized the *şehir emini*'s department into a general Muncipal Prefecture, still governed by the *şehir emini* but now with the help of a Prefecture Council (*Meclis-i Emanet*), which was to deal with daily affairs, and a General City Assembly (*Cemiyet-i Umumiye*), composed of delegates from each district of the city and assembled periodically to decide on more general questions concerning the municipality. Under the Prefecture, the city was divided into 14 districts (*daires*), including separate ones established along the European shores of the Bosporus at Beşiktaş, Yeniköy, and Rumeli Feneri and on the opposite banks at Kanlıca, Üsküdar, Haydarpaşa, and the islands, thus more or less forming the boundaries of Istanbul city government that have remained to the present day. Each district was organized and governed along the lines of the sixth district, with its own municipal council of 8 to 12 members, who chose 1 of their number as chairman and 5 others to represent them whenever the General City Assembly was called into session. Perhaps most important of all, the regulations introduced at this time established popular, though limited and indirect, elections of public representatives on the district councils, thus applying to Istanbul the same kind of principles that earlier had been applied to the provincial administrative councils.

The new municipal government and its constituent district organizations were given extensive duties and powers – including all matters regarding the construction and maintenance of buildings and streets, laying drains and water conduits, and embellishment and cleaning of the markets, lighting streets and public buildings, the provision of public transportation, the maintenance and extension of the quays, the procurement and storage of supplies such as coal, wood, construction materials, and food, the establishment and maintenance of hotels, cafés, theaters, and other public gathering places, the safety of vehicles, the accuracy of weights and measures, the enforcement of price and quality regulations, the maintenance of public health, and the provision of public facilities for orphans, invalids, and indigents – thus assuming most of the functions traditionally handled by the guilds and *millet*s as well as the *ihtisap ağası* and other state officials. The *şehir emini* was given the power to regulate the guilds and also to confirm their leaders and council members, thereby enforcing his will far more directly than had been possible in the past. Municipal taxes were to be collected by the district councils with the assistance of appropriate experts provided by the Prefecture.[45]

Application of the new regulations outside the sixth district came slowly, however. The government was beginning to fall into the crisis of money, politics, and diplomacy that was to undermine the Tanzimat in its last years. In addition, the notables and people of the other areas of the city were much less willing to cooperate in what, to them, was a major change in the manner in which city life was organized. The guilds and *millet*s in particular were opposed to the transfer of most of their functions to agents of the city. Yet organization did proceed, and by 1876 municipal government was operating reasonably well in all parts of Istanbul.[46] In addition to paving the streets, the municipality established the first Ottoman tramline, connecting Galata and Beyoğlu with an underground tunnel; and concessions were given to private companies to operate tramlines in other parts of the city as well as to develop more modern conduits for the provision of water into newly settled areas.[47] City policemen (*cavuşlar*) were organized to supplement the army police and enforce city regulations.[48] A municipal budget system was introduced, with each district council submitting its own monthly budget to the *şehir emini* for his approval, while he in turn had to do the same thing once a year for the Council of State. Direct elections were introduced for members of the sixth district council, replacing the old indirect system,[49] and later they also were extended to the other districts. Finally, a new city building regulation established the municipality's control over all aspects of construction, maintenance, and cleanliness of all buildings, public and private, throughout the city.[50]

The municipal structure thus organized remained with little change until the end of the empire and formed the basis for the structure of urban government developed by the Turkish Republic. The greatest changes in the Tanzimat structure were introduced by the Parliament of 1877, which increased the number of Istanbul's districts to 20 and reduced the qualifications to vote and serve on the councils. But as part of the process by which Sultan Abdulhamit II restored the early Tanzimat tendency to seek autocratic executive control, the municipality was given its final and definitive revision in 1878 when it was redivided into ten larger districts, with the representative councils replaced by appointed directors (*müdürs*) in each district and the *şehir emini* and his council and staff ruling throughout the city far more directly than had been the case earlier.[51] At the same time also, a provincial structure, with a governor (*vali*) and provincial officers, was established in 1878 to perform the same functions within Istanbul that provincial authorities performed elsewhere in the empire, specifically to collect state taxes and enforce state laws within the area ruled by the municipality.[52] This system also remained with little change into the republican period.

Finally, the example set in Istanbul gradually spread to the other major cities of the provinces. The Vilayet Administrative Code of 1870, amplifying the provincial reform laws passed six years earlier, provided for the organization of municipal councils in the towns and cities to cap the system already begun with the local *muhtars* and to take over direction of urban affairs from the governors.[53]

This was elaborated in the Provincial Municipal Code (*Vilayet Belediye Kanunu*) adopted by the Parliament in September 1877, which stipulated that every town would have a municipal council, with 6 to 12 members according to its population and importance, and elections every two years to choose half the members and membership restricted by property and income provisions. One of the council members in each municipality was to be chosen as mayor (*belediye reisi*), but by the Ministry of the Interior, which was to supervise the entire system, rather than by the council or the local population. The ministry thus was able to maintain far more direct control over the provincial municipal activities than was the case in Istanbul, which had more autonomy. General policy and municipal budgets were, however, sanctioned by municipal assemblies (*Cemiyet-i Belediye*), which met periodically and were responsible to the Provincial General Councils (*Meclis-i Umumi-i Vilayet*), the new form of the old provincial advisory councils.[54]

The Tanzimat Tax System and Financial Problems

Intimately connected with both the provincial and municipal structures of government built up during the Tanzimat period was the new tax system developed to exploit the wealth of the empire and to finance the reforms that were being attempted. The tax system that the Tanzimat inherited was basically that organized during the sixteenth century on the basis of traditional Islamic financial practices. The produce of the land had been subjected to the tithe (*öşür*, pl. *âşâr*), whose collection was assigned in units called *mukata'a* to holders of the Ottoman equivalents of fiefs (*timar*) and tax farms (*iltizam*) and supplemented by customary taxes (*tekâlif-i örfiye*), subject to regional variations. Urban dwellers, particularly those of Istanbul, were spared many types of taxes, paying mainly the traditional market dues (*ihtisap resmi*) and customs duties imposed on goods imported and exported from the empire as well as passing from one place to another within its boundaries. Finally, of course, all non-Muslims able to pay were subjected to the head tax (*cizye*) imposed in return for their protection by the sultan, retention of their own laws and customs, and exemption from military service. Exemptions from state taxes also had been granted to religious foundations, private-property owners, and certain villages and districts in return for their performance of special services like providing labor for neighboring fortifications, roads, or forests or men for the army and navy.[55]

The tax reform policy of the Tanzimat involved efforts to supplant the indirect type of tax collection through tax farmers and fief holders with direct collection by salaried state agents so that all the revenue would go to the treasury. In addition, a major goal was to replace the customary charges with more uniform taxes levied directly in relation to income and to abolish the exemptions previously granted so that all would pay equally. Tanzimat tax aims actually were first stated late in the reign of Mahmut II, when after imposing a number of urban excise taxes to finance his new *Mansure* army (1826), he subsequently abolished them along with the urban market taxes and most of the rural excise taxes. In their place, as we have seen, and under Mustafa Reşit's influence, he ordered cadastral surveys of property values throughout the empire so that subsequent taxes could be assessed entirely according to the ability to pay (August 8, 1838). But the surveys had only begun in the districts of Bursa and Gallipoli when he died, so that real tax reform had to await the Tanzimat, as did so many other of the reforms that he had planned.

The basic aims of the reformers in the field of taxation were declared in an *irade* issued on February 23, 1839. All the traditional taxes imposed in the name of the *Şeriat* were abolished with the exception of the sheep tax (*ağnam resmi*) and the poll tax on non-Muslims (*cizye*). A tithe of exactly one-tenth of the value was imposed as the sole tax on the produce of the land. In place of the market tax and urban excise taxes, previously abolished, merchants and artisans were subjected to a profits tax (*temettuat vergisi*) according to the ability to pay, with the new taxes being levied in each area as soon as the cadastres begun in Mahmut's time were completed. In addition, as we have seen (see. p. 84), all these taxes were collected by salaried agents of the treasury called *muhassıls*. The census and cadastre takers spread quickly out into the countryside, and the *muhassıls* followed as the Men of the Tanzimat awaited the revenues they needed to carry out the remainder of their reforms.[56] The new urban taxes were imposed and collected with reasonable efficiency, and their regularity and relation to income seemed to stimulate trade and industry.

But the new system simply did not work in the countryside. Surveying was not the problem; within a short time cadastres sufficient for tax purposes were available in the main agricultural centers. Enforcement, however, was another problem. There were not enough new bureaucrats willing and able to act as *muhassıls*, turning all their collections over to the treasury and remaining content with limited salaries. The tax farmers were basically businessmen who had collected taxes for a profit, and the new arrangement certainly was not agreeable to them. Hence they hung back and watched the new *muhassıls* who were sent out fail due to their lack of local connections and knowledge and to the huge areas assigned them for collection. Tithe revenues fell so badly as a result that at the end of 1840 the treasury had to restore the tax farm system. In auctions held in the provincial and *sancak* capitals, two-year rights to collect taxes in specific *mukataʿas* were given to those tax farmers who promised the highest return to the treasury.[57] But this simply restored the problems that the Tanzimat had attempted to correct, with the tax farmers taking as much as they could from the cultivators by legal and illegal means, to recoup the amounts of their bids and make a profit before their terms were up. State revenues remained low, therefore, and the treasury finally was forced to attempt a novel device never before tried in the empire. Paper money (*kaime-i mutebere*) was issued with the backing of 160,000 gold pieces held by the treasury to raise sufficient funds to meet current expenses in 1840 and again in 1842. To increase the revenues from the tax farms a decree also was issued in 1847 authorizing their assignment for five years at a time in the hope that this would encourage the tax farmers to consider the long-term interests of the lands under their jurisdiction and avoid overtaxation in order to keep the cultivators on the land and preserve a steady rate of cultivation. In return for the long terms, usually given without auction, the tax farmers had to agree to a number of provisions stipulated to protect the cultivators. They had to lend the latter funds at nominal interest to enable them to buy tools, animals, and seeds without falling into the hands of the moneylenders. They could not force the cultivators to pay taxes before their harvests came in; and they had to evaluate crops surrendered for tax payments in kind at the current market rates in their localities.[58]

While the tax farmers thus were not eliminated in the early years of the Tanzimat, the new tax system protected the peasants from injustice far more than before. In addition, efforts were made to expropriate fiefs and endowment lands and to include them among the state lands, thus subject to the same taxes, and the former holders were retired on life pensions. This was a slow process, hindered by the opposition of the holders and the inability of the state to find suitable replacements for either cultivation or tax collection, but it was almost complete by the end of the century, adding to the treasury's revenues though the pensions paid in return comprised a large burden for some time.[59] In addition, other taxes retained from before the Tanzimat were standardized in accordance with its basic principles. The sheep tax had been traditionally levied in kind at the tithe rate of one head in ten for the needs of the palace and the army, with the remainder collected in cash by tax farmers or fief holders at the rate of 1/40 of the money value of the animals, and exemptions for animals used directly in agricultural labor and transport. But the basic tenth had been supplemented with numerous additional impositions over the centuries, including slaughterhouse taxes, grazing taxes, and the like. The initial reform in the sheep tax was made by Mahmut II, who ordered that the basic tax be collected only in kind to provide the meat needed by his new army while protecting the peasants from the oppression implicit in the cash collections. The Tanzimat went on to abolish officially all the extra taxes in 1840, replacing them with an all-encompassing rate of 5 kuruş per head basic tax.

The poll tax (*cizye*) imposed on non-Muslims in Muslim states had traditionally been collected from male heads of households in annual impositions divided into three classes according to the ability to pay, with all poor persons, single or widowed, women, children, and religious persons exempted along with the aged and the infirm. The tax was regularized according to the Ottoman system in 1592, but later the right to collect the *cizye* taxes in individual localities was organized into *mukata'as* and farmed out to collectors who imposed additional irregular fees as they did in other areas of taxation. Mahmut II tried to rationalize the system by ordering that only the legal taxes be collected (1830), but he also legalized the additional "costs of collection" given to census takers and town authorities to provide for their expenses. Since permission for such minor additional sums encouraged the tax farmers and their collectors to add their own illegal exactions as well, in 1833 a single tax of 60, 30, and 15 kuruş respectively from the three classes was imposed and all other additions prohibited. The tax farm system remained, however, with all its difficulties, until it was abolished for the *cizye* in 1839, with the *millet* leaders then being made responsible for collecting the taxes and turning them over to officials sent by the treasury.

Despite the reforms, treasury revenues continued to lag behind expenditures necessitated by increased centralization. So the government had to issue new bonds (*kaime*) or paper money, building up a fairly substantial debt and interest obligation, most of whose recipients lived within the empire at this time. The Crimean War made the situation worse. The cost of Ottoman participation as well as that of caring for the allied troops and establishments on Ottoman territory created a tremendous burden, far in excess of normal revenues, stimulating the treasury to a series of financial measures that, while meeting the needs of the moment, eventually undermined the empire's financial stability and, as we shall see, threatened its very existence by 1876. A new program of taking over the tax farms as their five-year terms ended and administering them through salaried *muhassıls* (1852–1855) proved ineffective. The treasury, therefore, was forced to issue a fourth series of bonds, under the name public assistance (*iane-i umumiye*), forcing most bureaucrats and merchants to buy them to pay for current war expenditures. In addition, two famous Galata moneylenders, Leon and Baltazzi, created the Istanbul Bank to provide loans to the government; and in 1856 the famous Ottoman Bank (*Osmanlı Bankası*) was founded for the same purpose largely with English capital, for the first time providing the government with foreign loans to help meet deficits in the budget.

Soon after the Crimean War ended, the government attempted to solve its financial problem by restoring the tax farm system once again for all land tax collections with a new regulation (December 20, 1855) that remained in force for much of the rest of the century. On the assumption that tax farmers could best be controlled by forcing them to reapply for their holdings at short and regular intervals, their terms were shortened to one or two years. To prevent them from building local power that they might use to evade the law, the *mukata'a*s were reduced to individual villages and tax farmers were prohibited from holding *mukata'a*s in adjacent villages or *sancak*s.[60] But as usual the ingenuity and perseverance of the tax farmers prevailed, and the new system worked no better than the old. With the short terms the tax farmers had no interest in the long-term prosperity of the holdings, so that they collected all they could before their terms expired, oppressing the cultivators even more than before. Within a short time the wealthier tax farmers were able to build up holdings encompassing entire *sancak*s and even sections of provinces, completely flouting the regulations, subfarming their holdings at the village and *sancak* levels, thus creating a hierarchy of middlemen who maintained themselves at the expense of both the treasury and the cultivators.[61]

Treasury revenues continued to be inadequate, therefore, and Ottoman finances became so perilous that when Mustafa Reşit Paşa contracted for a new foreign loan in 1858, his creditors insisted that in return he institute major reforms and also cash in most of the bonds and paper money that were rapidly losing their value and undermining what was left of the state's financial credibility. At the same time, however, the foreign creditors were able to force the empire to accept such onerous conditions of interest and discount that it had to pay as much as 60 percent on this loan alone, a process that continued with depressing regularity in subsequent years. In response to this situation a series of measures was introduced starting in 1858, mainly under the leadership of Fuat Paşa, to reform the finances of the empire so that further foreign loans might be avoided. The Ministry of Finance was reorganized and made more efficient. For the first time a real system of annual budgets was introduced, with the budgetary estimates of individual ministries subjected to the scrutiny and reductions imposed by the treasury in accordance with estimated revenues each year.[62] A Department of Land Cadastre (*Tahrir-i Emlak Nezareti*) was organized for the purpose of providing the tax collectors with a comprehensive inventory of wealth. The new census system was carried out successfully in the *sancak*s of Bursa and Janina, after which it was revised on the basis of this experience and extended to the remaining provinces, with the exception of Erzurum and the Arab provinces, whose surveys were not fully completed until 1908. The surveys were, of course, followed by efforts to improve the collection of existing taxes and to add a number of new ones in those areas where previously untaxed wealth had become apparent. In addition to the tithes on produce, an entirely new property tax (*arazi ve müsakkafat vergisi,* or land and dwellings tax) of 4/10 of 1 percent was imposed on all cultivated land, urban land plots, and buildings, whether used for dwelling by the owner or rented out, with an additional tax of 4 percent being added for rental income.[63] While most of this went to the treasury, a portion was set aside for the municipality in which it was collected. It was followed by a profits tax (*temettuat vergisi*) imposed on individuals engaged in trade, commerce, and industry, with a rate set at 3 percent in 1860 and subsequently raised to 4 and 5 percent later in the century. Foreign subjects were exempted from this tax, even for profits earned within the Ottoman Empire, despite the efforts of the Men of the Tanzimat to include them. Wages and salaries were not taxed in any regular way until well into the Young Turk period, thus leaving Ottoman entrepreneurs to bear the brunt of this tax, adding to the advantages already held by their foreign counterparts.[64]

In the rural areas the tithe continued to be the most important single state revenue, with renewed efforts to limit the tax farmers mainly unsuccessful until late in the century. A system introduced in Rumeli in 1860 forced the local notables to collect the cultivation tax, remitting to the treasury the average annual tithe collection based on the amount paid from their districts during the previous five years and keeping the rest for themselves. For all practical purposes, this was the tax farm system under another name, the only difference being that it was carried out by local notables instead of outside businessmen. The tithe of Anatolia continued to be collected by the tax farmers along with some areas of Rumeli that could not be organized according to the new system.[65] But even in Rumeli the system did not work. The notables kept as much for themselves as the tax farmers had done, while only slightly improving the lot of the cultivators. Thus starting in 1866 its revenues also were auctioned off once again to tax farmers, though in a new attempt to limit the abuses the auctions were carried out by the Ministry of Finance in Istanbul rather than locally.[66] This had little real effect; hence in the revised provincial system introduced in 1868 tax farm assignments were again given to the governors in the hope that their local knowledge and power would enable them to regulate the system better than the central government could, with local notables considered preferable to outside businessmen. All of these systems were, however, variations on the same theme with little concrete result.

The Tanzimat reformers were much more successful in other areas of taxation. The basic sheep tax reforms were introduced in 1856–1857. The classical tax had been on capital rather than income, since it was levied at a set amount per head regardless of the sheep's size, weight, value, or whether or not it was to be sold at all. Now the tax was extended to all farm animals, and it was altered to relate to the value of each according to local market conditions and the animal's actual use, as determined by the village council of elders. Each council had to figure how much revenue the cultivator could secure from the milk and/or wool of a sheep or goat of a certain size in their area during the year. All findings were sent to the Ministry of Finance in Istanbul, which then set the tax per head in each district according to the revenues expected. Taxes were originally set at 10 percent of the revenue expected from each animal in Edirne and the Danube province, where they were most profitable, down to 1.5 percent in eastern Anatolia and the Arab provinces.[67] The system remained more or less the same afterward with only the general rates being increased from time to time as the government's need for revenues changed. Both the cultivation and sheep taxes continued to be collected mainly through the tax farm system until it was abolished by an act of Parliament (enacted April 24, 1877), with a new Department of Tithe and Sheep Tax (*Âşâr ve Ağnam Emaneti*) being organized in the Ministry of Finance to organize direct collections. Even then, however, opposition from the large landowners and tax farmers caused delay, and it was only late in Abdulhamit II's reign that this was fully accomplished.[68]

Particularly important for the cultivators of the empire were the old military-service and road labor taxes, which were subjected to major changes during the

Tanzimat. By Ottoman tradition, as we have noted previously, non-Muslims were subjected to the head tax (*cizye*) in lieu of military service, but all Muslims had to serve when called. However, the feudal (timar) regulations specified that if the holder died and the eldest son was too young to serve, he could send a personal substitute or, later, provide money with which a substitute could be procured. The latter provision gradually opened the door for Muslim timar holders who were unable or unwilling to serve to pay a regular substitution tax instead. Under the new conscription system introduced by Mahmut II in 1838 and then reformed by the Tanzimat a decade later, all Muslim subjects except those living in the exempted cities of Istanbul, Mecca, and Medina were required to serve at least five years (ages 20 to 24) as active soldiers in the new *Nizamiye* army, two years (ages 24 to 26) in the active reserve (*ihtiyat*), then seven years in the inactive reserves (*redif*) (ages 26 to 32), and an additional eight years (ages 32 to 40) in the local defense forces (*mustahfiz*), subject to regular training and calls to service in emergencies. Mahmut II allowed these conscripts to provide personal substitutes only, but the basic Tanzimat conscription law of 1845 allowed the obligation to be transmuted into cash, a payment called the military-service cash payment (*bedel-i nakdi-i askeri*). In 1871 it was specified that those who chose to avoid service in this way had to be wealthy enough to raise the money without selling their plots of land, so as to discourage poorer families from becoming hired laborers to the wealthy simply to rescue their sons from the army.[69] In the new Conscription Law introduced by Abdulhamit II in 1885, a man who wished to substitute money for personal service was allowed to do so only after training for three months with the nearest military unit, after which he then could pay 50 gold pieces to avoid every subsequent call-up,[70] and this was the arrangement that prevailed thereafter.

In the meantime, an entirely separate arrangement was made for non-Muslims. Continuation of the head tax into the nineteenth century was not considered anything unusual, since the Muslims also were able to buy their way out of military service in the same way. But the Reform Decree of 1856 specifically promised full equality to non-Muslims, and this meant equality in liability for military service as well as for entry to government positions and schools. Neither Muslims nor non-Muslims wanted the latter to serve in the army, the former because of the long-standing tradition, the latter because they preferred the more profitable lives of civilians. But since the Porte had promised the powers to end the head tax as a distinctive and discriminatory tax, it was abolished in 1857 and replaced by a simple military-service tax (*bedel-i askeri*) imposed on non-Muslims who were liable for conscription under the law. According to the new arrangement, 1 out of every 180 male subjects of army age had to serve, meaning – according to the census reports of the time, which specified that there were about 3 million non-Muslim males of age – that 16,666 of them were liable, each of whom was charged 50 liras, less than the equivalent tax imposed on Muslims for exemption. While the population of the empire increased during the Tanzimat, the number of men required for the army was reduced by 25 percent which, along with the relative increase of Muslims to non-Muslims due to the arrival of thousands of refugees from Christian oppression, left only 12,500 non-Muslims liable each year.[71] Collections were made by the *millets* themselves until 1887, when special commissions were organized at the *kaza* level in response to complaints that the *millet* leaders were using the tax to oppress their followers and enrich themselves at the expense of the state.[72] Finally, immediately after the restoration of the Constitution (1909), military service in person was made an obligation for all subjects regardless of religion or *millet,* and conscription taxes were abolished altogether.

During the early years of the empire, major roads were built by the state at the expense of the Imperial Treasury, while local roads were constructed by tax farmers and fief holders, mainly by forced labor imposed on the cultivators living nearby. Certain villages, particularly those settled by Turkomans and Yörüks in Anatolia and Rumeli, provided men to the army who did nothing but build and repair roads and bridges, in return for which they and the villages were exempted from all taxes. But once the conquests were ended and the treasury revenues thereby limited, it no longer had sufficient money to support the construction and repair of even the main roads, while the breakdown of the timar system left no one to maintain the lesser roads, leading to a decline of the entire system in the seventeenth and eighteenth centuries. What repairs there were were carried out by kadis and some *sancak* beys, who invented special customary taxes and extended the corvée for the purpose. As time went on, these impositions became regular taxes, levied annually whether or not they were actually used for the roads. They consisted of special charges collected by tax farmers and others who simply set themselves up at strategic points along the road, collecting far more than they were legally entitled to do, in return for allowing travelers and merchants to pass, thus hindering internal trade as well as travel, although foreign subjects generally were exempt from them by terms of the Capitulations agreements.

These road taxes were among the customary charges that were abolished by Mahmut II in the early years of the Tanzimat, with the treasury assuming the full cost of road maintenance and contructions. But as the state's financial difficulties increased, there was little left for such purposes; therefore, the roads deteriorated even further, seriously injuring the empire's military as well as economic potential. Finally, in July 1867 an entirely new system was developed, based mainly on Midhat's experiments in the Danube province. One Public Benefits Bank (*Menafi Sandığı*) was established in each province to finance the paving of roads, repairing bridges, building local schools, and the like, with revenues coming from a small supplementary tax imposed on the tithe as well as from lending out the bank's funds to cultivators at reasonable rates of interest.[73] This in itself was not enough, however, to pay those hired for roads; thus in the Road Construction Regulation of 1869 every rural male subject between the ages of 16 and 60 was required to work on roads and bridges in his area 4 days each year, or 20 days every five years, providing his own animals and other beasts of burden as well as his food. Only the residents of large cities, provinces not yet surveyed, and priests, teachers, and old and infirm persons were exempted from what was, essentially, a restored corvée.[74] No one could be forced to work farther away than 12-hours traveling time from his home without a special decree issued by the Porte. All the costs of equipment and transportation were paid by the Public Benefits Banks, which were taken over by the Agricultural Bank (*Ziraat Bankası*) in 1887 and then by the treasury in 1907. Men were allowed to provide personal substitutes at first, but they could substitute only cash after 1889, when the labor obligation was replaced by cash payments required from all males in the provinces aged 18 to 60 at the rate of 3 or 4 kuruş per day for the service, which now was set at 25 days every five years.[75] Soon afterward, the residents of Istanbul and the other exempted provinces were subjected to the same tax on the grounds that the maintenance of the empire's roads was of value to them as well.

One of the traditional revenues of state in Islam was the mining tax. The basic *Şeriat* regulation allowed the state treasury to take one-fifth of the produce of all mines in the empire, whether they were on public or private land. This was retained by the Ottomans, and the mines on state lands were managed by paid agents or through tax farmers. According to the Land Law of 1858, all newly discovered mines belonged to the state regardless of who possessed the land on which they were located, but the Imperial Treasury had to pay compensation if exploitation of the mine prevented the landowner from fully exploiting his holdings for agricultural purposes. Mining operations were codified for the first time in July 1861,[76] and supplanted in April 1869 by a new regulation based mainly on the French Mining Law of 1810, which divided all mines into three categories – basic mines, surface mines, and stone quarries – with the concessionaries being required to provide from 1 percent of the minerals extracted from the former to 5 percent of the latter, according to the difficulty and expense of extraction and the profits derived from the result, in addition to the annual fees imposed for the permit and land rental.[77] This was supplemented by a new regulation in August 1887 that established for the first time a Department of Mines (*Maadin Nezareti*) in the Ministry of Public Works and allowed it to award mining concessions for terms from 40 to 99 years, with the tax on the extract being raised to as much as 20 percent in places where extraction was easy and the ore was in large concentrations. Before paying the tax the operators were allowed to deduct all the costs of smelting the ores and transporting them to factories or ports. For all mines on private or foundation land the state continued to collect one-fifth of the product, with the remainder going to the owners or their agents.[78]

One of the most lucrative of all the sources of revenue invented during the Tanzimat was the tax applied to documents involved in governmental or commercial business. The stamp tax (*damga resmi*) was originally imposed by the treasury in return for the insignia (*alamet*) or embossed stamp (*soğuk damga*) affixed by the *muhtesip* or other officials on Ottoman-manufactured textiles and other goods indicating their source or quality, or for the stamp of purity (*ayar damgası*) placed by the mint on articles of gold or silver. The tax was assessed on the value of the goods in question, usually at the rate of 1/40, 1 para per kuruş, and their sale or exchange was prohibited without these certificates of quality. It was considered an excise tax and was abolished along with the rest of them in 1839.[79] In addition, there always had been fees (*harc*) charged the recipients of decrees, salary documents, and the like, by the scribes issuing them, but these also were abolished with the other *örfi* taxes. Soon afterward, however, prompted by the need for new sources of revenue, the Men of the Tanzimat invented new stamp duties. On May 22, 1845, the treasury printed a series of official blank papers embossed with stamped seals of different values (*damgalı varaka-ı sahiha*, or stamped legal documents), which had to be used for all commercial and legal documents and contracts with the exception of judicial decrees and opinions issued by the religious courts. The documents were sold by local financial officials already stationed in the districts and towns to help make the annual tax collections.[80] The new system spread fairly quickly throughout the empire, but there were two major problems: (1) insufficient officials selling the documents and (2) insufficient documents bearing the correct tax rates, making it difficult or even impossible to make many transactions or sign legal contracts. As a result, on October 15, 1852, the job of selling the documents was turned over to private merchants.[81] Moneylenders and tobacconists in particular stocked the documents and gained new revenues, while ending the problem of supply. The system was in fact so successful, and the treasury was receiving so much money as the Ottoman commercial structure expanded, that Fuat Paşa reorganized and expanded it with a completely new Stamp Tax Regulation (*Resm-i Damga Nizamnamesi*) issued on September 2, 1861. The exemption on court documents was removed, the embossed papers were replaced by special tax stamps of different values, and their use was extended to almost all commercial transactions, leaving the tax in the definitive form in which it has continued to provide major revenues to the state throughout the Ottoman period and in republican times to the present day.

The other major treasury revenues during the Tanzimat were survivors from classical times, but in radically different forms. The customs tax (*gümrük resmi*) involved duties imposed not only on goods passed into and out of the empire but also those being shipped from one place to another within the sultan's dominions. There were four major customs duties in the empire: (1) the import tax (*âmediye resmi*) and (2) the export tax (*raftiye resmi*) administered by the Foreign Customs (*Harici Gümrük*) service; (3) the source tax (*masdariye resmi*) levied on certain goods produced and consumed locally, such as tobacco and fish; and (4) the transit tax (*müruriye resmi*) imposed on Ottoman and foreign goods shipped within the empire, the latter two administered by the Domestic Customs (*Dahili Gümrük*). The sixteenth-century Capitulations agreements lowered the general customs charges on foreign goods from 10 to 5 percent. Beginning with the new trade agreement with France in 1683, this was lowered to 3 percent for it and all the other powers benefiting from the most-favored-nation clause. As a result, native industry, already restricted by guild regulations, could not compete with foreign goods and the treasury was deprived of much of its customs revenue. These regulations were altered somewhat in the empire's favor starting with the commercial treaty negotiated by Mustafa Reşit Paşa with England in 1838, but at the same time foreign subjects were also allowed to import and export certain goods without any restriction. The import duty was retained at 3 percent, but an additional 2 percent was imposed when such foreign goods were sold in the empire, thus raising the total to 5 percent, still low but more meaningful than it had been. Exports now were taxed 9 percent when they reached the quay and 3 percent when they were loaded. Transit taxes of 5 percent were imposed on foreign goods sent through the empire for sale elsewhere, with charges based on tariff schedules compiled by the customs office for the goods of each country rather than on their actual market value in the empire. At the same time, Ottoman goods passing through the empire were charged 8 percent as land customs, placing them on an equal footing with their foreign rivals throughout the Tanzimat period.

Customs duties were mostly organized as tax farms through the centuries of decline, and the Tanzimat's effort to administer them by salaried *muhassıls* was no more successful in 1839 than it was for rural tithes. Thus starting in 1840 a new Customs Administration (*Emtia Gümrük İdaresi*) was organized in Istanbul with the job of farming out all the customs offices in the major ports and trade centers, at auctions for three-year terms.[82] This system was so profitable for both the treasury and the tax farmers that it was extended to all the excise taxes imposed on spirits, tobacco, snuff, and lumber, which were placed under the same administration and farmed out in the same way after 1859.[83] As part of Fuat Paşa's effort to raise the empire's revenues, in 1861 the Customs Administration was reorganized into a new Excise Tax Administration (*Rüsumat Emaneti*) entirely separate from the bureaucracy of the Ministry of Finance. The farming out of the customs and excise taxes was ended, and these thereafter were collected by a new corps of salaried officials of the new administration.[84] The transit duties were abolished entirely soon afterward (1870), a major step in building an Ottoman mercantile class, although it cost the treasury considerable revenue until increases in the other taxes charged to merchants of all nationalities compensated for it.[85] Import taxes, however, remained artificially low due to strong resistance to increases on the part of the Capitulatory powers until the early years of the twentieth century, when the Young Turks unilaterally imposed ad valorem duties on all goods, at the same time raising the import duty to 15 percent, more in line with what was being charged elsewhere at that time.

Since spirits were prohibited to Muslims by the Şeriat, there were no official spirits taxes on consumption in the early days of the Ottoman Empire. By tradition, however, the holders of timars and some tax farms did collect what was called a grape juice tax (şira resmi) from the growers of wine grapes after they were ripened and pressed into wine. In the seventeenth century also an official spirits tax (müskirat resmi) was imposed on non-Muslims who had been drinking wine unofficially (and without paying taxes) from time immemorial. But there was so much complaint from religious figures about the state benefiting financially from the consumption of wine that soon afterward the tax was abolished and replaced by an increase in the head tax imposed on non-Muslims. During the eighteenth century, various "customary" levies were imposed on grapes and wine as they were shipped, and a new prohibitions tax (zecriye resmi) was imposed on all wines and spirits sold in markets. Of course, it was farmed out to non-Muslims in the main cities so that Muslims would not be directly involved in what amounted to legal sanctioning of an act forbidden to them. The Tanzimat initially taxed all intoxicating beverages (müskirat) at 20 percent of their value, but this was lowered to 10 percent in 1861 on the assumption that they were intended only for non-Muslims. In addition, all sellers of spirits or wine by the glass or in containers in Istanbul and vicinity had to buy annual shop permits (ruhsatname) at a fee of 15 percent of their shop rent, with no permits being granted for locations in Muslim quarters or within 200 yards of mosques and dervish tekkes, and additional fees were paid as a stamp tax as well as for the registration of the rental agreements.[86] Subsequent regulations exempted monks and priests in monasteries from the payment of all taxes on wine made or bought for their personal use.[87] The administration of the spirits tax later was put under the administration of a Spirits Department (Zecriye Emaneti) established in the Ministry of Finance (1860) until it was absorbed into the new Excise Tax Department when it was organized in 1861. Through the remaining years of the empire the tax was regularly increased to enable the treasury to pay the foreign bondholders, with its administration ultimately being turned over to the Public Debt Commission along with the remainder of the excise taxes to provide the latter with one of its principal revenues.

In addition to tax revenues as such, the Men of the Tanzimat and their successors also provided the treasury with revenue from enterprises operated by the state as monopolies or under strong state control. Foremost among these in terms of revenues was that involved with the processing and sale of salt. As was the case of other kinds of mines, the state was entitled to collect one-fifth of all salt extracted from its land or waters even when these were within private property. Traditionally, this right was organized in tax farms for each salt mine or pit, with the tax farmers also acting as their supervisors. Under the Tanzimat these were taken over and administered directly by the state, but unlike most other tax farms they never were given back but remained under direct state administration, first by the Ministry of Public Works and then, after it was organized, by the Excise Tax Department, which had its own Salt Works Department (Memlehe Müdürlüğü).[88] The ownership, production, and sale of all salt in the empire was now made a government monopoly, with the revenues devoted primarily to retiring paper money and bonds, while the importation of salt was prohibited. District salt offices were established around the empire to supervise production and to sell salt in quantity to dealers, who were allowed to collect an additional fixed amount to provide a profit and compensate for transportation costs.[89] The salt tax revenues also were turned over to the Public Debt Commission late in the century to help pay off the foreign bondholders.

Tobacco traditionally was grown by private cultivators after its introduction into the empire in the sixteenth century. But in 1860 all foreign-leaf imports were prohibited and a government monopoly was established over its retail sale, with an additional transit tax (*mürüriye resmi*) being imposed on farmers bringing their crop to market. Foreigners were allowed to import manufactured tobacco as cigars, cigarettes, and snuff, but they had to pay a special import tax of 75 percent of the value in addition to the regular transit taxes.[90] The transit tax was so heavy, however, that it discouraged domestic production; thus in 1867 it was modified, with the tax lowered and varied according to the quality and sales price of each load. Tobacco sent to Istanbul was exempted from the regular transit tax but subjected instead to a larger entry tax on the theory that there were greater sales opportunities and profits in the capital. A new Tobacco Law in 1873 gave the farmers full freedom to grow smoking tobacco without official permission but provided a hierarchy of officials to supervise the markets and cigarette factories. Ottomans and foreigners now could operate tobacco factories, but they had to pay a new consumption tax (*sarfiyat resmi*), which varied according to the types of tobacco and cigarettes produced.[91]

The treasury also received revenues from the manufacture and sale of gunpowder, the postal and telegraph services, the Istanbul gas works, the bridge across the Golden Horn, steamships operating on the Tigris and Euphrates rivers, imperial properties (shops, baths, farms, and other properties belonging to the government) and forests, along with the annual tributes paid by Egypt and other vassal states. There also were revenues from state-owned railroads as well as from the profits of private railroad companies in the empire in which the treasury had a share. These, however, were relatively small proportions of the total. All the tax reforms and efforts to secure new income increased treasury revenues enormously in the decade following the Crimean War. It was not enough, however, to stem the ever-increasing expenditures required by the reforms and debt payments and the expanding role of government.[92] The resulting financial chaos, which threatened to bring the Tanzimat, and the empire, to a sudden end, will be examined later (see pp. 155–156).

Fabric of a New Society

Changes in the basic institutions of Ottoman government were accompanied by corresponding alterations in the Ottoman social fabric. The old Ruling Class of Ottomans was replaced by a new class of bureaucrats, the *memurs*, with the insecurity resulting from their position as slaves of the sultan replaced by a new assurance provided by their development into a secular bureaucratic hierarchy with legal protections that discouraged the rapid shifts of fortune endemic in the old order. The Subject Class also experienced increased confidence and power because of the guarantees provided by the Tanzimat, stability that came with the new legal order, and the emergence of a middle class able to exert its influence within the councils of state far better than could the old *millet*s and guilds. All Ottomans, high and low, were liberated from the isolation characteristic of traditionalist Ottoman society by the tangible progress made in improving communications. Increased awareness of the world outside the rule of the Porte and willingness to adopt some of its philosophy and institutions provided the bases for the secular and modern states that were to replace the Ottoman empire after the catastrophe of World War I.

Education and the New Bureaucracy

Keystone to the new society was a system of public secular education that could liberate both minds and hearts from the restrictions imposed by the old order. Selim III and Mahmut II had seen the need for secular education in certain areas. They had developed technical academies to train officers, administrators, engineers, doctors, and the like. But they had been seriously limited by a lack of students trained in the essential elements of mathematics, science, and foreign languages. The *mekteps*, which served as a basis of ulema power and which still taught the traditional subjects in, at best, the traditional ways, continued to monopolize elementary education for Muslims. Their graduates simply were not prepared for the new technical education. The solution was to establish a secular elementary school system, but even the Men of the Tanzimat knew this had to be done cautiously so as not to affront the ulema openly. Thus both the objectives and the main problems of Tanzimat education were noticeable even before 1839.

Leadership in the field of education fell first to Mahmut II's Council on Useful Affairs (*Meclis-i Umur-u Nafia*), which became an adjunct of the Ministry of Trade in the early years of the Tanzimat. Soon after the Gülhane decree, the council established a separate Temporary Commission of Education (*Meclis-i Maarif-i Muvakkat*) to develop a program for secular education. It in turn was transformed into the Council on Public Education (*Meclis-i Maarif-i Umumi*) within the Ministry of Trade in 1846, including among its members the still young Âli and Fuat. A Ministry for Public Schools (*Mekâtib-i Umumiye Nezareti*) followed a year later, and finally a full Ministry of Public Education (*Maarif-i Umumiye Nezareti*) took charge of the system in 1866. Educational programs were developed by specialized committees within the legislative bodies of the time, sometimes in cooperation with the ministry, sometimes quite independently. As a result, hundreds of plans, reports, and programs emerged, pointing toward the creation of a system of secular and utilitarian education to train all Ottomans from the elementary to the most advanced stages.

The new system of education developed slowly, however. Many Ottomans opposed the new schools simply out of reverence for the old or the quite justified fear of what the new schools might bring. As the myriad of reforms and wars also drained the treasury, the government was reluctant to devote large sums to education. As in many other societies, education and culture suffered the most from the financial crunch. The central government actually provided very little money for secular education. In most cases the establishment of schools in the provinces depended on the initiative of local administrative councils, who saw them as means of stimulating their own economic development and who provided most of the funds for buildings, equipment, and teachers once sanction and guidance had been obtained from Istanbul.

The first modern secular schools beneath the level of the technical academies were established by Mahmut II to train *mektep* graduates intending to go on to the latter. These came to be known as *Rüşdiye* (Adolescence) schools, and provided education for youths between the ages of 10 and 15. During the early years of the Tanzimat, *Rüşdiyes* were established first in Istanbul and then in the provinces, but their extension was slow for some time because of a serious shortage of trained teachers. This problem was partly solved by the establishment in 1846 of a teacher-training school for men (*Dar ul-Muallimin*) under the direction of Mustafa Reşit Paşa's protégé, young Ahmet Cevdet Efendi. In both the *Rüşdiye* schools and the *Dar ul-Muallimin,* the program was intended mainly to supplement the religious education given in the *mekteps* and to bridge the gap to the technical academies. Thus while courses in the social and physical sciences and the humanities were provided, religious education was also included, and the ulema were put in a position where they could and did block any instruction that seemed to them to violate the precepts of Islam. The major problems of money, buildings, and teachers slowed progress considerably, so that by the Crimean War there were only 60 *Rüşdiye* schools in the entire empire with 3,371 students, all male, while in Istanbul alone the Muslim religious *medrese* schools had 16,752 students and those of the non-Muslim *millets* trained an additional 19,348 students of both sexes.[93]

Despairing of the progress of the regular school system, the Seraskerate developed its own structure of secular education, starting with the School of Military Sciences (*Mekteb-i Ulum-u Harbiye*), also founded late in Mahmut's reign, which became the leading technical school in the empire. It provided advanced instruction in engineering, geometry, and mathematics in addition to the military sciences and produced graduates who served in many parts of the bureaucracy as well as in the army. To supplement the civilian schools at the lower levels, the army also developed its own secular school system beginning in 1855. Army *Rüşdiye* schools were opened at nine locations in Istanbul and its environs and in many other places around the empire, while *Idadi* (middle) schools were established in Sarajevo, Erzurum, and Baghdad to provide a new secondary level for students before they entered the School of Military Sciences. As time went on, each of the provincial armies provided at least one *Idadi* and a number of *Rüşdiye* schools in its district, giving the population an opportunity for secular education long before the civilian system was extended to them.

Following the Crimean War, both the military and the civilian secular school systems expanded rapidly. The army took the lead in developing secular education at the elementary level, a task that it assigned to its *Rüşdiye* schools, making its *Idadis* in turn into middle schools and the *Harbiye* into a secondary school and then establishing a new advanced school of military science, the School of the General Staff (*Erkân-ı Harbiye Mektebi*), to cap the system. The Ministry of Education, while forced by public opinion to recognize the Muslim *mekteps* as elementary schools, more and more began to establish its own secular *Sıbyan* (Children) or *Iptidaiye* (Elementary) schools, requiring them to be maintained in every town and village and every quarter of large cities, with the financial help and supervision of the local councils of elders as well as the *millet* leaders. Both Muslim and non-Muslim students were accepted for their four-year terms of study. In addition to lessons in religion, which were taught separately to students of the different faiths, these schools also provided lessons in arithmetic, Ottoman history, and geography, with the non-Muslims being taught in their own languages whenever necessary.

With Âli and Fuat firmly in control in the 1860s, the French minister of education Jean Victor Duruy came to Istanbul to advise the Ottomans on further educational development. His report, which proposed the establishment of inter-denominational secondary schools, a secular university, new professional technical schools, and a public library system, formed the basis for the Regulation for Public Education (*Maarif-i Umumiye Nizamnamesi*) issued in 1869, which not only systematized what had been done during the previous three decades but also laid out plans that were applied during much of the remainder of the century. Under the new law, elementary education was compulsory for all children until the age of 12. Methods of instruction were modernized. Measures were taken to raise the general cultural level of the teachers. State examinations were instituted for students graduating from each class and level. Cultural institutions were expanded with the help of the state. Villages with at least 500 houses were to have at least one *Rüşdiye* school; and towns were required to establish and maintain one *Rüşdiye* for every 500 households in their population, with separate schools being provided for girls and for Muslims and non-Muslims where the population was heterogeneous. The schools were organized in four-year terms, with lessons provided in religion (according to that of the students), the Ottoman, Arabic, and Persian languages, arithmetic and accounting, geometry and mathematics, world and Ottoman history, geography, and the most important local language in the area of the school. Towns and cities had to provide one *Idadi* school for every thousand households in their population, except those having military schools, which could rely on them instead. The term of study in the *Idadi*s was three years, with instruction provided in Ottoman and French, logic, economics, geography, world and Ottoman history, algebra, arithmetic, accounting, engineering, the physical sciences, chemistry, and draftsmanship. Above the *Idadi* level, each provincial capital also had to maintain a lycée, to be called the *Mekteb-i Sultani* (School of the Sultan). All graduates from the provincial *Idadi*s had to be accepted in the latter, but they charged tuition, so that only the wealthier families could afford to send their children, except for the very best poor students, who could attend without charge. Advanced programs included humanities, lessons in Arabic, Persian, French, economics, international law, history, and logic and science courses in engineering, algebra, trigonometry, the physical and natural sciences, and the measurement of land. Students were exempted from conscription while pursuing their studies and for one year after their graduation; and if they fulfilled their obligation to serve the government afterward, they were given permanent exemptions.

The cost of building and maintaining the elementary schools, as before, was born by the localities, while the cost for the *Rüşdiye* and *Idadi* schools was shared with the central treasury. The *Sultani* lycées were paid for entirely from the sultan's personal funds. The Ministry of Education provided teachers for all the schools, established and maintained standards, and arranged for writing or translating textbooks, but salaries were paid locally. The reforms were applied first in Istanbul and then spread to the provinces. The state now also assumed for the first time the right to supervise the study programs and procedures in the *millet* and foreign schools, with permits from the Ministry of Education being required for their continued operation so that they would not stray too far from the educational aims of the empire.

The first and most famous of the *Sultani* secondary schools was that established in the old Imperial School building at Galata Saray, in Beyoğlu, which was developed mainly along French lines by Âli under the influence and support of the French government. Leadership was provided by French officials and teachers. The language of instruction was almost entirely French, and the curriculum included the social and physical sciences, Greek, Latin, and Ottoman Turkish. Education was secular, but Muslims were allowed to worship in a small mosque attached to the school grounds, while non-Muslim students worshiped in churches and synagogues of their own faiths nearby. Tuition was charged, but the government also supported about 300 students who proved their ability by examination. Most of the instructors were foreign, but some also were Turks, Armenians, and Greeks. Despite the strong European flavor, most of the *millet* leaders opposed the attendance of students of their own faiths, as they did also for the regular state schools, because of the fear that faith and morals would be debased by exposure to secular influences. Muslims, on the other hand, often kept their children out because of the Christian flavor of the faculty and curriculum. In the end, however, the school gave the broadest general education available to Ottomans of all faiths at that time. Its graduates provided leadership in Ottoman governmental and commercial life until the end of the empire and then well into the republican period.

Above the *Sultani* schools were the teacher-training schools, with the *Dar ul-Muallimin* for men being joined by a Normal School for Women (*Dar ul-Muallimat*) in 1870 in response to the creation of a number of secular schools for women and the opening of many regular secular schools to them after the Crimean War. The teacher-training schools were expanded as the secular system grew. All graduates had to teach in state schools for ten years following their graduation, remedying the shortage of teachers experienced earlier.

In keeping with utilitarian goals in education, the Tanzimat secular school system was rounded off not by a university but by the higher technical schools, the War School (*Mekteb-i Harbiye*), the Civil Service School (*Mekteb-i Mülkiye*), the General Staff School (*Erkân-ı Harbiye Mektebi*), the Army Engineering School (*Mühendishane-i Berri-i Hümayun*), the Naval Engineering School (*Mühendishane-i Bahri-i Hümayun*), the Imperial School of Medicine (*Mekteb-i Tıbbiye-i Şahane*), and the Civilian Medical School (*Mekteb-i Tıbbiye-i Mülkiye-i Şahane*) – all maintained by the Ministry of Education. All of these developed sections on the humanities, the social sciences, and foreign languages, in addition to their specialties, to produce well-rounded students and also to provide for students who did not intend to enter the professions involved. Positions in the relevant ministry bureaucracies were reserved for graduates, with those of the *Mekteb-i Mülkiye*, for example, filling all the provincial posts of *kaymakam* and *müşir*, thus providing a much higher standard of administration than had been available earlier in the Tanzimat.[94]

A university, called *Dar ül-Fünun*, was planned by Mustafa Reşit Paşa as early as 1846, and a building was finished, but it was never staffed or opened because of the government's reaction to student participation in the revolutionary movements then sweeping Europe. In its place Reşit developed the Council of Knowledge (*Encümen-i Daniş*) in 1851, appointing some of the leading political and administrative figures of the time, mostly his protégés and allies, with the objective of promoting learning and scholarship and public knowledge of scholarly books. Each member had to be a specialist in at least one of the new fields of knowledge as well as know one foreign language, and although he had to know enough Ottoman Turkish to be able to translate works into that language, this was not a major requirement. Members were allowed to communicate in any language they wanted as long as they were advancing knowledge. As a practical matter, the council's work concentrated on sponsoring public lectures on university-level subjects and original works about the Ottoman Empire, mainly the Ottoman history and grammar books by Ahmet Cevdet. Cevdet in particular seems to have worked to use it to establish contact between some of the learned ulema and the new educated Men of the Tanzimat in the hope of ameliorating the bifurcation developing between them, but there is little evidence that he was successful. The council also planned a university including divisions for both the religious (*ilim*) and modern sciences (*fen*), but nothing was done before it disappeared during the Crimean War.[95]

Âli and Fuat still were very interested in a university. Soon after Abdulmecit's accession, they got his permission for a new Ottoman Society of Science (*Cemiyet-i Ilmiye-i Osmaniye*), very similar to the *Encümen-i Daniş* in structure but concentrating on the secular fields of knowledge, as the first step toward the secular code of laws they hoped to introduce in place of the *Şeriat*. The society published the *Mecmua-i Fünun* (Journal of Sciences) and presented a series of university courses in the form of public lectures from 1862 to 1865. Abandoning Ahmet Cevdet's old effort to include the ulema, the society emphasized Western thinkers such as Diderot and Voltaire and subjects such as chemistry, physics, engineering, and world geography. The Public Education Law of 1869 also provided for an Ottoman university, again called the *Dar ül-Fünun,* with faculties for philosophy and the humanities, legal studies, and science and mathematics, and including secular courses in some of the religious sciences, something that most certainly must have angered many members of the ulema. Buildings were set aside, a faculty appointed, and entrance examinations administered. Some 450 students were accepted, many apparently from the *medrese*s, though there also were many graduates of the Galata Saray Lycée and the Civil Service School. The university opened in February 1870; classes began and public lectures were given, but soon after Âli's death it was closed (1871), due largely to his successor's desire to use the money for the other purposes and his conviction that the technical schools were sufficient for the state of Ottoman public education at that time (1872). It was reopened between 1874 and 1881 through the efforts of the minister of education at the time, Ahmet Cevdet Paşa, with the organization and make-up of the faculties remaining mostly the same as those established five years earlier. The university was definitively opened in its modern form on September 1, 1900.[96]

With the penetration of foreign commercial and missionary interests in mid-century, foreign schools were established, including the American school, called Robert College (1863), and other institutions founded by Austrian, French, English, German, and Italian missionaries. Some were only on the elementary level; some extended to the secondary level as well and provided excellent Western-style training with large doses of proselytization among non-Muslim subjects. These schools were allowed to operate where they wanted. But their teachers, curriculums, lessons, and textbooks had to be certified by the Ministry of Education so that they would not teach anything which would violate Ottoman morals or politics, an injunction that was usually ignored. The *millet* schools, especially after their curriculums were modernized late in the century, and the foreign schools provided a superior education to that offered in the still developing state schools, but the general feeling of scorn for Muslims that they fostered among their students deepened the social divisions and mutual hatreds that were already threatening to break up Ottoman society and the empire.

Inspired by Midhat's success in the Danube province, specialized schools were established around the empire to provide elementary secular education and training as artisans to orphan (*Islahhane,* or Reform School) and poor boys (*Sanayi*

Mektebi, or Industrial School), contributing to the rebirth of native Ottoman industry. At the lycée level, in Istanbul this work was supplemented by trade schools for adults and the Naval School (*Bahriye Mektebi*) established in 1870 on Heybeli Ada, with one branch at Azapkapı in Istanbul, to train officers for the merchant marine. In addition, the Society for Islamic Studies (*Cemiyet-i Tedrisiye-i Islamiye*) offered adult extension classes for Muslims in the Bayezit section of Istanbul starting in 1870; and the *Dar uş Şafaka* was opened in 1873 in the Aksaray section of Istanbul to provide lycée education to Muslim orphans, with the financial help of the sultan and the khedive of Egypt.

Finally, a number of cultural institutions were established in accordance with the Education Law of 1869. A Museum of Antiquities (*Mecma-i esliha-ı atika ve mecma-i asar-ı atika,* or Assemblage of ancient weapons and antiquities) was established as early as 1847 in the St. Irene church, outside the Topkapı Palace, but it foundered until its collections were made the basis for the new Imperial Museum (*Müze-i Hümayun*) opened in the same locale in the late 1860s. Under a succession of foreign directors it took the lead in developing archeological studies in the empire, leading finally to the Antiquities Regulation (*Asar-ı Atika Nizamnamesi*) in 1874, which placed all archeological excavations in the empire under the control and supervision of the Ministry of Education and provided that foreign researchers could no longer ravage and remove from the empire what they found but instead had to leave the best one-third of their discoveries to the state, as selected by the museum. Since the St. Irene church was by now far too small for the hundreds of antiquities that would come to the museum under the new law, the museum was transferred to the ancient Çinili Köşk, built by Mehmet the Conqueror in the gardens beneath the Topkapı Palace (1874), where it has remained, expanded by several new buildings constructed in its environs, to the present day. A school to train Ottoman archeologists and museum specialists was opened in the museum in 1875.

The Ministry of Education was unable to coordinate and manage all the institutions placed under its control until the Public Education Law of 1869 provided it with a professional General Council on Education, which worked through a Cultural Department, in charge of writing and translating textbooks, providing public lectures, and the like, and an Administrative Section, charged with appointing teachers and supervising public schools all around the empire. Policy was made by a central council composed of the chiefs of the two sections, all the members of the legislative and judicial councils, other leading members of the Ruling Class, and one religious leader from each of the major *millets,* which met twice a year under the chairmanship of the minister of education. Provincial education councils also were organized in every provincial capital under the direction of an educational director (*maarif müdürü*), with a Muslim and non-Muslim assistant, staff, and inspectors to tour the province to examine operations and enforce standards. The councils were given the state funds available for educational purposes. It was up to them to decide how and for what purposes they should be spent, providing money for buildings, salaries, books, libraries, and the like, as they saw fit. They also administered annual examinations for students graduating from each level of school as well as those needing certificates of ability (*rüus*), which entitled them to continue their education or to enter the bureaucracy, thus attempting to impose relatively similar standards in each province and throughout the empire.[97]

The effectiveness of the Tanzimat's new secular school system is difficult to measure. There were numerous problems. Teachers trained in the large cities were unwilling to serve in the countryside. There were not enough textbooks, and many of those available were in foreign languages that the students understood, at best, imperfectly. As in many other educational hierarchies in advanced countries, methods and systems were developed more to benefit and satisfy the administrators and teachers than the students. Non-Muslim subjects often refused to accept the new equality that was being offered, preferring to remain in their *millet* schools while complaining to their foreign protectors about the Tanzimat's failure to do more for them. Yet the system continued to expand. Numbers alone can be misleading, and are often difficult to uncover. Yet it is impressive to learn that between 1867 and 1895, a period of less than 30 years, the number of secular elementary schools and students attending them more than doubled, as Table 2.2 shows. About

Table 2.2. *The progress of Ottoman education, 1867–1895*[98]

	1858	1867	1895
Secular elementary schools	—	11,008	28,615
Secular elementary students			
boys	—	242,017	640,721
girls	—	126,454	253,349
Military *Rüşdiye* students			
boys	—	8,247	8,247
Millet elementary schools			
boys	—	—	239,449
girls	—	—	77,740
Foreign elementary schools	—	—	
boys	—	—	8,519
girls	—	—	8,160
Total no. of elementary students			
boys	—	—	896,936
girls	—	—	339,249
Total population of elementary school age			
boys	—	—	1,001,294
girls	—	—	924,175
Rüşdiye schools	43	108	426
Rüşdiye school students	3,371	7,830	33,469
Military *Idadi* schools[a]	—	—	9
Military *Idadi* students	—	—	5,492
Millet Rüşdiye schools	—	—	687
Millet Rüşdiye students	—	—	76,359
Foreign middle schools	—	—	74
Foreign middle students	—	—	6,557
Total middle schools	—	—	1,169
Total middle students	—	—	109,877
Male population of middle school age (10 to 15)	—	—	980,320

[a] The military *Rüşdiye* schools were equivalent to civilian elementary, and military *Idadis* were like civilian secondary schools.

Table 2.3. *Ottoman students in 1895*[99]

	Muslims	Non-Muslims	Total
State and Muslim elementary school students	854,841	80	854,921
State *Rüşdiye* school students	31,469	4,262	35,731
State *Idadi* school students	4,892	527	5,419
Army school students	15,338	13	15,351
Naval school students	1,734	—	1,734
Non-Muslim *millet* elementary school students	—	317,089	317,089
Non-Muslim *millet Rüşdiye* school students	—	76,359	76,359
Non-Muslim *millet Idadi* school students	—	10,720	10,720
Foreign *Rüşdiye* school students	—	6,557	6,557
Foreign *Idadi* school students	—	8,315	8,315
Foreign elementary school students	—	16,679	16,679
Civil Service Academy (*Mekteb-i Mülkiye-i Şahane*)	415	31	446
School of Law (*Mekteb-i Hukuk-u Şahane*)	334	38	372
Civil Medical School (*Tıbbiye-i Mülkiye-i Şahane*)	127	336	463
Normal School for Men (*Dar ul-Muallimin*)	125	—	125
School of Fine Arts (*Sanayi Nefise*)	57	86	143
School of Commerce (*Ticaret-i Hamidi*)	114	4	118
Galata Saray Lycée (*Mekteb-i Sultani*)	382	317	699
Normal School for Women (*Dar ul-Muallimat*)	350	—	350
School for Orphans (*Dar ul-Şafaka*)	421	—	421
School of Veterinary Medicine (*Mülkiye-i Baytar*)	51	9	60
Agricultural School (*Halkalı Ziraat Mektebi*)	59	14	73
Crafts and Arts School (*Mekteb-i Sanayi*)	220	32	252
Men's normal schools for elementary education	277	—	277
School for deaf mutes	16	—	16
Special and private schools in Istanbul	5,818		5,818
Total	917,040	441,468	1,358,508
Total population of school-going ages (5 to 25)			6,653,236
Total population of the empire (1895)	14,111,945	4,938,362	19,050,307

90 percent of school-age boys and over a third of school-age girls were attending elementary school by 1895, though the latter's formal education seldom went beyond this level. Out of a total population of 19 million (about 14 million Muslims and 5 million non-Muslims), 1.3 million were students at all levels, with a larger proportion of non-Muslims than Muslims attending school (see Table 2.3).

Combining the education and security provided by the Tanzimat with the surviv-. ing Ottoman bureaucratic traditions, the new bureaucrats (*memurs*) manifested an arrogance and reinforced feeling of independence in their positions as well as an assurance that only they knew what was best for the state and its people.

The New Middle Class

Domination of Ottoman government and society by the *memurs* was challenged by the new middle class, which was just becoming a significant political factor in the last half of the nineteenth century. With the bulk of wealth in traditional Ottoman society coming from the land and with its revenues considered the property of the sultan and his Ruling Class, capital and wealth among the subjects could be amassed only through trade and industry. Even when large portions of the imperial wealth were shifted to private hands, most of the possessors still continued to be members of the Ruling Class. But starting with the Celali revolts and the rise of the notables in the eighteenth century and continuing on an accelerated basis in the nineteenth century, new political and economic factors led to the rise of private landed as well as commercial wealth in the hands of what was to become a new middle class. The decline of the state's power led the provincial notables to take over many *mukata'as* and fiefs, thus building vast landed estates as the basis of their power. These revenues still were used primarily for political purposes, however, to build states and armies. But when Mahmut II crushed the notables in his later years and began to confiscate the fiefs, the large landed estates that nominally went back to the state in fact fell into the hands of private entrepreneurs who used the revenues as capital to develop economic and commercial enterprises that compounded their wealth. Whether originating and operating as merchants, moneylenders, government officials, or even as members of local garrisons or as fief holders, the new class of wealthy provincial notables, now called *ehali* (literally, "the people") or *eşraf* (notables), emerged to demand some kind of political influence commensurate with their economic power. This took place just when the Men of the Tanzimat were trying to extend the central government's power into the provinces at the expense of the older notables, the remnants of the Janissaries, the nomadic tribes, and the ulema, who resented the Tanzimat's encroachment into their operation of justice and education within the Muslim community. Using the newly developed "people" against the old elements of authority, the Tanzimat incorporated the former into the administrative councils, thus giving them the political power that they had sought.

The Land Law of 1858 (*Arazi Kanunnamesi*) was the first effort of the Tanzimat to consolidate its victories over the old holders of power. Originally, its intent was to reassert state ownership over the imperial possessions, which, over the centuries, had passed by one means or another out of government control. It covered not only lands now held privately but also lands whose taxes had been excused in return for special local services to the state and areas set aside as public pastures. As part of this process, all the old taxes on the land were replaced by a simple 10 percent tithe cultivation tax on all produce, regardless of where or by whom it was grown. The old Islamic categories of landownership were replaced by five new ones, reflecting the principal types of ownership then common: (1) private property (*mülk*), (2) state property (*miri*), (3) foundation lands (*vakıf*), (4) communal or public land (*metruk*), and (5) idle or barren land (*mevat*). A new Cadastral Regulation (*Tapu Nizamnamesi*) was prepared to enforce the land law, requiring all the land and property of each province to be surveyed as it was transformed according to the Tanzimat, with each person or institution claiming ownership being required to prove it with legal documents before it could be given a new ownership deed (*tapu senedi*) and the fact entered into the new cadastral registers.

Once ownership had been proved, however, the private owners were much freer than in the past to rent lands to others and leave them to heirs as long as they cultivated the land and paid their taxes. No practical limits were placed on the size of their holdings, nor in fact was any real state organization established to make sure that they lived up to their obligations in return for ownership. As time went on, the new rural notables were able to use the law to increase their power, using false documents to prove their claims, extending their rights to include the sale of such properties to others, leaving them to distant relatives, auctioning them off to the highest bidders, and maintaining these rights whether or not the lands in question were cultivated to the extent required by law. These evasions were sanctioned or overlooked by officials all too willing to accept the financial advantages that went with cooperation. Though much of the rural holdings had originated as imperial possessions, a vigorous application of the law would have dispossessed many members of the new middle class. But in practice the intent of the new cadastral regulation was overlooked, and in most instances there remained no practical difference between state and private lands. The holders of both were able to use and dispose of them as they wished, and there emerged larger and larger private estates controlled by wealthy individuals, now generally called *ağas*, and their families, whose economic and political power far exceeded that of even the greatest of the fief holders at the height of their power.

Far from resisting this tendency, the Men of the Tanzimat encouraged it to promote agricultural productivity. While the individual cultivators were supposed to be the prime beneficiaries of the measures taken by the Ministry of Agriculture to improve cultivation methods and tools, the establishment of the provincial agricultural credit banks (*memleket sandıkları*), though intended to help individual cultivators, in fact benefited mainly the large landowners who could utilize the assistance most effectively. Increased cultivation built up the wealth of the rural middle class as well as that of the treasury, adding to the power of the former as the century went on.

Emigration to the Empire: The Refugee Problem

The lands could not have been intensively cultivated and the rural middle class built up had it not been for a tremendous influx of refugees who provided the necessary labor. One must not forget that the Ottoman countryside had been largely depopulated since the seventeenth century as the result of misrule and the ravages of war, famine, and plague. But starting in the 1840s thousands of refugees flooded into the empire in flight from oppression and massacres. By the Refugee Code (*Muhacirin Kanunnamesi*) of 1857, immigrant families and groups with only a minimum amount of capital (stipulated at 60 gold *mecidiye* coins, about 1500 French francs at that time) were given plots of state land with exemptions from taxes and conscription obligations for 6 years if they settled in Rumeli and for 12 years if in Anatolia. They had to agree to cultivate the land and not to sell or leave it for 20 years and to become subjects of the sultan, accepting his laws and justice. Such immigrants were promised freedom of religion, whatever their faith, and they were allowed to build churches where they settled if suitable places of worship were not already available. News of the decree spread widely through Europe and met with a ready response from various groups unable to find land or political peace at home. To process the requests and settle the refugees a Refugee Commission (*Muhacirin Komisyonu*) was established in 1860, at first in the Ministry of Trade and then as an independent agency in July 1861.

These measures were in fact belated responses to an influx that had begun long before. Most of the refugees came from the Turkish, Tatar, and Circassian lands being conquered by the Russians north and west of the Black Sea and the Caspian. Even though there was no official Russian policy of driving these Muslims from their homes, the new Christian governments imposed in the Crimea (1783), in the areas of Baku and Kuban (1796), in Nahcivan and the eastern Caucasus (1828), and finally in Anapa and Poti, northeast of the Black Sea, following the Treaty of Edirne (1829), made thousands of Muslims uncomfortable enough to migrate, without special permission or attraction, into Ottoman territory. Even earlier, hundreds of Russian "Old Believers" had fled from the reforms of Peter and Catherine, settling in the Dobruca and along the Danube near the Black Sea. Between 1848 and 1850 they were joined by thousands of non-Muslim immigrants, farmers as well as political and intellectual leaders fleeing from the repressions that accompanied and followed the revolutions of 1848, especially from Hungary, Bohemia, and Poland. While many of these were absorbed by Ottoman urban life, as we shall see, many also settled on the land as farmers or managers of the farms being built by the large landowners, contributing to both estate building and the improvement of cultivation.

The flow became a torrent after the Crimean War due not only to the Refugee Code but also to new persecutions elsewhere in Europe. The war itself led the Russians to change their relatively tolerant policy toward the Tatars and Circassians into one of active persecution and resettlement from their original homes to desolate areas in Siberia and even farther east. The result was mass migration into Ottoman territory, often with the encouragement of the Russians, who were glad to get rid of the old population to Russianize and Christianize the southern portions of their new empire. We do not have overall figures of the total numbers of refugees entering the empire at this time, but from individual accounts we can assume that the number was immense. Some 176,700 Tatars from the Nogay and Kuban settled in central and southern Anatolia between 1854 and 1860. Approximately a million came in the next decade, of whom a third were settled in Rumeli, the rest in Anatolia and Syria. From the Crimea alone from 1854 to 1876, 1.4 million Tatars migrated into the Ottoman Empire. In addition, the Slavic migration begun before the Crimean War also intensified. Taking advantage of the Refugee Code, Cossacks who fled from the Russian army settled as farmers in Macedonia, Thrace, and western Anatolia. Thousands of Bulgarians – some of whom had earlier been settled in the Crimea by the Russians to replace the Tatars – themselves now reacted to the alien environment and secured permission to return to their homes in the Ottoman Empire. The mass migration of Muslims continued, though at a somewhat less intense pace, during the early years of Abdulhamit II, mostly in consequence of the Russo-Turkish war of 1877–1888, the autonomy given to Bulgaria and Rumania, Austrian control of Bosnia and Herzegovina, and the cession of northern Dobruca to Rumania and northern Macedonia to Serbia. According to the official statistics compiled by the Refugee Commission, over 1 million refugees entered the empire between 1876 and 1895 (as shown in Table 2.4). As a result, the number of male Muslims doubled during the years from 1831 to 1882 (as shown in Table 2.5), with the proportion of Muslims to non-Muslims increasing substantially.

The immigrants settled widely through the empire, many being placed in villages that had been abandoned and some settling in eastern Anatolia, particularly in Cilicia, leading to conflict with the nomads there. Many of the settlers became paid laborers for the large landowners. Others settled on plots given them in accordance with the Immigration Law of 1857. But most of the latter eventually had to turn their holdings over to the large landowners, as poor cultivation methods, bad management, disease, nomadic attacks, hostility on the part of the older cultivators

Table 2.4. *Refugees entering the empire, 1876–1896*[100]

Year	Total people	Total households
1876	276,389	69,000
1877	198,000	49,000
1878	76,000	19,100
1879	20,763	5,324
1880	13,898	3,460
1881	23,098	3,780
1882	33,941	6,396
1883	13,748	2,690
1884	13,522	2,816
1885	13,365	2,807
1886	12,084	2,614
1887	10,107	2,092
1888	11,753	2,506
1889	28,451	6,135
1890	23,220	4,835
1891	13,778	3,024
1892	18,437	3,901
1893	18,778	3,715
1894	14,040	2,888
1895	6,643	1,237
1896	5,846	1,224

Table 2.5. *The male population of the Ottoman Empire, 1831–1906*[101]

Year	Anatolia males			Rumeli males		
	Muslims	Non-Muslims	Totals	Muslims	Non-Muslims	Totals
1831	1,988,027	395,849	2,383,876	513,448	856,318	1,369,766
1843	3,101,980	n.a.	n.a.	873,077	n.a.	n.a.
1882	5,379,225	1,262,600	6,641,825	946,659	810,525	1,757,184
1895	6,084,419	1,221,209	7,305,628	1,237,325	1,186,615	2,423,940
1906	6,846,340	1,481,836	8,328,176	1,179,151	1,186,880	2,366,031

and notables, and the latter's use of their positions on the administrative councils made it almost impossible for the small landowners to survive. The situation was not helped when the Circassians and some of the Nogay Tatars settled in Bulgaria and central Anatolia reverted to their old nomadic pursuits, attacking the new settlers and old cultivators alike. Some of the Muslim settlers, remembering the persecution that had driven them from their homes in Christian lands, began to take vengeance from their non-Muslim neighbors in a manner hitherto unknown in the Ottoman Empire. Though landowners secured cheap labor, the undesirable consequences of mass settlement of refugees in the countryside led to new conflicts among the subject classes, and hostilities between cultivators and nomads were to last well into the present century.

Judicial and Legal Reforms

Many of the Crimean and Balkan settlers were notables and merchants who had converted at least part of their former holdings into gold and other valuables, which they used to establish themselves in trade and industry in their new homes, making themselves a prominent and dynamic element in the emerging Muslim urban middle class. A number of factors contributed to this development. The Gülhane decree, with its emphasis on the protection of life and property, made investment and capital enterprise a much more attractive occupation for Muslims than had been the case in an age when government solved its financial problems by confiscating the properties of the rich, with only the foreign merchants and their protégés safe from its grasp. The establishment of the Ottoman Bank (*Osmanlı Bankası*) in 1856 provided the chief source of venture capital as well as emergency funds needed by the government. The new spirit of enterprise was reinforced by provisions of the 1856 decree:

All trade and criminal cases that arise between Muslims and Christians or other non-Muslim subjects or between Christian subjects and other non-Muslim subjects attached to the different *millet*s shall be transferred to mixed tribunals (*muhtelit divanlar*). The sessions convened by these tribunals to hear the cases shall be public. The plaintiffs and defendants shall confront each other, and the witnesses will give testimony and swear oaths according to their own religions and sects. Cases concerning civil affairs shall be heard according to the laws and regulations in mixed councils (*muhtelit meclisler*), in the presence of the governor and the local kadi, in accordance with the *Şeriat* and regulations; and cases in all these courts and councils shall be carried out publicly. When private cases such as inheritance matters arise between two parties who are Christians or other non-Muslim subjects (of the sultan), they can be transferred to the jurisdiction of the bishops or the *millet* leaders and councils at the request of the parties. . . .[102]

Starting even before the decree, a whole series of secular law codes, based mainly on European counterparts, was enacted, leaving the subjects, Muslim and non-Muslim alike, with a feeling of security and confidence that they would be spared the exactions of the past and allowed to retain whatever profit they could amass from their own enterprise and skill. This was especially the case with the Penal Code (*Ceza Kanunnamesi*) of 1843 (revised in 1851 and 1857), which restricted the authority of the bureaucrats in interpreting the law. The Commercial Code (*Ticaret Kanunnamesi*) of 1850 (revised in 1861) and the Maritime Commerce Code (*Ticaret-i Bahriye Kanunnamesi*) of 1863 established a secure environment in which trade could develop. A separate system of mixed commercial courts was begun in 1840 to enforce these statutes and was reorganized in 1862 after the re-enactment of the Commercial Code. The tribunals thus organized were composed of three judges appointed by the government and four assessors representing the merchants, Ottoman and European alike. In cases involving Ottoman subjects and foreigners, the advocates of the latter selected two of the assessors from important members of their own communities to make certain that their interests and the codes were adequately considered in making judgments. The courts had unlimited jurisdiction in all commercial cases, while in mixed civil cases not involving real estate they had jurisdiction in cases whose value exceeded 1000 kuruş. In applying European-style law codes in courts organized essentially on European lines and with European procedures, the mixed commercial courts thus provided experience in the concepts of secular judicial practice. The mixed courts were so successful that following the Crimean War, in order to live up to the promises of equality for all subjects provided in the Reform Edict of 1856, they were reorganized and expanded, and separate mixed courts were established to hear civil and criminal cases involving Muslims and non-Muslims. The elaboration of secular justice was culminated in 1869 when a secular *Nizamiye* court system was begun under the direction of Ahmet Cevdet Paşa, serving as minister of justice at the time. A hierarchy of secular courts was created, starting with the *nahiye* council of elders at the lowest level and going on through courts in the *kaza, sancak,* and *vilayet capitals.* The new system reduced the authority and jurisdiction of the religious courts, but the ulema were mollified by the *şeyhulislam*'s continued right to appoint and supervise its judges. New codes of procedure for the commercial courts were issued in 1861, followed by similar codes for the criminal (1880) and civil courts (1881), all mainly inspired by French and Italian practice. The new courts were so effective for the mass of the people, Muslim and non-Muslim alike, that not even the ulema, whose traditional monopoly of justice was disappearing, ventured to make too strenuous an objection.

The commercial and industrial activities of foreigners in particular were further stimulated by the enactment (June 10, 1867) of a law allowing them to own real estate in the Ottoman Empire, with the European powers in return conceding that in cases involving such property, foreign subjects would be tried by the same laws and court procedures as the subjects of the sultan, thereby limiting the Capitulations privileges. The Ottoman system of justice was transformed not only by the introduction of the new courts but also by the issuance of the Ottoman Code of Public Laws (*Düstur*) starting in 1865 and the Ottoman Civil Code (the *Mecelle*), which modernized and codified the Hanifite interpretation of the *Şeriat,* accomplished by Ahmet Cevdet's commission between 1866 and 1888.[103]

Modernization of Communications

The development of private capital enterprise in the Ottoman Empire could not have taken place without a substantial improvement of communications. The Men of the Tanzimat were slow in realizing the importance of improved communications to increase the efficiency of government as well as to help the economy. Almost nothing was done, in fact, before the Crimean War, with the sole exception of a new postal system begun with a route between Istanbul and Izmir in 1823 and gradually extended, first to Edirne and then to the other major cities of the empire by 1856, with stations built along the main roads and the roads kept in reasonable condition so that postal schedules could be maintained. Little was done for other roads, however. Steamships were able to offer far more rapid and regular service, at least to the main ports, and their introduction during the nineteenth century can be compared with the twentieth-century development of airplane traffic. Mahmut II purchased a steamship for his own use on the Bosporus and the Sea of Marmara. He also built and purchased several steamships for an Ottoman fleet, which – subsequently organized as the *Fevaid-i Osmaniye* Company by the Egyptian prince Mustafa Fazıl Paşa (1844) – began regular service from Istanbul into the Black

Sea and the Aegean as well as to the Marmara islands. After various changes of name, this native company has survived into republican times as the *Denizcilik Bankası* (Maritime Bank). Competition was offered right from the beginning by steamships of the Austrian Lloyd starting in 1825 as well as by French, Russian, and English companies, which ran their ships not only between Ottoman and European ports but also on domestic runs between Ottoman ports. The *Fevaid-i Osmaniye* also began a subscription service to the Bosporus area for wealthy Ottoman statesmen and businessmen who maintained their homes there. There were British and Russian competing lines to the Bosporus also, but these were eliminated with the foundation of the Ottoman *Şirket-i Hayriye* steamship company by Hüseyin Hâki Paşa, with the assistance of Mustafa Reşit Paşa, which was given a monopoly of this service. The name survived well into the years of the Turkish Republic, even after it also was absorbed into the Maritime Bank.

It was only after the Crimean War that significant progress was made in improving other types of communication. The telegraph, invented by Samuel F. B. Morse in 1837, was introduced into the empire during the Crimean War by the British and French (1854), who laid an underwater cable from Balaclava in the Crimea to Istanbul, an underwater line from Istanbul to Varna, and then another line via Bucharest to Vienna, with a second line built by the Ottoman government and the French to Sofia, Belgrade, and Paris to get the war news to western Europe as quickly as possible. Following the war the equipment and trained telegraphers became the nucleus for the Ottoman telegraph service, which Reşit placed initially in the grand vezir's office at the Porte so that it could be used to keep the central government in direct and immediate contact with its provincial officials. Only some time later was it developed into a public service with the establishment of a Telegraphy Department in the Ministry of Public Works. Lines were built through much of Rumeli and Anatolia during the next decade. Submarine cables connected Istanbul with Anatolia and Alexandria, thus creating an overall network running from London to Tehran. Messages at first were sent in both French and Ottoman, with the latter transcribed into Latin letters until an Ottoman script machine was invented (with 428 characters) for the task. The basic Ottoman telegraph regulation (October 13, 1859) required the department to give precedence to governmental messages (carried free) and then, in descending order of importance, to the messages of foreign representatives, merchants, and private individuals, with ciphers allowed only for official messages. A telegraphy school was established along with a repair and guard service to build, maintain, and guard the lines around the empire. Within a short time, therefore, the Men of the Tanzimat had means to supervise and direct the officials of the empire regardless of the state of surface transportation, enabling them to maintain far more direct control than had been possible in the past. The telegraph also helped the Ottoman economy, particularly by enabling merchants to buy and sell their goods and arrange for other transactions without the long delays that had previously hindered their efforts.[104]

The postal and telegraphy systems were developed mainly with Ottoman capital, and the Ottoman steamship companies were able to compete reasonably successfully with their European counterparts. But railroad building following the Crimean War fell almost entirely to foreign financiers, since it required the kind of capital and technical expertise that the Ottoman government and capitalists were unable to provide. Concessions were issued to foreign investors, therefore, who were granted monopolies to operate the lines that they built for a certain number of years, and the government guaranteed sufficient profits and agreed to make up deficiencies as well as to provide the builders with certain sums for every kilometer built. These obligations became immense burdens on the treasury, as we shall see, but they did help the development of an empire-wide railroad network that would have been impossible otherwise. Construction of the major Anatolian and European lines began late in the Tanzimat and was completed only in the reign of Abdulhamit II. During Abdulmecit's reign only 452 kilometers were built, half in Rumeli, between Varna and Rusçuk in Bulgaria (66 kilometers) and Çernavoda and Köstence in Rumania (93 kilometers), and half in southwestern Anatolia, between the port of Izmir and the towns of Kasaba (159 kilometers) and Aydın (73 kilometers). Once the government began guaranteeing monopolies and profits in return for construction, however, a number of foreign financial organizations entered the field, extending these small beginnings all over the empire. The famous Oriental line, built by a company headed by the Belgian banker Baron de Hirsch, was completed from Istanbul to Edirne and Sofia (562 kilometers), with a branch from Edirne to Dedeağaç (Alexandroupolis) on the way to Salonica (1874). But travelers coming from Europe still could come by train only as far as Varna, thereafter going to Istanbul by sea until the Oriental line was completed via Belgrade to the Austrian border and direct service to Paris opened in 1888.

The main Anatolian Railroad was built from Haydarpaşa, on the Bosporus opposite Istanbul, to Izmit (1873), the first step of the railroad which was to go on to Ankara (1892), Konya (1896), and eventually to the Persian Gulf with the construction of the famous Baghdad Railroad, mainly by German interests. Another new line was built from Mudanya to Bursa (1873) by a French company. The Izmir–Aydın line opened the greater and lesser Menderes river valleys to the Aegean when it was finished in 1866 and then extended to Dinar in 1889. The Izmir–Kasaba line reached Afyonkarahisar in 1900, thus opening much of southeastern Anatolia as well as the Gediz and Bakır valleys. Under Abdulhamit II the Edirne–Dedeağaç line was extended to Salonica and then Monastir (1897), thus restoring direct communication with the Balkan provinces remaining under Ottoman rule.[105]

To connect the areas not yet reached by the railroads with the main market centers in their regions, or at least with the closest railheads, new roads were constructed in the decades following the Crimean War. Progress varied depending on the interest and energy of individual governors, but work proceeded fairly regularly, with macadamized surfaces being used on important roads, particularly in the Danube province in Rumeli and in the Amasya, Samsun, and Kastamonu areas of Anatolia. A Road Reforms Commission was established in 1866, but its work was limited mainly to widening and repairing Istanbul's streets, while a separate Roads Regulation (1867) put all provincial road work under the general direction of the Ministry of Public Works. To overcome the shortages of funds for road building, the corvée, or road labor tax, was used to secure the necessary labor without cost, as we have seen (see pp. 101–102). Roads now were standardized in four categories according to their widths. The imperial roads, connecting the provincial capitals with each other, seaports, railroads, and Istanbul, were given widths of 7 meters; the provincial roads, connecting the provincial and *sancak* capitals, were 5.5 meters wide; the *sancak* roads, connecting the *sancak* and *kaza* capitals and uniting them with the railheads and seaports, were set at 4.5 meters; and lesser roads, generally unpaved and not intended for carriage use, were no less than 3.5 meters wide. Most of the roads were built by public enterprise and capital, but a few particularly important areas were connected by privately constructed toll roads, including those built between Beirut and Damascus, and Bursa and Mudanya by French companies. By 1876 the empire certainly had a much better road system than earlier, and many of the major provincial centers were connected, but the lesser-road network remained incomplete and inadequate.[106]

Trade and Industry

In response to the new and favorable conditions created by the Tanzimat and the general encouragement of private enterprise, trade and industry expanded in the years before 1876, though very little was done about agriculture. Of course, foreign merchants were always ready to buy Ottoman raw materials and sell their own manufactures. Following the trade agreements signed with England and the other major European commercial powers between 1838 and 1840, hundreds of foreign merchants came to the empire, settling down to buy and sell goods and forcing out the relatively inexperienced and undercapitalized native Ottoman merchants. During the next two decades, trade with England and France increased almost fivefold, with imports and exports somewhat balanced, but after the Crimean War the balance shifted so radically that by 1876 the Ottomans had a considerable trade deficit (as shown in Table 2.6) with these as well as other nations of the world.

Quite surprising is the fact that, given the superiority of European manufactures and the continued restrictions imposed by the Capitulations, the Ottomans still were able to develop a nascent industry of their own. The old craft industries had declined in the face of foreign competition and the limitations imposed by the powerful guilds. Modernizing the economy involved the creation of entirely new factories, outside the old manufacturing centers and away from the influence of the guilds. Already in the time of Mahmut II, factories were built at government expense to manufacture the uniforms and headgear required for his new army. Under Abdulmecit technicians and machines were imported from Europe, and by the end of his reign there were a number of factories. Many still produced clothing, cloth, and headgear, but there were also artillery and rifle shops at

Table 2.6. *Imports and exports in 1876*[107]

	Ottoman imports from (in kuruş)	Ottoman exports to (in kuruş)
Great Britain	971,067,060	352,177,010
France	325,292,158	256,560,576
Austria	288,515,715	81,975,996
Italy	53,993,450	14,236,884
Greece	31,901,739	32,163,140
Russia	142,390,942	34,375,036
United States	41,629,335	9,112,633
	1,854,790,399	780,601,275
Total for all countries, including others not specified here	2,000,923,048	839,650,454

Tophane; the Beykoz army factory made shoes, boots, cartridge belts, and the like, and a glass factory was opened at Inceköy. But these were poorly run and inefficient, however, and failed to meet even the needs of the army and state.

Private factories established by both Ottoman and foreign capitalists in various parts of the empire contributed to economic growth as the nineteenth century continued. The old Ottoman silk industry, which had been driven out of business two decades earlier by British competition, was revived. In 1845 a Swiss industrialist named Falkeisen established a steam-powered factory to make silk thread in Bursa, and after some initial difficulties due to the reluctance of workers to enter a factory with machines, it expanded rapidly, with such business and profit that by 1876 there were at least 14 such factories in Bursa alone. In the Lebanon there were nine silk manufacturing plants in 1853, which sold their products mainly to France. In Izmir there were several carpet-weaving factories that employed about 1000 workers, and there was another near Konya. Flour mills and olive-oil extracting plants were built on Midilli island and in Syria. French interests established a candle and glass plant at Paşabahçe on the Bosporus. A canning factory was built at Kartal with Swiss capital. Paper and glass factories arose at Beykoz with British stimulus. There were cotton-gin plants built by British businessmen in Tarsus and Adana; carpet thread factories at Afyon and Izmir; and cotton yarn factories at Adana, Tarsus, and Izmir. There were two cloth factories at Mudanya, three at Bilecik, all established on the European model; silk works at Konya, Diyarbekir, Damascus, and Aleppo; and rug factories at Bursa, Karaman, Damascus, Vidin, Bosna, Salonica, Aydın, Sivas, Silistria, and Niş, though in the face of European competition not all of them survived very long.

Finally, capitalism also rose around the exploitation of Ottoman mineral resources, mainly in Anatolia. The Mines Regulation of 1861 (see pp. 101–102) ended the state monopoly of mines and allowed owners of private land with mines to exploit and develop them on their own, leaving only those found on state and foundation land to be exploited for the benefit of the state. Even here, since the government lacked the necessary capital and know-how, it could lease them to private companies to exploit them for mutual benefit. Private investors were quickly attracted, resulting in the development of a major coal mine at Zonguldak, iron, lead, silver, and copper mines in both Rumeli and Anatolia, lignite mines near Bursa and Kastamonu, manganese mines near Çanakkale, copper mines near Malatya, Aydın, and Çanakkale, and argentiferous lead mines on the island of Imroz, near Janina, and near Konya. But while the state treasury did benefit from the taxes and royalty charges imposed on these operations, most of the product was shipped out of the empire to feed the industries of Europe rather than contributing to the development of heavy industry at home.

Tanzimat economic development thus was partial at best. It did, however, encourage the rise of a small urban middle class, composed of shopkeepers and merchants, artisans and moneylenders, many Muslim as well as non-Muslim, with similar economic concerns and social aspirations.

Secularization and the Millets

The rising economic status of the new middle class challenged the traditional religion-based power structure of the community, the *millets* into which the subjects of the sultan were organized. Demands for lay participation and impatience with the exclusive control of community life by the religious and noble aristocracies led to increased secularization of Ottoman society. In the Muslim *millet* the move away from the dominance of the Religious Institution was the direct product of the Tanzimat reforms, which undermined the ulema's monopoly of justice and education and replaced their foundation revenues with direct state salaries. Secularization of the non-Muslim *millets* was furthered by the Reform Decree issued in 1856. After asserting the continuation of guarantees covered by the Imperial Rescript of Gülhane, the sultan called on his non-Muslim subjects to review their institutions and recommend changes:

Every Christian or other non-Muslim community shall be bound, within a fixed period, and with the concurrence of a commission composed of members of its own body, to proceed, with my approval and under the supervision of my Sublime Porte, to look into its actual immunities and privileges and to discuss and submit to my Sublime Porte the reforms required by the progress of civilization and the age.

The decree also indicated that the Porte intended to modify some of the administrative and financial arrangements of the *millets*, though without in principle revoking the traditional status and powers of the religious leaders:

The powers conceded to the Christian patriarchs and bishops by Sultan Mehmet II and his successors shall be made to harmonize with the new position which my generous and beneficient intentions ensure to those communities. The principle of appointing the patriarchs for life, following revision of the election rules now in force, shall be carried out exactly in conformity with the fermans which invest them. All the patriarchs, metropolitans, archbishops, bishops, and rabbis shall take an oath on their entrance into office in accordance with a form agreed on by my Sublime Porte and the spiritual heads of the different religious communities. The ecclesiastical dues, of whatever sort or nature they may be, shall be abolished and replaced by fixed revenues given to the patriarchs and heads of communities and by the allocation of allowances and salaries equitably proportioned in accordance with the rank and dignity of the different members of the clergy.

While the ecclesiastics were brought under increased administrative control, the subjects' participation in *millet* administration was also encouraged. Freedom of religious worship and security of person and property were emphasized as complimentary aspects of the Porte's benevolent and concerned attitude toward the subjects:

The property, real or personal, of the different Christian ecclesiastics shall remain intact; the temporal administration of the Christian and other non-Muslim communities shall, however, be placed under the safeguard of an assembly to be chosen from among the members, both ecclesiastics and laymen, of these communities. In the towns, districts and villages where the whole population is of the same religion, no obstacle shall be set to prevent the repair, according to their original plan, of buildings set aside for religious worship and for schools, hospitals, and cemeteries. The plans of these buildings, in the case of new construction, shall, after approval by the patriarchs or heads of communities, be submitted to my Sublime Porte, which will approve of them by my Imperial order or make known its observations on them within a certain time. Each sect, in localities where there are no other religious denominations shall be free from every species of restraint as regards the public exercise of its religion. In towns, districts and villages where different sects are mixed together, each community, inhabiting a distinct quarter, shall, by conforming to these regulations have equal right to repair and improve its churches, hospitals, schools, and cemeteries. . . . My Sublime Porte will take energetic measures to ensure to each sect, whatever the number of its adherents, entire freedom in the exercise of its religion.

Every distinction or designation tending to make any class whatsoever of the subjects of my Empire inferior to another because of their religion, language, or race shall be forever effaced from the laws and regulations of the empire. Laws shall be put into force prohibiting the use of any injurious or offensive term, either among private individuals or on the part of the authorities. As all forms of religion are and shall be freely professed in my dominions, no subject of my Empire shall be in any way annoyed on this account and no one shall be forced to change his religion. The nomination and choice of all functionaries and other employees of my Empire being wholly dependent on my sovereign will, all subjects of my Empire, without distinction of nationality, shall be admissible to public employment and qualified to fill them according to their capacity and merit. . . . All the subjects of my Empire, without distinction, shall be received into the civil and military schools of the government if they otherwise satisfy the conditions of age and examination specified in the regulations of these schools. Moreover each community is authorized to establish public schools of science, art, and industry, provided that the method of instruction and choice of professors in schools of this class shall be under the control of a mixed Council of Public Instruction, the members of which shall be named by my sovereign command.[108]

The provisions of the Reform Decree were mostly directed to the non-Muslim *millets* and aimed at ending their desire for autonomy or independence. The actual reform measures that followed varied according to the special situation and needs of each *millet*.

The Armenian Millet. Reform came first to the Armenian Gregorian *millet,* whose patriarch, while mainly independent of his spiritual superiors, the Catholicos of Echmiadzin and of Sis, was part of the small clique of wealthy Armenian notables who dominated the *millet* while serving in high positions of government, especially after the Greeks of the empire fell into distrust as a result of the Greek Revolution. Armenian merchants were among the first to benefit from the new industrial and commercial development in the empire. As early as 1838 the Armenian moneylenders, artisans, and merchants of Istanbul challenged the rule of the oligarchy, gaining a *ferman* (1841) that specified that civil affairs in the *millet* should be controlled by an elected council of laymen. But in the end the notables prevailed due to their strong financial position. Lay pressure continued, however, and in 1847 the patriarch responded by establishing a separate secular council, including both notables and artisans, while the old religious council was limited to religious affairs.

Although the new arrangement had some effect, continued lay dissatisfaction with the Gregorian establishment led many young Armenians to accept the teachings of Jesuit missionaries in the empire. About 1727 a young Gregorian Armenian priest named Mekhitar converted to Catholicism, established his own order and monastery on St. Lazare island, near Venice, and began to send out missionaries to convert his fellows within the Ottoman Empire, establishing a community of Armenian Catholics who were so persecuted by the Gregorian establishment that they finally secured French intervention to gain the sultan's recognition of their own *millet* in 1830. At the same time, during the early years of the nineteenth century Protestant missionaries from Great Britain and the United States also converted many Armenians, resulting in the establishment of a Protestant *millet*, mainly through British intervention, in 1850. The two new *millets*, aside from undermining the patriarch's authority, stimulated linguistic and historical studies, contributing to the new feeling of Armenian nationalism that was to disturb the Ottoman state later in the century. Leading the revival were missionaries who encouraged Armenian ethnic identity. An American Protestant missionary named Elias Riggs wrote a grammar book to teach Armenian to those *millet* members who spoke only Turkish. Mekhitar's monastery in Venice became a study center, and an east Anatolian Armenian named Garabed Ütücian, after 1840, published the newspaper *Massis* to spread modern ideas among Armenians in the empire. Many wealthy Armenians also sent their children to Europe to secure the kind of secular education that was not yet available in the Ottoman Empire. Soon the pressure of the new *millets*, combined with the effects of the cultural revival among the youths of the Gregorian *millet*, led to demands for further secularization of the latter and to continued rejection of the oligarchy's domination, causing strife within the *millet* during and after the Crimean War. This situation so threatened the social order of the empire that Âli Paşa finally intervened and forced the patriarch to call a joint lay-religious conference. It prepared a new *millet* constitution, promulgated by the sultan on March 29, 1863, which provided lay participation and representative government to the Armenians. The *millet* organization throughout the empire was developed under the leadership of the central organization in Istanbul. Within the central structure the council of religious leaders was retained only for matters of clerical organization and conduct and religious doctrine. The powers of the lay council were extended to *millet* taxation, health, education, and welfare. These councils were subordinated to a new general council of 140 elected members, of whom only 20 were clerics, leaving the lay element dominant. The majority of the Armenians then in the empire were concentrated in eastern Anatolia, but most of the representatives came from the more educated and advanced community of Istanbul, an arrangement that was to cause difficulty later. The electoral provisions for the new *millet* assembly were limited, with the vote being given only to men who paid a certain amount of *millet* taxes. The provincial *millet* councils elected their members locally and dealt with the same affairs within the provinces that the General Council handled in Istanbul, electing one of their religious leaders as metropolitan to represent the patriarch locally.[109]

The Greek Millet. There was less pressure for reform in the Greek Orthodox *millet*, probably because its priests had more power, it was associated much earlier with Greek nationalism, and the tyranny of the Greek priests over their non-Greek, mainly Slavic, followers led the latter to their own national movements rather than efforts to reform the *millet*. Here also an oligarchy dominated, with the patriarch of Istanbul helped by a synod of priests in both his secular and religious duties and influenced greatly also by the wealthy Phanariotes of Istanbul and the Principalities. Subordinate to him were the bishops in the provinces and the priests in villages. At the village level, community affairs were controlled by councils of elders and the *kocabaşıs*, elected by vote of all males, who collected taxes to support the local schools and churches and exercised all the other *millet* functions carried out by the patriarch in Istanbul.

While there was very little internal pressure for reform, Âli felt that something had to be done to protect the mass of Orthodox subjects from the tyranny of their leaders if the empire was in fact to live up to the Reform Decree. When the patriarch and the synod refused his requests for a constitution to provide lay rule, Âli sent the archbishops back to their dioceses and forced the patriarch to convene a constitutional committee that produced a series of regulations starting in 1860 that effectively constituted the equivalent of the Armenian Constitution. The results were not the same, however, since with very little lay pressure the patriarch and bishops were able to retain far greater power than did the clerics in the Gregorian *millet*. There was also a General Assembly with a lay majority, but it was not permanent, being called together only to choose new patriarchs, and then only from lists of candidates submitted by the bishops, while the Porte remained free to veto its candidates for reasons of its own. Once the patriarch was elected, he carried on affairs as before with the advice of the synod. But its authority now was limited only to church and religious matters, while secular affairs were handled by a mixed council of 12, with 4 bishops of the synod and 8 lay members elected by and from the Greek population of Istanbul. Members in the provinces though were not represented. There also were provincial assemblies with lay majorities, but they also lacked authority over their bishops, leaving the latter with continued power at that level. Hence in fact little was achieved to end the misrule and corruption that had prevailed in the *millet* for so long.[110]

The Jewish Millet. The Jewish *millet* was seriously divided during the Crimean War period. Its merchants and bankers, in opposition to the orthodox rabbis, demanded a more secular and progressive system of education and considerably more lay control of the *millet*. The same kind of strife that had prevailed among the Armenians finally forced Fuat Paşa to intervene and order the grand rabbi to convene a council that finally produced a constitution promulgated in 1865. Here the results were more like those of the Armenians rather than the Greeks, with the lay leaders emerging to dominate the *millet* organization. The grand rabbi remained the secular head of the *millet* throughout the empire and the spiritual head of the Jews of Istanbul, but he now had to accept the advice of secular and religious councils selected by an assembly of 80 with a lay majority elected by *millet* members residing in Istanbul and vicinity. The assembly also elected the grand rabbi from a list of candidates drawn up by its rabbi members, who were joined for this purpose by rabbi delegates from the provinces. Since the Jews lacked the strong clerical hierarchy of the Gregorian and Orthodox churches, however, there were no regulations for the clergy or for provincial organization, and the new structure was used mainly in Istanbul. But as head of the Jewish *millet*, the grand rabbi continued to be recognized by the Porte as secular leader of the empire's Jews, and while by Jewish law that did not extend to religion, he remained the main channel of communication with the Porte for all the rabbis and Jewish communities elsewhere in the empire.[111]

The reform provisions regarding equality for non-Muslims were carried out by developing the new doctrine of Ottomanism, which provided that all subjects were equal before the law. A series of laws followed to put this concept into effect. Non-Muslims were subjected to conscription and military service, and the head tax, long imposed in its place, was ended. Non-Muslims were admitted to the secular schools and allowed to serve in the bureaucracy after graduation. But such reforms encountered opposition from all sides. The leaders of the non-Muslim *millets* opposed the provisions regarding lay rule and cooperated as little as possible. While non-Muslims in general were willing to accept the benefits of equality, they opposed its price. They preferred, for example, to pay the head tax and remain free to develop their own careers rather than serving the empire by accepting conscription, and in consequence this particular effort was abandoned. Since these reforms also had come because of foreign pressure, the *millets* fell into the habit of securing foreign intervention whenever difficulties arose, thus bringing the powers into Ottoman domestic affairs and leading many Muslims to associate the minorities with foreign attack and even treason. Assuming that whatever delays and failures there were in the reforms affected only them, rather than the Muslims as well, the minorities got the powers to force the Ottoman government to emphasize reforms affecting mainly the Christian areas, leaving the Muslims feeling, with considerable justice, that the Tanzimat was, indeed, intended to place the minorities into a position of dominance in the empire and that it was singling out the non-Muslims for special treatment. The new regulations, therefore, did not make anyone particularly happy or end the clashes between religious and secular interests in the *millets*. But as time went on and generation followed generation, the overall effect of the Tanzimat's secularization programs began to be felt, and the religious communities lost their hold over the individual, both Muslim and non-Muslim.

The New Intelligentsia

The emergence of an Ottoman middle class in turn produced an intellectual awakening and was paralleled by the development of a new Ottoman intelligentsia, which displaced the ulema in their traditional role of cultural leadership in the Muslim community. Ottoman intellectual reorientation manifested itself in many different ways. Its most general characteristic was the displacement of both forms and themes of traditional Ottoman literature, produced largely by and for the Ruling Class, and the substitution of different ones imported from the West – plays, novels, operas, short stories, essays, and political tracts, treating not merely themes of love and passion and the lives and interests of the rulers but also presenting the great political, economic, social, and religious problems and ideas that were of concern to everyone in the empire.

Popularization of modern forms and ideas was made possible by the development of the Ottoman printing press beginning in 1835. In response to the increased literacy created by the secular schools, innumerable public and private Ottoman presses and publishing houses were established in Istanbul and the other major cities, producing almost 3000 books during the next half-century. This is not to say that all the books represented the new forms and themes. Of subjects treated at this time, religion still was most important (390 books, or 13.45 percent), followed by poetry (356 books, or 12.27 percent), language (255 books, or 8.79 percent), and history (184 books, or 6.34 percent). There were only 175 novels and short stories, both in original form and in translation (6.03 percent), 135 government publications (4.65 percent), 92 plays (3.17 percent), 77 books on science (2.65 percent), 76 on mathematics (2.62 percent), and 23 on economics and finance (0.79 percent). Nevertheless, the vehicle was there for those wishing to use it.[112]

More important, perhaps, than the books themselves were the newspapers and other periodicals produced in increasing numbers by the new presses. The monopoly of the official newspaper, *Takvim-i Vekayi*, was broken in 1840 by the first private Ottoman paper (published until 1860), the *Ceride-i Havadis* (Chronicle of

Events), founded by an English journalist and correspondent, William Churchill. Other important Tanzimat papers were the *Tasvir-i Efkâr* (Description of Ideas) (1861–1870), the *Ceride-i Askeriye* (The Army Newspaper), founded by the Seraskerate in 1863, *Muhbir* (The Informant) (1866–1868), *Hürriyet* (Liberty), published in London between 1868 and 1870, *Basiret* (Understanding) (1870–1877), and many others of shorter duration.

The theater also served as a vehicle of new ideas. Theatrical performances were staged at various embassies as early as the period of the French Revolution, but these were of interest mainly to foreign and non-Muslim residents of the capital even after they were attended occasionally by Mahmut II and by Abdulmecit and their retinues. Soon, however, Ottoman theaters were built. By 1839 there were three theaters, which produced Italian plays mainly for foreigners. The first real Ottoman theater, known as the French Theater (*Fransız Tiyatrosu*), was built in the heart of Beyoğlu by an Italian named Giustiniani, with the financial support of the Ottoman government as well as several foreign embassies (1840). Management later fell to an Italian magician named Bosco, who in addition to his own performances put on French plays and foreign operas for mixed audiences of Ottomans and foreigners. In 1844 the theater was taken over by a Syrian actor, Mihail Naum, who founded a repertory theater that continued actively until 1870, presenting operas, musicals, and plays such as the masterpieces of Molière to audiences that at times included the sultan. As the Tanzimat continued, countless other theaters were built and operated for shorter periods of time, but with productions mainly in foreign languages, they remained mainly for non-Muslims, with just a few Turkish guests and no wide penetration or interest among the masses.

The first Ottoman-language theater, called the Ottoman Theater (*Tiyatro-i Osmani*), was founded in 1867 at Gedik Paşa, in old Istanbul, by an Armenian repertory company directed by Agop Vartovyan, known as Güllü Agop (1840–1902), who in 1870 received from Âli Paşa a monopoly of the right to produce Turkish-language dramas in the capital for 15 years in return for opening similar theaters in other parts of the city. A year later, in Âli's presence, the Gedik Paşa theater inaugurated years of repertory performances of both Armenian and Turkish plays, including Namık Kemal's controversial patriotic play, *Vatan Yahut Silistre*. It remained active until the building burned to the ground in 1885. One of Agop's early collaborators, Mardiros Minakyan (1837–1920) then continued his work in his own theater, also called the Ottoman Theater, becoming the leading force in Ottoman drama until the end of Abdulhamit's reign. He often staged the translated works of foreign writers to avoid the censorship regulations of the time. Abdulaziz also encouraged the development of a popular Turkish folk theater (*Tuluat Tiyatrosu*), first in the palace and then in small theaters in the Muslim quarters of Istanbul. Here the actors used characters and stories from everyday life, improvising to match the interests and moods of their audiences, using the so-called *Orta Oyunu* technique, which became very popular as the century went on.

Simplification of the written Ottoman language to make it comprehensible to the mass of the people also encouraged literacy and the spread of new ideas. Already in 1845 the advisory commission created to develop a system of secular education recommended elimination of many Arabic and Persian words and expressions and their replacement with Turkish counterparts. In 1855 the Porte decreed that official documents should be written in simpler Ottoman Turkish, and this was already evidenced in the style of the Reform Decree of 1856. There were several attempts also to develop a system of orthography and spelling to make the Arabic script, ill fitted to the needs of Turkish, more understandable to the new reader by devices such as diacritical marks, the use of specified vowel letters to indicate pronunciation, and the development of standard spellings.[113]

What of the writers themselves? The intellectuals of the late Tanzimat period were of as many persuasions as the new freedom of thought made possible, but in general they came to be known as the Young Ottomans (*Yeni Osmanlılar*). Originally, the group consisted of several young men familiar with Western representative institutions and impatient with the pace of the Tanzimat. They were most active between 1865 and the adoption of the Ottoman Constitution a decade later. Those associated with the movement were products of the Tanzimat, educated in the new secular schools or sent abroad to finish their education but, unlike the *memurs* who found their places in life in the bureaucracy, unable to find good positions in the Tanzimat system. They became the self-appointed critics of the system and through their use of the press began to create public opinion while introducing concepts such as parliamentarianism, nationalism, and patriotism into the Ottoman political consciousness.[114]

The originator of the new movement in Ottoman literature was Ibrahim Şinasi (1824–1871). Born in Istanbul, he was the son of an artillery sergeant killed in the Ottoman-Russian war (1829) when Ibrahim was only five; and he was raised by his widowed mother during the last decade of Mahmut II's reign. After receiving a traditional *mektep* education, he entered one of the scribal departments at the Army Arsenal (*Tophane*), since there still was no *Rüşdiye* school to take him beyond the elementary stages. He was introduced to the classics of Islamic literature by one of his elder colleagues, but at the same time he learned about the West from several foreign officers working in the Arsenal and began to study French. Thus was laid the foundation for the passion for both East and West that was to characterize many of his later writings. He slowly rose within the Arsenal scribal hierarchy and in 1849 convinced its director and Mustafa Reşit Paşa to send him to Europe to perfect his French. After spending some time in Paris, he became an apprentice in the French Ministry of Finance, acquiring financial expertise, something that Reşit sorely needed at the time. Şinasi now attended the literary soirees of writers such as Lamartine and Ernest Renan and entered into contact with leading French Orientalists of the time. On his return to Istanbul, he resumed his work in the Arsenal and also became a member of the new Council on Education (1855). If this had taken place a decade earlier, Şinasi, as a protégé of Reşit might well have become a leading Tanzimat bureaucrat. But Reşit now was in his last years, and Âli Paşa, himself threatened by the possible ambitions and aspirations of this promising young man, arranged for his dismissal whenever he was in power. Şinasi eventually did gain the protection of another leading man of the Tanzimat, Yusuf Kâmil Paşa, but in consequence of Âli's opposition, he never held a significant position in the bureaucracy.

Frustrated, Şinasi turned to literary activities, beginning with a *Tercüme-i Manzume* (Translation of Poems), which presented excerpts from the classic French poets, including Racine and La Fontaine. He then published his own collection (*Divan*) of poems and presented his first play, the *Şair Evlenmesi* (Marriage of the Poet) in the sultan's theater (1860). In collaboration with a friend, Agâh Efendi, a young newspaperman trained on the *Ceride-i Havadis*, Şinasi founded the newspaper *Tercüman-ı Ahval* (Translator of Events) (1860–1865), subsequently using help from Prince Murat (later Murat V) and the Egyptian Prince Mustafa

Fazıl to establish his own paper, *Tasvir-i Efkâr* (Description of Ideas) (1861–1870), which soon became the leading forum for the expression of new literary forms and political ideas. His *Müntehebat-ı Esar* (Selections of Works), included praise of Mustafa Reşit Paşa but very little about the sultan and enough "subversive" ideas to cause Fuat to dismiss him from the Council on Education (July 2, 1863), specifically because of his demand for no taxation without representation, that is, for a representative Parliament.

Şinasi did not give up his hopes of resuming his government career, however. He modified the political approach of the paper, regaining the friendship of Fuat, who during his short term as *serasker* got his help in starting publication in 1864 of the *Ceride-i Askeriye* (The Army Newspaper) the second official Ottoman newspaper. Şinasi also asked Âli for a position on the newly established Supreme Council of State, but when he was rejected again, he came out in opposition to the Tanzimat leaders and, leaving the *Tasvir-i Efkâr* to a young colleague, Namık Kemal (June 1864), fled to France, spending the next four years in literary pursuits. He returned to Istanbul only shortly before his death of a brain tumor in September 1871.

All of the intellectuals associated with Şinasi in the Young Ottoman society were driven to opposition by Âli and Fuat. Another outstanding member of the group was the already mentioned Namık Kemal (1840–1888), who had entered the Translation Office (*Tercüme Odası*) in 1857 through Reşit's influence but had been thrown out by Âli, leading him to join Şinasi's circle in 1862 and very soon to become a prolific writer of essays on administrative and social reforms, and even on foreign policy, especially after Şinasi went to Paris. Ziya Paşa (1825–1880) was educated in one of Mahmut II's new *Rüşdiye* schools and also rose in the Translation Office with the help of Reşit. But after the latter's death he also was persecuted by Âli, who followed Ziya's every action with a personal interest in the hope of uncovering some misdeed that could be used to evict him from government altogether. Ziya in turn became the opponent of a governmental system that allowed this kind of autocratic behavior, and he used his literary talents to satirize Âli's policies. Also in sympathy with the Young Ottoman impatience with the Tanzimat administrators was Ali Suavi (1839–1878), who rose as a teacher in the new secular school system but was driven from government service due to conflicts with the governor of Filibe. And there were others, with very similar educational backgrounds and thwarted careers in the bureaucracy.

Once the Young Ottoman Society was organized in 1865, its members propounded their ideas in the *Tasvir-i Efkâr* and other newspapers and periodicals of the time, in pamphlets, and in plays performed in the new theaters. When the Tanzimat government began to suppress them in the fear that such opposition would undermine the reform movement, they fled to Europe, continuing to write and sending their works in through the foreign post offices, which by the terms of the Capitulations were beyond the control of the Ottoman government. Some returned in the hope of securing government positions, and those who were successful abandoned their intellectual and political opposition to the system. While in Paris and London the voluntary exiles supported one another financially, but the most significant assistance came from Prince Mustafa Fazıl, who was attempting to pressure the sultan to appoint him as crown prince and heir to the current khedive of Egypt.

On the whole, most of these liberal intellectuals were more conservative on religon than were the Men of the Tanzimat, feeling that the radical Western reforms introduced since 1839 had undermined the moral and ideological base of

Ottoman society without providing a suitable substitute. Proposing a new emphasis on Islam to fill the gap, they became the first Muslim thinkers to try to reconcile Western political institutions with traditional Islamic and Ottoman theory and practice, seeking to promote the principle of representation by establishing historical precedent. Their emphasis was on the progressive rather than the conservative aspects of Islam. There were complaints about the bureaucratic tyranny that had resulted from the powerful centralized government created by the Tanzimat, and criticism that the new bureaucracy, the new rural aristocracy, and the non-Muslim merchants and industrialists were dominating the ruler and his subjects to an unprecedented degree.

While the Young Ottomans were united in opposition to the Tanzimat, their proposed solutions varied widely. But there were at least three basic ideas on which they agreed: constitution, Parliament, and Ottomanism. First they wanted to limit the power of the bureaucracy through a constitution that all would have to obey regardless of rank or status in Ottoman society. They maintained that no matter how benevolent the reformers, their rule was still autocratic and arbitrary and led to a more extensive tyranny than was possible under the traditional Ottoman system. There was nothing to restrain the sultan and the Ruling Class from undermining the Tanzimat reform program when they wished to do so. A constitution was needed to protect the individual from arbitrary government action and to ensure the permanence and continued success of the reforms. Their second demand was for a representative, popularly elected Parliament as the instrument of constitutional control, to make sure that all the administrators functioned properly within the limits of the law. Many went on to argue also that the basic distinction between the Ruling and the Subject Classes harmed the empire by depriving it of the services of most of those who lived within its boundaries. A Parliament, then, was also the best means of securing the services of all the best people in the empire for the good of the state.

But the Ottoman Empire differed at least in one respect from the European nations whose parliamentary systems the Young Ottomans studied and admired. It was a highly heterogeneous state composed of many peoples who differed widely in language, race, and religion. The old *millet* system had kept the peace by separating them, but now many of the *millet*s were being affected by nationalism. The Men of the Tanzimat sought to counter the problem by reforming the old *millet* structure internally and providing sufficient legal equality to prevent nationalism from upsetting social stability and breaking up the empire. They feared that representative government would only focus on and deepen the old divisions. The Young Ottomans, on the other hand, felt that such a Parliament would provide a harmless outlet for national feelings by giving the different groups a voice in shaping government policy. They believed that participating in a parliamentary system of government would nourish in non-Muslim as well as Muslim subjects a feeling of belonging to the same fatherland (*vatan*), weakening parochial interests and ending their desire to form separate national states. Some Ottoman liberals went further than this, saying that true Ottomanism could be achieved only by abolishing the *millet*s altogether as legal entities, ending all the distinctions among them and their members, and providing in their place a single Ottoman nationality where all the sultan's subjects would have the same rights and obligations regardless of differences in race, religion, and language.

The second generation of the Men of the Tanzimat, liberals such as Âli and Fuat, who had succeeded Reşit after the Crimean War and introduced reforms during the next two decades, thus found themselves condemned as reactionaries by a new generation of liberals who were their ideological children as much as were the *memurs* who carried on their work in the government. Âli and Fuat themselves were far from being opponents of democratic and social reforms. Âli had been in contact with Napoleon III, who was liberalizing his own regime at the time and who influenced Âli to do the same thing by measures such as the provincial representative councils and the High Council of State. But both Âli and Fuat basically felt that their aims could best be achieved through the centralized and tightly controlled government they had created; that representative government would only delay modernization by making government less efficient; and that true democratic reforms could come only after the state was modernized and could afford such a luxury. The Constitution and Parliament introduced in 1876 and again in 1908 were the direct results of the agitation of the Young Ottomans, but one must remember that they could not have been achieved without the preparatory reforms carried out through the years by the dedicated Men of the Tanzimat whom the Young Ottomans criticized so vigorously. Reşit, Âli, and Fuat had to achieve modernization against the opposition of conservatives, and the measures they adopted were partly a response to this. The very fact that a vigorous intellectual generation such as the Young Ottomans could emerge is really a testimony to the success of their basic reforms.

Foreign and Domestic Difficulties

While striving to institute reforms, the Men of the Tanzimat were faced by a succession of external crises and internal revolts that consumed much of their energy and resources. Most of the revolts that convulsed the empire during the later years of the nineteenth century were products of long-nurtured national aspirations, but the conflicts might have been resolved within the empire had it not been for the intervention of the great powers of Europe, which often stimulated and used nationalism to extend their own influence. Based on the assumption that the Ottoman Empire could no longer hold itself together, friend and foe alike engaged in subtle calculations of power politics and considerations of how the spoils would be shared when the time came. The so-called Eastern Question thus was the outsiders' assessment of the troubles facing the Ottoman Empire and how they might benefit from the results. It has been the subject of numerous excellent studies and was, in any case, more part of European than Ottoman history; thus only its more important facets can be summarized here.

The Lebanese Crisis, 1840–1846

The first major crisis to engulf the Tanzimat came from the Lebanon, which had long maintained autonomy under native princes. Its population was composed of many different groups, including the Catholic Maronites, the heretical Muslim Druzes, who lived mainly on Mount Lebanon itself, and the Sunni Muslims, who dominated in Beirut and the lowlands. The ruling Şihabi family, led for many years by Emir Başir II, maintained a tenuous balance among them. This balance had been upset during the Egyptian occupation, when Ibrahim Paşa had used the Maronites against the Muslims, most of whom continued to support the sultan. The superior education provided in the Christian schools established a trend toward Maronite domination of Lebanon's life, and this continued after the Egyptians left, leading to resentment by the Muslims and increased conflicts. The difficulties were exacerbated by the efforts of the wealthy Druze landowners to use Başir II's deposition (1840) to regain their former power, and of the Maronites to expand southward into the predominantly Druze districts. When Başir's weak successors converted to Christianity, Muslim fears of a Christian takeover were intensified, with the antagonisms compounded by British support for the Druzes to counter what it feared would be French domination if the Maronites won. When Başir II's successor, Başir III, began to repress the Druzes, they besieged his capital at Dayr ul-Kamar (October 1841), leading the sultan to depose him and attempt to establish direct Ottoman rule in the area. The Druzes used this occasion to attack the Maronites, while the Christians of the mountain divided further, with the Orthodox supporting the Druzes against their old enemies, the Sunni Muslims, and villages on all sides being ravaged. The powers forced the sultan to introduce a new system of autonomy in an effort to end the fighting. Lebanon was divided into Maronite and Druze *sancaks* along a line drawn from Beirut to Damascus (1843), all under the Ottoman governor of Lebanon, who now was stationed in Beirut instead of Acre.

The system broke down quickly, however, over the question of who should dominate the mixed villages of the south, where Christians reacted to the rule of Druze administrators by attacking the Druze peasants, and the latter replied in kind. The definitive solution finally was imposed in 1845 by the new Ottoman foreign minister, Şekip Paşa, who arranged for a system by which the division between the Druze and Maronite *sancaks* was supplemented by local representatives of each faith collecting taxes and carrying on other administrative responsibilities in the villages inhabited by their coreligionists. In addition, each district was given a mixed council composed of salaried full-time representatives of all the different religious groups, which had the power to hear appeals from court decisions, apportion taxes and regulate their collection, and advise the district administrators, thus replacing the ruling families as leaders of their communities. France at first objected to the arrangement in the fear that it would lessen the power of its Maronite protégés, but Mustafa Reşit Paşa finally came to Lebanon and secured general agreement to the proposals (October 18, 1846), which forced the French and the Maronites to accept them without further protest.

Origins of the Crimean War: The Revolutions of 1848

The Crimean War was basically a conflict between Russia on one side and Britain and France on the other to see who would dominate the Middle East politically and economically as the Ottoman Empire declined. It was stimulated by Britain's gradual shift away from its eighteenth-century support for Russian ambitions in the area due to its realization that any Russian takeover would upset the European balance of power and also damage Britain's economic interests in the Middle East. The low Ottoman customs duties maintained by the Capitulations made the sultan's dominions an ideal market for British manufactured goods as well as a major source of cheap raw materials and food. Britain, therefore, did all it could to help the empire defend itself by promoting reforms, mainly by supporting Mustafa Reşit Paşa, while actively defending it from those who would destroy it. Czar Nicholas I of Russia, on the other hand, was convinced that the Ottoman Empire was the "Sick Man of Europe," that it was bound to collapse, and wished only to make sure that Russia would be in a good position to take more than its share of the spoils. But his determination to retain the friendship of Britain as well as Austria and Prussia against the threat of revolution in Europe, still symbolized by France, made him reluctant to follow his ambitions to their logical conclusion.

The revolutions of 1848, however, upset the concord between Britain and Russia. The events that affected the Eastern Question in particular started in Budapest, where the Chamber of Deputies declared Hungary virtually independent of the Habsburg Empire, joined with Austria only by the personal rule of the emperor (March 1848). This stimulated an uprising that forced him to flee from Vienna as well. The new emperor, Franz Joseph I (1848–1916) then regained Austria and Budapest (January 1849), but the Hungarian diet fled and declared its own republic, with Louis Kossuth as president, which lasted until Nicholas sent in troops who suppressed the rebels (August 9, 1849) and forced their leaders to flee, mostly into Ottoman territory.

Events in Wallachia also had their influence on the Porte at this time. The Russians occupied the Rumanian Principalities for five years after the Treaty of Edirne (1829–1834), ostensibly because of the sultan's inability to pay the war indemnities all at once. During the war, Russian occupation had been quite harsh, with many nobles and peasants deported, crops and livestock confiscated, and peasants subjected to forced labor. But when peace came, Russian administration became very enlightened under the government of Count Paul Kisselev. This was the first time the Principalities were ruled by a single government, so that nationalistic aspirations were encouraged. Kisselev established order and security, built up a medical service, developed a native police force under Russian-trained officers, and replaced the old feudal taxes and obligations with a single tax system based on the cultivators' ability to pay. He encouraged industry and commerce and removed the old restrictions on native traders. Most important were the Organic Regulations, promulgated for each Principality in 1829 on the basis of recommendations by committees organized in accordance with the Treaty of Edirne. Ottoman sovereignty was nominally restored, but with real control left to the boyars, who were under Russian protection and influence. Each Principality was given a prince, elected for life rather than for short periods by a special assembly with a majority of boyars but also with representation for the merchants and bourgeoisie. The princes had very limited power, since they could not dissolve the assemblies and could suspend them only in proven cases of sedition or grave disorders, and the final decisions on the promulgation of laws were left to the Russians and the Porte. Government in both provinces was to be highly centralized, and the princes still had to come from among the boyars. The Organic Regulations set down the boyars' rights in relation to the cultivators, mostly for the benefit of the former. The boyar was the owner of the land. The cultivator could keep only part of the crop and had to contribute even more free labor than before to the boyar. The peasant was not legally tied to the land but had to give advance notice and pay all back taxes before he could leave, attaching him to the land in fact and leaving him much worse off than before, laying the background for peasant participation in the 1848 revolutions.

After Russia was sure that it had control of the sultan through the Treaty of Hünkâr Iskelesi, it evacuated the Principalities early in 1834 in return for agreement on the Porte's payment of the remaining war indemnity, Ottoman acceptance of the Organic Regulations, and recognition of Russia as spokesman in Istanbul for the princes. Russia did agree to allow the sultan to appoint the first princes under the new regime, but the candidates of the boyars were to be accepted thereafter. The first princes were Alexander Ghica in Wallachia and Michael Sturza in

Moldavia. The latter was relatively successful though under strong Russian and boyar influence, opening the province to new ideas and carrying on Kisselev's reforms, including a flood-control system to end the Danube's periodic overflow of its banks. He eliminated brigands and built schools to educate peasant children as well as those of boyars. In Wallachia, however, things did not go as well. Ghica was ineffective and entirely under the control of the boyars and Russians, so that opposition to the new regime arose primarily here, mainly among children of merchants and boyars who had been sent to Paris for their education. One of these, George Bibescu, eventually replaced Ghica and improved conditions, also making an effort to end the customs barriers between the Principalities (1847), paving the way for a fiscal unity that was to lead to political unity in subsequent years.

Both Principalities developed economically. Their grain became a major element in Ottoman trade with Europe, and the steamship transit on the Danube put them into close touch with Europe. Intellectual awakening led to a national movement that demanded not only some sort of union and independence but also an end to the oligarchic oppression of the peasants by the boyars and the establishment of civil rights and a constitution. It is not surprising, therefore, that the revolutionary fever of 1848 affected the Principalities. The resulting uprising in Moldavia was poorly organized and had little support due to Sturza's able rule, but in Wallachia it was more successful, driving out the Russian advisers and forcing Bibescu to accept a revolutionary constitution that provided an assembly representing all classes and a prince who could come from any group. Feudal privileges and social distinctions were ended, and the unity and independence of Rumania were proclaimed (June 21, 1848).

As the Ottomans were no happier about this than was Czar Nicholas, the sultan accepted the latter's offer to suppress the Wallachian revolt, which his troops did as they marched against the Hungarian revolutionaries. Suppression of the revolt was easy, since the boyars still were powerful and many of the rebel leaders were themselves members of boyar families, costing them peasant support despite their programs. Britain accepted Russian intervention at first, but the very success of the repression undermined their cooperation, with Britain now seeing that its basic interests in the Middle East were in fact much closer to those of France than Russia. Hundreds of revolutionaries now fled into Ottoman territory, not only from Hungary and Wallachia but also from Poland, leading to a major international crisis. The Russians demanded extradition of the rebel leaders. When Mustafa Reşit Paşa firmly resisted their demands, relations were broken (September 17, 1849) and war threatened, leading both Britain and France to send their fleets to the Dardanelles to be in position to support the sultan if he was attacked. But when Fuat went to Petersburg to negotiate, the czar backed down, forgoing extradition in return for promises that the refugees would be kept distant from his borders. The crisis was over, therefore, but it displayed all the elements that were to lead to war over the Eastern Question when enmeshed with the religious passions engendered by problems in the Holy Land.

The Holy Places Dispute

The dispute over the Holy Places in Palestine, while providing the spark that set off the Crimean War, was laid in tinder that had been spread some time before. The powers sought to reinforce their influence over the sultan's non-Muslim subjects by providing particular protection for the priests of their protégés in the

Holy Land, with France supporting the Catholics and Russia the Orthodox. In Palestine the different religions and sects focused their rivalries on ambitions to control every act connected with the Holy Places of Christianity, with the right to repair a particular place or hold the key to a particular door symbolizing control of access and of rituals that formed the basis of the relative power and position of each group. Over the centuries a balance of power had been established among the sects, with the different rights established by custom and sanctioned by the Porte, whose main interest was to keep the bickering priests from upsetting the harmony of the *millets*. But the balance was upset after 1829 when Russia began to champion the rights of the Orthodox priests against the Latins supported by France. Russian pilgrims began to flood into Jerusalem after Czar Nicholas rebuilt two old Orthodox monasteries for their use (1841). In 1843 the Orthodox patriarch of Jerusalem obtained Ottoman assent for his separation from the patriarch of Constantinople, and he began to build his own power with the czar's help and support. In reaction the French government promoted the interests of the Latin priests, demanding new privileges for them (1850), partly also because of the desire of Louis Napoleon to use the religious fervor of his subjects to gain popular support at home. Thus began three years of demands and counterdemands on the sultan, who sought only to maintain a neutral position so as not to antagonize any of the powers.

At first France prevailed, securing several new concessions for the Latins, including control of the keys to the Church of Bethlehem. This gave Napoleon much prestige at the time when he overthrew the French Republic and established himself as emperor (November 2, 1852). Now he was willing to compromise with Russia on the questions of the Holy Places, but the czar was left in a position where he had to gain new concessions so as not to lose face. As a preliminary to new demands, he tried to restore the old cooperation with Britain by making an agreement for division of the spoils if the Ottoman Empire broke up. Russia did not want Istanbul but would not allow any other power to control it. Serbia, Bulgaria, and the Principalities would become independent under Russian influence, while Britain in compensation could take Crete and Egypt (January 1853). The two would cooperate to keep France out. No agreement actually was signed, but Britain's failure to reject the plan openly seems to have misled the czar into assuming that he had London's support for efforts to counter the French in the Holy Land. Hence he made new demands on the sultan, not only for Orthodox concessions in the Holy Places but also for a new treaty recognizing Russian protection over all the sultan's Orthodox subjects in return for promises of support against France (May 1853). With both the British and French ambassadors at home getting instructions, the sultan at first gave in to the Russian demands. But as soon as the British ambassador, Stratford de Redcliffe (1842–1858) returned, he got the sultan to restore Mustafa Reşit Paşa as foreign minister (May 15, 1853) and then persuaded the latter to reject the Russian demands.

The czar felt betrayed by Britain as well as by the Porte and was ready to declare war. But his foreign minister, Nesselrode, pointed out that if he attacked, he might have to fight the rest of Europe as well. Instead, the czar sent an ultimatum to the sultan (May 31) warning that his troops would occupy the Principalities unless the earlier demands were accepted. Britain encouraged Ottoman resistance by ordering its fleet to gather at Besika Bay, at the mouth of the Dardanelles, with Stratford given the authority to summon it to Istanbul if the Russians attacked. Mutual underestimation of the enemy led to a general European war. The czar felt the British would back down; therefore, on July 2 his troops crossed the Pruth and began to occupy the Principalities. Mustafa Reşit Paşa's determination to resist was buoyed by popular anti-Russian fervor as well as the presence of British and French warships. Britain really did not want to fight Russia, however; thus Stratford got the Ottomans to make a unilateral compromise statement confirming the "ancient privileges of the religion professed" by the czar, thereby hoping to avoid a bilateral agreement that would authorize the Russians to intervene.

In the meantime, the ambassadors of the powers were meeting in Vienna to find a compromise. Discarding the Ottoman declaration, which they felt the czar would not accept, they formulated the Vienna Note (July 28, 1853), by which the sultan would reaffirm the provisions of the Küçük Kaynarca and Edirne treaties regarding his Christian subjects, with Russia and France jointly guaranteeing their continued fulfillment. The czar accepted at once (August 5, 1853). But the Porte – emboldened by continued anti-Russian demonstrations in the streets of the capital and the arrival of a supporting fleet from Egypt (August 12), and resentful of the fact that the note was drawn up without Ottoman participation and sent to the czar before it was sent to the sultan – refused to accept unless it was altered to make clear that the privileges of the Orthodox priests and subjects were derived only from the sultan and not as a result of agreements with Russia. But this the czar was unwilling to accept. The British cabinet, hoping to avoid war by pressuring the Ottomans to accept a compromise, ordered its fleet to leave the Dardanelles, but it was too late. With the strong support of public opinion the Ottomans were determined to attack unless the Principalities were evacuated, and only Stratford's strong representations kept them from an immediate declaration of war.

The Crimean War

On October 4, 1853, the Ottoman commander at Şumla, Ömer Paşa, presented an ultimatum to the Russian commander in the Principalities, Prince Gorchakov, demanding evacuation of the Principalities on the threat of war. When there was no reply, the Ottomans crossed the Danube and attacked (October 27–November 3, 1853), thus beginning the conflict without waiting for official declarations. At the same time, in eastern Anatolia the Ottoman provincial army based in Erzurum and Kars moved into the southern Caucasus against Russian troops already weakened by a local Muslim uprising led by Şeyh Şamil. The sultan's fleet also sailed into the Black Sea, apparently in fear that the Russians were about to enter the Bosporus. When it could not find the enemy, it anchored at Sinop for the winter, only to be destroyed in the harbor by a powerful Russian squadron (November 30), an event which so inflamed public opinion in Britain and France as well as in the Ottoman Empire that it corroded further resistance to war. On December 23, 1853, the British government sent orders to its fleet to protect "the Ottoman flag as well as Ottoman territory" and to compel all Russian ships then in the Black Sea to return to Sevastopol. Russia refused this ultimatum as well as that of the Ottomans to leave the Principalities and broke relations with Britain and France (February 6, 1854), which in turn declared war (March 28, 1854), thus commencing the international conflict that came to be known as the Crimean War.

Ottoman public opinion supported the war, and thousands rushed to enlist in the army. The Russians launched a major offensive across the Danube. They took Ibrail, Ismail, Hirsova, and Köstence, occupied the Dobruca, and followed Ömer

Paşa's retreating army toward Şumla, Varna, and Silistria, which were built up as the main points of Ottoman resistance. A large French army reached Gallipoli on March 31, 1854, with Prince Napoleon himself landing with his troops. A British army arrived under the command of Lord Raglan, Wellington's chief aide at Waterloo, and it was quartered in the Selimiye barracks at Üsküdar while preparations were made to send it to the Principalities. Before the British and French could move to the front, however, the Russians took the city of Silistria (June 23), though the fort continued to hold out. In the meantime, Prussia joined Austria in pressuring the czar to leave the Principalities to avoid a general war. The Russians seemed agreeable even after an Ottoman-Austrian treaty (June 14) turned the Principalities over to the occupation of the latter for the duration of the war in return for its support against the Russians. The czar did not want the Austrians to have the Principalities, but he did not wish to wage war with them either. By leaving the Principalities to Austria rather than to the sultan he could remove the basic cause of the war without losing as much face as would have been the case had the Ottomans taken them back directly. In mid-June, then, his troops left the Principalities on the condition that the Austrians who replaced them keep the Ottomans, British, and French out.

These events altered the entire course of the war. The British and French troops were moving toward the Principalities and were intending to cross the Danube toward Odessa. Austrian occupation of the Principalities made this impossible, so that the allies now decided instead to attack the Crimea to destroy Russian naval power in the Black Sea and deprive it of a base it might use to attack the Ottomans from the north. Austria refused to join the alliance, fearing a struggle with the Russians in Galicia, but Prussia did join, hoping for new gains in the north. The war then became primarily a conflict in the Crimea between Russia and an allied European expeditionary force. The first allied landings took place near Sevastopol on September 14, 1854, and the allies made their preparations for the siege of the city. By the time the attack came in mid-October, the Russians were ready for an extended resistance, and the harsh winter months caused terrible suffering among the attacking forces. In the face of the British losses, the Ottomans signed an agreement (February 3, 1855) to provide 20,000 soldiers and all needed supplies to help them fight on. The death of Czar Nicholas I (March 2, 1855) and the accession of Alexander II stimulated peace negotiations, but in the meantime the war continued. The Ottomans supported the allied forces at terrible expense while Florence Nightingale and her colleagues established hospital service at the Selimiye barracks in Üsküdar.

The battles in Crimea during the summer of 1855 were inconclusive, but in mid-June the Russians advanced on Kars, clashing directly with the Ottomans. With eastern Anatolia threatened, the Porte asked for allied assistance. But the latter were determined to carry on in the Crimea alone and did not particularly care what happened in the east. The Ottomans had to defend Kars by themselves against a series of Russian assaults. Back in the Crimea a general assault on Sevastopol began in late August. Although the British failed to take the outpost at Redan, the French finally broke through, forcing the Russians to abandon the great port after sinking their fleet and blowing up their ammunition. Sevastopol's ruins were occupied by the allies on September 9, 1855, after a siege of just less than a year. The Russian attack on Kars continued, however, and it fell on November 25, 1855, thus exposing Anatolia to a major new push, though it was postponed by the arrival of winter.

Negotiations continued while the fighting and suffering went on. French and British differences over the settlement contributed to delays as much as did Russian recalcitrance. Palmerston, who had become prime minister in 1855, was building up the British armed forces and wanted the war to continue until vengeance could be gained for the defeat at Redan and the Russian army forced to surrender. France, on the other hand, was eager for peace since the emperor had secured the glory he wanted and now felt he was fighting more for British interests than his own. Austria supported the French position, while the Ottomans, still under British influence, held out in the hope of gaining concessions from the Russians. Finally, late in December, Palmerston joined in a note to Russia threatening Austrian intervention unless it agreed to negotiations on the basis of the Vienna Note together with the neutralization of the Black Sea against the warships of all powers and the return of Bessarabia to the Ottomans. The Principalities and Serbia would remain autonomous under Ottoman rule, but under the guarantees of the powers. The Danube would remain open to all nations, and the sultan would agree to protect the rights of his Christian subjects. As if to demonstrate in advance Ottoman agreement to these terms, but by decree alone of the sovereign sultan rather than by foreign dictate, the Reform Decree was issued on February 4, 1856, guaranteeing equality and reforms for all subjects. Soon afterward, on February 25, the czar accepted the allied demands, thus setting the stage for the conference called to meet in Paris to settle the war and the problems that had caused it.

The Peace of Paris

The peace conference opened in Paris on February 25, 1856 with all the belligerents represented, along with Austria and Prussia, and the Ottoman delegation led by Âli Paşa. He tried to keep the powers from settling their disputes at Ottoman expense, but it soon was very clear that this is what they were going to do despite the fact that the sultan had already declared his intention of instituting reforms on his own. The agreement of Paris, finally signed on March 29, 1856, purported to establish perpetual peace among the belligerents.[115] All sides agreed to evacuate territory taken during the war. The Russians left eastern Anatolia and the allies surrendered the Crimea and areas of the Black Sea coast. The signatories declared their joint guarantee of the territorial integrity and independence of the Ottoman Empire, promising also to mediate jointly any quarrels that might subsequently arise among any of them and the Ottomans. The sultan communicated the text of his Reform Decree, and the powers declared their full support, with no provision being made for individual or joint intervention to secure Ottoman fulfillment of these promises. The Straits were to remain closed to the warships of foreign powers and the Black Sea was to be neutralized, open only to merchant ships. Both the Ottomans and Russians would keep only small warships needed to defend their coasts, but their larger warships would be removed and all naval shipyards operating in the Black Sea would be closed. The Danube and the Straits also would be opened to the free navigation of the merchant ships of all countries. An International Danube Commission was established to enforce this provision and to organize measures to keep its channels dredged and open to shipping and to organize and enforce navigation rules and maintenance along the entire length of the river. Southern Bessarabia would be ceded by Russia to Moldavia, thus ending its direct access to the Danube, and the occupants of the province would be allowed to emigrate to Russia if they wished. The Principalities of Moldavia and Wallachia would regain their former autonomous status under the sultan but would be under the joint guarantee of the powers, which promised to refrain from intervention in the future. The sultan promised to organize an administrative council in each Principality with representatives of all elements of their populations, not only the notables, to consider necessary economic and social reforms. Serbia also would retain its autonomy under Ottoman suzerainty and under the joint guarantee of the powers. The Ottomans, however, retained the right to station garrisons in its territory, and the powers in turn promised to mediate in any Ottoman-Serbian dispute. The peace settlement thus established was reinforced by a separate treaty (April 15, 1856) by which Britain, Austria, and France guaranteed Ottoman independence and integrity, obviously against Russia, though France by this time was already tending toward some kind of agreement with it to restore Europe's balance of power against the dominance now achieved by Britain.

Results of the War and Peace Settlement for the Ottoman Empire

The Crimean War and the peace settlement that followed had tremendous impact on the Ottoman Empire. On the negative side, financial strain on the new Tanzimat treasury forced the Ottoman government to take a series of foreign loans at such steep rates of interest that, despite all the fiscal reforms that followed, it was pushed into insolvable debts and economic difficulties that continued for the rest of the century. On the positive side, the arrival of thousands of refugees from all parts of Europe, particularly from Hungary and Poland, and their settlement in the major cities offered the sultan and his ministers a new reserve of expert foreign advisers. Moreover, the presence of large numbers of foreign officers and soldiers and their families in the streets of Istanbul in particular familiarized the local population with European manners and made the work of Âli and Fuat and their associates much easier in the years that followed. The guarantees of the powers also freed the Men of the Tanzimat to push ahead with all their reforms without having to fear imminent attack from outside.

Union of the Principalities

The Peace of Paris protected the Porte from direct attack, but there was nothing to prevent those powers wishing its destruction to continue their old game of encouraging nationalistic feelings among the subject minorities to destroy the empire from within. The results came first in the Principalities, whose educated youths for some time had been developing the idea of a Rumanian nation on the basis of common origins among the Dacians of Roman times. The Russians encouraged this feeling during the occupation, and the Organic Regulations' removal of the old financial and trade barriers between the two provided economic stimulation for what had been no more than an idea. Napoleon III also emerged as a champion of European national movements as a device to extend French influence. He encouraged the Rumanians while trying to convince the sultan that union would build the Principalities against future Russian aggression. The idea, however, was opposed by the Ottomans and British, who feared that it would be the first step toward independence, thus further weakening the Porte, and by Austria, who feared the example might stimulate similar demands from its own subject nationalities.

But the Peace of Paris had provided for a popular referendum in the Principalities as well as further consultation among the powers to determine what their future should be. While the powers haggled in the International Danube Commission, their agents agitated the various partisan groups in the country, with France supporting the unionists and Austria the separatists. The new prince of Wallachia also supported union, since it would give his province supremacy because of its size, while the Prince of Moldavia opposed it from the same consideration. When elections were held for the advisory councils (September 1857), both had substantial majorities of unionists. Within a short time they developed charters that provided for a united state of Wallachia and Moldavia under the rule of a prince from one of the reigning dynasties of Europe and a single representative assembly. The powers were divided on how to meet this request, but a compromise agreement to replace the Organic Regulations finally was reached in Paris (August 19, 1858). It left the Principalities separate, each with its own prince, ministry, assembly, and militia, and under Ottoman suzerainty as before, but with a joint commission chosen by the princes and councils to draw up common law codes and other legislation needed by both, which then would be approved by the separate councils. The latter still would be elected by limited franchise, guaranteeing continuation of boyar control. Soon afterward, both councils did the one thing the powers had not anticipated: They elected the same man as prince of both Principalities, the boyar Alexander Cuza, then minister of war in Moldavia, thus bringing both together in a personal union. The Porte and Austria objected, but Cuza remained in power, mostly with French support, and the Austrians were too diverted by their own war with France in Italy to do much about the situation. Britain, which was preoccupied with the Indian Rebellion, finally devised a compromise, getting the sultan to accept the situation with the stipulation that it was exceptional, recognized only to help the Principalities recover from the war and without binding effect on the future (September 25, 1859), and this was accepted by the powers. But increased French influence at the Porte resulted in a new *ferman* (December 2, 1861) that created a single ministry and assembly for both Principalities as long as Cuza continued to rule. The seat of government was united at Bucharest, previously the capital of Wallachia. This gave it the expected dominance in the new state, which remained intact thereafter despite internal tensions.

Crisis in the Lebanon

Once the Crimean War had been settled the Ottomans were free to resume their reforms, and the Lebanon had first priority. Actually, it was easier to introduce reforms here than elsewhere in the empire, since the way had been prepared by the various foreign invasions as well as the reforms of Emir Başir and Ibrahim Paşa. The arrangement introduced in 1846 worked well for some time, with the governors enforcing the general Tanzimat reforms, including centralization, whittling down the authority of the local notables and chiefs. Though the Druzes were able to remain united and had considerable autonomy in their own areas, the Maronites were weakened by internal divisions resulting from reactions against feudal control in the north. Here the great Maronite families had ruled their lands, held as *mukata'as*, with little outside intervention as long as they paid their taxes. But now the Maronite peasants, stirred on by the clergy, became restless. In 1858 they revolted under the leadership of a blacksmith named Taniyus Şahin and established a peasant republic. The district leaders and Maronite clergy secretly supported the republic, since anything that weakened the feudal families helped them. The governor was happy to sit back and use Maronite divisions to increase central authority. Meanwhile, Muslim sentiment was reacting to the provisions for equality for non-Muslims made in the Reform Decree, and Britain also stirred things up by sending arms to the Druzes to counter French influence among the Maronites. Relations among the communities were further strained when the Druzes and the Sunni Muslims, encouraged by the Maronite divisions, tried to use the situation to restore their own domination. The explosion came on May 27, 1860, when a group of Maronites raided a Druze village. Massacres and countermassacres followed, not only in the Lebanon but also in Syria. In the end, between 7,000 and 12,000 people, of all religions, had been killed, and over 300 villages, 500 churches, 40 monasteries, and 30 schools were destroyed. Christian attacks on Muslims in Beirut stirred the predominantly Muslim population of Damascus to attack the Christian minority, with over 25,000 of the latter being killed, including the American and Dutch consuls, giving the event an international dimension.

It was at this point that Fuat Paşa, now foreign minister, came to Syria to solve the problems, which he did by seeking out and executing the culprits, including the governor and other officials. Order was restored, and preparations made to give Lebanon new autonomy to avoid European intervention. But the powers were determined, under the pretext of helping the Ottomans and supporting the Peace of Paris, to use the situation to intervene even though the problems had been solved. France sent a fleet, and Britain joined to prevent a unilateral intervention that could help French influence in the area (September 5, 1860). The Ottoman government was required to help the foreign force while it was in the Lebanon, and the latter's commander was supposed to cooperate with Fuat. In the end only the French actually landed troops, while Britain and the other powers manifested their presence with warships in the harbor of Beirut. The French soon found that Fuat had, indeed, settled the problems and that they were not needed. An international conference then was assembled to make a new settlement, and it met first at Beirut and then Istanbul under Fuat's chairmanship. The French troops had to withdraw (June 1861), and the Beyoğlu Protocol was signed (June 9, 1861) giving Lebanon a new Organic Statute that made it a privileged and independent province, with administrative, judicial, and financial autonomy to satisfy all elements of the population, though the arrangement was limited to the mountain itself, excluding Beirut and other Muslim coastal areas. Lebanon was thereafter headed by a Christian governor general (*mutassarıf*), who was to be a Catholic designated by and responsible to the Porte but approved and supervised by the powers, and he was to be helped by the old Administrative Council (*Meclis-i İdare*). The new government would control its own judicial system and militia; no Ottoman troops would be stationed anywhere in the Lebanon, nor would tribute be sent to Istanbul. All subjects were to have equality before the law regardless of religion; local taxes could be used for local needs, but deficits had to be made up locally and not by the Ottoman treasury.

The new organization was successfully carried out during the long administrative terms of the governors Davut Paşa (1861–1868), the Italian Rüstem Paşa (1873–1883), the Italian Vasa Paşa (1883–1892), and others, who developed a system of government that took over most of the powers of the notables while introducing the best features of the Tanzimat. Within the Maronite community the decline of the feudal notables was followed by the ascendancy of the ecclesiastical hierarchy, and while the divisions among the various religious and social groups were not entirely healed, the strife that had led to foreign intervention ended and Lebanon was left to develop in its own way for the remaining years of Ottoman rule.

Autonomous Lebanon was not wealthy; it had lost the great seaport of Beirut and the agricultural lands of the Bika'a to the north. But its governors and people were unusually resourceful, and as a result it achieved a prosperity, security, and cultural development unmatched anywhere else in the empire. The disasters of 1860 did more than establish Lebanese autonomy; they also attracted various Christian missionary groups that established churches, hospitals, and schools. Lebanon developed a high rate of literacy and became a center for the development of Arabic literature. But despite all the prosperity and literacy, the bloody events of 1860 never have been forgotten and to the present day leave a legacy of communal antagonism and bitterness that remains a principal motivating factor in Lebanese society and politics.

The Developing Autonomy of Egypt, 1849–1879

In the meantime, after the death of Muhammad Ali in 1849 Egypt developed an independent position, gradually increasing its political and economic autonomy from the Porte but remaining close to the sultan through family and financial ties. Under Ibrahim Paşa's sons Abbas I (1849–1854) and Sait (1854–1863) Egyptian policy reflected their grandfather's experience that the powers would not allow it to break up or take over the Ottoman Empire. Therefore, they renounced territorial aspirations and resumed the role of faithful vassals, restoring payments of tribute and accepting all the legal and financial restrictions imposed in the settlement of 1841. Relations with France also cooled, while Britain developed an important commercial as well as political presence in the country just as it was doing elsewhere in the empire. Internally, the government relaxed the stringent policies of Muhammad Ali, such as those regarding forced labor and monopolies, while continuing the progressive spirit of his reform program and adopting other reforms introduced by the Tanzimat. The powers now concentrated their rivalries on economic exploitation, making loans, gaining the right to exploit raw materials, and securing new markets for their own industries.

Economic and financial problems created by Muhammad Ali's agricultural and health programs, discernible under Sait and Abbas, became important under their successor, Ismail (1863–1879). Muhammad Ali had replaced land previously used for food with crops sold abroad, such as cotton, sugar, and indigo, but there still was enough land for food as long as it was farmed intensively. But the large estates that he had turned over to members of his family and other members of the upper classes were hardly organized to provide the kind of efficient cultivation needed. In addition, the health services begun early in the century now were having a measurable effect on cutting down the death rate, leading to a population increase and resulting problems of food shortages and unemployment. Proposals from France and England seemed to provide plausible solutions. A French financial group headed by Ferdinand de Lesseps, who had made friends with Sait while serving as French consul in Cairo, offered to build a canal through the isthmus of Suez, with thousands of peasants conscripted for forced labor on the project. Thus the Suez Canal Company was formed. Britain, needing new sources of cotton for its textile industry because of shortages caused by the American Civil War, also convinced Sait that he could provide employment and gain profit by turning to cotton as a major new staple. The cultivation of cotton utilized land and labor previously used by the Suez Canal Company, to which large amounts of money were paid in compensation. The early results were deceptive. With the general rise of cotton prices on the world market there was a new prosperity for Egypt. But the increase in cotton production left Egypt with a food deficit, requiring it to import food while leaving it dependent on the vagaries of international economic factors and in particular the price of cotton. De Lesseps in the meantime substituted machines for the men he had given up and went on to build the Suez Canal despite the opposition of Britain, which feared that under French control it would restore French power in the Levant. On November 17, 1869, the canal was opened with a lavish ceremony provided by Ismail, in the presence of some of the crowned heads of Europe led by Princess Eugenie of France, but at a cost that drove new nails into the financial coffin of Egypt.

Ismail now worked to make himself a worthy successor to Muhammad Ali. Already in 1866 he had secured Ottoman permission to establish succession from father to son instead of by seniority, which had been stipulated in 1841, in return providing assistance against the revolt in Crete as well as a substantial increase in the annual tribute paid to the sultan. The next year (June 8, 1867) he gained a status above that of the normal governor with the old Persian title of khedive coined to signify his right to issue his own decrees without confirmation by the sultan. He still had to limit the size of his armed forces, however, and to submit his annual budget to the Porte for approval, conditions insisted on by Britain to restrict what it considered to be a French vassal. Once the canal was opened, however, France had much less need to support him than in the past. Ismail increased his close relations with the sultan and after Âli Paşa's death was able to secure a new *ferman* that increased his autonomy and power (June 8, 1873), with the order of succession again modified so that it would go to the eldest son of the khedive, or if there were no sons to the eldest nephew, with a regency to rule if the heir was a minor. In return for new increases in tribute he was also given the hereditary governorship of the strategic Red Sea ports of Sawakin and Massawa, full administrative independence, the right to conclude nonpolitical treaties and loan agreements with foreign countries and banks, and to increase his army and navy without prior approval of the Porte. For all practical purposes, then, Egypt was almost completely independent, with only the tribute and the continued presence of an Ottoman commissioner reminding the khedive of his ties with his suzerain.

Ismail then moved rapidly to modernize the country. Mixed courts were introduced here too, applying new law codes that restricted the legal rights of the Capitulatory powers and of their subjects living in the country. Peasants were given full rights of ownership in the land, though high taxes, conscription, and forced labor made this of limited benefit and the great landowners continued to predominate and extend their holdings. A semiparliamentary body was established in November 1866. The members were chosen by indirect election from among the village headmen to provide at least a semblance of popular participation in government, though there are indications that it really was created to balance the power of the Turko-Circassian aristocracy rather than to limit the khedive's powers. A secular education system was rapidly built up, and an independent press began to develop, stimulated mostly by Lebanese immigrants. A new system of irrigation canals increased agricultural production, and sugar cultivation and processing added to Egypt's foreign trade. Foreign merchants and industrialists were encouraged to settle, thus strengthening the community of Levantines that dominated much of Egyptian life until the revolution of 1954. Docks and harbors, railroads, and telegraph lines opened up the country, very much as the Tanzimat programs had done elsewhere in the empire. With assistance from British officers, attempts were made to extend Egyptian rule southward into the Sudan between 1869 and 1876. Hostilities also were begun against Abyssinia (1875–1877), but the Egyptian armies were defeated, and it was only because of Abyssinian internal divisions that Ismail finally was able to capture the hinterlands of Massawa, Sawakin, and Harar.

But the new agriculture and industry simply did not produce enough money to pay the cost of Ismail's programs of modernization and conquest, particularly since they were accompanied by his own extravagance. With the right to make loans without Ottoman approval, Ismail contracted loan after loan, at high rates of interest, building a huge debt in a relatively short time. To secure more revenues he resorted to all kinds of expedients, collecting taxes years in advance, making internal loans with no intention to repay, and, finally, selling his shares in the Suez Canal Company to the British government (November 1875), thus giving the latter substantial control of the enterprise, which it had originally opposed because of French involvement. In 1876 his financial problems became so acute that he withheld interest payments to the international bondholders, reduced government salaries, and doubled cultivation taxes. The immediate crisis was solved when the Mixed Commercial Court in Alexandria forced him to pay the bondholders by sequestering his palace at Ramla, forcing him and his relatives to give more of their estates to the state and to accept the control of a Public Debt Commission with foreign members, which organized the collection of sufficient revenues to pay the interest on bonds regularly. British and French experts also were appointed to control the ministries of finance and public works, thus establishing foreign control over his government's major policies. Eventually, Ismail was deposed because of foreign and internal pressure (1879) and replaced by Tevfik Paşa (1879–1892), under whose rule Egypt's terrible financial situation ultimately led not only to foreign control within the government but to the occupation of the country by Britain in 1882 (see pp. 193–195).

The New European Concert

The concert of Europe established in 1856 was shaken in 1859 when France and Austria fought over Italy. It came apart completely as a result of Bismarck's wars to create a united Germany, with Prussia defeating Austria in 1866 and France in 1870, thus establishing itself in place of Austria-Hungary as the dominant power in Central Europe as well as the entire Continent. Britain, worn out by its participation in the Crimean War and diverted by the Irish question and the whole complex of problems created by the Industrial Revolution, chose not to intervene again to restore the European balance. Bismarck now was satisfied with the new situation he had created and did not wish a breakup of the Ottoman Empire to create rivalries that might lead to war. So he took up the czar's earlier suggestion that arrangements be made in case the empire fell apart, creating the Three Emperors' League with Austria and Russia to keep France isolated on the Continent. France under Napoleon III responded by supporting self-determination movements, particularly if they concerned the three emperors or the sultan. Thus revolts in Poland against Russia and national aspirations in the Balkans were encouraged by France. Nor was Russia happy with the status quo. Thus it worked to regain its right to maintain a fleet on the Black Sea and vied with the French in gaining influence in the Balkans by using the new Pan-Slavic idea that all Slavs should be united under Russian leadership. This could be done only by destroying the two empires where most of the non-Russian Slavs lived, the Habsburg and the

Ottoman. The ambitions and rivalries of the Russians and French in the Balkans surfaced in Serbia, which was experiencing its own national revival and had ambitions that partly conflicted with those of the powers. How had Serbia come to this stage, and what were the consequences?

The Developing Autonomy of Serbia

Serbia had gone through perilous times since it was made autonomous by the Treaty of Edirne. Under the new regulations no Ottomans could live in the country except the soldiers who garrisoned its forts and people already resident in the main cities. All the timar holders were expelled, their properties sold to Serbs and the returns paid to the Istanbul government, which could provide compensation to the former *Sipahis* if it wished to do so. Serbs now manned the administration of the province. Taxes went to the Serbian treasury, and a fixed annual tribute was forwarded to the Porte. The Greek Orthodox patriarch of Istanbul remained supreme, but he could do no more than confirm the choice of native Serbian priests to replace the Greeks whom he formerly appointed.

In August 1830 Miloş Obrenoviç was chosen hereditary prince by the Serbian assembly and confirmed by the sultan. When Mahmut refused to surrender six border districts promised the Serbs in the treaty, Miloş waited until the Ottomans were diverted by Muhammed Ali's invasion of Anatolia in 1833 and then occupied them, increasing the principality's size by one-third and giving it boundaries that were to remain unchanged until 1878, bounded by the Danube in the north, the Drina and Timok in the west and east, and Alexinatz and Niş in the south. Under Miloş Serbia's problem was similar to that of Wallachia, namely, which class would rule. Traditionally, power had been held by the *knezes*, and there were also new provincial military leaders produced by the long years of revolution. In addition, the people had been accustomed to the traditional Ottoman decentralized government and resisted the kind of centralized authority Miloş attempted to impose. When the assembly reflected this opposition, Miloş began to act autocratically, calling it only on rare occasions and interpreting the law as he wished. Meanwhile, he built up his personal wealth by illegal means. To conciliate the cultivators he began to confiscate the fiefs that had been given to Serbian notables who had joined the fight against the Ottomans. The resulting discontent over Miloş's rule led to a revolt against him in 1835 that forced him to accept a new constitution. The prince now had to accept the advice of a committee of six leaders chosen by the assembly. The arrangement did not last very long. Neither the Russians nor the Austrians liked such democratic institutions, however limited they were. Miloş also became even more autocratic despite the committee, building up a highly centralized government to break down the power of the provincial notables and traditional assemblies, using as his instruments better-educated Serbs from Hungary and excluding native Serbs from government service. To build Serbia as a buffer against the Russians, particularly after Russia's diplomatic victory in Istanbul through the Treaty of Hünkâr Iskelesi, Palmerston encouraged Miloş's autocracy. On the other hand, Russia persuaded Mahmut II to replace the constitution of Serbia with a new statute that put power in the hands of a council of 17, appointed by the prince for life. It now had the right to approve all laws and taxes before they became law, though the prince still retained his final right of veto. Absolutism thus was ended, but Miloş reacted by stirring the peasants to revolt with stories that the new regime had been instituted to help the nobles restore feudalism and raise taxes. The revolt was suppressed, and on June 13, 1839, Miloş was forced to abdicate in favor of his eldest son, Milan Obrenoviç. Miloş fled to Austria.

Milan died soon afterward; he was replaced by his younger brother Michael under the control of a regency until he came of age in 1840. Once in full power, Michael worked to modernize the agricultural and educational system but angered the peasants and clergy, who disliked the innovations. To pay for the reforms he modernized the tax system, doubling the rates. The result was another revolt (1842) which forced Michael to follow his father to Austria. The national assembly (September 14, 1842) then elected Alexander Karageorgeviç, son of the old Kara George, Miloş's rival, perpetuating the old quarrel between the two dynasties. Alexander managed to retain power until 1858 despite the strong opposition of Russia. But since he had never been given the right of hereditary succession, he ruled cautiously, with gradual internal development. Serbia remained neutral during the Crimean War, and the Peace of Paris ended the Ottoman right to station garrisons in the countryside. Secretly, however, Alexander had supported Austria, so that after the war the French and Russians supported the opposition. When he tried to assert his own power over that of the assembly, the Obrenoviçes joined the agents of the Russians and the sultan in forcing his abdication (December 23, 1858), with Miloş finally being recalled. The latter, however, though now 79 years old, had not forgotten his old ways, and resumed his arbitrary methods of rule, dissolving the assembly, banishing his opponents, putting his favorites into important positions, and increasing his personal wealth at the expense of the people.

Miloş died two years later and was succeeded by Michael once again, who in his second reign (1860–1868) ruled far more wisely and effectively than before. He now proclaimed the supremacy of the law and got the assembly to introduce a number of important modernizing measures including new systems of taxation and conscription, a modern school system, and a national militia. In addition, Michael skillfully used clashes between the remaining Ottoman garrisons and the Serbian population to get the powers to pressure Abdulaziz into withdrawing the remaining Ottoman troops and residents (April 18, 1867) in return for no more than a provision that the Ottoman flag be flown jointly with that of Serbia over the Belgrade citadel. For all practical purposes, therefore, Serbian independence was achieved.

Michael's last major effort was the creation of an alliance of the newly independent and autonomous Balkan states against the Ottomans. With Russian encouragement, he agitated for a Pan-Slavic movement to free the southern Slavs not only from the Ottomans but also from the Habsburgs and to form them into a united state under his leadership. The Greeks were willing to help, since they had their own ambitions against the Ottomans in the Epirus and Macedonia as well as in Crete, where they had just stimulated a revolt against the Porte. Austria was opposed to such a union, but it had just been defeated by Prussia (1866) and hence was not in a position to do anything. Michael, therefore, was able to develop a system of alliances, first with Rumania (1865) and with Montengro (1866). These were followed by an agreement with a group of Bulgarian revolutionaries claiming to represent popular opinion in that province, which was still under direct Ottoman rule (1867), stipulating the ultimate union of Serbia and Bulgaria. An alliance with Greece (1867) provided that the latter would get Epirus and Thessaly in return for allowing Serbia to annex Bosnia and Herzegovina. Thus Michael created the prototype of the coalition of Balkan states that ultimately was to attack the Ottomans in 1912. Nothing happened immediately, however, because the states involved lacked sufficient armed force, and by the time they were ready, the Ottoman diversion in Crete had come to an end and Prussia and Austria were again at peace. In addition, the Pan-Slavic efforts to rid themselves of the domination of the Greek Orthodox church alienated Greece, which now moved to block Slavic nationalistic moves in the Balkans. Russia in any case provided only ideological and moral support, not practical assistance, and Austria soon returned to its former policy of opposing all revolutionary activities in the area. Finally, when Michael died by the hand of an assassin (1868), the coalition fell apart, with the partners thereafter pursuing their own national interests, often in the form of conflicting ambitions in Macedonia and other areas still under Ottoman rule.

Because Michael himself had no children, succession went to a distant relative, Milan Obrenoviç (1868–1889), who was studying in Paris at the time. He was given much more power than his predecessors, with a constitution that provided that one quarter of the assembly's members would be appointed by the prince while the rest were elected by limited suffrage. The prince could nominate anyone he wished, convoke and dismiss the assembly at will, and only he could initiate legislation. For the first time the Obrenoviç family got the hereditary right to rule, but Milan proved to be more interested in personal luxury and failed to provide real leadership. While Serbia's economic and social conditions continued to improve, therefore, the intrigues of the politicians and the exiled dynasty and its supporters left its political life in chaos. There were few positive accomplishments until Serbia was involved in the great Eastern Crisis of 1875.

Problems in Herzegovina and Bosnia and Revolt in Montenegro, 1858–1869

In the meantime, Russian and Serbian intrigues were having their effect to the west, leading to discontent and uprisings in both Bosnia-Herzegovina and Montenegro. In the twin provinces, half the population was Muslim, albeit of Slavic origin.[116] Their self-image as the last remaining frontier area facing the Habsburgs as well as the principal locale of the old feudal families forced from Hungary reinforced a situation in which the notables resisted any concessions to the Christian minority or to those foreign powers who acted as protectors. The Tanzimat reforms were opposed here with more vehemence than in any other part of the empire, with many of the large landowners retaining their timars, or where they had been transformed into tax farms, controlling the latter. They collected more than their due from their cultivators while withholding most of it from the treasury, so that Bosnia and Herzegovina, though major agricultural areas, lagged behind most of the other Balkan provinces in terms of actual revenues sent to the Porte.[117] While the Muslim peasants suffered from feudal tyranny every bit as much as did the Christians, it was the latter whose cause was taken up by the politicians of Britain and France and by the Pan-Slavic agitators, who tried to stimulate a revolt that would massacre or drive out the Muslims and establish Slavic Christians in their place.

Local revolts stimulated by the feudal landowners prevented the introduction of significant reforms into Bosnia until the governorship of Ömer Lütfi Paşa (1860–1861), a former Austrian officer born in Croatia who suppressed and killed most of the rebel leaders and applied the Tanzimat reforms, breaking up much of the political and economic power of the feudal families. The Tanzimat provincial organization was introduced, with the district *kaymakams* being given military power to enforce the reforms. Sarajevo became capital instead of Travnik, which was the center of the landlords' power. Ömer Paşa's attempts to replace tax farming with direct tax collection failed, however, as it had elsewhere in the empire.

The mostly Christian principality of Montenegro, ruled now by Prince Bishop (*Vladika*) Danilo, was drawn into the conflict. Danilo had responded to Russian agitation during the Crimean War by revolting against the sultan before giving in to Ottoman pressure because of the czar's failure to send actual assistance. Subsequent Austrian intervention on his behalf in Istanbul, however, persuaded the sultan to leave him in power (March 3, 1853), in a position to use tensions in Bosnia and Herzegovina to his own advantage. Danilo tried to get the conference of Paris to recognize Montenegran independence and allow it to take a number of border territories from Herzegovina, but this was nullified by strong Ottoman opposition. The Porte then offered him new privileges, but he refused and declared his independence unilaterally (1857). The Ottomans invaded the Principality, but the powers moved to settle the problem collectively, with an international commission deciding to support Montenegran autonomy within its existing frontiers. Danilo resisted at first, but a new Ottoman expedition finally forced him to accept the arrangement (November 8, 1858).

Danilo continued to push his ambitions, now with the help of the Pan-Slavic committee established in Moscow in 1856. It spread its message through the Russian consulate at Mostar, urging the Slavs to demand complete freedom to repair their churches and build new ones, the replacement of Ottoman with native policemen, and Greek with Slavic priests, and the lowering of cultivation taxes and their collection by local representatives in place of the Ottoman collectors. Within a short time the Christians of Herzegovina were also agitating in support of these demands.

Danilo was assassinated (August 11, 1860), but his nephew and successor, Nicholas Petroviç, was active in encouraging the Slavs of Herzegovina. Montenegran groups began to go into Herzegovina, massacring Muslims and capturing several small villages near the border. Ömer Paşa finally routed the rebel forces at Piva, for all practical purposes ending the affair (November 21, 1861). When Montenegro mobilized its own forces and threatened to intervene, Ömer Paşa invaded the Principality as well, routing the rebels and forcing them inland. At this point, however, the powers intervened to force a settlement at Işkodra (August 31, 1862). Montenegro's previous boundaries and autonomy were restored in return for promises to cease helping the Herzegovinian rebels, and the Porte was recognized as the sole mediator in any border disputes that might arise between Montenegro and its neighbors.

Major reforms were introduced into Bosnia-Herzegovina during the long governorship of Topal Osman Paşa (1861–1869). The province was divided into seven *sancak*s under *kaymakam*s with military as well as administrative powers. A provincial advisory council composed of representatives of the major religious and economic groups was formed (1866). Secular schools were opened for Muslims and Christians alike, health and sanitation facilities were improved, roads built, the cities modernized, and the first railroad opened from Banya Luka to Novi (1872). Commerce and trade developed, though much of the new prosperity benefited Serbian immigrants, who used their situation to encourage agitation against Ottoman rule. But the old timar holders also continued to maintain their power, using various devices to convert their lands into private estates and absorbing what peasant free holdings remained from earlier times. With Bosnia and Herzegovina reasonably quiet, the Ottomans were able to turn their attention to a new danger arising out of Greek ambitions in the Mediterranean.

The Revolt in Crete, 1866–1869

The revolt that broke out in Crete in 1866 was the culmination of four decades of Greek agitation to annex the island. Crete had been in a state of pending revolt since 1821, when its Greek majority massacred their Muslim neighbors in the hope of joining the new Greek kingdom, only to be suppressed by the army of Muhammad Ali and then prevented from union with Greece by Britain for strategic reasons. Sporadic uprisings followed, with the Ottomans turning the island over to the governorship of Muhammad Ali as part of the arrangement by which he also was given Syria (1830–1840). The island then reverted to the Porte, but once the Egyptian troops had gone, the rebels resumed their activities, starting two decades of massacre, suppression, and renewed massacre, which kept the island in turmoil long before the revolt itself actually took place.

When the revolt finally broke out in 1866, it included the whole island and was coordinated and well supplied by Greece. It began on May 14, 1866, when a group of local citizens demanded that the governor lower taxes and make the court system more favorable to them. The governor promised compliance, but correctly fearing that such radical demands were in fact only a pretext for war he sent his soldiers throughout the island to protect its Muslim inhabitants from renewed Greek massacres. The Greeks, however, used this as a pretext for an open rebellion. The Greek press immediately played up what it called Muslim massacres of the Greeks. The word was spread throughout a Europe ready to believe the worst of Muslims. Thousands of Greek volunteers were mobilized and sent to the island, with the Greek government demanding intervention by the powers on behalf of the rebels (August 14). In response the sultan sent two regiments from Istanbul, with additional forces coming from the khedive to show his loyalty.

In the meantime, the international politics of the time favored the Porte in Crete. Napoleon III had been willing to support the rebels to get Russian support against Prussia following the Austro-Prussian war (1866). He even had gone so far as to propose that Thessaly and Epirus be given to Greece along with Crete in return for Russian support in western Europe. But now Russia was busy with internal unrest and with new plans to expand into Central Asia, and it also feared that any enlargement of Greece would help its closest friend, France. Britain and Austria continued to oppose any move that would weaken the Ottomans and thus help Russia. The Porte, therefore, was able to go ahead without fear of foreign intervention in Crete. As soon as its forces had quieted the disturbances, Âli Paşa went to Crete to provide a permanent solution.

Âli wanted to establish a model regime in Crete that would satisfy all of its inhabitants and make them willing to remain under the rule of the sultan, ending their susceptibility to the lures offered from Athens and St. Petersburg. A reformed regime in Crete might well form a basis for similar policies that could contain the remaining Christian provinces of the empire. After declaring an amnesty (October 4, 1867), he summoned a general assembly composed of two Muslim and two Christian delegates from every district on the island, asking them to communicate the complaints of the people and to offer solutions. The island's security system was reorganized and its fortifications strengthened to prevent

Greece from starting a new revolt before a settlement could be reached. Âli sought to conciliate the people by declaring that their taxes would be lightened considerably whatever the assembly proposed. Working closely with the assembly, he drew up a new organization for Crete. By a decree issued on February 14, 1868, the island was divided into two new districts according to population. The districts in turn were divided into *kazas* ruled by *kaymakams*, whose religion generally reflected the majority of its inhabitants. As elsewhere in the empire, representative administrative councils were formed at the vilayet, district, and *kaza* levels, with each including popularly elected Muslim and non-Muslim representatives. The mixed law courts were developed, and the villages were turned over to councils of elders chosen by the people. Christians were not required to serve in the army, nor did they have to pay the conscription tax. The tithes for the previous and subsequent two years were cut in half, and a new cadastre system was introduced so that taxes would be levied thereafter according to the ability to pay. Also, to lower prices on the island the customs duties were reduced.[118]

Execution of the reforms was left to the new governor, Hüseyin Avni Paşa, one of Mustafa Reşit Paşa's last protégés, who subsequently was to become minister of war and a major participant in the events that led to the overthrow of Abdulaziz. Quiet was restored, but the powers were unhappy that the Porte had achieved a settlement without the kind of support that would require gratitude and new concessions in return. Thus when Greece again began to send "volunteers" to the island and appeal for a revolt and Âli reacted with a threat of war (December 1868), the powers intervened to put their imprint on the settlement. Napoleon summoned a new conference, which met in Paris (January 20, 1869) and ordered the Greeks to stop sending "volunteers" and to compensate all Ottoman subjects who had been injured by the revolt it had started. Since the revolt in any case had been suppressed, Greece accepted. Hence the crisis came to an end, with the Ottomans more victorious than they had been or would be in almost any other diplomatic confrontation during the century.

Opening of the Straits

Much of the Ottoman victory was, however, dissipated by the powers. To secure continued Russian support for the League of the Three Emperors and to keep France isolated, Bismarck now supported Russia's longstanding ambition to denounce the Black Sea provisions of the Peace of Paris (1856), securing the agreement of an international conference held in London (January 17, 1871). Russia was allowed to fortify its harbors and build a fleet on the Black Sea once again, and in return for this the Porte was allowed to open the Straits in peacetime to warships sent by its friends if needed to assure enforcement of the other clauses of the Peace of Paris. Âli thus was able to secure a concession in return for his agreement, while the British again transformed a unilateral Russian action against the Porte into an international agreement to be maintained by joint action. Nevertheless, Russia had won a major diplomatic victory, and soon this was to lead to a new and more menacing relationship with the Porte.

Undermining the Tanzimat

The death of Fuat Paşa in 1869 and of Âli two years later presaged a major shift in the political power structure that had dominated Istanbul since 1839. The events that followed threatened to undermine the Tanzimat reform program and led to the deposition of Abdulaziz and his ultimate replacement by Abdulhamit II, the introduction of a constitution, the trial and death of Midhat Paşa, and the establishment of a new era of autocracy that effectively restored the main trends of the Tanzimat program and brought it to culmination.

The Tanzimat was characterized politically by the domination of Porte over palace, established by Reşit and enforced and even extended by Âli and Fuat. Neither of the reigning sultans had been able to challenge the leadership of the Men of the Tanzimat despite their earnest desire to do so. Both functioned as figureheads, signing decrees, meeting foreign dignitaries, and cooperating in leading society toward westernization. Abdulmecit had little choice to do otherwise, but with the death of the Porte's dominant leaders, Abdulaziz had a good opportunity to regain power for the palace. A general Ottoman reaction to Âli's policies in particular helped him. In his later years Âli had, indeed, become the terror of Ottoman politics, striking out against those who violated his concept of the Porte's prerogatives, alienating many supporters of reform.

After Âli's death on September 7, 1871, Abdulaziz began to build his own political group. His principal instrument was Mahmut Nedim Paşa (1817–1876), one of Reşit's protégés, who had fallen from the master's favor and in consequence did not rise rapidly in the bureaucracy. Establishing connections with the palace, he had secured some administrative assignments. He became governor of Damascus (1854–1857) and then of Izmir (1857–1858), served for a short time as Fuat's acting foreign minister when the latter went to the Paris Peace Conference, and then as minister of trade (1858–1859). During most of the decade of domination of the Porte by Âli and Fuat, because of his support of the palace, Nedim was in honorable exile from Istanbul as governor of Tripoli, in Libya (1860–1867), returning finally at the sultan's insistence and with the help of some of the Young Ottomans. In 1867 he became a member of the Supreme Council and then minister of justice (1867) and of the navy (1867–1871), using the sultan's interest in naval affairs to become a close confidant and the latter's chief candidate to replace Âli.[119]

Nedim grasped the opportunity for power, bringing with him into the Porte like-minded politicians, who used the situation to rise to the top, although at the price of allowing power to flow back to the palace. Within a short time Âli's chief supporters were sent into exile. Upon his refusal to increase contributions to the central treasury, Midhat Paşa was dismissed from his governorship at Baghdad. But plans to exile the great provincial reformer failed when Midhat secured an audience with the sultan, leading to Nedim's dismissal and Midhat's first appointment to the grand vezirate (July 31, 1872). Abdulaziz now returned to his father's traditional policy of rapidly changing grand vezirs and ministers to prevent them from building bases of power. He was a reformer, but he wanted to lead reform. Midhat in turn was hardly one to allow anyone, even a sultan, to dominate him; after only two months in office he was replaced by a series of lesser figures, including Mütercim Mehmet Rüşdü Paşa (October 19, 1872–February 15, 1873), Âli's protégé Şirvanizade Mehmet Rüşdü Paşa (April 15, 1873–February 13, 1874), *Serasker* Hüseyin Avni Paşa (February 15, 1874–April 25, 1875) and finally Nedim once again (August 26, 1875–May 11, 1876), with corresponding shifts in the ministries. Meanwhile, the sultan built his personal machine centered at the new Yıldız Palace, high on the hills overlooking the Bosporus.

Reform Efforts, 1871–1876   ~Look over~

The new power group also supported reform, wanting only to change the political balance in its own favor. Nedim introduced a number of major administrative changes, though in most cases they were based on political as much as reform considerations. His first step on assuming the office was to order all the provincial governors to rule with justice and make sure that the advisory councils were freely elected. Soon afterward he remitted an extra tax that had been added to the tithe and excused many cultivators from at least part of their arrears obligations. On December 12, 1875, he promised major reforms in the tax and judicial systems and the improvement of conditions for members of the non-Muslim *millets* to enter government service. On February 21, 1876, he repeated his insistence that elections to the provincial councils be free and called for measures to improve the provincial police and the prisons.[120] He went on to establish a Reduction and Economy Commission (*Tensikat ve Tasarrufat Komisyonu*) to perform the urgently needed task of rationalizing the vast bureaucratic structure built up during the Tanzimat and of eliminating those offices that no longer performed needed functions. While this would help the state budget, it would also serve to root out those who did not support Nedim and his policies.

Nedim also tried to adjust the vilayet provincial system established in 1864, reducing the size of some of the larger provinces to provide greater efficiency, thus taking Sofya from the Danube province, Şebin Karahisar from Trabzon, and Maraş from Adana and making them into separate provinces, and also taking Herzegovina from Bosnia and joining it with Novipazar in a new province. When he found Âli's appointees and the friends of Midhat too entrenched in the Council of State, he used its admitted organizational problems to reorganize it, reducing its membership and the number of its departments from five to three: the Reform Legislation Department (*Tanzimat Dairesi*), which prepared all legislation and agreements with foreign companies, the Interior Department (*Dahiliye Dairesi*), and the Justice Department (*Muhakemat Dairesi*). This plan in fact was prepared by one of the grand vezir's Young Ottoman friends, Namık Kemal, who along with a number of colleagues formerly in exile now accepted an offer to join the service of the state. The new organization effectively rationalized the unwieldy Council of State, but in the process, of course, the membership was replaced by men more willing to accept the will of the palace and the grand vezir. Nedim then went even further, abolishing the council's administrative and judicial functions on the grounds that they duplicated the activities of the relevant ministries and courts, transferring its remaining legal and judicial duties to the *Divan-ı Ahkâm-ı Adliye,* and leaving it only with its legislative functions and the duty to approve all appointments of senior provincial officials below the rank of governor. The council's administrative duties and some of its legislative functions were soon transferred to a new Reform Commission (*Islahat Komisyonu*), which the grand vezir created to supervise all legislation and administration and manned with his own supporters.[121]

Succeeding Nedim, Midhat used his short term as grand vezir to attempt major reforms at the central level. Abolishing the Reduction and Economy Commission and the Reform Commission, he replaced them with a restored Council of State, which retained the Reform Legislation and Interior departments created by Nedim, leaving the *Divan-ı Ahkâm* with judicial duties, and added an Accounting Department (*Muhasebat-ı Umumiye Dairesi*), which took over most of the Reduction and Economy Commission's duties of auditing the accounts and activities of all departments and provinces.[122] Midhat also recalled the exiles, appointing Hüseyin Avni as *serasker* and Ahmet Cevdet as minister of education, and encouraged them to develop reform programs in their own departments. Midhat went on to modernize the collection of tithes, extend education into the provinces, plan an extension of the railroads, systematize the handling of business at the Porte, and further the conversion of the empire to the metric system. He restored the budget cuts that Nedim had made in the provinces and began to undo much of the confusion that had resulted. But when he began to look into corruption on the part of Nedim and his associates, many of whom were close friends of the palace, they were able to convince the sultan to dismiss him.[123] Of Midhat's successors as grand vezir only Hüseyin Avni really tried to resume the reforms, though he devoted most of his attention, and an increasing proportion of the treasury's resources, to the army.

Financial Chaos

Aside from the rapid political shifts, the ever-worsening financial situation undermined reform efforts. The Men of the Tanzimat were not particularly good economists or financial leaders. The development of agriculture and industry had never been pushed with sufficient intensity to provide the state with an adequate tax base to pay for all the reforms. Though the new tax structure had increased revenues, expenditures rose so much that instead of the slight surplus of 170.3 million kuruş, 10 percent of the revenues, which Fuat had projected in the reform budget of 1862–1863, after 1864 there was a chronic deficit, reaching 72.8 million kuruş, or 4.5 percent of the revenue in 1866–1867. The Porte achieved a surplus on paper afterward only by adding domestic and foreign loans, taken at very high rates of interest, so that however much Âli was able to increase revenues (to 1.7 billion kuruş in 1869–1870, over 7 percent more than Fuat's collections in 1866–1867), the proportion of expenditures that the treasury had to devote to paying off the bonded debt rose from 21 percent (313.1 million kuruş) in his first budget to 34 percent (570.7 million kuruş), more than absorbing the revenue increase and leaving little to pay for state expenditures.

The new period of palace power after 1871 only compounded the financial problems. Between 1871 and 1874 there was an overall revenue increase of 20 percent. The difficulty was that expenditures increased even more. This was caused not, as has been claimed, mainly by Abdulaziz's extravagance. He did throw money to the winds, buying new warships and rifles, building palaces, and distributing lavish gifts; but most of the money for this came from his private treasury. The amount devoted to palace expenses by the state treasury, though it increased from 101.3 to 131.5 million kuruş between 1869–1870 and 1874–1875, was a decreasing proportion of the total expenditures, falling from 6 to 5.25 percent during this time. Even expenditures for the Seraskerate went up only slightly, from 379.6 to 415.9 million kuruş while falling from 21.9 to 16.7 percent of the total budgeted revenues. The percent of total revenues spent also on other parts of the regular budget also fell in relative terms. The budget of the Foreign Ministry increased from only 14.3 to 17.5 million kuruş; that of the Ministry of the Interior, which financed most provincial administration, from 179.7 to 284.3 kuruş, or 10.8–11.4 percent of the total. Even though the pension list as such doubled from 32.7 to 64.4 million kuruş, it still comprised only 2.5 percent of the total, hardly sufficient to justify the accusation made by the foreign bondholders and their representatives that these segments were eating up the budget.

The trouble really was caused by the treasury's failure to collect budgeted revenues, which led in turn to increased foreign borrowing at exorbitant rates of interest and discount. Collections were hurt not so much by defects in the system as by Nedim's policy of rapidly changing the governors and his attempts to alter the provincial system and to reduce the gendarmerie. In addition, there were severe agricultural crises, with drought and famine in Anatolia during much of the period between 1872 and 1875 and in Rumeli in 1872 and 1873 – all severely reducing tax collections. The amount of the budget devoted to the bonded debt, therefore, increased from 313.1 million kuruş (18.8 percent budgeted revenues) in 1862–1863 to 570.75 million kuruş (33 percent) in 1869–1870 and to 1.089 billion in 1874–1875, the latter figure being 43.9 percent of all revenues. Continuation of these conditions, combined with the loss of several provinces during the wars of 1875–1877, led to a budget deficit in the financial year 1877–1878 of 974.5 million kuruş, almost 50 percent above the budget revenues, while an additional extraordinary budget of 2.59 billion kuruş, used to support the Ottoman armed forces and to feed and house the millions of Turkish refugees driven into the empire by its enemies, forced the government to suspend temporarily all payments on the external debt, a sum that in the same budget had reached the astronomical figure of 1.7 billion kuruş, only slightly less than the anticipated total state revenues for the whole year![124]

Of course, all the figures quoted were only *anticipated* revenues and *expected* expenditures. When revenues did not live up to expectations, the representatives of the powers made very certain that what money there was went to pay the foreign bondholders. Only what was left was given to the civil servants and army, whose salaries were in as much of a state of arrears as were all the various tax revenues of the state. A faulty system of tax collection, the inability to meet budgeted estimates, and a huge and pressing burden of indebtedness to foreign bondholders, as well as the Ottomans' own financial mismanagement, made foreign fiscal intervention seem inevitable.

Foreign Policy Shifts

The assumption of increased power by the palace after 1871 also led to major changes in Ottoman foreign policy. Âli and Fuat had supported British and French policy and had been helped by their ambassadors in Istanbul in return. Mahmut Nedim, therefore, backed by Abdulaziz, sought to base the new regime on friendship with Russia, which had gained a major diplomatic victory in 1871 by forcing the powers to restore its military position in the Black Sea. Principal agent of Russian policy in the empire was Count Nicholas Ignatiev, ambassador to the Porte from 1864 to 1877. Ignatiev long was involved in promoting Pan-Slavic sentiments among the Porte's remaining Slavic subjects; but he now achieved such an ascendancy and influence over Mahmut Nedim that the grand vezir came to be called "Nedimov" in the streets of the capital while the latter in turn gained the appellation "Sultan Ignatiev."[125]

Internal Discontent

The Tanzimat seemed to founder, the Russians were in ascendancy, the financial crisis had left thousands of civil servants without salaries and thousands more shopkeepers without customers, the countryside suffered from drought and famine, and the Balkan subjects were being stirred up by outside agents. With the sultan seemingly doing nothing to remedy the situation, internal opposition to the regime developed, and ideas on a constitution, Parliament, Ottomanism, and the like, promoted by Midhat and his friends, were discussed in the newspapers and journals. The liberal upsurge was highlighted by a new play written by Namık Kemal, *Fatherland or Silistria (Vatan yahut Silistre)*, produced early in 1873. It opened on April 1 to cheering throngs, with a new emphasis on Ottoman patriotism and the need to work together to save the empire from its enemies. For the first time, people reacted by speaking of the possibility of putting Prince Murat on the throne, leading the authorities to arrest the author and many of his friends and exile them to Cyprus and elsewhere, while closing the play and newspapers that supported the liberal ideas. The exiles, however, continued to propound their ideas and publish their works in one way or another, evading what was a fairly inefficient and vastly overworked censorship department. Namık Kemal and his friends remained in exile until Abdulaziz was dethroned, but their work remained influential.

A different kind of opposition came from the conservatives, led by the ulema. As a result of the financial, judicial, and educational reforms introduced since the Crimean War, they lacked the power to threaten the secularist policies of the Tanzimat, but they did continue to exist, and the conditions after 1871 enabled them to build mass support for the idea that it was the secularization imposed by the Tanzimat, the influence of foreigners, the intrusions of the foreign representatives, the resulting "equality" given to non-Muslims, and the agitation of the latter for increased privileges and even independence that had caused the empire's difficult situation. These feelings, shared in part by many Young Ottomans, generated a new wave of Muslim revivalism. Influential in the revival was Cemalddin al-Afgani, who because of his prestige in Islamic religious circles was brought to Istanbul by Âli and put on the Council of Education created in 1870 in the hope that he would represent religious feeling without actually stirring up and leading the Ottoman ulema. Soon after, he began a series of public lectures at the newly opened university and at the mosques of Aya Sofya and Sultan Ahmet. But Âli really did not know what he was getting into. Al-Afgani's ideas of reviving Islam, using the artifacts of the West to combat the West and uniting the Muslims of the world against the West and its supporters, stimulated such public support for the ulema that Âli asked him to leave, causing him to enter the service of Khedive Ismail in Egypt (1871), where he remained until called back to Istanbul two decades later by Abdulhamit II.

The appeals of al-Afgani struck a particularly vibrant chord in Istanbul because the plight of the Turks of Central Asia in the face of Russia's implacable advance had already stirred public sympathy. A revolt of the Chinese Muslims in Yunnan province in the 1860s, Yakup Bey's establishment of a Muslim state in Turkistan, stories of massacre and suffering inflicted on the Turkish inhabitants of Taşkent, Samarcand, Buhara, and Hiva as they were conquered by the Russians, and the masses of refugees entering the empire as a result of these and other Christian conquests of Muslim territories had turned the attention of the masses to the plight of Turks and Muslims outside the empire. Ali Suavi and others now began to advocate a Turkish national movement, the political and cultural union of all the Turks of the world under Ottoman leadership. This feeling also coalesced with the urgings for union with other Muslims, which had been stimulated by al-Afgani, with the newspaper *Basiret* taking the lead in popularizing the new ideas.

These feelings and movements were taken up and used by the opponents of the

Tanzimat. Some began to emphasize the role of Abdulaziz as caliph of all the Muslims. Others began to think of coalescing the Muslims of British India and Russian Central Asia into a gigantic world movement under Ottoman leadership. These ideas were later taken up and used by Abdulhamit II. The foreign representatives in Istanbul were still strong enough to get the government to suppress them, particularly when the supporters of Pan-Islamism combined their fervor with strong criticism of the reforms. One identifiable aspect of the movement was hostility to foreigners in the empire, including efforts to remove foreign instructors from the schools. The Galata Saray Lycée was partly Turkified. Restrictions were imposed on the activities of the foreign missionaries, many of whom in the course of their proselytizing expressed a hatred of Muslims and of Islam that contributed greatly to the development of hostility among the *millets* in Ottoman society. In 1874 the government prohibited the sale of the Christian scriptures in Ottoman Turkish and put into law the longstanding unofficial restrictions against the conversion of Muslims to Christianity. The Ministry of Education began to restrict foreign schools, particularly those aspects of their curriculums that emphasized Christian superiority and anti-Muslim hatred. For the first time since Selim III foreigners were attacked in the streets. Many Ottomans began to wear more traditional clothing, or at least modified forms of the Western garments worn since the Crimean War. And strong agitation rose to end the Capitulations and the privileged position given not only to foreigners but also to the urban Christian minorities who had attached themselves to their foreign counterparts, strengthening each others' scorn of all things Muslim. These feelings were reinforced by what happened in the Balkans as the Tanzimat lost momentum.

Crisis in Bosnia-Herzegovina

The spark that set off both a domestic and diplomatic crisis came first from Bosnia and Herzegovina, where continued foreign agitation led the Christian peasants into uprisings against the large landowners. Ignatiev's agents were attempting to raise the Slavic Christians not only against the Porte but also against Austria-Hungary. Supporting them were the Hungarian elements in the dual monarchy, led by Prime Minister Count Julius Andrassy. They urged Russian annexation of Bosnia-Herzegovina to prevent Austria from taking over an area that would increase the Slavic population in the empire and thwart Hungarian ambitions. But the emperor himself listened to complaints from Bosnian Slavs and was sympathetic to adding territory to his dominion despite the Hungarian objections.

The revolt began in several small villages in Herzegovina, where the tax farmers had been demanding full payment of the cultivation and sheep taxes despite a bad harvest in 1874. Peasant attacks on the tax collectors led to intervention by the provincial garrisons, with Muslim deaths being ignored as usual while the deaths of many Christian rebels were trumpeted as massacres. Many of the rebels were able to secure arms and ammunition from Montenegro, which they used to raid roads, capture bridges, and attack and massacre Muslim villages (starting July 24, 1877), leading to bloody replies in kind, and the crisis soon escalated. Grand Vezir Ethem Paşa sent negotiators to talk with the rebels, promising to solve all their problems if only they laid down their arms, but the rebels felt they could get better terms by appealing directly to the foreign consuls in the area, complaining in particular of high taxes, forced labor, and the continued feudal attitudes of the great landowners. Within a short time the revolt spread to all parts of Bosnia and

Herzegovina. Arms came mainly from Habsburg territory in Hungary and Dalmatia, since the Russian leaders were too divided on what should be done. Prime Minister Gorchakov opposed Ignatiev's efforts in the fear that they would only upset the European balance and lead to new troubles, while the Pan-Slavs in Russia and certain military elements strongly supported the ambassador. France, still seeking to restore its influence in Europe by supporting national uprisings, began to organize a general European conference to force a settlement that would favor the rebels, and this proposal was accepted in mid-August.

In the meantime, Esat Paşa had been replaced as grand vezir by Nedim, who brought in Hüseyin Avni as minister of war and Midhat Paşa as minister of justice in the hope that a combination of force and reform would end the trouble before it led to international complications (August 26, 1875). To meet the emergency, interest payments on foreign bonds were reduced. The British and French ambassadors agreed to this only on condition that their own bondholders be exempted. When the grand vezir went ahead and cut the interest rates on all bonds to 5.5 percent, the foreign bondholders reacted strongly, adding to the general disfavor in which the Porte was held in Europe as a result of the massacre stories spread earlier in the year. The League of the Three Emperors attempted to prevent a war with the Ottomans by holding a new conference in Berlin and agreeing on the Andrassy Note to the Porte (December 30, 1875), which demanded that the Ottomans abolish tax farming in Bosnia and Herzegovina, provide religious freedom (!), and help the peasants buy their own lands from the lords to reduce the tension that had led to the crisis. The sultan would establish mixed administrative councils in both provinces, including Muslims and Christians, to supervise execution of these reforms. Taxes would be lowered, and the foreign consuls would make sure that the promises would be carried out. With Nedim under Ignatiev's influence, the Porte accepted the proposals (February 13, 1876) even though they involved direct foreign intervention in Ottoman administration. In protest, Midhat Paşa resigned as minister of justice, and was replaced, ominously enough for him as we shall see, by Ahmet Cevdet Paşa.

The Porte was willing to accept the proposed reforms because they were no more than those of the Tanzimat, with only the foreign intervention added. But enforcing them in Bosnia against the hostility of the large landowners and the unwillingness of the rebels to put down their arms unless they received far stronger guarantees from the powers was more than the Porte could handle. Ignatiev in fact undercut the Berlin settlement by sending his agents to the rebel areas and encouraging them to fight on to gain greater concessions. The Ottoman government at first hoped that its acceptance would end the rebellion and that Russia and Austria would also cease their aid to the rebels. Thus it pardoned all those who laid down their arms and returned to their homes, promising them tax exemptions for two years and free lumber to help repair their homes. But when the rebellion continued, the Porte responded with force, sending Ahmet Muhtar Paşa, later to become one of the greatest Ottoman military heroes of the last quarter of the century, who sealed off the borders of the provinces and used force to restore order. Thousands of Christians from the affected provinces began to flood across the border into Serbia, Montenegro, and Austria. In the first two, mass Slavic feelings reacted with demands for open intervention, which were not taken up only because their rulers realized they still lacked sufficient military strength to attack the Ottomans. But their demands for assistance from Russia and Austria invoked the danger of a general war involving half of Europe.

In the face of this crisis the foreign ministers of the League of Three Emperors again met at Berlin (May 13, 1876) and drew up a new reform memorandum elaborating on the earlier Andrassy proposals. There would be an armistice of two months to allow a general cooling off of emotions in the states involved, followed by negotiations between the Porte and the rebels. A more specific reform program was set down, in many cases incorporating what the Porte had already proposed, financial assistance to resettle rebels and refugees and tax and administrative reforms. But the rebels were to be left in possession of their arms, and the foreign consuls were to supervise the implementation of the reforms. The agreement also included stipulations that if the reforms failed and the Ottoman Empire broke up, Austria would take part of Bosnia while Russia would be compensated with southern Bessarabia, and the powers might use force to compel Ottoman acceptance of the demands. France and Italy subsequently supported the agreement. In England, however, Benjamin Disraeli (elected in February 1874) had just purchased the khedive's share of the Suez Company bonds and he refused to join, not so much because of the threat of foreign intervention in Ottoman affairs, but rather because Britain had not been involved in preparing the note.

The Bulgarian Crisis

Just as the Berlin proposals were sent to Istanbul, the crisis was intensified by a new uprising in Bulgaria, where the situation was complicated by the unhappiness of the Orthodox subjects with the Greek Phanariote control of the Bulgarian Orthodox Church since the eighteenth century. The situation of the Bulgarian peasants, Christian and Muslim alike, was no better or worse than that of subjects elsewhere in the empire during the long centuries of decline. As with the Turkish Celalis in Anatolia, the Bulgars had responded with their own bandits, called *hayduts* locally, who had been joined by thousands of discontented rayas as well as Muslim and Christian soldiers deserting from the Ottoman army. Though the powerful notables of the late eighteenth and early nineteenth centuries had been eliminated late in Mahmut II's reign, the bandits continued to raid town and country alike from strongholds in the Rhodope and Balkan mountains. The early Tanzimat reformers divided Bulgaria into the eyalets of Niş (including Sofia), Vidin, and Silistria, with representative provincial and district councils advising the governors and their subordinates. Here as elsewhere in the Balkans, however, the great landowners, called *ağa*s when Muslim and *gospodar*s when Christian, managed to build great estates and continue to misrule the peasants, Muslim and Christian alike. The resulting discontent was frequently fanned into rebellions by agents from Serbia and Wallachia, the worst of which took place in the northwest (1835), at Niş (1841), Ibrail (1841–1842) and Vidin (1850). The Greek Revolution had caused the Ottomans to suspect the loyalty of the Greeks who remained in the empire, enabling Armenians and many Bulgarians to replace the Phanariotes in the mercantile life of the province. Bulgaria grew prosperous by providing grain, honey, and cattle to all parts of the empire as well as supplying textiles for the new armies being built during the Tanzimat. In addition, unlike in Bosnia and Rumania, the landlords here were much more willing to sell land to the peasants, giving rise to a substantial native landholding class that benefited greatly from the new prosperity.

Prosperity, however, does not necessarily breed contentment, and in this case the new wealth soon stimulated movements demanding not only freedom from the Greek church but also national independence. Secret Slavic schools were developed outside the Greek-controlled *millet* schools to stimulate a national uprising. Trade schools established by merchants offered subjects such as history, geography, and mathematics, exposing young men to European political thought as well. National liberation movements followed. Stimulated by the achievement of religious autonomy in Serbia and the Principalities (1845), the first step was a demand for independence from the Greek church. The patriarch's opposition was supported by Russia, which hoped to use him as an instrument for its own influence at the Porte and therefore did not want him weakened in any way. He continued to refuse the Bulgar demands for Slavic priests and bishops but consented to the printing of religious books and secular works in their own language. Insisting on holding services in Bulgarian, the Bulgars finally took over the Orthodox church in the province, drove out the Greek priests, and appointed native priests in their place. The Porte had long supported the patriarch to keep the *millet* in order, but it now gave in to the Bulgars to keep them from joining the Bosnian rebels and issued a decree that recognized a separate Bulgarian Exarchate (1864), with jurisdiction also over those areas of Macedonia in which at least two-thirds of the population voted to join. Thus, Greece, Serbia, and Bulgaria began the territorial contest there that was to go on a half-century.

Through the monumental work of Midhat Paşa, at first in the province of Niş (1861–1863), and then in the Danube province, the Ottomans tried to stem the call of Slavic nationalism in Bulgaria. Midhat attempted to find out and remedy the reasons for the discontent and banditry and to establish security for Muslims and Christians alike. He built roads and bridges, created a new provincial gendarmerie, pardoned back taxes, and prevented immigrants from Serbia and Wallachia from entering to stir up trouble. He made Bulgaria into a model province, building its economy and also including Bulgarians in the advisory councils at all levels. He organized agricultural banks to rescue the peasants from the moneylenders, established steamship lines on the Danube and a postal system, and developed secular schools on all levels, including special schools for orphans and the poor.

It was a remarkable achievement, but far too late. Efficient tax collection only led to new discontent despite the prosperity that resulted from Midhat's work. The Bulgarian Exarchate further stimulated the movement for political as well as religious autonomy, despite the fact that as many as one-third of the Bulgars were Muslims, including the native Slavic Pomaks who had accepted Islam in the sixteenth and seventeenth centuries and lived mainly in the Rhodopes. Adding to the traditional sources of discontent at this time were the thousands of Crimean Tatar and Circassian refugees settled in Bulgaria by the Ottoman government and who, bitter at the Russians who had driven them from their homes, found the Slavic Bulgars convenient foils for their anger. Russia, which had forced the immigration of the Tatars and Circassians in the first place, now took the lead in criticizing the Ottoman government for failing to control them. The Ottomans did what they could, but financial problems prevented the large increases needed in the provincial garrisons and gendarmeries, forcing them to turn to provincial volunteers, the *başıbozuk*s, many of whom were Dobruca tribesmen as well as new immigrants from the Crimea. Little mercy could be expected from them, and the Ottoman government found it very difficult to control the manner in which they treated the rebellious Bulgars.

Despite Midhat's reforms and the general prosperity thereupon, there was continued Bulgarian opposition to the Porte. Most of the native Slavic agitators were sons of well-to-do Bulgars, young men who had been educated in the new Tanzimat schools as well as those of the missionaries. As Midhat suppressed all efforts at revolt, the Bulgarian nationalists fled to Serbia and the Principalities, where they planned their uprising, though often differing on questions such as whether to demand autonomy or independence, what kind of foreign help they should get, and what kind of constitution the new Bulgarian state should have. A series of Bulgarian revolutionary committees was organized to stimulate and lead a mass Bulgarian uprising against the Ottomans, and they waited for the opportune moment. In 1870 the different nationalist groups joined in the new Bulgarian Revolutionary Central Committee and agreed that violence and revolution rather than negotiation should be used to gain independence.

The new group was based mainly in Serbia. It developed very slowly, since it could find very few supporters in Bulgaria other than the Russian consuls in Rusçuk and Filibe and a few intellectuals. An attempt finally was made to begin an incipient uprising in the Balkan Mountains near Filibe and Pazarcık (May 2, 1876). Ignatiev played a double game, stimulating Nedim to suppress the rebels harshly on one hand and to appoint incompetents to handle military and political affairs on the other, thus instigating further revolts that the Ottomans could not suppress. The revolts now spread, leading to the massacre of hundreds of Muslims and the seizure of the main Ottoman forts in the Balkan passes nearby. With the local garrison at Filibe far too small to do anything, the governor had to resort to employing volunteer *başıbozuk* militias, which joined what regular troops there were to defend the Muslim villages and put down the revolt (May 11–June 9, 1876). Some massacre and countermassacre between Muslim and Christian villages followed, with Ottoman regular forces striving to restore order and security for all. But now the forces of European propaganda went to work. While no more than 4,000 Bulgarian Christians had been killed (and considerably more Muslims), the British press trumpeted the charge of "Bulgarian horrors," claiming that thousands of defenseless Christian villagers had been slaughtered by fanatical Muslims. American missionaries estimated that as many as 15,000 Christians had been killed, and the Bulgars leaped ahead to estimates of from 30,000 to 100,000! William Gladstone successfully defeated Disraeli by repudiating the latter's Turkophile policies of the previous two decades, accusing the Muslims in Bulgaria and Bosnia of all kinds of atrocities while ignoring the fact that Muslims also had been slaughtered and that the Ottoman troops were acting to restore order. Public opinion in England was so stirred that it was impossible for Disraeli or anyone else to propose British intervention to save the Ottoman Empire if the Russians now intervened. Adding more fuel to the fire was an incident in Salonica on May 6 when a Bulgarian Christian girl who had converted to Islam was seized by a group of Greeks at the railway station, who tore off her veil and clothes. A Muslim mob came into the streets to avenge the insult. In the melee both the French and German consuls were killed, and while the murderers were immediately hanged, this not only failed to end the din in the European press but also led to new problems in Istanbul.

Revolt of the Softas

All the news that had been coming to Istanbul, of the massacres of helpless Muslim villagers in Bosnia and Bulgaria, of the distortion of events in a European press seemingly thirsty for Muslim blood, and of the diplomatic interventions in favor of the Balkan rebels stirred Muslim passions throughout the empire. Though the Istanbul press was placed under strong censorship, rumors spread that Nedim was planning to bring in Russian troops to keep order. Shopkeepers began to sell weapons to anyone who could pay. Europeans and Christians feared Muslim reprisals, closing their shops and even sending their families on extended vacations to Europe. Ignatiev fortified the Russian embassy. Midhat Paşa, now out of the government, and Hüseyin Avni, former *serasker,* were the heroes of the moment, not only among the liberals but also the ulema and religious students who turned to them to save the empire and their brethren in the Balkans from the Russians.

On May 8, 1876, the students of the religious schools (*softas*) left their classes and joined popular meetings at the main mosques and public squares of Istanbul, denouncing the government for cowardice in the face of large-scale massacres of Muslims and European intervention. Abdulaziz at first tried to appease the demonstrators, replacing the *şeyhulislam* with a reform partisan, Hafız Hayrullah Efendi, but the students were merely encouraged to demand the dismissal of Nedim as well, and this was done on May 12. The sultan still tried to control the situation by appointing his own man, Mütercim Rüştü Paşa, as grand vezir, with Midhat as minister without portfolio and Hüseyin Avni as minister of war. To get popular support the new ministry rejected a recent financial arrangement negotiated with foreign bankers to settle the debt by issuing new low-interest bonds on the grounds that the issuance of new bonds, whatever the interest, would only give profits to the latter, who secured commissions from each bond brought in and sold. The financial crisis remained unresolved, therefore, further disturbing the Porte's relations with the powers at this crucial moment.

The Deposition of Abdulaziz

Abdulaziz's continued desire to hold the reigns of power brought him into conflict with the new ministry. Hüseyin Avni seems to have taken the lead in advocating his deposition in favor of Prince Murat. Midhat, while not opposing the idea, seems also to have tried to persuade the sultan to agree to a constitution to avoid such an eventuality. As head of the army, Hüseyin Avni expected to take the lead in any coup and thus emerge as the leading figure of the new regime, and he secured the help of Süleyman Paşa, head of the *Harbiye* Military Academy and a strong supporter of a constitution and reform. Fear of disclosure led to execution of the plans earlier than planned. Early on the morning of May 30, the Dolmabahçe Palace was surrounded by two battalions commanded by Süleyman Paşa as well as several naval ships off shore. At first Murat refused to leave his apartments, fearing that he was being lured to his own assassination, but he finally agreed to go to the ministry of war and take the throne after receiving written word that the grand vezir awaited him. Murat's agitation continued even when after his accession Abdulaziz was sent off to the Topkapı Palace.

Murat's First Days

Despite his initial nervousness, Murat V at first seemed to live up to the promise of his youth as an intelligent and a forward-looking man. The vast store of valuables found in the Yıldız Palace was turned over to the treasury, balancing the state budget for that year at least. While no public pronouncement regarding a constitution was made, Murat as well as Mehmet Rüştü, still grand vezir, seemed to presage its adoption by mentioning the "will of the people" in speeches referring to the new regime. That Murat was sincerely interested in reform seemed indicated by his initial decree, which ordered major changes in the organization of the Council of State as well as several ministries and also voluntarily ended all treasury contributions to his personal purse, a sum of some 30 million kuruş per year. The *Şeriat* was to be protected, but all subjects were to be free and equal as Ottomans, without distinction as to religion or race, to work together for fatherland, state, and nation. But all was not well with Murat. The events of his accession seemed to have upset him more than appeared at first. Midhat subsequently pointed out that he remained in the palace for two nights after Murat's accession because the new sultan did not wish to be left alone. Adding to the pressure on him was a split among the coalition of ministers who had put him on the throne, with Midhat now producing the draft of a constitution that would provide for an elected Parliament and ministerial responsibility while the grand vezir and Hüseyin Avni pleaded with the sultan to reject the idea for the moment.

In the meantime, Abdulaziz lived on, in good health, with Murat reacting to his ministers' disputes with the fear that the old sultan's supporters might put him back on the throne. Murat's exchange of correspondence with his predecessor only strengthened these fears and led him to transfer Abdulaziz to the Feriye Palace, located in a section of the harem at the Çırağan Palace (June 1, 1876), where he would be close enough to Dolmabahçe to be watched at all times.

But on Sunday, June 4, 1876, Abdulaziz was found dead on the floor of his new apartment, with his veins cut and one artery slashed, apparently the victim of suicide with a small pair of scissors that had been provided to trim his hair and beard. The ministers accompanied grand vezir Mehmet Rüştü to the scene, an investigating committee of 19 eminent doctors, including several attached to the foreign embassies, confirmed the verdict of suicide, and this seemed the end of the matter. It was not long, however, before rumors began to circulate that Abdulaziz had been assassinated, perhaps by Hüseyin Avni and Midhat, to prevent his eventual restoration to the throne. But whatever the cause of Abdulaziz's death, the event was disastrous for Murat. Already distraught by the events that had led to his accession, his condition grew worse.[126]

The Çerkes Hasan Incident

Ottoman politics soon were disturbed by another violent incident that increased the sultan's fears and broodings. On June 15, 1876, Çerkes Hasan, brother of Abdulaziz's second wife and a member of Prince Yusuf Izzeddin's personal staff, broke into a ministerial meeting at Midhat's house and killed both Hüseyin Avni and Foreign Minister Raşit Paşa, wounding several others as well, apparently because of some personal affront administered to him previously by the *serasker* as well as to gain revenge for what he considered the latter's role in Abdulaziz's death. Çerkes Hasan soon was tried, convicted, and hung (June 18, 1876), but the rumor then spread to the conservatives that the whole incident had been arranged by Midhat to remove the only minister strong enough to prevent him from dominating the cabinet and securing approval for the Constitution.

Approach to Constitution

Despite the clamor that followed Hüseyin Avni's death, Midhat pushed the cabinet toward open support of the Constitution that was being prepared. Midhat's Young Ottoman friends, recalled from exile, helped generate and sustain public interest in constitutionalism. Ziya Bey was appointed as undersecretary of education. Namık Kemal and his colleagues began to publish freely, attacking the conservatives and defending parliamentarianism. With the encouragement of the British ambassador, Midhat worked not only in the cabinet but also with the ulema leaders, getting their agreement for a representative council on the central level, more or less like the Council of State and even including Christians, but only to control the government's financial policies and help balance the budget.[127]

The First Balkan Crisis

These efforts were temporarily frustrated by the international crisis, intensified by allegations by the European press of large-scale massacres in Bulgaria. The wild reports inflamed not only the British and the French but also the masses of Serbia, who felt close to their Bulgarian brothers. At first Prince Milan hoped to avoid war, but under Russian pressure he signed an alliance with Montenegro (May 26) and then secretly declared war on the Porte (May 30), with his ally following suit. Aside from a few border clashes, however, things remained quiet. By June 9 the grand vezir was able to inform Milan of the suppression of the Bulgarian revolts and promise that all rights would be respected. But Milan sent an ultimatum regarding Bosnia and Herzegovina, claiming that the Ottoman suppression there had hurt Serbia's trade and economic interests as well as national pride. He demanded that he be appointed its governor so that Serbian troops could occupy the province and restore order, and that Herzegovina be turned over to Montenegro at the same time! As might be expected, the Ottomans refused to comply. On July 2 Milan proclaimed war publicly, and Nicholas followed suit the next day on the pretext that Ottoman troops in Herzegovina had violated his southern boundary in pursuing rebels. Thus began the first Balkan crisis. The war declarations forced Russia and Austria to coordinate their reactions and ambitions at Reichstadt (July 8), in southern Bohemia. The agreement provided that they would stay out of the conflict for the moment. But if the Ottomans defeated the Serbs and Montenegrans, they would step in to assure that the sultan would not benefit but would instead give Montenegro independence while establishing Bosnia and Herzegovina in the manner envisaged by the earlier Berlin memorandum. The texts differed on what would happen if the Ottomans lost. The Austrian version stated it would get Bosnia and Herzegovina in return for Russian gains in Bessarabia and northeastern Anatolia and Serbia's acquisitions would be limited to Novipazar and Old Serbia, while the Russian version provided parts of Bosnia and Herzegovina for Serbia and Montenegro, with the Habsburgs getting only Ottoman Croatia and parts of Bosnia near the Austrian border to balance the Russian gains.

Russian public opinion was wildly enthused by the actions of Serbia and Montenegro, but since the czar was not yet willing to intervene openly, sympathy was all the Pan-Slavs could give, though hundreds of Russian volunteers went to Serbia and a Russian general, Chernayev, was appointed commander of the Serbian army. But the Balkan alliance already had broken down. King Carol of the United Principalities stayed out, not wishing to help any of his neighbors to expand, though he tried to use the crisis to increase his influence in Istanbul, demanding that his nation now be called Rumania and that he be allowed to station his own commissioner in Istanbul to represent him with the Porte and the foreign ambassadors. Greece also remained neutral though it used the situation to get the Greeks of Crete to refuse to cooperate in the elections then being held for the administrative councils, in the hope that the Porte would be forced to grant them representation in proportion to their numbers rather than mere equality with the Muslims. Serbia was not ready for a war, particularly against an Ottoman army that had been built up and given modern rifles and cannon during Abdulaziz's later years. Milan also chose to divide what forces he had, hoping to join with the Montenegrans in the conquest of Bosnia while resisting Ottoman forces entering Serbia from Bulgaria and Macedonia. But this so reduced the forces led by Chernayev that the Ottomans were able to destroy them in a week-long battle at Alexinatz (August 19–24, 1876), though they did not follow up the victory because of fear of foreign intervention. The Montenegrans had been relatively successful along the Bosnian border against the Ottoman garrisons commanded by Ahmet Muhtar Paşa, but with the Serbian defeat they soon withdrew, and so the crisis eased.

The Deposition of Murat V

In Istanbul, Midhat still was working on his draft constitution, but the popular passions against Europe required his immediate attention. The arrival of reinforcements from Egypt and Tunisia created a frenzied religious atmosphere in the capital. Meanwhile, the temporary loss of revenues from Bosnia and Bulgaria – when combined with the cost of the new mobilization and the flood of refugees from the rebellious provinces – made it impossible for the government to even attempt to pay the interest on the bonds; therefore, in July Mehmet Rüştü suspended all debt payments, causing a tremendous reaction in European banking circles. In desperation the grand vezir appealed to the subjects for voluntary tax payments and loans, which in many places were in fact required regardless of ability to pay. New paper money was printed without any real backing. It soon began to depreciate, dragging the entire Ottoman financial system down with it. With thousands of men in the army, many crops were left unharvested in the fields, further hurting the financial situation as well as causing famine and distress around the empire.

Strong leadership was needed to face internal and external crisis, but Murat V's condition showed no sign of improvement. A Viennese doctor who had once treated Queen Victoria visited Istanbul on August 10 and was invited by the government to examine the sultan, whom he reported was depressed and nervous but able to recover if only he abstained from drinking and tried to rest. But Murat still was head of state. His signature was required to validate laws and decrees, diplomatic agreements, and other major decisions. It was difficult for the government to function without him. Suggestions now were put forward that Prince Abdulhamit take the throne, or at least accept a regency in place of Murat. There was no Ottoman precedent for a regency, however, and Abdulhamit insisted that he would agree to rule only after a medical examination certified that Murat was incurable. Abdulhamit seems to have been quite ready to gain the throne. He was an intelligent and ambitious prince, well read, conversant with liberal ideas, and convinced that he could save the empire. To get Midhat's support he met with him outside the palace, at a private mansion, and promised that if he was made sultan, he would approve the Constitution, act only with the advice of his ministers, and appoint their men as palace secretaries. Midhat accepted, since he saw in the new arrangement the promise of a parliamentary regime.

So it was that on August 31 the cabinet decided to depose Murat. The *şeyhulislam* issued a *fetva* justifying the act on grounds of insanity, which was supported by a medical statement signed by several Istanbul physicians declaring that it was unlikely that Murat could ever recover. The next day all the notables assembled in the Imperial Council rooms of the Topkapı Palace. Murat was deposed, and all swore loyalty to Abdulhamit II as the new sultan. Murat then went off to live in the Çırağan Palace. His mental condition improved as soon as the cares of state were removed, leading him to dabble somewhat in politics and engage in several unsuccessful efforts to regain his throne until he died of natural causes on August 29, 1904. The unstable Murat thus was succeeded by the man who was to dominate Ottoman life for the next 33 years.

Notes to Chapter 2

1 Lütfi, VI, 41–42.

2 Kaynar, p. 100.

3 Ercüment Kuran, "Reşit Paşa," IA, X, 701–705.

4 Lütfi, VI, 60, 64–65.

5 The original Ottoman text, now found in the Treasure Room of the BVA in Istanbul, was published in TV 187 (15 Ramazan 1255). A facsimile can be found in *Tanzimat*, Istanbul, 1940, I, opposite p. 48. Copies are in *Düstur*[1], I, 4–7, and Lütfi, VI, 61–64. Transcriptions to Latin letters are in Kaynar, pp. 172–173, Karal, OT, V, 263–266, and *Mufassal Osmanlı Tarihi*, V, 2182–2185. The official French translation is reproduced by A. Ubicini, *Lettres sur la Turquie*, 2nd ed., Paris, 1853, I, 527–530; Young, *Corps de droit Ottoman*, Oxford, 1905–1906, I, 29–35; Engelhardt, *La Turquie et le Tanzimat*, 2 vols., Paris, 1882–1884, I, 257–261. A contemporary, but only partial, English translation appears in F. E. Bailey, *British Policy and the Turkish Reform Movement*, Cambridge, Mass., 1942, pp. 277–279; Hurewitz, *Diplomacy*[2], I, pp. 269–271 (translation by Halil Inalcık). The translation here is our own.

6 Davison, pp. 83–93.

7 The name was changed from *sadr-ı azam* to prime minister (*baş vekil*) by Mahmut II in 1838, restored to grand vezir in 1839, remained that way through the Tanzimat period, was changed to prime minister and back again in 1883. For a list of the Tanzimat grand vezirs, see pp. 438–440.

8 *Dahiliye Nezaretinin vezaif-i esasiyesini havi kararname* (Decision on the basic duties of the Ministry of the Interior), 16 Zilkade 1285/February 28, 1869, Istanbul University Library 83306.

9 BVA, Bab-ı Asafi section, Dossier collection, file 60 no. 116; BVA, Irade/Meclis-i Mahsus 3169.

10 TV 191 (17 Zilkade 1255); BVA, Maliyeden Müdevvere 8999, pp. 38, 40.

11 BVA, Maliyeden Müdevvere 8999, fol. 54–55.

12 BVA, Bab-ı Asafi, Teşkilât-ı Devair 16/6; Meclis-i Tanzimat, I, 72–73; Irade/Meclis-i Vâlâ 53, 12 Cemazi I 1275.

13 BVA, Bab-ı Asafi, Teşkilat-ı Devair 16/19.

14 Maliye Nezareti, *Ihsaiyat-ı Maliye. Varidat ve Masarif-i Umumiyeyi Muhtevidir*, vol. I (1325/1909–1910), Istanbul, 1327/1911–1912, pp. 4–6; TV 566 (26 Rebi II 1275/1858), 567 (18 Cemazi II 1275/1859); BVA, Irade, Meclis-ı Vâlâ 1788.

15 BVA, Mesail-i Mühimme 10, Irade dated 8 Rebi II 1256/1840; Irade, Meclis-i Mahsus 1588, *nizamname* dated 26 Zilkade 1286/February 27, 1870; Teşkilat-ı Devair 11/25; TV 173 (28 Şaban 1254), 176 (21 Zilkade 1254), 180 (6 Rebi II 1255), 237 (26 Zilhicce 1257), 282 (4 Rebi I 1261), 302 (14 Cemazi II 1262), 405 (14 Cemazi II 1265), 426 (8 Şaban 1266), 167 (14 Rebi II 1254), 170 (13 Cemazi II 1254), 192 (26 Zilkade 1255).

16 BVA, Teşkilat-ı Devair 19/1, 25/2, 19/2, *irades* of 3 Zilkade 1283, 5 Zilkade 1283, and 11 Zilkade 1283.

17 This discussion is based primarily on S. J. Shaw, "The Central Legislative Councils in the Nineteenth Century Ottoman Reform Movement Before 1876," IJMES, 1 (1970), 51–84.

18 BVA, Meclis-i Tanzimat, I, 4–6; TV, 519.

19 Shaw, "Ottoman Legislative Councils," pp. 54–63.

20 September 26, 1854. BVA, Irade, Meclis-i Mahsus 79; Meclis-i Tanzimat, I, 1–3, 6–10; TV 519 (14 Cemazi I 1271).

21 Shaw, "Ottoman Legislative Councils," pp. 63–69.

22 Shaw, "Ottoman Legislative Councils," pp. 69–73.

23 April 2, 1868; BVA, Teşkilat-ı Devair/Meclis-i Mahsus no. 11; Lütfi, XI, 176–178; *Düstur*[1], I, 703–706; TV 963; Young, I, 3–5; *Levant Herald,* May 8, 1868.

24 Shaw, "Ottoman Legislative Councils," pp. 73–84; BVA, Teşkilat-ı Devair 1/25; Lütfi, XIV, 29a–b.

25 TV 1490 (22 Rebi I 1289), 22 (15 Zilkade 1247), 103 (15 Safar 1251), 116 (12 Recep 1251), 197 (12 Safar 1256), 297 (18 Safar 1262), 343 (3 Şaban 1263), 360 (5 Muharrem 1264), 751 (end of Zilhicce 1280), 795 (28 Zilkade 1281), 798 (5 Zilhicce 1281), 845 (2 Muharrem 1283).

26 TV 427, 690, 691, 692, 884, 885, 886, 887.

27 TV 191 (17 Zilhicce 1255), 193 (13 Zilhicce 1255); Lütfi, VI, 152–156; Kaynar, pp. 226–254.

28 Kaynar, pp. 254–258; Lütfi, VI, 93; BVA, Mesail-i Mühimme 2, 23 Şevval 1255.

29 Shaw, "Origins of Representative Government," pp. 53–142; BVA, Irade Dahiliye 356 (29 Cemazi I 1256); Cevdet Dahiliye 14547, 12226, 4893.

30 Shaw, "Origins of Representative Government," p. 53.

31 Istanbul University Library, TY 8975/b.

32 BVA, Maliyeden Müdevvere 9061, pp. 35–42; Lütfi, VII, 35, 52; TV 238, 240; Inalcık, "Tanzimatın uygulanması," p. 638; BVA, Irade Dahiliye 2710.

33 September 22, 1858; BVA, Cevdet Dahiliye 2299; TV 566–574, 576, 578, 618; BVA, Irade Meclis-i Mahsus 2371.

34 *Düstur*[1], I, 201; Aristarchi, I, 170; Young, VI, 93–100; BVA, Irade Dahiliye 3507.

35 BVA, Irade Meclis-i Mahsus 886, 4976.

36 TV 576, 578.

37 Ezel Kural Shaw, "Midhat Pasha, Reformer or Revolutionary?" unpublished Ph.D. dissertation, Harvard University, Cambridge, Mass., 1975, pp. 77–95; *Düstur*[1], I, 608–624; TV 773; Aristarchi, II, 273–295; Young, I, 36–45; Testa, VII, 484–493; Davison, pp. 146–151.

38 BVA, Name-i Hümayun, XI, 361; Lütfi, II, 173, III, 165; Ergin, *Belediye,* I, 338–354, 978–980; BVA, Mesail-i Mühimme 167 (27 Safar 1264), 177/1–2 (9 Şaban 1274); Irade, Meclis-i Vala 1544; Şerafettin Turan, "Osmanlı teşkilatında hassa mimarlar," *Tarih Araştırmaları Dergisi,* I/1 (1963), p. 178; Cengiz Orhonlu, "Mesleki bir teşekkül olarak kaldırımcılık ve Osmanlı şehir yolları hakkında bazı düşünceler," *Güney-doğu Avrupa Araştırmaları Dergisi,* 1, 93–138.

39 TV 536 (Muharrem 1267); *Boğaziçi, Şirket-i Hayriye, Tarihçe, Salname,* Istanbul, 1330/1912, pp. 2–8.

40 Ergin, *Belediye,* I, 1376–1403. November 1855.

41 Ergin, *Belediye,* I, 1403–1456.

42 Ergin, *Belediye,* I, 1403, 1415–1423; Aristarchi, III, 63; Young, VI, 149–151; Lütfi, IX, 151–152; *Düstur*[1], II, 460–462; BVA, Meclis-i Tanzimat, I, 39–42, 52–59 (11 Cemazi II 1274).

43 BVA, Meclis-i Mahsus 886.

44 BVA, Meclis-i Vâlâ 23276.

45 BVA, Meclis-i Tanzimat, II, 183–190; *Levant Herald,* 25 Cemazi II 1285; TV 1008, 1009; Young, VI, 149–150.

46 Lütfi, XIV, 45; BVA, Meclis-i Mahsus 8695.

47 TV 1218 (28 Muharrem 1287/May 1, 1870).

48 TV 1327 (5 Zilhicce 1287/February 26, 1871) ; TV 1510 (16 Cemazi II 1289).

49 TV 1436 (20 Ramazan 1288), 1576 (10 Rebi I 1290).

50 TV 1716 (12 Safar 1292/March 20, 1875).

51 September 23, 1293; BVA, Meclis-i Tanzimat, V, 28–38; *Düstur*¹, IV, 520–522; Young, VI, 151–155; BVA, Yıldız Palace Archives, K37 Z47 Kutu 112, no. 302; Ergin, *Belediye*, I, 1457–1555.

52 BVA, Meclis-i Tanzimat, V, 39–51; Irade Meclis-i Mahsus 1402; Young, I, 69–84; *Düstur*¹, IV, 528–570.

53 29 Şevval 1287, BVA, Meclis-i Tanzimat, III, 14–38; Young, I, 47–69; *Düstur*¹, I, 625.

54 27 Ramazan 1294; BVA, Meclis-i Tanzimat, V, 39–51; Irade, Meclis-i Mahsus 480; *Düstur*¹, IV, 528; Ergin, *Belediye*, 1556; Lewis, "Baladiyya," EI², I, 972–975.

55 This discussion is a summary of S. J. Shaw, "Ottoman Tax Reforms," pp. 421–459.

56 BVA, Kanun-u Kalemiye, Muhtelif 38, pp. 1–5.

57 BVA, Buyuruldu IV, 40 (Cemazi I 1262).

58 BVA, Cevdet Maliye 10658; Irade, Meclis-i Vâlâ 5609; Meclis-i Vâlâ, 7366; Irade, Dahiliye 13563.

59 BVA, Kanun-u Kalemiye, Muhtelif 38, pp. 5–8, 97; Irade, Meclis-i Vâlâ 19710.

60 BVA, Irade, Meclis-i Vâlâ 9828, 13897; Meclis-i Mahsus 232.

61 BVA, Irade, Meclis-i Mahsus 532.

62 Young, VI, 93–100; *Düstur*¹, I, 200–208; BVA, Irade, Meclis-i Mahsus 886. On the budget system introduced by Fuat, see Shaw, "Ottoman Tax Reforms," pp. 449–451.

63 BVA, Irade, Meclis-i Mahsus 910.

64 BVA, Irade, Meclis-i Mahsus 2606; *Düstur*¹, IV, 810–812; Young, VI, 120–123.

65 BVA, Irade, Dahiliye 31455; Meclis-i Mahsus 1270.

66 *Düstur*¹, II, 41; BVA, Meclis-i Tanzimat I, 48, VII, 132–144.

67 BVA, Irade, Meclis-i Vâlâ 13897; Meclis-i Mahsus 1190.

68 *Düstur*¹, II, 41, 49, IV, 804; BVA, Meclis-i Mahsus 2554, 3077.

69 BVA, Irade, Dahiliye 45606; Meclis-i Mahsus 1663; Dahiliye 47558; Kanunname-i Askeri, IV, 10, 17, 46.

70 BVA, Meclis-i Mahsus 3669; Young, II, 396–402.

71 *Düstur*¹, IV, 407; *Ihsaiyat-ı Maliye* I 45–46.

72 BVA, Meclis-i Mahsus 4063.

73 BVA, Irade, Meclis-i Vâlâ 35822 (18 Safar 1284).

74 18 Cemazi II 1286; BVA, Irade, Meclis-i Vâlâ 25822; Meclis-i Tanzimat, I, 247.

75 BVA, Nizamat, IV, 55; Irade, Meclis-i Mahsus 4706, 4795.

76 BVA, Meclis-i Tanzimat, III, 14; Irade, Meclis-i Vâlâ 13.

77 *Düstur*¹, III, 318; BVA, Irade, Meclis-i Mahsus 1517.

78 *Düstur*¹, V, 886, 971; BVA, Nizamat, II, 323; Young, VI, 17; BVA, Meclis-i Mahsus 3927. For separate regulations on rock quarries, dated 24 Rebi I 1305, see BVA, Nizamat, II, 29, and *Düstur*¹, V, 971; also Meclis-i Mahsus 4022.

79 BVA, Buyuruldu, II, 144.

80 BVA, Irade, Dahiliye 5210.

81 BVA, Irade, Dahiliye 4; Meclis-i Vâlâ 15679, 15247.

82 21 Rebi II 1259. BVA, Irade, Meclis-i Vâlâ 56981.

83 BVA, Irade, Meclis-i Mahsus 5087.

84 *Düstur*¹, II, 565; BVA, Meclis-i Mahsus 946.

85 BVA, Irade, Meclis-i Vâlâ 5378.

86 8 Zilkade 1278; BVA, Buyuruldu, III, 179–181.

87 *Düstur*¹, II, 712; BVA, Meclis-i Mahsus 37.

88 21 Cemazi II 1278/November 24, 1861. BVA, Irade, Meclis-i Mahsus 1045.

89 BVA, Irade, Meclis-i Mahsus 1206; Meclis-i Vâlâ 22148; Meclis-i Tanzimat, II, 286–287, III, 6–7.

90 BVA, Irade, Meclis-i Mahsus, 1081, 1219.

91 BVA, Irade, Meclis-i Vâlâ, 812, 74; Şurayı Devlet, 108.

92 For detailed figures on the various state revenues and the budgetary situation in the nineteenth century, see Shaw, "Ottoman Tax Reforms," pp. 451–459.

93 *Salname-i Devlet-i Aliye*, Istanbul, 1268/1852.

94 BVA, Meclis-i Vâlâ 17787/2; Meclis-i Tanzimat, I, 70–72.

95 TV 453, 449; Berkes, pp. 177–178; Fatma Aliye, *Cevdet*, pp. 60–68.

96 Faik Reşit Unat, *Türkiye Eğitim Sisteminin Gelişmesine Tarihi Bir Bakış*, Ankara, 1964, pp. 49–57.

97 BVA, Meclis-i Tanzimat, II, 221–245; TV, 1125–1129; *Düstur*[1], II, 184–185; Young, II, 355–373; Aristarchi, III, 277–278; "Maarif Nezaretinin Tarihçesi," *Salname-i Nezaret-i Maarif*, Istanbul, 1316/1898–1899, pp. 16–32; Faik Reşit Unat, *Türkiye Eğitim Sisteminin Gelişmesine Tarihi Bir Bakış*, Ankara, 1964, pp. 92–119.

98 The figures for 1858 and 1867 are from the official government yearbooks, *Salname-i Devlet-i Aliye* for those years. Those for 1895 are from the official statistical presentation, *Istatistik-i Umumi*, pp. 13, 18, 53–87.

99 *Istatistik-i Umumi*, pp. 53–87; BVA, Irade, Dahiliye 3087.

100 *Istatistik-i Umumi*, p. 27; BVA, Irade, Meclis-i Vâlâ 367.

101 The figures for 1831 come from E. Z. Karal, *Osmanlı Imparatorluğunda Ilk Nüfus Sayımı, 1831*, Ankara, 1943; those from the 1843 conscription census are in Ahmet Cevat, *Tarih-i Askeri-i Osmani*, vol. III, MS TY 4178, Istanbul University Library, pp. 33–34. The complete 1882 census is in the Istanbul University Library, TY 4807. The 1895 census is in *Istatistik-i Umumi*, pp. 1–21; the complete 1906 census is in MS TY 947, Istanbul University Library; figures are adjusted from the later census to account for lost provinces and shifted territories.

102 *Düstur*[1], I, 11; Young, I, 29–33; Hurewitz, *Diplomacy*,[2] II, 315–318; the translation is our own.

103 Hıfzı Veldet, "Kanunlaştırma Hareketleri ve Tanzimat," *Tanzimat*, pp. 139–209; Ebül'ulâ Mardin, "The Development of the Sharî'a under the Ottoman Empire," S. S. Onar, "The Majalla," and H. J. Liebesny, "The Development of Western Judicial Privileges," in *Law in the Middle East*, M. Khadduri and H. J. Liebesny (eds.), vol. I, *Origin and Development of Islamic Law*, Washington, D.C., 1955, pp. 279–333.

104 TV, 579; BVA, Meclis-i Vâlâ 16565: Ottoman Ministry of Foreign Affairs archives, BVA, dossier 1258; FO 78/1254, no. 12, 24; FO 78/1255, nos. 76, 77, 102, 110; FO 78/1258, no. 264; FO 78/1634; Aziz Akıncan, *Türkiyede Posta ve Telgrafçılık*, Edirne, 1913; Young, IV, 345; Şekip Eskin, *Posta, Telgraf ve Telefon Tarihi*, Ankara, 1942.

105 Young, IV, 245–253; *Düstur*[1], II, 310; BVA, Irade, Dahiliye 3162.

106 Farley, *Modern Turkey*, 1st ed., London, 1866, pp. 140–191, 2nd ed., 1872, pp. 272–296.

107 *93 Senesi martı ibtidasından nihayetine değin bir sene zarfında memalik-i mahruse-i şahane mahsulat-ı arziye ve sinaiyesinden diyar-ı ecnebiyeye giden ve bilcümle diyar-ı ecnebiyeden memalik-i mahruse-i Şahaneye gelen eşyanın cins ve mikdarını mübeyyin tanzim olunan istatistik defterlerinin hulasa-ı al-hulasa cedvelidir*, Istanbul, 1294/1877.

108 English tr. from U.S. Congress, spec. sess. (March 1881), Senate Exec. Doc. III/3; see also Young, II, 3–9; Aristarchi, II, 14–22; Hurewitz, I, 149–153; *Düstur*[1], I, 7–14.

109 Davison, pp. 114–126; Young, II, 79–92; *Düstur*[1], II, 938–961; L. Arpee, *The Armenian Awakening: A History of the Armenian Church, 1820–1860*, Chicago, 1909.

110 *Düstur*[1], III, 902–961; Davison, pp. 126–129; Young, II, 21–34; BVA, Irade Dahiliye 1403.

111 Davison, pp. 129–131; Young II, 144–155; *Düstur*[1], II, 962–975; BVA, Irade, Şurayi Devlet 507.

112 Jale Baysal, *Müteferrika'dan Birinci Meşrutiyete kadar Osmanlı Türklerinin Bastıkları Kitaplar*, Istanbul, 1968.

113 Davison, pp. 176–182.

114 Şerif Mardin, *The Genesis of Young Ottoman Thought*, Princeton, 1962.

115 *Muahedat Mecmuası*, IV, 242–244.
116 *Salname-i Bosna*, 1287/1870, pp. 44–45.
117 Cevdet "Maruzat," TTEM, no. 2 (79), p. 107.
118 BVA, Girid Mesalihi dosyası, Irade no. 279.
119 Inal, *Son Sadrazamlar*, I, 259–314. Pakalın, *Son Sadrazamlar*, I, 1–188; Ali Fuat (Türkgeldi), *Rical-i mühimme-i siyasiye*, Istanbul, 1928, pp. 1529–1555.
120 Davison, pp. 314–315.
121 TV 1497 (11 Rebi II 1289/June 18, 1872); BVA, Teşkilat-i Devair 10/22, 8 Rebi II 1289/June 15, 1872.
122 BVA, Teşkilat-i Devair 19/25, 4 Cemazi II 1289/9 August 1872; *La Turquie*, August 5, 11, 1872; Pakalın, *Son Sadrazamlar*, p. 217; Lütfi, XIV, 29a–b; Shaw, "Ottoman Legislative Councils," pp. 83–84.
123 Davison, pp. 287–289; Midhat, *Tabsira-ı Ibret*, pp. 134–137; Mahmut Celaluddin, *Mirat-ı Hakikat*, I, 37–38.
124 These figures have been secured from the budgets cited in S. J. Shaw, "Ottoman Tax Reforms" pp. 449–450.
125 Davison, p. 283.
126 Davison, pp. 317–346; Mahmut Celaluddin, *Mirat ul-Hakikat*, I, 96–106; Haluk Şehsuvaroğlu, *Sultan Aziz, Hayatı, Hal'i, Ölümü*, Istanbul, n.d., pp. 86–205; I. H. Uzunçarşılı, *Yıldız*.
127 Davison, pp. 346–349; *Levant Herald*, July 17, 1876.

3

Culmination of the Tanzimat: The Reign of Abdulhamit II, 1876-1909

Abdulhamit II came to the throne at the youthful age of 34, having been born to one of Abdulmecit's concubines, Tirimüjgân Kadın, soon after his father's accession, on September 21, 1842. During his years as prince, he seems to have distinguished himself among his brothers by avoiding the new style European frivolity that was entering the palace under his father's influence, avoiding extravagance to the point of parsimony. He also spent a great deal of time outside his apartments in the Dolmabahçe Palace at a summer house on the Bosporus above Tarabya, a small pleasure palace at Kâgıthane, on the Golden Horn, at his mother's house in Maçka, in the country outside Beyoğlu, and in the palace of his sister, using the opportunity to contact Ottomans of all ranks and some foreigners, discussing with them the problems of the empire and how they could be resolved. Particularly close to him in these early days were an Englishman named Thompson, who owned a farm next to his at Tarabya, and two lesser Tanzimat bureaucrats, Ibrahim Ethem Efendi and Mehmet Esat Saffet Efendi, most famous of the nineteenth-century ministers of education, both of whom subsequently served him for a time as grand vezirs. His personal finances were handled by a well-known Armenian Galata banker, Hagop Zarifi Bey, from whom he gained a knowledge of finance and economics that was to serve him well in later times. The young prince was thus a sincere though somewhat dour and persistent young man who was determined to prepare himself as best he could for the task of rescuing the empire.

The International Crisis

The beginnings of his reign were hardly propitious. Prince Milan responded to the disaster at Alexinatz, which had occurred only a week before Abdulhamit's accession, with peace proposals. However, Ignatiev's agents in Belgrade stirred up a new war fever despite the fact that back in St. Petersburg the czar and most of his ministers by this time had rejected the idea of spreading Russian influence through Serbia, advocating instead a large and independent Bulgaria, which would be created at the expense of Serbian ambitions in the south and would serve as the keystone of Russian power in the area. The ambassadors in Istanbul advised the Porte to be cautious and to accept Milan's overture, but the Ottoman reply, delayed by the events of the new accession, stated that the Serbs were using Ottoman restraint to rearm and that the powers would have to guarantee the empire against a renewed attack before it would agree to peace. Despite the Pan-Slavic agitation, Milan went on to offer loyalty to the new sultan, to allow Ottoman forces to occupy four main forts in the country, at Belgrade, Böğürdelen, Semendria, and Feth ul-Islam, to disband the Serbian national militia and return the Bulgarian nationalists who had fled to Serbian territory, and to increase the tribute to compensate the Porte for the damages caused by the war. Finally, Milan offered to complete the Belgrade – Niş portion of the Rumeli Railroad, which would allow the Ottomans to have direct rail communications with Europe, an ambition long frustrated by the Serbs. The powers supported all Milan's proposals except those concerning the limitation on his armed forces and establishment of Ottoman garrisons on his territory. Britain wished to add provisions to force the Porte to grant autonomy to Bosnia and Herzegovina and promise major reforms in Bulgaria, but these finally were excluded in order not to delay resolution of the immediate crisis.

But while the Russian ambassador in Istanbul accepted the new proposals, Chernayev, still head of the Serbian army, and the Pan-Slavs in Belgrade forced Milan to reject them. The Serbs attacked the Ottoman positions at Alexinatz twice (September 22/23 and September 28) and were routed, with many of the Russian officers losing their lives. Milan mobilized every able-bodied man he could find in Belgrade and set out for the front at the head of a ragged brigade. In Istanbul, Ignatiev intervened, threatening a Russian attack unless the Serbs were left alone. The ultimatum prevailed; the Ottoman army was called back from Serbia (November 3, 1876); and the provincial levies and militia were sent home to reduce the tremendous financial burden.

The possibility of Russian intervention threatened a war with Austria, which had its own ambitions in the western Balkans. Such an event would destroy the League of the Three Emperors, which Bismarck had maintained to counter French revanchist ambitions in Europe. To rescue the European balance of power that he had established, Bismarck therefore proposed a division of the Ottoman Empire in a way that would satisfy both Austria and Russia. The former would acquire Bosnia and Herzegovina, the latter not only southern Bessarabia but also some kind of domination over Rumania and Bulgaria. France would be compensated with Syria and Britain with Egypt and some of the Mediterranean islands. Disraeli, however, while limited in his ability to support Ottoman integrity because of Gladstone's "Bulgarian horrors" campaign, worked to frustrate this solution to avoid the increase in Austrian and Russian power that it would have brought regardless of any compensation to Britain and France. Finally, when the Ottoman push into Serbia threatened Russian intervention and a war with Austria, Bismarck backed down and accepted a proposal of the British for an international conference at Istanbul to settle the matter (November 4, 1876).

The Porte disliked the idea, since it involved British insistence that it restore the prewar boundaries of both Serbia and Montenegro and promise local autonomy and reforms in both Bulgaria and Bosnia-Herzegovina, but British threats to allow the Russians to attack and defeat the armies of the sultan finally forced him to go along. Much of the actual negotiations took place among the foreign representatives in the early weeks of December as they gathered in Istanbul for the conference. After some discussion and argument, they agreed to leave the boundaries of Serbia and Montenegro as they were, with only minor territorial adjustments in their favor at the expense of Bosnia. Now virtually autonomous, Bosnia would be united with Herzegovina in a single province and would be ruled by a governor appointed by and responsible to the sultan but with the advice and consent of the powers. Ignatiev now reflected the new desire of Russia to base its position in the Balkans on the support of a large Bulgaria by advocating that it get much of southern Serbia and lands all the way to the Aegean and the Black Sea, still under Ottoman suzerainty, but with a Christian governor appointed by the sultan for life and with

Russian military occupation to arrange its new administration. The British were able to persuade the Russians to abandon the desire for a Bulgarian outlet to the Aegean.

The Constitution of 1876

Midhat used the conference to justify the immediate promulgation of a constitution that would establish parliamentary government. He argued that its proclamation would dissuade the powers from intervening in Ottoman affairs under the pretext of enforcing reforms. On the other hand, once on the throne Abdulhamit wished to regain power for the palace, and he was in no hurry to issue such a document. Instead of the men desired by Midhat, therefore, he appointed to his personal palace service his brother-in-law, Damat Mahmut Celaleddin Paşa, previously minister of trade, as chief of the palace inner service (*mâbeyin müşiri*), with the latter's slave Bahrem Ağa as chief eunuch and two of his protégés, Ingiliz Sait (Sait the Englishman) as his aide-de-camp, and Küçük Sait (Sait the Younger) as his chief scribe, thus forming his own palace coterie, with Ahmet Cevdet and *Serasker Redif Paşa* as his principal political advisers.

Midhat Paşa still retained his ascendancy in the cabinet, though only as president of the Council of State. In response to his continued requests, Abdulhamit (October 7) ordered the establishment of a Constitutional Commission to work on the drafting of the Constitution. The commission was put under Midhat's chairmanship and had 28 members in all, including 16 bureaucrats, 10 ulema, and 2 members of the military. The presence of men such as Cevdet meant that Midhat no longer had the kind of dominance here that he maintained in the cabinet. Drafts came from a number of members, including Midhat. In October, after considerable debate, it approved the Parliament, to be composed of an elected chamber of 120 members, both Christians and Muslims, serving three year terms, with one-third being replaced each year. The upper house, to be appointed by the Porte, would have between 30 and 50 members. The proposal was published in the newspapers, officially approved by the notables of the empire on October 10 and promulgated on October 28, with the governor being ordered to prepare at once for elections. It is highly unlikely, therefore, that the representatives of the powers who came together in Istanbul a month later were as unaware of the Ottoman reform efforts as they later claimed to be.

Mehmet Rüştü, still grand vezir, joined with the sultan's men in rejecting clauses that tended to limit the powers of the sultan, so that final acceptance was delayed while the commission had to go back to work. But the imminence of the international conference gave Midhat the lever he needed to force compromises so that the final Constitution could be produced before the powers actually met. The final draft was ready on December 1 and discussed vehemently the next few days. Provisions making the major minority languages official and equal with Ottoman Turkish were rejected on the grounds that this would make the Parliament a veritable Tower of Babel. Abdulhamit's desire to strike out the clauses regarding ministerial responsibility also was accepted despite Midhat's objections, thus removing the heart of the latter's original plan. Though only Midhat and Rüştü supported an article guaranteeing freedom of the press, it finally was accepted to avoid a crisis in the commission just as the representatives of the powers were assembling. On December 6 the cabinet gave final approval to the commission's work, but promulgation was held up by the sultan, who insisted on the inclusion of a royal prerogative allowing him to exile anyone whom he considered dangerous to the safety of the state. While this seemed to contravene many of the guarantees of justice contained in other parts of the Constitution, the cabinet finally accepted it, and article 113 was added to obtain the sultan's approval.

With the commission's work completed, Midhat was appointed grand vezir for the second time (December 19, 1876). The Constitution, proclaimed on December 23, 1876, consisted of 119 articles divided into 12 sections but was not really the Western-style document depicted at the time or subsequently by Western observers, and it incorporated previous Ottoman experience and practice much more than appeared on the surface. It provided for separation of powers much more in form than fact, and the institutional changes reflected evolution rather than a radical departure from past practice. (The sources for the Constitution are discussed on page 454.)

The Sultanate

Not even the most liberal member of the commission suggested the establishment of a republic or any basic diminution in the sovereign rights of the sultan. Thus Ottoman sovereignty was declared to include the supreme caliphate of Islam, and it continued to be vested in the eldest member of the dynasty of Osman (articles 3 and 4). The person of the sultan was sacred, and he was responsible to no one for his acts (article 5), thus leaving the entire Constitution dependent on his continued good will. He had the sole right to appoint and dismiss ministers, thus making them responsible to him rather than the Parliament, to coin money and have his name mentioned in the Friday prayers, to conclude treaties and declare war and peace, command the armed forces, promulgate all secular laws, supervise the enforcement of the *Şeriat*, commute judicial penalties, convoke and dissolve the Parliament, and make arrangements for the election of deputies (article 7). The sultan not only promulgated parliamentary decisions to make them into law but also could continue to enact any decree without its approval, though this had rarely been done during the previous half-century. He could declare a state of siege and temporarily suspend all the guarantees of the Constitution whenever he considered it necessary and banish anyone whom he felt dangerous to himself and the state (article 113). For all practical purposes, then, Abdulhamit II remained as powerful as his predecessors, with Midhat Paşa himself soon to be the first victim once the international danger had passed.

The Executive

Midhat originally wanted to restore the title prime minister in place of grand vezir as part of the process establishing ministerial responsibility to the Parliament. But the final draft of the Constitution not only retained the latter title but also deprived the holder of the office of effective power by allowing the sultan to appoint, dismiss, and thus control individual ministers. The grand vezir could call and preside over meetings of the Council of Ministers (article 28) and care for matters not falling within the competence of individual departments (article 29), but without any real power over the ministers he remained even less than first among equals. Each minister was responsible for the acts of his department, but demands for trial, requiring a two-thirds majority vote of the Assembly, had to be sanctioned by the sultan before a trial could occur (article 31). The cabinet could initiate legislation, including proposals to modify existing laws. If the Assembly rejected an important proposed law, the sultan could dissolve the Parliament and order a re-election within a limited period (article 35). In addition, in cases of "urgent necessity, if the General Assembly is not sitting, the Minister may issue orders with a view to preserving the State against danger and protecting the public security," though such laws did have to be submitted subsequently to the Parliament as soon as it met (article 36). Every minister could attend sessions of both houses or be represented by a subordinate, and he also could speak before them whenever he wished (article 37). If the Assembly summoned him for explanations, he had to appear personally or send a representative, but he also could "reserve his defense" if he wished, leaving the Assembly without any coercive power (article 38).

The Parliament

The Parliament itself was divided into two houses, a Chamber of Deputies (*Meclis-i Mebusan*) and a Chamber of Notables (*Meclis-i Âyân*), which were to meet annually from November 1 to March 1 (articles 42, 43) unless the sultan acted to "advance the time of opening or abridge or prolong the session" (article 44). The opening ceremony was to take place in the presence of the sultan or of the grand vezir as his representative as well as the ministers and other notables, with an imperial speech "showing the situation of the home affairs of the Empire and the state of foreign affairs during the course of the past year and indicating the measures whose adoption are necessary for the following year" (article 45). All members of the Parliament were to be free to express their opinions and vote, and were not to be prosecuted for these "unless they have infringed the rules of their chamber" (article 47). They were immune from arrest and suit while in office unless their chambers chose to waive this immunity by majority vote (articles 48, 79). They could not serve in both houses or in an executive position at the same time (articles 50, 62). Individuals wishing to petition for legislation could do so through the appropriate ministry. Laws approved by the two houses had to be ratified by the Council of Ministers and the grand vezir before being submitted to the sultan (articles 52–54), and all debates had to be held in Ottoman Turkish (article 57), with votes secret or open depending on the circumstances (article 58).

The Chamber of Notables was to be appointed directly by the sultan, with members equal in number to no more than one-third of the Chamber of Deputies (article 60). Members had to be at least 40 years old and to have performed considerable state service. They were appointed for life but had to resign if "called by their own desire to other offices" (article 62). The number of deputies was fixed "at the rate of one deputy to fifty thousand males of the Ottoman nationality" (article 65), to be selected by secret ballot according to a system to be determined by special law (article 66). Terms were for four years, and each deputy represented the whole nation and not only his constituency (article 71), but he did have to reside in the district originally to become a candidate (article 72). The sultan was to pick the council's president and two vice presidents from lists submitted to him by the members (article 77).

The Council of State (*Şurayı Devlet*) was retained in both of its former functions, as supreme court of appeal for decisions in cases of administrative law and as the body in charge of preparing bills for proposals initiated by ministries, the Chamber of Notables, or the Chamber of Deputies, based on the "information and explanations furnished by the proper departments" (article 53). Thus the Council of State provided experience in the drafting of laws, while Parliament served as an avenue of popular representative input before the laws were promulgated.

Reflecting the supervisory function conceived for Parliament by supporters of constitutionalism was the real power given the Chamber of Deputies on fiscal matters. It had the right to vote on the annual budgets, which were to be submitted by the Council of Ministers immediately after the sessions opened each year (article 99). The government could not collect taxes or expend funds not authorized in the budget (articles 97, 100), and even the sultan could not override or ignore the Parliament's decision in this area as he could do in the case of normal laws. To assist its financial operations the Chamber of Deputies was to organize its own Council of Accounting (*Divan-ı Muhasebat*), which was to audit the accounts of all government departments and officials, and while its members were to be appointed for life by the sultan, they could be dismissed by a majority vote of the Chamber of Deputies. These provisions gave the Parliament considerable control over the government's operations, but this power was limited by provisions that enabled each ministry to apply the previous year's budget if under "exceptional circumstances" it failed to obtain the Parliament's approval for the new year before the session was over (article 102). In addition, the Constitution also provided that, when the Chamber of Deputies was not in session, "in urgent cases, arising from extraordinary circumstances, the ministers may . . . create, by Imperial decree, the necessary resources, and cause an outlay unforeseen in the budget," on condition only that they inform the Parliament during its next session (article 101), leaving matters more or less as they had been previously.

Individual Rights

Ottomanism was now the official policy of the empire, embodying the concept of equality contributed by the Tanzimat and endeavoring to eliminate the separatism of the *millet* system. "All subjects of the Empire are, with distinction, called Ottomans whatever religion they profess" (article 8). "All Ottomans enjoy individual liberty on condition that they do not interfere with the liberty of others (article 9). "All Ottomans are equal in the eyes of the law. They have the same rights and duties toward the country without prejudice regarding religion" (article 17). It was asserted that admission to public offices depended only on ability and on knowledge of the official state language (articles 18, 19). Every Ottoman was guaranteed free pursuit of his religion on condition only that "no breach of public order or good morals be committed" (article 11). Nevertheless, Islam remained the official religion of the state. Taxes were to be levied in proportion to the wealth of each taxpayer (article 20), and private property could no longer be confiscated, except for public purposes and with adequate compensation (article 21). The privacy of the home was declared inviolable: "Authorities may not forcibly enter any residence, to whomsoever it belongs, except in cases determined by law" (article 22). Other articles attempted to eliminate arbitrary treatment of subjects: "No sum of money can be gathered as a duty or a tax, or under any other denomination except in accordance with the law" (article 25), and "the rack and torture in any form are completely and absolutely prohibited" (article 26).

System of Justice

To enforce these rights the entire secular court system developed by the Tanzimat was incorporated into the Constitution. Judges were to be appointed for life (article 81), the courts organized according to law (article 88), and no interference was allowed (article 86). The *Şeriat* courts were retained for Muslim religious matters, while non-Muslims went to their own *millet* courts in such cases. Finally, a new High Court (*Divan-ı Âli*) was created to hear accusations against members of the government, both in the executive and the Parliament, with ten members each coming from the Chamber of Notables, the Council of State, and the High Court of Appeals. The court was to be convoked by decree of the sultan, as needed, to judge "ministers, the president and members of the Court of Cassation, and all others accused of the crime of *lèse-majesté* or of attempts to destroy the safety of the State."

Provincial Administration

Finally, under Midhat's inspiration the vilayet provincial system of 1864 was incorporated, with provincial, district, and county representative councils performing the duty of "debating on subjects of public utility, such as the establishment of means of communication, organization of agricultural interests, development of trade, commerce, and agriculture, and extension of public education" as well as lodging complaints and gaining redress for acts committed in violation of the law (articles 109, 110).

The Subjects

The Tanzimat reforms imposed on the *millet*s also were included, with each *millet* being bound to organize its own elected lay council on the central and local levels to care for internal affairs as well as the relations of its community with the government and the administrative councils. The municipal organizations previously developed in Istanbul and the provinces also were to be maintained by separate regulations (article 112), but, as an outcome of Midhat's experiences as provincial governor, the Constitution included a provision that "the administration of the provinces will be based on the principle of decentralization," with details to be determined and fixed by law in the future.

In sum, therefore, the Constitution of 1876 contained, in a form understandable to the West, the provisions for human rights and basic institutions that had been developed during the previous half-century by the Tanzimat. A Western-style Parliament was created to assist the Council of State in the legislative process and provide a counterbalance to the Porte. In structuring modern government out of Ottoman experience, the members of the Constitutional Commission, sharply watched by the new sultan, produced an instrument that was intended to carry on the work begun by the Tanzimat.

Conclusion of the Istanbul Conference

Declaring the Constitution was, of course, timed to coincide with the official opening of the Istanbul Conference, held at the Ministry of the Navy offices at the Imperial Dockyard on the Golden Horn. As the first session met, the delegates were startled to hear the booming of the cannon that accompanied the proclamation. Saffet Paşa, the sultan's old friend and now foreign minister, immediately informed the conferees that the reforms demanded by the powers were no longer an issue, since they had been incorporated into the Constitution. For the same reason, every proposal previously developed by the ambassadors was rejected. The new territories to be taken from Bosnia for Serbia and Montenegro could not be given up, since the Constitution declared the empire to be an integral whole. Distinctions could not be made between Muslim and non-Muslim subjects, since the Constitution provided for equality. Foreign supervision and control were not provided for in the Constitution. The creation of local armed Christian militias would only disturb the harmony the Constitution was creating. Separate religious courts for non-Muslims would destroy the secular courts enshrined by the Constitution, and so forth.

Abdulhamit actually sent Midhat his own plan to be presented to the powers. An international commission would be convoked to examine the complaints of the Bulgars and make recommendations for changes, itself judging all officials found responsible for any atrocities. The Ottoman government would promise quick fulfillment of the reforms envisaged in the Constitution, with the powers at the conference as guarantors. But Midhat in fact was more strongly opposed to foreign involvement than was his sultan, probably as a result of his experience with them in the Danube province; thus he treated Abdulhamit's proposals only as suggestions, did not present them to the conference, and continued to maintain a hard line against all its proposals.[1] Faced with complete Ottoman rejection of the compromise proposals, Lord Salisbury – far more favorable to Russia and the aspirations of the Balkan states than were his cabinet colleagues and Disraeli – secured agreement on a modified program that proposed Bulgaria's division into two vilayets, east and west. New courts of appeal would be organized there as well as in Bosnia-Herzegovina, the judges would be appointed for life in conjunction with the powers, and the local languages would be used in the courts as well as Ottoman Turkish. The provincial governors also would be chosen with the participation of the powers, and in Bulgaria the choice would be limited to Christians. The tobacco and customs taxes would go to the central treasury, but all other taxes would be left for provincial expenditures, with the tithe being replaced by a new land tax. Muslim soldiers would remain only in the major cities and forts, while Christian and Muslim militias would be organized to police the countryside in the areas where their coreligionists were in the majority. All Circassian refugees would be sent to Anatolia; a local gendarmerie would be formed under European officers; and a force of 5000 Belgian soldiers would be sent to help in Bulgaria, with a program instituted to transfer lands held by Muslims to Christian cultivators, all under the supervision of mixed commissions.[2]

Clearly the new proposal was no more acceptable to the Porte than the old. Salisbury threatened that if the plan was rejected, Russia would attack and Britain would do nothing to help the Porte defend itself.[3] Three days later, Midhat presented the plan and the accompanying warnings to a general assembly of notables convened in Istanbul, explaining that the Ottomans might well have to fight alone, but emphasizing that capitulation would mean the end of Ottoman independence. Midhat's words seem to have caught the passions of the notables as well as the masses in the streets. Even the *millet* leaders spoke strongly against the proposals for foreign intervention, so that in the end they were rejected almost unanimously, with Midhat then offering the powers no more than the basic Tanzimat provincial reforms already promised.[4] Midhat apparently was encouraged in this obduracy by Sir Henry Elliot, British ambassador in Istanbul, who with Disraeli opposed Salisbury's policies and planned to do what they could to save the Ottomans. The sultan, apparently not informed of the latter communications, regarded Midhat's decision to reject the proposals without further negotiations as an unnecessary invitation to war and began to have second thoughts about his new grand vezir. Salisbury and the German representatives made one last effort to secure an agreement, scaling down the proposals for a Christian governor of Bulgaria and a Belgian gendarmerie, but Midhat rejected these too, and the conference then broke up in utter frustration (January 20, 1877).

Midhat's Dismissal

In many ways it was the failure of the conference rather than the operation of the Constitution that inspired Abdulhamit to scheme for restoration of power to the palace. The sultan in any case had never liked Midhat, seeing very clearly the political objectives of the Constitution and resenting the fact that credit for the reforms was going to his grand vezir, who was lionized by Ottomans and foreigners alike. The sultan's palace intimates, led by Mahmut Celaleddin and his wife, Cemile Sultan (the sultan's sister), used every incident to stir the sultan against Midhat, in particular his attachment to the Young Ottomans, attributing all their statements to his influence. Midhat's plans to admit Christian students to the War Academy and his repudiation of Mahmut Nedim's program of refinancing the public debt also stirred the sultan's ire. Finally, holding Midhat responsible for the failure of the conference, Abdulhamit decided to send him on an extended trip to Europe (February 5, 1877) shortly after the foreign plenipotentiaries left Istanbul. Midhat, deprived of the seal of the grand vezirate, was cited by article 113 of the Constitution and had to board the ship that was to take him to exile. The sultan's confidant Ibrahim Ethem Paşa, previously chairman of the Council of State, became grand vezir. Abdulhamit himself now chaired meetings of the Council of Ministers, determining government policy on foreign affairs as well as on the suppression of demonstrations by students of religion and, ominously enough, students in the War Academy. The sultan soon managed to submerge further protest in the general passions that accompanied the parliamentary elections and the new international crisis that followed.[5]

Diplomatic Efforts to Avoid War

In the meantime, Midhat had been negotiating a separate peace with Serbia and Montenegro to undermine the position of the powers at the Istanbul Conference and to remove the bases for the Russian threats. Right after Murat's deposition Prince Milan had accepted the Ottoman conditions, and the peace agreement was signed on February 28, 1877, providing that Serbia return to its prewar status. It promised not to build any additional fortifications along the Ottoman boundaries or to support any of the terrorist bands operating within Ottoman territory. The Ottoman flag would continue to fly over the fort of Belgrade but without any Ottoman garrison; and in return Serbia would recognize the religious freedom of all Muslims, Jews, Armenians, and Catholics within its territory. Efforts to secure a similar peace with Montenegro proved fruitless, however, since the latter was under Russian influence to continue the war in order to give the czar the pretext he wanted for direct intervention.

The stage was being set for an attack on the Ottomans regardless of what the Porte arranged with its recalcitrant vassals. In 1854 the threat of Austrian intervention had forced Russia to leave the Principalities. Now the czar had to get

Vienna's cooperation if his troops were to pass through Rumania to attack the Ottomans in the Balkans. For some time he had been trying to get the emperor to clarify the vague Reichstadt stipulations regarding Austria's position in the event of a Russo-Ottoman war, but the disorganized state of the Austrian armies had held the latter back despite his inclination to cooperate against the sultan. The failure of the Istanbul Conference, however, finally enabled the czar to secure the desired agreement, at Budapest (January 15, 1877). Austrian benevolent neutrality was promised in case of a Russo-Ottoman war in return for its being allowed to occupy Bosnia and Herzegovina when it wished, with Serbia, Montenegro, and the *sancak* of Novipazar remaining neutral and not to be occupied by either of the signatories. Russia would get Bessarabia, and the allies would support each other against any objections by the other powers. No specific provisions regarding Bulgaria were included, though the agreement did prohibit any large state being formed in the area. If the Ottoman Empire broke up completely, Istanbul would be a free city rather than going to Russia or Greece, but the latter would be compensated with Crete, Thessaly, and southern Epirus. Russia thus gained a free hand against the Porte, while Austria secured considerable territory as well as assurance that it rather than Russia would dominate Serbia – all in return for simple neutrality.

The Ottoman Parliament

Midhat had felt that it would be very advantageous for the Porte if the new Parliament, the most visible evidence of the Constitution, could meet in Istanbul in the full view of the foreign representatives and press while the Istanbul Conference still was in session. In addition to the Constitution, then, the commission also drew up a temporary electoral law, which was announced on October 28, 1876. Because of the need for haste the regulation provided that, for this time only, the deputies would not be elected by the people but instead by the members of the provincial and district councils already elected under the Tanzimat provincial regulations. The Porte would specify the number of delegates from each province, presumably in proportion to population, with its governor determining the ratio of Muslims to non-Muslims. Special regulations now assured predominately Christian delegations from Christian areas.[6] The vassal provinces — Rumania, Serbia, Montenegro, Egypt, and Tunisia – were not involved, since they had their own governmental systems. Lebanon and Crete also refused to participate in order to preserve their own autonomy, though the Porte assured them that participation would in no way diminish their new powers of self-government. Elections started in November and continued into the new year except in Bosnia and Salonica, where the governors simply appointed whom they wished to represent the different communities. Istanbul followed separate regulations, since it was not yet a province, with the 20 municipal departments serving as electoral districts and each choosing two electors, one Muslim and one non-Muslim, according to the votes cast by all residents of the districts regardless of religion. While the Constitution required an equal ratio of representation for all the provinces of the empire, to impress the powers with the new privileges being given to Christians the European provinces were considerably overrepresented, receiving one deputy for every 82,882 males, while the Anatolian provinces had one for every 162,148 males and those in Africa one for every 505,000. The Jews were given one for every 18,750 males (4 deputies in all); the Christians, one for every 107,557 males (44 deputies in all), and the Muslims, one for every 133,367 males (71 deputies in all). The proportions were similar for the second assembly, which met late in 1877.[7] The sultan appointed 26 members of the Chamber of Notables, of whom 21 were Muslims.

The Parliament officially opened on March 19, 1877, with an elaborate ceremony held in the reception hall of the Dolmabahçe Palace attended by all the ministers, notables, and representatives as well as foreign dignitaries. Presiding was Ahmet Vefik Paşa, chosen president of the Parliament by the sultan regardless of the election rules, which provided that the choice be made by and from among the deputies. The sultan's speech, read by his secretary Küçük Sait, stressed the earlier reform failures, the difficulties caused by foreign attacks, and the bonded debt. It stated that the sultan had granted the Constitution in order to "use the system of deliberation as a useful means to improve the administration of the country," and he asked the delegates' cooperation in producing the legislation the empire needed. He promised that the government would soon submit many new law codes and regulations, emphasized the need to improve agriculture, justice, and the bureaucracy, and stated his intention of establishing a new Civil Service School (*Mekteb-i Mülkiye*) to produce administrators able and willing to administer the new laws with efficiency and honesty.[8] Meeting later in its own building, the old university across the road from the Aya Sofya Mosque, the Parliament replied with a statement that eulogized the sultan for his having convoked it and promised it would work to "eliminate the last traces of abuses, the heritage of the regime of despotism." It also declared strong opposition to foreign intervention and the hope that Montenegro as well as Serbia would accept the Porte's terms.[9]

The two houses now set to work, the deputies in public sessions and the notables in secret as prescribed in the Constitution. In general, the former turned out to be mostly members of the councils that had elected them, thus representing the new ruling and middle classes produced by the Tanzimat in the provinces, while the latter consisted mainly of bureaucrats who had served for many years in the departments and councils of the government, and a few members of the ulema. In a true sense, then, the two houses represented the respective ruling classes of the provinces and the capital rather than the sultan or the general public. With so many deputies representing the different peoples and religions of the empire, all speaking the common Turkish of the people rather than the flowery official language used in the capital, they soon developed a feeling of brotherhood and devotion to the Constitution. A truly Ottoman institution, in the sense the term "Ottoman" was used in the Constitution, had thus come into being.

The Russo-Turkish War, 1877–1878

The Ottoman transition to a constitutional regime was no deterrent to Russian ambitions, but the czar had to consider the state of his own military. His army, preparing to march southward through the Principalities, was equal to that of the sultan in numbers while inferior in equipment due to Abdulaziz's lavish purchases late in his reign. Despite this, however, the Russians were convinced – correctly as events were to prove – that they still would win because of superiority of command. The Ottoman officer corps still had not been fully developed, and it was divided by the same kind of political rivalries that had hindered the work of the Men of the Tanzimat. Thus while Russia obtained Rumanian permission for transit of the czar's army through its territory (April 16, 1877), it spurned the offer of troops as, indeed, it declined similar assistance offered by Greece, Serbia, and Montenegro. The Russian ambassador informed the Porte that his government had declared war

(April 24) and immediately left the capital. Abdulhamit asked for the help of the signatories of the Peace of Paris, but this was of little use. Disraeli – still hindered by Gladstone's political forays against "the terrible Turk" – attempted to nullify the czar's agreement with the emperor by concluding an Anglo-Austrian alliance to limit any Russian gains that might result; but Andrassy was willing to act openly only if the Russians violated the Budapest Convention. Disraeli, therefore, was unable to gain cabinet support for England to intervene and had to leave the Ottomans to fight alone.

The principal aim of the Russian campaign was to cross the Balkan Mountains and approach Istanbul and the Straits as rapidly as possible in the west while also moving into northeastern Anatolia and taking Kars, Ardahan, and Erzurum to force the Porte to accept the proposals it had rejected at the Istanbul Conference. Once the czar was in position to control the Black Sea and push across Anatolia to Alexandretta, he would gain free access to the Mediterranean. The Slavic states of the Balkans would also be severed from Ottoman control and left under strong Russian influence, and the czar's position in the European alignment of states would thus be strengthened. In defense the main Ottoman line was established at the Danube, with the area between Varna and Vidin heavily fortified and major reinforcements gathered at Silistria, Rusçuk, Nicopolis, and Vidin. The Balkan Mountains formed the second line of defense from bases at Varna, Şumla, and Sofia. The Dardanelles were fortified in case the Russian Baltic fleet was again sent into the Mediterranean, and in the east the garrisons at Kars and Erzurum were heavily manned. Since Russia had no time to rebuild its Black Sea fleet, the Ottomans had no fear from this direction but instead planned to send only light ships to the Danube to help supply their defense forces there.

The Russians moved in the west in June 1877 with a twin attack across the Danube, one force moving into the Dobruca and the other passing between Rusçuk and Nicopolis and taking Sistova with the help of its mainly Bulgarian population, slaughtering most of the Muslims (June 27). It then went on to take Tirnovo (July 1) to breach the Balkan passes and move onto Sofia and Edirne. The Ottomans' second line of defense thus was broken quickly. The Russian moves into northern Bulgaria were accompanied by large-scale massacres of Turkish peasants to make certain that they would not disrupt troop and supply movements. Nicopolis held out valiantly until it fell under a series of enemy assaults (July 16), with a heavy loss of men and equipment. Istanbul was shocked by the series of disasters. Abdulhamit replaced all the principal commanders who survived, appointing Süleyman Paşa, former commander of the Military Academy and now leading the troops in Montenegro, to take over the defense of the Balkan passes. To gain the necessary popular support Abdulhamit declared himself the gazi, fighter for the faith against the infidel, getting the ulema to declare the conflict a Holy War. Taking the standard of the Prophet from its storage place in the Topkapı Palace, he soon excited popular passions sufficiently not only to secure the needed men but also to raise money through personal contributions to help finance the tremendous war costs, beginning the kind of appeal that was to be heard again and again during the subsequent half-century of Ottoman existence.

Süleyman Paşa brought his men by sea to Dedeağaç (Alexandroupolis), quickly marched overland into northern Bulgaria, and drove the advanced Russian forces back through the Şipka Pass, which he took over and fortified. The right wing of the Russian advance had followed the victory at Sistova with the capture of Vidin, but it was held back at Plevna by a strong defense commanded by Osman Paşa, who was reinforced with volunteers sent from Istanbul. The Russians thus were stymied in the west, the expected quick push to Istanbul being denied them by the Ottoman resistance at Şipka and Plevna.

The eastern campaigns followed a similar pattern. At first the Ottomans were hindered by the need to divide their defense forces among all the forts that the Russians might possibly attack between the Black Sea and Lake Van. They could provide little resistance, therefore, when the Russians attacked and took the main forts, one after the other, first Ardahan (May 18, 1877) and then Doğu Bayezit (June 20). The Ottomans suffered heavy losses of men and rifles. The Russians used the latter, as in Bulgaria, to arm the local Christians and stimulate massacres of the Muslim villagers to thwart local resistance. Kars now became the center of Ottoman defenses, with the remaining troops in the area being pulled together under the command of Ahmet Muhtar Paşa, who soon brought the Russian advances to a halt.

With quick victory thus denied him, the czar had to face renewed political and diplomatic pressures that threatened even the limited fruits of his early gains. He had given in to the Pan-Slavic war pressures at first. But Gorchakov and others still feared European intervention and possible revolution at home if the war went on too long. They now advised that it be ended on the basis of the status quo ante, with an autonomous Bulgarian state that would extend only to the Balkan Mountains, while the Austrians would be compensated with Bosnia-Herzegovina. Disraeli (now Lord Beaconsfield) had more or less secured cabinet support to save the Ottomans, but since the cabinet was unwilling to engage in war in Europe without the alliance of at least one other Continental power, its efforts were directed more toward sending the British fleet to keep the Russians out of Istanbul and the Straits (June 30). The new British ambassador, Sir Henry Layard, achieved a very close rapport with the sultan that he was to retain for much of the remainder of his mission. Disraeli and Layard now envisioned a possible British expedition into eastern Anatolia to drive the Russians back. Jingoistic war fever swept England as the mob demanded war to save India as well as the Middle East from Russian imperialism, with the Ottoman heroes of Plevna and the Şipka Pass being featured in the popular British press. Disraeli, however, was still unable to gain the hoped-for agreement with Austria, which insisted on some of the original Russian claims, including occupation of the right bank of the Danube and creation of a large Slavic state under Russian protection in return for its support to end the war.

Thus the war continued. The czar now reversed his earlier refusal of the help offered by his Balkan friends. Serbia agreed to enter the war, though it did not actually do so until the subsequent capture of Plevna assured it of a Russian victory. The Greeks also were asked to divert the Ottomans by attacking in Thrace; but by now they were quite impressed by the Ottoman army and the threat of British intervention, and so they refused to give assistance without a Russian guarantee that they would gain both the Epirus and Thessaly. Rumania, however, was in no position to refuse or even stall the Russians. Its army therefore helped the Russians in a new siege of Plevna, which continued to hold out. In appreciation of their heroic resistance to the Russians, Abdulhamit awarded the title of gazi to its commander, Osman Paşa, as well as to Muhtar Paşa for his work in the east.

The Parliament at Work

In the meantime, the Parliament had been performing its legislative duty. A new law revised the Provincial Regulation of 1864 after considerable debate between the Muslim and non-Muslim deputies over the composition of the advisory councils. The rural delegates united to restrict the powers of the administrators over the councils and also to prevent the municipality of Istanbul from getting any more taxes to meet its needs than the smaller towns were allowed to keep for similar purposes. Major municipal regulations were passed, elaborating on the urban structures that had begun to emerge late in the Tanzimat.

The measure that stirred much debate was a Press Law proposed by the grand vezir, which allowed censorship and the closing of publications that violated government regulations. In the end, however, most of these provisions were included, with the deputies succeeding only in reducing the monetary penalties provided, and then getting the Council of State to reconsider the entire draft to such an extent that the bill was lost in the legislative process and never was promulgated while the Parliament was in session. In addition to regulations for the Chambers of Deputies and Notables,[10] the Parliament also passed the basic election law for the empire, providing one deputy for each 50,000 male inhabitants in each *sancak,* with indirect elections for electors, more or less according to the system used in Istanbul in 1877. The vote was given to all subjects of good reputation aged 25 or over who were not convicts or bankrupts. The deputies had tried to establish a direct system of election and to deny the vote to delinquent taxpayers, but these provisions were removed by the notables, again demonstrating the interests of the groups who controlled each body.[11] This bill also was never promulgated, since by the time it reached the sultan, he had dissolved the Parliament.

The deputies did show independence in considering the budget, reducing the number of civil servants and the sums proposed for their salaries before passing the 1876–1877 proposal. They did, however, accept all the heavy expenditures required for the war, which produced a substantial deficit, and they approved increases in income, property, and animal taxes to compensate. They also approved a compulsory internal loan requiring property owners and civil servants alike to purchase government bonds according to their wealth and means.[12] Aside from this the deputies did not deal directly with the conduct of the war, but they did confer the title of gazi on the sultan. On May 22 they unanimously asked that Mahmut Nedim be tried for getting the empire into the crisis, but this was never acted on by the sultan. There was no particular criticism of the conduct of the war in the Parliament, but Ismail Kemal Bey, a Foreign Ministry official and close friend of Midhat, tried to get liberal support outside Parliament for a plan to establish a war committee in the Chamber of Deputies to organize and direct the war, something that most certainly would not have been accepted by the sultan and that conflicted with the Constitution on several points.[13] Ismail Kemal also got 90 deputies to ask the sultan to reinstate Midhat (May 22), but the attempt was dropped two days later when the students of theology protested the loss of Ardahan by demanding the resignation of *Serasker* Redif Paşa, surrounding the Parliament building and demanding the right to participate in the discussions when he was interrogated by the Assembly (May 24). The sultan reacted by proclaiming Istanbul in a state of siege, in accordance with his prerogatives in the Constitution, and sent the students into exile.[14] These events, though not directly related to the Assembly's work, did excite suspicion in the sultan's mind, leading to his subsequent decision to dispense with it altogether.

The first session ended finally on June 19, 1877, considerably beyond its original deadline due to the need to pass the budget and emergency bond bills. Elections were ordered for the second session, though since the electoral bill still had not been passed and the November opening date of the new session was close, the Provisional Electoral Regulation again was used. The elections were carried out in September and October, with the results about the same as before, though there were fewer Muslim deputies from Anatolia due to problems caused by the war.[15] The Parliament again was opened with a speech from the throne, but only on December 13, 1877, and with very little ceremony or popular emotion due to the serious news then coming in from the war fronts. The sultan expressed his regret that his Balkan vassals had revolted without cause and praised the courage of his army, especially that of the non-Muslims in the provincial militias. He promised that the deputies would receive new regulations being prepared by the Council of State on elections, judicial reform, and the code of civil procedure, and said also that he would return to them the Press Law, the provincial regulation, and the tax bills passed at the previous session so that they could consider the objections that had been raised.[16] But in their reply the deputies used what was to be a formal occasion to express their discontent with the progress and handling of the war, creating a sensation at the Porte. The grand vezir offered to resign, and in the palace Abdulhamit finally decided that the Chamber of Deputies would have to go.

The New Crisis

The war had, indeed, taken a turn for the worse as the long Russian sieges of the main Ottoman defense points in both east and west finally took their toll. On October 14, 1877, 6,500 Ottoman soldiers had to surrender at Aladağ, and on November 14 Muhtar Paşa abandoned Kars, though he was able to withdraw most of his men and heavy equipment in good order back to Erzurum. All of eastern Anatolia seemed open to the enemy, with only winter providing temporary protection. In the Balkans likewise Gazi Osman Paşa was forced to give in to the suffering of his men and to surrender the 42,000 survivors at Plevna on January 10, 1877, thus breaking open the western front. King Milan of Serbia now gained the courage he needed to proclaim his independence (January 24) and declare war (January 28), occupying Pirot, on the Bulgarian border, and besieging and taking Niş (February 11). The defenders of the Şipka Pass were overwhelmed on January 9, 1878, costing the Ottomans another 32,000 men and 103 large cannons. Süleyman Paşa himself was able to escape, and he took over the defense of Sofia. But the Ottoman forces were now too scattered. Soon it fell also, and Edirne followed (January 20), with no real resistance. At the same time, with the Ottoman garrisons of Montenegro engaged in the east, the Montenegrans also declared war and captured Bar (January 15) and Ülgün (January 19).

The rapid Russian advances into Bulgaria alarmed Britain and Austria, which now realized that the large Bulgaria envisioned by the czar could only be an instrument for Russian domination of Southeastern Europe. Franz Joseph wrote to Czar Alexander II warning that he would oppose such a creation and demand Bosnia and Herzegovina even if Russia took only southern Bessarabia, and he insisted that all the powers, not only Russia, participate in the peace to be made with the Ottomans. Britain followed with a similar warning. But the Russian troops, commanded by

Grand Duke Nicholas, pressed ahead toward Istanbul, forcing the Porte to ask for an armistice, which was concluded at Edirne on January 31. Before the peace conference took place, the Ottomans gave up the remaining Bulgarian forts of Vidin, Rusçuk, and Silistria, agreed that Bosnia-Herzegovina and Bulgaria would receive autonomy, with reforms introduced under European supervision, that Russia would have full rights to use the Straits, and that the Porte would pay a war indemnity. In short, this was an unconditional surrender to the victors. A conference between the Ottomans and the Russians was arranged, at San Stefano (Yeşilköy), outside Istanbul, to conclude a new treaty without the intervention of the powers.

Dismissal of the Parliament

Parliament had continued to work on the resubmitted bills and also on two new ones regarding the reorganization of the secular courts. But the deputies' attention was diverted by the military disasters and rather than concentrating on legislation, they turned to criticizing the government, attacking the conduct of campaigns, the incompetence of officers, and the overall management of the war effort, most probably with some justification.[17] Suggestions that Midhat be brought back hardly endeared the deputies to the sultan. In addition, the Armenian and Greek delegates urged their compatriots to refuse the sultan's invitation for them to serve in the army, while groups of liberal and non-Muslim deputies began to circulate petitions of nonconfidence in some of the ministers as well as the palace entourage.[18] The last straw came on February 13 when the sultan convoked the Chamber of Notables, including members of the Parliament, to consult with them on inviting the British fleet to enter the Sea of Marmara to help protect Istanbul against a possible Russian advance. After most of the deputies declared their approval, one of them named Naci Ahmet, himself only a baker and head of his guild, declared to the sultan: "You have asked for our opinions too late; you should have consulted us when it was still possible to avert disaster. The Chamber declines all responsibility for a situation for which it had nothing to do."[19] This was the end. The next day Abdulhamit dissolved the Parliament, stating simply that it had done its duty but that the current situation was "not suitable for it to properly perform its functions."[20] Abdulhamit had at first also ordered the arrest of the deputies who had most strongly criticized the government, fearing that they would undermine popular and military morale. But at the insistence of Ahmet Vefik he modified the order, requiring instead that they return to their homes at once. Though some of the deputies then protested on the grounds that he had violated the Constitution, Parliament was nonetheless dissolved.[21] Disappointing as this abrupt end was, in his actions and his ruling without Parliament in the following three decades the sultan was acting in accordance with the powers granted him by the Constitution. He had simply used the crisis to apply the provisions that Midhat and his colleagues had accepted in order to protect the Constitution from conservative reaction. With Parliament gone and the Porte weakened, Abdulhamit established the bases of the autocracy that was to dominate Ottoman government for the remaining years of his reign.

The Treaty of San Stefano

Back in England Queen Victoria, supported by public opinion, got the cabinet to agree to Disraeli's desire to send the fleet to Istanbul. As soon as the sultan's permission arrived, it passed the Dardanelles and anchored opposite the capital. It did not, however, land troops because Disraeli had not yet reached an agreement with Austria, though the latter had protested the terms of the Edirne armistice to the czar. Bismarck still hesitated to do anything that would divide the League of the Three Emperors. In the meantime, Russian troops advanced to Çatalca, immediately outside Istanbul. The inhabitants of Istanbul, including Ahmet Vefik, now grand vezir, feared Russian occupation of the capital. But in St. Petersburg the conservatives had gotten the czar to agree that if the British did not land troops, his men would not move to take Istanbul or the Straits. Neither side wanted to to prolong the war. The campaigns had drained the Russian treasury, and the czar had resorted to the issuance of new paper money, leading to inflation and discontent. Rumania had been disillusioned by its ally's ambitions in Bessarabia. Austria, though opposed to the Russian plans, also stayed out because of its own precarious finances. Britain's reluctant and delayed involvement also cost it some loss in prestige.

It was under these circumstances that the peace conference of San Stefano proceeded. From the outset the Ottomans agreed with Russia in opposing any European protest that might follow its conclusion. The treaty (March 3, 1878) was based on the truce terms signed at Edirne a month earlier and basically fulfilled the demands of the Pan-Slavs. Montenegro and Serbia were to be independent, though the latter, because of its poor war performance, was to get only a few additions along its southern border, including Niş, the Drina valley, and part of the *sancak* of Novipazar. The Porte would recognize Rumania's declaration of independence and pay it some war compensation, accept Russian annexation of southern Bessarabia, and compensate Rumania with parts of the Dobruca. Most important of all, Bulgaria would become autonomous, still acknowledging Ottoman suzerainty but with its own prince, soldiers, and administration. Its territories would extend from the Danube to the Aegean, including the provinces of Monastir and Salonica and a considerable Aegean shoreline but excluding the ports of Dedeağaç and Salonica themselves, since their populations were mainly Muslim and Jewish. Bulgaria thus was expanded three times and given a population of 5 million. Its prince would be chosen by the people, confirmed by the powers, and accepted by the sultan. Russian troops and a Russian commissioner would remain in the new Principality for two years to help it organize its government and militia, while all the Ottoman officials and soldiers would retire. The Porte would introduce all the reforms demanded at the Istanbul Conference for Bosnia and Herzegovina after consulting with Austria and Russia. The new system of government introduced in Crete in 1868 would be carried out and also extended to the Epirus and Thessaly, though these territories were still left to the Ottomans rather than being given to Greece.

Inspired by Russian propaganda, Armenian nationalist feeling had been stirred up among some intellectuals in the Ottoman Empire, and the Armenian patriarch of Istanbul, Nerses, went to San Stefano to ask the Russians to help create an independent Armenian state in eastern Anatolia in return for their help against the Ottomans during the war. But the Russians were much happier with discontented Armenians within the Ottoman Empire than with an independent state that might soon stimulate their own Armenians and other nationalities to make similar demands. Instead, they secured Ottoman promises for reforms in the areas of Anatolia claimed by the Armenians along with guarantees against Kurdish and Turkoman nomadic attacks. Thus was born the Armenian Question, which the Russians were to develop and use with much skill in later years.

The sultan agreed to pay a huge war indemnity of 1.4 billion rubles (equal to 24 billion kuruş, four times the annual state revenues), of which less than half would be paid off by surrender of large areas of the Dobruca, the islands of the Danube, and the east Anatolian districts of Kars, Ardahan, Batum, and Doğu Bayezit. All those wishing to leave the new Russian territories were to be allowed to sell their properties within three years, thus assuring a continuing flow of refugees into the Ottoman Empire during the remainder of Abdulhamit's reign. All the sultan's Orthodox subjects, churches, and priests would be under Russian "protection." The Ottomans were able to resist only Ignatiev's desire for joint protection and administration of the Straits, but the terms remained very severe, with the financial obligations alone assuring Russian domination and influence in the future.[22]

Reaction in Istanbul

The population of Istanbul had already been doubled by the Muslim refugees who had fled from Bulgaria. They were very hostile to Christians as well as to the sultan who had given in to the hated enemy. While the old residents of the city reacted to the defeat with numb sorrow, many having lost loved ones in the terrible catastrophes and many also their homes and incomes as a result of the accompanying inflation, the refugees were almost fanatical in their determination to force the empire to carry on the struggle against the Russians. Rising to lead them was Ali Suavi, once a Young Ottoman and now a strong Pan-Turkist as well as a Muslim mystic. Arming some 30 refugees, he led a raid on the Çırağan Palace with the aim of rescuing Murat V and restoring him to the throne and then upsetting the San Stefano settlement. But the palace guards killed most of the attackers and frustrated the plot (May 20, 1878). Ali Suavi was tried and hanged, and the only immediate result of the affair was to fortify the sultan's determination to establish an absolute regime that would prevent similar occurrences in the future. His principal aide, Ingiliz Sait Paşa, was implicated in the plot and dismissed. He was replaced with the hero of Plevna, Gazi Osman Paşa, who, as soon as he was released by the Russians, hurried home and became a powerful conservative influence in the palace during much of the remainder of Abdulhamit's reign.

Diplomatic Maneuverings

Ignatiev had rushed through the settlement with the Porte in the hope of presenting Britain and Austria with a *fait accompli* that they could not change. He had not, however, reckoned with the strength of the European reaction that followed, not only from Disraeli and the emperor but also from Germany, where Bismarck now saw the need to act to prevent a war between his Russian and Austrian allies. The czar also realized that such a war would be inevitable unless he agreed to a European conference to review the results of San Stefano; therefore, he accepted Bismarck's proposal to hold it in Berlin. He did not, however, expect his erstwhile allies to join Britain in demanding that all the provisions be reviewed, but when they did, he had to accept to avoid war. Austria demanded that the new Bulgaria be reduced in size to lessen Russian power in eastern Europe and that Russia accept Austrian annexation of Novipazar as well as Bosnia and Herzegovina. As soon as Russia agreed to these points, the emperor was not as willing to support British demands for a general revision as he had been earlier. This forced Britain in turn to deal directly with the Russians and, through Bismarck's intermediacy, to accept a compromise limiting the new Bulgaria to the area north of the Balkan Mountains. The rest would be returned to the Ottomans as an autonomous province called East Rumelia, and would be given immediate reforms. Most of eastern Anatolia would be returned to the Porte in return for compliance with the remainder of the San Stefano agreement, but Russia would retain Kars, Batum, and southern Bessarabia (May 30, 1878).

The bases for revision of San Stefano thus were laid even before the Congress of Berlin actually met. Britain, however, was not satisfied. In eastern Anatolia the Russians still were in a position to make a subsequent advance to the Mediterranean or to the Persian Gulf or to stimulate Armenian uprisings. To guarantee the integrity of the remaining Ottoman possessions in Anatolia, Disraeli proposed British occupation of Cyprus so that its military forces could respond to any crisis at a moment's notice. The sultan was not at all enthused about the idea, but in the face of a British threat to leave San Stefano as it was, he had no choice but to sign the Cyprus Convention (June 4, 1878), which provided that Britain would occupy and administer the island in the name of the sultan. All surpluses of revenues over expenditures were to be paid to the treasury in the form of tribute, and the Ottomans would continue to control the island's institutions of justice, religion, and education. Britain in return promised to provide all necessary aid to defend eastern Anatolia if the Russians attacked.[23] Thus were laid the bases for Disraeli's final triumph at Berlin.

The Congress of Berlin

In spite of all the arrangements, when the congress actually met, it was not easy to reach a settlement. The Russian armies and treasury were exhausted, but Russia still did all it could to evade fulfillment of the agreements it had already signed. There also were problems raised by interests not directly represented at the congress: the Bosnian and Herzegovinan Christians, the Bulgarian Christians, the Bulgarian Muslims, who strongly resisted the idea of Christian rule over them, and the Armenians, who believed they could get the powers to force the Ottomans to turn over large Muslim territories to them. The Greeks were demanding Crete, Thessaly, and the Epirus. The Ottomans were represented by a Christian public works minister, Karatodori Paşa, as well as the ambassador to Berlin, Sadullah Paşa. The powers simplified matters by concentrating on their own aspirations and not paying much attention to those of the states whose lands were being manipulated.

The Congress of Berlin concluded on July 13, 1878. The Big Bulgaria envisioned by Russia at San Stefano was broken into three parts, with autonomous Bulgaria extending only from the Danube to the Balkan Mountains and remaining under Ottoman suzerainty, with a Christian prince, an army, and Christian administrators, but paying an annual tribute to the sultan. The prince would be chosen from one of the great houses of Europe, confirmed by the powers, and sanctioned by the sultan. Organization of the new regime would be supervised by commissioners representing Russia, the Porte, and the other signatory powers, but they would remain no longer than nine months. The remaining portions of Big Bulgaria were divided into two sections. The area south of the Balkan Mountains remained under the sultan's rule as the province of East Rumelia, with direct Ottoman political and military control but a special administrative system, and the area of Macedonia between Niş and the Greek border was returned to direct Ottoman administration with promises for reforms. Although East Rumelia had a large Muslim population, it would be administered by a Christian governor appointed by the Porte for a five-year term with the sanction of the powers. He would have a Christian militia but could call on the help of Ottoman soldiers stationed in garrisons to maintain internal order and defend the province against external attack. The Russian army in Bulgaria and East Rumelia would number no more than 55,000 men and remain no longer than nine months. Crete would remain under Ottoman rule, with the 1868 reforms being fully applied. The powers would mediate any border disputes that arose between the Ottomans and Greeks in Macedonia. Bosnia and Herzegovina, though under Ottoman rule, would be occupied by Austrian troops and administered by Austrian civil servants for an indeterminate time according to regulations to be drawn up in subsequent negotiations between the two powers. Montenegran independence would be recognized, but its prince would promise to provide equal treatment for subjects of all religions. Serbia also was to be independent, with its territory extending southward as far as Niş and east to Pirot; both it and Montenegro had to promise to assume a portion of the Ottoman debt in return. Rumania would be independent, ceding to Russia the parts of Bessarabia received at Paris in 1856 and being compensated with islands in the Danube delta as well as the Dobruca. It also had to agree to destroy the fortifications along the Iron Gates of the Danube and to allow free communication along its entire length while prohibiting the entry of foreign warships.

In the east the Ottomans had to leave Kars, Ardahan, and Batum to Russia. Batum became a free port, and the czar promised not to fortify it. The Eleşkirt valley and Doğu Bayezit, gained at San Stefano, were returned to the Ottomans. The Porte promised to introduce reforms in areas settled by the Armenians and to confirm complete civil and religious freedom in the empire. The provisions of the 1856 and 1871 agreements regarding the Black Sea and the Straits were to be continued. The Ottoman government still would have to pay a war indemnity to Russia, now set at 802.5 million francs, to be paid at a rate of about .35 million kuruş annually, and it also agreed to accept further Russian territorial demands if it could not complete the payments.

In sum, the Ottoman Empire was forced to give up two-fifths of its entire territory and one-fifth of its population, about 5.5 million people, of whom almost half were Muslims. It also lost substantial revenues, though it was partially compensated by the tribute paid by the remaining vassals and the agreement of the newly independent states to assume portions of the Ottoman public debt. Insofar as Britain was concerned, the Russian threat had been weakened, but for the Ottoman Empire the Congress of Berlin was a terrible defeat, depriving it of territory, people, and finances and making it difficult for what was left to survive.

Foreign and Domestic Difficulties, 1878–1908

In the years following the Treaty of Berlin, while Europe groped to establish a new balance of power, the Ottomans were exposed to a series of foreign interventions in their internal affairs under the pretext of helping the sultan's minority subjects.

Austrian Rule in Bosnia-Herzegovina

A relatively easy problem to deal with involved Bosnia-Herzegovina, which Austria occupied immediately after the Congress of Berlin. The Muslim population of the provinces, comprising at least one-half the inhabitants, resented the arrangement by which they were placed under Christian control and strongly resisted the occupying troops, leading Austria to establish a military regime in its new province. Though Abdulhamit felt strongly about Bosnia-Herzegovina due to longstanding Muslim traditions in the provinces, there was little he could do, since his direct connection with them was tenuous. On April 21, 1879, therefore, he agreed to accept Austrian rule for an indeterminate period, stipulating only that revenues from the area be used locally, that the Muslims be allowed to practice their faith freely, that the name of the caliph-sultan continue to be recited in the Friday prayers, that natives be employed in the administration, and that those Muslims wishing to leave be allowed to do so.

French Occupation of Tunisia

The example of European occupation of the sultan's more distant territories proved very contagious, however. The Ottomans never had held Tunisia too closely. In the sixteenth century it had been controlled by the local military and naval corps, whose ascendancy was based mainly on piracy and the slave trade. After these were stamped out in the early nineteenth century, it came under the influence of European investors and merchants, followed by their governments, who saw in Tunisia's strategic location a key for their Mediterranean and North African ambitions. First came the French, who following their occupation of Algeria in 1830 established financial institutions in Tunis, lending money to the beys, and investing extensively as the first step toward building an African empire. French primacy was not challenged until 1870, when the achievement of Italian unity encouraged Italian agricultural and industrial investment in Tunisia in the hope of establishing it as the first link in a new mid-Mediterranean empire. Britain also began to move in, seeking opportunities for raw materials and investment as well as protection for its strategic concerns in Central Africa. The beys now maintained themselves mainly by accepting loans and other considerations from the competing foreign interests, playing them off as best they could, but eventually finding themselves inextricably caught in financial difficulties.

Following the Crimean War the Men of the Tanzimat had been fairly successful in pulling the Tunisian beys back into the Ottoman orbit, securing their agreement to apply the Tanzimat laws and to contribute taxes and ships in return for recognition of a position very similar to that of the khedives of Egypt. The principal agent of Ottoman influence in the country for many years was Hayreddin Paşa, originally a slave of Mustafa Reşit Paşa, who had been sold to one of the beys and then rose in the service of his master and his successors. He used his influence to maintain Ottoman as opposed to foreign interests, stimulating the hostility of the foreign consuls and enabling his political rivals in the Tunisian court to secure his dismissal and exile. His departure from Tunis and subsequent entry into the service of Abdulhamit led to a rapid deterioration of Tunisia's ties with the Porte.

Just as in Cairo and Istanbul somewhat later, the bey's financial difficulties and foreign debts led to European intervention. In 1869 an International Debt Commission was organized and given control over Tunisia's major revenues to consolidate the debts and arrange for regular payments. Under its supervision foreigners gained control of most of Tunisia's public services and raw materials, adding to the province's economic difficulties. Tunisia also became involved in the European diplomatic maneuverings that followed the Berlin settlement. Italy, unhappy at the failure of the powers to provide it with what it considered adequate compensation, was enraged by Britain's offer of Tunisia to France in return for its acquiescence in the Cyprus Convention. France was not overly anxious for a new colonial adventure at this time, but it did not want to allow what had been offered to it to fall to the Italians by default; hence it used as pretext a Tunisian border raid into Algeria to occupy the entire country, forcing the bey to accept French "protection" (May 12, 1881). The Ottomans protested the situation to all the powers that had guaranteed Ottoman integrity at Berlin, challenging the validity of a treaty signed by the bey. But no one bothered to reply, and the Ottomans had to accept the situation as a *fait accompli*.

The British Occupation of Egypt, 1882

Egypt's financial difficulties and the economic and political rivalries of the powers led it to a situation very similar to that of Tunisia, with similar results. Sait and Ismail had granted hundreds of concessions to foreign investors, giving them virtual control of Egypt's economy. Their own expenditures left the government in debt to foreign bondholders. They had to accept huge discounts and exorbitant interest rates to secure the money needed to continue operations, devoting as much as two-thirds of the entire state budget to the payment of interest alone by 1876. This culminated in the establishment of the *Caisse de la Dette Publique* (May 1876), with foreign controllers collecting state revenues from customs duties, railroads, tobacco, and other excise taxes and using them to pay off the debt. In 1878 Ismail was compelled to accept a cabinet headed by the Armenian nationalist Nubar Paşa, with an English expert as minister of finance and a Frenchman as minister of public works. When he tried to replace this with one composed mainly of native Egyptians, the British and French forced him to abdicate (July 26, 1879) in favor of his weak son Tevfik Paşa, who accepted the Law of Liquidation, which separated the debt payments from the other obligations of the Egyptian treasury and gave the former first call on all revenues. Egypt's finances were at least stabilized but at the cost of placing them under direct foreign control and using them to foreign advantage.

While foreign intervention might have been justified by the rules of international finance then in vogue, it stimulated a strong nationalistic reaction among the native Egyptians. They began to condemn the economic policies that had placed the mass of the people under the control of the landed Turko-Circassian aristocracy and the foreign bankers and merchants who controlled the urban economy. Resentment in the army was stimulated by the domination of the scions of the aristocracy and a small group of Western-educated officers, who discriminated against those attempting to rise from the ranks. This led to an uprising in September 1881 by an army group led by Ahmet Urabi Paşa, one of the few natives who had managed to rise into the officer corps. The soldiers took over the government, began to end the foreign domination, and sent troops to Alexandria to guard against any possible foreign invasion. The British position was complicated by its current role as protector of the Ottoman Empire as a result of the Cyprus Convention. While there were some elements in the army and cabinet who wanted to intervene, Prime Minister Gladstone formulated a policy to avoid intervention except in conjunction with the Ottoman army and at the invitation of the sultan. The French, on the other hand, were anxious to intervene, not only to protect their bondholders and add to their African empire but also to break Britain's new relationship with the

Porte. Abdulhamit encouraged the khedive and Urabi to restore the foreign control system, which was very similar to an arrangement being contemplated for introduction in Istanbul. To forestall direct intervention Gladstone arranged for a new conference of ambassadors in Istanbul (June 1881). Grand Vezir Sait Paşa and the Ottoman cabinet wanted to join the conference, but Abdulhamit refused, feeling that this would only legitimize foreign intervention. His view finally prevailed, and the ambassadors agreed that the Ottomans should try to settle Egypt's problems by themselves and that there should be no unilateral foreign intervention "except in case of unforeseen circumstances."

Abdulhamit immediately complied with the directive by bringing Urabi and several of his colleagues to Istanbul and sending Derviş Paşa to negotiate a settlement with the khedive. But while the negotiations were in progress, the arrival of foreign ships outside Alexandria's harbor stimulated some of its inhabitants to attack and kill several foreigners in the streets. This event and continued fortification of the Alexandria harbor led the commander of the British ships, Admiral Seymour, to send an ultimatum demanding the restoration of order and an end to the construction. This was ignored; so he bombarded the undefended city (July 13, 1882), although the French squadron backed out at the last minute on the pretext that such an action had not been approved by the Chamber of Deputies.

Following the bombardment, the negotiations came to a sudden end. The Egyptian nationalists now had support from most classes of the population. The British cabinet was divided on what should be done. The Porte, in conjunction with ambassadors in Istanbul, decided that the sultan should send 4000 of his own troops to solve the situation. Abdulhamit, however, refused on the grounds that such a force would be too small to force Urabi to do anything. He would rather negotiate a settlement of the financial difficulties so that Ottoman control could be substituted for that of the foreigners and the Egyptian nationalists could be put in charge of introducing the sultan's reform measures in the province.[24]

While Abdulhamit's agents went off to Cairo once again, the interventionists in Britain gradually gained the upper hand under the leadership of Joseph Chamberlain, then president of the Board of Trade, who wanted to occupy the country and crush the nationalists in order to protect the interests of the British bondholders as well as to procure more and cheaper cotton for the textile manufacturers of Chamberlain's home city of Manchester. The French opposed any kind of occupation, feeling it would simply bring Britain into the Levant and end French economic and cultural domination of the area. With Gladstone ready to retire, however, the interventionists in London won out. Landings at Alexandria were followed by a climactic victory over the Egyptians at Tell el-Kebir (September 13, 1882). Cairo was occupied four days later, thus beginning British rule of the country, which was to last, in one form or another, for some 70 years. The Ottomans protested but lacked the power to reverse the situation; and when Britain stipulated that it had come to Egypt only temporarily to solve its immediate problems, the sultan accepted the situation, reaching an agreement (October 24, 1885) by which his suzerainty was maintained along with regular payments of the Egyptian tribute. The Ottomans and British were to maintain their own high commissioners in the country to advise the khedive on his domestic policies and to help make peace in the Sudan. Britain subsequently would stipulate when it would leave.[25]

Britain built its own domination of Egypt, establishing a kind of joint rule under the direction of its high commissioner and Governor General Evelyn Baring

(Lord Cromer) (1883–1907), who placed British "advisers" beside Egyptian officials and modernized the economy and physical plant of the country while neglecting the kind of education that might enable the Egyptians to displace their British masters. Britain was now in an awkward position, having some responsibility in finding a solution to the country's financial problems. Britain's subsequent intervention against the Sudanese nationalists, led by the Mahdi (1884–1885), further worsened Egypt's financial situation and led to a new international control system that allowed French participation and modified Britain's dominant position.

In 1885 Britain sent Sir Henry Drummond Wolff to Istanbul to arrange for British evacuation and restoration of direct Ottoman control. Though Abdulhamit long had agitated for British departure, he was in no position to assume the consequent financial and military burden. Thus while he considered an agreement for Britain to leave within three years, with the right to send in troops if required by domestic turmoil or foreign danger, he finally decided that this would only enable the British to increase their influence in Istanbul and did not ratify it.[26] Britain therefore remained in Egypt. Abdulhamit was unable to control his vassal province, but he remained in touch with its political and intellectual leaders through his high commissioner, Ahmet Muhtar Paşa, and the Egyptian ruling family. The Egyptian aristocracy also developed very close relations with the "motherland," sending their children to Istanbul for their education, maintaining summer homes along the Bosporus, and intermarrying with the Ottoman upper classes to such an extent that the latter had far more influence in Egypt than was apparent to the British, who remained largely on the surface of Egyptian life through their long years of political and military control.

The Balkan Tinderbox

For all practical purposes the Treaty of Berlin ended the Ottoman Empire as a significant European power and created the morass of petty Balkan states whose rivalries created a tinderbox, drawing the great powers into the confrontations that culminated in World War I. Greece, Bulgaria, Rumania, Serbia, and Montenegro now were independent or so autonomous that they were independent in everything but name. Bosnia and Herzegovina were under an Austrian occupation that was considered temporary only by the Ottomans. All the sultan had left in Europe was a strip of territory south of the Balkan Mountains extending from the Black Sea to the Adriatic and including Macedonia, Thrace, Thessaly, and Albania – organized into the provinces of Edirne, Salonica, Kosova, Janina, Monastir, and Işkodra – a far cry indeed from the mighty European empire that had once stretched all the way to the gates of Vienna. Millions of Muslim refugees had lost everything to their victorious Christian neighbors and now were wending their way to a homeland they never had seen. But autonomy or independence was hardly satisfying to the emerging Balkan states. Each soon aspired for further territory, becoming passionately nationalistic and imperialistic, demanding all the lands ruled by its people at any time in history, regardless of the fact that others had comparable historical claims and the areas were currently inhabited by different peoples. The result was constant aggression against what was left of the Ottoman Empire in Europe, wiping out defenseless Muslim villages and, occasionally, open conflict over how the spoils should be divided.

Each of the Balkan states had something to complain about in the Berlin settlement. Greece had gained new territories in Thessaly and the Epirus, but determination of the new boundaries had been left to negotiation with the Porte, which resisted the award of any territory inhabited by a large number of Muslims. In July 1881 the powers pressured the Ottomans to surrender most of Thessaly and the district of Arta in the Epirus, but Greece seemed insatiable, demanding Crete, the Aegean Islands, Istanbul, and much of Anatolia, in short, the realization of the *Megalo Idea,* or the "Great Ideal," of gaining all the territories once ruled by the Byzantine Empire. The original Treaty of San Stefano had divided the *sancak* of Novipazar between Serbia and Montenegro, giving the former access to the Adriatic. But the Ottomans had regained the district at Berlin, not only hurting the Serbian economy but also preventing their direct access to the southern Slavs in Montenegro. The Rumanians in turn were angered by Russia's desertion at both San Stefano and Berlin, forcing them to surrender Bessarabia, a major grain-producing area that also commanded the mouths of the Danube, and to accept instead the far poorer Dobruca, filled with Tatars who did not fit in a truly national Rumanian state. Finally, there was the new small Bulgaria squeezed between the Danube and the Balkan Mountains and with access only to the Black Sea. It had lost Macedonia and East Rumelia as well as the access to the Aegean that it had gained at San Stefano. Bulgaria nurtured a feeling of revanche not only against the Ottomans but also against the Serbs and the Greeks over the question of who should rule Macedonia.

Of the powers, Russia was the most unhappy about the Berlin settlement, though the czar had accepted it because he knew the other powers would concede nothing more without war. In place of the League of Three Emperors, Bismarck formed an alliance with Austria (1879), leaving Russia in diplomatic isolation. Instead of approaching France, as he might have, the czar took his hat in hand and rejoined his old partners in a new Triple Alliance (1881), whose purpose was, as before, to maintain the status quo regarding the Ottoman Empire to avoid future conflicts that might upset their unity against France and Britain. The allies agreed that there would be no further modification of Ottoman territory without unanimous consent, meaning that each would consult the other two before taking more. Russia accepted the Straits settlement, which prevented it from sending warships into the Mediterranean. Germany and Russia agreed to allow Austria to annex Bosnia-Herzegovina outright when and if it wished; and all the partners agreed to allow Bulgaria to annex East Rumelia, which Bulgaria would do very shortly.

Although Austria was allied with Russia, it used the Berlin Treaty to extend its influence over those Balkan states that had been deserted by the czar, signing alliances with Serbia (1881) and Rumania (1883) by which it offered protection in return for economic and political concessions and promises, particularly by Serbia, not to support or encourage Pan-Slavic agitation in Austrian territories. Extending its commercial and economic activities in the area, Austria built a network of railways that was to culminate with the opening of the direct line between Istanbul and Vienna in 1888, giving it a far stronger position in Southeastern Europe than seemed possible only a short time earlier.

Bulgarian Annexation of East Rumelia

Russia, indeed, had based its entire position in the Balkans on support of Bulgaria, and while it had not been able to retain all the territories set aside for the Bulgars at San Stefano, it still expected gratitude in return for its role in securing independence, helping build the new state, and strengthening it by the continued presence of the Russian army. But the Bulgars turned out to be nationalists above all else. They did not wish to exchange Ottoman for Russian rule, and they resented the airs of superiority of the czar's bureaucrats. In a surprisingly short time, therefore, gratitude changed to hostility and suspicion, undermining Russian policy in the area.

In 1879 the Russian commissioner summoned an assembly of notables and gave it a draft constitution to establish the kind of autocratic government that the czar preferred. But the assembly turned out to be under the control of liberal and nationalist politicians who discarded the Russian draft and formulated one that provided for a one-chamber legislature elected by universal male suffrage. Ministerial responsibility was to the assembly rather than to the prince. The limited power the prince had in appointing ministers was to lead to struggles for power with the assembly and affect Bulgaria's political life during the next several decades. Despite Russian protests, the constitution was accepted. Prince Alexander of Battenberg was chosen as prince, seemingly an ideal choice, since he was German but related both to the British and Russian royal families, and he took over in April 1879. But Alexander turned out to be highly autocratic and in favor of Russian predominance in Bulgaria, leading to continuous clashes with the assembly and the government. Though the prince hoped for direct Russian intervention, Czar Alexander II refused, wanting to give the constitution a chance to work. But the assassination of the latter (March 1881) gave the prince his chance, since the new Czar Alexander III strongly opposed constitutionalism and liberalism. The prince and his Russian supporters carried out a coup in May 1881, suspended the constitution, dismissed the liberal ministers, and, against the threat of abdication, forced the assembly to give him autocratic powers for seven years. Rigged elections enabled him to have an assembly that let him rule autocratically. However, the Russian generals assumed that their role in the coup gave them the right to control the prince, leading him gradually to join with the liberals and conservatives against the Russians. To regain popular support he restored the original constitution (1883) and concentrated on plans to annex East Rumelia.

The autonomous Ottoman province of East Rumelia had been organized by an international commission and, in accordance with the Treaty of Berlin, provided with a substantial regulation (April 26, 1879) that detailed every aspect of its internal organization and administration. Recognizing the sultan's suzerainty, the province paid him a regular annual tribute. The governor, appointed by the sultan with the sanction of the powers, had to be a Christian and to govern with the assistance of Christian directors of justice, education, trade, agriculture, and public works. The sultan was to appoint European officers to direct finance, the gendarmerie, and the militia, who turned out to be German, British, and French respectively. He could build and man forts and send troops when requested by the governor. The latter had to build up a native militia through conscription, with its officers, however, to be appointed by the Porte. A provincial assembly was established, with 36 elected representatives, 10 appointed by the governor and 10 more serving ex officio by virtue of their positions as judges, religious leaders, and financial inspectors. Its decisions had to be sanctioned by the sultan to become law, but if he did not do so within two months, they became law anyway. It was supposed to send representatives to the Istanbul Parliament when it met again.

The Ottoman treasury received all revenues from customs duties, the postal and telegraph services, and two-thirds of all other revenues, while the provincial treasury got the balance. The Muslims had been in a large majority in East Rumelia before 1875, but the large-scale massacres carried out by the Bulgars and their Russian allies and forced emigration had left a Christian majority. Turkish, Bulgarian, and Greek were the official languages.

The first governor of the province was Aleko Paşa, son of the Greek governor of Samos. He was a man of the Tanzimat who had risen through the bureaucracy, but in his new office he did all he could to ingratiate himself with the advocates of union with Bulgaria, appointing Bulgars to administrative positions in far greater numbers than their proportion of the population warranted and protecting the Bulgarian agents sent to stir the Christian population to upset the settlement in Bulgaria's favor. In addition, he intimidated Muslim landowners who had fled during the war and now wanted to return, threatening to impose large back-tax claims and forcing those who did come back to sell their lands to pay, with Bulgarian peasants taking over their properties. Despite these difficulties, Abdulhamit was not too unhappy with the arrangement, since he secured considerable revenue without having to pay for any of the administrative expenses. Thus he acquiesced in Aleko's blatant violations of the provisions of equal treatment for all, while the powers said nothing as long as it was the Muslims who were being persecuted. However, his resistance to Russian intervention led the Russians and their allies in Bulgaria to advocate his dismissal. Since the Porte in any case had not been too happy with his conduct, he finally was replaced by a compromise candidate, a Bulgarian named Gavirel Krestovic (Gavril Paşa), who was believed to be weak and therefore acceptable to everyone. Gavril, however, turned out to be even more nationalistic than Aleko, openly pushing Muslim peasants across the border into Thrace, appointing Bulgarian nationalists to key positions, and protecting the Bulgarian unionist agents sent into East Rumelia.

On September 14, 1885, a unionist revolt broke out near the capital, Filibe. In response to severe Russian pressure Gavril moved to suppress it, but he was imprisoned by a group of deputies led by Stefan Stambulov, who was to become a leading Bulgarian political figure. Stambulov declared union with Bulgaria in the name of the assembly, inviting Prince Alexander to come and take over. Once again the powers who had guaranteed the terms of the Treaty of Berlin had an opportunity to live up to their obligations, and once again they failed to do so. The Porte had the right to intervene with troops on its own, but Abdulhamit was confident that the powers would move to maintain the empire's integrity. The League of the Three Emperors originally had supported the idea of union, but the czar now refused to go along because of his dislike of the prince, demanding his removal as the price for agreement. Fears, however, rose that union might lead Greece and Serbia to try to compensate themselves by taking parts of Macedonia, which, in turn, would lead Austria to annex Bosnia-Herzegovina, causing trouble with both the Russians and Ottomans. To prevent this a new conference of ambassadors was held in Istanbul (November 1885), with the representatives of the three emperors following the Russian line in opposing unification. Britain, however, now supported an enlarged Bulgaria, thus regarding it as a bulwark against Russian influence in the Balkans. France continued to support the Balkan nationalists. Rather than be accused of "massacre" again, the Ottomans wanted the sanction of the powers to intervene, but they could not get it and nothing was done.

The only direct action was taken by Serbia, which declared war on Bulgaria to gain territorial compensation for its anticipated gains. Most observers expected an easy Serbian victory, since the Bulgarian army had lost its Russian officers and in any case was concentrated on the borders of East Rumelia. But a few detachments kept the Serbs away from Sofia until Alexander arrived with most of his army just in time to rout the enemy at Slivnitza, just outside Sofia (November 17–19). In the end Austrian intervention prevented any permanent Bulgarian occupation of southern Serbia. Peace was reached (March 3, 1886), with Bulgaria remaining in control of East Rumelia. Abdulhamit emerged with less revenue and almost no respect for the powers, which had repeatedly failed to live up to their obligations. He therefore moved to use Alexander's quarrel with the czar to pry Bulgaria away from Russia and thus prevent further Russian expansion. Bulgaria again recognized the sultan's suzerainty, and Prince Alexander accepted the appointment as governor of East Rumelia for five years. A personal union then was established between the two provinces, and tax payments to Istanbul were restored (March 24, 1886). Abdulhamit thus secured a much better settlement than might have been expected, though neither Alexander nor the powers really expected Ottoman suzerainty there to be maintained for long.

The new arrangement was, however, opposed by the Bulgarian nationalists, and the czar used this to get rid of the prince finally. With the connivance of the Russian representatives in Sofia, a few army officers and politicians arranged for Alexander to be kidnapped and forced him to abdicate (August 20, 1886). Stambulov established a popular government and, despite Russian pressure, named another German prince, Ferdinand of Saxe-Coburg, who ruled from 1887 to 1914, though under Stambulov's strong influence in the first part of his reign (1887–1894). Ferdinand finally used the death of Alexander III and Czar Nicholas II (1895) to restore the old friendship with Russia, subsequently gaining recognition of the union of East Rumelia with Bulgaria. His ambitions eventually were to lead to the rise of a major new conflict with the Porte and his Balkan neighbors over Macedonia.

Problems in Albania

Abdulhamit also faced serious difficulties in Albania, though it was only much later in the century that these became acute. The Albanians on the whole seemed quite satisfied with their position in the empire, with many serving in the Ottoman Ruling Class, while in Albania the Catholic and Muslim mountain tribes of the north and the Greek Orthodox of the Suli and Hamari regions of the south enjoyed almost complete autonomy. But this situation changed when, beginning at San Stefano, the powers started awarding parts of Albanian territory to the new Balkan states. Albanian national consciousness began to develop. Discarding their religious and tribal differences, they defended themselves against their Slavic brothers. The Albanian League was created at Prizren in 1878 with at least the tacit approval of the Ottoman government. The league was disappointed by the Berlin Treaty, which left some Albanian territories to Serbia and Montenegro; thus when the sultan pressured the league to accept the new arrangement, it turned against him as well as its Balkan neighbors, demanding recognition of Albanian territorial integrity and some kind of autonomous status within the empire. Following the Congress of Berlin the Ottomans divided Albania into four vilayets, Janina, Monastir, Üsküp, and Işkodra, whereas the league and its supporters sought to unite them into a single province, thus initiating a movement toward Albanian solidarity. According to the *millet* system, all Muslim Albanians were taught only

Turkish and Arabic, while the Christians were educated in Greek under the watchful Orthodox *millet* leaders. There was no recognition of the Albanian language or culture, and this also was a grievance that the nationalist leaders now sought to remedy. Cultural nationalism and a desire for autonomy within the empire turned to aspirations for independence after the Porte ceded Dulcigno to Montenegro in 1880. Albanian rebel bands rose in the mountains, attacking Ottoman officials and troops. Villages resisted tax collectors, and the railroads were attacked. The Ottoman garrisons still were able to suppress most of the brigands and to maintain general control, but nationalist agitation continued to build, creating a problem that was to become increasingly serious in the early years of the twentieth century.[27]

The Armenian Question

Frustrated in their hopes of dominating Southeastern Europe through a Bulgarian satellite, the Russians sought an alternative instrument to chisel at the Ottoman Empire and turned to one of the minorities that had not sought to revolt against the sultan, the Armenians. There had been no difficulty with the Armenians previously because they had been integrated fully into traditional Ottoman society, with their own Gregorian *millet* maintaining religious and cultural autonomy under the Armenian patriarch of Istanbul. What misrule there was had been the consequence of domination by the religious hierarchy, as had been the case in some of the other non-Muslim *millet*s. The few Armenians who reacted expressed their discontent in religious terms, converting to Catholicism or Protestantism. Ottoman acceptance of the Catholic and Protestant *millet*s in the Tanzimat period gave the Armenians in the Gregorian *millet* alternatives, challenging the traditional authority structure. The community had long been dominated by the wealthy Armenian officials and bankers in conjunction with the religious leaders, but the new competition, when combined with Tanzimat pressure, forced it to accept the same kind of democratization that had been introduced in the other *millet*s. Lay members secured a far greater voice in *millet* affairs than had been the case in the past, though the wealthier members continued to dominate in many ways.

Armenians had always played an important role in Ottoman trade and industry, specializing, in the usual Middle Eastern manner, in money changing, goldsmithing, jewelry, foreign trade, construction, medicine, and the theater. In addition, after the Greek Revolution, Greeks remaining within the empire had been mostly supplanted in the schools and government by Armenians. Because of their knowledge of foreign languages and finance and experience in trade, they rose in all branches of the elaborate Tanzimat administration, particularly in the ministries of Finance, Interior, Foreign Affairs, Education, Justice, and Public Works; in the postal, telegraph and census services, and the railroads. Though some European travelers and missionaries claimed that there were over 2 million Armenians in the sultan's dominions, the Ottoman census department, which maintained a continuous record of population in conjunction with the identity card system, found some 988,887 Armenians in the Gregorian *millet,* both men and women. If one assumes that about two-thirds of the 160,166 Catholics and 36,339 Protestants in the empire were of Armenian origin, one could conclude that there were about 1,125,500 Armenians in the empire, only 5.5 percent of the total population of 20,475,225 (excluding those portions of the empire not yet surveyed, the Yemen, Hicaz, Tripoli, Bengazi of Libya, Egypt, and Tunis). Even in Istanbul, which had by far the largest

Armenian urban community in the empire, there were only 97,782 Gregorians, 407 Catholics, and 340 Protestants, or 18 percent of a total population of 542,437 in the 1878 census. In addition, in the Byzantine period and continuing into the Turkish settlement of Anatolia starting in the eleventh century the Armenian communities had been scattered widely, and by 1882 they formed small minorities in all the provinces and *sancak*s of the empire, even in those six (see Table 3.1) that their nationalists were later to claim as their own. Even on the *kaza* level (see Table 3.2.) in the rural areas where most of the Armenian provincial population lived it was very rare for them to have a majority.

Thus in none of the provinces and in only two of the *kaza*s in the empire did the Armenians have a numerical majority. Outside the main cities they were interspersed with the Muslim cultivators and nomadic tribesmen, the latter of both Turkish and Kurdish origin, whose condition was no worse but certainly no better than that of their Armenian brothers. If there were economic and social problems, these involved the misrule of the bureaucrats and great landowners and the age-old tendency of the tribesmen to raid the cultivated areas, but these conditions affected Muslims and Christians alike. Whatever unhappiness existed among Armenians, it was absorbed within the structure of their *millet,* whose leaders supported the status quo to maintain themselves in power. The Armenians were as free to lead their own lives as were all other subjects of the sultan. Their churches,

Table 3.1. *The Armenian population of the six provinces, 1882*

Vilayet	Gregorians	Catholics	Protestants	Total	Total population	Armenian (%)
Erzurum	101,138	6,730	1,970	109,838	659,155	16.6
Bitlis	101,358	4,948	1,498	107,804	276,998	38.9
Van	60,448	—	—	60,448	269,860	22.3
Diyarbekir	46,833	9,955	3,981	60,769	289,591	20.98
Mamuret ul-Aziz	73,178	1,915	4,971	80,064	481,346	16.6
Sivas	116,256	3,223	1,994	121,473	926,564	13.1

Table 3.2. *The Armenian population of major* kaza*s in eastern Anatolia, 1882*[28]

Kaza	Gregorians	Catholics	Protestants	Total	Total population	Armenian (%)
Erzurum	9,730	791	329	10,850	38,684	28.04
Erzincan	12,686	—	88	12,774	54,503	23.43
Adana	9,622	348	636	10,606	70,665	15.00
Sis	14,026	56	87	14,169	20,523	69.03
Haçin	10,204	145	682	11,031	24,057	45.85
Kayseri	25,250	765	1,315	27,330	130,899	20.87
Diyarbekir	12,083	2,560	983	15,626	62,870	24.85
Sivas	20,466	1,592	89	22,147	88,375	25.06
Trabzon	9,546	1,209	91	10,846	117,563	9.22
Van	33,053	—	—	33,053	51,149	64.62

schools, and hospitals were maintained and operated to meet the needs of the people. There was no significant dissatisfaction.

During the early years of the nineteenth century, however, partly stimulated by Western missionary activity, there was an Armenian national cultural revival, particularly in the new Catholic and Protestant communities. They developed their own cultural centers, reviving the study of classical Armenian, publishing bibles in the vernacular rather than the classical church language, and developing a new literary language that the masses could understand. In response to this the Gregorian *millet* in turn experienced a cultural awakening at the same time that it was democratizing under government pressure, with lay influence leading to the introduction of secular education into the *millet* schools. Many wealthy Armenians sent their children to study in France, where they were influenced by French culture. Upon their return they advocated not only radical reform within the *millet* but also secularization and autonomy. During the 1860s, some of these Armenian nationalists joined the Young Ottomans and worked successfully in the dissemination of the concept of representative government within both the *millet* system and Ottoman society. The few who advocated independence for the Armenians under the sultan's dominion were opposed by the Gregorian *millet* establishment and by the wealthy Armenian merchants and officials who prospered under Ottoman rule; hence the former's influence was limited to intellectuals.

The international crisis that culminated at the Congress of Berlin contributed to changes in outlook within the Armenian *millet*. The achievement of independence by Bulgaria and Serbia stimulated many Armenians to hope for the same. The Russian invasion of eastern Anatolia in 1877 was spearheaded by Armenian officers and administrators who had risen in the czar's service since his absorption of the Caucasus earlier in the century. They contacted many of their brothers in the Ottoman Empire to secure their help against the sultan. The mass of Ottoman Armenians remained loyal subjects, but the deeds of the few who did not left a feeling of mistrust. This was magnified by Patriarch Nerses' efforts at San Stefano and Berlin to gain European support for an Armenian state in the east as well as subsequent Russian efforts to develop Armenian nationalism as a means of undermining the Ottoman state. The Armenians as well as the Ottomans thus became pawns in the struggles for power in Europe.

With Russian encouragement, most Armenian nationalists emphasized political goals. When the European powers did not pay attention to their demands for autonomy or even independence, they turned from persuasion to terrorism in order to achieve their ends. Armenian revolutionary societies sprang up within the sultan's dominions, particularly at Istanbul, Trabzon, Erzurum, and Van, among wealthy Armenians in the Russian Empire, and also in the major cities of Europe, publishing periodicals and broadsides and sending them into Ottoman territory through the foreign post offices. The most violent of the nationalist societies was that established in Tiflis, which sent rifles and ammunition into Ottoman territory from Batum to Rize, while Armenians living in Tabriz sent agents across the border to terrorize Muslim villagers. The Armenian demands were weakened by the fact that, unlike the situation with the Serbs and Bulgars, there was not a single large area in the Ottoman Empire where the Armenians were in a clear majority. In addition, Czar Alexander soon realized that the efforts to undermine the sultan were being accompanied by radical doctrines that might well stimulate revolt among his own subjects as well, and he soon withdrew his support.

Faced with these difficulties, the Armenian nationalists became increasingly violent, using terror to force wealthy Armenians to support their cause and to stimulate Muslims to the kind of reprisals that would force the governments of Britain and Russia to intervene. They strove to undermine the sultan's faith in his Armenian officials by forcing the latter to support the national cause. The revolutionary nationalists formed their own terror bands in the east, attacking Ottoman tax collectors, postmen, and judges, massacring entire villages, and forcing the Armenian peasants and merchants to hide and feed them on pain of death. But on the whole their numbers were too small, the mass of Armenians too disinterested, and Abdulhamit's provincial police too efficient for them to make much headway. The Muslims were kept from responding in kind, though the sporadic Armenian raids increasingly poisoned the atmosphere and made it more and more difficult for Armenians and Muslims to live side by side as they had for generations.

With the failure of the Armenian revolutionaries inside the Ottoman Empire, the stage was left to those outside. Two groups dominated the movement, the Bell (Hunchak) organization of Armenian students in France and Switzerland, founded in 1886, and the Armenian Revolutionary Federation, or Dashnaks, established in 1890 in Russia to unite all the Armenian nationalists after they had been suppressed by the czar as part of a policy aimed at eliminating radicalism in his empire. Their programs involved the creation of action groups to enter Ottoman territory, terrorize government officials and Armenians alike, and stimulate massacres. This would bring about foreign intervention and help the nationalists secure an independent, socialist Armenian republic, presumably in the six east Anatolian provinces from which all Muslims would be driven out or simply killed. The Dashnaks established a number of cells in Istanbul, Trabzon, and Van, but they really did little prior to 1895. On the other hand, the Hunchaks were quite successful in and out of the empire, establishing centers at Erzurum, Harput, Izmir, and Aleppo as well as at Geneva. They cooperated with the other national groups agitating against the Ottomans, particularly those from Macedonia, Crete, and Albania. Revolutionary literature was sent into the empire, again through the foreign postal systems; bombs were exploded in public places; officials were murdered at their desks, and postmen along their routes. Within a short time, despite all the efforts of the government to keep order, the Hunchaks had what they wanted, reprisals from Muslim tribesmen and villagers. It should be recalled that the new wave of Armenian terrorism came just when millions of Muslim refugees were flowing into the empire from Russia, Bulgaria, and Bosnia, bringing tales of how their loved ones had been murdered and their homes and properties stolen; therefore it did not take too much to stir up the Muslims, with the refugees in fact taking the lead. Abdulhamit had been close to many Armenians in his early life, but he now changed his attitude, playing into the latter's hands by accusing Armenian officials of disloyalty and ordering the government to crack down on the Armenian merchants of Istanbul to lessen their undeniable economic power, and also by organizing the local *Hamidiye* tribal gendarmes to help the army suppress terrorism in the east.

Terrorism and counterterrorism went on for three years (1890–1893), with the government acting sternly, albeit sometimes harshly, to keep order. The Hunchaks were, however, denied the kind of harsh reprisal that they really needed to make their case in Europe. They then organized a major coup at Sasun, southwest of Muş, the strongest area of Armenian population, where there were many marauding tribesmen who had caused trouble to the cultivators in the past. When the local governor tried to collect tax arrears, the Hunchaks had the cultivators greet the collectors with rifles and swords. The army arrived to enforce order, and the rebels fled into the mountains, ravaging the Muslim villages in the area as they went, knowing that the remaining Armenian peasants would suffer the consequences. And suffer they did, as the regular troops and *Hamidiye* regiments ravaged Sasun after having seen the tragedies left in the nearby Muslim villages, where the entire population had been wiped out.

The countermassacre had been undertaken entirely on the initiative of the Ottoman troops and local commanders and without any order to this effect from the central government. But the deed had been done, and the network of revolutionary propaganda was put into action to develop popular European reaction similar to that which had followed the earlier events in Bulgaria. Once again the circumstances were ignored and the provocation forgotten. The Ottoman government was accused of ordering the destruction of 25 villages in the area and of the execution of 20,000 Armenian villagers! Detailed investigations made by a mixed Ottoman and foreign commission demonstrated the exaggerated nature of the claims, but European public opinion, followed closely by its politicians, was ever ready to believe the worst of Muslims. The sultan attempted to conciliate Europe and make it easier for their politicians to accept what they knew to be true by promising once again to make the reforms he was, in fact, already making in the east, and the powers therefore declined to intervene.[29]

Because the response of the powers disappointed the Hunchaks, they tried again, this time in Istanbul, to create a disturbance everyone would see. On September 30, 1895, a demonstration was organized to protest the commission's report, marching first to the major foreign embassies and then to the Porte. This inflamed the masses of the capital, then thronged by thousands of homeless and jobless refugees from Bosnia and Bulgaria passing through the city on their way to Anatolia. Rumors about the death of an Ottoman policeman trying to control the demonstrators stimulated a general riot, leading to communal massacre and countermassacre, which helped the terrorist cause. Abdulhamit prepared to send in police to restore order, but the ambassadors complained that the measure was intended only to suppress the Armenians. Nothing was done, therefore, until the disturbances threatened to spread to the areas where the Europeans lived, at which time they finally allowed the government to establish a martial law and bring in the army to end the troubles (October 9). Similar communal disturbances followed at Trabzon and several other cities and towns. Again the cry went through Europe that Muslims were slaughtering Christians with government connivance. But with the British cabinet too divided to act and Russia opposed to any action that would bring Britain into control of the Straits, there was no intervention and the terrorists were disappointed once more.

The winter of 1895–1896 witnessed large-scale suffering throughout Anatolia as general security broke down, but little could be done until the army was brought in during the spring. In Istanbul the Armenian terrorists, still hoping to force foreign intervention, struck again. On August 26, 1896, a group of Armenians took over the main Ottoman Bank in Beyoğlu.[30] Bombs were planted throughout the building, some of the bank employees were held as hostages, and preparations were made for a lengthy siege in the hope of rousing European interest. Soon after, a second group forced its way into the Sublime Porte, wounding several officials and threatening the grand vezir with a pistol. Revolutionary units ran through the old quarter of Istanbul, throwing bombs and firing wildly with rifles and pistols, killing and wounding a number of innocent bystanders. Another bomb was thrown at the sultan as he was going to the Aya Sofya mosque for the Friday prayer, with more than 20 policemen guarding him being killed. Demands were delivered to the European embassies calling for the dispatch of a new investigation commission to the eastern provinces, the appointment of Christian governors and *kaymakam*s to administer them, of Christian police, gendarme, and militia forces to replace those of the government, pardoning of all taxes for five years and their reduction by four-fifths thereafter, increases in state expenditures in the area for schools and other local needs, a general pardon for all Armenians accused and/or convicted of crimes during the previous incidents, and restoration of all confiscated property. Abdulhamit could not accept these demands if he was to retain any authority in his empire – so he rejected them. After a day-long siege the bank occupiers were captured and the other demonstrators driven off. To reduce the tension and prevent further clashes the sultan soon afterward decreed a general amnesty and began to appoint Christian administrators in the east, even though the Christians were minorities in most of the districts involved.

At this point Lord Salisbury attempted to get the support of the new czar, Nicholas II (1894–1917), for the British fleet to come to Istanbul to persuade the sultan to give the Armenians what they wanted. Russia, however, feared this would increase British control in the empire and joined France in opposing unilateral intervention to pressure the sultan. Salisbury's initiative was frustrated, and nothing was done; and with no foreign support likely the Armenian terror groups themselves broke up in internal quarrels. With the provocations soon forgotten, relations between Muslims and Armenians in the empire for the most part returned to normal. Armenian officials again were appointed to high positions in the bureaucracy, and Armenian merchants and cultivators resumed their activities. But the terrible events had taken their toll. The harmony that had prevailed for centuries was gone. Those Armenians who could – that is, wealthy urban merchants and also many revolutionary society members and intellectuals – reacted to the continued unwillingness of the Armenian masses to join or even support their movement. They left the Ottoman Empire, going to Iran, Egypt, Europe, and especially to the United States, where they settled and devoted their energies and ability to making new lives for themselves and their families. By 1897, then, the Armenian Question was exhausted and lay dormant until World War I. It is interesting to note, however, that during these last years the Armenians of the empire actually increased in population (see Table 3.3) and as the empire lost territory in the Balkans, they became a larger percentage of the total population.

Table 3.3. *The Armenian population of the Ottoman Empire, 1882–1914*[31]

Year	Gregorians	Catholics	Protestants	Total Armenians	Total population	Armenian (%)
1882	988,887	100,160	36,339	1,125,386	17,375,225	6.47
1895	1,042,374	80,334	44,360	1,167,068	19,050,307	6.12
1906	1,140,563	90,050	53,880	1,280,493	20,947,617	6.10
1914	n.a.	n.a.	n.a.	1,294,831	18,520,016	6.11

The Greco-Turkish War

One of the most surprising facets of Ottoman foreign relations during the nineteenth century was the relatively minor role of Greece. Of all the Balkan states it was the only one to claim the Ottoman capital as well as parts of Rumeli and western Anatolia. Greeks constituted the largest minority in the empire, in 1895 numbering 2,569,912, or 13.49 percent, with clear majorities or substantial minorities in a number of important provinces.[32] Greek subjects of the sultan had in time shaken off the accusations of disloyalty resulting from the Greek Revolution and had again achieved high governmental positions, and they had a far more extensive and wealthy merchant community than that of the Armenians. Whereas the Armenians were divided on important national questions, the Greeks almost unanimously supported the idea of a restored Greco-Byzantine Empire. But little was done toward achieving this end either by the kingdom of Greece or by the sultan's Greek subjects. There was, indeed, a national irredentist society, the *Ethnike Hetairia,* formed in 1894 among Greek army officers, but it did not resort to violence to achieve its aims. Having achieved independent statehood and international recognition as heirs of an ancient civilization, perhaps the Greeks did not feel frustrated enough to resort to extreme measures. The mild attitude of Greece can also be attributed to a lack of money to build an army large enough to achieve its ambitions and the existence of bitter internal political rivalries. The liberals, led by Charilaos Tricoupes, were supported by the urban middle class, and the conservatives of Theodore Deligannes were supported by the notables and the army. The former group introduced reforms while in power and the latter repealed them, attempting to divert the resulting dissatisfaction by renewed emphasis on the Great Ideal. Greece could achieve its ambitions only gradually by expansion north into Thessaly and Epirus, east into Macedonia, and south into the Aegean Islands, including Crete. Most of the territories mentioned had sizable Greek majorities, with the exception of Macedonia, which had large Muslim and Slavic populations and also was coveted by Serbia and Bulgaria. In 1881 the powers had given Greece much of Thessaly and Epirus, but the creation of Bulgaria, when added to the existing threat from Serbia, had thwarted Greek ambitions in Macedonia. In 1885 when Bulgaria took East Rumelia, Deligannes tried to appease Greek feelings by securing the rest of Epirus in compensation, but the powers forced him to desist by blockading his ports. A decade later, especially with the formation of the *Ethnike Hetairia,* Deligannes attempted to satisfy national ambitions by gaining control of Crete.

In Crete conditions had improved with the application of the Organic Regulation of 1868, but Greek instigation had led to a general revolt between 1875 and 1878. To remedy the situation Abdulhamit sent his trusted adviser, the Greek Karatodori Paşa, to govern the island. He signed an agreement with the consuls of the powers at Haleppa (October 1878), promising the island a representative assembly with a Greek majority. But Greek bands continued to penetrate the island, stimulating renewed attacks on tax collectors and occasional bloody clashes. Finally, in 1889 the sultan suspended the Organic Regulation as well as the Haleppa Pact, governed directly through Muslim governors, and mainly abandoned the representative institutions in order to restore order and introduce reforms directly. More disturbances followed, however, with the Greek nationalists sending in men and supplies and the Russians leading the powers in urging the sultan to restore the old arrangement to bring peace. Late in 1896 Abdulhamit agreed to replace the Organic Regulation with a new statute providing government by a popular assembly and a

Christian governor, with general amnesty for all who had participated in the disturbances. But the clashes between Muslims and Greeks continued, and the Greek government was under nationalist pressure to intervene. Then late in January 1897 a group of rebels from Crete was joined by Greeks from the mainland. They openly revolted against the sultan and declared the island's union with Greece. On February 3 a Greek force of 10,000 men was sent to occupy the island under the leadership of Prince George. They cut a swath of devastation, slaughtering thousands of Muslims. The powers tried to intervene to secure a settlement but the massacres continued, forcing the governor to flee on a Russian warship while the Ottoman soldiers responded by slaughtering Greeks as well as defending the Muslims. It was this act alone that seemed to catch the eye of the European press. The powers proposed a settlement with full autonomy for Crete and with all the Ottoman soldiers withdrawn. The sultan could not agree to this, and the crisis continued. The Muslims besieged Hanya and Candia and shut off all sources of food and other supplies.

Greece now tried to use the situation in Crete to expand its hold in Thessaly, starting a war which lasted for a month and proved to be a complete disaster for it. Prince Constantine led a small force across the border near Janina (April 10), but the far larger and better-equipped Ottoman army of Monastir not only pushed it back, but also moved deep into Greek Thessaly, routing the Greek army, taking Terhala, Larissa (Yenişehir), and Tirnovo and advancing to the Gulf of Volo (May 5). Athens panicked, and it seemed possible that Greece might again fall under Ottoman rule. Neither the powers nor the Ottomans, however, wanted this. By this time Britain was basing its Middle East position more on its control of Egypt than on the continued survival of the rest of the Ottoman Empire, and Russian attention was turned to the Far East. Therefore, they intervened to force an armistice and peace agreement by which the Ottomans agreed to leave Thessaly and the Greeks promised to pay a small war indemnity as well as allow Muslims to emigrate to Ottoman territory, starting a new flow of refugees. The powers thus protected Greece from suffering the consequences of its attack and then went on to reward it by forcing Abdulhamit to establish a new autonomous regime in Crete (December 19, 1897), still under Ottoman suzerainty but with a Christian governor appointed by the sultan with the sanction of Athens. Ottoman soldiers were withdrawn, and the governor promised to protect all Muslims remaining on the island, but with a Greek militia this meant very little. The powers soon surprised the sultan by appointing the Greek Prince George as their high commissioner for Crete, thus giving Greece control of the island for all practical purposes, though it was not formally annexed until 1912. Again the settlement was followed by the now familiar sight of weary lines of Muslim refugees leaving everything they owned for an uncertain future in Anatolia as the only alternative to the persecution that they knew would otherwise be their fate. Greece had achieved a victory through diplomacy, but the king and the government suffered the stigma of the military defeat for some time. They responded with measures to modernize their army and tried to gain some restoration of prestige by participating with special vigor in the increasingly serious situation then evolving in Macedonia.[33]

The Macedonian Question

The most difficult, complicated, and long-lived problem faced by Abdulhamit II was the Macedonian Question, which resulted from the ambitions of his Balkan neighbors to rule Macedonia. From the Congress of Berlin until World War I the issue occupied Ottoman and European statesmen alike more than any other single diplomatic problem, contributing significantly to the rivalries and wars that engulfed the area early in the twentieth century. Macedonia itself stretched between Thrace and Albania, bounded in the south by the Aegean, in the north by the Sar Mountains, and in the west by Lake Ohrid. It was organized into the Ottoman provinces of Salonica, Monastir, and Kosova including in addition the cities of Serez, Ohrid, Üsküp (Skopje), and Bitola. Its population was mixed, with no single group having a majority and each disputing which elements should be counted with it. According to the Ottoman censuses taken during Abdulhamit's reign, it was equally divided between Muslims and Christians, as shown by Table 3.4.

Though the Serbs usually were counted with the Greeks in the Greek Orthodox *millet*, the Bulgars still had a clear majority of the non-Muslim population. In general, the cities were predominantly Muslim and Greek (with the exception of Salonica, which was mainly Jewish), while the countryside was Muslim and Slavic. Regardless of exact numbers at the time, however, most of the claims to rule were based more on emotion and pride, with each group looking back to the greatest extent of its national rule in the area – the Greeks to the times of Alexander the Great and the Byzantine Empire, the Serbs to the empire of Stefan Dušan, the Bulgars to their great empire of the past as well as to the Big Bulgaria established at San Stefano.

Macedonia was of strategic importance, commanding the communication route down the valleys of the Vardar and Morava and offering both Bulgaria and Serbia a vital outlet to the sea. It also had considerable agricultural wealth. With the existing balance of power, control of Macedonia would give any Balkan state just the strength needed to dominate the area. To the Ottomans Macedonia meant not only rule over more than 1 million Muslims but also substantial tax revenues and a buffer against Greek ambitions for Ottoman territories farther east. The powers were attracted to the controversy by Macedonia's closeness to Istanbul and the Straits. Greece had a weaker army than its Slavic rivals, but it seemed to have the inside track to Macedonia through its control and use of the Orthodox church. The establishment of the Bulgarian Exarchate (1870) created a balance that, when combined with Bulgaria's financial and military resources, seemed to presage a

Table 3.4. *The population of Macedonia, 1882-1906*

	1882	1895	1904	1906
Muslims	1,083,130	1,137,315	1,508,507	1,145,849
Greek Orthodox	534,396	603,249	307,000	623,197
Bulgarian Orthodox	704,574	692,742	796,479	626,715
Catholics (Greek)	2,311	3,315	—	2,928
Vlachs	—	—	99,000	26,042
Serbs	—	—	100,717	—
Jews and others	151,730	68,432	99,997	30,594
Totals	2,476,141	2,505,503	2,911,700	2,455,325

Sources: The figures for 1882, 1895, and 1906 come from the regular Ottoman census reports cited in note 31. Those for 1904 come from a special survey made by Inspector Hüseyin Hilmi Paşa, cited in Bayur, *Türk Inkilabı Tarihi*, Istanbul, 1940, vol. I, p. 152.

victory for it. Serbia was in the weakest position, since it was difficult for it to prove that it had any adherents in Macedonia at all and it lacked the kind of religious instrument of penetration that its rivals were able to use. Its main strength, however, was Austria, whose ambition to extend its influence to the Aegean could be achieved only through a Serbian triumph. Rumania also put in a claim on the basis of the presence of Vlachs, but they were such a small minority that this can be seen only as an effort to keep Bulgaria from expanding its power. As the dispute developed, there also emerged a Macedonian separatist movement whose adherents claimed that they were neither Bulgars, Serbs, nor Greeks but an entirely separate Slavic people, with a distinct dialect of their own that entitled them to independence from all who claimed to rule them. And, finally, there were the Muslims, many of them refugees from lands to the north, who formed the largest single *millet* in Macedonia and opposed any claim that would again place them under the control of Christians, who had treated them so badly in the past.

The battle was fought in various ways. First, for purposes of indoctrination each of the competing Balkan states had its own organization to provide leadership in churches, schools, and cultural activities. Spreading nationalist propaganda were the Bulgarian Cyril and Methodius Committee (1884), the Serbian Society of Saint Slava (1886), and the Greek *Ethnike Hetairia* (1894). If these had been the only instruments of rivalry, neither the disputants nor the Macedonians and Ottomans would have suffered so much. But the Balkan nationalists also formed terrorist societies, on the Armenian model, to spread their messages. Most violent of these were the Internal Macedonian Revolutionary Organization (IMRO) established by Bulgarians in Macedonia (1893) to lead their people against the Ottomans and all others who opposed the Bulgarian claim, and the rival External Macedonian Revolutionary Organization (EMRO), established in Sofia to train Macedonian exiles for the same kind of objective. IMRO was reflective of Macedonian viewpoints, aiming at the establishment of an autonomous province, associated federally with Bulgaria and Serbia, while the EMRO was more Bulgarian in its goals, advocating union with Bulgaria once the Ottomans were driven out. The Serbs and Greeks had their own terrorist organizations, on a smaller scale. Supporting these groups, in and out of Macedonia, were the governments and consuls of the nations concerned, who provided not only money and encouragement but also arms and ammunition and at times legal protection to the terrorists.

Starting in 1900 the different groups began their campaigns, ravaging the countryside, slaughtering officials as well as Muslim and Christian subjects who refused to accept their points of view. Trains and postal carriages were intercepted, foreigners and wealthy natives kidnapped for ransom, churches blown up. Macedonia became a common expression of horror in the foreign press, particularly when incidents involved foreigners or Christians. Though the Ottoman government only strove to restore order and protect all elements of the population, somehow it was blamed for everything the terrorists did, with the sufferings of the Christians emphasized almost exclusively while the Muslims were mostly forgotten. The signatory powers of Berlin pressured the Ottomans to make "reforms" in Macedonia in the hope that this might satisfy the terrorists. In response, Abdulhamit organized a new province, called the Three Provinces (*Vilâyet-i Selase*), including Salonica, Kosova, and Monastir, whose regulation was to be drawn up by a special Rumeli Provinces Reform Commission on the basis of investigations made by Hüseyin Hilmi Paşa, former governor of the Yemen. It provided for mixed police and gendarmerie forces, special new departments to deal with public works and foreign affairs, mixed courts, a Christian governor, new schools, and a large part of the province's tax revenues to be used to develop its own economy.[34] But neither the terrorists nor the Russians or the Austrians were satisfied with a plan that would enable the Ottomans to keep Macedonia. When the reform plan was proclaimed and officials were sent out to put it into effect, the IMRO fought back with a general uprising centered at Monastir, taking over most of the province and attacking Muslims as well as Christians not wishing to join the movement, while the Ottoman army replied in kind. Thousands of terrorized Muslims fled toward Istanbul, and an equal number of Christians moved toward Sofia. The Bulgarian government, fearing that the IMRO activities might draw it into an unwanted war, finally took steps to curb it, at least by preventing it from operating in Bulgarian territory (September 1903).

Russia and Austria opposed any settlement that the Ottomans might impose by direct negotiation with the Balkan states. On February 21, 1903, they issued their own reform proposals in Vienna. They demanded that the provincial inspector continue his work, that no soldiers be used locally without special permission, that new reforms be introduced to satisfy the different elements of the population as well as the powers, that the local police and gendarmerie be composed of Muslims and Christians in proportion to their numbers in the population, and that tax reforms be carried out, including replacement of the tithe with a regular land tax. Even though the administration was thus to be carried out partly under the control of foreigners, the sultan was satisfied because direct foreign intervention would be avoided. But, as earlier, the terrorists did not want a settlement that left the Ottomans still in control of Macedonia. Nor were the Macedonian Muslims happy with an arrangement that allowed Christian soldiers and policemen; hence they began demonstrations in Kosova that cost the lives of many of their Christian countrymen as well as that of the Russian consul of Üsküp. The Serbian and Bulgarian terrorists began to raid from their mountain fastnesses, encouraging the Christians of Macedonia to join a general uprising against the Ottomans. The IMRO terrorists copied the Armenians by attacking and blowing up the Ottoman Bank at Salonica. Only the Greek terrorists, not wishing their Slavic rivals to gain full control of the province, held back and at times cooperated with the Ottomans to restore order.

In response to the new difficulties, Czar Nicholas and Emperor Franz Joseph issued a new reform program at Mürzteg (October 9, 1903), presenting it to the Ottomans after gaining the approval of all the Berlin Treaty signatories. They now demanded that the Ottoman inspector general be accompanied and advised by Russian and Austrian officials, who would investigate the complaints of Christians and root out all instances of misrule and oppression. A general amnesty would be proclaimed. The Ottoman government would give financial assistance to help the villagers restore their homes and fields. Mixed administrative councils and courts would be introduced in all localities where the populations were mixed, and the Russian and Austrian consuls would supervise all the reforms. Abdulhamit disliked many of the provisions involving foreign supervision, but he did not want the Macedonian problem to lead to a more general war, and he was willing to let the foreigners try out reforms he knew would not satisfy the terrorists. Within a short time the reforms were begun. But now the Greeks and Vlachs, supported respectively by the patriarchate and the Rumanian government, became far more active than they had been earlier, opposing a settlement that they feared would favor the Slavs. In addition, while Bulgaria signed a separate agreement with the Porte

(April 8, 1904) reaffirming its intention to stop the terrorist bands, it was unable to do so. Political murders continued throughout the province until the end of Abdulhamit's reign, and it was only in 1909 that a reformed gendarmerie and police finally were able to bring some order.

In the meantime, the powers also proposed new financial reforms to be carried out through the Ottoman Bank and its branches in Macedonia, which would, in essence become the financial departments of each of the three provinces. But Abdulhamit refused to accept such direct foreign participation in the Ottoman financial process. An International Finance Commission was formed to supervise Macedonia's finances (May 8, 1905), but the Porte refused to accept its intervention. An international fleet of five ships then was sent to take over the island of Midilli (November 26, 1905). It went on to capture the customs offices at Limni (December 5, 1905) before Abdulhamit finally caved in. The Germans arranged a compromise: The International Finance Commission now was composed not of inspectors but only of advisers, including one appointed by the Ottomans. It would prepare the budgets of the three provinces in Macedonia, but they would have to be sanctioned by the sultan before they could be put into effect. All proposals for further financial reforms would have to go through the regular Ottoman legislative process.

The reforms began after the withdrawal of the powers from Limni and Midilli. To close deficits in the provincial budgets the Ottoman government proposed that instead of raising taxes on the inhabitants the customs duties be increased from 8 to 11 percent. But the powers, always willing to demand reforms as long as their own interests were not involved, agreed only in return for commercial concessions elsewhere, with the British gaining an extension of the concession for the Izmir–Aydın railroad until 1940, the Germans securing an addition to the guarantee money paid by the Ottomans to their bankers for the Anatolian Railroad, and so forth. The financial reforms were then put into effect. The continued activities of the terrorist bands, now led by the Greeks with the connivance of the Greek government, were the main obstacle because they left the provincial government with a hand-to-mouth existence for the remainder of Abdulhamit's rule.

The last phase of the Macedonian Question came when the king of England and the czar of all the Russias met at Reval, in Estonia, on June 9, 1908, to arrange an alliance against the rising power of Germany on the Continent. As part of the program to settle all differences between them, they agreed that the governor of Macedonia, though an Ottoman subject, should be appointed only with the agreement of the powers and that he should be helped by a large staff of European administrators paid out of the provincial revenues. The agreement at Reval was opposed by Austria, still hoping to expand to the Adriatic through the agency of Serbia, and by Germany, which hoped to displace England as the major European power with influence at the Porte. In response to the rapprochement of England with Russia and, soon afterward, with France, thus forming the Triple Alliance, Austria and Germany engaged in a new era of cooperation that contributed to the escalation of rivalries and ultimately led to World War I.

The Structure of Autocracy

Though Abdulhamit II came to the throne promising to support constitutionalism, the dynastic considerations surrounding his accession, his lack of confidence in the integrity or ability of statesmen associated with the Porte, and the internal and external crises that convulsed the empire led him to adopt an increasingly personal, autocratic, and absolutist policy of administration. His memory of Abdulaziz's fate and knowledge of Murat V's improved mental condition subsequent to the dethronement made him feel insecure. He also believed that all Ottoman statesmen were self-seeking and corrupt and that there was a lack of civic-mindedness among Ottoman bureaucrats. The Russo-Turkish War of 1877–1878 and the turmoil that followed the Congress of Berlin, the activities of the terrorist bands, and the threats of the Balkan neighbors as well as European powers convinced the sultan that effective administration could be achieved only through centralized rule, not by diffusion of power.[35]

The pattern of autocracy through which the sultan was to achieve his aims was discernible even before the Congress of Berlin when, reacting to the political criticism of the war effort, he used the powers given him by the Constitution to send Midhat Paşa into exile and dismiss the Parliament. Abdulhamit considered himself to be, and was in fact, a reformer, but like the Men of the Tanzimat he felt that in the context of the time democratic representation embodied in the Parliament led only to delays, inefficiency, frustration, internal weakness, and further defeats and disintegration. Abdulhamit generally followed the example of Abdulaziz in his later years, centering power in the palace rather than the Porte and bureaucrats. He developed a structure of personal control that, with the centralized system of administration created by the Tanzimat, made possible a far more extensive and complete autocracy then anything ever achieved previously by the greatest of the sultans. Through this autocracy Abdulhamit managed to restore and defend his shattered empire, revitalize its society, and bring to a successful conclusion most of the reforms that had been threatened after 1871, thus making himself the last man of the Tanzimat. He did so at a price, however, stifling the slow evolution that had been taking place toward basic political reforms, intended to provide representative institutions that would enable the subjects to participate in the process of rule. We must now proceed to examine the sultan's system of autocratic rule and see whether the results were worth the price.

Abdulhamit II's Concepts of Rule

It is a mistake to assume that Abdulhamit came to the throne with the intention of establishing his autocracy and that he worked to undermine the Parliament right from the outset. In fact, he initially reversed Abdulaziz's personal rule by accepting the Constitution, adding only sufficient guarantees to ensure that the Porte would never again establish the kind of domination it had achieved during the Tanzimat. There is every indication that, at this time, Abdulhamit was still young and impressionable, willing to learn and to test Midhat's ideas to save the empire. During his first year, he was far more open to new ideas than any of his immediate predecessors, praying with the common people during the Friday services, talking with Ottomans and foreigners about the problems of the state, summoning bureaucrats, scribes, intellectuals, and even the Young Ottoman leader Namık Kemal, to whom he said "Let us work together, Kemal Bey, let us raise this state and sultanate to a higher condition than before."[36]

His turn toward autocracy was determined by the events and conditions he witnessed following his accession. Abdulhamit believed that Midhat's refusal to allow the refinancing of the Ottoman debt to go forward and his rejection of the mediation of the Istanbul Conference – regardless of the consequences, simply because of his dislike of foreign intervention – had left the empire in a financial and diplomatic dilemma. He observed the ambitions and intrigues of the politicians on all sides and the Parliament's delaying role in the legislative process, imposed as it was on the existing structure between both the Council of State and the Council of Ministers. It was difficult to unify various groups whose interests often clashed, in the sultan's opinion, with the interests of the empire as a whole. Abdulhamit was also disillusioned by the attitude of the powers, which ignored the sufferings of the thousands of Muslims being persecuted and massacred in Bulgaria and Bosnia while presenting the suffering of Christians as evidence of Muslim barbarism, and by their exploitation of the ambitions of the Balkan states more as instruments of their own imperial goals than to meet the needs of the people of the area. The rise of groups within the Parliament that used the war disasters to put forward their own views and needs rather than supporting the war effort was only the final element in a long series of events that convinced the young sultan that the empire was not ready for democracy and that autocracy was the only way for it to survive in troubled times:

> I made a mistake when I wished to imitate my father, Abdulmecit, who sought
> to reform by persuasion and by liberal institutions. I shall follow in the foot-
> steps of my grandfather, Sultan Mahmut. Like him I now understand that it is
> only by force that one can move the people with whose protection God has
> entrusted me.[37]

Center of Power: The Palace

At the center of power after 1878 was the palace of the sultan, who built the relatively simple *mâbeyin* structure developed at Yıldız by Abdulaziz into a complex bureaucracy, itself directing, supervising, and investigating many aspects of government and society that had been mainly autonomous in previous years. Beneath the dominating presence of the sultan there were several major figures who shared the reins of power by advising him on the problems that came to his attention and controlling his access to individuals and information.

On one side there was the pervasive influence of the hero of Plevna, Gazi Osman Paşa (1832–1897), who as chief of the palace service (*mâbeyin müşiri*) and chairman of the Privy Council (*ser Yaverân-ı Ekrem*) not only directed the sultan's personal staff and finances but also was his chief executive officer. Representing the ulema and the military and leading the reaction to Western ways, he exercised a conservative influence on Abdulhamit's policies and took the lead in reinvigorating the institutions of Islam. Gazi Osman remained the sultan's *müşir* even when at times he left the palace to serve as minister of war, acting as the sultan's eyes and ears and, in many ways, the real power in the state as long as he lived. Sharing Gazi Osman Paşa's influence in the spheres of administration, finance, and foreign affairs were the sultan's scribe (*baş kâtip*) and assistant scribe (*kâtib-i sani*), who expanded their official roles of presenting to the sultan all communications and proposed laws and decrees into a power to dominate his relations with the departments and officials of government, telling them what the sultan's desires and policies were and communicating to him their versions of the results. Most powerful of the chief scribes was Küçük Sait Paşa, originally appointed due to the influence of the sultan's brother-in-law, Damat Mahmut Paşa, but subsequently appointed to serve as grand vezir several times as well as minister of various departments, thus becoming Abdulhamit's principal agent in the government. His successors as chief scribe were Ali Fuat Bey (1878–1881); Süreyya Efendi (1881–1894); and finally Tahsin Paşa, who, following Gazi Osman Paşa's death more or less replaced him as chief adviser and remained with Abdulhamit until his deposition in 1909. The position of second scribe was purely a subordinate one until it came to be filled after 1893 by Ahmet Izzet Paşa, who acted as the sultan's chief of staff after Gazi Osman's death, meeting with the grand vezir and ministers to convey the sultan's wishes and receive their reports. He chaired many of the important commissions that the sultan had established on matters of particular concern, such as those to reform Ottoman finances, build and administer the Hicaz Railroad, and deal with the diplomatic problems that arose over the presence of the British in Egypt and their intrusion into the Red Sea area. Ahmet Izzet subsequently rose to be grand vezir for Mehmet VI Vahideddin following the collapse of the Young Turks and end of World War I (1918). With the first and second scribes gaining increased influence in Gazi Osman's declining years, following his death the position of *müşir* was left vacant so that they could continue to dominate the palace.

Under the general authority of the *müşir* and the scribes there were several other influential individuals and institutions within Abdulhamit's personal system of government. Insofar as his women and slaves could influence him, they did so mainly through the eunuch of the Sublime Porte (*dar us-saade ağası*). Two holders of this office, Gânî Ağa and Hafız Behram Ağa, were given the rank of vezir, placing them higher than the *müşir* and the scribes and equal in official protocol only to the grand vezir, the *şeyhulislam,* the khedive of Egypt, and the prince of Bulgaria. The Privy Council (*Yaverân-ı Ekrem*), composed of current and retired government and military leaders appointed to the newly established high rank of imperial aide-de-camp (*yaver-i ekrem*), was responsible for advising the sultan on public policy and for inspecting the army and civil service to ferret out dishonesty, disloyalty or inefficiency. There was a secret police (*hafiye*) organization in the palace under the sultan's personal control, directed first by Ahmet Celaleddin Paşa, one of his personal slaves, and subsequently by another protégé, Fehim Paşa, who remained until dismissed by the Young Turks. Under their direction was an army of spies as well as informants (*jurnalcıs*); they were appointed to every department of the government to ascertain and report on the actions and thoughts of individual bureaucrats in memorandums (*jurnals*), which were used to promote, dismiss, or even imprison those thought to be treasonous under article 113 of the Constitution. Recommended by the director of the Ottoman Bank to Abdulhamit while he still was a prince, an Armenian banker, Hagop Zarifi Paşa, handled the sultan's personal finances and advised him on economic and financial policy. The Greek Alexander Karatodori Paşa, after representing the sultan at the Congress of Berlin and serving as foreign minister, retired to the palace, where he advised Abdulhamit on important internal foreign affairs and supervised the work of the Foreign Ministry. There was a palace Press Department, headed first by an Armenian named Nişan Efendi and then by his brother Sefer Efendi, who prepared summary translations of important news items in the foreign and domestic press and also translated foreign novels for the pleasure of the sultan. And there were the directors of some of the older departments – the chief chamberlain, the chief imam, the chief doctor, and the head of the sultan's personal guard (*Ser Yaverân-ı Harp*) – all of whom exercised some influence by virtue of the sultan's isolation and dependence on them for news and opinions.

Finally, starting in 1879 an entirely new corps of palace servants was created to help the sultan and his advisers in the palace, while the old departments and staffs at the Topkapı Palace and elsewhere were drastically reduced. The young men employed in this service were graduates of the *Rüşdiye* schools. Some also were sent for further training to the Civil Service School (*Mekteb-i Mülkiye*) or the military academies after which they entered careers in the civil service and army, where they were expected to keep the sultan informed of the latest trends. Thus did Abdulhamit II adapt the old Ottoman system of protégés, effectively utilized earlier by Mustafa Reşit Paşa, to become the instrument for palace control of the entire system of government.[38]

Beyond the palace the sultan's will was enforced at several levels. In 1880 the police and gendarmes of the empire, formerly directed by a Control Commission (*Zabtiye Meclisi*) in the Ministry of the Interior, was organized into a separate Ministry of Police (*Zabtiye Nezareti*) and extended into a highly organized hierarchy throughout the empire, mainly on the French model. Commissioners (*komisers*) under the direct control of the minister supervised and directed police activities in each district of Istanbul and the other large cities as well as in each province. The urban and rural police forces were now put under united control, almost independent of the administrative authorities in the area. To give the police the power not only to control crime but also to supervise society, the ministry was given a number of functions formerly exercised by other departments, including control of the operation and activities of the press and theater and supervision of travel within the empire, requiring all subjects and foreigners to register whenever they changed residence or traveled from one place to another.[39] The old *polis müşiri*, who formerly commanded the police of Istanbul under the authority of the *serasker* as well as the minister of the interior, was supplanted by the minister of police, a post that the sultan gave to his most trusted confidants, first Hafız Mehmet Paşa, one of his military aides-de-camp (1880–1884); then Kâmil Bey (1884–1890), a scribe; followed by the most famous of them all, Nazım Paşa (1890–1897), one of the sultan's protégés, who previously had served as tax collector and member of the secret police in Beyoğlu; and finally Şefik Paşa, formerly chief judge of the Court of Cassation (*Temyiz Mahkemesi*), who served until the Young Turk Revolution. The secret police, stationed in the palace, was nominally under the authority of the Ministry of Police but was in fact independent, with the sultan thus maintaining two police forces to spy on each other as well as everyone else.

Supervision of the bureaucracy was accomplished through two organizations. In 1878 the Civil Service Commission (*Memurin-i Mülkiye Komisyonu*) was established to appoint, promote, supervise, transfer, and retire all bureaucrats, more or less in the Western manner. In addition, the Commission to Register the Affairs of Civil Servants (*Ahval-ı Memurin Sicili Komisyonu*) had branches in each ministry and department and kept detailed biographies and records of the activities, statements, and opinions of all bureaucrats, with a large staff of investigators and scribes contributing to the maintenance of each individual's record. Acting directly under the grand vezir, both commissions provided the sultan with as complete a means of controlling the mass of bureaucrats as did the police for high officials, foreigners, and the remainder of his subjects.[40]

All civil servants had to get prominent subjects to post bonds to guarantee their good behavior as well as the efficient and honest conduct of their duties.[41] There were laws that regulated the operations and output of all presses, authors, and newspapers, with publishers and writers alike required to pay large annual permission fees and to post bond and provide outside guarantors to assure their good behavior. The basic press law issued in 1856 was rigorously enforced after 1878 and then replaced by a new and more extensive law in 1885.[42] and when that was not enough, by another one in 1888.[43] Writers were regulated separately in 1870 and in a series of laws promulgated by Abdulhamit.[44] A separate law was introduced for booksellers in 1894.[45]

Individuals suspected of seditious thought or behavior were dismissed from their positions, sometimes exiled, and even executed. The most notable example was the case of the well-known reformer and the major proponent and author of the Constitution, Midhat Paşa. After his return from exile in 1878, he served for two years as governor of Syria (1878–1880) and then for a short time at Izmir (1880–1881) before his continued concern for the restoration of the Parliament finally led the sultan to have him tried and convicted (1881) of the crime of murdering Sultan Abdulaziz on the basis of rather flimsy evidence and testimony built up by a committee headed by Ahmet Cevdet. He was sent to imprisonment in the Yemen, where he died three years later at the hand of an unknown assassin. Midhat's fate became a warning to others who might choose to resist the will of the sultan.[46]

The Structure of Government and Justice

The policies and programs desired by the sultan were carried out by the ministries established during the Tanzimat. There was the Ministry of the Interior (*Dahiliye*), which, while no longer concerned with the police, still dealt with provincial and local government, the Ottoman-language press, the census, and the settlement and maintenance of refugees. The Ministry of Foreign Affairs (*Hariciye*) lost its Imperial Council departments to the grand vezir's office and its functions regarding the *millet*s to the Ministry of Justice, so that it concentrated now on foreign affairs, and its only additional duties involved the supervision of the foreign-language press and the mixed courts, matters of nationality, foreign trade, and the supervision and care of all foreign officials living in the empire. The office of the *şeyhulislam* was expanded into a committee to interpret and execute the Holy Law (*Bab-ı Vâlâyı Fetva Heyeti*), with an undersecretary (*müsteşar*) in charge of financial and administrative matters, supervising endowments assigned to the maintenance of the ulema, organizing and assigning all judges, administering the property of orphans, supervising religious publications, controlling the religious schools and caring for their students and teachers, and maintaining the mosques and other religious institutions. The *şeyhulislam* himself, while nominally the equivalent of the grand vezir, was left with little power or authority.

The Seraskerate, still not quite called the Ministry of War, was now given a General Staff (*Erkân-ı Harbiye*) to carry out its functions. It had a far more elaborate and complex hierarchy than before because of reforms introduced by Prussian advisers between 1885 and 1895, with separate departments for matters such as military operations, statistics, encampment and barracks, military arts, infantry, cavalry, schools, veterinary medicine, artillery, military courts and prisons, supply, construction, fortification, health, and communications as well as special departments to supervise the activities of each of the provincial armies. The Ministry of the Navy (*Bahriye Nezareti*) remained unchanged except for the addition of a general staff that directed operations under the authority of the minister. The Imperial Dockyard (*Tersane*) was now directed by an officer with the rank of field marshal (*müşir*) whose relationship with the *serasker* was about the same as those of the marshals who directed the provincial army. The Ministry of Justice (*Adliye Nezareti*), established as such in 1870, was now also given all functions concerned with the non-Muslim *millets*; thus its name was changed to the Ministry of Justice and Sects (*Adliye ve Mezahib Nezareti*). It continued to supervise and control the entire complex of *Nizamiye* secular courts, including the appeals courts developed in Istanbul. The Ministry of Finance (*Maliye*) was constantly changing its structure to accomplish the difficult task of keeping the empire's finances afloat. In addition to the usual departments to care for specific categories of revenues and expenditures, there also were special sections to help finance military institutions (*Tesisat-ı Askeriye Iane Komisyonu*), supervise the Public Debt Commission (*Düyun-u Umumiye Muhasebesi Kalemi*), administer the cadastres of property and property taxes, and control the mint. Other ministries that continued with little change from the Tanzimat period were those of education (*Maarif-i Umumiye Nezareti*), Foundations (*Evkaf-ı Hümayun Nazareti*), and Trade and Public Works (*Ticaret ve Nafia Nezareti*), the latter also dealing with railroads, roads and bridges, industry, and statistics.

In addition, there were several formerly subordinate departments that were expanded into full-fledged ministries: the Hicaz Railroad Ministry; the Ministry for Military Equipment (*Techizat-ı Askeriye Nezareti*), established by the sultan to raise money outside regular treasury sources to supply the army; the Accounting Council (*Divan-ı Muhasebat*), set up to check the accounts of all ministries and departments including that of Finance; the Ministry of Property Records (*Defter-i Hakanî Nezareti*), and those of Excise Taxes (*Rüsumat Nezareti*), Forests, Mines, and Agriculture (*Orman ve Maadin ve Ziraat Nezareti*), Health (*Sıhhiye Nezareti*), Telegraph and Post (*Telegraf ve Posta Nezareti*), Police (*Zabtiye Nezareti*), the Civil Servants' Retirement Fund (*Mülkiye Tekaüt Sandığı Nezareti*), and the Military Retirement Fund (*Askerî Tekaüt Sandığı Nezareti*).

At the top, the Office of the Grand Vezir (*Sadaret-i Uzmâ Daire-i Celilesi*), constituting the Sublime Porte (*Bab-ı Âli*), was organized into several specialized departments that coordinated the affairs of state. The old offices of the Imperial Council, now gathered as the *Âmedi* Department of the Imperial Council, supervised administrative matters, and the Scribal Department of the Grand Vezir (*Mektubî-i Sadr-ı Âli Odası*) handled scribal and financial affairs, though there was considerable overlapping as time went on. It was the latter that took care of correspondence between the grand vezir and all other government departments, keeping its files in the Archives of the Sublime Porte (*Bab-ı Âli Evrak Odası*), which today provides us with our principal records of the period. The *Beylikçi* department and the *Mühimme Odası*, charged with keeping important records belonging to the Imperial Council, once included in the Foreign Ministry and then transferred to the Porte, continued to perform their old functions. In addition, the grand vezir chaired a number of commissions established by the sultan, with their staffs adding to the general crowding at the Porte. These included the Imperial Commission on Refugees (*Muhacirin Komisyon-u Âli*), nominally chaired by the sultan himself, the Retirement Assistance Fund of the Porte (*Bab-ı Âli Teşkilat Sandığı*), and the Administrative Commission of the Hicaz Railway.

Finally, now thoroughly integrated into the structure of the Porte under the grand vezir was the Council of State (or *Şurayı Devlet*), again the main legislative organ as well as the high court of appeal for administrative cases. Soon after the Parliament had been dissolved, a series of regulations (1878–1880) reorganized the council, restoring its original functions except for its role as an appeals court for the *Nizamiye* courts, which the Constitution had given to the Court of Cassation (*Temyiz Mahkemesi*) in the Ministry of Justice. The council's internal organization developed by Mahmut Nedim during his last grand vezirate was partly revived, with separate Departments of Legislation (*Tanzimat*), Administrative Regulations (*Dahiliye*, or Interior), and Administrative Justice (*Muhakemat*). Its manner of composition was changed, however, with the old election system being replaced by appointment of former civil servants and military officers by the grand vezir, making them thus an integral part of the bureaucracy of the Porte. The Chamber of Notables (*Meclis-i Ayan*) created by the Constitution continued in existence: one of the ministers served as its chairman and the membership included the other ministers and additional appointees. Under these circumstances the occasional clashes of opinion between the Council of State and the Council of Ministers that had delayed legislation in the past now took place, if they did at all, within the former before details of draft laws and regulations were drawn up, and confirmation with little change by the latter was almost assured. Thus legislation could proceed more efficiently, though it was at the cost of eliminating the popular input formerly provided by the council's elected members and later by the elected members of the Chamber of Deputies.

The Council of State continued to maintain its administrative courts to hear appeals as well as cases of first instance originating in the central government. A supplementary regulation issued in 1885 provided that when its decisions conflicted with those of the Court of Cassation, a special High Appeals Committee should be established, with three members from each, under the chairman of the Council of State.[47] In 1895 the administrative courts of the council were reorganized into primary (*bidayet*), appeal (*istinaf*), and final appeal (*temyiz*) bodies and put under the supervision of the Ministry of Justice even though they remained structurally within the council.[48] Two years later the remaining portions of the council were given their final organization, with a new Financial Department (*Maliye*) being added while the Interior Department was limited to civil service affairs (and thus was changed in name to *Mülkiye Dairesi*, or Civil Service Department), with the job of investigating the activities of departments, ministries, and individual bureaucrats and drawing up new regulations on such matters, while the Tanzimat Department was given the additional task of drawing up all agreements that gave foreign companies concessions in the empire.[49]

Abdulhamit's Bureaucrats

The departments now were staffed almost entirely with graduates of the secular schools, providing a competent and efficient group of civil servants. Of course, policy now emanated from the palace rather than the Porte, with grand vezirs and ministers alike being no more than instruments of the sultan's will. On the other hand, in such a vast bureaucratic structure it was impossible for the sultan and his palace group to control or supervise every aspect of administration. Abdulhamit tried to prevent a resulting increase in the bureaucrats' control of the administration, not only by his orders to ministers and his spy and reporting system, but also by rapidly shifting bureaucrats from one position to another. As long as they did not incur his displeasure, they usually managed to secure equally good positions in other departments, thus playing a continuous game of musical chairs. The sultan shifted high administrators even more frequently at times, to make the foreign ambassadors think they were influencing him in one way or another or to make specific changes in the general policies of the departments concerned.

Throughout Abdulhamit's reign, then, there was a group of high-ranking bureaucrats, the fourth generation of Men of the Tanzimat, who carried on the functions of government, drawing up the laws and regulations and putting the sultan's reforms and other policies into effect. One of the earliest was Ibrahim Ethem Paşa (1818–1893), born early enough to have been one of Husrev Paşa's group of slaves and protégés. He was Abdulhamit's first grand vezir after Midhat Paşa and directed the government through the Russo-Turkish War, subsequently serving as minister of interior (1883–1885) before falling into disfavor. Ibrahim Ethem established the first modern Ottoman government printing press (*Matbaa-i Âmire*) in the walls outside the Topkapı Palace. His articles on geology in the popular press helped stimulate the development of Western scientific thought among Ottoman scholars and intellectuals, and his sons, Osman Hamdi, Ismail Galip, and Halil Ethem, also made major contributions to Turkish scholarship and culture well into the republican period.[50] Ahmet Vefik Paşa (1823–1891), originally a protégé of Mustafa Reşit Paşa and subsequently a major figure in developing the Tanzimat secular judicial and educational systems, served as chairman of the Chamber of Deputies during its short existence (1877–1878), as grand vezir (1878), and then as governor of Bursa (1878–1882). He devoted his retirement to compiling the first scientific dictionary of Ottoman Turkish (*Lehçe-i Osmani,* first edition, 1876; second revised edition, 1888) as well as a history of the Ottoman Empire for the *Rüşdiye* schools (*Fezleke-i Tarih-i Osmani*). He translated and published 16 comedies of Molière as well as a number of old Turkish classics, with his house and most of his land subsequently going to Robert College to house faculty and students.[51]

Most prominent among the sultan's ministers and protégés was Küçük Sait Paşa (1838–1914). After serving Abdulhamit II for a short time as chief secretary (1876–1878), Küçük Sait became his chief instrument in the cabinet, for a time in rivalry with Ahmet Vefik. As minister of justice, he introduced the institution of public defender in the *Nizamiye* courts and also developed new commercial and criminal codes. At the request of the sultan he drew up a major program of reform in the army's financial system to reduce its drain on the central treasury. He also provided the sultan with a program to restore centralized control of the provinces, reversing the trend of decentralization discernible in the later years of the Tanzimat. In seven terms as grand vezir (1879–1880, 1880–1882, 1882, 1882–1885, 1895, 1901–1903, 1908), he carried out the sultan's programs more faithfully than anyone else, balancing the budget and increasing tax collections, negotiating the public debt settlement with the powers (1881), creating the Istanbul Chamber of Commerce to develop native trade and industry, building up the secular school system, organizing the police, and making the courts independent of the executive so that they could make their decisions without being subject to government intervention. It was Küçük Sait who further modernized the civil service system, instituting a system of examinations and establishing pension funds so that aged bureaucrats could retire without fear of poverty. In his later years, however, Sait incurred the sultan's suspicion, and he remained in retirement to avoid Midhat Paşa's fate. After having been away from the public eye, then, he was able to rise once again during the Young Turk period, serving twice as grand vezir with the support of the Committee of Union and Progress (1911, 1912) and finally as chairman of the Chamber of Notables (1913) before retiring.[52]

Sait's principal rival and regular replacement as grand vezir was Mehmet Kâmil Paşa (1832-1913). Born in Cyprus, he rose in the Egyptian civil service and served for many years in the Ottoman provincial bureaucracy (1860-1879). His efforts to counter British intrigues in the Lebanon while governor of that province drew the sultan's attention, and, after serving in various cabinet positions, he rose to the grand vezirate for the first time in 1885 when Sait was dismissed due to the Bulgarian annexation of East Rumelia. During the next six years (1885-1891) of his first term, Kâmil stabilized Ottoman finances following the creation of the Public Debt Commission and encouraged foreign companies to build up the empire's railroads and industries to enable the treasury to pay off the debt. In 1895, during his second and final grand vezirate, however, he attempted to gain foreign support against the sultan's efforts to intervene in the government, resulting not only in his dismissal but also threats of death. He was sent into exile as governor of Izmir, where he remained for a decade. During the Young Turk period, he served two more times as grand vezir, replacing Sait (1908-1909) when the latter resigned in protest against the army's resistance to civilian control. His *Tarih-i Siyasiye-i Devlet-i Osmaniye* (Political History of the Ottoman State), when combined with Sait's publications, provide major source material for the period.[53]

Perhaps the most unusual of Abdulhamit's leading ministers was Hayreddin Paşa (1822-1890), originally a Circassian slave in Istanbul, subsequently given to the bey of Tunis, who raised and educated him and entered him into his service. After serving his master and his successors in Tunis for many years and arranging a number of the European loans that caused the latter to fall into debt, he finally succumbed to court politics and fled to Istanbul, where he gained Abdulhamit's favor by his work on the Financial Reform Commission established in 1878 to reform the empire's tax and budget systems. Hayreddin served as grand vezir only for a short time, in 1878-1879, and for the most part was ineffective because his origins outside the Ottoman system created resentment among his colleagues. In addition, while he readily gained the favor and confidence of the British and French ambassadors, his attempt to achieve some independence in his office and to make his ministers responsible to him soon led to his dismissal. It was really after this time that he made his greatest contributions. Staying at his mansion in the Nişantaşı section of Istanbul, he rejected a second term as grand vezir in 1882 and instead contented himself with writing a series of memoranda to the sultan on all aspects of the Ottoman system, inspiring some of the later reforms. Hayreddin urged the sultan to develop the Civil Service School (*Mekteb-i Mülkiye*) and also to raise salaries and provide opportunities for able men to rise quickly in order to attract such men into governmental service.[54] He said that the Parliament could serve the empire well only if it was elected by means that would assure the selection of the ablest and most objective persons, and directed to consider only the problems brought before it.[55] He again urged the sultan to establish some kind of system of responsibility to the grand vezir within the cabinet and made a detailed exposition of the Porte's machinery, stimulating a general overhaul during the sultan's later years.[56] He also proposed the restoration of the Council of Ministers in place of the sultan's Privy Council as the principal debating and policy-making body of the central government, but this was never put into effect.[57] Hayreddin later became one of Küçük Sait's main advisers, helping plan a series of administrative reforms enacted during the latter's subsequent terms as grand vezir.[58]

Modernization of the Ottoman Empire

Through all the many difficulties experienced during his reign Abdulhamit remained in his palace, devouring the reports of his administrators, spies, and secret police, instructing his ministers and legislators on the policies they should pursue, reading every piece of proposed legislation, and approving or modifying them according to his own concepts of how the state should be run. Late in his reign, however, as the terrorist threats and foreign attacks mounted, his fears of personal assassination or dethronement led him to subordinate his concentration on reform to his desire to destroy treason and revolt within the empire. Even then the institutions of legislation and administration established by the Tanzimat and reinvigorated during Abdulhamit's early years continued to pour out and apply an enormous number of laws and regulations that gradually completed the work of modernizing the Ottoman system.

Most of Abdulhamit's reforms were directed toward carrying out a program that he developed himself and communicated to his ministers in 1879, soon after the Parliament was dismissed and immediate foreign danger was removed by the Congress of Berlin. Every aspect of the Ottoman system was included – the military, the central administration, the provinces, the law courts, finance, the economy, public works, education, fine arts, and the administration.[59] To a surprising extent, the measures enacted during much of the remainder of his reign adhered quite closely to the program elaborated at its beginning. What were his reform plans? How were they implemented? What was the end result?

Finance

Basic to the success of any reform program in the Ottoman Empire was finding a solution to the financial problems that had plagued the Men of the Tanzimat since the Crimean War. The central issue was the debt owed to the foreign bondholders, which because of financial mismanagement as well as the excessively high rates of interest had come to absorb 80 percent of the revenues of state by the time of Abdulhamit's accession. Mahmut Nedim's plan to resolve the problem by paying off the old high-interest loans with a new issue of low-interest bonds seemed to offer financial solvency, but it had been scuttled by Midhat Paşa, who had proposed instead that the interest payments be suspended at first and then reduced by half, an idea that appealed to his followers but was certain to destroy Ottoman credit and endanger availability of foreign capital and expertise in the future. The Constitution attempted to solve the financial problem by requiring that the Chamber of Deputies approve new budgets. It did, indeed, go through the budget line by line and reduce the salaries and pensions of those who were as usual most accessible, the civil servants. It also established its own budget commission to scrutinize the government's budget requests regularly in the future. The legislature avoided raising taxes, fearing that this would further weaken the economy. Instead, it asked the government to expand agriculture, trade, and industry and to improve the empire's exploitation of natural resources so that revenues would naturally increase and provide for the state's needs.

But the empire was in the midst of a war, and however much the legislature could economize at the expense of the bureaucrats, it still had to provide for extraordinary military expenses that reached as much as 2 billion kuruş above normal revenues, which had fallen drastically because of the loss of several provinces to the enemy, of cultivators to the army, and of tax collectors due to the disruption of the economic system. These funds were provided in a separate extraordinary budget, thereafter a standard feature of the Ottoman financial system, with a series of forced loans and popular subscriptions arranged to pay the cost of what was an increasingly popular though disastrous war. In return for approving these loans and expenditures, however, the deputies were emboldened to demand detailed information from the ministries about their regular financial operations and budget requests, leading to the recriminations that fortified the sultan's subsequent decision to eliminate the Parliament altogether. Abdulhamit took over and applied the policy of pruning the bureaucracy, though he waited until the war was over so as not to hurt morale at a critical time.[60]

Once the Assembly had been dissolved and peace secured, Abdulhamit was free to develop his own financial policies. His aim was to balance the budget without further foreign loans as a first step toward solving the state's financial crisis. He began by trimming the bureaucracies of the Topkapı Palace and the Ministries of the Interior and of Foreign Affairs. The army was left alone because of continued foreign threat. All the princes and other members of his family as well as important ministers were forced to accept reductions in salary. Palace expenditures were removed from the treasury and paid mostly from the sultan's privy purse, which was placed under the efficient management of Hagop Paşa. The state budget was subjected to the scrutiny of an expert Financial Reform Commission (*Islahat-ı Maliye Komisyonu*) before it reached the Council of Ministers. Each member of the commission was rated according to the number of budget items he could reduce with "no serious damage to the state." But since members were themselves bureaucrats who tended to defend the interests of their own departments, and the latter were quite adept at arranging their budgets in a way so that little could be cut out, the result was disappointing.

In any case, the Ottoman financial crisis had not been caused by extravagance in the normal expenditures of state. Salaries of most bureaucrats were low even by Ottoman standards. Neither the army nor the palace took a larger proportion of the state revenues in 1876 than they had earlier, and only by eliminating literally thousands of positions, virtually paralyzing the state, could any significant change have been made in this direction. The main problem came rather from the foreign debt, to which the new war indemnities owed to Russia added an almost intolerable burden. Abdulhamit asked the czar to lower the amount by as much as three quarters and pointed out that if the empire collapsed, neither the czar nor anyone else would get their money, and the resulting crisis might well lead to a new war. Czar Nicholas was amenable to this idea, but when he asked Ottoman support for Russian diplomatic policies in return, the sultan reneged, not willing to accept such foreign dictation no matter what the rewards. Therefore, in 1881 he agreed to pay the 35 million kuruş per year stipulated at Berlin for 100 years, with only the czar's willingness to forgo the payment of interest easing the burden in any way.

It was the bonded debt, then, that had to be reduced. By 1878 the debt consisted of 9.5 billion kuruş in capital remaining from 24.4 billion kuruş borrowed between 1854 and 1876. In addition, there were about 4 billion kuruş outstanding in internal bonds, bringing the total to 13.5 billion kuruş, with over 1 billion kuruş required just to pay the interest, 44 percent of the 1874 budget. By 1876 the prosecution of the war had forced the treasury to assume an additional burden of 7.45 billion kuruş of debt, adding 433.8 million kuruş to the amount that should have been paid annually just to service the debt.[61] The treasury was empty. It could hardly pay the civil servants, whose salary arrears reached back as much as four or five years. The treasury's credit was so low that new loans could be made to meet daily obligations only at huge discounts, which raised the interest even higher, with a loan contracted in London and Paris to keep the state going after the loss of Plevna bringing in only 60.9 percent of the borrowed amount after the discount was paid! By 1881, then, it seemed very likely that the autocratic state that Abdulhamit had created might succumb to foreign financial control and military occupation. Similar situations had led to this outcome in Tunisia and Egypt. At the Congress of Berlin the Russians had actually proposed such an action so that the Ottoman government could meet its bonded obligations, but the other powers had refused because they were afraid of allowing Russia into the Ottoman Empire, even in conjunction with their own forces.

This feeling in the end dictated the solution for the Porte's financial problems. Abdulhamit informed the powers that unless the debt was consolidated and its service reduced, no one would get anything, thousands of bondholders throughout Europe would lose all, and a general financial catastrophe would ensue. The European financial and political leaders agreed to consolidation only if their own representatives were given control over certain Ottoman revenues, which they would administer and collect and then devote entirely to the service of the debt. This was the basis of the agreement reached late in 1879. Abdulhamit II put it into effect with a series of decrees issued between then and 1882. The first of these, issued on November 22, 1879, ordered that the Ottoman state thereafter would be required to pay no more than 135 million kuruş annually to service its debt. For this purpose all the excise taxes levied on spirits, salt, hunting and fishing licenses, silk, tobacco, and documents would be turned over to a commission composed of representatives of the Ottoman Bank and the major Galata banks for administration through the tax farm system. To this the treasury was to add: (1) revenues received from the tributes paid by the princes of Montenegro, Serbia, and Bulgaria, (2) one-third of the projected 3 percent customs tax increase, and (3) any other new taxes that might subsequently be created. The commission in turn agreed to divide with the government any increased revenues that might result from its improved system of administration. Abdulhamit persuaded the European powers to include the Russian war indemnity payments as part of the foreign debt that they would service under the new arrangement. A series of meetings held in Istanbul culminated in Abdulhamit's famous Decree of Muharrem, issued on November 23, 1881. By its terms the remaining Ottoman public debt, both domestic and foreign and including interest owed but not paid since 1876, was evaluated at 21,938.6 million kuruş. This was reduced by almost half, to 12,430.5 million kuruş, by applying a complicated system to the various loans, reducing the oldest ones, going back to 1858, by as much as 85 percent, and the most recent ones by 50 percent for the foreign loans and 41 percent for the domestic ones. To service the balance the Public Debt Commission (*Düyun-u Umumiye Komisyonu*) was established outside the Ministry of Finance, including one delegate each from England, the Netherlands, France, Germany, Italy, Austria-Hungary, and the Ottoman Empire, as well as a special representative of the Galata bankers, each serving a term of five years. The delegates were to be assisted by their own staffs of financial experts, about 5000 men in all, of whom 2 percent would be foreign and the remainder Ottoman, with no more than 7 percent of the latter being Ottoman Christians. The Public Debt Commission thus was established as a separate Ottoman treasury with the purpose of servicing the remaining Ottoman public debt, including not only foreign and domestic bonds as such but also the Russian indemnity and the various government obligations to retired bureaucrats and former owners of timars and *mukata'as*. It would administer and collect all the taxes and revenues previously turned over to the Galata bankers together with a number of additional ones, including the excise taxes on salt, smoking tobacco, chewing tobacco, and spirits, formerly cared for by the Excise Tax Department, the tithe levies on silk production, whatever new revenues might be derived from increases in the profits tax, plus the possible institution of a new kind of income tax (*patent vergisi*). East Rumelia, Cyprus, Greece, Bulgaria, and Montenegro were to pay their tributes directly to the Public Debt Commission as their share of the debt payments. The debt obligation thus reduced took about 20 percent of the current state budget, a quite bearable burden. Abdulhamit then proceeded to apply his financial reform program so that the balance of the state's revenues could be increased to compensate for lost revenues and the government and army could be supported without incurring further debts.

The sultan's first objective in his 1879 reform program had been the "establishment of a regulation for the internal organization and operations of the Ministry of Finance."[62] This was accomplished in a series of measures that reorganized the ministry's departments established in the early Tanzimat period. Between 1880 and 1887 separate committees were created to coordinate the work of administration, inspection, and financial control. Financial functions previously exercised by officials in other departments – especially the provincial and municipal governors and lesser officials with mainly administrative duties under the authority of the Ministry of the Interior – were transferred to the Ministry of Finance. To unify their activities the sultan proposed the "organization of a Department of General Collections (*Tahsilat-ı Umumiye Nezareti*) in the Ministry of Finance," the "appointment of a Collections Administrator (*Tahsilat Müdürü*) in each province and a Collections Administrator Assistant (*Tahsilat Müdür Muavini*) in each county and district." "Tax collectors rather than military officers would collect the revenues according to published regulations which would indicate collection time for state revenues, the duties of the collection committees, and the preparation of receipts to be given to the taxpayers."[63] The sultan's wishes were carried out in the Collection of Revenues Regulation (*Tahsil-i Emval Nizamnamesi*) enacted on November 11, 1879, together with additional regulations that specified the powers and duties of the independent tax-collecting service itself. To centralize the state's financial operations and prevent the ministries and departments from developing their own financial and accounting systems, the Financial Reform Commission was established in the Ministry of Finance to coordinate the financial operations and budgetary processes of all the departments of government and to bring them together in the annual budget before it went to the Council of Ministers. Again, as proposed by the sultan, for the "preparation of a general procedure for the establishment of accounting methods for the state" and "organization of an accounting department to direct it,"[64] a Central Auditing Council (*Divan-ı Muhasebat*) was, established outside the Ministry of Finance (November 18, 1879) with the power to audit the financial operations of all the departments, including that of Finance, thus bringing the ministries and departments under real central financial control for the first time. Finally, to coordinate all the different divisions and departments in the Ministry of Finance and Auditing Council and to secure the advice of financial specialists from the private sector, a Committee on Financial Consultation (*Heyet-i Müşavere-i Maliye*) was set up (February 3, 1897), and at regular meetings thereafter it provided guidance on the operations of all governmental and nongovernmental bodies concerned with finance.[65]

In addition, the sultan stimulated a series of tax reforms, extending the profits tax throughout the empire, including Istanbul, though his effort to supplant it with an income tax applied to the earnings of foreigners in the empire as well as those of Ottomans was frustrated by the opposition of the European ambassadors, who represented their mercantile communities. Other major reforms were made in the tithe, sheep tax, property tax, and the military-service taxes, the major sources of revenue left to the treasury after the excise taxes were taken over by the Public Debt Commission.

The end result of Abdulhamit's financial reforms and the efforts of the Public Debt Commission was a substantial increase in total state revenue collections, from 1615 million kuruş in 1880–1881, the last year before the Decree of Muharrem, to 1722.7 million kuruş in 1898–1899 and 2290.5 million kuruş in 1906–1907, a relatively small increase of 7.4 percent in the 17 years to the first date and then, as the reforms fully caught hold, a rapid rise bringing the total increase to 43 percent during the quarter-century to 1907. It is interesting to note that the Public Debt's share of these revenues increased only marginally, from 6.02 percent of the total in 1881–1882 to 7.7 percent in 1898, hardly enough to warrant the imposition of European control (see Table 3.6). During the same quarter-century, the budgets of many departments were substantially decreased, but increased expenditures for the army, the grand vezir's office, and the imperial princes still left the treasury with a regular annual deficit (see Table 3.5).

Special expenditures – for settling refugees, building the Hicaz Railroad, financing the Red Crescent society, and paying for military equipment such as new

Table 3.5. *Changes in Ottoman departmental budgets between 1880 and 1907 (in millions of kuruş)*

Department	Budget in 1880–1881	Budget in 1907–1908
Navy	98.9	60.8
Police	185.1	130.6
Privy purse subsidies	105.9	57.7
Legislative bodies (excluding Council of State)	11.3	1.32
Finance	107.2	99.3
Excise tax (including Public Debt Commission)	43.1	40.1
Army	547.4	898.1
Grand vezir (including Council of State and Ministry of Interior)	56.9	114.09
Support for imperial princes	22.2	35.7
Justice	42.6	51.9
Ilmiye	18.6	27.4

Sources: The Budget of 1296/1880–1 is in BVA, Yıldız K36/156/11; that of 1322/1906–7 is in *Düstur*[1], VIII, 476–493.

Table 3.6. *The budget of the Ottoman Empire under Sultan Abdulhamit II,*
1877–1906 (in millions of kuruş)

Fiscal year	Revenues	Expenditures	Balance	Extraordinary budget deficit	Total balance	Percent of revenues devoted to public debt	
1877–1878	1972.5	2947.1	−974.6	−2587.8	−3562.4	1740.4	59.05
1889–1890	1793.9	1873.3	−79.4	−338.1	−417.5	533.8	29.75
1890–1891	1776.7	1828.5	−51.8	—	—	554.0	31.18
1897–1898	1829.1	2244.8	−415.7	—	—	648.3	35.44
1904–1905	2025.8	2123.2	−97.4	—	—	733.1	36.18
1905–1906	2229.1	2297.1	−68	—	—	733.1	32.88

Sources: Ihsaiyat-ı Maliye, vol. I, pp. 402–403; the Budget of 1296/1880–1 is in BVA,
Yıldız K36/156/11; that of 1297/1881–2 is in Yıldız K36/142/156; that of 1314/1898–9 is
in BVA, Bab-ı Âli Evrak Odası 104786; that of 1324/1906–7 is in BVA, Irade Maliye 1324
Safar no. 42. Information on the collections of the Public Debt Commission is in BVA,
Bab-ı Âli Evrak Odası 106313, 13 Şaban 1317. A full list of the budgets involved, along with
additional information on the treasury revenues, is in S. J. Shaw, "The Nineteenth Century Ottoman Tax Reforms and Revenue System," IJMES, Vol. VI (1975), pp. 421–459.

battleships and rifles – were entered into a special annual extraordinary budget.
Administered mostly by the Agricultural Bank, which sometimes used its surplus
to pay off the deficit, this budget spent as much as 200 to 300 million kuruş
annually. Special taxes were added to the regular ones to raise additional funds.
But when deficits persisted, they were paid by the already depleted treasury.

To pay all these deficits the government again had to turn to foreign lenders,
whose confidence in Abdulhamit's reforms and the presence of the Public Debt
Commission made them willing to invest in the empire. Between 1886 and 1908, 19
new loans were contracted, bringing a total of 12 billion kuruş of foreign funds,
of which only 10.8 billion kuruş were actually received, since the balance was
discounted.[66] As a result, the amount of state revenues devoted to the payment of
the debt rose from 28.83 percent of revenues in the budget of 1881–1882 to 31.16
percent of revenues in 1906–1907. The situation was better than that which had
existed in 1875 but was not the result expected by Abdulhamit and the powers when
they arranged the empire's financial affairs in 1881.

Nevertheless, the sultan did more than contract loans to balance the budget. He
encouraged economic development to broaden the taxable base of the empire. With
the help of the Public Debt Commission, he was able to interest many European
industrialists, bankers, and merchants in investing in specific areas, such as public
works, that would contribute to the rapid growth of the economy.

Railroads

Begun soon after the Crimean War but left half-finished because of the financial
crises of the early 1870s, railroads were an important area of European investment
during Abdulhamit's reign. Most of the early railroads had been built by European

companies stimulated by Ottoman government guarantees, but by 1888 there were only 1780 kilometers of track operating in the empire. Except for a short line in the Adana plain, all had been built in Thrace or the westernmost provinces of Anatolia to link fertile valleys with the coast or to connect Istanbul with the remnant of its European empire. Abdulhamit sought to develop the empire's economy by resuming railroad construction on a large scale. Since the empire lacked both capital and experience, the sultan turned to private European companies for extensive railroad construction. To divert political and imperial rivalries into economic ones he encouraged the powers to compete for the right to develop his empire. So it was that on September 27, 1888, the longstanding predominance of Britain, France, and Austria in the Ottoman economy was challenged by the signature of an agreement for the Deutsche Bank's participation in the construction and ultimate operation of a new line to extend the old Haydarpaşa–Izmit line to Ankara and eventually to Baghdad and the Persian Gulf. Britain and France reacted so strongly to the "affront" that they also were included in the consortium. The Ottoman government guaranteed a minimum amount of gross income per kilometer of track constructed and put into operation, supplementing the railroads' revenues only when they fell below the agreed amounts. To finance the guarantee the government set aside revenues not under the control of the Public Debt Commission – usually the tithes or sheep taxes collected in the areas benefiting from the railroad construction – on the assumption that total treasury revenues from those areas would rise as a result. Since the foreign financiers really did not trust the efficiency of the Ottoman government, these revenues usually were administered for them by the Public Debt Commission. After making up for the deficit in the revenue from each railroad line, the balance was delivered to the Treasury. As a result of these arrangements, the number and extent of railroads operating in the empire increased enormously, along with treasury revenues, during the balance of Abdulhamit's reign. Total trackage increased 5883 kilometers by 1907–1908, over three times what it had been when he came to the throne. At the same time, government revenues from railroad operations increased almost tenfold, from 80.5 million kuruş in 1887–1888 to 740.04 million kuruş in 1907–1908. The most spectacular addition to the Ottoman railroad network was the famous Hicaz Railroad, built by the government through popular subscription and treasury subsidies and with German technical help, to connect Syria with the Holy Cities. The extension of the Anatolian Railroad from Ankara to Mesopotamia, not fully completed by the end of Abdulhamit's reign, nor by the end of World War I, contributed to economic and political change, though its exact impact on the Ottoman economy and society as well as governmental operations remains to be studied and quantified.

Paved Roads

The railroad system was supplemented by construction of other communications networks in the empire. Forced labor, restored in 1869, continued to be used for road building and repairs until 1889. It then was replaced with an equivalent tax levied on villages adjacent to the roads (see p. 101). First the Agricultural Bank and then the Ministry of Public Works used this tax to finance major road operations, though in many cases villagers continued to supply labor and animals in place of their cash obligations.[67] Total funds used for road building rose during Abdulhamit's reign from 14.39 million kuruş in 1891 to 31.5 kuruş in 1907–1908, and as a matter of fact to 60.7 million kuruş only four years later during the early years of the Young Turk period. Between 1881 and 1897, the only years for which detailed figures are available, an average of 823 kilometers of new roads was built each year and 450 kilometers repaired. The total road network increased from 6,500 kilometers in 1858 to 14,395 in 1895 and 23,675 in 1904. This still was not very much in an empire that had some 20 million inhabitants and covered 3,272,354 square kilometers of land, but with most people still using animals and carts for their transportation, dirt tracks sufficed more or less as they had for centuries. The new roads were intended to facilitate the tax and military operations of the government as well as its efforts to expand agriculture and internal trade.[68]

Steamship Lines and Harbor Works

Abdulhamit did not pay too much attention to water transportation, and what steamships there were depended mainly on the initiative of private European and Ottoman companies that had operated in the empire since the start of the Tanzimat. There was a government fleet, called the *Idare-i Mahsusa* (Reserved Administration), which was originally organized by Abdulaziz as his private line, operated by his privy purse. Abdulhamit turned its administration over to a private Ottoman company, with some foreign capital and management but under the supervision of the Ministry of the Navy. At the end of the century it had no more than 95 ships of all sizes operating within the empire and to Egypt. In addition, there was the old *Şirket-i Hayriye*, a private Ottoman company that operated passenger steamships along the Bosporus and to the Marmara islands, with foreign lines providing most of the service to the Anatolian shores of the Black Sea and the Sea of Marmara as well as to more distant ports in and out of the empire. In 1895 there were about 50,000 vessels flying the Ottoman flag, of which only 3,047 were propelled by steam. By 1905 this had risen to 68,769 vessels, including 4,756 steamships.

The maintenance of quays and harbor facilities was left to private concessionnaires. For instance, the Istanbul Quay and Entrepot Company, established in 1890, developed the quays that are still in use between the Golden Horn and Tophane. These and other companies provided the treasury with a regular annual income and also made it possible for steamships to use Istanbul and the other major ports. Though the number of sailing ships calling at Istanbul fell from 46,531 in 1888 to 37,567 in 1904, that of steamships almost trebled during the same period, from 1548 to 5161, and in tonnage from 711,882 to 2,375,430.[69]

Postal and Telegraph Service

Facilities for sending messages in and out of the empire improved during Abdulhamit's reign, making up for the relative failure to extend the road system. Telegraph lines went along with the railroads, with the length of land lines increasing from 23,380 kilometers in 1882 to 49,716 kilometers in 1904, while underwater lines remained about the same, 610 kilometers in the former year and 621 kilometers in the latter. Within the same period the number of telegrams sent increased from about 1 million to 3 million, while revenues went up from 39.2 to 89.38 million kuruş. Though at least half of this was eaten away by costs, the treasury was still left with a considerable profit.[70] The Ottoman telegraphs were operated mainly by foreigners in the years immediately after the Crimean War, but schools to train Ottoman telegraphers soon produced an able and extremely dedicated body of specialists that assumed operation of the system, with the exception of the foreign services, after 1876.

Expansion of the Ottoman postal system was more difficult because of strong competition from the foreign post offices operating in the empire. Since there was no Ottoman postal service until 1841, the foreign operations were at first welcomed. As long before as 1721 Austria had been given the right to operate a regular postal service between its embassy in Istanbul and Vienna, and Russia received the same right early the next year. Initially these services were only for official correspondence, and the communications were carried by Ottoman postal messengers (*tatars*) protected by special Janissary detachments in the sultan's territory. In 1729 the British and Austrian merchants residing in the empire secured the right to use these services for their own mail as well. In 1739 the Austrians gained permission to use their agents to carry and guard the mail, and the Russians followed suit in 1783. At this point all the Europeans, and the Ottomans who wished to do so, were using the Austrian post, and to a much lesser extent that of the Russians, for mail going outside the empire, while internal communications were carried only by private *tatars*. In the nineteenth century the other major European powers secured the right to establish their postal operations in the empire – France in 1812, Britain in 1832, Greece in 1834, Germany in 1870, Egypt in 1873, and finally Italy in 1908. While they were supposed to carry mail only between Istanbul and their own countries, soon they also began to receive mail deposited at their consulates within the empire, and not only for Europe but also for addresses in Istanbul and Izmir in particular, thus providing internal service as well. Because of this kind of competition after its establishment in 1841, the Ottoman post office found it difficult to develop its service and secure sufficient customers to meet costs. It was only after postage stamps were used in place of seals affixed at the post offices, starting in 1863, that any real progress was made. A private company, Lianos et Cie, operated a separate city post in Istanbul between 1865 and 1873, but it then was abolished and the service taken over by the Ottoman post office. In addition, competition for service in the empire was provided by the foreign and domestic steamship lines, but these also were taken over by the post office shortly after Abdulhamit came to power.

The Ottoman postal service expanded considerably during the early years of the reign, from 11.5 million letters and packages carried in 1888 to 24.38 million in 1904. But the Ottoman government was convinced that profit for the treasury would increase even more if the competition was ended. This feeling was strengthened by its desire to stop the sending of subversive materials into the empire without interception by the Ottoman police, who were restricted by the Capitulations and had jurisdiction only over mail sacks belonging to the government post office. The first attempt to end competition was made in 1874, but it was abandoned because of the strong opposition of the powers. In 1881 the Egyptian and Greek post offices were abolished and the Ottoman post office began operating its own foreign services, sending mail by sea to Marseilles, Brindisi, and Varna and then overland by rail. The Porte also attempted to stop the foreign post offices by refusing them permission to send their own mail sacks into the empire, but pressure from the ambassadors in Istanbul undermined the effort once again.

Beginning in 1901, the Ottoman post office tried a new approach, seeking to compete with its foreign rivals by providing better service, selling stamps at discounts if bought in bulk, and numbering the stamps and giving their holders opportunities to win prizes at public raffles. The foreign post offices responded in kind and also built separate branches in Istanbul and Izmir and around the empire, providing complete domestic as well as foreign service, so that Ottoman postal revenues actually went down after 1904. It was only as a result of the Bosnian Crisis that the Ottoman government was able to abolish the Austrian post office in 1909 along with all the foreign post offices outside Istanbul and Izmir. The beginning of World War I finally enabled the Porte to take these over as well on October 1, 1914. Foreign postal services certainly had hindered the development of the Ottoman post office, while the resistance of the powers to nationalization violated the principle of state postal monopolies already established in their own countries. On the other hand, the existence of competing systems did give the subjects of the sultan a kind of service that they probably would not have been able to enjoy through the operations of the Ottoman post office alone.[71]

Experimental telephone service was established in Istanbul in 1881 by the Ottoman post office between its branch offices at Galata and Eminönü, in the new and old sections of the city respectively, but because of the sultan's strong fear of electricity all services making use of it were forbidden for private use for the remainder of his reign. It was only after 1909 that electricity, with its many benefits, was spread widely in Istanbul as well as elsewhere in the empire.

Agriculture

It took some time for agriculture to get the attention it deserved from the Ottoman government. Until 1893 a subordinate agriculture director (*ziraat müdürü*) within the Ministry of Trade and Public Works supervised agriculture policies. There was only one director during this period who was really active, the Armenian Amasyan Efendi (1880–1888). He sent agricultural inspectors to the provinces to advise cultivators on methods and crops and dispatched young Ottomans, mainly Armenians, to be trained in European agricultural schools. In 1893 agriculture was transferred to the new Ministry of Forests, Mines, and Agriculture (*Nezaret-i Orman ve Maadin ve Ziraat*), in which it had primary importance. The position of minister was held by Selim Melhame Efendi, a Syrian Catholic who could make his policies prevail and secure funds because his brother Necib held high rank in the secret police. Selim built a staff of professional agricultural experts, with the Armenians prevailing, but an increasing number of Muslims and Greeks were also sent to Europe for training. As they returned, the system of agricultural inspectors was extended to most provinces, though until there were enough men many had to serve more than one area and it was difficult for them to operate effectively. Once there were enough Ottomans to staff it, the Halkalı Agricultural School was established just east of Istanbul, at Küçük Çekmece (1892). Soon its graduates returned to their homes to carry on the ministry's work. Courses were given in agricultural theory and practice, chemistry, mathematics, and land and tax law as well as in subjects such as the use of agricultural machines and tools and the cultivation of different crops. Veterinary medicine was added in 1895. The ministry also intended to establish more elementary agricultural schools elsewhere in the empire, but in fact only two were set up, at Salonica and Bursa, both mainly with local funds. Their graduates joined those of the Halkalı school in spreading modern agricultural methods around the empire. In addition, in order to help the inspectors disseminate agricultural information, model farms were established at Adana, Sivas, Konya, and Izmit in Anatolia, at Damascus and Aleppo in the Arab provinces, and at Monastir in Europe. These served as locales for experimentation and demonstration of new cultivation techniques and equipment.[72]

Societies for both trade (*Ticaret Cemiyeti*) and agriculture (*Ziraat Cemiyeti*) had been established as early as 1876 to promote economic development. Nonsalaried members drawn from among leading cultivators and merchants in each area joined these advisory and promotional bodies. They met weekly and sent the Istanbul government regular reports and recommendations on how trade and agriculture could be developed locally and throughout the empire.[73] The results were limited, however, so in 1880 Sait Paşa reorganized them into chambers of commerce (*Ticaret Odası*) and agriculture (*Ziraat Odası*) in each provincial capital, with similar membership, organization, and regulations, but under the control of the governors in the hope that they would receive guidance and provide effective leadership.[74] Voluminous reports that were sent by these chambers to the ministry formed the basis for many of the regulations issued in subsequent years. The Istanbul chamber published the *Journal de la Chambre de Commerce de Constantinople* starting in 1885, providing a major source of economic news. Ottoman chambers of commerce also were established in various European capitals to encourage the sale of Ottoman goods abroad, thus promoting trade as well as agriculture in the early years of the twentieth century.[75]

All these organizations, however, had little effect on the most important problem of Ottoman agriculture, that of providing the cultivators with sufficient funds to obtain seed and equipment without having to suffer the burden of the excessive interest rates traditionally charged by the moneylenders. As early as 1844 the government had ordered the provincial councils to give low-interest loans to cultivators, but without capital reserves or encouragement these efforts had very little effect. After 1864, as part of the provincial reforms, cooperative district funds (*Memleket Sandığı*) were established in many *kaza*s of the Danube province during Midhat Paşa's governorship to provide low-interest loans to cultivators. By 1871 these had spread to all the provinces where the reforms had been introduced.[76] In 1883 the funds were put under the control of the Ministry of Trade and Public Works as well as the Ministry of Agriculture, and funds also were provided from a surtax of 1 percent imposed on the tithe as a Benefits Donation Share (*Menafi Iane Hissesi*). But with increased resources, the problems also increased. Wealthy local notables continued to control the councils and direct loan policy to favor their own interests, raising the rates on smaller loans while granting themselves large loans for long terms at low interest, leaving even less for the cultivators than before.[77]

Finally, therefore, in 1888 the Agricultural Bank (*Ziraat Bankası*) was created to take over and reform the entire system of agricultural credit. It subsequently developed not only into the major source of agricultural capital in the empire but also into its largest bank, a position that it retains in the Turkish Republic to the present day. Still under the control of the Ministry of Trade and Public Works, it was managed by an administrative council that included representatives from the Council of State, the Auditing Council, and from the Istanbul chambers of commerce and agriculture, as well as high officials of the ministry. Taking over the benefit funds system, it soon had over 400 branches, each headed by directors from Istanbul advised by unsalaried local councils. Capital came from the proceeds of the surtax, private deposits (which earned interest at the rate of $4\frac{1}{2}$ percent), and interest received from loans, with surpluses going to the central treasury. Loans could be made only to cultivators at first, but this definition continued to include not only those who worked the land personally but also those who hired others to do so. Big landowners still secured the bulk of the loans and left most of the small cultivators dependent on the moneylenders. The bank relaxed its requirements for collateral only at times to help those hurt by natural disasters or who wanted to buy new machinery.[78]

It was the Agricultural Bank that took over the task of financing agricultural improvement and education. To finance the schools, model farms, the salaries of the teachers and inspectors, to buy seed and equipment for the model farms as well as for some cultivators, and to pay for demonstrations, the bank allocated funds to the responsible ministry. Division of responsibility between the Ministry of Trade and what eventually became the Ministry of Forests and Agriculture caused trouble, however, with the former encouraging the Agricultural Bank to develop commercial and industrial interests and to take over collection and distribution of the Educational Share surtax established to help the Ministry of Education fund new schools and teachers, the Military Equipment Assistance Share imposed to help the government buy modern equipment for the army and navy, and the Refugees Assistance Stamp affixed to all official documents in addition to the stamp tax to help finance refugee settlement. It also came to administer the road labor system and the tax introduced to replace forced labor, sometimes turning the receipts over to the local officials in charge of road building, but at times itself managing this far-flung operation. All these activities diverted staff and funds from the agricultural operations that were supposed to be its raison d'être. Its revenues were often diverted to pay off the annual deficits of the central treasury as well as the supplementary budget.[79] Such measures were justified when the only alternative was foreign loans, but the manner in which they were introduced made agriculture in particular the chief contributor to maintaining the entire system, thus limiting the development of the backbone of the economy.

Nevertheless, Ottoman agriculture developed considerably during Abdulhamit's long reign. It was helped by the railroads and by agents of foreign equipment companies, who were anxious to sell their products. The cultivators were far less conservative than one might imagine once the use of the new machines was demonstrated and means provided for their purchase. Newly settled refugees were particularly receptive, perhaps because they were not hindered by local custom and practice. Much depended on the encouragement of the local officials as well as the agricultural and trade bodies. Customs-tax exemptions on imported agricultural machinery helped keep prices down, and though they lapsed in 1885 pressure from the rural councils caused them to be restored in 1890. The larger equipment from England and the United States was used at first, but Germany gradually gained a dominant hold on the Ottoman market because of its manufacturers' willingness to modify their products and produce smaller and lighter machines to meet the needs of the rather rocky and uneven Anatolian fields. Once again, however, it was the large landowners who were best able to buy the machines or secure the loans for them; hence the trend toward development of large estates was accelerated.[80]

Grain production was encouraged by the distribution of improved-quality American wheat and barley seed, the latter to take advantage of a new Ottoman taste for beer. Anatolian grain growers were directed to develop markets in Istanbul, which traditionally had depended on Balkan sources because of their accessibility and abundance. Grape production was encouraged, not only to provide wine for the empire but also as a substantial export crop, which at times (in the form of raisins) comprised as much as 20 percent of the empire's total exports. There was a constant struggle against the phylloxera infestation, which had decimated the French vineyards in the 1870s. Importation of the same American vines that enabled the French to restore their grape industry finally resulted in success in the

Ottoman Empire as well. The silk and tobacco industries were under the direct control of the Public Debt Commission. The silk industry developed through importing high-quality silkworm eggs and cocoons and the use of the methods developed by Pasteur to prevent their succumbing to disease, with training provided in the agricultural schools and the Silk Raising Institute (*Harir Dar ut-Taalim*) opened in Bursa in 1888. In 1883 the Public Debt Commission turned the tobacco monopoly over to a private German-French company called the *Régie cointéressée de tabacs de l'Empire Ottoman,* which paid a fixed annual fee of 75 million kuruş in return and then divided the profits with the Ottoman treasury. The *Régie* had the sole right to buy and process all tobacco sold in the empire and regulate its cultivation. It provided interest-free loans to tobacco growers but in return secured their crops as collateral. Before the harvest its agents and the planters inspected and registered the crops in the fields so that nothing could be harvested and sold illegally. The tobacco then was stored in the *Régie* warehouses, and the sales price was fixed by negotiation with the planters, with disputes settled by arbitration. The *Régie* was in charge of selling tobacco products in the empire, setting its own prices and choosing its shops, and other shops selling foreign tobacco products operated only when licensed by it. The treasury expected to receive annually at least the same amount as the fee that the *Régie* paid the Debt Commission, about 75 million kuruş, but in fact it rarely did, averaging no more than 42 million kuruş between 1884 and 1907. This was the result of the *Régie*'s exorbitant charges for storing, manufacturing, and selling the tobacco, deducted from the gross income before the profit shares were determined.

The other major new crop developed in the late nineteenth century was cotton, grown mainly in southern Anatolia around Izmir and Adana. It was first introduced, as in Egypt, in the 1860s to take advantage of the world shortage caused by the American Civil War. Production declined afterward due to the renewed competition of the fine American cotton, but the government encouraged its continuation by distributing American seeds and also providing tithe exemptions. Finally, when world demand for cotton once again exceeded the supply after 1900, the Ottomans were ready to participate in the world market, with exports increasing as much as 25 percent during the last decade of Abdulhamit's rule, though at the expense of cereal production, making it necessary at times to import food to meet internal needs.

Because of the inadequacy of agricultural statistical surveys for the early years of Abdulhamit's reign, it is difficult to give an exact quantitative account of the development of the different crops. However, an increase in the tithe collections from 425.7 million kuruş in 1887–1888 to 690.5 million kuruş in 1908–1909, about 60 percent, can be attributed to the success of the policy.[81] The gradual shift from the tax farms to direct collection might explain some of the increase in tax revenues, but crop export statistics, with the value of grains shipped from Anatolia increasing from 465 million kuruş in 1877–1878 to 753.9 million kuruş in 1907–1908, also indicate increased agricultural production.[82] Loans made by the Agricultural Bank also rose from 10,842 loans worth 16.2 million kuruş in 1889 to 47,097 loans worth 109.7 million kuruş in 1907.[83] By the end of Abdulhamit's reign, grain continued to dominate Ottoman agriculture in terms of the area cultivated, as well as the value of total produce (see Table 3.7).

Attention was paid to the development of animal husbandry during the Tanzimat, so that in about four decades related taxes increased by over 50 percent, from 72.8 million kuruş in 1839 to 183.9 million kuruş in 1876. But interest declined during

Table 3.7. *The major Ottoman crops in 1909*

	Tithe paid (in millions of kuruş)	Value of crop (in millions of kuruş)	Kilograms produced (millions)	Area cultivated (in millions of acres)
Grain	660.5	5,500.3	149.9	11,900,000
Olives	20.0	202.9	65.5	701,766
Silk	26.9	198.1	n.a.	n.a.
Nuts	12.3	144.5	72.3	741,365
Cotton and poppies	14.3	109.6	41.2	991,287
Fruits and vegetables	12.4	81.6	124.1	1,300,000
Grapes	9.5	50.2	66.8	743,882
Tobacco	29.5	n.a.	33.7	119,068

Source: *Ihsaiyat-ı Maliye*, I, 78–85.

the remainder of the century, however. Taxes from animal husbandry therefore rose only to 186 million kuruş in 1907–1908, making this area a far less important part of the Ottoman economy than had been the case earlier.[84]

Mineral Resources

Exploitation of Ottoman natural resources increased during the nineteenth century as foreign concessionaries worked to provide their own countries with the needs of their emerging industries. Mines traditionally were assigned to tax farmers by the Ottoman government, with the treasury receiving one-fifth of the product. But it was only with the promulgation of the first Ottoman Mines Law in 1861 and its revision in 1869 that conditions were made sufficiently favorable for foreign operators to develop Ottoman mines on a large scale. The latter regulation gave the state only from 1 to 5 percent of the minerals extracted according to the extent of the mine and the difficulty of extraction. As a result, exploitation increased markedly in the late Tanzimat period. The coal mine at Ereğli, the copper and iron mines at Ergani, the gold and silver mines at Bulgardağ, the silver mines at Gümüş and Hacıköy, the stone quarries at Eskişehir, and the clay pits at Ankara were most productive. The Mines Department then began a successful campaign to attract new foreign operations, securing a regulation in 1887 that allowed them longer leases, up to 99 years, in return for the payment of taxes to the treasury, amounting to as much as 25 percent of the value of the extract. An additional land tax also provided the state with more revenues than under the previous regulations but left the exploiters with sufficient profits to encourage them to continue and even expand their operations.[85] By the end of Abdulhamit's reign a total of 43,234 tons of minerals were being extracted, including 19,586 of chrome (45 percent), 7,343 of borax (17 percent), 6,396 of emery (14 percent), 5,733 of manganese (13 percent) and lesser quantities of lead, gold, lignite coal, and arsenic, most of which was exported to Britain and to a far lesser extent to Germany.[86] Thus advances were made, but mineral exploitation still was limited because of inadequate transportation facilities and the lack of Ottoman factories able to utilize them. Sait Paşa in particular was aware of the problem, but little in fact was done to remedy these difficulties until the republican period.[87]

Salt continued to be intensively extracted to meet the needs of the empire's own population. Traditionally, it had been exploited by tax farmers, but the profits were so attractive to the government that in 1840 it took over direct control of the system by establishing a state monopoly, which continued thereafter. Directors were appointed to buy the salt from those processing and extracting it, mainly from the major salt lakes found in central Anatolia. The distribution and sale of salt was under the general control of the Excise Tax Department (*Rüsumat Emaneti*) at first and the Public Debt Commission after 1881. Production increased by 66 percent during Abdulhamit's reign, from 205.2 million kilograms to 340.9 million kilograms between 1885 and 1912, while exports increased sixfold, from 17.9 million kilograms to 114.6 million kilograms between 1892 and 1909. Treasury revenues from salt just about doubled during the reign, from 65.6 million kuruş to 115.3 million kuruş between 1887 and 1908, regularly contributing about 5 percent of total state revenues.

Forestry

With the Ottoman forests the problem was not so much to increase exploitation, but rather to conserve what was left following the unrestrained use of timber and the ravages of fires. Traditionally, all forests belonged to villages, private individuals, or religious foundations. Even the forests left to the state, mostly those in mountainous areas, which were difficult to reach, could be used by private persons without any obligation to pay taxes; thus the forests were depleted fairly rapidly. The Tanzimat established a forestry department in 1846, but like the departments concerned with agriculture and education it was passed around to different ministries, from Finance to Public Works and Trade and, finally, to Mines and Agriculture, but never with sufficient staff or political support to enable it to become effective.

The Land Law of 1857 attempted to control the unrestricted use of forests by imposing the tithe on those taking wood from state and village lands. But exemptions were given to the village residents living nearby who provided for the needs of the armed forces and in return were allowed to continue to cut as much as they wanted without any tithe payments or restrictions.[88] In 1870 a Forestry Academy (*Orman Mektebi*) was established, and the first Ottoman Forest Regulation (*Orman Nizamnamesi*) put all forests under the control and supervision of the Forestry Department regardless of who owned the land. It established strict regulations on tree cutting, and extended the tithe to include timber and produce from forests on village lands as well as those of the state.[89] In addition all those holding plots of forest land on state properties were subjected to a special new land tax (*icar-ı zemin*) and required to accept the regulations of the Forestry Department in exploiting their holdings. A forestry service was established, with inspectors sent to forested districts of the empire to enforce the law, giving permits, collecting taxes, and supervising tree cutting. However, it was badly undermanned. The forests continued to be heavily cut despite the law, and conservation or reforestation policies were not developed. The worst culprit was, in fact, the government. In 1897 there were 4.27 million acres of forest land in the empire, mainly in the provinces of Aydın (753,136 acres), Kastamonu (677,013 acres), and Salonica (639,910 acres). While only 1.14 million cubic meters of timber were cut annually for private use, at least legally, 9.9 million cubic meters were being cut for the armed forces, railroad construction, and state buildings.[90] It is not surprising, therefore, that in 1909 there were only 3.2 million acres of forest left in the empire, with 319,340 acres in Aydın province, 289,791 acres in Kastamonu, and 304,256 acres in Salonica.[91] An effective conservation policy had to await the establishment of the Republic.

Industrial Development

The emphasis on agriculture and raw materials fitted in nicely with the prevailing free-trade ideas of the Manchester School, which dictated that each country should do what it could accomplish best. Britain thus manufactured and prospered while the underdeveloped countries concentrated on producing raw materials and purchasing British goods. In the face of the competition of European industry, even the craft industries that had been most developed under the Ottomans suffered. Ottoman policy makers and thinkers wanted to reverse this trend and build Ottoman industry so that the empire and its people could also share in world prosperity. Abdulhamit therefore developed the existing armaments and clothing factories, created originally to provide for the needs of the armed forces. The cloth and porcelain factories established by Abdulaziz to meet the needs of the palace were set to work to manufacture goods that the public would buy. Private capital was encouraged to develop factories to compete with those of Europe. As a result, by the end of Abdulhamit's reign Istanbul had a few private factories making bricks, cotton cloth, tile, and glass. There were leather factories in Istanbul, Diyarbekir, and Mosul. Salonica had tile, beer, brick, and cotton cloth factories. Izmit had fairly substantial paper and cloth factories as well as one making woolen and cotton thread. There were rug factories in Urfa, Gördes, and Uşak and silk factories in Bursa, Izmit, Aleppo, and Edirne. And there were about 1500 other small plants of various kinds around the empire.[92] But they were still small-scale operations and could not really compete with European manufactures either in quality or cost. Moreover, the powers opposed Ottoman attempts to protect infant industries by increasing tariffs on imports and raising the cost of Ottoman raw materials. The Capitulations were used to "keep the Turk in his place." The powers also failed to provide the kind of investment and stimulus to industry that they so readily gave to Ottoman communications, raw materials, and agricultural products because the latter benefited them in one way or another. Ottoman industry remained underdeveloped, therefore, leaving the people of the empire almost completely dependent on Europe for clothing and other manufactured goods.

Trade and Commerce

Foreign trade consequently flourished. Hundreds of European and Ottoman merchants made fortunes by shipping Ottoman raw materials to Europe and receiving and selling manufactures in return. Government promotion, though present, was not important. There was a Ministry of Trade and Public Works under Abdulhamit, but most of its activities were directed toward developing railroads and roads, and trade was covered by a small department having little more than a director and his secretary. Centrally organized encouragement for trade came mainly through the activities of the chambers of commerce started by Âli Paşa in the 1860s, with the one in Istanbul coordinating the activities of 13 other chambers located at the main provincial centers.[93] Constituted basically as merchant guilds, they regulated the standards and activities of their members, pressured the government at all levels to

Table 3.8. *The major Ottoman exports
in 1897 (in millions of kuruş)*

Agricultural goods		Other goods	
Grapes	177.5	Silk	135.8
Figs	67.8	Rifles	64.8
Olive oil	62.7	Minerals	47.0
Opium	61.5	Drugs	23.1
Nuts	57.7	Salted fish	10.0
Cotton	48.0	Sponge	8.1
Barley	47.5		
Wool	46.9		
Sheepskins	34.7		
Sesame seeds	31.8		
Coffee	29.7		
Indian corn	27.3		
Lentils	24.4		
Tobacco	24.0		
Salt	23.6		
Dates	19.4		
Hazelnuts	17.7		
Wheat	14.8		
Citrus fruit	13.5		
Dried fruit	13.2		

Source: Istatistik-i Umumi, pp. 110–112.

facilitate trade by building or repairing quays and roads and simplifying customs-tax systems, and secured the abolishment of the internal customs duties. They promoted the use of the decimal system in measurements and opened trade and commerce schools to help beginners understand European trade laws and methods. They opened stock exchanges, insurance companies, and banks and urged the government to facilitate banking and business by legislation.

During the reign of Abdulhamit, exports – stimulated far more by increasing European profits at the expense of the Ottoman Empire – increased by more than 100 percent, from only 839.6 million kuruş in 1878–1879 to 1.9 billion kuruş in 1907–1908. The main exports (see Table 3.8), as one might expect, were agricultural goods, led by grapes, figs, olive oil, and opium, with silk, rifles, and minerals also making a significant contribution. The leading purchasers were England and France, followed by Austria, Italy, Germany, and Russia. But imports from these countries increased even more (see Table 3.9), as the thwarted Ottoman industry left the subjects to buy most of their clothing and textiles and other necessities, such as medical supplies and sugar, from Europe. Imports therefore increased from a value of 2 billion kuruş in 1878–1879, with a trade deficit of 1.1 billion kuruş, to 3.4 billion kuruş in 1907–1908, with a deficit of 1.5 billion kuruş. Only France kept a reasonable trade balance with the Ottoman Empire during those years, while Britain, Austria, and Italy in particular built such substantial surpluses that it was impossible for the Ottomans to achieve any kind of favorable balance (see Table 3.10).

238   *The Rise of Modern Turkey, 1808–1975*

Table 3.9. *The major Ottoman imports in 1897 (in millions of kuruş)*

Agricultural goods		Textile goods		Other goods	
Sugar	157.5	Coarse cloth	139.4	Timber	36.4
Coffee	102.7	Cotton yarn	117.8	Coal	27.0
Rice	78.8	Calico	69.5	Drugs	22.7
Flour	78.3	Petticoats	64.1	Paper	20.6
Wheat	62.2	Gauze	56.2	Copper	17.3
Oxen	28.6	Kashmir cloth	41.8	Spirits	16.7
Clarified butter	19.9	Muslin	40.2	Glass	16.1
Vanilla	5.8	Linen	35.1	Morocco leather	15.8
		Felt	31.9	Nails	12.6
		Ready-made clothing	24.4	Earthenware	11.9
		Homespun cloth	21.0	Cognac	9.4
		Fezzes, hats	20.9	Matches	8.9
		Handkerchiefs	12.0	Cord	7.4
		Blankets	12.0	Watches	7.0
		Linings	10.1	Bricks	6.0
		Lace	7.6		

Source: Istatistik-i Umumi, pp. 110–112.

The leading port of the empire by far was Izmir, which in 1897 handled 501.6 million kuruş of imports and exports, followed distantly by Istanbul (258.4 million kuruş), Beirut (142.2 million kuruş), Salonica (95.1 million kuruş), Baghdad (80.5 million kuruş), Alexandretta (73.6 million kuruş) and Trabzon (67.7 million kuruş).[94]

Ottoman Society in the Age of Abdulhamit II

The total population of the Ottoman Empire in 1897 was 39,096,294 if one includes provinces such as Egypt, Tunisia, Bulgaria, Cyprus, Bosnia-Herzegovina, and the Lebanon, which remained under the sultan's suzerainty but outside his administrative control. But if one excludes all the provinces not yet counted by the census administration, principally the latter together with the Yemen, Hicaz, Libya, and parts of the east Anatolian and Arab provinces, the actual population counted for tax purposes came to 19,050,307, of whom 14,111,945 men and women, or 74 percent, were Muslims, and 4,938,362, or 26 percent, were non-Muslims (see Table 3.11). It was a fairly old population, with 3.6 million persons, almost 19 percent, under the age of 10, another 9.7 million, or 50.1 percent, between the ages of 10 and 40, and 6.7 million, or 31 percent, above 40. The birth rate was only 3.75 percent per year, with the Muslim rate slightly higher than the other *millet*s in relation to the proportion of Muslims in the population as a whole. The death rate was 2.12 percent, leaving a natural increase of about 1.63 percent, only 310,000 persons in all.[95] In fact, population in the empire increased considerably less than that amount during Abdulhamit's reign, from 17,143,859 in 1884 to 19,050,307, in 1897, an average of 7/10 of 1 percent, while the empire remained intact, due most likely to the decimation of all elements of the population because of terrorist activities and countermeasures to suppress them (see Table 3.12). If one recalls

Table 3.10. *The Ottoman trade balance, 1878–1912 (in millions of kuruş)*

Year	Value of exports	Value of imports
1878–1879	839.6	2,000.4
1879–1880	876.0	1,941.7
1880–1881	849.7	1,784.7
1881–1882	1,139.5	1,948.6
1882–1883	1,096.4	2,019.2
1883–1884	1,239.0	1,975.7
1884–1885	1,279.8	2,063.7
1885–1886	1,207.6	2,000.3
1886–1887	1,270.7	2,070.3
1887–1888	1,128.9	2,010.5
1888–1889	1,304.6	1,945.6
1889–1890	1,527.2	2,104.1
1890–1891	1,283.6	2,291.4
1891–1892	1,537.0	2,455.3
1892–1893	1,557.2	2,446.6
1893–1894	1,326.2	2,410.8
1894–1895	1,375.3	2,407.5
1895–1899 (average)	1,457.7	2,321.3
1899–1907 (average)	1,672.2	2,655.2
1907–1908	1,921.3	3,476.3
1908–1909	1,843.9	3,143.2
1909–1910	1,829.9	3,593.6
1910–1911	2,193.9	4,125.7
1911–1912	2,471.2	4,499.0

Sources: For 1878–1895, *Istatistik-i Umumi*, p. 109; for 1895–1911, *Ihsaiyat-ı Maliye*, I, 164–165, III, 130–131.

that during the same years 202,822 Muslim refugees entered the empire (an additional 812,193 had come between 1878 and 1884) and that large numbers of Christians were fleeing to Bulgaria and Greece due to the troubles in Macedonia, it becomes even more apparent that it was the Muslims far more than the non-Muslims who suffered the greatest loss of population.

That these trends continued through the remaining years of the empire is demonstrated by the later census reports (see Table 3.13). The decrease in the 1914 figure to 18.5 million reflects the loss of Macedonia and Janina during the Balkan Wars. But if one adds the population of the lost territories as they appeared in the 1906 census, 2,455,329, to that of 1914, the resulting 20,975,345 is comparable, particularly in the light of the 1910 total figure of 20,706,170. This is supported by comparing the figures of the Bulgars and Greeks who left the empire plus those of

Table 3.11. *Composition of the Ottoman population in 1897*

Millet	Males	Females	Total	Percent
Muslim	7,499,798	6,612,147	14,111,945	74.07
Greek	1,341,049	1,228,863	2,569,912	13.49
Armenian Orthodox	546,030	496,344	1,042,374	5.47
Bulgarian	449,286	380,903	830,189	4.36
Catholic	65,912	54,567	120,479	0.64
Jewish	117,767	97,658	215,425	1.13
Protestant	22,963	21,397	44,360	0.24
Latin	12,280	10,055	22,335	0.12
Maronite	15,262	17,154	32,416	0.17
Keldani	3,866	1,902	5,768	0.03
Syriac	19,500	16,054	35,554	0.18
Gypsy	10,309	9,241	19,550	0.10
Totals	10,104,022	8,946,285	19,050,307	100.00

Source: Istatistik-i Umumi, pp. 15, 16; the figures come from the official Ottoman census/identity card counts that were constantly kept up to date in the Census Department and Police Ministry – see BVA, Teşkilat-ı Devair, Dosya 26/1–3.

Table 3.12. *Ottoman population by religion, 1884–1897*

Year	Muslims	Non-Muslims	Totals
1884	12,590,352	4,553,507	17,143,859
1885	12,707,638	4,578,774	17,286,412
1886	12,824,924	4,603,041	17,427,965
1887	12,942,210	4,637,308	17,579,518
1888	13,059,496	4,661,579	17,721,075
1889	13,176,782	4,685,842	17,862,624
1890	13,294,068	4,701,109	18,400,177
1891	13,411,354	4,734,376	18,145,730
1892	13,411,361	4,763,381	18,174,742
1893	13,578,647	4,776,738	18,316,295
1894	13,645,903	4,804,942	18,450,845
1895	13,763,249	4,832,149	18,595,398
1896	13,890,910	4,848,849	18,739,759
1897	14,111,945	4,938,362	19,050,307

Source: Istatistik-i Umumi, p. 15; Istanbul University Library, TY5651.

Table 3.13. *Ottoman population by*
religion in 1906 and 1914

	1906	1914
Muslims	15,518,478	15,044,846
Greeks	2,833,370	1,792,206
Armenians	1,140,563	1,294,831
Bulgars	762,754	14,908
Jews	256,003	187,073
Protestants	53,880	—
Others	332,569	186,152
Totals[a]	20,897,617	18,520,016

[a] The total for 1910 was 20,706,170, a
decrease of over 240,000 from the 1906
figure.

the Jews who remained in Salonica. The total of 1,918,010 itself accounts for much
of the population loss when one also considers that thousands of Muslims fled to
the Ottoman side. Using, then, the figure of 20,975,345 for 1914, we find that the
total population increase averaged 0.6 percent from 1897, about the same as it had
been in the previous years.[96]

Urban Life

Urban life changed markedly during Abdulhamit II's reign. In Istanbul, Izmir,
Edirne, Salonica, and the other main cities, streets and sidewalks were now paved
and lit with gas lamps and kept clean and safe. Horse-drawn public streetcars were
operated, usually by foreign concessionaries. There were thousands of small
merchants selling goods and luxury items from every corner of the earth. The
myriad of post offices, telegraph lines, and steamships provided internal as well as
external communication. Modern medical services eliminated the plague as a major
threat, giving the average subject a far more pleasant and secure existence than had
seemed possible only a century before.

Above all the urban conglomerations in the empire loomed the great city of
Istanbul, still capital of a vast empire, perhaps the most cosmopolitan city in the
world, where the many peoples of the empire mingled with foreign residents and
visitors coming from halfway around the globe. Privileged among the cities of the
empire, in mood and appearance it reflected the modernization imposed on the
empire during the previous half-century. Istanbul, however, had its own problems,
mainly that of attempting to assimilate a rapidly expanding population, which increased from about 391,000 men and women in 1844 up to 430,000 in 1856, right
after the Crimean War, 547,437 in 1878, and then in another burst to 851,527 in
1886, over 100 percent in all in only 40 years. This included about 100,000 foreign
subjects who came to reside in the city during the same period. The birth rate in
Istanbul was no higher than elsewhere, and its rapid growth came not only as the
natural result of the rapid expansion of government and business in the principal
city of a great empire but also in consequence of the crowding in of thousands of

Muslim refugees, with Istanbul acting as a funnel for all those fleeing from Europe, Russia, and even Algeria. The government kept pushing them into the countryside as rapidly as they could be settled, but this still meant that at any one time there were as many as 200,000 refugees milling in the streets of the capital, restless, usually jobless, supported by pittances from the government and the mosques, taxing the city's resources and sanitary facilities to the utmost, and always ready to rise in expression of their sufferings and frustration. The problem persisted through much of Abdulhamit's reign, as indicated by the later population figures for the city, 903,482 in 1897, 864,566 in 1906, 855,976 in 1910, and 909,978 following an influx in the aftermath of the Balkan Wars. In 1927, after the wars decimated the Ottoman population and destroyed the empire, the population figure for Istanbul went down to 690,857 before it began climbing again during the years of the Republic.

All the elements of the population shared in Istanbul's growth between 1878 and 1886 (see Table 3.14), the only years for which we have detailed analyses. The Muslims increased by 90 percent, the Greeks by 60 percent, the Armenians by 53 percent, and the Jews by 131 percent.

Government service remained mainly a Muslim monopoly, with 95.4 percent of the positions being held by Muslims and only 4.6 percent by members of the minorities. In fact 11.4 percent of all Muslims resident in the city worked in some way for the government. While a quarter of the Muslim population was engaged in trade and industry, this came to only 39 percent of all those involved in these occupations compared with 61 percent of the minorities. Among the latter, almost all the Bulgars resident in Istanbul (81.4 percent) were in trade and industry, as were 43 percent of the Armenians, 36.8 percent of the Greeks, and 31 percent of the Jews. The desire for education among the Christian minorities is also evident

Table 3.14. *The religious make-up of Istanbul, 1844–1886*

	1844 (estimate)	1856 (estimate)	1878	1886	Ratio of females to males in 1886 (%)
Muslims	195,836	214,229	203,148	384,836	91
Greeks	75,994	97,136	96,044	152,741	66
Armenians	85,438	80,179	97,782	149,590	78
Bulgars	—	—	2,521	4,377	10
Catholics	10,303	10,874	5,610	6,442	101
Jews	24,083	26,047	19,223	22,394	97
Protestants	—	468	511	819	82
Latins	—	1,241	396	1,082	110
Foreigners	—	—	122,202	129,243	—

Sources: The figures for 1844 and 1856 come from Istanbul University Library, TY8949; those for 1878 and 1886 from *Bâ Irade-i Seniye-i Cenâb-ı Padişahi buda icra olunan Tahrir-i sabık yoklaması mucibince Der Saadet ve Bilad-ı selasede mevcut nüfusun İstatistik Cetvelidir,* Istanbul, 1302, hereafter abbreviated as *Der Saadet nüfus,* pp. 2–4. The census reports for 1844 and 1856 include only male subjects, since they were for tax and conscription purposes; thus to provide comparative figures with the later tables, the same ratios of men and women found in the 1886 report have been used to estimate a female population figure and calculate an estimated total figure in the two earlier reports.

from their occupying 52 percent of all the student openings available in the city despite their smaller numbers. Forty-one percent of the Greeks and 38.6 percent of the Armenians were students, while only 36 percent of the Muslims and Jews were occupied in this way (see Table 3.15).

Administration

There were a number of other areas in which the reforming hand of the sultan was felt. In administration the beginnings were made during the short era of the Parliament when major regulations were promulgated for provincial and municipal organization. The Provincial Regulation of 1876 was delayed by demands from the non-Muslim deputies for equal representation for their coreligionists in the advisory councils regardless of their small proportion of the total population, but this was finally rejected in favor of proportional representation for the major religious and economic groups. The most important contribution of the new regulation, and the first major modification of the 1864 provincial system, was the creation of a new level of government, the township (*nahiye*), composed of adjacent villages in a *kaza* having between 5,000 and 10,000 people. It was given its own administrator (*müdür*) and advisory council and acted on matters regarding tax assessment and collection, local public works, agriculture, and education. The provincial councils now also became general assemblies composed of representatives elected in the *sancak*s for terms of four years.[97]

A new municipal law was provided for Istanbul, more or less preserving the previous organization. The mayor (*şehir emini*) was assisted by a council of six members; but the city was now divided into 20 departments, each administered by elected councils of from 8 to 12 members who helped the *muhtar*s and police commissioners carry out their work.[98] The large number of districts soon was found too unwieldy and expensive, and in 1880 they were reduced to ten.[99] In addition, a provincial Municipal Law was introduced, providing a municipal organization for every city and town in the empire, under the supervision of the Ministry of the Interior. Local administrative councils chose the mayor (*muhtar*) from among their own members, and municipal assemblies, including representatives of the government and councils, met twice a year to approve the municipal budgets.[100]

In response to the increased intervention of the representatives of the powers in Ottoman administrative affairs, Abdulhamit moved to centralize control over the governors and civil servants throughout the empire, often establishing direct lines of communication between them and the palace in addition to their official ties with the Ministry of the Interior. The latter in turn developed a highly centralized system that allowed no deviations from central regulations, with even the smallest expenditure or action requiring prior authorization from Istanbul. In his reform program of 1879 Abdulhamit had emphasized the need to develop government service into the kind of honored career that it once had been and also to institutionalize the vast bureaucratic structure built up by the Tanzimat while improving its efficiency and effectiveness. To assure that bureaucrats were well trained the secular education system was expanded. At the top, the Civil Service School (*Mekteb-i Mülkiye*) was reorganized and expanded, and new schools were opened to train bureaucrats expert in the law (*Mekteb-i Hukuk*) and finance (*Mekteb-i Maliye*), with their graduates being given first preference whenever there were vacancies in the provincial civil service. The establishment of the Civil Service Commission and the Commission to Register the Affairs of Civil Servants may

Table 3.15. *The occupational make-up of Istanbul's population in 1886*

Millet	Government service		Trade and industry		Students		Religious and children		Total interviewed
	Number	Percent of total population	Number	Percent of total population	Number	Percent of total population	Number	Percent of total population	
Muslims	22,984	11.4	51,073	25.4	73,199	36.4	54,083	26.8	201,339
Greeks	348	0.04	33,866	36.8	37,717	41.0	19,873	21.6	91,804
Armenians	494	0.06	35,979	43.0	32,399	38.6	14,998	17.8	83,870
Bulgars	1	—	3,238	81.4	634	15.9	104	2.6	3,977
Catholics	155	4.9	1,783	55.5	845	26.3	426	13.3	3,209
Jews	99	0.04	6,984	31.1	8,067	36.2	7,244	32.3	22,394
Protestants	3	0.06	123	25.3	218	44.7	144	29.4	488
Latins	28	5.3	251	47.5	140	26.5	109	20.7	528
Totals	24,112		133,297		153,219		96,981		407,609

Source: Der Saadet Nüfus, p. 6.

have discouraged initiative, but the general standards of efficiency and honesty improved.[101] A complicated salary system was set up. It arranged all bureaucrats in a series of salary steps according to rank and position, ending the favoritism that often had enhanced the revenues of a favored few. The grand vezir was given a salary of 25,000 kuruş monthly, the ministers 20,000 kuruş, the undersecretaries 10,000 kuruş, local directors (*müdürs*) from 3,000 to 10,000 kuruş according to the importance of their departments, and the scribes of the bureaucracy down to 1,000 according to the importance of their positions. The provincial governorships were divided into three salary ranges receiving 20,000, 17,000 or 15,000 kuruş monthly. Similar high salaries were given to members of the military and religious classes to remove the temptation of demanding bribes, though the latter again became a serious problem once the government's financial problems made it impossible to pay these salaries on time and in full.

Military Development

During the early years of his reign, Abdulhamit devoted a great deal of attention to modernizing his armed forces. Perhaps the most important change was the sultan's active resumption of the old military role of his ancestors. He retained the position of commander in chief provided in the 1876 Constitution, relegated the *serasker* to a mainly subordinate position, and exercised his powers directly through a series of military commissions. The High Commission of Military Inspection (*Teftiş-i Umumi-i Askeri Komisyon-u Âlisi*) was organized under the sultan's personal chairmanship to investigate the military and legislate necessary changes. Gazi Ahmet Muhtar Paşa served as executive director, and membership went to some 40 experienced army officers, including a number who were secret protégés of the sultan, acting as his eyes and ears in the army. Foreign technical assistance came mostly from Germany, considered more objective toward the Ottomans because of its lack of direct interests in the Middle East. Helmuth von Moltke, now German chief of the General Staff, sent a number of his best officers, among them Von der Goltz, who served the sultan for over a decade, later returning to command the army of the Arabian provinces during World War I.

The sultan had originally intended to modernize all his armed forces, but financial stringencies compelled him to emphasize the traditional Ottoman reliance on land power. The navy, strengthened under Abdulaziz, fell into a state of relative decay, and the empire relied primarily on German industry for cannons and other weapons. Between 1885 and 1888 huge cannons manufactured by Krupp were put into place to guard the Straits as well as the Çatalca defense line north of Istanbul.[102] The modern German Mauser rifle soon replaced the archaic carbines previously used by the Ottomans.[103] The General Staff (*Erkân-ı Harbiye*) was reorganized and limited mainly to preparing staff studies and collecting data and statistics on the army, while a Second General Staff (*Maiyet-i Seniye Erkân-ı Harbiye*) was established to convey the sultan's wishes directly into the military structure.

In 1886 the conscription system was reorganized and made more comprehensive. The army districts became recruiting regions as well, and the reserve (*redif*) centers took over the task of assigning and processing the recruits and making sure that only able-bodied men were taken. Efforts were made to extend the obligation of service to all Muslim males of age 20 and above, though the traditional exemptions given to inhabitants of Istanbul and its environs were retained along with those for Albania, the Hicaz and Necd in Arabia, and Tripoli and Bengazi in North

Africa. The nomadic Turkomans, Kurds, and Arabs were exempted, but the immigrating Turkish refugees were included in the obligation, providing a major new source of men for the army.[104] The provision of personal substitutes (*bedel-i şahsi*) was finally abolished, but exemption by payment continued (see pp. 100–101). Students in the religious and secular schools were exempt as long as they continued their studies. Only three years of active service were now required, followed by six years in the active reserves (*ihtiyat*), nine in the inactive reserves (*redif*), and two in the home guard (*mustahfız*).

An important addition made to the army during the latter years of Abdulhamit's reign was the *Hamidiye* cavalry (1891), composed of Kurdish and Turkoman tribesmen from eastern Anatolia. Initially it was organized to counter the Russian Cossack forces in the Crimea[105] and also to control the tribes themselves by making the new organization responsible for them. The cavalry was formed first in the nomadic areas adjacent to the Russian border in the provinces of Van, Bitlis, and Erzurum, with some 50,000 men being called to service and grouped into regiments of between 768 and 1,152 men each.[106] Each tribe provided one or more regiments, and smaller tribes furnished joint regiments. Men called up were paid only when they were on active duty, but they and their families also were exempted from all taxes except the tithe and the animal tax. Arms were supposed to be provided only when they were engaged in combat, but in fact most of them managed to keep their traditional arms.[107] Youths usually entered at the age of 17, served as apprentices for three years, then served in the regular force (*nizam*) until the age of 30, after which they joined the reserve units until they were 40. The regiments were commanded by the tribal chiefs, but regular army officers also went along to train the men and make sure that the overall commands were carried out. A Tribal School (*Aşiret Mektebi*) was organized to train native Turkoman and Kurdish officers, but no more than 15 men graduated in any given year. Some noncommissioned nomadic officers also were sent to the regular cavalry and military schools for training, after which they returned to their home units, providing most of the commanders. The new *Hamidiye* tribal force grew fairly rapidly, to 40 regiments in 1892, 56 in 1893, and 63 in 1899, and it was used to suppress terrorism in eastern Anatolia. However, proposals to apply similar methods to other parts of the empire were never carried out,[108] and the system fell into disuse after Abdulhamit's deposition.

Justice

The most difficult aspect of the judicial sphere was its lack of unity. There were at least four court systems operating in the empire, supervised by different governmental authorities. Each dispensed justice to different groups of people according to different methods and different laws. The secular *Nizamiye* courts handled criminal and civil cases among Ottoman subjects, except those matters of marriage, death, divorce, and inheritance that were still cared for by the *millet* courts. The consular courts had jurisdiction in trade disputes involving their own subjects and other matters reserved for them by the Capitulation treaties. The mixed trade courts handled commercial disputes arising between Ottoman and non-Ottoman subjects or among non-Ottomans of different nationalities. The *Nizamiye* courts and the mixed trade courts were under the jurisdiction of the Ministry of Justice; the Muslim religious courts were under the *şeyhulislam*'s office; the non-Muslim religious courts were under the Foreign Office at first and then the prime minister's office; and the consular courts remained under the supervision of the Foreign Office. Each supervisory body applied and enforced different regulations and standards, further complicating the situation.

Within this complex structure there were many difficulties. The judges in the *Nizamiye* and Muslim religious courts were paid mainly by the litigants in the form of fees, with no salaries coming from either the religious foundations or the Imperial Treasury. Financial independence, however, did not eliminate administrative influence, since the government exerted control through its power to appoint and dismiss the judges. Moreover, the judges themselves were encouraged to supplement their incomes by bribes from the parties. The Men of the Tanzimat pledged repeatedly that the courts would be independent of the government, but the Council of State and appeals courts in Istanbul remained under the direct control of the grand vezir, while the provincial courts were supervised by the governors and their subordinates. Nor can it be said that the consular courts were free of vice, since those who could pay were often favored. On top of everything else the *Nizamiye* courts were very crowded. Cases often were delayed for months, with the accused being held in jail without the possibility of bond. Though the opportunity of appeal existed, it was so subject to influence by the original judges as well as the officials of government that the convicted person rarely was able to present his case before he had served many years of his sentence.[109] There were no schools to train judges in the secular law systems applied in the *Nizamiye* courts, and the Tanzimat hesitated to interfere with the Muslim religious courts in fear of alienating the ulema.[110] Most judgments were carried out by the provincial armies, giving the subject little chance to exercise his rights. And of course it was for this reason that foreigners in the empire insisted on remaining under the jurisdiction of their own consular courts.

The Constitution of 1876 had recognized these difficulties but did little to solve them. It professed general principles that everyone's rights should be protected, the judges kept independent of government control, and public defenders provided for the poor. It was left to the Parliament to elaborate on these principles, but when it was dissolved, judicial reform was left to the sultan. In his 1879 reform program Abdulhamit specified a number of important judicial reforms that he wished to enact:

1. Full action to carry out the Law on the organization and duties of the secular courts; 2. Preparation of a Law on procedures in the primary courts; 3. Preparation of a Law on procedures in the appeals courts; 4. Preparation of a Regulation on the execution of legal judgments; 5. As has already been done in Istanbul so also in the staffs of the courts of first instance of every province, county and district, appointment of special officials to execute court judgments to take out of the hands of army officials the important task of executing legal judgments; 6. Appointment of judicial inspectors to every province; 7. The appointment to the provincial appeals courts of public prosecutors and to the courts of first instance of the counties of assistant public prosecutors; and by appointing as public prosecutors in the lower courts of qualified persons, ending the fear of the courts on the part of accusers and defendants alike; 8. Breaking up the appeals and primary courts in the provinces into two divisions, called Civil and Criminal, and the appointment of sub-chairmen for each of the appeals courts.[111]

These aims and more were accomplished in a series of laws put into effect during the next few years.

The first step was the reorganization and expansion of the Ministry of Justice, originally established by Âli in 1870. A major new regulation issued on May 4, 1879, gave the ministry the right not only to control the *Nizamiye* courts but also the appeals courts in the Council of State and the religious courts, with the sole exception of the Muslim courts, which remained under the *şeyhulislam*. The ministry was divided into departments to handle criminal and civil justice, the *millet* courts of non-Muslims, and the mixed trade courts. The minister was made a member of the Council of Ministers for the first time, giving him and his advisers power to develop their own legislation.[112]

The new School of Law (*Mekteb-i Hukuk-u Şahane*), established in 1878 to train civil servants as well as judges for the *Nizamiye* courts, expanded rapidly during the next decade, producing as many as 100 well-trained graduates each year. As new judges became available, the *Nizamiye* court system was extended to the more distant provinces, with the criminal and civil courts divided into primary (*bidayet*) and appeals (*istinaf*) courts, capped by the Court of Appeal (*Mahkeme-i Temyiz*) in Istanbul. New trade courts (*Ticaret Mahkemesi*) were opened in major trade centers.[113] A series of regulations followed to assure that only the ablest legal experts were appointed as judges, that they received the salaries and promotions they deserved, and that the incompetent and corrupt were removed and punished.[114]

In 1880 and 1881 two laws were enacted to fulfill the sultan's desire for standard and regular procedures to be followed in the criminal and civil courts, providing the subject with assurance that he would be tried fairly without the intervention of state officials or anyone else.[115] The rights and duties of plaintiffs and court officials were spelled out, and public defenders were provided. Additional laws stipulated the duties of lawyers. Judges and their subordinates were assigned salaries, and they were allowed to keep no more than one-fifth of the court fees, sending the balance to the treasury. Provincial and municipal police were made responsible for the enforcement of court decisions, and the army was prohibited from intervening. Special regulations were introduced to protect the subject from arbitrary search and seizure in his home unless authorized by the courts, echoing articles of the Constitution. As fast as they graduated from the law schools, judicial inspectors were sent to the provinces to ensure that the new regulations were obeyed. New primary and appeals courts were opened in the more distant provinces, and the backlogs of cases were brought to an end. Court charges were strictly regulated; the courts thus were made available to even the poorest of subjects.[116]

Not all the abuses and injustices were removed from the Ottoman judicial system any more than they have been from those of other states. But, on the whole, a standard of honesty and efficiency unequaled in Ottoman history was established for all subjects regardless of religion. Under the direction of a series of able ministers of justice, most prominent of whom was Ahmet Cevdet Paşa, the new laws were put into practice. Justice was institutionalized, and the average subject protected. But intellectuals and rebels found the system restrictive, and when they were accused of violating the law, they protested that it was the fault of the judicial organization. Most Europeans in the empire and the minorities dependent on them were too prejudiced against Muslims to allow themselves to be tried in the Ottoman courts regardless of the latter's improved state. The powers therefore refused to accept the applicability of the regulations to the mixed and consular courts, keeping the system divided and claiming that Muslims were incapable of judging non-Muslims fairly and honestly. Though some prominent individuals suffered from palace intervention, such cases were hardly ever tried. This was of little relevance to the way justice was dispensed to the mass of the people, whose rights were protected far more extensively than in the past.

Education

To those committed to the Tanzimat program of reform and modernization, secular education was a practical goal, needed to produce the kind of people needed to run the government, the courts, and the army. In his 1879 reform program Abdulhamit urged: "If there are any deficiencies or gaps in the existing organization of public education they should be brought to an end." Accordingly, he offered an extensive program to develop schools on all levels throughout the empire.[117]

Very little was done, however, during the early years of his reign. The old Tanzimat system by which schools were built with local funds and on local initiative had resulted in a relatively haphazard development around the empire. The existence of several independent school systems run by the state, the *millets*, and various foreign organizations prevented the kind of unity that might have facilitated reform of the educational system. There were not enough teachers and certainly not enough funds. Without an extensive system of secular primary schools there were not enough qualified students to benefit from the technical and specialized training offered in the new higher schools, and hence progress was slow.

The real breakthrough came in 1883 when the sultan developed the old Assistance Surtax (*Iane Vergisi*) of one-tenth levied on the tithe since 1866 to provide capital for the agricultural banks into a surtax of about 39 percent (literally one-seventh and one-fourth). Two-thirds of the sum was devoted to agricultural development and the remaining one-third, called the Education Benefits Share (*Maarif Hisse-i Ianesi*), provided for the construction of new public schools.[118] With such assistance public secular education expanded rapidly (see pp. 112–113). We do not have complete statistics regarding all the higher technical schools in Abdulhamit's reign, but we do know that the Civil Service School graduated 620 students between 1878 and 1897; the Imperial Law School, 502 between 1885 and 1897; the Imperial Medical School, 882 from 1874 to 1897; and the Industrial Arts School, 352 during the same period. After it was founded in 1891, the Imperial Veterinary School's average yearly enrollment in its first seven years was 42 students, and 40 students graduated during the same years. The Halkalı Agricultural School averaged 77 students annually between 1892 and 1898 and graduated 39 of them. The concentration of schools in Istanbul presented a problem that was resolved by spending the tithe surtax all over the empire so that by 1897 1 percent of the elementary schools, 7 percent of the *Rüşdiye*s and 3.6 percent of the *Idadi*s were in Istanbul.[119]

By the end of 1897 the military school system had 29 *Rüşdiye*s, including 6 in Istanbul and 1 in each of the other provinces, with 8,247 students. The higher military schools had 15,351 students, of whom 15,328 were Muslims, 11 Jews, 10 Greeks, and 2 Armenians. From 1873 to 1897 the War Academy graduated 3,918 students, the Imperial Engineering School 669, the Army Medical School 3,602, and the civil service section of the Army Engineering School 126, totaling 7,313 in all, a larger number than those who graduated from the civilian higher academies during the same years.[120] The navy maintained a much smaller school system, including one *Rüşdiye* school with 303 students, a Merchant Marine School (*Kapudan-ı Ticaret Mektebi*) with 107, the Naval Academy (*Bahriye-i Şahane*) with 429, a Scribal School (*Munşa-i Küttap*) with 20, and a Projectiles School

(*Heydehane*) with 974 students. From 1876 to 1897 these schools graduated 1,758 students, averaging 160 students per year.[121]

The various non-Muslim *millets* maintained 5,982 elementary schools in 1897, with 8,025 teachers and 317,089 students; 687 *Rüşdiyes* with 2,274 teachers and 23,192 students, and 70 *Idadi*-level schools, with 584 teachers and 10,720 students. Like the public schools, they were spread widely around the empire, with only 2.4 percent of the elementary schools, 14.7 of the *Rüşdiyes*, and 24 percent of the *Idadis* in Istanbul.[122] With regard to the *millets*, the Greek Orthodox maintained by far the largest number of schools (4,390), followed by the Bulgarians, reflecting their strong interest in Macedonia (693), the Armenian Gregorians (653), the Jews (331), the Armenian Protestants (198), the Serbs (85), the Vlachs (63), the Greek Catholics (60), and the other Catholics (50).[123]

Finally, there were the schools sponsored by foreign missionaries, of which 246 were on the elementary level, with 728 teachers and 16,629 students; 74 on the *Rüşdiye* level, with 551 teachers and 6,557 students; and 63 on the *Idadi* level, including secondary schools such as Robert College, run by Americans, with 464 teachers and 8,315 students. Missionaries from the United States sponsored the largest number of schools (131), followed by those from France (127), England (60), Germany (22), Italy (22), Austria (11), and Russia (7). While they provided excellent educations, they were established mainly for the purpose of conversion. Therefore, most of the students were non-Muslims who, in the course of their studies, developed an attachment to Western cultural values and ways of thinking and disdain of things Muslim. The missionary groups used the influence of their governments to resist all efforts of the Ottomans to supervise, let alone control, their curriculums, while at times they sympathized with the minorities and encouraged their nationalist aspirations.

The new state secular school system also had problems that were never entirely resolved. The vast hierarchy of education often was quite inefficient and wasted a great deal of money. Nevertheless, an effective supervision system was established when the power to distribute the *hisse* funds as well as to hire and fire teachers was placed in the hands of the local educational councils, which had a far greater knowledge of local conditions and needs and of the ability of the teachers than did the bureaucracy in Istanbul. This was one of the few instances in Abdulhamit's reign when he decentralized authority. There were few Ottoman textbooks, and the Ministry of Education had to prepare and publish thousands of translations to meet the needs of the students. In the process it also had to develop a technical vocabulary and a written language style the students could understand. Despite the difficulties, the system succeeded. It taught a substantial number of subjects to read and write. Though it emphasized the old rote method of instruction then being questioned in Europe for the first time, it still taught many to think for themselves, with the generation educated in Abdulhamit's time becoming the founders of the Turkish Republic. Perhaps the most serious damage came from the fragmented nature of the system. The state schools, the *millet* schools, and the foreign schools gave their students entirely different ways of thinking, with different methods and objectives, and produced several educated classes, parallel to one another yet hostile, unable to understand or appreciate each other, preventing the kind of national unity and cohesiveness needed to hold the empire together. Again, this problem was resolved only during the period of the Turkish Republic.

Capping the new system of secular education was the Ottoman University (*Dar ül-Fünun-u Osmani*), completely reorganized and reopened, mainly at the instigation of Sait Paşa, on August 12, 1900, to celebrate the beginning of the 24th year of the sultan's reign. The university was organized in four faculties under the general direction of the Ministry of Education: the Faculty of Religion (*Ulum-u aliye-i Diniye*), the Faculty of Mathematics (*Ulum-u Riyaziye*), the Faculty of Physical Sciences (*Ulum-u Tabiiye*), and the Faculty of Literature (*Ulum-u Edebiye*). The imperial schools of law and medicine were now considered to be adjunct faculties. Students wishing to enroll had to be at least 18 years old, of good character and morals, not convicted of crime or crippled by illness, graduated from any of the *Idadi*s or lycées or any of the higher technical academies or able to show equivalent knowledge through examination. Enrollment was limited to 24 to 30 students yearly in each faculty, with competitive examinations being used when necessary. Examinations were held at the end of each year, and only those who passed were admitted to the next level. Classes were held daily throughout the year except on Fridays and Sundays, during Ramazan, for one month after the examinations, and special state holidays. The Faculty of Religion gave courses in Koranic study and interpretation, the tradition of the Prophet, jurisprudence, philosophy, and religion. The Mathematics and Physical Sciences faculties jointly provided courses in mathematics, algebra, engineering, accounting, physical science, chemistry, biology, agronomy, and geology. The Faculty of Literature offered courses in Ottoman and world history, philosophy and logic, Ottoman, Arabic, Persian, and French literature, general and Ottoman geography, archeology,ˈ and education. For the first time the empire thus had a functioning university, starting a revival of higher learning that was to continue unbroken to the present day.[124]

Cultural Development

Increased literacy during Abdulhamit's reign contributed to the growth of cultural activity. Many public libraries were built. The Ottoman press flourished, with thousands of books, journals, newspapers, and pamphlets flooding into the hands of an eager public. By using the press, authors supplanted the ulema as leaders of culture and contributed to general mass education.[125]

Ironically, the cultural explosion was accompanied by a tendency toward censorship, not only by the autocratic sultan but also by the democratically elected delegates to the Parliament, who were also quite sensitive to criticism. Newly enacted legislation prohibited public criticism of officials, held the press financially responsible for errors made in reporting statements made by officials, and prohibited publication of satirical journals altogether.[126] Abdulhamit established a censorship department in the Ministry of Education to enforce the various press and publication laws. Criticism of the sultan was forbidden, but not that of his ministers as long as it was not too violent. The writings of some "seditious" authors were banned, including those of Namık Kemal and Ziya Paşa, and of European authors such as Racine, Rousseau, Voltaire, Hugo, and Zola. Certain suggestive words could not be used, such as "anarchy," "liberty," "strike," "constitution," "revolution," "assassination," "socialism," "dynamite," and "Murat." Newspapers and presses were fined and/or suspended whenever they violated the law. But in fact the sheer mass of publications so overwhelmed the censors that the laws were enforced sporadically, arbitrarily and with much heavy-handedness to be sure, but without any of the efficiency that has come to distinguish such efforts around the world in recent times. Newspapers and books prohibited under one name would appear under new names. Truly seditious materials often evaded the censors. Many works continued to be written abroad and sent in through the foreign post offices. Most writers managed to meet the needs of the reading public without offending the law, resulting in a myriad of novels, essays, tracts, and other books so extensive and varied that the era did, indeed, become one of the most lively cultural periods in Ottoman history, exceeded, perhaps, only by the period that followed in the early decades of the twentieth century.

Public Education and Ahmet Midhat Efendi

During the Age of Abdulhamit, the expansion of printing, the emphasis on education, and the technical as well as economic and political impact of Europe created a thirst for knowledge. Popular newspapers of the time like *Sabah* (Morning), *Vakit* (Time), and *Tercüman-ı Hakikat* (Translator of the Truth) as well as periodicals, books, and plays came in abundance to satisfy this need.

Outstanding among the Ottoman popularizers was Ahmet Midhat Efendi (1855–1912), who wrote in all these media during his lengthy career. Born in Istanbul of a poor family he accompanied his bureaucrat brother to Bulgaria and then to Niş, where he was educated in the secular schools, entering the service of Midhat Paşa (and taking the name of his patron) in 1864 in the Danube province and later in Baghdad, editing the provincial newspapers and yearbooks and serving generally to popularize the provincial reforms among the masses. When Midhat returned to Istanbul, Ahmet Midhat came along, becoming editor of the new army newspaper *Ceride-i Askeriye* (The Army Journal) when his master became grand vezir. In the meantime, Midhat Efendi educated himself in the new knowledge and began to nourish literary ambitions, founding his own small press and two short-lived newspapers. He published a literary journal, *Dağarcık* (The Pouch), presenting contributions by a number of liberal political writers. The disapproval of the censors led to his exile to Rhodes, where he spent four years as a teacher in a *medrese* before returning to Istanbul following Abdulhamit's accession.

Midhat now decided that his function in life was educating the masses, not stirring them to revolution. On his return, then, he decided to accept the political order as it was and to work through the existing system to achieve his aims. He gained the favor of the sultan publishing his *Üss-i İnkılâp* (Origins of the Revolution), in which he described the political maneuverings that accompanied and followed the sultan's accession and acceptance of the Constitution and more or less justified the suspension of the Parliament. He was rewarded by being appointed director of the Imperial Press (*Matbaa-i Amire*) and editor of the official newspaper *Takvim-i Vekayi* (Calendar of Events). Soon afterward, in 1878, with the financial assistance of the sultan, he founded the *Tercüman-ı Hakikat* (Translator of Events) newspaper. With a literary section edited by his son-in-law, Muallim Naci, also a well-known writer, the newspaper soon became one of the most widely read periodicals of the time, publishing the short stories and articles not only of its editor but also of leading writers like Ahmet Rasim, Ahmet Cevdet, and Hüseyin Rahmi (Gürpınar), many of whom were to continue writing well into the period of the Republic. Midhat was a prolific author. He wrote 33 substantial novels as well as works on history, science, philosophy, and religion, always educating while entertaining. He used a simple language and style so that even those with a limited education could understand what he said, and he did not hesitate to digress from the story to give extensive encyclopedic information. Always aiming to disseminate knowledge, he wrote popular works including *Tarih-i Umumi* (General History),

Kâinat (Existences), a 13-volume history of the different European countries, and numerous novels of romance and adventure. He also continued to serve the government in special assignments, as chief scribe of the Quarantine Service for a time and later as Ottoman delegate to the International Congress of Orientalists held in Stockholm in 1888. His travels in Europe were subsequently described in his *Avrupada bir Cevelan* (A Trip in Europe). Though his books were widely read, because of his very popularity and simple style he was scorned by the intellectuals. At the same time, his closeness to the palace led the Young Turks to despise him and, soon after their deposition of Abdulhamit, to force him from his newspaper. He later tried to resume his writing career but was frustrated by the liberal press of the time and also by changes in popular taste, which now demanded more sophisticated works. He was, however, allowed to teach Ottoman history at the university and the Normal School (*Dar ul-Muallimin*), where he remained in obscurity until his death.[127]

The Beginnings of Modern Research: The Work of Şemsettin Sami

While Ahmet Midhat sought to educate the new reading public, other writers began to develop the tools and disciplines of scientific research and to apply them to the social sciences, linguistics, and particularly to the study of Ottoman civilization. Among the founders of modern research in the Ottoman Empire and Turkey was Şemsettin Sami (1850–1904). Born of a feudal landowning family in Albania, he and his brothers spent much of their early lives in the employ of their elder brother, who operated the family holdings. His early education at Janina, at least partly in a Greek *millet* school, gave him a good knowledge of Greek, French, and Italian, and he gained Arabic and Persian from private tutoring. Thus he had a wider horizon than the average Muslim boy of that time. After entering the scribal profession in Janina, he went to Istanbul (1872) and became a scribe in the censorship department of the Ministry of the Interior. He also began a literary career, working for several liberal newspapers until they were closed and the leading Young Ottoman writers were sent into exile (April 6, 1873). Like Ahmet Midhat, the young Şemsettin decided that his role in life was to inform the public rather than suffer the endless chain of exile and return to which the liberal political writers were being subjected. Therefore, he abandoned his newspaper work and returned to the ministry. He began publishing his own literary work, at first translating French novels and plays and then publishing his own. His tragic play *Besa* (Enough!), relating to the situation in Albania, was produced at the Gedik Paşa Theater in April 1874. He served for two years as editor of the Tripoli newspaper *Trablusgarp*, returned to Istanbul after Abdulhamit's accession, and assumed the editorship of the journal *Muharrir* (The Writer) while its owner and editor, Ebüzziya Tevfik, shared the liberals' fate of exile in Rhodes.

While working on *Muharrir*, Şemsettin made the acquaintance of a wealthy Greek merchant named Papadopoulis, who was financing Ebüzziya's operations, and within a short time they joined in founding the newspaper *Sabah* (Morning), which was to become one of the most famous and certainly the longest-lived daily newspapers of the empire, continuing to appear every morning for 10,821 issues (1876–1916). Şemsettin, however, quarreled with his wealthy partner and left the newspaper after only 11 months, becoming seal bearer (*mühürdar*) of the governor of Rhodes and then a member of the Military Consignment Commission (*Sevkiyat-ı Askeriye Komisyonu*) established to facilitate the movement of army supplies during the Russo-Turkish War. On his return to Istanbul, he founded and became the editor of another newspaper, the *Tercüman-ı Şark* (Translator of the East), emphasizing reports on the Congress of Berlin and the newly rising Albanian Question, being drawn close to the Albanian nationalists by his origin and the activities of his brother. He wrote a number of articles defending the Albanian point of view until the newspaper was closed by the censors in October 1878. Şemsettin joined the Albanian Cultural League in Istanbul, not only advocating Albanian national claims but also publishing a number of grammars and dictionaries to develop a Latin alphabet and separate literary tradition for the Albanian language.

Şemsettin then secured backing from one of the former owners of *Sabah* and *Tercüman-ı Şark*, Mihran Efendi, to publish a series called Pocket Library (*Cep Kütüphanesi*), which provided the public with the classics of Ottoman and Islamic literature as well as books on more modern subjects, thus forming in essence an encyclopedia in serial form. It was this series that attracted him back to the favor of the palace. Abdulhamit made him scribe and later member of the Military Inspection Committee established to keep the army under close supervision, a position he retained for the rest of his life. With the backing of the palace, Şemsettin turned his attention from the promotion of the Albanian language to the study of Ottoman Turkish, which occupied most of his attention thereafter as he produced a series of dictionaries and reference works. His monumental *Dictionnaire turc-français,* later developed into *Kamus-i Turki* (The Turkish Dictionary), reflected more than any other work the Ottoman literary language developed by the modern writers of the nineteenth century. Perhaps his greatest achievement was his *Kamus al-A'lâm* (Dictionary of Proper Names), which was no less than an encyclopedia of all the historical, geographical, and scientific knowledge of the time along with biographies of the major political and literary figures. Şemsettin did not just repeat his sources but engaged in exhaustive and careful comparison and analysis. He also was intensely interested in Turkic history, especially of the pre-Ottoman Turks and the Ottoman Turkish dialects used in the provinces. He now was recognized as a major scholarly figure in Istanbul, and his home at Erenköy, on the Anatolian shores of the Sea of Marmara, became a center for literary and scientific discussions until his death at the age of 54 (June 18, 1904). Many of his plans remained unfulfilled, though he had, indeed, set the pattern for the historical, linguistic, and literary research that was to be followed in later years.[128]

Elitism and Symbolism: The Servet-i Fünun Movement

There were other, quite different, reactions to Abdulhamit's repressive political policies. This was the period of the famous periodical *Servet-i Fünun* (The Wealth of Sciences), founded in 1891 by Ahmet Ihsan to become the vehicle for the new literature. It published the early writings of many distinguished writers, including the poets Tevfik Fikret (1867–1915), himself its editor during its greatest days, Abdulhak Hamit (1853–1937), Cenap Şehabettin (1870–1923), and Süleyman Nazif (1870–1927), and the novelists Halit Ziya Uşaklıgil (1865–1945) and Hüseyin Cahit Yalçın. The writings of this school came to be known as *Servet-i Fünun* literature.

Under the influence of the French Parnassian School, Fikret and many of his associates emphasized art for art's sake, preferring poetry to prose, and dwelling on technique and form rather than content. Their aloofness from the present, delight in describing scenes of natural beauty, resort to symbolism for artistic purposes, and choice of obscure Arabic and especially Persian vocabulary for poetic effect were well suited to the need to evade censorship. Though they avoided easily discernible social and political criticism, their writings often carried a melancholy and pessimistic note. Occasional writings that protested the autocratic regime of Abdulhamit, such as Fikret's *"Sis"* (Fog), that complained of the depressing atmosphere hanging over Istanbul, did so symbolically. The novels, also written for an elite readership, reflected the social and intellectual malaise of the period and analyzed upper-class Ottoman society experiencing the impact of the West. The sophisticated style of the *Servet-i Fünun* writers was difficult for the censors to comprehend – thus much of what they said went officially unnoticed. Though lacking in mass appeal and not interested in reforming society, this genre nevertheless was highly reflective of Abdulhamit's reign.

This literary movement, however, was very short-lived. Disputes between Tevfik Fikret and Ahmet Ihsan began the downfall that was completed when the palace began to grow suspicious of poetry and prose that could be interpreted in more than one way and suspended the periodical in 1897. By the time Ahmet Ihsan revived it in 1901, the group had dispersed. Many of its former writers went on to distinguished literary careers in the Young Turk and republican periods, but the *Servet-i Fünun* ceased to be a major literary journal.[129]

Political Protest: The Young Turk Movement

While the educational explosion during Abdulhamit's reign produced hundreds of educated bureaucrats, doctors, officers, and writers willing to work within the system, it also introduced some Ottomans to the liberal political thought of western Europe. Like the Young Ottomans of the previous generation, they rejected a basic premise of the Tanzimat, as extended by Abdulhamit, that true modernization could only be imposed by an elite class from the top. They argued that physical reforms, however successful, were liable to failure and collapse unless they were accompanied by fundamental political and social reforms.

Consisting of many protest groups under different names in and out of the empire during much of Abdulhamit's reign, these liberals gradually came together in a loosely formed coalition called the Young Turks throughout Europe. One of them, the Committee of Union and Progress, was finally able to force the sultan to restore the Parliament in 1908 and subsequently to abdicate.

The Young Turks came from different backgrounds and expressed their opposition in different ways. Many were from the most distinguished of Abdulhamit's academies, the pampered and prized students of the Imperial Lycée of Galata Saray, the Imperial War Academy at Pangaltı, the Civil Service Academy, and the Army Medical School. Many of the Young Turks were frustrated Young Ottomans, disappointed by the failure of Midhat Paşa's grand vezirate and the Constitution. They had gone into exile in Paris, London, Geneva, Bucharest, and, after the British occupation, Egypt, expressing their opposition in a series of small news letters among which *La Jeune Turquie* – published in Paris by Halil Ganim, a Lebanese Maronite and former deputy to Parliament in 1877 – survived long enough to give its name to the movement in Europe.

In Abdulhamit's early years the censorship was not severe enough nor the police system strong enough to prevent an increasing number of intellectuals, students, and bureaucrats from expressing their opposition to the regime. The ferment became particularly strong in the late 1880s when the sultan attempted to balance the budget by reducing the staffs of the ministries and the army, thus setting loose many graduates of his schools who, after having achieved their education, felt that they had a right to government employment at comfortable salaries. Real organization came first in the Imperial Medical Academy in May 1887 when Kâzım Nami Duru and five fellow students formed a group called the Society of Union and Progress (*Ittihat ve Terakki Cemiyeti*). It does not seem to have lasted long, but two years later, in May 1889, one of its first members, an Albanian Muslim named Ibrahim Temo, joined with a Circassian student, Mehmet Reşit, and two Kurds, Abdullah Cevdet and Ishak Sükûti, to reconstitute the group first as the Ottoman Union Society (*Ittihat-ı Osmani Cemiyeti*) and then as the Ottoman Society of Union and Progress (*Osmanlı Ittihat ve Terakki Cemiyeti*). They called for a program of constitutionalism, Ottomanism, and freedom, to be achieved by replacing the sultan with one of his brothers, either the former sultan, Murat V, or the man who ultimately was to succeed, Mehmet Reşat. Other groups rose and fell depending on fluctuations in the interest of their membership rather than actual government suppression.

As the time went on, however, a hard core of dedicated liberals emerged, determined to end the absolutist regime regardless of their personal careers. Working at first inside the empire, eventually they had to carry on their activities abroad. An early leader among them was Ahmet Rıza (1859–1930), son of an Austrian mother and Anglophile Ottoman father, both quite wealthy. After his education in France he entered the Ministry of Agriculture in the hope of improving the condition of the Ottoman peasant. When he realized that agricultural develoment was impossible without educating the peasants, he transferred to the Ministry of Education and served as director of education in Hüdavendigâr province before the lure of luxury offered by his family's wealth led him to remain in Europe after going to Paris to visit the International Exposition of 1889. He soon became a follower of the positivist movement of Auguste Comte. But it took five years of intellectual contemplation before he returned to any direct interest in Ottoman affairs, in 1894 publishing a series of memorandums to the sultan demanding a constitutional regime to assure government for the benefit of the people instead of what he called the whims of the bureaucrats. Justifying his demand for a Parliament on the basis of the old Islamic and Ottoman tradition of consultation (*meşveret*), in 1895 he joined with Halil Ganim and used his personal wealth to publish a bimonthly and bilingual (Ottoman Turkish and French) newspaper, *Mechveret*. He gathered around him many Ottoman exiles and formed one of the most important Young Turk groups in Europe, demanding fulfillment of the positivist dream, order and progress (*intizam ve terakki*). Entering the empire through the foreign post offices, the *Mechveret* began to circulate in intellectual circles, stimulating liberal thought and action within the empire as well.

Second only to Ahmet Rıza in developing the Young Turk movement was Mehmet Murat Efendi (1853–1912), a Caucasian Turk from Dağıstan, on the Caspian, who after a lycée education in imperial Russia had fled to the Ottoman Empire in 1873 because of the feeling that he as a Muslim would have far greater opportunities. He soon found employment in Istanbul, first on the staff of the Public Debt Commission (1874) and then as a teacher in the Civil Service School (1878). He came into contact with several liberal writers and began to publish his own works, a six-volume general history (*Tarih-i Umumi*) and a one-volume Ottoman History (*Osmanlı Tarihi*). He followed with an autobiographical novel, *Turfanda Mı Yoksa Turfa Mı* (First Fruit or Forbidden Fruit?), going on to submit

several reform proposals to the sultan. But he soon despaired at seeing them fulfilled and went abroad in 1895, going first to Egypt. With the encouragement of the
long-time (1895–1906) Ottoman high commissioner, Muhtar Paşa, he began to
publish his own newspaper, *Mizan* (Scale). He then went to Europe and acquired
his own group of followers. The *Mizan* also found its way into the empire through
the British and French post offices and stirred considerable reaction on its own.

Within the empire the Committee of Union and Progress continued to develop,
including not only teachers and students but also some bureaucrats, army officers,
and even members of the ulema. Ibrahim Temo began to organize chapters in the
major cities of Rumania, Bulgaria, and Albania. But near the end of 1895 a premature attempt at a coup made with the cooperation of the commander of the
Istanbul garrison, Kâzım Nami Duru, led to the suppression of the Istanbul group,
and those who could fled abroad. The new influx of members from Istanbul greatly
increased the strength of the movement elsewhere. In Egypt Ishak Sükûti organized a new chapter and began publishing several newspapers. He then went on
to Geneva, where in collaboration with "Mizancı Murat" (Murat, of *Mizan* fame)
and Abdullah Cevdet he inaugurated a new branch of the society and started
publishing the *Osmanlı* (Ottoman). Ahmet Rıza also received a number of new
collaborators who strengthened his group. But while the different Young Turk
groups abroad agreed in their opposition to the sultan, they found it very difficult
to get together because of personal as well as ideological differences. Ahmet Rıza
was the most conservative and moderate of the major leaders. He supported the
Ottoman political and social systems more or less as they were, hoping simply to
get the sultan to democratize the administration and remove the corrupt bureaucrats. Murat went further, emphasizing the need for major reforms in all areas to
save the empire from Christian aggression and blaming Abdulhamit for the government's impotence in the face of terrorism, but still advocating peaceful change
through consultation rather than revolution. They continued also to support the
empire's integrity and unity against the claims of the minority nationalist groups
that were also active in Europe, but their opposition to the sultan increased in
direct proportion to their frustration.

Nor did the sultan neglect his critics. Always considering himself a reformer, resentful of those who idled uselessly in Europe while avoiding the hard work needed
to modernize the empire, Abdulhamit did all he could to get their European hosts
to suppress them, but a sympathetic European public opinion and the Young
Turks' ability to travel freely from one place of exile to another frustrated these
efforts. Much more effective was an opposite approach. Since so many of the
exiles had gone into opposition simply because of frustration in their work or
failure to secure high positions and ranks, Abdulhamit began to offer them opportunities to put their ideas to work in the government. In 1897 he sent one of the
leading members of his secret police, Ahmet Celaleddin Paşa, to Europe to recall
the dissidents to duty, using the recent Ottoman victory against Greece as a selling
point and promising them high positions if they abandoned their opposition and
came home. The first to accept was Murat, who convinced many of his friends to
go along, including the two early founders of the movement, Abdullah Cevdet and
Ishak Sükûti. By the end of 1897, then, the Young Turk movement was scattered
and dispirited, with only Ahmet Rıza still holding out in Europe.

The movement was revived in 1901 when Damat Mahmut Paşa (1853–1903),
grandson of Mahmut II and husband of the sultan's sister, defected from the sultan's side. His support for the Constitution and later involvement in the Ali Suavi

affair had led to his removal from the palace and appointment to positions far inferior to those that he felt that his rank and prestige entitled him. Escaping on a French freighter, Damat Mahmut was accompanied by his two sons, Princes Sabaheddin and Lütfullah, and he resisted all efforts of Ahmet Celaleddin and others to get him back. Soon after, the émigrés were further stimulated by the arrival of Ismail Kemal Bey Vlora, an Albanian Muslim who had occupied high Ottoman positions before joining the Albanian nationalist movement. While Damat Mahmut at first paid homage to Ahmet Rıza for his long service in the forefront of the Young Turks in Europe, soon he, and especially his son Prince Sabaheddin (1877–1948), emerged as rival leaders. Sabaheddin founded his own group, the Society of Personal Initiative and Administrative Decentralization (*Teşebbüs-ü Şahsi ve Adem-i Merkeziyet Cemiyeti*), whose views he published in his own newspaper, *Terakki* (Progress). Far more radical than the other Young Turks, he advocated fundamental social changes in the empire as well as the deposition of the sultan. He wanted not merely to end the distinction between the Ruling and Subject classes but also to abandon the centralized institutions of government created by the Tanzimat and to restore the old Ottoman decentralized system. Local bodies would care for tax collection, municipal, and judicial affairs and would make decisions on the basis of local problems and needs. Individual and local initiative would be developed by what he called the Anglo-Saxon emphasis on individual effort, with the motive of private profit encouraging individuals to develop the resources of the empire as the best means of restoring its power and defending it against its enemies. Ahmet Rıza and Murat abhorred European intervention as well as revolutionary action, but Sabaheddin and his group advocated the use of all available means, including revolution and pressure from the powers. Since his ideas seemed to coincide with the demands of many of the national groups for autonomy in their own areas of the empire, he welcomed their support as well. Sabaheddin joined them to get British and French help to force the sultan to abdicate and secure the desired reforms, leading his Ottoman opponents to accuse him of treason.

Shortly after Damat Mahmut's death, Prince Sabaheddin attempted to resolve the differences by calling a general Congress of Ottoman Liberals, which met in Paris from February 4 to 9, 1902. The first of its kind, the congress included not only the various Young Turk liberals scattered around Europe but also the minority national groups. Ahmet Rıza and his group also attended, though they were not too happy at being a small minority among the non-Muslim Ottomans. Sabaheddin tried to conciliate the groups by emphasizing general resolutions that blamed all the empire's difficulties on Abdulhamit's regime, stressed the Ottoman ideal of equality among all the peoples and races of the empire, and promised continued loyalty to the house of Osman and the idea of the territorial integrity of the empire. But the minority delegates secured the addition of a resolution declaring the congress's support for the full execution of all the "reforms" imposed on the empire by the treaties of 1856 and 1878. This was too much for Ahmet Rıza, who saw in it an invitation for European intervention, and too little for the Armenian nationalists, who demanded more specific efforts to secure foreign intervention to gain autonomy or independence for their people in eastern Anatolia. None of the minorities in fact was willing to support a constitutional regime and reforms that might strengthen the empire. The congress broke up without any final agreement, therefore, deepening the rivalry between Sabaheddin and Ahmet Rıza.

In reaction to the activities of the Young Turks and to help strengthen the empire against all internal and external dangers, Abdulhamit fostered two movements: (1) Islamism, which emphasized a return to the values and traditions of Islam as a religion and culture and a desire to restore unity among Muslims all over the world, and (2) Turkism, which stressed the Turkish traditions in Ottoman culture and sought to create a feeling of unity among the Turks of the world.

Islamism and Pan-Islamism

The most widespread ideological force in the Ottoman Empire during Abdulhamit's years was Islamism, calling for a return to the fundamental values and traditions of the civilization of which the empire was the most modern manifestion. Though encouraged and used by the sultan, this movement transcended him in both time and scope. It began in the late Tanzimat period, mostly in reaction to the manner in which millions of Muslims were being treated by the Russians as well as the newly independent Balkan states. Stories of persecution and savagery from the Crimea to Belgrade and Sarajevo were mingled with accounts of oppression from India to Algeria and contrasted with the toleration and good treatment provided for non-Muslims in the great Muslim empires, including that of the Ottomans. The Tanzimat movement also was accused of undermining the ulema and abandoning the basic ideals, traditions, and institutions of Islam by imitating European ways. The Ottoman financial plight, which included European use of the Capitulations to destroy the traditional Ottoman industries and the debilitating dependence on high-interest loans, added to a general feeling of distrust. The French occupation of Tunis followed by the British occupation of Egypt confirmed the feeling. The last straw was provided by the press and politicians of Europe, who seemed to resurrect medieval religious fanaticism by clamoring over the deaths of a relatively few Christians in the sultan's empire while ignoring the large-scale massacres of Muslims in the Balkans and Russian Central Asia. Namık Kemal and the other Young Ottomans therefore preceded Abdulhamit in reacting to European bigotry with an Islamic emphasis, becoming as critical of Western influences and foreign penetration as were some of the most reactionary of the ulema. Reacting in particular to Ernest Renan's claims that Islam was the enemy of science and philosophy, Kemal cited the tremendous advances that had been made in all aspects of culture and civilization under the great Islamic empires of the past. Soon these feelings were translated into a movement to establish contacts with all the oppressed Muslims of the world, including those in British India and Egypt, Russian Central Asia, and French Algeria and Tunisia, with the aim of forming a union of Muslims to help defend them and their ways against the inroads of the West.

Abdulhamit thus only took over an idea that was already popular among all classes of his Muslim subjects and used it to strengthen his hand against enemies both at home and abroad. Under the leadership of his palace *müşir,* Gazi Osman Paşa, the resources of the state treasury as well as of the sultan's own privy purse were used to build up the Muslim schools to enable young Ottoman Muslims to compete successfully with their non-Muslim counterparts. Pensions, salaries, and other revenues paid to the ulema were increased. Mosques and other religious monuments were repaired and restored. Islamic holidays were emphasized once again, and their public celebration was officially encouraged. The use of Western translations of Ottoman and Arabic terms on public buildings and street signs was discouraged. Lessons in Islam and the Arabic language were added to the curriculums of the secular schools. The use of Arabic as a language of culture and even administration was encouraged, though Sait Paşa did divert the sultan from his desire to raise it to equality with Ottoman Turkish as an official language. Arabs from Syria and Lebanon were brought in to serve in high positions of government, often in preference to their counterparts from the Balkans. Abdulhamit sought to establish a role as caliph of all Muslims. He began to use his long-standing right to appoint religious officials in former Ottoman territories now under foreign rule in order to maintain his influence among their Muslim populations. He thus personally selected and appointed kadis, teachers, and other ulema sent to Egypt, Cyprus, the Crimea, Bosnia-Herzegovina, and Bulgaria. The Ottoman government protested and intervened officially whenever there was news of misrule or oppression of Muslims no matter where they lived. Influential Muslim leaders from all over the world were brought to Istanbul for extended visits to establish contacts that later could be and were used to extend the sultan-caliph's influence. The British, Russians, and French were warned, with some vehemence, that aggression against the Ottoman Empire or their own Muslim peoples might lead to a united Muslim uprising against them with full Ottoman support. Islamism thus became an ideological weapon wielded by the sultan to counter the imperialism of the Western powers as well as the minority nationalist movements that threatened his empire.

The sultan was remarkably successful in this endeavor. Despite all the complaints about his regime, his own person and the institution of the sultanate-caliphate were highly revered by the mass of the subjects. Despite their subsequent professions to the contrary, Islamism also did intimidate the Powers. They took the movement very seriously at the time, treating every Muslim visitor to Istanbul from outside the empire and every Ottoman visitor to the Muslims of their own empires as dangerous spies who threatened to undermine the stability of their rule. The fact that European aggression against the Ottomans mainly stopped after the British occupation of Egypt and that the imperialist rivalries of the powers were diverted from military to economic competition during the remaining years of Abdulhamit's long reign can be attributed at least partly to the success of his use of Islam as a weapon to ward off the aggressors.

Turkism and Pan-Turkism

Many of the same factors that stimulated Pan-Islam also led to the rise of an incipient Turkish nationalism. The very idea of nation, as it had been developed in nineteenth-century Europe and advocated by so many nationalists of the Ottoman minorities, cannot have been ignored entirely by Ottoman intellectuals. Though Ottomanism promoted the idea of the motherland, with all subjects, regardless of religion and race, equal before the law and loyal to the same Ottoman dynasty, the refusal of the minority nationalists to accept that equality, the success of national unity movements in Germany and Italy, and nationalist aspirations of non-Turkish Muslim groups in the empire led to an increased awareness of the Turkish identity and almost forced the germination of Turkish nationalism.

Much of the rationale came from European philosophers and Orientalists. The Frenchman de Gobineau had developed the idea of blood and race as the most important influences on human development and history, with some races naturally superior to others. A number of European Turcologists began to discover the Turkish past, their great Central Asian civilizations, and the role of their language and culture in history A. J. de Guignes showed the Turks in the mid-eighteenth century that they had accomplished great things for the world long before the Ottoman Empire came on the scene. A. L. David's *Grammar of the Turkish Language* (London, 1832) presented the first systematic study of the Turkish element in Ottoman Turkish and added a strongly eulogistic survey of the various Turkish dialects as well as the accomplishments of Ottoman culture, previously ignored by Ottomans and Europeans alike. In 1869 the theme was taken up by Mustafa Celaleddin Paşa, a Polish convert to Islam, whose *Les Turcs anciens et modernes* (Istanbul, 1869) emphasized the unique racial qualities of the Turks, whom he said were part of the "Touro-Aryan" race rather than the Mongol, and stressed their contributions to world civilizations. By providing a racial connection between the Turks and Indo-Europeans, he provided an argument that might well reduce the longstanding European prejudice against the Turks. Extremely influential at the time was Arminius Vambery (1832–1913), a Hungarian anthropologist and Turcologist who spent many years in the Ottoman Empire and Central Asia and was a close friend and adviser of the sultan himself. Vambery included the Turks, Hungarians, Finns, and Estonians in the Turanian linguistic and racial group, publishing widely in Europe (with translations into Ottoman) about the language, culture, and civilization of the Turks. Leon Cahun (1841–1900) contacted the Young Ottomans in Paris in the 1860s, developing an interest in the Turks in his *Introduction a l'Histoire de l'Asie,* where he also included the Turks among the Turanian people and stressed their role in transmitting elements of Chinese culture into that of the Persians and into Europe as well. He described the great Turkic civilizations in a manner sure to engage the interest and belief of Europeans and Ottoman Turks alike. The more detailed researches into the inscriptions left by the ancient Turks by scholars like Radloff, Thomson, and others also awakened a feeling that there was much about Turkish history and the Turkish contribution to world civilization that had been ignored or forgotten.

Ottoman awareness of the non-Ottoman Turks was also excited by the flow of refugees into the empire and the stories of persecution and oppression that followed the Crimean War. This was compounded by a tendency among the Turks remaining under Russian rule to strengthen their contacts with the motherland by sending their children to Istanbul for their education and by visiting Istanbul, establishing close connections and interchanges of information. Especially important among these visitors were many Central Asian intellectuals, who began to flow into the empire and to stay long enough to teach the history and languages of their people. There was considerable Turkish intellectual activity in the Russian Empire, centered mainly in the Crimea and Kazan, which was influenced by Western liberal thought as well as the writings of the Young Ottomans and Young Turks. Leading these intellectuals was Ismail Bey Gasprinski (1851–1914), whose newspaper, *Tercüman* (The Translator), established in the Crimea in 1883, emphasized the unity of all the Turks in the face of Russian nationalism and tried to develop a common literary dialect that could be understood by all. He came to Istanbul in 1874 and 1875 to spread his message. The Azerbaycani writer Mirza Fath Ali Ahundzade (1812–1878) published a newspaper in Baku and wrote Turkish plays even before that genre had spread very widely in the Ottoman dominions.

Another Azerbaycani, Ağaoğlu Ahmet (1869–1939) studied in Paris, contacted the Young Turks, and then also published his newspaper in the Caucasus, conveying the Young Turk message as well as his own desire for Turkish unity against the Russians. Eventually, he was to take an important role in developing Turkish nationalism in the Ottoman Empire after Abdulhamit's deposition. There were Çagatay and Uzbeg Turkish writers from the Volga area, who worked mainly in dervish monasteries and whose linguistic and historical studies also provided a major impetus to Turkish nationalism in the Ottoman Empire. Later they came to Istanbul and established their own *tekke* in Üsküdar, which became the first center of Turkic studies within the empire. Leading them was Buharalı Süleyman Efendi, whose *Lügat-ı Çağatay ve Türki-i Osmani* (The Çagatay and Ottoman Turkish languages) (Istanbul, 1928) told its Ottoman readers about the Çagatay dialect for the first time, stressing its close connection also with early developments in the Ottoman Turkish language.

Finally, one of the most important of the Russian-Turkish intellectuals who came to the Ottoman Empire was Yusuf Akçura (1876–1933), born in Simbirsk, on the Volga, having a Kazan background similar to that of his fellow townsman Nikolai Lenin. Yusuf came to Istanbul in his youth and was educated in Abdulhamit's military schools. He then began writing about his Turkish brothers back in Russia and joined the Young Turk movement, leading to his banishment to Libya for a time. He fled to Paris, became a student in the School of Political Science, and joined Prince Sabaheddin's radical movement, adding to it, however, the need to struggle to assure Turkish domination as against the former's desire to include all the minorities in a decentralized empire. Reacting to the Ottomanist tendency of the Young Turks, he returned to Russia, where he published his famous *Üç Tarz-ı Siyaset* (Three Kinds of Policy) and other treatises, emphasizing Turkish nationalism and unity. He sent his publications into the Ottoman Empire through the Russian post office and gained a wide following which he used to become one of the leading advocates of Turkish nationalism in the empire as soon as he was able to return to Istanbul following the revolution of 1908.

Of course Turkish nationalism, if brought to its logical conclusion, contradicted both Ottomanism and Islamism. If the Ottoman Empire was made into a Turkish national state, there would be no room not only for most of the non-Muslims but also for the non-Turkish Muslims who supported the empire because of their position as Muslims. Abdulhamit suppressed the Turkish nationalist writings, therefore, though he shared their feelings in many respects. Despite this, however, expression of Turkish sentiments appeared at times in newspapers and periodicals. For the first time, the word "Turk" began to be used with pride, gradually losing its less desirable connotative meaning (a country lout), very much as the term "Arab" had been used for bedouins in the eastern provinces. The adjective "Turkish" now began to replace "Ottoman" in many newspapers, very often as subordinate headings on their banners. The term "Turkistan," a direct translation of the word "Turkey" which Europeans long had applied to the Ottoman Empire, now was commonly used, and "Ottoman" came to be used to distinguish the Turks of that empire from those living elsewhere. The term *millet*, formerly denoting the religious communities of the empire, now also was given the modern connotation of "nation," with *milliyet* signifying "nationality."

The connection of the Ottomans with the ancient Turkish nomads of Central Asia began to be treated in history books. Whereas the earlier nineteenth-century Ottoman historians, including Namık Kemal, started their presentations of Ottoman history with their settlement in Anatolia in the eleventh century, the Ottoman historians of Abdulhamit's time went much further back. In the introduction to his study of the empire between 1774 and 1826, Ahmet Cevdet Paşa stated that classical Islam had been ruled by two *millets*, the Arabs and the Turks, with the Turkism (*Türklük*) of the Ottoman Empire providing much of its greatness.[130] Ahmet Midhat Efendi was the first popular Ottoman writer to present a detailed history of the pre-Ottoman Turks and to stress their connection with the Ottomans as well as their role in the development of world civilization,[131] while making an effort to discount any Ottoman connection with Greek civilization. Mizancı Murat also brought in the great Turkish empires of Central Asia in his general history,[132] stressing their role in reviving Islam in the tenth century and thereafter.

While the new Ottoman history books developed these themes of Turkish nationalism and the importance of the Turks in contributing to the grandeur of Islamic civilization and the long duration of the Ottoman Empire, the popular press began to publish accounts of Turks living in the Crimea, in China, and in Samarcand, welcoming every sign of Turkish national awakening among them with enthusiasm and publicizing the work of the well-known Turcologists of the time. It was only when they emphasized the need to defend the Turks against the Russians that Abdulhamit's censors drew the line, fearing to raise hopes that could not be fulfilled and of stimulating a new Russian attack on the Ottoman Empire. Stifled in this direction, Turkish nationalism developed a kind of Anatolian nationalism, stressing it as the real homeland (*vatan*) of the Turks and concluding that it had been the addition of southwestern Europe and its peoples to the empire that had caused the empire's decline. For the first time the Turkish peasants of Anatolia were glorified as the real strength of the Turkish state. It was the Turkish language as used by the Anatolian peasant that had to be studied and even imitated if the Turks were to escape from the domination of the Arabic and Persian vocabulary and phrases used in the Ottoman language. The Anatolian peasant became the focus of patriotic sentiment, particularly during the wars fought with the Balkan states. Anatolia, above all else, had to be preserved if the Turkish nation was to survive attacks from outside.

To reform the Ottoman language and in particular to develop its Turkish elements, the *Encümen-i Daniş* (Academy of Learning) commissioned Ahmet Cevdet and Mehmet Fuat to write their Turkish grammar. Inspired by David's work, they made a distinction among the Turkish, Arabic, and Persian elements in the language (1851). Many of the Young Ottoman writers used simpler language in order to communicate their ideas. In 1877 the statesman Ahmet Vefik published a new Ottoman dictionary, stressing its identity as a distinct Turkish dialect.

Other grammars and dictionaries followed, culminating in the massive work of Şemsettin Sami. Of course, this movement was strongly resisted by the state and others who advocated the official Ottomanist policy emphasizing that the empire and its language were, indeed, amalgams of all its peoples and their languages and cultures. Hence it was only after Abdulhamit's fall that the advocates of Turkish really prevailed.[133]

Prelude to Revolution

While the sultan's police kept the Committee of Union and Progress (hereafter referred to as the CUP) well suppressed in and around the capital after 1897, conditions nurtured and strengthened its cause. For one thing Abdulhamit's schools were producing an increasing number of bureaucrats, officers, and intellectuals who, unlike most of the Young Ottomans and Young Turks who preceded them, came from the lower classes, were not related to the existing Ruling Class establishment, and were willing to change the system by force if necessary to achieve their ends. Especially in the army the lower officer ranks came to be filled by educated and political-minded officers from the Subject Class, who were frustrated by the long years of unsuccessful struggles against the Macedonian and Armenian terrorists. Though Abdulhamit had limited his military expenditures because of financial problems, most of these young officers were convinced, with some justice, that the sultan kept the army from developing because he was afraid of them. They believed that if a more favorable regime was established and the old politicians swept away, they could eliminate the terrorists and reestablish order. Many of them also espoused programs of social reform in response to the preachings of the CUP intellectuals, but this was secondary to their immediate desire to end what they considered to be the politicians' hinderance of the army's work.

Similar frustration and discontent also spread among the bureaucrats as the twentieth century began to unfold. Reforming legislation continued to pour out, and it was widely applied. But as terrorism and the attacks of the Young Turks increased, the sultan became more and more suspicious, extending the activities and power of his police, watching over the bureaucrats more intensely than ever, spreading fear even among his grand vezirs, and centralizing authority and power in the palace to such an extent that no one could act without its direct permission. While the sultan had been equal to the task of supervising every detail of government in his early years, his concentration on plots against him, the terrorist attacks of the minorities, and his general mistrust of all bureaucrats caused him to neglect his administrative duties more and more. The whole structure of government began to bog down as the administrators waited for palace orders before acting. Graft and corruption also tended to increase. Continued budgetary deficits and terroristic activities made many begin to feel that, perhaps, three decades of rule were enough.

It was in the provinces, though, and mainly among the army officers that the movement of rebellion developed in the early years of the twentieth century. In Damascus a group of young officers of the Fifth Army, including a young lieutenant named Mustafa Kemal, who had just graduated from the War Academy in January 1905, organized a secret group known as the Fatherland (*Vatan*) Society. Branches were established among brother officers in Jerusalem and Jaffa and manifestos were drawn up demanding that the sultan fully observe the Constitution and establish a governmental regime that could deal efficiently with the needs of the army and other organs of the state. The name of the group soon was changed to Fatherland and Liberty (*Vatan ve Hürriyet Cemiyeti*), and a number of provincial bureaucrats also were included. There was little immediate action because their senior officers opposed revolution despite their own discontent. Syria, in any case, was too far from the capital for them to have major influence, and there was no local following, since the Arabs themselves were not yet rebellious against the sultan.

It was most likely Mustafa Kemal who suggested that the group work to gain adherents among fellow officers in his home city, Salonica. As one of the leading cities of Macedonia, Salonica was a far more likely center for revolutionary activity than was Damascus. It had traditionally been in closer contact with Europe than any other Ottoman city, and many of its citizens were far more aware of European intellectual currents than were their Ottoman counterparts elsewhere. It had a substantial Jewish population as well as a large group of Jewish converts to Islam called *dönmes*, who while ostensibly accepting the dominant faith of the empire secretly retained some of their old beliefs and practices, creating a situation that hindered their full acceptance into the Muslim community. Merchants living in this trade center felt very keenly the economic and financial difficulties of the time. Salonica also was one of the centers of the Third Army of Macedonia and was filled with officers who were bitter at their inability to suppress the terrorists and at the consequent deaths of hundreds of their comrades – all of which they blamed directly on the Istanbul government. In addition, because of its distance from the capital and the presence of the gendarmerie imposed on the empire by the powers, Salonica was far less susceptible to the activities of the sultan's police than was Istanbul.

Thus when Mustafa Kemal came to spread the word of Fatherland and Liberty early in 1906, he was welcome. He found a number of kindred spirits in the Third Army, including Cemil Bey, adjutant of the military governor of Macedonia, and Talat Bey, a local postal official later to become a major Young Turk figure. He formed them into a branch of the Damascus society but with a different name, the Ottoman Liberty Society (*Osmanlı Hürriyet Cemiyeti*). Mustafa Kemal had left his post in Syria without permission and had to return before his absence was discovered officially. He subsequently secured official permission to transfer to the Third Army and returned to Salonica in June 1907 to find that leadership there had been assumed by others in the meantime, leaving him with only a subordinate role in the events that were to follow.

The Ottoman Liberty Society had expanded rapidly among officers and bureaucrats in the Macedonian provinces. Organized in small cells on the model of those of the Bulgarian terrorists, the new organization seems to have held its meetings in the lodges of the masonic order and to have received financial and other assistance from *dönmes* who hoped that its triumph might alleviate their situation in Ottoman society. The organization also contacted the Muslim Albanian national groups organized to the north, putting their common opposition to the sultan above differences about the ultimate organization of the empire. In February 1907 relations were also established with the Young Turks in Paris, generally with those of the Ahmet Rıza faction, and the two groups were amalgamated under the name of the Paris organization, the Committee of Union and Progress (September 27, 1907), with the goal of restoring the Constitution. The Salonica group retained its own organization and independence, with Ahmet Rıza agreeing to interfere with its decisions only through persuasion.[134]

On December 27–29, 1907, the Second Young Turk Congress met in Paris in a new effort to secure cooperation against the common enemy. This time it was chaired jointly, not only by Ahmet Rıza and Prince Sabaheddin, but also by K. Maloumian, of the Armenian Revolutionary Federation (Dashnaks), who hoped to use the Young Turks to gain their own national objectives. In many ways it was the Armenians who carried the day as the Young Turks were convinced to accept a far more violent program of action than they had been willing to espouse in the past. The final declaration stated that the sultan had to be deposed and the existing regime replaced by a constitutional and representative government, and any means, including revolutionary violence if necessary, would be used to achieve the goal. Within the empire, armed resistance to oppression had to be organized along with peaceful resistance in the form of strikes, refusal to pay taxes, circulation of propaganda, and arrangements for a full-scale revolt if all else failed. To keep the organization together Ahmet Rıza at first reluctantly agreed to the statement. But he soon reacted to the boasting of the Armenians that the Turks had in fact accepted the methods that they had used in eastern Anatolia, split with Prince Sabaheddin once again, and returned to his original position. The reconciliation of the different groups in Europe thus proved illusory, and, in the end, they played no active role in the Young Turk revolution when it came.

The Young Turk Revolution

When it finally did take place, the Young Turk Revolution was one of the strangest events of its kind ever seen in history. It was not planned, at least in the manner and at the time it finally broke out – it really did not even happen, and it certainly did not depose Abdulhamit. Yet it forced him to recall the Parliament and, for all practical purposes, to give up most of his powers.

The revolution was in fact only the last of a series of small uprisings that had been taking place throughout the empire since 1907 because of financial rather than ideological reasons. The harvests in Anatolia had been bad. Taxes were coming in very slowly; therefore, salaries were in arrears, and most promotions had been suspended. Many soldiers and officers as well as bureaucrats were manifesting their displeasure by leaving their jobs. There had been some CUP propaganda in Anatolia and Rumeli, but with little effect. The troops in Macedonia were especially unhappy, since there had been a recent upsurge of Christian terrorism, now supported by the Greek churches in the area. The CUP leaders in Salonica attempted at first to use the situation simply to inform the powers of the committee's existence and ability to bring order to Macedonia if only it was given proper sanction (May 1908). Stating that all the peoples of Macedonia were suffering from the sultan's oppression, they concluded that the recall of Parliament would solve the Macedonian problem. All the elements of the empire would be able to work for the common good. There would be equality under the law, and the powers would no longer need to intervene to protect the sultan's subjects.[135] The representatives of the powers ignored this request, which, after all, had come from an unknown and presumably illegal organization of Muslim Turks, and so the countdown toward revolution continued.

Abdulhamit sent a number of agents to Macedonia to investigate the situation and find those who had caused the unrest. One of them, former Police Chief Nazım Bey, was shot and wounded in Salonica on June 11 just before he was to return to Istanbul with his report. The sultan then sent a full commission of inquiry, ostensibly to inspect the Third Army's efforts against the IMRO and Greek terrorists, but in fact to uncover the revolutionary leaders and bring them to justice. The commander in chief of the Third Army and his chief assistants also were blamed for the army's discontent and replaced by officers considered more loyal to the palace. Several spies were sent to discover revolutionary activities in the ranks. One of them seems to have uncovered the CUP cell of Adjutant Major Ahmet Niyazi Bey, who immediately fled into the hills with his men (July 3, 1908) and began a kind of guerrilla resistance movement against the provincial authorities near Ohrid and Monastir, ordering the people to pay their taxes to him instead of the government until the Constitution was restored. Other junior army officers, including young Enver Bey, followed his example. The sultan sent one of his principal military aides, Şemsi Paşa, as special commander with the job of leading the Macedonian army in crushing the rebels, but he was assassinated in

Monastir (July 7, 1908) by a CUP agent. The supporters of the sultan were demoralized and adherents of the CUP encouraged by the government's inability to protect one of its leading generals.[136]

Now matters really got out of hand. Troops brought to Macedonia from Anatolia to suppress the rebels joined them instead, while more of the sultan's agents were caught and killed. Joint military and civilian uprisings took place at Monastir, Firzovik, Serez, Üsküp, and other towns and cities, proclaiming their support for the constitution in mass meetings held between July 20 and 23 and sending telegrams to the sultan expressing their demands. The CUP in Salonica, not having planned an open revolt at this time, was caught unawares and was planning to follow suit only on July 27 when it was caught up in the rapid course of events. At this point the master politician Abdulhamit, who for three decades had maintained himself and his empire against powerful opponents within and without, moved to forestall the rebels. After all, it had been he who had promulgated the Constitution. He could argue that through all the years of autocracy he had ruled through its provisions. It had never been suspended. He felt he had allowed the CUP to gain adherents by posing as the defender of his Constitution. His solution, then, was to anticipate their next move by recalling the Parliament, thus, essentially, restoring the representative organ of government provided for in the Constitution and meeting the demand agreed on by all the rebel groups. The recall of Parliament was the major immediate sign of change from autocracy to a constitutional government. Without any real revolution, then, without any soldiers storming the palace, and without bloodshed, the Young Turk Revolution in fact had taken place (July 23, 1908). The sultan declared that he had suspended the Parliament until the work of modernization was completed and that the time had now come for it to meet again so it could share in the difficult task of saving the empire from its enemies. In a true sense, however, in giving in to the rebels at this point, the sultan had surrendered. The age of Abdulhamit II was over, though the sultan was to remain on the throne for another ~~year, and~~ the era of the Young Turks was about to begin.[137]

Notes to Chapter 3

1 Mahmut Celaleddin, *Mirat-ı Hakikat,* I, 227–230; Ahmet Midhat, *Zübdet ul-Hakayik,* Istanbul, 1295/1878, pp. 89–91; Karal, OT, VIII, 30.

2 FO 198/42, no. 157, Salisbury to Derby, January 11, 1877.

3 FO 198/42, no. 158, Salisbury to Derby, January 12, 1877.

4 Ahmet Midhat, *Zübdet ul-Hakayik,* pp. 91–118, FO 198/42, no. 159, Salisbury to Derby, January 12, 1877.

5 Davison, pp. 394–402; Mahmut Celaleddin, *Mirat-ı Hakikat,* I, 266–268; Karal, OT, VIII, 9–14; Shaw (E. K.), "Midhat Paşa," pp. 287–383, has a detailed analysis of the Constitution as well as the Istanbul Conference.

6 BVA, Yıldız Doc. 1/2, 10 Şevval 1293/1876.

7 Devereux, pp. 123–145; BVA, Bab-ı Âli Evrak Odası, 10762.

8 *Zabıt Ceridesi,* I, 7–12; Devereux, p. 113; Ali Haydar Midhat, *Life of Midhat Pasha,* pp. 157–160.

9 *Zabıt Ceridesi,* I, 44–60; Devereux, pp. 186–187, M. K. *Türkiyede Meclis-i Mebusan,* Cairo, 1293/1876, pp. 251–263; BVA, Irade Dahiliye 4726.

10 *Düstur*[1] IV, 20–58; BVA, Irade Meclis-i Vala 1324.

11 *Zabıt Ceridesi,* I, 231–232, 248–259, 294–297, 326–327.

12 *Zabıt Ceridesi,* I, 338–344; *Levant Herald,* June 9, 12, 20, 1877; Devereux, p. 206.

13 *Zabıt Ceridesi,* I, 271–278; BVA, Irade Dahiliye 5347.

14 *Zabıt Ceridesi,* I, 280–282; Devereux, pp. 193–194; BVA, Irade Dahiliye 3625.

15 Devereux, pp. 136–145.

16 *Zabıt Ceridesi,* II, 7, 10; *Levant Herald,* December 14, 1877; Sait Paşa, *Hatırat,* I, 14; Devereux, pp. 117–118.

17 *Zabıt Ceridesi,* II, 31, 86–91, 70–73, 104, 181–187.

18 *Stamboul,* November 26, December 10, 12, 26, 27, 1877; Devereux, pp. 223–224, 236–242.

19 *Zabıt Ceredesi,* II, 401; tr. by Devereux, pp. 243–244.

20 *Zabıt Ceridesi,* II, 406.

21 Mahmut Celaleddin, *Mirat-ı Hakikat,* III, 60–62; *Zabıt Ceridesi,* II, 410–411; *Levant Herald,* 20, 21 February 1878; Devereux, pp. 247–248.

22 *Muahedat Mecmuası,* IV, 183–186.

23 Mahmut Celaleddin, *Mirat-ı Hakikat,* III, 134–137; Karal, OT, VIII, 71–72.

24 Inal, VII, 1013; Karal, OT, VIII, 96–97; Ali Vehbi Bey, *Pensées et Souvenirs d'Abdul-Hamid* (Paris, 1910), p. 96.

25 Bayur, *Kâmil Paşa,* p. 132; Karal, OT, VIII, 98–9; Bab-ı Âli, Hariciye Nezareti, *Mısır Meselesi,* Istanbul, 1334; W. L. Langer, *European Alliances and Alignments, 1871–1890,* New York, 1956, pp. 251–280.

26 Bayur, *Kâmil Paşa,* p. 134.

27 Skendi; Halil Inalcık, "Arnawutluk," EI², I, 653–658.

28 The 1882 census figures are found in Istanbul University, TY4807; for a complete discussion of the census, see pp. 239–243.

29 The reports of the investigatory commission are found in BVA, Yıldız Palace Archives, K22/Z153/415, K9/Z72/1072, K11/Z120/1222, K14/Z126/390; the subsequent reforms are described in BVA, Yıldız Palace Archives, K31/Z158/1727, K31/Z158/2016, K31/Z158/2020, K31/Z158/2021, K31/Z45/1915M, K31/Z45/2023; and K31/Z111/985; Langer, *Diplomacy of Imperialism,* pp. 145–166.

30 The building is now used as the Istanbul Men's Lycee (Istanbul Erkek Lisesi), just off Taksim Square in the new part of the city.

31 The 1882 population records are in the Istanbul University Library, TY4807; for 1895 in *Istatistik-i Umumi,* pp. 1–26; for 1906 in the Istanbul University Library TY 947; and for 1914 in *Tableaux indiquant le nombre des divers éléments de la population dans l'Empire Ottoman au 1 Mars 1330 (14 Mars 1914),* Constantinople, 1919. The Armenian terrorist activities are described in the report of Nazım Paşa to Abdulhamit II, *Ermeni Tarih-i Vukuatı,* Yıldız Palace Archives BVA, K36/Z131/139(80), partly duplicated, but with additional information, in a report of the Ministry of Security (*Nezaret-i Zabtiye*), dated 9 Şaban 1312/February 6, 1895, in Yıldız K35/Z50345. The activities of the groups outside the empire, especially in Russia, are described in K35/Z50/334M. The best scholarly account of the situation is Langer, *Diplomacy of Imperialism,* pp. 145–166, 195–212.

32 Eighteen percent (161,867) in Istanbul, 29.3 percent (288,968) in Edirne, 15.5 percent (229,598) in Aydın, 88.25 percent (286,716) in the Aegean Islands, 38 percent (272,203) in Monastir, and 53 percent (287,812) in Janina.

33 *Mufassal Osmanlı Tarihi,* VI, 3368–3383; Karal, OT, VIII, 112–125; Langer, *Diplomacy of Imperialism,* pp. 315–320, 355–378, 383–384.

34 BVA, Yıldız Palace Archives, K37/3576.

35 FO 78/2951, no. 442, 28 May 1879; quoted in Shaw, "Promise of Reform," pp. 364–365.

36 Inal, III, 1277–1278.

37 *Zabıt Ceridesi,* II, 401, tr. in Devereux, p. 244; Sait Paşa, *Hatırat,* II, 32–34, 83–84.

38 Abdulhamit's palace organization and policies are described in the reports of the Reform Commission (*Islahat Komisyonu*) established in 1879 to reorganize the palace service, found in BVA, Yıldız Palace Archives no. 140 (63) and 140 (64). See also the memoires of his last chief scribe, Tahsin Paşa, *Abdülhamid ve Yıldız Hatıraları,* Istanbul, 1931, pp. 18–26, 118–121; Osman Nuri, *Abdul-Hamid-i Sani ve Devr-i Saltanatı,* Istanbul, 3 vols, 1327/1911, II, 496–532, 537–563; Karal, OT, VIII, 264–265.

39 The principal Police Regulation and Instructions, dated March 16 1296/19 Rebi II 1298, is in the Yıldız Palace Archives, no. 2290/(47)80. A description of the Ottoman police system by Bonin, a French adviser, dated March 7, 1300/1884, is in Yıldız K14 no. 88/27. See also the Police Regulation of 1907 (5 Rebi I 1325) in *Düstur*[1], VIII, 666–693; and Derviş Okçabol, *Türk Zabıta Tarihi ve Teşkilâtı Tarihçesi*, Ankara, 1940, pp. 71–75.

40 *Düstur*[1], IV, 63–66, V, 965, VI, 3; BVA, Yıldız Palace Archives, nos. K37, 47/37, and K36, 47/36; for reports on these commissions, see Yıldız, K14 nos. 1239 and 1339.

41 *Düstur*[1], IV, 692–694; BVA, Irade, Şurayı Devlet 2735.

42 BVA, Irade, Meclis-i Vâlâ 16095 (12 Cemazi II 1273/1857); *Düstur*[1], V, 992–1000.

43 BVA, Nizamat, VI, 3.

44 *Düstur*[1], II, 229, III, 931, V, 263; *Maarif Nezareti Salnamesi*, Istanbul, 1916, pp. 170–90.

45 *Düstur*[1], VI, 1544.

46 Uzunçarşılı, *Yıldız*.

47 BVA, Yıldız K14 no. 2061, doc. 17, 18, 19, 13, 14, 16; *Düstur*[1], V, 1076–1077.

48 29 Recep 1311; BVA, Nizamat VI, 344; *Düstur*[1], VI, 1459, 1474; Young, I, 6–7; Aristarchi, II, 38; BVA, Teşkilat-ı Devair, Dosya 25/2, doc. 23/1, 24.

49 11 Şaban 1314; *Düstur*[1], VII, 150; BVA, Nizamat, VII, 273; BVA Teşkilat-ı Devair, Dosya 26, 26/1, 26/2.

50 E. Kuran, "Ibrahim Edhem Pasha," EI[2], III, 993; Inal, II, 600–635; Pakalın, *Son Sadrâzamlar*, II, 403–477.

51 Ahmet Hamdi Tanpınar, "Ahmet Vefik," IA, I, 207–210; Murat Uraz, *Ahmet Vefik Paşa*, Istanbul, 1944; Inal, II, 651–738; Pakalın, *Son Sadrâzamlar*, III, 45–359.

52 E. Kuran, "Küçük Said Paşa as a Turkish Modernist," IJMES, I (1970), 124–132; idem., "Said Paşa," IA, X, 82–6; Pakalın, *Son Sadrâzamlar*, V (1948); Sait Paşa, *Hâtırat;* Ali Fuad Türkgeldi, *Görüp Işittiklerim*, 2nd ed., Ankara, 1951, pp. 8–112.

53 Bayur, *Kâmil Paşa;* Inal, III, 1347–1372.

54 Yıldız Archives, K31/Z97/1520.

55 Yıldız K31/Z97/1526.

56 Yıldız K31/Z97/1520.

57 Yıldız K31/Z97/2252.

58 Inal, II, 895–960, Pakalın, *Son Sadrâzamlar*, IV, 313–377.

59 Shaw, "Promise of Reform," pp. 359–365.

60 *Zabıt Ceridesi*, I, 335, 338–339; Karal, OT, VIII, 416–419.

61 *Maliye Vekâleti Mecmuası*, VI, 5.

62 Shaw, "Promise of Reform," p. 361.

63 Shaw, "Promise of Reform," p. 362.

64 Shaw, "Promise of Reform," p. 361.

65 The regulation reorganizing the Ministry of Finance is in *Düstur*[1], IV, 716; The Administrative Committee of the department received its regulation on 9 Safar 1297/January 22, 1880 – *Düstur*[1], III, 674–716; the ministry's administration was reorganized and an Inspection Committee established on 18 Şeval 1301/August 14, 1884 – *Düstur*[1], V, 75–78; the Financial Control Committee was established on 17 Safar 1306/October 24, 1888 – *Düstur*[1], VI, 231, BVA, Irade Meclis-i Mahsus 4293, Nizamat, I, 40. The Department of General Collections was organized by the Collection of Revenues Regulation (*Tahsil-i Emval Nizamname*), issued on November 11, 1879/25 Zilkade 1296 – BVA, Irade, Meclis-i Mahsus 3031, Meclis-i Tanzimat, VI, 1; *Düstur*[1], IV, 382; it was amended on 19 Muharrem 1304/November 18, 1886 – *Düstur*[1], V, 664; Nizamat, II, 193; Irade Meclis-i Mahsus 3668; and on 1 Şaban 1311/February 7, 1894 – *Düstur*[1], VI, 1461; Nizamat, VI, 211. The initial regulations on collections were issued on 11 Şevval 1299/August 26, 1882 – *Düstur*[1], Zeyil 2, pp. 8–12, 24 Şaban 1302/June 10, 1885 – BVA, Irade Meclis-i Mahsus 3466, and 11 Şaban 1320/November 13, 1902 – BVA, Irade Maliye 1320 Şaban no. 9. The basic regulations for the Financial Reform Commission were issued on 2 Zilkade 1295/October 28, 1878 – BVA, Irade Dahiliye 63157, with

270   *The Rise of Modern Turkey, 1808–1975*

Ohanes Efendi as its first director. It was reorganized on 15 Cemazi I 1321/August 10, 1903 – BVA, Bab-ı Âli Evrak Odası 163982, with new additions issued on 7 Şaban 1322/ October 17, 1904 – *Düstur*¹, VIII, 90–92; BVA, Nizamat, X, 170. The Central Accounting Council was originally established by the Tanzimat in 1863 (BVA, Buyuruldu, V, 71–74), but was disbanded after a year. Abdulhamit restored it on 3 Zilhicce 1296/ November 18, 1879 – BVA, Irade, Meclis-i Mahsus 1397; Teşkilat-ı Devair, Dosya 16/4, 16/5, 25/2.

66 *Maliye Vekâleti Mecmuası*, VI, 6–7.

67 Heidborn, *Manuel de droit public de l'Empire ottoman*, 2 vols. Vienna, 1908–1912, II, 264–266; Quataert, p. 54.

68 *Istatistik-i Umumi*, p. 152; *Ihsaiyat-ı Maliye*, I, 52–54, III, 48–49.

69 *Istatistik-i Umumi*, p. 145; Devlet-i Osmaniye, *Liman Istatistikleri*, Istanbul, 1323.

70 *Istatistik-i Umumi*, pp. 162–163, 157; Devlet-i Osmaniye, *Telgraf Istatistikleri*, Istanbul, 1323.

71 Ali Nusret Pulhan, *Türk Pulları Kataloğu*, vol. XII, Istanbul, 1974, pp. 35–104, 927–982; also Aziz Akıncan, *Türkiyede Posta ve Telgrafçılık*, Edirne, 1913; *Istatistik-i Umumi*, pp. 157–158, 162–163.

72 Quataert, pp. 92–128.

73 *Düstur*¹, III, 570–572, Aristarchi, V, 270–271.

74 Sait Paşa, *Hatırat*, II/2, 4–5, II/1, 176.

75 Quataert, pp. 64–69.

76 Atasağun, pp. 2–4, 7; Du Velay, p. 205.

77 De Velay, pp. 205–210; Atasağun, pp. 5–11; Sait Paşa, *Hatırat*, I, 175.

78 Quataert, pp. 132–136; Atasağun, pp. 115, 166–167, 205–209, 229–230, 274–275.

79 Atasağun, pp. 329–332; Quataert, pp. 150–153.

80 Quataert, pp. 155–186; *Düstur*¹, II, 437; Vital Cuinet, *La Turquie d'Asie*, 4 vols., Paris, 1890, I, 28–29, III, 406–412, IV, 440–441; BVA, Bab-ı Âli Evrak Odası, 128387, 131438, 151706, 159642, 180317, 231847, 190774, 203203.

81 *Ihsaiyat-ı Maliye*, I, 86, III, 64.

82 Quataert, p. 261.

83 Quataert, pp. 375–376.

84 *Ihsaiyat-ı Maliye*, I, 66–69.

85 The Mines Regulation of 1861 is found in BVA, Meclis-i Tanzimat, II, 14, and BVA, Irade Meclis-i Vâlâ 13; that of 1887 is in *Düstur*¹, V, 886, BVA, Nizamat, II, 323, BVA, Irade Meclis-i Mahsus 4927, and Young, VI, 17. Stone quarries were regulated in a separate law found in *Düstur*¹, V, 971, BVA, Irade Meclis-i Mahsus 4022, Nizamat, II, 99; the new Mines Regulation of 1906 is in *Düstur*¹, VIII, 438, BVA, Nizamat, XI, 109, and Irade, Kavanin ve Nizamat, 1324 Safar no. 4.

86 *Istatistik-i Umumi*, pp. 99–101; *Ihsaiyat-ı Maliye*, I, 98–104; Karal, OT, VIII, 455–458.

87 Sait Paşa, *Hatırat*, II/2, pp. 7–8, 19, 401; Karal, OT, VIII, 455–458.

88 *Düstur*¹, I, 165; Young, VI, 45–83.

89 *Düstur*¹, II, 404; BVA, Meclis-i Tanzimat, II, 266.

90 *Istatistik-i Umumi*, pp. 102–6.

91 *Ihsaiyat-ı Maliye*, I, 278–279, 92–97.

92 *Istatistik-i Umumi*, pp. 139–140.

93 *Istatistik-i Umumi*, p. 140.

94 *Ihsaiyat-ı Maliye*, I, 164–165; *Istatistik-i Umumi*, pp. 109–110.

95 *Istatistik-i Umumi*, pp. 19–21, 24–25.

96 The population figures for 1884–1897 come from *Istatistik-i Umumi*, p. 15; for 1906 from Istanbul University Library, manuscript TY 947; for 1910 from *Ihsaiyat-ı Maliye*, III, 8–9; and for 1914 from *Tableaux indiquant le nombre des divers élémens de la population dans l'Empire Ottoman au 1er Mars 1330/14 Mars 1914*, Constantinople, 1919.

97 *Zabıt Ceridesi*, I, 62–66, 82–87, 91–98, 105–113, 122–129, 132–136, 160–168, 191–194;

Sait Paşa, *Hatırat*, I, 208–210; *Düstur¹*, III, 93; Aristarchi, V, 50; BVA, Meclis-i Tanzimat, V, 10; Meclis-i Mahsus 2382; because the Assembly was proroged, the bill was put into force as a temporary decision (*Kararname*) of the sultan, a new kind of law, and it was not actually promulgated until 1896; Young, I, 99–105; *Düstur¹*, III, 120, VI, 224; BVA, Yıldız K37/Z47/47).

98 27 Ramazan 1294/October 5, 1877 – BVA, Meclis-i Tanzimat, V, 28–38; *Düstur¹*, IV, 420–553; Ergin, *Belediye*, II, 31; Young, VI, 151–155 (omits articles 10–62); Yıldız K37/Z47/302.

99 BVA, Irade, Şurayı Devlet 346.

100 *Düstur¹*, IV, 528–570; Young, I, 69–84; BVA, Meclis-i Tanzimat, V, 39–51; Devereux, 198–199; *Zabıt Ceridesi*, I, 276–282, 300–320, 364–365.

101 *Düstur¹*, IV, 823; BVA, Meclis-i Tanzimat, VI, 67; BVA Irade, Meclis-i Mahsus 2974. 24 Muharren 1297/January 11, 1880 – *Düstur¹*, IV, 491, 753; BVA, Irade Şurayı Devlet 2735.

102 Von der Goltz, *Generälfeldmarschall Colmar Freiherr von der Goltz Denkwürtigkeiten*, Berlin, 1929, pp. 124–125; Griffeths, pp. 68–69.

103 FO 195/2053, 22 May 1890.

104 Young, II, 395; Griffeths, pp. 75–84; *Asakir-i Nizamiye-i Şahanenin Suret-i Ahzını Mübeyyin Kanunname-i Hümayun*, Istanbul, 1302.

105 FO 195/1718, May 5, 1891.

106 FO 195/1718, May 5, 1891.

107 FO 195/1981, December 30, 1897; Griffeths, p. 122.

108 Griffeths, pp. 123–124.

109 Karal, OT, VIII, 342–343.

110 Karal, OT, VIII, 344.

111 Shaw, "Promise of Reform," p. 361.

112 *Düstur¹*, IV, 125–131; BVA, Meclis-i Tanzimat, VI, 83–87, Irade, Şurayı Devlet 2471.

113 BVA, Yıldız K35/Z44/2250.

114 The basic regulations on the choice of provincial judges were issued on 6 and 25 Şeval 1296/September 23 and October 12, 1879 – BVA, Meclis-i Mahsus 3025 and 3007; they were revised on 7 Rebi II 1300/February 13, 1883 – *Düstur¹*, V, 1058–1062; Young, I, 182–184; BVA, Nizamat, III, 103; BVA, Irade, Meclis-i Mahsus 4079. Judges also were closely watched over by the *Sicil-i Ahval* Commission, and records were kept of all their decisions as well as any mistakes made during their careers; 22 Cemazi II 1305/March 5, 1888 – *Düstur¹*, V, 1058–1062; BVA, Irade, Meclis-i Vâlâ 4079; Istanbul University Library, TY3398.

115 Both laws were promulgated on 19 Cemazi II 1296/June 13, 1879. That of Civil Procedures is in BVA, Meclis-i Tanzimat, VI, 16, and of Criminal Procedures in BVA, Meclis-i Tanzimat, VI, 98 and Irade, Meclis-i Mahsus 508; the latter was revised on 10 Cemazi I 1313/October 29, 1895 – *Düstur¹*, VII, 31.

116 BVA, Yıldız K35/Z14 no. 4.

117 Shaw, "Promise of Reform," p. 363.

118 27 Rebi II 1301/February 26, 1884 – text not located.

119 *Istatistik-i Umumi*, pp. 62–63.

120 *Istatistik-i Umumi*, pp. 74–75.

121 *Istatistik-i Umumi*, pp. 80–81.

122 *Istatistik-i Umumi*, pp. 82–83.

123 *Istatistik-i Umumi*, pp. 83–85.

124 BVA, Irade, Makatib Dosya 58, file 3.

125 *Istatistik-i Umumi*, p. 67; *Salname-i Devlet-i Aliye-i Osmaniye, 1326* (1910–1911) *sene-i maliye*, pp. 402–425.

126 *Zabıt Ceridesi*, I, 144, 171, 201, 224; *Düstur¹*, II, 229, 231, 431, 444; BVA, Meclis-i Mahsus 2659.

127 Bernard Lewis, "Ahmed Midhat," EI², I, 289–290; Sabri Esat Siyavuşgil, "Ahmed Midhat Efendi," IA, I, 184–187; Ahmet Hamdi Tanpınar, XIX. Asır Türk Edebiyatı Tarihi, I (Istanbul, 1956), pp. 433–466.

128 Ömer Faruk Akun, "Şemseddin Sami," IA, XI, 411–422; Hikmet Dağlıoğlu, Şemseddin Sami, Istanbul, 1934.

129 Nihat Sami Banarlı, Resimli Türk Edebiyatı Tarihi, Istanbul, n.d., pp. 299–329; Hasan Ali Ediz, "Servetifünun," Aylık Ansiklopedi II, 729–731; Tahir Alangu, Serveti Fünun Edebiyatı Antolojisi, Istanbul, 1958.

130 Cevdet¹, I, 14.

131 Mufassal Tarih-i Kurun-i Cedide, Istanbul, 1303/1885–1886, I, 122.

132 Muhtasar Tarih-i Umumi, Istanbul, 1302/1884–1885, pp. 21–25.

133 The rise of Turkish cultural nationalism in Abdulhamit's period is best described by David Kushner, The Origins of Turkish Nationalism, London, 1977. See Karal, OT, VIII, 550–564; Berkes, pp. 313–322; H. N. Orkun, Türkçülüğün Tarihi, Ankara, 1914.

134 Bayar, I, 126–131, 239–251.

135 Niyazi, pp. 50–60.

136 Bayar, I, 132–138.

137 E. Ramsaur, The Young Turks: Prelude to the Revolution of 1908, Princeton, N.J., 1957; and Ahmad, pp. 1–13.

4

The Young Turk Period, 1908–1918

The Young Turk era deepened, accelerated, and polarized the major views that had been gathering momentum in the Ottoman Empire during the nineteenth century: Ottomanism and nationalism, liberalism and conservatism, Islamism and Turkism, democracy and autocracy, centralization and decentralization – all to the point where the empire might well have blown up had this not been accomplished by the events of World War I. This era, almost more than any other, has attracted scholars of modern Ottoman history, and it has been studied in such detail that it is difficult to believe that it was so short. Yet the politics, wars, and personalities of the period have so diverted its scholars that, to the present time, almost nothing has been done to study the modernization that it brought in even the darkest days of war. During this tragic period, four major wars decimated the population of the empire, raised its internal tensions to the breaking point, and threatened to destroy all the efforts of the sultans and reformers who had sought valiantly to save it during the previous century. Nevertheless, it was a time of regeneration during which the accomplishments of the Tanzimat and of Abdulhamit II were synthesized in a manner that laid the foundations of the modern Turkish Republic.

Reaction to the Revolution

The Young Turk Revolution had involved a cooperative effort of the CUP and various nationalist groups in Europe, so that the immediate internal reaction to the sultan's restoration of the Constitution was a wave of mass demonstrations, without equal in the empire's long history, in Istanbul and other major cities. Happy mobs of Turks, Arabs, Jews, Greeks, Serbs, Bulgars, Armenians, and Europeans embraced in the streets and made eternal vows of brotherhood for the common good. "Men and women in a common wave of enthusiasm moved on, radiating something extraordinary, laughing, weeping in such intense emotion that human deficiency and ugliness were for the time completely obliterated. . . ."[1] But what were they shouting for? "Tell us what constitution means," shouted the crowd. "Constitution is such a great thing that those who do not know it are donkeys," answered a speaker.[2] Constitution had been advertised as such a general panacea that everyone assumed the recall of the Parliament would immediately solve all the problems that had crept in during the era of autocracy, including the terrorism of the minority national groups and their demands for autonomy or separation from the empire. The Armenian and Greek nationalist groups, on the other hand, tended to think that because they had cooperated with the Young Turks in Paris, the new regime would grant all their demands. To all, thus, it seemed that the millennium had come, the tension was over, and the empire would in fact be preserved.

The Constitutional Monarchy of Abdulhamit II

The joy was premature. In subordinating their desires to the immediate objective of restoring the constitutional regime, the different nationalist groups had ignored the many inherent contradictions in their programs. Achievement of the immediate goal ended the loose coalition of divergent interests, and the old differences and hostilities were revived.

The "revolution" had been made by the CUP, whose active members in the empire were mostly in the army. But it also suffered from internal divisions. While some of its members had advocated the Constitution in support of their brothers in Paris, most simply hoped that it would gain them promotions and higher pay as well as sufficient support from the Istanbul government to enable them to wipe out the provincial rebels. The CUP itself, therefore, never had drawn up a real political program beyond the restoration of Parliament. Nor was there any unity on the question of what to do with the sultan. Few of the liberals had gone as far as to advocate his overthrow, let alone the destruction of the dynasty. And whatever sentiment there had been to replace him was largely overwhelmed by the mass gratitude to him for restoring the Constitution. Abdulhamit remained on the throne, therefore, apparently determined to make *his* Constitution work. The CUP, whose members were not yet known to the public, remained in the background, mostly in Salonica, acting only as a pressure group to ensure the success of the new regime. It did, however, dispatch to Istanbul a Committee of Seven, including three figures who later were to become most important – Staff Major Cemal Bey (later Minister of War Cemal Paşa), Talat Bey (later Minister of the Interior Talat Paşa), and Cavit Bey (later Minister of Finance and Public Works Cavit Paşa) – to represent it as steps were taken to establish a new government and to hold elections for the Parliament. But government itself remained in the hands of the old politicians, with the grand vezirate being held first by Sait Paşa (July 22–August 4, 1908), now a hero because of his criticism of the sultan's autocracy in its latter days, and then Mehmet Kâmil Paşa (August 5, 1908–February 14, 1909), who had held the office twice before, in 1885–1891 and again for a short time in 1895.

The CUP's decision not to take over the government but to influence it through the Committee of Seven, thus in a sense to keep power without taking responsibility for its exercise, created a difficult political situation. No one knew exactly where power and authority lay. Did they still belong to the sultan? Were they to be exercised by the grand vezir? Or would the Parliament assume the leading role once it was convened? Inevitably, the result was confusion and conflict. In the provinces, political activists used the situation for their own purposes, getting the government to dismiss governors and other administrators whom they accused of corruption and misrule, sometimes with justice but more often simply to settle old scores. The government in Istanbul, unsure of its powers and the will of the CUP, usually complied, administering without having a policy of its own.

All these disputes came to a focus following the imperial decrees of August 1 and 3, 1908, modifying article 113 of the 1876 Constitution, which had allowed and even encouraged Abdulhamit's autocracy. The secret police now was abolished. The remaining police forces could act only in accordance with the Constitution. Other statements reasserted what already was in the Constitution. All Ottomans would have the same legal rights regardless of religion. No one could be arrested or imprisoned without cause. The courts were to be free entirely from outside interference. Subjects were guaranteed complete inviolability of their domiciles except with the authority of the courts and according to law. They could travel to foreign countries for any purpose whatsoever without any longer having to secure special permission. The government no longer would examine and censor publications before they were issued (publishers, however, were still subject to subsequent action if they violated the press or publication laws). More specific promises went beyond the provisions of the 1876 Constitution. The government could not thereafter examine and seize private letters and publications in the mails. Teaching and studying were to be free, without any kind of control. Bureaucrats no longer could be assigned to positions that they did not want (military officers excepted), and they were free to refuse to obey orders that they felt violated the law or the Constitution. All ministers, governors, and members of the Council of State were to be chosen by the grand vezir with the assent of the sultan, and all lower bureaucrats were to be appointed by the responsible ministers and governors in a similar way, with promotions and dismissals still subject to confirmation at the higher levels. Only the *şeyhulislam* and the ministers of war and the navy were exempted from this procedure and instead were to be chosen directly by the sultan with only the advice of the grand vezir and the Council of Ministers. The budget was to be published annually, and separate regulations were to be drawn up to reorganize the ministries and the provincial administration.[3] Immediately there were disputes over the question of appointing the ministers of war and the navy. To resist the efforts of the Committee of Seven to control the two ministries, the sultan and Sait Paşa introduced special regulations aimed at preserving civilian control over the armed forces, but the CUP finally prevailed, and Sait was soon replaced by the more compliant Kâmil Paşa. The Committee of Seven then retired behind the scenes, with the CUP declaring that it would do no more than attempt to guard the Constitution while leaving actual administration to the government.[4]

It was the government of Kâmil Paşa, then, that cared for administration during most of the remaining months of Abdulhamit's reign, apparently with the full cooperation of the sultan. On August 16, 1908, it issued a detailed program promising financial reforms, reorganization of the administration and armed forces, and an effort to balance the budget. Treaties also would be renegotiated and measures taken to develop the economy. Education and science would be encouraged, and to secure the full equality of races promised in the Constitution, non-Muslims as well as Muslims would be conscripted and the military substitution tax ended as rapidly as possible. The special privileges enjoyed in the empire by foreigners by virtue of the Capitulations would be ended by agreement with the powers and by reforming the government so that foreigners would be willing to accept its authority. The separate privileges of the *millets* would gradually be brought to an end as all subjects, of all religions, would be given the same rights and legal status.[5]

A whole series of laws and regulations followed to fulfill these promises. Political prisoners were pardoned and released, while prisoners held for nonpolitical crimes were released if they had served at least two-thirds of their sentences or longer than 15 years. The special martial law courts established in Macedonia to deal with rebels were abolished. A new advisory council was established in the Ministry of Forests, Mines, and Agriculture to recommend what measures the Parliament should take to improve the economy. Measures were taken to reorganize the bureaucracy and reduce the number of bureaucrats to meet the immediate budgetary crisis, but this was met with such strong protest that it was never fully carried out. The government was left with an extremely difficult budgetary problem, often lacking money to meet its daily expenses. Kâmil Paşa did what he could, however, abolishing many of the smaller ministries that Abdulhamit had created for special purposes, like those for Health and Military Supplies, and turning their functions over to the regular ministries. General salary reductions were imposed (except for the army), and new commissions were established to unify government purchases, saving considerable amounts in a relatively short time. Quotas were set up to limit promotions in the administration and the Religious Institution, and the army was warned to limit its expenditures as much as possible. A special committee was set up to recommend means to reduce the annual interest payments made to the bondholders, and the extraordinary budget was abolished along with the special taxes imposed on the wages of civil servants and military officers to finance it. The Council of State was reorganized into four departments, Legislation (*Tanzimat*), Civil Affairs (*Mülkiye*), Finance (*Maliye*), and Education (*Maarif*), so that it could better prepare legislation for consideration by the Parliament, and the Ministries of Trade and Public Works were united, again eliminating the jobs of many civil servants.[6] Finally, election laws were promulgated, and preparations were made for the convening of Parliament.

In the meantime, with a freedom of press and political association hitherto unknown in the Ottoman Empire, newspapers and political parties blossomed and the empire experienced a real political campaign. Two major political groups emerged to fight for power. First there was the CUP itself, which, while it did not actually form a party, issued a general manifesto of its policies and supported those candidates who promised to follow it, thus forming them into a group that came to be known as the Unionists (*Ittihatçılar*). Included in their number were Ahmet Rıza, now returned from Paris and soon to be named president of the Chamber of Deputies, Talat, and Enver, among the few CUP members to reveal themselves, Abdullah Cevdet, Ahmet Muhtar, and others who campaigned in general support of modernization and westernization, though with some differences as to detail. The basic CUP program at this time included political reforms, popular freedom, strengthened national sovereignty and unity, agricultural and industrial development, and just taxation.[7] The main opposition came from the Ottoman Liberal Union Party (*Osmanlı Ahrar Fırkası*), formed by Prince Sabaheddin as soon as he returned from Paris. The Istanbul newspaper *Ikdam* was the principal organ of this group, which included the grand vezir and others who supported the prince's call for decentralization and full equality for the minorities, thus gaining the support of the latter as well. The Liberal Union, however, was organized only on September 14, 1908, and therefore had very little time to participate in the campaign. The more conservative elements, representing the Islamic views previously favored by the sultan, did not actually form a group because they feared the CUP, but they did speak quietly about the need to retain Islam as the basis of state and empire. Debate in the campaign proceeded mainly on the questions of westernization and modernization and centralization versus decentralization, with Islamism and Turkism as well as the minority aspirations being de-emphasized under the assumption that the new freedom and equality would satisfy all.[8]

The prospects of democracy in the empire were, however, destroyed by the greed of the powers and the empire's neighbors, who proved to be as hungry for democratic, constitutional, Young Turk territory as they had been for that of the despotic Abdulhamit. Even as the campaign went forward, they took advantage of the temporary vacuum of power in Istanbul to strike while there seemed little chance of an immediate Ottoman response. On October 5, 1908, Austria annexed Bosnia-Herzegovina outright and Bulgaria proclaimed its independence, both renouncing the sultan's suzerainty and stopping the payment of tribute to his treasury. The next day Greece took advantage of the powers' evacuation of Crete (completed on July 27) to annex it. In all these cases Ottoman protests to the signatories of the Treaty of Berlin, supposedly bound to guarantee its provisions, were met with no response. The Porte finally was compelled to solve the crisis on its own. It adopted measures to prevent internal uprisings against the minorities and made direct settlements with those who had violated their obligations. By the terms of the agreement signed on February 26, 1909, Austria would evacuate the *sancak* of Novipazar in return for Ottoman recognition of its rule over Bosnia and Herzegovina, pay monetary compensation of 200.5 million kuruş, and help the Porte secure the agreement of the other powers to the abolition of the foreign post offices and all the Capitulatory privileges in the empire. A settlement with Bulgaria followed (April 19, 1909). Russia secured an agreement by promising to cancel 40 of the last 74 payments owed by the Ottomans for the war indemnity, and the Bulgars were to pay their compensation owed the sultan to Russia instead. In both cases the sultan, as caliph, would continue to control the lost provinces' Muslim religious life, appointing the kadis and religious teachers as well as the chief muftis, who would represent him in religious matters and care for the interests of Muslims in the provinces. Austria and Bulgaria promised to finance the maintenance of Muslim schools and mosques and to facilitate the free exercise of the Islamic religion. Thus the matter was settled. The real losers were Serbia and Montenegro, whose ambition to reach the Adriatic had been thwarted by the Austrian acquisition of Bosnia and Herzegovina. Nor was Russia very pleased, since Austria had fulfilled its ambitions without compensation to keep the balance of power in Central Europe. The czar therefore finally withdrew from the old League of the Three Emperors and moved toward the Triple Entente with Britain and France, finally completing the diplomatic alignments that were to lead directly to World War I.

The diplomatic settlement hardly assuaged Ottoman public feeling. In a very short time the new regime had lost more territory than Abdulhamit had been forced to give up since 1882. The new era of cooperation and hope was suddenly gone. The Muslims who had assumed that the Constitution would end the European efforts to break up the empire now began to turn toward the old sultan once again. The minority nationalists saw in the government's anguish at the loss of these territories a denial of their own hopes for autonomy or even independence. The mass of subjects saw in the latter's reaction the ephemeral nature of the hope that they might finally work together for the preservation of the empire. All the old divisions and hatreds returned despite the efforts of the government to keep everyone together. And the palace, which earlier had sat back in the hope that the Constitution would be able to solve the problems it could not solve, now itself began to encourage and support those elements that sought to use the situation to restore the sultan's power.

The time between the territorial losses and the elections was, however, too short for any major political shift to take place, particularly since the CUP and the army, in league with the government, were in real control of the country. The elections went ahead in November and early December 1908 under an electoral law issued by the government. Elections still were indirect, with the people choosing electors and the latter naming the actual deputies. The campaigns went ahead smoothly except in Macedonia, where the Greek government and the patriarch intervened to secure candidates favorable to their views. Mizancı Murat, now out of prison, strongly supported the Liberal Union, though it was accused of receiving funds from the Greek government, the Dashnaks, and even the patriarch in return for its support of minority aspirations. The Greek ambassador declared that there were 6.5 million Greeks in the empire and demanded that they be given one quarter of all the seats in the new assembly and that Greek be made an official language. The Dashnaks made similar demands for the Armenians. In reaction the Muslims turned more and more to Islamic and Turkish views, though since the latter had no candidates the CUP prevailed, winning all the 288 deputy seats but one, which went to the Liberal Union. The Turks gained a bare majority, with 147 seats, while 60 seats went to the Arabs, 27 to Albanians, 26 to Greeks, 14 to Armenians, 10 to Slavs, and 4 to Jews.[9] The voting had been honest, all the *millets* were represented in proportion to their actual population, and it seemed possible at least that democracy in the empire might well be given a second chance. The upper house, or Chamber of Notables (*Meclis-i Ayan*), was soon appointed by the Council of Ministers, and the Parliament and government seemed fully prepared for the new Ottoman constitutional regime.

On December 17, 1908, the old city of Istanbul witnessed one of the most remarkable scenes in its long history. Sultan Abdulhamit drove through the narrow streets in an open carriage, waving to the crowds assembled as he went to open the new Parliament, assembled in the Ministry of Justice building behind the Aya Sofya mosque. With his first secretary reading his speech, the sultan explained why he had not recalled the Parliament since 1878, stating that his advisers had recommended postponing this part of the Constitution until the empire was ready for it, the people better educated, and the basic reforms well established. "Being satisfied that the fulfillment of this wish would promote the present and future happiness of my Empire and Country, I proclaimed the Constitution anew without hesitation in spite of those who hold views and opinions opposed to this," he explained.[10] In response, both councils praised the sultan for restoring the Constitution and criticized those of his advisers who had misguided him in the past. Then they went on record to support the government's efforts to regain the recently lost territories.[11]

But the new regime had little chance of success. The Parliament simply helped focus attention on the divisions and rivalries that had been momentarily extinguished. The minority delegates did what they could to paralyze action until their demands were granted. The Muslim delegates and ministers were divided on whether to follow the CUP or the sultan or to develop an independent policy. Endless debates soon stalled most of the laws prepared by the Council of State. After he saw how unsuccessful the Porte had been in countering foreign aggression and how ineffective the Parliament was in facilitating the passage of legislation, Abdulhamit did not hesitate to intervene. The supporters of Islamism began to agitate openly, possibly but not definitely with the support of the sultan. Reacting to the secularism of the Constitution, the appearance of unveiled women on the streets, and the new equality recognized for non-Muslims, the Muslim religious conservatives began to campaign openly against the Constitution, declaring that the empire's decline had been caused by its departure from basic Islamic foundations and that Islam could be adapted to meet the demands of a modern age; Islam could provide the laws to regulate every aspect of the empire's social and political life, while only the technology of the West need be borrowed. Sympathizers were found everywhere, not only among the ulema, but also in the bureaucracy and the army, the dervish orders, and among the masses. The attempts of the new government to make provincial government more efficient and to conscript everyone also irritated the tribes of eastern Anatolia, which had always insisted on autonomy. Leading the movement in Istanbul was Kâmil Paşa, joined by all those who were unhappy with the new order, including officials and army officers who had been dismissed and former palace spies. Soon joining them were the mass of Istanbul's Muslim population – artisans and merchants, proprietors of coffeehouses and public baths, porters, fishermen, peasants in the capital to sell their crops, recent refugees – all easily susceptible to a religious appeal.[12]

Opposed to the conservatives were the modernists, holding views similar to those of Ahmet Rıza, but now led by men such as Abdullah Cevdet, Ahmet Muhtar, and Celal Nuri. Some of them advocated full imitation of the West to secure its support and respect. Most, however, felt that Ottoman modernization had to be more selective, taking what was best in the West and modifying it to meet the special needs of Islam and the Ottoman community. Enlightenment through education had to accompany the reforms so that the general population would support them and benefit from them. The modernists, however, were divided. Those who were unwilling to accept the CUP's direction in the Unionist Party or the decentralist policies of the Liberal Union joined the General Welfare Club (*Selamet-i Umumiye Kulübü*) in 1908 and later the Ottoman Democratic Party (*Osmanlı Demokrat Fırkası*). Led by such old Young Turks as Ibrahim Temo, Abdullah Cevdet, and Ibrahim Naci, the new group did not actually participate in the 1908 elections, but it was able to get several CUP assembly members to represent its views while publicizing them in the newspaper *Türkiye* as well as in papers in Izmir, Monastir, and Aleppo, indicating the wide extent of support and organization.[13] In addition, the Greek and Armenian delegates to the Assembly formed their own political groups dedicated to the autonomy or independence of Macedonia and the provinces of eastern Anatolia, seeking to accomplish their aims mainly by disrupting the Parliament in the hope that political anarchy would lead to fulfillment of their desires.

In the midst of these conflicts and resentments Kâmil Paşa tried to play off the different groups to build his own power at the expense of palace and Parliament as well as the CUP. At first the CUP refrained from opposing him, feeling he was the best alternative for the moment, but he assumed that this was the result of CUP weakness and thus attempted to use the situation to appoint his own men as ministers of war and the navy (February 10, 1909). The CUP then did show its real power. It secured an Assembly vote of no confidence against him, leading him to resign in favor of a CUP man, Hüseyin Hilmi, who became the new grand vezir. The CUP tried to conciliate the opposition, but the sultan and conservatives were alarmed at its demonstration of power, and events were set in motion that presaged major political changes.

The Counterrevolution of April 13, 1909

The modernists were too divided to take serious action against the CUP. But for the conservatives it was quite different. It seemed to them that the replacement of Kâmil Paşa, if not protested, would end the sultan's power to control the government and, thus, their own ability to curb its "irreligious" actions. Tension mounted in the capital. Students of religion massed here and there demanding an end to the Constitution. The army soldiers grumbled openly in the barracks with support from their officers. Many artisans and laborers, themselves under the influence of orthodox and mystic religious leaders, talked with increased fervor about the threat to the Şeriat and the danger of Christian domination.

It was one Hafiz Derviş Vahdeti who focused this discontent into an attempt at counterrevolution. Apparently a member of the *Bektaşi* order, he began to publish a newspaper called *Volkan* (Volcano) on November 10, 1908, presenting a mixed message of mystic and popular Islam and strong opposition to the secularism of the government as well as the influence of the minorities and foreign representatives.[14] Within a short time he formed the Society of Islamic Unity (*Ittihad-ı Muhammedi Cemiyeti*), intended to replace the Constitution with the *Şeriat* and use Islam to modernize and rescue the empire. The secular schools and courts would be replaced with their Islamic counterparts and the authority of the sultan restored as the best means of rescuing the empire. While Abdulhamit apparently refused to provide financial support for the new organization and newspaper, it appears that it was helped by other elements in the palace, with one of the sultan's sons, Burhaneddin Efendi, actually becoming a member.[15] *Volkan* now began an active campaign against the government. The Society of Islamic Unity declared its intention to establish a regime that would fulfill the basic duties of Islamic government – to protect and promote the *Şeriat* and the basic practices of Islam, spread the light (*nur*) of Divine Unity throughout the empire, and free Muslims all over the world from the tyranny of non-Muslim oppression. Its immediate aims were to promote the interests of Muslims, support the Islamic principle of consultation (*meşveret*) as the basis of government, secure wider application of the *Şeriat* in the *Mecelle* code used in the secular courts, and to encourage the development of Muslim morals and traditions in the daily lives of all Muslims in the empire.[16]

On April 3, 1909, the society held its first mass meeting at the Aya Sofya mosque, using the celebrations of the birthday of the Prophet to gain further popular support. Vahdeti harangued the crowd with appeals for struggle against secularism, stating that the Muslims had the same right as non-Muslims to organize to defend their ideals and rights.[17] Chapters were organized in other cities, and these in turn began to send popular petitions to the government demanding that the *Şeriat* be restored. The society soon had members in the First Army of Istanbul, key to gaining control of the city. It cooperated with the Liberal Union group and campaigned against the government. A groundswell of mass support soon pushed the conservatives to open action.[18] During the night of April 12/13, the soldiers of the First Army joined the students of religion before the Sultan Ahmet mosque, marched to the nearby Parliament building, and surrounded it. The grand vezir had been aware of the rising tension but had not expected such a sudden explosion; thus when he heard of the affair, he sent only his chief of police to see what was happening. The demonstrators presented him with a series of demands: the government would have to resign and send many deputies into exile; the rules of the *Şeriat* would be obeyed in full; all military officers removed by the government would be recalled, and the CUP influence in the army brought to an end. Ahmet Rıza would be removed as president of the Chamber of Deputies and a "true Muslim" appointed in his place. Word of the demands was sent to the deputies gathered in the building, but since they had no authority to comply, the tension mounted. The mob began flooding into the Parliament buildings, and as the deputies fled in terror two were killed, apparently under the mistaken impression that they were Ahmet Rıza and Hüseyin Cahit Bey, editor of the pro-CUP paper *Tanin*. The government faced a crisis. The minister of war refused to order the army to disperse the rebels. Grand Vezir Hüseyin Hilmi was powerless; he rushed to the Yıldız Palace and presented his entire cabinet's resignation to the sultan. Abdulhamit not only accepted the resignations but also sent his first secretary to Aya Sofya with an order accepting all the rebel demands. The CUP in any case had never been strong in Istanbul; its authority was based mainly on the threat of action on the part of the Macedonian army, and now it seemed completely defeated. CUP members who were in Istanbul fled, and its party and newspaper headquarters were sacked. Whether or not the sultan actually had participated in the planning of the counter-revolution, he now used it to restore his old powers, appointing his own men as ministers of war and the navy and thus reestablishing control over the armed forces. Ahmet Tevfik Paşa was appointed grand vezir with a new cabinet, though he was able to get the sultan to accept his own men in the key ministries as a price for his cooperation. Those deputies still in Istanbul were called to meet once again. Ismail Kemal was elected new president of the Chamber, while Mizancı Murat, long an Islamicist at heart, provided full support to the new regime, thus giving it the backing of the Liberal Union as well.[19]

The sultan was back in power again, and the CUP in Istanbul was shattered. Senior army officers in Macedonia, not necessarily CUP members, took the lead to restore order under the leadership of the Third Army commander, Mahmut Şevket Paşa, his chief of staff, young Mustafa Kemal, and several officers who later were to make their mark both militarily and politically, including Ismet (Inönü) and Enver Bey. The CUP tried to rally its supporters around the empire, appealing also to the minority national groups with which it had cooperated in 1909. The only result of this was an Armenian uprising in Adana that stimulated a severe repression on the part of the local garrison, with massacre and countermassacre following until as many as 20,000 people of all religions were killed (April 14, 1909). Mahmut Şevket interpreted this to mean that the political solutions offered by the CUP would not work and that open military intervention alone could resolve the situation. In this he was supported in particular by Mustafa Kemal, who, since his rejection by the CUP leaders after his initial organizing successes, had abandoned it and opposed military participation in politics. Mustafa Kemal now organized the Macedonian army for the move on the capital, loading its men on trains and organizing what he called the "Operation Army" (*Hareket Ordusu*), which now moved toward Istanbul under the command of Hüseyin Hüsnü. Since this was not a CUP operation, though some of the officers involved had been CUP members, and since the Operation Army was operating in the name of the army to restore order, Abdulhamit at first accepted and welcomed the move. But the Operation Army soon took a turn quite different from what he expected. Most deputies and members of the Chamber of Notables joined members of the former and current cabinet to go to meet the advancing military train outside Istanbul at Yeşilköy (San Stefano) in the hope of gaining an agreement to restore the Parliament and defend the Constitution without any conflict. On April 22, 1909, they met together secretly as the National Public Assembly (*Meclis-i Umumi-i Milli*) under the chairmanship of former Grand Vezir Sait Paşa, now president of the Chamber of Notables. In order to assure the army that they had not participated in the counterrevolution and did not support the new government, they decided to depose Abdulhamit, though to lessen the danger of resistance in Istanbul they kept this part of their decisions secret. On the morning of April 24 the Operation Army reached the Istanbul railroad station and occupied the capital. The sultan ordered that there be no resistance, but some of his supporters set up barricades and fought vigorously near the Porte and at their barracks at Taksim and Üsküdar. By the end of the day, however, they were crushed. Mahmut Şevket declared martial law and summary courts tried, executed, or exiled those found responsible for the counterrevolution or the resistance that followed the arrival of the Operation Army. Military officers were sent to the provinces to collect taxes so that the government could carry on. Thus, in the name of the Constitution and democracy the army assumed autocratic control.[20]

The final step came three days later. On April 27 Parliament again met as the National Public Assembly, this time at the Aya Sofya mosque and under Sait Paşa's chairmanship. Obtaining a *fetva* that justified the sultan's deposition on the grounds of complicity in the counterrevolution and the deaths that resulted, as well as of the theft of state funds, the National Assembly declared him deposed in favor of his brother, Mehmet V Reşat.[21] The sultan and his family were immediately placed on a special train and sent to Salonica the same night so that the next morning the public and the sultan's supporters were presented with a *fait accompli* against which there could be no real opposition. After 33 years on the throne, then, still now only in his 66th year, Abdulhamit accepted the events as the will of God and lived on quietly in Salonica until he was recalled to Istanbul in 1912 due to the fear that he might fall to the enemy in the Balkan Wars. He then resided in the Beylerbeyi Palace, on the Anatolian side of the Bosporus, until his death six years later, on February 10, 1918. Thus ended in obscurity and disgrace the life of one of the most eminent of all Ottoman sultans.[22]

The Ottoman Constitutional Democracy, 1909–1911

It long has been assumed that the revolutions of 1908 and 1909 ushered in a period of direct rule by the CUP. However mistaken this assumption was for Abdulhamit's last year of power, it was even less true in the period of constitutional democracy that followed until the disastrous war with Italy in Tripolitania. As we have seen, the counterrevolution of April 1909 disrupted and scattered the CUP and its supporters, and it was the senior officers of the Macedonian army who restored the Parliament and deposed Abdulhamit to preserve order. This in turn inaugurated not a new period of CUP dominance but, rather, a mainly constitutional and democratic regime influenced from behind the scenes by Mahmut Şevket Paşa, who became martial-law commander of Istanbul as well as inspector of the First, Second, and Third armies, thus inaugurating a limited kind of army participation in politics that has been exercised from time to time ever since.

In response, the CUP itself emerged mainly as a civilian political party. It worked to restore its previous authority by developing an empire-wide membership and political organization as well as a program that could appeal to the masses. So it was that while its first congress, held in Salonica in 1908, was secret, with its public statement still limited to support of the as yet unstated aims of the Macedonian CUP, the one held on November, 13, 1909, and all subsequent party congresses were quite public. The secret "patriotic clubs" previously established in the provincial centers now openly emerged as its party centers, all, however, still under the strong control of its leaders in Istanbul and Salonica. Its military members did not participate actively in politics, but their influence still was felt from behind the scenes. The CUP program was strongly secularist and reflective of the modernist policies of the intellectuals. It favored the existing organization of Parliament, with a Chamber of Notables partly appointed by the sultan and partly by the Chamber of Deputies. The vote was to be given to Ottoman male subjects over the age of 20 who possessed some property. Elections still would be indirect, but article 113 would be abolished altogether. All Ottomans would be equal before the law, free to assemble publicly and discuss political issues as long as the public order was not disturbed. Censorship would be abolished, but the press still would be subject to regulations. Public primary education would be compulsory and free, with instruction being given in the language of the majority of the students in each school. But in the intermediate and higher levels, education would be voluntary and instruction only in Turkish. New laws would regulate the relations between workers and their employers. The tax system would be reformed to reflect economic and social needs. Efforts would be made to develop the economy of the empire and to encourage ownership of the land by the cultivators. All these were programs that could very easily have been accepted by Abdulhamit and the Men of the Tanzimat. The strong Turkish nationalism, which was to develop later, was as yet absent; there was a continuation of the practice that Ottoman Turkish was the official language of state.[23]

With both the Liberal Union and the Islamic Unity parties wiped out by the events of 1909, only the small Ottoman Democratic Party remained to provide the CUP with some opposition in the elections and Parliament. For the most part, then, the main struggle for power in the government was between Mahmut Şevket, representing the military, and the CUP. Mahmut Şevket generally prevailed, though the CUP exercised some influence through the appointment of two members, Cavit Bey (deputy from Salonica) and Talat Bey, to the key positions of minister of finance and minister of the interior respectively. Şevket worked to keep army members out of politics and out of the CUP. But he also resisted the efforts of the government to supervise the army budget and, thus, to control the army. With such pulls from both sides, the members of the CUP's parliamentary group found it impossible to stay together. In February 1910 some of them formed their own parliamentary group, the People's Party (*Ahali Fırkası*), thus bringing the divisions into the open.[24] There soon followed the Ottoman Committee of Alliance (*Heyet-i Müttefika-i Osmaniye*), which included members of the minority national groups as well as those members of the banned political parties who were still active in politics and advocating a decentralized empire.[25] There also were the Liberal Moderates (*Mutedil Liberaller*), led by Ismail Kemal and including deputies from Albania as well as the Arab provinces.[26] But none of these could participate too openly in politics due to the continued martial law; thus they acted merely as parliamentary groups, cooperating in opposition to the CUP and to the government when it supported CUP policies and representing a more conservative approach to public policy combined with a desire to meet the nationalist demands by a decentralized type of government. In November 1911 all the opposition groups joined in the Freedom and Accord Party (*Hürriyet ve İtilâf Fırkası*), led by Ismail Hakkı Paşa, deputy from Amasya, Damat Ferit Paşa, member of the Chamber of Notables, and Rıza Nur, deputy from Gümülcine.[27] There also were two radical underground groups. The Ottoman Radical Reform Party (*Islahat-ı Esasiye-i Osmaniye Fırkası*), formed in Paris at the end of 1909 by the Ottoman ambassador to Sweden, Şerif Paşa, advocated revolutionary action to topple the regime by assassinating the government leaders, ending the martial law, and forming a new Parliament through elections.[28] There also was an Ottoman Socialist Party (*Osmanlı Sosyalist Fırkası*) formed in Istanbul in 1910 under the leadership of Hüseyin Hilmi, publisher of the newspaper *Iştirak*, which gained its main support from the Armenian and Bulgarian groups in the Parliament. But both right and left were suppressed by the army and forced to transfer their activities to Europe, after which they had little influence on politics within the empire.[29]

The amendments to the Constitution of 1876 constituted the most important legislation passed in the years before the Italian War. After a long series of debates in the Chamber of Deputies, a new law (August 21, 1909) fundamentally altered the balance of power in the government. The powers of the sultan and palace were severely reduced. The sovereignty vested in the House of Osman in the Constitution now was made contingent on the sultan's fulfillment of his accession oath made to the National Assembly promising to respect both the *Şeriat* and the Constitution and to be loyal to the fatherland (*vatan*) and nation (*millet*), thus giving the Parliament the right to depose him if it wished to do so (article 3). He still was allowed to retain his private treasury, wealth, and estates (article 6). But the ministers and the grand vezir were made responsible to the Parliament rather than to the sultan, and he was bound to call it into session within a certain number of days after each election and to allow it to meet at least for a certain amount of time, thus greatly limiting his actual authority to control the affairs of government. Even these limited rights were further restricted in subsequent articles. His right to conclude treaties was made subject to the ultimate approval of the Parliament. He could choose only the *şeyhulislam* and the grand vezir, whereas the latter alone could choose the rest of his cabinet subject only to the sultan's sanction (article 27). The presidents and vice presidents of the two chambers now were elected by their own members instead of being appointed by the sultan, and he could do no more than sanction them (article 77). Article 113 was altered to allow the government to proclaim martial law when needed and to suspend the normal laws and protections, but without any participation on the part of the sultan. Finally, the sultan's secretary and chief *mâbeyinci* and their staffs were to be appointed by and responsible to the cabinet rather than the sultan, making it very clear that he could no longer build a government within the palace as Abdulhamit had done.

The Constitution also was modified to limit the power of the Porte in relation to the Parliament. Ministers were made responsible to the Chamber of Deputies rather than the grand vezir (article 29). If the cabinet disagreed with the Chamber on any matters, including finance, it was the latter that prevailed, and the former had to resign if it did not accept the situation (article 30). If it did resign and the same grand vezir or a new one formed another cabinet that failed to accord with the will of the deputies, the sultan had to dissolve the latter and hold new elections. But if the new Chamber upheld the will of its predecessor, then the cabinet in the end simply had to conform (article 35). The Chamber of Deputies had the right to interpellate the grand vezir or any minister, and if it disapproved of his conduct, the minister had to resign. If it was the grand vezir who was thus rejected, the entire cabinet fell and a new one had to be appointed (article 38).

When the Parliament was not in session, the cabinet could have its decisions promulgated directly by order of the sultan, but only for grave emergencies threatening the state or public order, and subject always to the ultimate approval or disapproval of the Parliament as soon as it could gather in regular or special session (article 36). The right to initiate legislation was extended to both chambers of the Parliament, whose decisions went directly to the sultan for promulgation without the sanction or intervention of the cabinet. The sultan had to promulgate the law within two months or return it. It then could be passed only by a two-thirds vote of the deputies, in which case the sultan had to promulgate it (articles 53–54). Thus the sultan's veto had only a delaying power. Both houses had to meet from November 1 to May 1 each year and to assemble without the call or sanction of the government or the sultan. Their terms also could be extended through the normal process of legislation and promulgation (article 43). The deputies retained their right to approve the annual expenditure budget and to interpellate the ministers on its contents, but only the cabinet could determine how the revenues would be assessed and collected (article 80).

Finally, rights previously in the Constitution were made more specific. Subjects were now to be free from search, seizure, or imprisonment except in conformity with the law (article 10). Publications were to be free, and there was to be no censorship before publication (article 12). The post could not be opened or searched except with the authorization of the courts (article 119). But while Ottomans were to be free to organize themselves into societies, all secret societies organized to destroy Ottoman territorial integrity, disturb public order, divide the races of the empire, or violate the Constitution were prohibited (article 120).[30]

But with the political leaders in Parliament spending most of their time in political maneuvering, there was little opportunity to develop a concentrated program of legislation to put any of the different groups' ideas into effect. Far fewer laws were passed during the three years preceding the Italian War than in the later years of the autocracy, and the bulk of these was concerned with fulfilling the Parliament's constitutional responsibility of authorizing the annual budget and providing supplementary funds when necessary.[31] Further efforts were made to balance the budget by reducing the bureaucracy, salaries, and promotions.[32] A new system of financial inspectors was created to go around the empire to ensure that taxes were collected on time and in full and that government resources were not squandered.[33] The tax collection service and its methods were again revised.[34] A Financial Reforms Commission (*Islahat-ı Maliye Komisyonu*) was established in the Ministry of Finance to recommend changes in organization and collection methods to maximize revenues and reduce expenditures.[35] State tax collectors assumed the job of collecting and distributing the surtax shares intended for public works and education, and the treasury received its own share to help meet its financial obligations.[36] A new central accounting system was organized to provide more efficient control over the handling of public funds by officials, ministries, and departments.[37] Individual taxes also were reorganized and generally increased. Under the constant prodding of the legislature and the Accounting Office, revenue collections increased dramatically to almost 100 percent of assessed taxes, but expenditures increased even more rapidly, particularly for the army (which increased from 596.7 to 849.8 million kuruş between 1901 and 1910), the navy, (from 50.06 to 115.2 million kuruş), the gendarmes and police (from 120.4 to 166.1 million kuruş) and the Parliament itself, which now cost some 100 million kuruş for salaries and other administrative costs. As a result, the deficit increased steadily through the Young Turk period, as shown in Table 4.1.

Most other legislative actions were devoted to meeting the terroristic attacks that arose in Macedonia and eastern Anatolia following the counterrevolution. The "Law on Vagabonds and Suspected Criminals" (May 8, 1909) was passed to enable the government to deal with anyone suspected of acting against the interests of the empire. Persons apprehended without any visible means of support could be turned over to the public prosecutor and sentenced from two to four months to work of public utility. Suspected criminals could be held up to 48 hours by the police, and if proof of illegal acts or plans was discovered, they then could be turned over to the public prosecutors for punishment according to the law. Anyone found carrying arms could be imprisoned for six months. Those who actively participated in armed bands were to be imprisoned for ten years, and their leaders

Table 4.1. *Ottoman revenues and expenditures, 1908–1911*

Fiscal year	Total collections (kuruş)	Percent of assessment	Expenditures (kuruş)	Balance (kuruş)
1324/1908–9	2,519,791,592	92.16	n.a.	n.a.
1325/1909–10	2,692,693,836	96.44	2,775,263,363	−82,569,527
1326/1910–11	2,878,303,078	98.14	3,374,511,319	−496,208,241

Source: Ihsaiyat-ı Maliye, vols. I, III, especially I, 402–433.

and organizers were to be executed. The families of those participating in such bands also were subject to punishment, and their property could be confiscated by the state. The army was ordered to establish "pursuit battalions" to capture and disarm the terrorist bands, and all subjects were required to report the presence of such groups and to cooperate with the army's efforts against them.[38] A Law on Public Gatherings required that permits be obtained to hold any public gathering, indicating the time and place, the subjects to be discussed, and the names of its sponsors, so that they would be available for punishment if the law was violated. No public gatherings could be held within 3 kilometers of the Porte or Parliament while they were in session. Gatherings could not disturb the regular flow of traffic in the public thoroughfares or sidewalks. Government officials had to be admitted to all gatherings so that they could ascertain that the law was being observed.[39] The Societies Law provided for the registration of all associations and also prohibited the formation of groups based on nationality or race or which advocated action to violate the law or public morality, disturb public order, or attack the empire's unity.[40] A new Press Law more or less confirmed those of Abdulhamit, making each newspaper legally and financially responsible for publishing information that might disturb public order, harm individuals, or incite violations of the Constitution.[41] Printing presses and publishers were restricted in the same way.[42] Istanbul and its environs were organized into a new province, side by side with the municipality, with a police organization (*Emniyet-i Umumi Müdürlüğü*) established under the governor and, thus, the central government, to police the capital more efficiently than its own forces had done in the past.[43] Ottoman society thus was far more restricted in the name of public order after the Constitution had been restored than under Abdulhamit.

These restrictions were intended primarily to discourage the terrorists and the more extreme elements of the right and the left. The system of justice, as it related to the vast majority of subjects, continued to improve. The Ministry of Justice was enlarged and reorganized so that it could better supervise the courts and ensure that judges were able and honest.[44] A new system of judicial inspectors made certain that the courts were not subjected to interference and that judgments were made in accordance with the law.[45] In addition, the provincial courts were completely removed from the authority of the governors, and separate courts were provided in most places for civil, criminal, and commercial cases on both the primary and appeal levels.[46]

The new regime took steps to modernize the armed forces, which had been neglected in Abdulhamit's later days. New guns, cannons, battleships and other equipment were purchased on a large scale, mainly from Germany, Britain, and the United States. Foreign advisers were brought in to train the Ottomans in their use, and a series of new laws modernized the army. A new Advisory Military Council (*Şurayı Askeri*) was established at the Seraskerate, and it prepared a large number of regulations to modernize the organization and operations of the army.[47] The reserves were reorganized and given additional equipment and training.[48] The army medical and veterinary services were expanded and modernized.[49] But reforming the army was a difficult task, with the vast morass of military bureaucrats reacting very slowly to the changes that were made, while the political rivalries among the CUP officers and their opponents made it difficult for them to cooperate for the common good.

With financial stringency pressing all the other departments and with the Parliament bogged down in politics when the army or finances were not involved, little else was done until the end of 1911. A few laws were passed to encourage the construction of urban tramways and public roads and the extension of the railroads.[50] The Istanbul trams were, at long last, electrified,[51] and public steamship service was provided into the Golden Horn.[52] The secular school system continued to expand and modernize with the help of the education surtax, but no major changes were made in the basic organization and regulations inherited from the time of Abdulhamit. The only major new schools established were for noncommissioned army officers and infantry riflemen.[53] Only lip service was paid to developing the economy, and new regulations were prepared to encourage the cultivation of rice,[54] reorganize the forestry system[55] and the chambers of commerce[56] and to transfer the Agriculture Department from the Ministry of Trade to that of Forests, Mines, and Agriculture, thus ending the longstanding conflicts that had arisen because of its position astride the two ministries.[57] The retirement provisions for bureaucrats were liberalized,[58] employment of foreign experts restricted to provide more room for trained Ottomans,[59] and an organization of civil service inspectors established to make sure the bureaucrats were obeying the law and respecting the rights of the subjects.[60] But that was all, and the limited accomplishments were a far cry from the aspirations of the CUP and most of the people.

Internal Dissent and the Albanian Revolt, 1910–1912

The new regime failed to produce miracles, and relations among the races in the empire continued to grow worse. The Armenian Dashnaks launched a new wave of terrorism in eastern Anatolia and intensified their European propaganda campaign accusing the Ottomans of massacre. And the Greek terrorists in Macedonia were equally active. Popular opinion in Istanbul was convinced that terrorists had caused the fire that had destroyed the Çırağan Palace, only recently converted for use of the Parliament, though apparently an electrical short circuit was responsible (January 1910). Parliament lost its archives and papers and had to move to the much less spacious building of the Fine Arts Academy in the Fındıklı section of the capital (now the Atatürk Girls' Lycée), where it remained until the end of the empire. Continued Greek claims for Cyprus and demands of the Greek representatives in Parliament for substantial quotas of Greek army officers and provincial officials further inflamed the situation.

Another source of trouble was Albania. Since many Albanians had been involved in the Young Turk movement, men such as Ibrahim Temo and Ahmet Niyazi, its nationalists assumed that the triumph of constitutionalism would mean achievement of all the ambitions which they had nourished since the Congress of Berlin.

But Ottomanism, as it was developed in the Young Turk period, meant essentially cooperation in a united empire, not the kind of autonomy that the Albanian nationalists wanted. The Young Turks did not hamper the activities of the Albanian nationalist clubs at first, but they also established in Albania, as elsewhere in the empire, their own party headquarters, which in advocating Ottomanism campaigned against the nationalists. In reaction, the latter renewed demands for autonomy, development of the Albanian language, and appointment of Albanians to key positions in the province. Ismail Kemal Vlora came to Istanbul as parliamentary deputy for Berat and acted as their principal voice in the capital. The participation of Albanian soldiers in the 1909 counterrevolution and Ismail Kemal's cooperation with the Liberal Union contributed to the misunderstanding. The Young Turks assumed that all the Albanian Muslims supported the central government against the Christians, but the issues were complex. Many Muslims supported the nationalists, putting their Albanian identity above all else, while many Christians, especially the Gheg tribes of the north, opposed them because they feared losing their traditional privileges in an autonomous Albania.

The Albanian revolt, when it finally came in the winter and spring of 1910, was as much a campaign against the new efforts at efficiency and centralization as it was a national movement. The new census and tax regulations struck especially at mountaineers who had long treasured their independence and avoided conscription. The laws against vagabonds and national societies struck Albania in particular because of its traditional armed bands, which had dominated the mountains for centuries. These laws transformed general resentment against government controls into open support of the nationalists. The harshness of Mahmut Şevket's suppression of the initial revolts won new supporters for the nationalists. Montenegro began to support the rebels, not only shielding and arming Albanian refugees but also pleading their case in Europe, demanding that the sultan give a general amnesty, compensate for all confiscated weapons and property, and that all municipal and district chiefs in the province be Albanians. During the winter of 1911, the trouble mounted, and the nationalists demanded the limitation of Albanian tax revenues to expenditures in Albania. The revolt was begun by the Catholic Albanians, but thousands of Muslims soon joined in the demand for "liberty, justice, and autonomy." In June 1911 the sultan himself visited Kosova to calm the situation, signing a decree of amnesty and introducing many concessions, including Albanian schools, military service to be performed only in the province, suspension of all conscription and taxes for two years, and the use of officials conversant in Albanian. But while these measures calmed the north, the revolt in the south intensified, with a national Albanian committee formed at Vlora demanding union of the provinces of Işkodra, Kosova, Monastir, and Janina into a single Albanian province governed by its own Parliament and administration and with its own army (May 15, 1911). The government finally gave in to most of the demands (August 1911), but the solution again proved temporary. By this time Ismail Kemal and his associates were convinced that they could secure far more than autonomy as a result of the Ottoman-Italian war in Tripoli and the promises of assistance from the latter as well as from Montenegro. By June 1912 Albania was again in open revolt, with the rebels now demanding a united Albania, fully autonomous, administered by and for Albanians.

The Beginnings of Turkish Nationalism

It was the Albanian revolt, more than any other event, that convinced the Turks that it would be impossible to conciliate different national interests and attain a unified empire. While the conservatives reacted by turning back to Islam, the secularists who supported the Constitution turned instead to Turkish nationalism. The Turkist groups, which had been quiescent since the counterrevolution, became active once again and attracted extensive popular support. In January 1909 the Turkish Society (*Türk Derneği*) had been formed to coordinate their activities, publishing a journal by the same name to advocate its views, and it had gained little response. But now with the new public interest, its leaders transformed it into the Turkish Homeland Society (*Türk Yurdu Cemiyeti*) (August 31, 1911) and developed it into a major movement. Under the leadership of Yusuf Akçura and Ahmet Ağaoğlu it began to publish its message in the famous periodical *Türk Yurdu* (The Turkish Homeland). They initiated a national campaign to simplify the Ottoman Turkish language to reflect the spoken language of the people, and they strove to promote the political and economic interests of Turks all over the world as well as those within the sultan's dominions.[61] The CUP itself, long the principal supporter of Ottomanism, also began to give up hope that the minorities could be kept within the empire and itself turned strongly toward Turkish nationalism.[62]

The Tripolitanian War

The Young Turks' transition to Turkish nationalism had only begun, however, when it was given a final thrust forward by a new wave of foreign attacks on the empire starting with that of the Italians in Tripoli and Bengazi late in 1911. The kingdom of Italy dreamed of an empire that would revive the glory of the old Roman Empire. Most of the African territories contiguous to the Mediterranean had been already taken by Britain and France, and only Tripoli seemed reasonably available. Ottoman rule there was nominal. The garrisons were weak, the government limited and inadequate, and the economic situation poor. The interior, inhabited by bedouins, had recently come under the control of a Muslim pietistic movement led by the Senusis, further undermining the sultan's suzerainty. On the other hand, Tripoli was close to Italy. Italian merchants had been active there for some time, and their complaints about mistreatment as well as the difficult conditions in the country provided a pretext for armed intervention. Nor were the Italian ambitions particularly secret. In 1900 France had agreed to allow it to take Tripoli in compensation for the expected acquisition of Morocco. Two years later Austria had followed suit in return for Italian support of its ambitions in Bosnia-Herzegovina. Britain joined the agreement as part of its effort to gain Italian participation in the emerging Triple Entente. In 1909 Russian approval was secured in return for Italian support of its ambition to force the Porte to open the Straits to its warships. Though Germany and Austria feared Italian aggression into the Ottoman Empire might cause a major new crisis, they did not wish to alienate Italy and push it even closer to Britain and France. Thus once the French position in Morocco was secured and the Italian press and public agitated for compensatory action in Tripoli, the Italian government decided to go ahead.

The Italian government for some time had complained about "mistreatment" of its subjects in Tripoli and Bengazi, and the Ottomans had tried to satisfy them with guarantees and other promises in order to avoid a war. The Italians, however, who had already decided to attack, rejected the Ottoman offers.[63] On September 29, 1911, war was declared. A day later Tripoli was put under naval blockade. Britain declared its neutrality. On October 4 Tripoli was bombarded and an Italian expeditionary force landed at Tobruk. The Ottoman garrison in both provinces numbered only 15,000 men at best. Because of the situation in the Balkans the government in Istanbul decided to send only limited reinforcements, but these were put under the command of two of its brightest young officers, both CUP members, Enver Bey, recently married into the imperial family, who was made commander at Bengazi, and Mustafa Kemal Bey, placed in command at Tripoli and Derne. Even before they arrived, however, the Italians overran the entire coastal area; Kemal and Enver landed their forces and took them into the interior, where they took command of the remaining Ottoman garrison and joined the Senusi tribesmen in preparing to resist the infidel in a Holy War.[64] On November 4 Italy officially proclaimed its annexation of both Tripoli and Bengazi, but its control remained limited to the coast while the Ottomans and Senusis began an effective guerrilla resistance from the interior. In response the Italians began to send arms and ammunition to Montenegro and Albania and encouraged new adventures against the Porte.[65]

The Rise and Fall of the CUP

In Istanbul the immediate political result of the Italian victories was a rapid decline in the fortunes of the Unionists, leading to the resignation of Grand Vezir Ibrahim Hakkı Paşa (September 28), who had prided himself on his good relations with the Italians. Several groups split off from the CUP to form the *Hizb-i Cedit* (New Party), which demanded that the government support the caliphate and sultanate while adhering to the democratic procedures provided in the Constitution.[66] In reaction, a more liberal group, the *Hizb-i Terakki* (Progress Party), was formed within Unionist ranks.[67] Mahmut Şevket, now minister of war, blamed the entire catastrophe in Tripoli on CUP intervention in the army, and the CUP also suffered from its previous advocacy of friendship with Germany, since Germany was allied with Italy.[68] The CUP tried to regain its popularity by organizing a public boycott of Italian goods and getting the Parliament to abolish the Italian Capitulatory rights and dismiss Italians in Ottoman service. Only partially successful in restoring its prestige, the CUP was forced to accept a coalition government with a number of opposition representatives under the leadership of Sait Paşa as grand vezir (September 30, 1911). Sait asked Britain to help in Tripoli and offered to join the Triple Entente in return, directly contravening the CUP policy, but his overtures were ignored. Russia, fearing that the war would lead the Ottomans to close the Straits, attempted to mediate by demanding that the Porte recognize the Italian conquests and threatening new troubles in Albania and Macedonia in the spring if the war went on; but Sait Paşa rejected the plan, and hence nothing was done.

The victory of the Liberal Union Party, now restored as the Party of Freedom and Accord (*Hürriyet ve Itilaf Fırkası*) in a parliamentary by-election in Istanbul late in 1911 encouraged it to demand a general investigation of the government's inability to defend Tripoli, while several more CUP members joined the opposition. Since the Parliament thus was getting out of hand, the CUP got Sait Paşa to try to dissolve it by modifying article 35 of the Constitution to restore the sultan's right to dissolve the Chamber of Deputies without the excuse of a dispute between it and the cabinet. The Liberal Union opposed elections at the time, since it realized that the CUP was the only party with a political apparatus, but it was difficult for its deputies to oppose Sait's idea, because they previously had advocated just such a measure to strengthen the sultan's authority. Nevertheless, the modification was defeated by the Chamber of Deputies on January 13, 1912. This, however, triggered the dispute between the Chamber and the cabinet that provided the pretext for the sultan to dissolve Parliament, which he did two days later.[69] A full-scale electoral campaign followed, but the new press, public gathering, and society laws were applied to favor the CUP candidates, and with the additional advantage of its empire-wide organization it had little trouble winning an overwhelming victory, with many of the Liberal Union members of Parliament being defeated.[70] The Italians now tried to pressure the Ottomans to settle the stalemate in Tripoli by occupying the Dodecanese Islands (April 24–May 20) and bombarding the forts at the entrance to the Dardanelles, leading the Porte to close the Straits, as Russia had feared would happen. But this act strengthened public support of the CUP as the only political force able to organize national resistance, so that it emerged stronger than ever. When the new Parliament met again in mid-May, more CUP members were appointed to Sait Paşa's cabinet, including Cavit Bey in the key position of minister of finance. In addition, the CUP now was able to push through the constitutional amendments that increased the sultan's power and thus gained the victory they had sought to achieve by dissolving Parliament.[71]

But in gaining the victory the CUP lost the basis of its original political support. Now mostly composed of civilian politicians working to maintain their position, its actions alarmed not only the opposition but also many in the army who had supported it to prevent just the kind of autocratic control that it now wielded and who feared it was using its victory to destroy many of the achievements gained in 1909. As a result, a number of liberal officers formed their own Group of Liberating Officers (*Halaskâr Zabitan Grubu*) with the objective of ending the CUP's autocracy and eliminating politics from the army.[72] Working with the Liberal Union they threatened some sort of violent action unless the CUP stepped down. Mahmut Şevket resigned as minister of war to support their campaign, and a new coup seemed very likely. Thus despite a strong vote of confidence from the CUP-controlled Chamber of Deputies, Sait Paşa resigned (July 17, 1912) and the government fell.[73] Sultan Mehmet Reşat tried to resolve the situation by criticizing the officers for intervening in politics and then replacing Sait with the elderly hero of the Russo-Turkish War, Gazi Ahmet Muhtar Paşa (1839–1918), for some time president of the Chamber of Notables and a distinguished elder statesmen considered above politics.[74] Ahmet Muhtar tried to establish a cabinet above party, including in his cabinet a number of former grand vezirs, Kâmil Paşa (now president of the High Council of State), Damat Ferit (minister of the interior) and Hüseyin Hilmi (minister of justice), hoping thus to unite the empire's politicians to face the difficult crisis at hand while weakening the CUP by removing the cabinet members associated with it.[75]

The Liberating Officers, however, had achieved only part of their objective. The CUP was out of the government, but it still controlled Parliament. They began to demand its dissolution and the holding of new elections. Ahmet Muhtar responded by submitting the amended article 35 of the Constitution to the Chamber of Notables. He had no difficulty securing its approval, since it was now manned mainly by former officers sympathizing with the Liberating Officers. This was followed with an amendment to article 43 to provide that if Parliament was dissolved, the new Chamber of Deputies could be called to an extraordinary session for two months and that this in turn could be prolonged if necessary. The sultan then dissolved the Parliament (August 5), and new elections were called, with the general feeling being that this was the end of the CUP.[76] Now it was the CUP that was restricted by the government during the campaign. Its principal newspaper, *Tanin,* was suspended entirely. The CUP at first considered condemning the entire procedure as illegal and refusing to participate in the election, but when Talat convinced his colleagues that this would only lead to its destruction, they decided to participate and the campaign went on.

Background to the Balkan Wars

At this point politics was overshadowed by a new threat from the empire's Balkan neighbors. Austrian annexation of Bosnia stimulated the aggressive desires of the Balkan states to gain compensation and also ended the cooperation between Russia and Austria that had previously kept the peace. Serbia, encouraged by Russia, began to demand new territory and proposed a new Balkan alliance to prevent Austria from making further advances. Though continued rivalries in Macedonia prevented such an alliance right after Bosnia was annexed, the Italian attack on Tripoli convinced the Balkan leaders that their rivalries in Macedonia had to be subordinated to take advantage of the Ottoman preoccupation across the Mediterranean. The first alliance reached was between Serbia and Bulgaria (March 13, 1912) on the basis of autonomy for Macedonia as a means of settling their dispute as to which should control it. In the case of victory over the Ottomans, Serbia would receive the *sancak* of Novipazar and the district of Niş and Bulgaria would get the lands east of the Rhodope Mountains and the Struma. In addition, if Macedonian autonomy proved impractical, then Bulgaria would get Monastir and Ohrid, Serbia would take over northern Macedonia, and the balance, including Komanovo and Üsküp, would be divided between the two by arbitration of the czar. A Greco-Bulgarian alliance followed (May 29, 1912), the Macedonian problem simply being ignored while the two agreed on joint assistance in case of an Ottoman "attack." Bulgaria was to remain neutral if the Ottomans and Greeks again fought over Crete. Montenegro completed the ring around the Porte by reaching similar military agreements with Bulgaria (September 27) and Serbia (October 6), the latter actually specifying that hostilities would commence with the Porte no later than October.[77]

The Ottomans hardly were in a position to fight all their Balkan neighbors. The attempt to vitalize the army after its neglect late in Abdulhamit's reign had only begun to produce results. Thousands of cannon and rifles lay in storehouses, and the men were still untrained in their use. Political dissent in the officer corps had destroyed much of the morale and unity that had been encouraged in Abdulhamit's early years. Furthermore, Mahmut Şevket's resignation as minister of war had been followed by a general replacement of most of the officers on the General Staff, and the new departmental chiefs had not yet been able to familiarize themselves with the mobilization and war plans that had been prepared. The diversion in Tripoli had not been as serious as the Balkan allies expected, simply because the Italian blockade had prevented the Ottomans from sending more than a few detachments to support the guerrilla war. Even then, however, the Porte had no more than 250,000 men under arms, far fewer than the combined Balkan armies.

Clearing the Decks: Ending the Tripolitanian War and the Albanian Revolt

Ahmet Muhtar and his new cabinet conceived their main job to be that of stalling for time until the powers could intervene to forestall the Balkan attack or until the Ottoman army was fully mobilized. Therefore, the government made an attempt to settle the Albanian Question first. On August 9, 1912, the Albanian rebel leaders in the north presented a new series of reform proposals: the establishment of an autonomous system of administration and justice; military service to be performed in Albania except in time of war; the use of officials knowing the local language and customs, but not necessarily being Albanians themselves; the establishment of new lycées in the main cities and agricultural schools in the larger districts, reorganization and modernization of the religious schools, the use of Albanian in the secular schools, freedom to open private schools and societies, the development of Albanian trade, agriculture and public works, a general amnesty for all those captured during the rebellion, and, finally, the court martial of the Istanbul ministers who had attempted to suppress the Albanian revolt in the first place.[78] The Albanians themselves were divided, some supporting the CUP and others the Liberal Union, with some even wishing to return to Abdulhamit's autocracy. Thus the proposals represented a compromise with which not only they but also the Ottoman government could live. Therefore, with only the final point being ignored, on September 4, 1912, the government accepted the proposals and the Albanian revolt was ended.

Ahmet Muhtar then moved to settle the war with Italy, which had become increasingly embarrassed by its failure to crush the Ottoman resistance in the interior of Tripoli after its initial victories along the coast. Negotiations were difficult at times, with the Italians resisting the Ottoman efforts to limit their control to Tripoli. The Triple Entente powers attempted to get Italy to compromise, but it threatened to retain Rhodes and the Dodecanese and to stir the Albanians and Montenegrans to further aggression unless the Porte accepted its full demands. Finally, on October 15, 1912, an agreement was reached at Ouchy, near Lausanne, following the same formula that had established Austrian rule over Bosnia-Herzegovina. The Ottoman army would evacuate all its remaining units from both Tripoli and Cyrenaica. In return Italy would leave the Dodecanese, acknowledge the sultan's religious position in the provinces, allow his name to be read in the Friday prayers, accept the religious teachers and judges whom he appointed, preserve the religious foundations, and accept an Ottoman agent to represent all the Muslims now placed under Italian control. The boycotts imposed against Italian goods and individuals were ended, and the Italian Capitulations and postal rights in the empire were restored, but Italy promised to help the Porte gain European agreement to their total abolition. Italy also assumed the burden of its new province's share of the Ottoman public debt.[79] Italy in fact did not evacuate the Dodecanese Islands, on the pretext of protecting them from the Balkan War, which broke out soon afterward, but at least the Porte was freed to face the onslaught of its neighbors without further diversion.

The First Balkan War

Montenegro started the war by moving into northern Albania as well as the *sancak* of Novipazar on October 8, 1912. Soon after, its allies sent identical ultimatums to the Porte demanding the autonomy of its remaining European provinces, redrawing the boundaries on ethnic lines, with Christian governors, provincial elective administrative councils, free education, native militias and gendarmes, new reforms under Christian supervision, and the immediate demobilization of the entire Ottoman army. Clearly, Ottoman agreement was not expected, and war declarations from all sides followed during the next few days. Greece went on to announce its formal annexation of Crete.[80]

The war was disastrous for the Ottomans, particularly since the Greek fleet was able not only to take a number of the Aegean Islands but also to prevent reinforcements from being sent from Anatolia through the Aegean to the beleaguered garrisons in Rumelia. The Bulgars wanted to move immediately into Macedonia, but fear of an Ottoman offensive from Istanbul compelled them to send most of their forces toward the Ottoman capital, allowing the Greeks and Serbs to conquer and divide Macedonia before they could get there. The Bulgars moved rapidly into eastern Thrace, routing the main Ottoman defense forces at Kırklareli (October 22–24) and putting Edirne under siege. With the CUP officers and their political enemies fighting over strategy as well as politics, the Ottoman army retreated in disorder to a new defense line at Lüleburgaz, where the Bulgars routed it again (October 22–November 2) and then advanced to Çatalca, the last defense point before Istanbul. After only a month of war, then, all of Thrace was gone and the Bulgars were besieging Edirne and Istanbul.

To the west the Serbs quickly took much of northern Macedonia, including Kosova (October 23) and then joined the Montenegrans in taking Priştina and Novipazar and routing the remaining Ottoman forces at Komanova (October 23–24). They then occupied much of northern Albania and put Işkodra under siege. In the south the Greeks pushed west and north into Macedonia, taking Preveze (November 3) and, finally, the great prize of Salonica (November 8), getting there just ahead of the Bulgars. Another Greek force took the Epirus and put Janina under siege, taking most of southern Albania as well. In two months, therefore, the Ottomans had lost all their remaining territories in Europe with the sole exception of the four besieged cities.[81]

In Istanbul the defeats, the food shortages, and the government's inability to pay the salaries of bureaucrats and teachers led to a series of violent demonstrations, which soon spread to the other major cities of the empire. For the first time in modern memory the young men of Istanbul and of the provinces were fighting and dying together on the battlefields, with hardly a family being spared. Those who had long held properties in the remaining European provinces had lost them, and many were reduced to poverty. Thousands of refugees streamed in from the north. Misery and tragedy stalked the streets, and the government was blamed. The CUP emphasized its role as a coalition of patriotic officers and bureaucrats who sought to restore and modernize the empire. It now advocated a cabinet above party so that all could cooperate for the common cause. But the Liberal Union and the Group of Liberating Officers, though strongly critical of Ahmet Muhtar and his government, were determined not to allow the CUP to share power in any way.[82] When the Muhtar cabinet resigned, then, the opposition got the sultan to replace him with Kâmil Paşa, ostensibly so that he could use his British connections to secure foreign intervention but actually just to keep the CUP out.[83] The new arrangement did little good, however. The Triple Entente was unwilling to push the Balkan states into the hands of Austria by opposing their advance, and the CUP abandoned its patriotic stand for a new exertion of violence to secure control of the government. Kâmil Paşa's first move was to propose that the powers bring their fleets to Istanbul to save it from the advancing Bulgars (November 6). The CUP, fearing that he was about to capitulate, advocated resistance, leading the grand vezir to send the police to suppress its clubs and newspapers as well as all popular demonstrations. Unionists were arrested and imprisoned, and some fled to Europe.[84] Abdulhamit was brought back to Istanbul just in time to escape the Greek attack on Salonica. And with the CUP at least temporarily dispersed and the Bulgarians still stalled at Çatalca, the government was able to obtain the agreement of all the remaining parties for a truce proposal (December 3).

Peace negotiations began in London on December 16, with British Foreign Secretary Sir Edward Grey acting as mediator. The Balkan states demanded full Ottoman cession of all its European possessions and the Aegean Islands. The Ottomans, emboldened by their resistance to the Bulgars at Çatalca and by the rapid increase of their men under arms, rejected this proposal and countered with a plan to cede the conquered territories except the provinces of Edirne and Albania, which would become autonomous under an administration to be set up by the powers. The Aegean Islands would not be ceded, but the Porte would accept a decision of the powers on Crete. Macedonia would become an autonomous province under the rule of a member of the Ottoman family. This time, however, the Balkan states demurred and the conference threatened to break up. Grey then got the powers to propose a compromise by which the Ottoman Empire would retain only those parts of eastern Thrace that lay south of a line drawn between Midye on the Black Sea, and Enez, located where the Maritsa flows into the Aegean. Edirne thus would go to Bulgaria, and the powers would make a final decision on the Aegean Islands.[85] At this point the Ottoman army felt that the Bulgarians had been so extended and its own force so built up that if the war went on, eastern Thrace could be regained and Edirne relieved. The cabinet, however, decided that it could not simply reject the powers' offer outright, since it had wanted foreign intervention previously. So it accepted the proposal, but with the proviso that Edirne remain in the empire, since its population was mostly Muslim and that the area between it and the Dardanelles be formed into a neutral and an independent principality that would constitute a buffer zone to protect the Straits from direct Bulgarian incursion.[86] The CUP, however, began to fear that Kâmil Paşa was going to give away the sacred city of Edirne to get peace. On January 23, 1913, it organized the famous "Raid on the Sublime Porte." Enver led an army band into the Porte building, burst into a cabinet meeting, and forced Kâmil to resign at gunpoint.[87] That the CUP was acting mainly to save Edirne rather than to secure full power is indicated by its actions during the next few days. Cemal Bey was made commander of the First Army in Istanbul, and he issued a conciliatory proclamation asking for cooperation of all and promising that political groups could continue to meet as long as they did not violate the law. When Enver went to see the sultan, he asked only for a cabinet of all the parties. The able and nonpolitical soldier Mahmut Şevket Paşa became grand vezir, with the assignment of doing what was needed to save eastern Thrace.[88] In the new cabinet only three Unionists were appointed, and the grand vezir himself became minister of war. The CUP's return to power thus was nonintrusive, with interests of the empire being put first.[89]

The new government took over under difficult conditions. What tax revenues could be secured from Anatolia hardly were enough to compensate for the loss of those from Rumeli. The army had been shattered, and the public was in despair. Kâmil's dismissal had made the conference delegates in London very suspicious that the Porte might break the truce. Mahmut Şevket's task was to insist on the retention of Edirne and eastern Thrace but to keep the London Conference going at least long enough for him to restore the army and appease the public at home. He proposed a compromise to the powers, agreeing to cede only the portions of Edirne on the right bank of the Maritsa, retaining the main part of city on the left bank, where most of the Muslim population as well as the ancient mosques and tombs were located. The powers could decide the fate of the Aegean Islands, but the Porte would have to retain some, since they were necessary for the defense of Anatolia. Finally, he added something new – that in return the powers allow the empire to set its own customs duties, apply the same taxes to foreigners in the empire as to Ottomans, and, eventually, to abolish the rest of capitulatory provisions (January 30, 1913).[90] But the Bulgarians refused the territorial proposals, and the London Conference broke up.

The armistice ended on February 3, and the bombardment of Edirne resumed. The Bulgars now began a campaign of slaughtering thousands of Turkish peasants in Thrace, sending hundreds more toward the capital to disrupt further its ability to support the war. The Bulgars also began a general assault at Çatalca, but they were beaten back again after two weeks of continuous fighting (March 18–30). However, Mahmut Şevket was unable to restore the army because of lack of money. On March 28 Edirne was starved into submission, leading to a reign of terror from which the city has never fully recovered. Already on March 6 Janina had fallen to the Greeks. İşkodra fell on April 22, thus finally ending Ottoman rule in Europe with the exception of Istanbul. Kâmil Paşa tried to use the situation to organize a countercoup that would totally eliminate the CUP and restore the Liberal Union to power. Traveling to Cyprus and Egypt, he seems to have secured British support in return for promises to surrender the key administrative and financial positions in the government to foreign experts.[91] His plans were discovered by the government, however, and on his return to Istanbul he was arrested (May 28, 1913). In the meantime, in the face of all the disasters Mahmut Şevket had to offer a restoration of the truce and full acceptance of the powers' peace terms (March 31, 1913). The armistice was restored on April 16, negotiations resumed on May 30, and ten days later the Treaty of London was signed, with the Midye–Enez line being established as the new Ottoman boundary and with Thrace and Edirne in enemy hands. The Porte surrendered all rights in Crete and left the settlement of the Aegean Islands and the Albanian boundaries to the powers.[92]

Kâmil Paşa remained under arrest, but the Liberal Union plans for a coup continued and were actually intensified by the Treaty of London. Plans were made to assassinate not only the grand vezir but also the major CUP men to gain revenge for the attack on the Porte and removal of Kâmil. In the end, however, only Mahmut Şevket was gunned down, at Bayezit Square while motoring from the Ministry of War to the Porte. Cemal Paşa immediately put the capital under martial law. Several of the assassins were caught and the ringleaders put under arrest. The CUP took full control after the assassination. Members of the Liberal Union not implicated in the murder were arrested and sent into exile. A court martial convicted and sentenced to death 16 Liberal Union leaders, including Prince Sabaheddin (in absentia) and a number of soldiers involved in the assassination.[93] The CUP appointed one of its members, Mehmet Sait Halim Paşa, an Egyptian prince and a grandson of Muhammad Ali, as grand vezir, and four other committee members were assigned key cabinet positions. Thus began the CUP dictatorship that was to carry the empire to disaster in World War I (June 12, 1913).[94]

The Second Balkan War

The war with the Balkan states was not yet finished, however, because disputes among the allies over division of the spoils soon altered the military balance. Arrangements made among the Balkan states prior to the war were upset by the Albanian Question. As the war went on and the Ottomans were defeated repeatedly, the Albanians began to feel they might achieve full independence instead of the autonomy granted by Mahmut Şevket. On November 28, 1912, a National Assembly of Muslims and Christians met at Avlonya (Valona) and declared Albania's complete independence, with Ismail Kemal Vlora as president. The Albanians quickly got the support of Italy, which hoped to use the new state as a base for its power in the Adriatic, and of Austria, which hoped to use it to keep Serbia from extending its power by securing a direct outlet to the sea. On December 12, 1912, even before the Ottomans returned to the conference table, the ambassadors of the powers meeting in London accepted Albanian independence, pressuring Serbia and Montenegro to withdraw from those of its territories that they had taken from the Ottomans. Once the Treaty of London was signed and the occupiers withdrew, Albania finally achieved its independence, though conflicts between Austria and Italy over who would predominate led to the choice of a weak German prince, William of Wied, and to internal difficulties that left the country bitterly divided in the years preceding World War I.

But with Serbia excluded from Albania, it felt it had the right to demand compensation in the Macedonian territories previously assigned to Bulgaria, particularly areas that it had occupied south of Ohrid and Veles. In this the Serbs were supported by Greece, which, happy to keep the Bulgars as far from Salonica as possible, agreed to cooperate to secure a common frontier in Macedonia west of the Vardar, leaving only the eastern portions of the province to Bulgaria. Russia tried to mediate the dispute, inviting all the parties to meet in St. Petersburg. The Bulgars refused to attend; thus the settlement went against them, setting the stage for a fratricidal conflict that could only help the Ottomans.

The Bulgars were furious. They had done most of the fighting in the First Balkan War, but now their allies were attempting to satisfy their own ambitions at Bulgaria's expense. On the night of June 29–30 the Bulgars, therefore, made a surprise attack on their two main allies in Macedonia, Serbia and Greece. The latter soon were joined by Rumania and Montenegro, however, and the Bulgars, surrounded and outmanned, soon succumbed. In the meantime, the CUP led the Ottoman press and public in advocating restoration of Edirne. The cabinet was divided, with some members fearing that such an advance would only lead to a disastrous new war. In the end, however, Talat and Enver prevailed. On July 21 the Ottoman army was able to reoccupy all of eastern Thrace and move into Edirne without meeting any resistance, since the Bulgarians had withdrawn their army to meet their former allies. In response to the Ottoman push the latter soon made peace, though at Bulgarian expense, in the Treaty of Bucharest (August 10). Greece was able to extend its territory in Macedonia north of Salonica and beyond Kavala in the east, and took all of the Epirus, including the districts of Janina claimed by Albania. Serbia took Old Serbia and most of northern Macedonia, thus doubling its size, though it had to divide Novipazar with Montenegro. Bulgaria got only a small part of eastern Macedonia, but it did at least secure an Aegean coastline of about 80 miles including the port of Alexandroupolis (Dedeağaç), giving it direct access to the open sea.

The boundaries thus established were ratified in a series of separate treaties signed with Bulgaria (September 29, 1913), Serbia (November 14, 1913), and Greece (March 14, 1914), which also regulated the status of Ottoman-owned property and of Muslims resident in the lost territories. All Ottoman subjects were given four years to decide if they wished to remain under Christian rule or to emigrate; if they did leave, they were to be allowed to sell their property and transfer their assets to Istanbul. Those remaining were to have the same civil and political rights as their Christian neighbors. Their new governments would give them freedom to practice their religion and maintain their own culture, with secular schools teaching Turkish as well as the state language. Religious affairs would be controlled by chief muftis chosen by the local ulema, who would supervise and control Muslim schools and foundations under the general guidance of the *şeyhulislam* in Istanbul. Every town or village with a substantial Muslim population could also elect its own Muslim community (*millet*) council to care for local affairs such as schools and administration of religious endowments and to represent the Muslims with the central government.[95] With the exception of the Bulgarian territories on the Aegean, which went to Greece after World War I, the boundaries thus established in Thrace and Macedonia have held to the present day. The Macedonian Question thus came to an end. Albania was independent, though with not quite all the lands that it had expected. Bulgaria had been enlarged by almost 30 percent, and it had gained an outlet to the sea. Serbia's territory had been increased by 82 percent and its population by over half. Greece and Montenegro had experienced comparable gains. Only the Ottomans had really suffered, losing 83 percent of their land and 69 percent of their population in Europe as well as much of the revenues and food that had come into Istanbul each year. The Balkan allies thus had accomplished a tremendous amount for themselves, but frustrations and rivalries remained, leading to new difficulties as World War I approached.

The CUP in Power

The recapture of Edirne stimulated a mass Ottoman exaltation so intense that the CUP's right to rule unopposed was accepted and confirmed without further discussion or opposition. The main political opposition, the Liberal Union, had in any case been dissolved because of its involvement in the assassination of Mahmut Şevket. The empire was facing terrible problems that required some kind of strong leadership. Public buildings such as mosques and schools were overflowing with the war wounded, and thousands of refugees were flooding into Istanbul from the lost provinces. Many families had lost their properties, homes, and breadwinners and had to adjust to entirely new lives in the lands left to the empire. The economy had to be rebuilt and the system of supplying food to the cities reorganized. The administration had to be adjusted and reduced to meet the needs and capabilities of a much smaller state. The tax system had to be revised once again. The armed forces had to be rebuilt to meet possible future aggressions on the part of the empire's neighbors. Ottoman society had to be restored and its morale raised after the tremendous shocks inflicted on it during the war. Only the CUP had the organization, manpower, and program to accomplish these ends, and so it was to the CUP that the nation instinctively turned, allowing it to assume a kind of autocracy in times of crisis that no individual or group had ever achieved in the empire before.

Power now lay in the hands of the Porte, with both the sultan and the Parliament acceding to its will with little protest. The latter, in any case now filled almost entirely with CUP protégés, met infrequently; most items of legislation were put into effect by decree (*irade*) of the sultan as temporary laws (*kanun-u muvakkat*) or governmental decisions (*kararname*) until they could be confirmed by the Parliament, but in fact they remained without change as permanent parts of the Ottoman legal system.

Nominally leading the nation during these crucial times was Grand Vezir Sait Halim Paşa (1913–1917), himself a CUP member, but real power in the cabinet fell to the CUP leaders who had emerged before and during the Balkan War crises and whose authority had been established and confirmed by their strong actions at crucial times. No longer children of the Ruling Class or the Tanzimat bureaucracy, the new generation of national leaders had emerged from the lower classes through the army and bureaucracy and was determined to modernize the empire in such a way as to benefit all classes, not just those in power. Secularist and modernist, in many ways far more ruthless than the old generations of reformers, the leaders of the CUP at this time started to lay the foundations for the new era that was to follow. First and foremost among them was the brilliant party leader and strategist Talat Paşa (1874–1921). Following the death of his father, he had been forced to abandon his early army education in order to make a career in the postal bureaucracy. He had joined the Young Turks in his birthplace, Edirne, and then in Salonica, using his official position to circulate their communications in Macedonia and emerging as a leading party strategist. In December 1908 he came to Istanbul as one of the CUP deputies to Parliament from Edirne, and it was he who got the members who survived the counterrevolution to go to Yeşilköy and make their peace with the army. He was actively involved in government after Abdulhamit's deposition, serving mostly as minister of the interior during the remainder of the Young Turk era.[96]

The second major figure of the CUP triumvirate that increasingly dominated the state after 1913 was Cemal Paşa (1872–1922), who had risen in the army. He had used his position as inspector of railways in Macedonia to help spread the CUP message and organize its cells very much as Talat had done in the post office. After the revolution he had become a member of the CUP executive committee under Talat's chairmanship and had led several army units that came to Istanbul in the Operation Army, subsequently rising because of his role in suppressing the counterrevolution as military governor of Istanbul in 1909 and 1910 and again in 1912 after the attack on the Porte and assassination of Mahmut Şevket.[97]

Finally, the most vibrant personality among the CUP leaders was Enver Paşa (1881–1922), a military career officer who, as we have seen, had fought valiantly against the terrorists in Macedonia and the Italians in Tripolitania. He went as Ottoman military attaché to Berlin in 1909, and again in 1910–1911, establishing close contacts with senior German military officials and developing an admiration for German militarism that was to dominate and influence the remainder of his life. His recent marriage to Emine Sultan, daughter of Prince Süleyman Efendi, and subsequent service in Tripoli, seems to have caused a rivalry with his fellow officer Mustafa Kemal, which was to keep the latter out of the CUP leadership. Enver rose to first rank among the CUP leaders, however, only when he led the famous Raid on the Porte (January 23, 1913) and commanded the Ottoman troops that retook Edirne during the Second Balkan War, actions that gained him the position of minister of war during the crucial year that preceded World War I.[98]

The members of the CUP triumvirate had different personalities. Talat, by far the most brilliant and calculating, was the master politician, "a man of swift and penetrating intelligence, forceful when necessary but never fanatical or vengeful."[99] Cemal's role in suppressing the opposition stamped him as a skillful professional soldier, absolutely ruthless and without pity when dealing with enemies. Enver, finally, was the soldiers' soldier, the people's hero, quick, energetic, courageous, loyal to his colleagues and friends, honestly patriotic and devoted to the nation, a good soldier and an extremely able administrator. Together their talents brought them to almost absolute power within the councils of state, particularly after the empire was once again engulfed in war.

The program of the CUP was clearly set out in its congress declarations made almost annually until 1913. Government was to be made more efficient by the "extension of responsibility" of individual bureaucrats, giving them the authority to act without having to secure authorization for every move from superiors, and by the "separation of duties" among the different bureaus, departments, ministries, and individual officials of the central government and between it and the equivalent provincial bodies. The nation was to be given economic independence, the Capitulations abolished, and foreigners made subject to the same laws as Ottomans so that the government could develop financial and economic policies related to the empire's good and not that of the foreign powers. The Parliament was to be given more power, and both the deputies and notables were to receive higher salaries. Deputies who were members of the administration or the police would have to resign before entering the Parliament to ensure their independence in policy making. Greatly increased low-interest loans were to be made available to cultivators to help the advance of agriculture, and they were to be allowed to form their own cooperatives and other organizations to protect themselves in marketing their goods. Artisans were to be allowed to protect themselves by developing their guilds into craft unions. The tithe was to be reduced once again to no more than one-tenth, with the surtaxes ended and education and public works financed from other sources. The tax farm system was to be abolished once and for all and the profits tax extended into a full-fledged income tax so that all would share in the burden of government according to their means. The animal taxes were to be reduced and imposed only when the cultivators could pay in cash rather than being forced to surrender their animals in payment. Efforts also were to be made to improve animal husbandry, to develop industry and trade, and to facilitate the formation of corporations. Above all, the government would have to be reorganized and systematized. All corruption, favoritism, and protection were to be ended. The communes (*nahiye*) would be allowed to develop their own police, education, and public works according to local needs. Strong efforts were to be made to develop public health and to wipe out the diseases that had so troubled the population. Municipalities were to be given sufficient money to meet local needs without calling on the central government for help. Private, religious, and foreign schools were to be supervised by the government and elementary education made free and compulsory, with Turkish used in all schools in order to promote the unity of Ottoman society. More teachers were to be trained, and they would go where they were needed in the countryside rather than remaining in the big cities. Students and teachers who excelled in their work were to receive salary supplements and bonuses as further encouragement. The religious schools were to be reformed to meet the needs of the modern world and new arrangements made to support the religious and cultural institutions previously maintained by foundations. Foreign experts would be brought to the empire as needed to help develop the higher technical academies and schools.[100]

Ziya Gökalp and the Foundations of Turkish Nationalism

With the definitive loss of the major non-Muslim territories in the empire and with the continued ambitions of the Balkan states and czarist Russia, Ottoman public opinion joined the CUP in abandoning Ottomanism in favor of Turkism. Particularly influential in developing the ideological basis of Turkish nationalism, both in and out of the CUP, was the great Ottoman sociologist and philosopher Ziya Gökalp (1876-1924), whose work contributed to the intellectual development of the empire in its latter days and of the Turkish Republic that followed.

Born in Diyarbekir in the first year of Abdulhamit's reign, Gökalp grew up in a mixed Kurdish-Turkish area, speaking both languages but very early emphasizing his Turkish background and connections and acquiring an abiding interest in the subjects of race and national culture. In his youth Ziya received both religious and secular education and became acquainted with the philosophies of a number of intellectuals exiled from Istanbul by the sultan, including one of the founders of the CUP at the Istanbul Army Medical School, Abdullah Cevdet, who roused his interest in the French sociologists. Soon after going to Istanbul to further his education (1896), Ziya became involved in Young Turk political activities and was imprisoned and sent back to his home within a year, thus ending his higher education before it really had begun. By this time, Ziya's father, a minor bureaucrat, had died, but the latter's pension and the modest wealth of his wife enabled him to devote his full time to studying philosophy, psychology, and sociology, abstaining for some time, however, from publication so as not to attract the attention of the sultan's police. After Abdulhamit had been deposed, Gökalp began to lecture at the local CUP branch, editing several local newspapers, publishing his own works, and building a reputation as a forceful thinker.

Gökalp's rise to the national stage came suddenly, in the fall of 1909, when he represented Diyarbekir at the first CUP congress in Salonica. His writings and speeches apparently impressed the leaders, since he was elected a member of the party's executive council, a position he retained until it was dissolved in 1918.

Gökalp stayed in Salonica and started teaching at the CUP-sponsored lycée, becoming the first teacher of sociology in the empire. He also served as the director of the party's youth department. Within a short time he was the most influential of the CUP party philosophers, writing widely and giving lectures to disseminate the ideas he had formulated during the long years of study. He carefully avoided an active political life, preferring philosophical and scholarly activities over holding government positions. He settled in Istanbul only after the CUP party headquarters was transferred there during the first Balkan War. At this time he shared the CUP's early enthusiasm for Ottomanism, making the transition to Turkish nationalism only in disappointment at the failure of the minorities to cooperate. Ziya became the first professor of sociology at the University of Istanbul, joined the Turkish Hearth (*Türk Ocağı*) organization, and helped Yusuf Akçura publish its *Türk Yurdu* (The Turkish Homeland). He urged the CUP to sponsor major reforms in education and stimulated and in certain instances formulated its strongly secularist policies during the war. Many of his disciples at this time, including the historian Fuat Köprülü, the novelist Halide Edip, the poet Yahya Kemal, the writer Ömer Seyfeddin and the journalists Ahmet Emin Yalman and Falih Rıfkı Atay, went on to distinguished and influential careers during the Republic, though Gökalp himself spent his last years at his home in Diyarbekir and in Ankara, supporting the Turkish national revival by producing his own *Küçük Mecmua*

(Small Journal). His death on October 25, 1924, deprived the young Republic of the continued stimulation of a dedicated ideologist.

Reforms draw their strength either from the ability of the authorities to impose them, as was the case during the periods of the Tanzimat and of Abdulhamit, or from the receptivity of society. Ziya Gökalp's ideas created an intellectual movement that provided the inspiration needed for a change in popular mentality from empire to nation, from religious to secular, from East to West. The rapid succession of reforms that followed, from 1913 through the first decade of the Republic, was reinforced, and in many ways made possible, by the ideological basis and support Gökalp's writings provided. Thus changes that had been accepted (and resented) previously as inevitable adjustments needed for survival were transformed into goals that were considered desirable by the mass of the people. The Ottoman Empire, by his time, was in a position where it could not be preserved. But instead of bemoaning the loss, his ideas provided the means to build a new nation with firm roots in the past and trust in the future. This optimism and constructive approach was the light (Turkish *ziya*) that led to the building of a new society.

Gökalp began writing at a time when Islamism and Ottomanism were the predominating trends of thought. There had been signs of an awakening Turkism, but the latter lacked a real body of philosophy to give it life and force. Gökalp believed in nationalism based on a foundation of social science, one that drew its strength from the traditions, customs, art, folklore, language, and social consciousness of the people that formed the nation. He launched his program on two fronts: (1) the positivist-sociological approach that brought out his scholarship and gave his ideas as part of a systematic, learned, closely reasoned argument; and (2) the publicist aspect of his work, often written as didactic poetry, to facilitate the transmission of ideas through memorization and repetition. He wrote children's stories inspired by old legends, in the process creating a new pride in the Turkish past and awareness of historical ties with the Turks of Central Asia. This ideological imperialism offered an escapist consolation at a time when the actual boundaries of the Ottoman Empire were contracting.

Gökalp maintained that nations developed through three stages. First there were tribal communities, in which language and race had precedence. Then there were the religious communities, based on religious unity. And, finally, there was the nation, in which the basic concepts of culture and civilization had to exist. Culture belongs to the nation, he argued, whereas civilization is international. A nation may change from one civilization to another, but it cannot change cultures without losing its identity. A nation must preserve its culture, therefore, and use it as an inspiration for further artistic and creative developments. In dealing with nationalism, Gökalp drew his examples from Turkish history, sociology, and folklore. He expressed his belief in a nationalist education but rejected racism and blind attachment to the past. The past, traditions, and the Islamic background could provide the Turks with a stable base for participation in contemporary Western civilization. "Turkification, Islamicization, and Contemporarization" were thus compatible, with all joining together to strengthen both state and society.

Gökalp aimed at eliminating the dualisms that led to philosophical and practical inconsistencies and hindered progress. He favored the adoption of Western models and technique without abandoning elements of national culture and identity. His concept of culture (*hars*) was based on folk tradition and feeling, and he viewed it as the core of national strength. Aesthetics, arts and crafts, literature, music, and ethics drew their inspiration from the people (*halk*). Accordingly, the complex Ottoman language, with its Arabic and Persian elements, had to be replaced by the simple Turkish language and grammar of the people, although Arabic and Persian vocabulary already absorbed into the language might be kept as enriching elements. Some of Gökalp's students and successors were to extend these ideas into a doctrine demanding complete purification of the language through the elimination of all non-Turkish words. In poetry he felt that the old *aruz* meter, based on a system of short and long syllables, was not easy to adopt to the smooth flow of the Turkish language and that it should therefore be replaced by the syllabic meter, based on counting syllables. A collection of his poetry, *Kızıl Elma* (Red Apple), published in 1914–1915, contained only one poem using the old meter, and in spite of the fact that many of his brilliant contemporaries, like Yahya Kemal, Mehmet Akif, and Ahmet Haşim, continued to use the old *aruz* with mastery, he started a trend toward the syllabic meter that has continued to the present day.

Gökalp criticized the Tanzimat for having failed to develop the cultural base of the nation. It had borrowed automatically from Europe without attempting to distinguish what really was needed and what could be taken from the Turkish national tradition. It had imitated the external manifestations of Europe civilization without penetrating to its philosophical and scientific foundations. It had introduced secular schools and courts without eliminating or reforming the traditional institutions developed by Islam, thus leaving a dangerous dualism that undermined whatever successes it might have achieved. Instead of unifying the nation, it had widened the gap between the rulers and the common people.

Gökalp's approach to the religion of Islam was an attempt to keep what was essential and discard those elements that prevented the progress of Turkish society. In developing a rational approach to religion, he thus started a movement that, although modified by the much more secularist approach of the Republic, has gradually reimposed itself on Turkish life in the modern world. To him, Islam was most important as a source of ethics and it was fully capable of being modified to meet the needs of the time. To rescue religion as well as the nation they had to be separated, making possible the retention of Islam's fundamental values and principles side by side with a modern and Turkish national culture. Legislation had to be rescued from the limitations of the religious law, and religion left to the ulema. The *şeyhulislam* himself had to be as independent from the control of the state as the legislature would be from him. The religious endowments also had to be eliminated, since they diverted much of the wealth of the nation and allowed funds to be mismanaged in the hands of incompetent trustees. The religious schools and courts had to be abolished to end the longstanding dualism between secular and religious elements that existed in Ottoman society. The religious law had to be supplanted by secular law. The position of women had to be restored to the high place it had enjoyed in ancient Turkish society. However much Islam had developed its practices toward women to save them from discrimination, its modern manifestation had held them down, prevented them from taking their rightful place in the Turkish nation. Women should be given the same education as men; they had to be allowed to earn their living in the same way as men; they could no longer be subjected to the degradation that was inherent in polygamy, which was allowed by traditional Islam. The family had to be developed as a basic unit in society, and toward this end family names had to be adopted as was done in Europe. Islam would remain, therefore, but only as a national religion, supplementing the national culture. It could be used to retain the connections with the Muslim brothers in the Arab world, Central Asia, and the Far East, but the interests of the Turkish nation had to be uppermost. Islam had to be Turkified. Arab traditions had to be replaced by Turkish traditions, rituals and prayers had to be carried out in the Turkish language and in the Turkish way, and the Koran had to be taught in Turkish, so that the people would understand their religion and appreciate God far more than they could when reciting phrases in a foreign tongue.[101]

The Islamicists and Pan-Islam

Though the CUP emphasized Turkish nationalism, the strong Islamicist feelings nurtured during Abdulhamit's reign were not forgotten. The fact that the Turks now shared the empire primarily with Arab Muslim brothers even strengthened the feelings of many that for survival they should emphasize Islam rather than Ottomanism or Turkism. This group, however, lacked effective leadership. The major Islamicist group, the Society for Islamic Unity, had come to a sudden end following the failure of the counterrevolution in the spring of 1909. Its basic message had been that Islam had to be maintained as the religion of the state; no matter how the regime was established and whether it was autocratic or constitutional, its primary duty was to enforce the Muslim religious law; and because the Young Turks were not following the *Şeriat*, they were secularists and atheists and had to be overthrown. Though the party ceased to exist, its philosophy was kept alive by Sait Nursi (1867–1960), who led a group of religious reactionaries called "Followers of Light" (*Nurcu*) and favored the reestablishment of religious autocracy until the day of his death, well into the republican period.[102]

Another influential Islamicist group was the Society of Islamic Learning (*Cemiyet-i Ilmiye-i Islamiye*), which, starting in 1908, published its ideas in its monthly periodical, *Beyan ul-Hak* (Presentation of the Truth). It was led by Mustafa Sabri, who achieved his greatest notoriety during the Allied occupation of Istanbul following World War I (1918–1923), when he led a number of ulema who cooperated with the British in abolishing the secular measures introduced by the Young Turks. Sabri led those who felt that Islam could in fact itself become the principal vehicle for the empire's modernization; Muslims had to unite to reform their religion on its own terms as well as to repel the attacks by non-Muslims.[103]

The most intellectual Islamicist group was that led by the poet Mehmet Âkif (1870–1936) and a group of conservative intellectuals who published their ideas in the monthly *Sirat-i Müstakim* (The Straight Path), later called *Sebil ur-Reşad* (Fountain of Orthodoxy). Claiming that Abdulhamit's autocracy had violated the simple faith of the Prophet and the Orthodox Caliphs as much as had the secular Young Turks, Âkif and his followers emphasized the perfect conformity of the Constitution with the democracy of Islam, with the Parliament representing the earliest Muslim practices of consultation among believers. But they differed with the reformers over those policies that attempted to introduce Western institutions and to give equality to non-Muslims. Those policies that emphasized union with the Turks of the world at the expense of universal Muslim ties also were condemned. Western civilization had corrupted the Islamic ethic, and Muslims would have to return to their old values and unity if they were to be rescued from imperialism. Islam could take only the science and technology of the West, rejecting the elements of government that would weaken the Islamic community. There was a tremendous gap between the so-called educated people and the mass of the people. The former attempted to imitate the West, but the latter knew that this was in fact the cause of their fall. Intellectuals could not yet see that nations had to follow different roads to progress according to their own backgrounds and experience and that the road of the Islamic world was not that of the West.[104]

The Modernizers

In the precarious situation of the empire, however, and under the joint influence of the CUP and the intellectual message provided by Ziya Gökalp, it was those who advocated modernism who dominated Ottoman life during the later Young Turk years. Basing their ideas on the need for unity with both the Turks and the Muslims outside the empire, they felt that the empire simply had to modernize if it was to survive and that the West was the only model from which this modernization could be taken. Leading the secular modernizers was the poet Tevfik Fikret, who attacked the idea of Islamic domination of state and society rather than the religion of Islam as much. But since, for the orthodox, Islam covered all aspects of life and since the traditional Islamic state was based on religion, this still brought down on him the attacks of the conservatives. Another persistent advocate of modernization was one of the early CUP founders, Dr. Abdullah Cevdet (1869–1932), who had first published his ideas in the *Içtihat* (Struggle) in Geneva. He criticized all those who would return to the past and showed impatience with those who fell short of his expectations. Under Abdulhamit he found fault with the people for allowing such an autocracy; he attacked the Young Turks when they failed to live up to their democratic ideals. To him the only civilization of the modern world was that of Europe. The trouble with the Tanzimat, the Young Turks, and Abdulhamit was that they had not gone far enough, they had left too much of the old for the new to work efficiently. What should have been done, what had to be done, was to destroy the old and replace it with European civilization, thus making the Ottoman Empire part of the West. He accepted the Tanzimat idea that reform had to be imposed from on top and said that people had to be driven to modernize themselves. Thus along with Ziya Gökalp he provided much of the impetus for Mustafa Kemal's reforms during the early years of the Republic.[105]

Modernization Under the Young Turks, 1913–1918

Under the stimulus of their own party program as well as the intellectual and mass demand for rapid modernization to save the empire, once in full power in 1913 the CUP began a frantic push toward secularization, which continued, with little pause, right through World War I until its leaders were forced to flee due to the empire's defeat and occupation. The reforms of the later CUP period often are overlooked by those who see only the autocracy and the war itself. As during the period of Abdulhamit, the autocracy harmed only those who actively opposed the regime, but to most intellectuals as well as to the mass of Muslims now forming the bulk of the empire's population, it was absolutely essential if they and the empire were to survive.

In direct fulfillment of the CUP party program of 1913, modernization of the apparatus of government came first. For the first time since the early years of the Tanzimat, the ministries were reorganized and modernized. Divisions of authority and responsibility were more clearly defined. Civil servants were encouraged to take the initiative, and the bureaucratic structure was rationalized to better serve the needs of a much smaller empire than that which the Men of the Tanzimat had ruled.[106] A new Financial Reform Commission (*Islahat-ı Maliye Komisyonu*), established in 1912, drastically reformed the tax system, with the tax farms on the tithes definitively abolished and the rates raised sufficiently to balance the budget in the face of rising costs.[107] The road-labor tax was increased and its application extended to Istanbul and the other large cities that had been exempt, thus spreading the burden and leaving the rural populace with less to pay than in the past.[108] Income taxes were introduced to provide the municipalities with needed funds.[109] The financial activities of all civil servants were placed under the supervision of a newly established Financial Inspection Commission.[110]

A new Provincial Administration Law (March 15, 1913) strengthened the governors and extended bureaucratic reforms similar to those introduced in Istanbul.[111] Reforms in the financial and judicial systems in the provinces assigned increased responsibility to those in positions of authority.[112] The police also were reorganized and placed entirely under civilian authority, with more personnel and equipment to enable them to enforce the laws limiting the activities of the terrorist groups.[113] An entirely new gendarme organization was established, on the model of that created by the foreign advisers in Macedonia, and its control was transferred from the Ministry of War back to that of Interior, again strengthening the civilian authorities in the provinces.[114]

Istanbul's municipality was reorganized and modernized, with a City Council (*Şehir Emaneti Encümeni*) provided to help the mayor; councils of law, health, accounting, and police were introduced to provide the necessary technical advice and direction to municipal operations.[115] With the municipality now securing sufficient funds, especially from the new income taxes, it was able to carry out a vast program of public works, paving streets and sidewalks, installing electric lights and a new sewage and drainage system, and reorganizing the police and fire departments. The major city communication services, the telephone, trams, the tunnel between Beyoğlu and Galata, and the electric, water, and gas services also were modernized and extended so that by the commencement of World War I, Istanbul had caught up to the major European cities. The municipality also worked to solve the city's population problem. The refugees who had crowded in since 1908 and the new refugees coming after the Balkan Wars were resettled outside Istanbul as rapidly as possible. But new problems were to appear in consequence of the population dislocations of World War I.[116]

In addition, a series of even more drastic reform proposals made by Ziya Gökalp to further Ottoman secularization were brought to culmination during the darkest days of the war. On April 26, 1913, a new regulation established close state control over the ulema and the religious courts, requiring them to accept the authority of the secular appeals court (*Mahkeme-i Temyiz*) in many areas.[117] State standards of education and training were imposed on the kadis, and a new state-operated *medrese* was opened in Istanbul to train ulema wishing to serve as judges in religious courts.[118] State examinations administered by the *şeyhulislam* were imposed to test their training and competence.[119] All subordinate employees of the religious courts were placed under the control of the Ministry of Justice,[120] and new regulations limited the authority of the religious courts in favor of the secular ones.[121]

This was only the beginning. In 1915 Gökalp proposed the complete secularization of the religious courts, schools, and religious foundations and the limitation of the *şeyhulislam* to purely religious functions. This program was carried out by a series of measures enacted during the next two years. In late April 1916 the *şeyhulislam* was removed from the cabinet and his office changed from a ministry to a department. On March 25, 1915, all *Şeriat* courts as well as those organized by the Ministry of Religious Foundations to care for properties belonging to foundations and orphans were transferred to the authority of the Ministry of Justice, with decisions of the religious courts being subject to review by the secular Appeals Court. Kadis now were appointed, supervised, transferred, and dismissed by the Ministry of Justice in accordance with the same regulations and standards applied to the secular courts.[122] All other members of the ulema were placed under direct government control and put on a salary and pension scale comparable to that of other civil servants.[123] Religious foundation property was put under the control of the Ministry of Finance.[124] Religious schools were put under the Ministry of Education,[125] which sent its own directors to modernize their staffs and curricula. A new Department of Foundations was established under the Ministry of Finance to manage the financial affairs of foundation properties and the religious schools and mosques supported by them, with surplus revenue going directly to the Imperial Treasury for general use. The *şeyhulislam* thus retained only religious consultative functions, and even these were placed under a new department, called the *Dar ul-Hikmet ul-Islamiye* (School of Islamic Wisdom), associated with his office.[126] A Council of *Şeyh*s (*Meclis-i Meşayih*), organized to control all the dervish monasteries and lodges, made certain that their activities conformed fully with the law.[127] The rapid secularization of schools and courts promised an end to the dualisms that Gökalp and his disciples had criticized. Nor was this all. As the war came to a climax, on November 7, 1917, the Code of Family Law was promulgated. Though it included the basic regulations of the *Şeriat* as well as of Jewish and Christian law regarding matters of divorce, marriage, and other family relationships for subjects of those religions, the state's assumption of the legal power to enforce these regulations furthered the secularization movement considerably. The marriage contract became a secular contract and, despite the mention of the religious codes in the law, it was subject basically to secular regulations.[128]

Gökalp led the way in emancipating women during the CUP period, advocating legal reforms to give them a position equal with that of men in marriage and inheritance, educational reforms to give them a chance to secure the same kind of secular education as men, and social and economic reforms to allow them full and equal participation in society and economic life as well as in the professions.[129] Elementary and middle education for girls was greatly expanded by the Ministry of Education, and women were admitted to the higher schools. The first lycée especially for women was opened in 1911. Trade schools for women were established to teach them not only to cook and sew but also to give them training so that they could earn a living as secretaries, nurses, and the like. City women began to work in public, not only in textile and tobacco factories, replacing men taken into the army, but also in businesses and stores. They began to discard the veil in public and appear in European-style clothing long before such measures were decreed by the Republic. Associations to protect the rights of women were established in the major cities. Liberated women emerged to lead the fight for justice, led by one of Gökalp's most distinguished followers, the novelist Halide Edip (Adıvar). A 1916 law finally allowed women to obtain divorces if their husbands were adulterers, wished to take additional wives without the first wife's consent, or violated the marriage contract, thus undermining the traditions based on *Şeriat* provisions.[130]

Women still were far from having full equality, however. They could not go to public places of assembly such as theaters and restaurants in the company of men, even their own husbands, but had to keep to areas especially set aside for them. In the higher schools and the university they could not attend joint classes with men but had to go to special classes or hear lectures in curtained-off sections of the classrooms. They could not smoke publicly or greet men of their acquaintance on the streets. Popular customs limiting the relationship of girls and boys and providing for arranged marriages remained in force. And women in the villages remained bound by their husbands' will according to the traditions of centuries. Yet the advances made for urban women still were tremendous, enabling the full emancipation of women decreed soon afterward by the Republic to take place quickly and completely and with little significant opposition.[131]

The empire was modernized in many other ways during the CUP period. Electricity and the telephone became common, at first in official and business buildings and later in the homes of the wealthy. Sanitation facilities and general cleanliness were greatly improved. Airplanes were introduced in 1912, and the Ottoman army had its own air force in World War I.[132] The dual system of Muslim and European calendars, based on the lunar and solar year respectively, which had been introduced during the time of Selim III and extended during the Tanzimat now was replaced by the latter, with the lunar-year calendar remaining in use only for strictly religious activities.[133] The Islamic systems of telling time and measuring, however, remained in force together with their European counterparts until their elimination by the Republic in 1926.[134]

After the Balkan War debacles the need to modernize the armed forces was recognized fully. A German military mission came to help the government. General Liman von Sanders initially was appointed commander of the First Army in Istanbul (November 1913), with the right also to direct the activities of all the other German officers in Ottoman service. But because of the fears of the other powers, led by France and England, that this would give Germany control of the Ottoman army, a compromise was reached by which he was instead appointed only inspector general of the First Army, and his colleagues also were made subordinate to their Ottoman colleagues. Though the Germans continued to play an important role in Ottoman military affairs before and during World War I, their appearance of arrogance soon became very grating to most of the Ottoman officers. The Entente's accusations that Germany actually controlled the Ottoman army were quite unfounded, since command remained in Ottoman hands under the jealous watch of Enver and his associates. With German help, however, the Ottoman army was rapidly modernized and reorganized. Its annual budget was almost doubled. Large quantities of new equipment were purchased in Europe, and the Imperial Arsenal and other military factories were modernized. All the senior officers who had led the army during the Balkan Wars were retired or transferred to nonmilitary duties, and the remaining junior officers were promoted, giving them an opportunity to display their knowledge and energy in command. Enver encouraged initiative among his officers and men, himself inspiring a spirit of confidence and vigor that had been sorely lacking since the time of Abdulaziz.[135]

Soon afterward, Cemal Paşa was assigned to modernize the navy in the same way. Von Sanders' appointment was balanced by the appointment of a British naval mission led by Rear Admiral Sir Arthur H. Limpus, which helped Cemal to reorganize the ministry completely. The previous tendency of departmental chiefs to avoid responsibility by deferring to the Naval Council was ended by abolishing the latter. The Admiralty then was reorganized into autonomous technical departments whose directors were made responsible for developing and carrying out reform plans, while the grand admiral was limited to matters of planning, training, and war command. The Imperial Shipyards at Samsun, Izmir, Beirut, and Basra also were set to work competing with one another to see which could build the most and best ships in the shortest time. As in the army most of the older officers were retired and command passed to the young and enthusiastic recent graduates of the naval academy. The British also were urged to speed up construction of two new battleships ordered some time earlier. To provide the last payments a popular subscription campaign was opened, with collection boxes set up in schools and hospitals and outside mosques, coffeehouses, and railway stations. Even schoolchildren made contributions to the campaign, and the ships were named after the first and then-reigning sultans (*Sultan Osman* and *Reşadiye*). Preparations were also made for lavish patriotic ceremonies when the ships were scheduled to be delivered, in August 1914, to cap off the forced draft program of rearmament that was intended to assure that the empire would never again be dishonored.[136]

The Young Turks, anxious not to allow any single power to dominate the empire, followed a careful policy of balancing the political, economic, and military influence of Britain, France, and Germany. If Germany seemingly was favored, as that country's European rivals often complained, it was because it was so far behind at the start. To be sure, a number of German firms were allowed to invest in the Ottoman railroads, particularly the new Baghdad Railroad, but despite a steady increase in German economic involvement in the Ottoman Empire, it still was well behind Britain and France in overall investment as well as in imports and exports. France still dominated the Ottoman Public Debt Commission, and joined with Britain in controlling the Ottoman Bank, which had a legal monopoly on the issuance of bank notes and regularly financed the cash flow deficits of the treasury. To further balance German and British predominance in the armed forces, French officers were employed to modernize the gendarmerie and to introduce new organization and methods into the Ministry of Finance during the last two years before the war.[137]

In response to the urgings of the Turkish nationalists and in reaction to the tragedy of the Balkan Wars, official and popular opinion moved strongly toward Turkish nationalism. On March 22, 1912, the Turkish Homeland Society (*Türk Yurdu Cemiyeti*) was supplanted by the Turkish Hearth (*Türk Ocağı*), incorporating many of the former leaders but also witnessing the emergence of many new ones, such as Halide Edip (Adıvar), Ahmet Ağaoğlu, Fuat Köprülü, and others, who were to lead the struggle for Turkish national rights in the years ahead. Organizing now on the pattern of the CUP itself, the Turkish Hearth established units in every city, school, and major public organization. The Turkish Hearth was mainly a nonpolitical organization. Its duty was to combat the ideas of Islamism and Ottomanism and to convince the Turkish people of the empire that they could survive only if they accepted the ideals of Turkish nationalism as developed mainly by Gökalp. Participation of Turks in the areas of the economy and government that previously had been monopolized by non-Turks was encouraged. Contacts were made with Turks outside the empire, and for the first time there was an attempt to counteract the propaganda of the minority organizations in Europe. The Hearth's chapters around the empire became adult education societies, educating cultivators and townspeople alike in the Turkish language and history and striving to develop an awareness of the Turkish cultural heritage. Pressure was applied on the government to increase the use of Turkish in official business and to squeeze out the many Arabs who had been introduced into the bureaucracy by Abdulhamit. The use of Turkish as the primary language of business in the foreign and minority commercial establishments and schools was encouraged. With the religious schools and courts coming under governmental control, Turkish rather than Arabic predominated.

As it was developed during the CUP period and came to be applied under the Republic, Turkish nationalism was mainly a constructive rather than a destructive force, seeking to convince its adherents to build their society and nation by their own efforts, aiming only to eliminate those elements of discrimination that kept them from doing so, and inviting all those ethnic groups that were not Turkish to accept the new nationality and to join in the struggle to build a new nation in place of the declining empire. This was not to be, however. As the Turks were beginning to seek their own national identity, the bases of Islamic unity in the empire were torn apart, and the Arab national movement developed to the extent that it facilitated the disintegration of the empire soon after the war began.

The Ottoman Empire Enters the War

Ottoman involvement in World War I, and on the side of the Central Powers, certainly was not inevitable. Despite the newly emerging patriotic fervor, most members of the cabinet and the CUP and many Turkish people realized that the empire was hardly in a state to support any major military effort so soon after the series of wars that had decimated its population and finances as well as its armed forces. Although Germany had been building up the army, it did not really expect the Porte to be able to make a significant military contribution even if it did decide to join the Central Powers. Modernization had only begun. Besides, most members of the CUP and the mass of the public still felt closer to Britain and France than to Germany. German autocracy and militarism appealed only to Enver and those officers who had received some training in Germany, but they hardly dominated Ottoman politics at the time, and whatever influence they had seemed to be countered fully by that of Cemal and the navy, which favored the Triple Entente, or even better, neutrality.

Behind the scenes, however, Enver was skillfully paving the way for an alliance with Germany. His argument was simple. If war came, Russia would most certainly attempt to extend its gains at Ottoman expense, particularly in the east, where it continued to foment Armenian terrorism and agitation. With Russia on the Entente side it would be difficult to secure protection from England and France. On the other hand, Germany had no territorial ambitions in the Middle East; its own strategic interests required limitation of further Russian expansion. While its Austrian ally long had coveted Ottoman territory, its acquisition of Bosnia and Herzegovina had increased its minority problems to such an extent that it hardly would be anxious to add further Slavic territories to its domains. Cemal actually made some approaches to the Entente early in 1914 to counter Enver's efforts, but Britain and France brusquely rejected the offer. Germany, on the other hand, alone among the major powers, seemed willing to join the Ottomans in open alliance. Since there remained so much popular opposition to an attachment with Germany, however, the negotiations were conducted secretly with only the grand vezir and foreign minister, Sait Halim, and Enver initially involved. The actual alliance treaty was signed only on August 2, 1914, after the war had already begun in Europe. It provided for Ottoman intervention in support of the Central Powers only if Germany's assistance to Austria in the Serbian crisis (Austria had declared war on Serbia on July 28) led it to war with Russia, an eventuality that did in fact take place only four days later, on August 6. The Ottomans agreed to leave the von Sanders mission "with an effective influence on the general direction of the army," and Germany in turn promised to help protect Ottoman territorial integrity against Russia. The treaty was kept secret and was to be disclosed only when the parties chose to invoke it.[138] Cemal and the other cabinet members did not know about the agreement until after it was signed, and while some demurred they finally were persuaded to go along, because it was already a fact and also because it did provide the empire with the protection against Russian ambitions that Britain and France had refused to supply.[139]

The main problem the government leaders now had was to get the empire to fulfill the obligations which they had agreed to in the face of general public opposition as well as the legal requirement that the agreement itself had to be ratified by the Chamber of Deputies as long as it was in session. The latter problem was solved by getting the sultan to send the Chamber home until the end of November as soon as it had authorized the 1914 fiscal year budget as well as various provisions for conscription in case of war.[140] The treaty continued to be kept secret in the hope of securing delivery of the battleships from Britain, with strict press censorship being established to make sure it would not leak out. With the deputies adjourned, the government could promulgate temporary laws with the sultan's assent, subject only to the requirement that they be approved some time in the future by the Parliament, so it now was able to go ahead with a series of laws and regulations preparing the way for full mobilization.[141] Public opinion remained a problem, but here Britain provided the Ottoman government with the help it needed. At the beginning of August the two ships being built in England were ready. Ottoman crews had been sent to pick them up. A "Navy Week" had been scheduled in Istanbul, with lavish ceremonies to welcome the largest and most modern ships of the fleet. On August 3, however, without any advance warning, and apparently without any knowledge of the Ottoman-German treaty that had just been signed, Winston Churchill, first lord of the admiralty, suddenly announced that in view of the emerging European conflict the ships had been commandeered for use by the British navy. Intense popular disappointment and anger swept the Ottoman Empire. Thousands of schoolchildren who had contributed money for construction of the ships swarmed through the streets to protest this example of what appeared to be British perfidy and bigotry.[142] It seemed very likely that if the German alliance had been announced at this moment, it would have been welcomed without demurral.

At this point, however, most of the ministers who had not been privy to the original agreement began to hold back. It was uncertain that Germany would in fact win in the west. Germany also was asking the Porte to support it and Austria actively against Russia, but Sait Halim was demanding formal protection against possible Balkan attacks in return, and even Enver was demanding compensation in the form of the Aegean Islands and western Thrace, with Greece and Bulgaria being compensated elsewhere.[143] At this point, however, two other battleships provided Germany and Enver with a convenient means of gaining the desired Ottoman entry. Two cruisers of the German Mediterranean squadron, the *Goeben* and the *Breslau,* had bombarded French bases in North Africa (August 3) and then fled into the eastern Mediterranean with the British navy in hot pursuit. Enver arranged for them to pass into Ottoman waters (August 11). When Britain protested that the Ottomans, as neutrals, either had to intern the ships and their crews or had to send them out to fight, the ships were transferred to the Ottoman fleet by a fictitious sale, being given the names *Yavuz Sultan Selim* and *Midilli,* with the squadron commander, Admiral Souchon, becoming commander of the Ottoman Black Sea fleet while his sailors were given fezzes and Ottoman uniforms and enlisted into the sultan's navy.[144] Most members of the cabinet continued to oppose entry into the war at least until the desired safeguards had been secured. Enver and Cemal advocated policies that would bring the empire into war on Germany's side, while Talat mediated between the two groups. Germany by now was anxious for the Ottomans to enter, proposing attacks into the Crimea or around the Black Sea against Odessa and toward the Suez Canal to divert the Russians and the British. Britain and Russia however began to encourage Ottoman neutrality and started negotiations to provide the long-desired guarantees of Ottoman independence and territorial integrity, even offering concessions regarding the Capitulations if only the Porte stayed out.[145] The relative stalemate that emerged on the western front and Russian victories in the east further strengthened the Ottoman advocates of peace and hindered Enver.

Enver and his allies therefore sought out and pushed through more provocations to force the Western allies to declare war on the Ottoman Empire. On September 7 the Capitulations were abolished, inflicting a major blow on the economic interests of the Entente powers in particular.[146] On September 14 Cemal, as minister of the navy, authorized Admiral Souchon to take his ships into the Black Sea and attack any Russian ships or bases he might encounter in the name of the Ottoman government, thus most certainly providing the desired war provocation, but this was countermanded by the cabinet.[147] On October 1 the Ottoman customs duties, traditionally controlled by the powers through the Capitulations, were unilaterally increased by 4 percent. The foreign post offices in the empire, including those of Germany, were closed and taken over. Foreigners in the empire were made subject to Ottoman laws and the Ottoman courts.[148] Enver personally ordered the Dardanelles and the Bosporus closed to foreign ships to prevent the Entente from intervening.[149] On October 11 the German ambassador secretly promised delivery of 2 billion kuruş of gold to the Ottoman government if war was declared,[150] and arrival of the gold on October 21 cleared the way for action. Enver and Cemal again gave Souchon authority to attack the Russians in the Black Sea to force a war declaration without consulting the remainder of the cabinet. On October 29 Souchon bombarded the Russian coast and destroyed several Russian ships. Sait Halim and Cavit were furious and got Enver to send a cease-fire order to Souchon as well as apologies to the Entente governments.[151] But it was too late. Enver's apologies included claims that the incidents had in fact been provoked by the Russian Black Sea fleet. On November 2 Russia replied with a war declaration on the Ottoman Empire. Britain and France followed three days later. Britain proclaimed the annexation of Cyprus and, soon afterward (December 18), the independence of Egypt under British protection. Khedive Abbas Hilmi, who was then visiting the sultain in Istanbul, was replaced with Hüseyin Kâmil Paşa, son of the old khedive, Ismail. Already on November 11 the sultan had replied with the Ottoman war declaration, using his claim to be caliph to add a proclamation of Holy War against the Entente and asking all Muslims, particularly those in the British and Russian possessions, to join in the campaign against the infidel. Interest payments on all the public debt bonds held by investors of the enemy nations were suspended also, thus relieving the Porte of a considerable financial burden, at least until the war was over, and adding one more crack to the crumbling order of European society (December 17, 1914).[152]

War Mobilization and German Military Control

In Istanbul the war declaration was followed by full mobilization. Heavy new war taxes were introduced and non-Muslims again were required to pay conscription exemption taxes. Pensions were provided for the families of bureaucrats called to the army. The Parliament was prorogued so that additional measures could be pushed through without delay. Enver decided to assume command of all Ottoman operations in eastern Anatolia and Cemal took control of Syria, both also retaining their ministerial positions and dominance in Istanbul. Liman von Sanders, who preferred an active role, was made commander of the First Army initially, caring for Istanbul and its environs, subsequently succeeding Cemal as commander in Syria while the latter concentrated on the ministry. Von Sanders' chief assistant, General von Seeckt, became chief of the Ottoman General Staff, von der Goltz succeeded von Sanders as chief of the First Army for a time and then of the Sixth Army in Mesopotamia; von Falkenhayn became adviser and then commander of the Ottoman army in Palestine; and German officers were put in command of the Ministry of War departments of Operations, Intelligence, Railroads, Supply, Munitions, Coal, and Fortresses.[153]

War Aims and Strategy

The Germans first considered Ottoman assistance mainly against those Balkan states that joined the Entente. But most of those states either remained neutral or joined the Central Powers. Rumania was being courted by both sides but had ambitions that included territories controlled by members of both : Bessarabia, held by Russia, and Transylvania, Bukovina, and the Banat, held by Austria, with each bloc promising it the territory held by the other to get its help, or the lack of same, against the Austrian invasion of Serbia and of Russian Galicia, which opened the war in August 1914. Serbia, under attack from Austria, had no choice but to join the Entente, hoping to be compensated with Bosnia and Herzegovina as well as access to the Adriatic. But the Ottomans could not reach Serbia, since Greece remained neutral, divided between King Constantine's desire to join the Central Powers because of his relationship with the kaiser and that of Prime Minister Venizelos to join the Entente in order to get Istanbul, which also was desired by Russia, a major member of the Entente. The real key to the situation was Bulgaria, which the Entente could only offer Ottoman territory in eastern Thrace and the parts of Macedonia held by Serbia since the Balkan wars. But since the Central Powers offered the Greek-held territories in eastern Macedonia as well as the parts of the Dobruca lost to Rumania in 1913, Bulgaria joined them instead on September 6, 1915. After Greece refused Serbia's request for assistance in accordance with their 1913 alliance, Entente forces invaded Greece (September 21, 1915) to help Venizelos prevail over the king, but they were forced to retire, enabling the Austro-German-Bulgarian alliance to invade and conquer Serbia from all sides (October 1915). The Austrians also took Albania, while a final Entente effort to enter Bulgaria through Greek Macedonia failed, and the Bulgars occupied most of Macedonia as a result.

With Bulgaria cooperating quite successfully with the Central Powers, German strategy therefore dictated that the Ottomans be kept away from their ambitions in the Balkans, where they would most certainly clash with the Bulgars, and instead be used mainly to serve the German interests of diverting the Russians and British from the main war theaters in Europe. The Ottomans therefore were to advance into Egypt and to invade the Caucasus, with an appeal for a Holy War enhancing their efforts in these campaigns as well as undermining the enemy's ability to mobilize its forces. Germany also attempted to secure the support of the Iranian government against Russia, but Russia responded with an occupation of the northern part of the country (November 1915), forcing the Germans to set up their own puppet government and army at Kermanşah. This stimulated the British to reply along the Persian Gulf in the south, with Sir Percy Sykes leading the South Persian Rifles, based in Shiraz, which, with some assent from the Tehran government, prevented the Germans from getting help from the Persian Gulf and so forced them to depend entirely on what they could get from the Ottomans and von der Goltz in Iraq.

The Ottoman war aims, as elaborated by Enver and his colleagues, were mostly but not entirely the same as those of the Germans. Enver really hoped to use the war to regain substantial territory in Macedonia and Thrace as well as in eastern Anatolia, Egypt, and Cyprus. As his ambitions developed, however, they also came to include the liberation of the Turkish people of the Caucasus and Central Asia from Russian and Armenian tyranny, the establishment of the influence of the sultan-caliph over all other Muslims in the world, particularly those of India, and the final liberation of the empire from the economic and political domination of all the powers, including the Germans.

The Northeastern Front, 1914–1916

German strategy prevailed at the outset, so that Enver had to concentrate first on his ambitions in the east. Almost as soon as he became minister of war he began to strengthen the Third Army, based at Erzurum, which covered the entire area of northeastern Anatolia from Lake Van to the Black Sea; thus it was ready to attack almost as soon as war was declared. Enver made a last effort to secure the support of the sultan's Armenian subjects, but a meeting at Erzurum with Armenian leaders from Russia as well as the Ottoman Empire was unsuccessful. Russia already had promised the Armenians an autonomous state including not only the areas under Russian rule in the Caucasus but also substantial parts of eastern Anatolia with, presumably, Russian help in finishing the job begun in 1877 of driving out or eliminating the Muslims who still comprised the vast majority of their populations. The Armenian leaders told Enver only that they wanted to remain neutral, but their sympathy for the Russians was evident, and in fact soon after the meeting "several prominent Ottoman Armenians, including a former member of parliament, slipped away to the Caucasus to collaborate with Russian military officials," making it clear that the Armenians would do everything they could to frustrate Ottoman military action.[154]

Still Enver decided that the Ottoman security forces were strong enough to prevent any Armenian sabotage, and preparations were made for a winter assault. Meanwhile, Czar Nicholas II himself came to the Caucasus to make final plans for cooperation with the Armenians against the Ottomans, with the president of the Armenian National Bureau in Tiflis declaring in response:

From all countries Armenians are hurrying to enter the ranks of the glorious Russian Army, with their blood to serve the victory of Russian arms. . . . Let the Russian flag wave freely over the Dardanelles and the Bosporus. Let, with Your will, great Majesty, the peoples remaining under the Turkish yoke receive freedom. Let the Armenian people of Turkey who have suffered for the faith of Christ received resurrection for a new free life under the protection of Russia.[155] Armenians again flooded into the czarist armies. Preparations were made to strike the Ottomans from the rear, and the czar returned to St. Petersburg confident that the day finally had come for him to reach Istanbul.

Hostilities were opened by the Russians, who pushed across the border on November 1, 1914, though the Ottomans stopped them and pushed them back a few days later. On December 21 Enver personally led the Third Army in a counterattack. He aimed to cut the Russian lines of communications from the Caucasus to their main base at Kars and to reoccupy it along with Ardahan and Batum as the first step toward an invasion of the Caucasus. Key to the envelopment operation was the border town of Sarıkamış, which lay astride the main route from Kars to the north. The Ottomans managed to occupy the town on December 26, but the Russians then retook it. A subsequent Russian counteroffensive in January caused the Ottoman army to scatter, with over three-fourths of the men lost as they attempted to find their way back to safety. Ottoman morale and military position in the east were seriously hurt, and the way was prepared for a new Russian push into eastern Anatolia, to be accompanied by an open Armenian revolt against the sultan.[156]

In the initial stages of the Caucasus campaign the Russians had demonstrated the best means of organizing a campaign by evacuating the Armenians from their side of the border to clear the area for battle, with the Armenians going quite willingly in the expectation that a Russian victory would soon enable them not merely to return to their homes but also to occupy those of the Turks across the border.[157] Enver followed this example to prepare the Ottoman side and to resist the expected Russian invasion. Armenian leaders in any case now declared their open support of the enemy, and there seemed no other alternative. It would be impossible to determine which of the Armenians would remain loyal and which would follow the appeals of their leaders. As soon as spring came, then, in mid-May 1915 orders were issued to evacuate the entire Armenian population from the provinces of Van, Bitlis, and Erzurum, to get them away from all areas where they might undermine the Ottoman campaigns against Russia or against the British in Egypt, with arrangements made to settle them in towns and camps in the Mosul area of northern Iraq. In addition, Armenians residing in the countryside (but not the cities) of the Cilician districts as well as those of north Syria were to be sent to central Syria for the same reason. Specific instructions were issued for the army to protect the Armenians against nomadic attacks and to provide them with sufficient food and other supplies to meet their needs during the march and after they were settled. Warnings were sent to the Ottoman military commanders to make certain that neither the Kurds nor any other Muslims used the situation to gain vengeance for the long years of Armenian terrorism. The Armenians were to be protected and cared for until they returned to their homes after the war.[158] A supplementary law established a special commission to record the properties of some deportees and to sell them at auction at fair prices, with the revenues being held in trust until their return. Muslims wishing to occupy abandoned buildings could do so only as renters, with the revenues paid to the trust funds, and with the understanding that they would have to leave when the original owners returned. The deportees and their possessions were to be guarded by the army while in transit as well as in Iraq and Syria, and the government would provide for their return once the crisis was over.[159]

The Entente propaganda mills and Armenian nationalists claimed that over a million Armenians were massacred during the war. But this was based on the assumption that the prewar Armenian population numbered about 2.5 million. The total number of Armenians in the empire before the war in fact came to at most 1,300,000, according to the Ottoman census. About half of these were resident in the affected areas, but, with the city dwellers allowed to remain, the number actually transported came to no more than 400,000, including some terrorists and agitators from the cities rounded up soon after the war began. In addition, approximately one-half million Armenians subsequently fled into the Caucasus and elsewhere during the remainder of the war. Since about 100,000 Armenians lived in the empire afterward, and about 150,000 to 200,000 immigrated to western Europe and the United States, one can assume that about 200,000 perished as a result not only of the transportation but also of the same conditions of famine, disease, and war action that carried away some 2 million Muslims at the same time.[160] Careful examination of the secret records of the Ottoman cabinet at the time reveals no evidence that any of the CUP leaders, or anyone else in the central government, ordered massacres. To the contrary, orders were to the provincial forces to prevent all kinds of raids and communal disturbances that might cause loss of life.[161]

In April 1915, even before the deportation orders were issued, Dashnaks from Russian Armenia organized a revolt in the city of Van, whose 33,789 Armenians comprised 42.3 percent of the population, closest to an Armenian majority of any city in the empire. While the local Armenian leaders tried to restrain their followers, knowing they would suffer in any prolonged communal conflict with the Muslim majority, they were overwhelmed by the agitators from the north, who promised Russian military assistance if only they showed their loyalty to the czar by helping to drive the Muslims out. The Russian army of the Caucasus also began an offensive toward Van with the help of a large force of Armenian volunteers recruited from among refugees from Anatolia as well as local Caucasian residents. Leaving Erivan on April 28, 1915, only a day after the deportation orders had been issued in Istanbul and long before news of them could have reached the east, they reached Van on May 14 and organized and carried out a general slaughter of the local Muslim population during the next two days while the small Ottoman garrison had to retreat to the southern side of the lake. An Armenian state was organized at Van under Russian protection, and it appeared that with the Muslim natives dead or driven away, it might be able to maintain itself at one of the oldest centers of ancient Armenian civilization. An Armenian legion was organized "to expel the Turks from the entire southern shore of the lake in preparation for a concerted Russian drive into the Bitlis vilayet."[162] Thousands of Armenians from Muş and other major centers in the east began to flood into the new Armenian state, including many who broke away from the deportation columns as they passed the vicinity on their way to Mosul. By mid-July there were as many as 250,000 Armenians crowded into the Van area, which before the crisis had housed and fed no more than 50,000 people, Muslim and non-Muslim alike.[163] Early in July, however, Ottoman reinforcements pushed the Russo-Armenian army back. It was accompanied by thousands of Armenians who feared punishment for the killings that had made possible the short-lived state. "The panic was indescribable. After the month-long resistance to Cevdet Bey, after the city's liberation, after the establishment of an Armenian governorship, all was blighted. Fleeing behind the retreating Russian forces, nearly two hundred thousand refugees, losing most of their possessions in repeated Kurdish ambushes, swarmed into Transcaucasia,"[164] with as many as 40,000 Armenians perishing during the flight. The number of refugees cited encompassed essentially all those Armenians of the eastern provinces who had not been subjected to the deportations. Those who died thus did so mainly while accompanying the retreating Russian army into the Caucasus, not as the result of direct Ottoman efforts to kill them.[165]

The Dardanelles Campaign

Ottoman fortunes varied widely during the war, sometimes exceeding the fondest hopes of Enver and his associates, at other times approaching the kind of catastrophes experienced during the Balkan Wars. In general, however, the army showed evidence of the modernization program carried out by the Young Turks and their German advisers just before the war, achieving far more success than its enemies and friends had expected until it was undermined by the general collapse of the Central Powers near the end of the war. Certainly one of the most spectacular and successful Ottoman operations came at Gallipoli, where an Allied effort to force the Dardanelles was beaten back with heavy losses almost at the start of the war.

The first impetus for the campaign came from Russia, which to facilitate its campaign into eastern Anatolia asked the British to mount some kind of operation to divert the Ottomans. After considerable debate the British decided in favor of an operation proposed by Churchill, a naval expedition "to bombard and take the Gallipoli Peninsula (the western shore of the Dardanelles), with Constantinople as its objective." Capture of the Straits would force the Ottomans from the war, frustrate German efforts to expand their influence in the east, facilitate planned British campaigns in Mesopotamia, safeguard the British position in Egypt, and open the way for supplies to be sent to Russia through the Black Sea.[166]

The first British squadron moved to the attack on February 19, 1915, expecting to force the Straits with ease and pass on to Istanbul. But the British were not aware that the Ottoman First Army, now led by von Sanders, had mined the waterway and mounted strong batteries on the surrounding hills; hence a month went by with their objectives unfulfilled and three battleships lost. As a result, the operation was changed to include landings by British troops from Egypt starting on April 25. In the meantime, however, von Sanders himself came to Gallipoli and strengthened the Ottoman defenses even more. Command over the Ottoman troops was given to the brilliant Mustafa Kemal, who now began to gain the popular reputation that was to serve him so well after the war. Against strong Ottoman opposition a force composed mainly of Australian and New Zealand contingents managed to establish a bridgehead north of Kabatepe on the western side of the peninsula. Landings at other points on the eastern side were only partly successful, and at very heavy cost, however, while the Ottomans remained in their fortifications and beat the British assaults back again and again. The French were able to land at Kumkale, on the Anatolian side of the Straits, but this had little strategic significance and they finally were recalled to help at Gallipoli.

Basically, however, there was a stalemate as summer approached. The only hope for the British commanders was additional reinforcements, the kind of major involvement that Britain really could not afford. Churchill now was relieved as first lord, though he remained on the War Cabinet. The British still felt they were too deeply involved to pull out; thus in an effort to sever the Ottomans' north–south communications down the peninsula from Istanbul, another landing was made farther north of Kabatepe at Anafarta Limanı (Sulva Bay) on the night of

August 6–7, while another force mounted the heights of the Kilid-i Bahr fort, which overlooked the Straits from the east. But again they were kept to the beaches by fierce Ottoman resistance, with heavy casualties, and as the year came to an end the War Cabinet decided to give up the entire operation. The only real British success of the campaign was, in fact, the evacuation, which took place on December 18–19 on the western banks and January 8–9, 1916, at the tip of the Gallipoli Peninsula. The attempt to force the Straits had failed. There were 213,980 casualties on the British side, and the Ottomans had 120,000 dead and wounded. The Ottomans remained in a position to move against the Russians or the British in Egypt. The Bulgars and Germans were encouraged to go ahead with their campaign against Greece. Russia continued to be isolated from British assistance. And the morale of the Central Powers was immensely improved.[167]

The Iraqi Front

The Ottoman action in Iraq was entirely defensive against British efforts to defend their oil wells and refineries in southern Iran, gain control of new ones recently discovered around Mosul and Kerkuk, in northern Iraq, and counter the Ottoman call for a Muslim Holy War. British operations here were carried out mainly by forces from India. Political affairs were directed by Sir Percy Cox, for many years British resident among the Arabs of the Persian Gulf. Overall Ottoman defenses were directed at first by Süleyman Askeri Bey, one of the young men promoted suddenly by Enver, having enthusiasm but no real experience. The British landed at Fao, where the Şatt ul-Arab runs into the gulf (November 6, 1914), beat back the resistance of a few Ottoman brigades, and took Basra (November 21) against little resistance, with the only Ottoman success being a raid across the river into Iran against the oil establishments at Abadan. General Sir Charles Townshend then led a British offensive up the river toward Baghdad with the ultimate objective of reaching the Russians in the Caucasus and joining in a common effort to overrun Anatolia and force the Ottomans from the war in the east. The British advance, however, was extremely slow. They made no effort to use Arab auxiliaries, as was done in Arabia and Syria, preferring to wait for supplies landed at Basra and transported up the river. The climate was difficult, and they avoided long marches during the summer months. British operations were hindered by the need to watch for a possible German offensive from Iran. While the British failed to move quickly to use their initial advantage, the Ottoman defense in Iraq was given to von der Goltz Paşa, one of the ablest German generals in the sultan's service, who soon formed the Iraqi army into an effective fighting force with the help of new contingents sent by Enver after the conclusion of the Caucasus campaign.

The British advance was so slow that they took Kut ul-Amara, 400 kilometers north of Basra, only on September 29, 1915. They then moved toward Baghdad, but now the Ottomans were ready. At Selman Pak, von der Goltz smashed the British (November 22), inflicting heavy casualties and putting them under siege at Kut. Townshend appealed for reinforcements, but they had to come all the way from India. In the meantime von der Goltz sent a detachment under Enver's uncle, Halil (Kut) Paşa, who fortified the course of the Tigris to the gulf, making it impossible for a British relief force to reach Kut quickly even if it had arrived on time. Townshend became so desperate that he asked for Russian help from Iran even though this would bring Russian influence into the areas of Iran and Iraq that Britain preferred to retain as its own sphere of influence. Von der Goltz died of typhus in Baghdad (April 6, 1916), but Halil Paşa pushed the siege at Kut to a successful conclusion, forcing the British to surrender their entire force (April 29, 1916) and causing them to suffer another major defeat soon after Gallipoli was evacuated.

Halil now wished to fortify the Tigris against a possible British return from Basra. But as Ottoman interests again were subordinated to those of the Germans, only a single brigade was left at Baghdad while Halil had to lead the main Ottoman force into Iran to help German ambitions there. The British were able to return, therefore, now under the command of Sir Frederick Maude, who took the offensive in December 1916. Unaware of how weak the Ottoman defenses were along the river, he made his way gradually up the Tigris in a series of outflanking maneuvers, forcing the Ottomans left behind to withdraw rather than to be cut off from the rear. The river was crossed and Kut recaptured on February 22, 1917. Halil then returned from Iran, but he was unable to reach Baghdad before its commander, Kâzım Karabekir, later to find fame in the War for Independence, had to evacuate it to avoid encirclement, enabling the British to take it without resistance (March 11, 1917). Maude moved rapidly north in order to join a Russian force advancing through northern Iran and the Caucasus to make a united effort against Mosul. But he had to stop because of the summer heat, and by the time he resumed his march the Russian army had dissolved because of the advent of the Russian Revolution. In September, however, he took al-Ramadi, on the Euphrates, thus assuring British control of central Iraq. Maude himself died of cholera, but his successor, Sir William Marshall, took the rest of Iraq except for Mosul. It too was occupied following Ottoman withdrawal because of the armistice of Mondros thus precipitating a struggle at the peace conferences to see who would control its rich oil deposits once the war was over.

The Egyptian Campaigns

The British in India and Egypt and the Russians in Central Asia were successful in suppressing the sultan's call for a Pan-Islamic movement. One might say, however, that to the extent that the powers had to maintain large garrisons at home to keep their Muslim subjects from revolting, the call had more success than has generally been admitted. Perhaps its greatest direct success came in Libya, where the Senusis responded by resuming their revolt against the Italians early in 1915, using Ottoman officers and German money to force the Italians to leave most of the desert areas and to concentrate in the coastal areas that they had taken in the early years of the Tripolitanian War. They also began to attack the British in Egypt's western deserts, and, though they were beaten in open battles, they carried on a destructive guerrilla warfare from a base at the Siwa Oasis until it was taken by the British late in 1916.

The Ottomans were encouraged to move into Egypt not only by the deposed Khedive Abbas Hilmi, who assured the sultan that his subjects would rise in revolt, but also by the British, who occupied the port of Akaba, at the northern tip of the Red Sea, thus posing a serious threat to the Ottoman positions in Syria as well as the Arabian Peninsula. In direct response Cemal Paşa was made governor of Syria with the job of organizing and leading an expeditionary force to drive the British from Egypt. After he arrived in Damascus, he started to introduce major reforms in the hope of securing Arab assistance, but emerging Arab nationalism led to local resistance. Cemal was therefore forced to take stern measures to prevent an open revolt from frustrating his plans for Egypt. Thus even as new roads and schools were built, leading nationalist agitators were imprisoned and executed and general suppression followed. His move against Egypt was no more successful than his effort to conciliate the Arabs. He marched a force of some 80,000 men across the wastes of the Sinai Desert in January 1915, but the British had successfully suppressed Arab movements in Egypt through a combination of force and promises for some kind of Arab independence in the future. So Cemal was not greeted with the expected Egyptian uprising, and strong British resistance forced him back from the Suez Canal without any success. Thereafter, the Ottoman threats to the canal and to Egypt were limited to a series of raids, mainly under the command of a Bavarian colonel, Friedrich Kress von Kressenstein. He was helped by a young German major, Franz von Papen, whose subsequent rise to power in Germany led him to a role in the Nazi triumph, after which he was sent back as German ambassador to the Turkish Republic during World War II.

Secret Wartime Promises

As the war went on, the Entente's need to secure allies against the Central Powers led it to make arrangements by which enemy territory, mainly that of the Ottomans, was promised in return for various forms of wartime assistance. This was entirely suitable to the Russians, who wanted to use the war to satisfy their ambitions at the Straits and in eastern Anatolia, but it was quite a change for its allies, who previously had supported Ottoman integrity to maintain the balance of power in Europe. The result was a series of agreements dividing the Ottoman Empire, some of which, particularly those involving the Arab nationalists and the Zionists, were contradictory. The promises were successful in securing effective wartime support, but they gave rise to new conflicts and bitterness in the postwar world.

There were three major agreements concerning the Middle East made during the war. The first, often called the Istanbul Agreement because it purported to settle the question of who should control the Ottoman capital, was concluded by an exchange of notes among Russia, England, and France on March 18, 1915. The principal object of the agreement was to allow Russia to take Istanbul and both Straits, with sufficient land on both sides and islands at their mouths to assure full control of all navigation as well as defenses against outside threats. Russia also was promised eastern Thrace to the Enos–Midye line, which was to be the boundary of Bulgaria, and the Anatolian hinterland of the Bosporus and the Sakarya River to the Gulf of Izmit. Istanbul, however, was to remain as a free port for all the Entente members, with Russia agreeing to allow free commercial navigation through the Straits as well as the British and French spheres of influence in Anatolian Turkey. The Muslim Holy Places in Mecca and Medina and the rest of Arabia and the Arab world would be detached from the Ottoman Empire and placed under independent Arab rule. The division of Iran between Russia and Britain, as agreed on originally in 1907, would be continued. The neutral zone formerly maintained as a buffer between them would go to the latter, with the exception of Isfahan and the eastern sections near Afghanistan, to be taken over by Russia.

The Treaty of London (April 26, 1915) concluded by the Entente powers with Italy allowed the latter to secure full sovereignty over the Dodecanese Islands, which it never had really evacuated. In addition all Ottoman rights in Libya were transferred to it along with a part of the Mediterranean coast of Anatolia, mainly the province of Adalya, in case Turkey in Asia was partitioned after the war.

Probably the best-known and most significant of the wartime secret agreements regarding the Middle East was that reached between Britain and France on May 16, 1916, as the result of a long series of negotiations carried on by Sir Mark Sykes and Georges Picot (and thus usually called the Sykes-Picot Agreement) to adjust their claims to the Asiatic portions of the Ottoman Empire. Britain also was negotiating with the Zionists and with Şerif Hüseyin of Mecca to secure their support against the Ottomans, promising the former a Zionist homeland in Palestine and the latter recognition of Arab national aspirations in return, and France wanted to make certain that its ambitions for rule in the Levant were not sacrificed in the process. By the terms of the agreement Britain was to secure southern Iraq, from Baghdad to the Persian Gulf, along with the ports of Haifa and Acre in Palestine. France in turn would get the coastal province of Syria, the province of Adana, and all of Cilicia. Palestine would be internationalized, while the remaining Arab territories between the British and French areas would be formed into an Arab state or confederation of Arab states. This area would also, however, be divided into spheres of influence, with France controlling the rest of Syria and northern Iraq, including Mosul, while Britain got the area stretching between Palestine and Iran. Russian acquiescence was secured with promises of compensation in much of eastern Anatolia, including Erzurum, Trabzon, Van, and Bitlis and a large part of northern Kurdistan, from Muş and Siirt to the Iranian border. The treaty was kept secret because the provisions concerning the Arabs and Palestine contradicted the promises then being made to the Arab leaders. Italian agreement was later secured at St. Jean de Maurienne (April 17, 1917), where Italy's area around Adana was defined to include most of southwestern Anatolia, including the provinces of Izmir and Konya and the districts of Menteşe, Adalya, and İçel, along with a sphere of influence in western Anatolia to the Bosporus. This also had to be kept secret since Venizelos of Greece was being wooed at the same time with promises of Izmir and parts of southwestern Anatolia. The only part of the Sykes-Picot Agreement that was subsequently altered was that concerning Mosul, which in December 1918, after the British occupied it, was surrendered to England by France in return for a share in the Iraqi oil fields once they were developed.

The promises made by the British to the Arab leaders involved those of Arabia rather than Syria, since the latter had been suppressed by Cemal Paşa. There were two main Arab leaders in the peninsula, Abdulaziz Ibn Saud, who had reestablished Saudi-Wahhabi power in the Necd in the early years of the century, and Şerif Hüseyin, who ruled the Holy Cities as an autonomous vassal of the sultan. The British agreement with Ibn Saud (December 26, 1915) was patterned on similar arrangements previously made with other Arab chiefs along the Persian Gulf. He was recognized as ruler of the Necd and its environs; Britain would pay him a subsidy and defend him against outside attacks. In return he promised only to be friendly with Britain, to refrain from attacking other British-supported chiefs, and to keep other foreign powers out of his lands. It was thus a passive arrangement, not requiring him to attack the Ottomans, but, by keeping him from attacking Şerif Hüseyin, it did encourage the latter to more open action. The British agreement with the latter was concluded in negotiations with Sir Henry McMahon in Cairo early in 1916. By its terms Britain promised to support full independence for almost the entire Arab world, from the 37th parallel to the Persian Gulf in the east, south to the Arabian Peninsula and the Red Sea, and west to the Mediterranean, but excluding coastal Syria west of Damascus, Homs, Hama and Aleppo, Lebanon, and possibly Palestine, though the exact definition was left vague in regard to the latter. Britain would help the new Arab governments establish themselves in return for the right to be their principal foreign adviser and for a special position in the provinces of Baghdad and Basra. It would guarantee the Holy Places against attack and provide Şerif Hüseyin with a subsidy and military assistance to help him organize what, in fact, became the Arab Revolt. Of course, these promises already had been violated by the Sykes-Picot Agreement and by similar wartime promises made to the Zionist leaders of England and America, incorporated into the Balfour Declaration, accepted by the British cabinet, and communicated to the Zionists on November 2, 1917, in which the British government stated that it would "view with favor the establishment in Palestine of a national home for the Jewish people" and "use their best endeavors to facilitate the achievement of this object, it being clearly understood that nothing shall be done which may prejudice the civil and religious rights of existing non-Jewish communities in Palestine or the rights and political status enjoyed by Jews in any other country."

Beginnings of the Arab Revolt

In the meantime, with McMahon's promises in hand Şerif Hüseyin proclaimed the Arab Revolt on June 5, 1916, soon following with a declaration of himself as "King of the Arab Countries," though Allied objections, particularly on the part of France, subsequently caused him to modify this to no more than "King of the Hicaz." The Ottoman army in Arabia was stationed in the Yemen, at the Holy Cities, and along the new Hicaz Railroad, which connected Medina with Damascus, and it assumed a mainly defensive role. Hüseyin organized the bedouins under his control into a guerrilla army entrusted to the command of his son, Emir Faysal, with the advice of several British officers, including T. E. Lawrence, whose later claims to have inspired the movement seem somewhat exaggerated. The immediate effect of the revolt was to cut the Hicaz Railroad and overrun the Ottoman garrisons at Mecca and Cidda. All the other towns in the Hicaz soon were also under rebel control with the exception of Medina, which remained under siege, and the Yemen was entirely cut off. Another Arab force commanded by Emir Faysal was organized to move north to assist a British push from Egypt into Syria. But with the barren wastes of the Sinai Desert as well as a strong Ottoman army in Syria, now commanded by von Sanders and Mustafa Kemal, the British took their time. Though the Arab Revolt concentrated in the Arabian Peninsula disrupted the Ottoman position there, it had yet to make the significant overall contribution the British expected.

The Russian Occupation of Eastern Anatolia

Despite the victory at Kut ul-Amara, the Ottomans were unable to react more actively to the Arab Revolt or the expected British push from Egypt because they were diverted by a Russian campaign into eastern Anatolia. One force moved southward around Lake Van and toward Muş while another, in the north, advanced directly from Kars toward Erzurum, which it besieged and took (February 16, 1916). The worst massacre of the war followed as over a million Muslim peasants and tribesmen were forced to flee, with thousands being cut down as they tried to follow the retreating Ottoman army toward Erzincan. Enver sent Ahmet Izzet Paşa, former minister of war, to organize a counteroffensive force near Erzincan with the help of men who had just arrived from their victory at Gallipoli. But his effort to retake Erzurum was frustrated by supply shortages, since many Turkish peasants in the area had been slaughtered or had fled, while most of the Armenians had been deported to Syria or had gone behind the Russian lines to avoid entrapment in the battle. The Russians went on to overwhelm Trabzon (April 18, 1916) and Erzincan (late July), cutting the Sivas–Erzurum road before they were slowed down by the arrival of winter. The Ottomans were more successful in the south, blocking the Russian push around Lake Van but at heavy cost, and the Russians were able to prepare for a general offensive toward Harput and Sivas as well as along the Black Sea coast as soon as spring came. Armenians throughout the world also were organizing and sending volunteer battalions to join the effort to cleanse eastern Anatolia of Turks so that an independent Armenian state could be established. But the Russians, while happy to use Armenian support, were no more anxious than were the Ottomans to see the lands of eastern Anatolia and the Caucasus formed into an independent state. Therefore, in the negotiations for the Russian annex to the Sykes-Picot Agreement, mention was made only about Russian acquisition of the northeast and that of France in Cilicia, with no mention at all about any obligation to give the Armenians autonomy or independence. Though eastern Anatolia was for a time under Russian occupation, the 1917 revolution in Russia freed the Ottomans to face new dangers confronting them in Iraq, Arabia, and Syria.

The Yıldırım Army

With the Russian offensive halted and the Arab Revolt still in the Hicaz, Iraq seemed to be the most pressing danger for the Porte during the winter of 1917. Enver at first tried to get the Germans to live up to their promises to send men and arms as well as money if Ottoman lands should be occupied or in danger, as was the case here. But when he received no definite reply, he decided to do what he could to organize a special strike force on his own, first to regain all Iraq and then to move against the British and Arabs in the west, giving it the name Thunderbolt (*Yıldırım*) to signify the intent of its structure and operations. Appointed to command the army were General von Falkenhayn and 65 German officers, who came with about 6000 selected German soldiers intended to weld it into a force with unlimited power and range. With Russia now convulsed in revolt, it was felt safe to reinforce the new army with selected regiments from eastern Anatolia as well as five divisions that had been fighting with the Germans in the west. By early 1917, the *Yıldırım* Army, now also known as the Seventh Army, had 14 divisions ready to go, and it was given several of the best Ottoman officers available, including Mustafa Kemal, who thus once again was in a key situation to demonstrate his abilities.

Resumption of the Syrian Campaign, 1917

The *Yıldırım* Army never got to Iraq, however. After a year of preparation the British expeditionary force in Egypt had finally begun its Syrian campaign, under the command of Sir Archibald Murray (December 1916). The Ottoman defenses were weakened by conflicts of jurisdiction between the *Yıldırım* Army, sent to defend Gaza, and the regular Fourth Army of Syria, which remained under Cemal Paşa. The British were initially beaten back at Gaza with heavy losses (March 1917), leading to Murray's replacement by Sir Edmund Allenby. But the advance then proceeded methodically, with the invaders going slowly enough to build a railroad to keep them supplied while Faysal's Arab army moved through the interior east of the Jordan, taking Akaba (July 6) and harassing the Ottomans with raids and other forms of sabotage.

Once the summer heat had passed, the British offensive resumed in October against Ottoman defenses stretching across much of Palestine from Gaza on the Mediterranean to Bir us-Sebi, at the edge of the desert. After a major week-long battle (October 26–November 1) the latter fell to a combined British-Arab assault, and Acre followed after a three-day siege. The Allies moved ahead on a wide front against Ottoman resistance, taking Ramla and Jaffa in mid-November and moving ahead along the coast while Jerusalem held out against several massive assaults before finally surrendering on December 9. The *Yıldırım* Army was forced to move its headquarters back from Jerusalem to Nasiriye, and then after the latter's fall (December 27) into Syria, causing Cemal to leave his command and return to Istanbul. Syria's defense and administration were left entirely in von Falkenhayn's hands, while Mustafa Kemal, never very anxious to accept German orders, resigned his post and returned to Istanbul to see if he could get the government to make better arrangements for the following year's campaign.

Political Changes in Istanbul

Meanwhile, in the capital, Grand Vezir Sait Halim resented the manner in which his colleagues had pushed the empire into war, and, after several unsuccessful efforts to counteract the power gained by Enver, he resigned (February 3, 1917). Talat's appointment in his place brought the CUP triumvirate into power in name as well as fact. The new grand vezir remained also as minister of the interior to add to his political control of the situation. The Russian invasion of eastern Anatolia, compounded by drought and the conscription of cultivators, affected agricultural productivity and led to severe food shortages in Istanbul and other major cities. The typhus epidemic that had begun among the warring armies in eastern Anatolia soon also began to decimate the civilian population. Large tax increases, government repression of opposition, and the news of German losses on the western front also caused severe morale problems that the government no longer could counter by patriotic appeals. The entry of the United States into the war also had a severe effect (though the Ottoman Empire never declared war on it), which was not really counteracted when Emperor Wilhelm II made a state visit to Istanbul in September 1917 followed by a return visit to Germany of Crown Prince Yusuf Izzeddin Efendi. Despite the censorship and police control, more and more people began to question openly why the Porte had become involved in such a long-drawn-out and disastrous war, and no clear answer could be given. Only the Russian Revolution seemed to give cause for hope.

The Bolshevik Revolution and the Treaty of Brest-Litovsk

The revolution of 1917 did, indeed, offer hope for all the Central Powers. Soon after the Bolsheviks had taken control, they published the secret agreements to partition the Ottoman Empire (November–December 1917), greatly embarrassing the Allies. Lloyd George attempted to nullify the effect by stating that Britain really did not wish to "deprive Turkey of its capital or of the rich and renowned lands of Asia Minor and Thrace . . . homelands of the Turkish Race," [168] while Woodrow Wilson stated in the twelfth of his Fourteen Points that "The Turkish portions of the Ottoman Empire should be assured a secure sovereignty," but there were few in the empire who believed them in the light of the Russian disclosures. Only the Bolsheviks clearly renounced Russia's rights under the agreements, declaring (December 5, 1917) that "the treaty for the partition of Turkey which was to deprive it of Armenia is null and void," though adding that "after cessation of military operations the Armenians will be guaranteed the right of free determination of their political destiny."[169]

Peace negotiations with the Central Powers went on at Brest-Litovsk after December 1917 despite the efforts of the Entente powers and some Soviet elements to keep Russia in the war to frustrate further German ambitions. The Ottoman representatives tried to regain the east Anatolian provinces in the process, with opposition coming more from Germany than Russia. Only Enver's strong protests at the last minute secured inclusion of a provision that in addition to the immediate evacuation of the provinces of eastern Anatolia and their return to Turkey, the districts of Ardahan, Kars, and Batum also would be cleared of Russian troops. Russia agreed also to abandon Iran and the Caucasus as well as Poland, Lithuania, the Ukraine, Finland, and the Baltic provinces and to demobilize the Armenian bands found in Russia as well as the occupied Turkish provinces. Enver got German agreement allowing him a free hand in the Caucasus and northwestern Iran, thus securing an opportunity to fulfill his Pan-Turkic ambitions in these areas.

Competition in the Transcaucasus

It was one thing for the Ottomans to reclaim their eastern provinces by treaty – it was another to actually occupy them. Enver hoped to replace the lost Arab provinces with a Turkish empire that would extend through the Caucasus into the Crimea and Central Asia. But the native national groups in the Caucasus, the Georgians, Azerbaijani Turks, and Armenians, had formed their own independent Transcaucasian Republic at Tiflis, with its own government and army (December 1917). And the British and Germans had their own ambitions to control the oil of Baku as well as the manganese and other ores of Georgia.

Following the revolution a truce was signed between the Republic and the Ottoman Empire at Erzincan (December 18, 1917), but the Armenian national units began a general massacre of the remaining Turkish cultivators in the southern Caucasus and eastern Anatolia, leaving over 600,000 refugees out of a former population of 2,295,705 Turks in the provinces of Erzurum, Erzincan, Trabzon, Van, and Bitlis before the war.[170] With the truce clearly violated, Enver responded with a general offensive. The Third Army forces around Diyarbekir and Muş commanded by Ali Ihsan Saip and those at Erzincan led by Kâzım Karabekir soon emerged as the early leaders of the Turkish War for Independence. On February 14 Kâzım took Erzincan, forcing the thousands of Armenian refugees who had gathered there to follow their army back into the Caucasus. Kâzım now became commander in charge of further operations to free the Muslims of the Caucasus just as the news came of Brest-Litovsk, and he went on to occupy Kars, Ardahan, and Batum as the Russians retired. When the Armenians at Erzurum refused to surrender, he took it by storm (March 12), thus breaking the Armenian hold in the north and forcing those concentrated at Van in the south to retreat without further resistance.

Peace negotiations with the Transcaucasian Republic began at Trabzon. Enver offered to surrender all ambitions in the Caucasus in return for recognition of the Ottoman reacquisition of the east Anatolian provinces at Brest-Litovsk. The Armenians pressured the Republic to refuse, however, so that hostilities resumed and the Ottoman troops overran new lands to the east as the Russians retired. Thousands of Armenians who had retired behind the battle lines expecting a victory which would enable them to settle in new homes in eastern Anatolia now were forced to flee into Armenia proper. Erivan became so crowded that "anarchy, famine and epidemic" were the result.[171] A new peace conference opened at Batum (May 11), with the Ottomans extending their demands beyond the Brest-Litovsk provisions to include a number of districts around Tiflis as well as Alexandropol and Echmiadzin, through which a railroad could be built to connect Kars and Julfa with Baku, key to Central Asia. In addition, Enver insisted that Ottoman merchants gain free right of passage through the Caucasus and that the Transcaucasian Republic reduce its armed forces to prevent future Armenian threats to Anatolia. The Armenian and Georgian members of the Republic's delegation began to stall, however, and so the Ottoman army moved ahead once again into areas of Russian Armenia that had not been under the sultan's control since the seventeenth century. Hundreds of pleas for help against persecution on the part of their Turkish inhabitants provided Enver with more than enough pretext. But the Germans, of course, also were interested in taking over the area. So in response to Armenian appeals channeled through German missionaries, they pressured Enver to keep his forces in eastern Anatolia against the possibility of British advances in Iraq and Syria. They even tried to get the Ottomans out of Batum, which as the terminus of the oil pipeline from Baku could become a center for the shipment of raw materials from Central Asia to the factories of Germany.

In the end, with German encouragement, the Georgians broke up the Transcaucasian Republic, forming their own independent state under German guarantees (May 26, 1918), with the Armenians and Turkish Azerbaijanis following suit soon afterward. Germany also agreed with Russia (August 27, 1918) to keep the Ottomans away from Georgia and Baku in return for Russian promises to send some of the latter's oil to fuel the kaiser's warships. It was at this point, however, that a British force came from Iran under the command of Major General L. C. Dunsterville (called "Dunsterforce") to keep the Caucasus out of German and Ottoman hands, reaching Baku in mid-August. Here the Russian Social Revolutionaries and Armenian Dashnaks had combined to drive the Bolsheviks out and establish their own regime, so the situation was quite fluid. Talat in the meantime succumbed to German pressure and signed an agreement (September 23) promising Ottoman withdrawal from the Caucasus and pressure to get the nascent Azerbaijani Republic to favor German economic and political interests. With Dunsterville in Baku, however, the Germans had to abandon their opposition to an Ottoman advance. Enver sent a new push through the Caucasus that took Derbend (September 10), cutting Baku off from the north. Dunsterville was forced to sail away, much to the unhappiness of the local Russians and Armenians, who were forced to flee to Erivan as the Ottomans occupied the city and made it into the new capital of the Azerbaijani Republic. In protest the Bolsheviks repudiated the Treaty of Brest-Litovsk with the Ottomans, but this was of little consequence, since by now they had no force to back up their claims.

Collapse of the Ottoman Empire, 1918

Enver's victories in the Caucasus were, however, gained at the expense of the other fronts. Even as his forces were advancing to the Caspian, the British were moving into the heartland of the empire from the south. Mehmet V Reşat died on June 28, 1918, and was replaced quietly by Abdulmecit's eldest son, Mehmet VI Vahideddin, who became even more of a puppet of the CUP than his brother had been. The capital was filled with starving refugees. There were massive food shortages and the inevitable typhus, and a new Allied blockade of the Dardanelles further increased these problems.

Almost as if on signal, the Allies began mopping up on all fronts. In Iraq the British occupation of the north continued, now in conjunction with their forces from Iran. Kerkuk fell on May 6 and the remaining Ottoman defenders were routed 40 kilometers to the north at Altın Köprü. A second force went up the Tigris, routed a series of Ottoman ambush efforts, and finally occupied Mosul soon after the armistice. In Syria the Ottoman resistance was stronger, with the army commanded by von Sanders, joined again by Mustafa Kemal, at least holding together as Allenby pushed it farther northward. The fall of Nablus and breaking of the Şeria River line (September 20, 1918) broke the organized Ottoman defenses, with Haifa and Acre both succumbing to the invaders on September 23. The Arab nationalists in Damascus openly revolted against its Ottoman garrison; thus it was evacuated (October 1), Aleppo and Homs fell without resistance a few days later. The French fleet soon occupied Beirut (October 6), and Tripoli and Alexandretta followed (October 14) as the Ottomans began to retire quickly into Anatolia toward Adana to make a new stand on home territory.

The Armistice of Mondros

There was, however, to be no further resistance. As Talat returned from Berlin, he saw the beginning of the end of the Bulgarian army, which led to its acceptance of the Allied surrender terms on October 2. With the direct Ottoman connection with Germany thus severed, the fate of the Ottoman empire was sealed. Within the Allied camp the British gained the right to send their forces from Salonica through Thrace to Istanbul, with their Allies gaining only token representation. This gave Britain control of Istanbul and the Straits on land and sea, enabling them to impose the final armistice terms on the Ottomans without consulting the other Allies to assure their control of the Ottoman capital as soon as the armistice was put into effect.

Talat initially joined the German efforts to make armistice overtures through President Wilson (October 5), relying on his Fourteen Points to save the empire from the kind of retribution advocated by the other Entente countries. Armistice overtures also went through other channels and were finally referred to the commander of the British Mediterranean squadron that had been blockading the Dardanelles, Admiral Calthorpe, who went to Mondros on October 11 to make final arrangements. Talat and the CUP cabinet already had resigned on October 8, but no one could be found to assume responsibility for a week until Ahmet Izzet Paşa, former commander in the east, finally accepted the grand vezirate. For the purpose of concluding peace he formed a new cabinet (October 14), which included several CUP members (in particular Cavit Paşa as minister of finance), though the triumvirate stood aside and soon afterward fled. The British delayed the final meeting at Mondros for two weeks to enable their forces to occupy Mosul and Aleppo and make sure that they, rather than the French, would dominate Istanbul and the Straits. The Ottoman delegation, now headed by the new minister of war, Hüseyin Rauf Orbay, was finally brought to Mondros only on October 27, and four days later the armistice agreement was concluded.

The Armistice of Mondros, signed ten days before the fighting stopped on the western front, provided for a total and unconditional surrender, a considerably harsher arrangement than that imposed on the Christian members of the Central Powers. The Straits were to be opened at once, their forts surrendered to Allied crews, and passage facilitated for Allied warships sailing into the Black Sea for action against the Bolsheviks in southern Russia. All mines were to be removed or their locations communicated to the Allied commanders. Allied prisoners, and all Armenians held in Ottoman prisons, no matter what their crimes, were to be freed immediately. Ottoman forces were to be demobilized and surrendered except where their presence was temporarily needed to keep order. Ottoman warships were to surrender, and all ports were to be opened to Allied ships. The Allies were to be allowed to take over important forts, railroads, telephone and telegraph facilities, harbors, quays, and the tunnels leading through the Taurus in Cilicia. Ottoman forces still operating in the east were to surrender to the nearest Allied troops. The Ottomans were to supply the occupation forces, without charge, with coal, food, and whatever other supplies they needed. German and Austrian military and civilian officials in the empire were to be turned over to the Allies and communications with the Central Powers cut. The Allies were put in charge of all food supplies for the empire's civilian population. Finally, "in case of disorder in the six Armenian provinces, the Allies reserve for themselves the right to occupy any part of them," with Sis, Haçin, Zeytin, and Ayıntap to come under immediate occupation.[172]

The armistice terms went into effect on October 31, 1918. Ottoman troops began laying down their arms, and the Allies prepared to occupy Istanbul and the other major cities. The Ottoman Empire thus was placed in the hands of the Entente Allies, led by Britain, who at long last were in position to do with it as they wished. The six eastern provinces already were being called Armenia. The Greeks came to Istanbul in the guise of victors in consequence of Venizelos' last-minute entry on the Allied side, and they were not very far behind in pressing their case. Vengeance was, indeed, for the victors.

The Allied Occupation

Ottoman compliance with the truce provisions went very quickly. Liman von Sanders turned his Syrian command over to Mustafa Kemal and returned to Istanbul. After the *Yıldırım* Army reached Adana and surrendered to the Allies, the latter also went back to the capital (November 13). Allenby's forces immediately spread out to occupy their share, and the French landed to take up the areas allotted to them in Cilicia, including Mersin, Tarsus, Adana, and all the Taurus tunnels.[173] The British took those parts of Mosul originally assigned to the French in the Sykes-Picot Agreement and surrendered later in return for oil concessions.[174] In the east it soon became apparent that the Allies were preparing to give the Armenians not only the six provinces specified at Mondros but also the three districts of Kars, Ardahan, and Batum, which had even smaller Armenian populations and had been returned to the empire by Russia only recently.[175] The British intentions seemed all too clear when, during February, Armenian officials assumed most civilian positions in the occupied eastern provinces.

In north-central Anatolia, efforts unfolded to establish a Greek state in the ancient Pontus region, encompassing the districts of Samsun, Amasya, and Sivas. A secret Greek society looking for such a state had been established in Merzifon in 1904, and it had developed into a widespread movement, giving the Greek government a golden opportunity to press its claims. On March 9, 1919, British forces landed at Samsun and went on to occupy Merzifon, leading Greek bands to revolt openly and to slaughter their Muslim neighbors in the hope of founding the new state. Order was partly restored, but with great difficulty, by the Ottoman police helped with some reluctance by the British.[176]

In the southwest the Allied occupation was a joint affair because of the conflicting claims for territory by the Italians by virtue of the wartime agreements, and the Greeks, who now sought to change the settlement to fulfill their old dream of restoring the Byzantine Empire. The Allied fleet that occupied Izmir (November 7) was commanded by a British officer, but it included ships and men sent by France as well as the disputing parties. The command of individual districts as well as the blockade still enforced against Anatolia was alternated among the different nationalities. Elsewhere in the southwest the Italians occupied Marmaris, Antalya, and Burdur to take the positions promised them in the treaty of St. Jean de Maurienne (January–April 1919) and tried also to establish a claim on Konya, though this was prevented by a British detachment that had earlier occupied the town.[177]

Finally, the greatest prize of all was Istanbul and the Straits, which after the withdrawal of the Russian claims had been without formal claimants until the British assured their own control preceding and following the armistice agreement. On November 13 a large Allied fleet sailed through the Straits and landed at Istanbul. The city was formally placed under Allied occupation, with military control mainly in the hands of British troops. Overall political and administrative control was given to Admiral Calthorpe as Allied high commissioner, governing with the help of a three-man High Commission, with British, Italian, and French members. The shores of the Bosporus were originally occupied solely by the British, but on November 15 the European side was turned over to French forces.[178] Allied authority in the Ottoman government was assured by appointing commissioners to supervise the ministries to make sure that the civilian authorities would do whatever the high commissioner wanted.[179]

The Allied forces entered the Ottoman Empire with an unshakeable belief in the truth of their own propaganda, that the Turks had slaughtered millions of Christians for no reason whatsoever, forfeiting their right to rule even themselves and demonstrating once again the essential superiority of Western civilization over that of Islam. Admiral Calthorpe himself stated that "it has been our consistent attitude to show no kind of favour whatsoever to any Turk . . ." and "All interchange of hospitality and comity has been rigorously forbidden. . . ."[180] That the minorities intended to use the Allied occupation for their own benefit was demonstrated time and again as the occupying troops marched into the major cities and were welcomed by throngs of Greeks and Armenians waving Allied flags and kissing and hugging their deliverers. The feeling was reciprocated by the Allies in hundreds of incidents. Turks and other Muslims were replaced by Christians in most of the local governments as well as in the railroads and other public utilities. Muslims were discriminated against in public places. When the state schools were reopened, only Christians were allowed to attend, while Muslim children had to remain in the streets. Perhaps most cruel of all, Christian missionaries were put in charge of the major orphanages and they often used their positions to identify as

Christian thousands of Turkish youths who had lost their families during the war, applying the general rule that the children were Armenian or Greek unless they could prove the contrary, a difficult task indeed in a land where records had been destroyed and entire families scattered.[181] In many of the occupation areas, especially in eastern Thrace, southwestern Anatolia, Cilicia, and the eastern provinces, the entire machinery of local governments, and in particular the local police forces, were turned over to the minorities in preparation for the final partition of the country. The latter in turn massacred large numbers of recently discharged Ottoman soldiers as well as thousands of civilians without any visible effort by the Allied forces to interfere. Only the Italians in the south made some efforts to control the minorities and protect the Muslim population.[182]

The Peace Conferences

As the Paris Peace Conference began to meet in January 1919, various plans were put forward to partition what was left of the Ottoman Empire, with only conflicts of interest among the victors rather than consideration of the national rights of the defeated delaying a settlement. The main differences between the British and French delegates came not so much over the Turkish area but, rather, over the Arab lands, with the former, now urged on by T. E. Lawrence, desiring to satisfy the Arab national claims mostly at the expense of the Syrian areas originally assigned to France, and the latter insisting on its share so as to retain its traditional position in the Levant. Emir Faysal came to the peace conference as the principal Arab representative, insisting on full recognition of Arab national rights and fulfillment of the wartime promises to the Arabs. When he visited England and France before coming to the conference, he learned of French resistance and, to get British support, signed an agreement with the Zionists (January 3, 1919) by which he welcomed Jewish immigration to Palestine and the establishment of the Jewish national home envisioned in the Balfour Declaration, but only in an Arab state made fully independent. Zionist representatives came to Paris to gain international recognition of the Balfour Declaration by including it in the peace treaties and also to prevent the establishment of an Arab state in Palestine, preferring instead British control, under which they felt they could develop the kind of home they had envisaged.

Greece had entered the war only at the last minute, and in return for Allied promises, which had been limited due to Italian interests in southeastern Anatolia and those of Britain in Istanbul. Now, however, the brilliant Greek Prime Minister Venizelos came to Paris with a claim to occupy Izmir and much of southeastern Anatolia because of a long historical link between the eastern and western shores of the Aegean and the possibility of their joint economic development as well. Britain supported the Greek claim because of the strong anti-Muslim sentiment at home, fully shared by Prime Minister David Lloyd George, and also a desire to have a friendly state in control of the Aegean to counter any possible future Russian move. The Armenians demanded full independence for their own state, which would stretch from the Black Sea to the Mediterranean as a reward for their "long centuries of suffering" as well as their contributions to the Allies, mainly in the service of the Russians.[183] Despite the exaggerations of these claims, the Armenians were able to gain British support, again in the hope of maintaining a friendly vassal state in eastern Anatolia to fulfill its longstanding hope of establishing a permanent rampart against Russian expansion to the Mediterranean from that direction. Early support received from France in this matter, however, soon turned to hostility when the claims were extended to include the French-occupied areas of Cilicia. The Arab delegations also had the same lands in mind for their independent state. The Kurds, Georgians, and Azerbaijanis disputed other parts of the Armenian claims along with the Turks, who had substantial majorities of the population in the entire area. Iran demanded the Caucasus regions lost to Russia during the nineteenth century, including Armenia and much of the Kurdish area in the southeast. The Republic of Azerbaijan sought the southern districts of Tiflis and Erivan as well as Baku and even Batum and Kars.[184] While the debates went on, the Armenian delegations strove to get Allied support for a plan to forbid the return of any Turks or Kurds to eastern Anatolia and to replace them with Armenian refugees so as to create an Armenian majority. While continuing to express sympathy publicly, Britain and its Allies in fact largely dropped their interest in satisfying these extensive ambitions.

At this point the position of the United States became crucial. It had not been involved in the wartime treaties and was not bound by them, as President Wilson made very clear in his Fourteen Points. His insistence on self-determination conflicted with all the claims being made at the peace conference, with the exception only of those of the Arabs and the Turks. The Armenians in the United States therefore mounted a large-scale campaign to force the President to abandon his principles and support their cause at the conference. Lloyd George began to develop the idea of replacing whatever obligation Britain had to help the Armenians by getting the United States to assume a mandate over the disputed provinces or all of Anatolia, officially proposing it in mid-May just as the Council of Ten decided on a mandate system for the Arab provinces of the empire. In response, Wilson sent two investigative commissions to the Middle East, one to Syria under the leadership of Henry C. King, president of Oberlin College, and Charles Crane, founder of a leading plumbing and toilet manufacturing company, and the other to Anatolia under Major General James G. Harbord. The King-Crane Commission toured Syria and Palestine in July and August 1919, concluding that almost all the Arab inhabitants wanted an independent and united Arab state, including the Lebanon, but that if full independence could not be achieved, they preferred a mandate controlled by the United States or Great Britain, with very strong opposition to France except from a few pro-French groups in the Lebanon. All expressed strong opposition to the establishment of a Jewish home of any kind in their midst. The delegations from Iraq demanded only independence, expressing no mandatory preference. The commission therefore recommended an American mandate over Syria, or otherwise that of Britain, which also would establish mandatory rule over Iraq while both would be constitutional Arab kingdoms. It opposed establishment of a Jewish state in Palestine, recommending instead that it become part of a united Syrian state, with the Holy Places being internationalized. The Harbord Commission toured Anatolia in the same summer. Its report, issued in October 1919, found that most of the existing population was, indeed, Turkish and recommended that in view of the minority claims a single mandate be established over the entire area, including the Caucasus, to provide political and economic unity and facilitate whatever settlement might be agreed on. Wilson, however, was in no position to get the United States into the League of Nations, let alone to assume such a burden, and thus this plan was dropped.[185]

Most of the final treaties dealing with former Ottoman territory were signed in 1919 and early in 1920. The Treaty of Saint-Germain (July 16, 1920) provided for a breakup of the Austro-Hungarian Empire and the surrender of its remaining Slavic areas to the new Confederation of Serbs, Croats, and Slovenes, soon to grow into the kingdom of Yugoslavia. Bulgaria was broken up by the Treaty of Neuilly (November 27). Its western districts went to Yugoslavia while those in the Rhodope Mountains and its stretch of Aegean coastline were transferred to Greece. Bulgaria was partly compensated with Ottoman territory north of Edirne, and it was allowed to maintain a merchant fleet in the Black Sea with free access to the Mediterranean through the Straits. By the Treaty of Trianon (June 4, 1920) Hungary had to cede Transylvania and most of the Banat to Rumania. The Arab portions of the Ottoman Empire were dealt with by a conference held at San Remo, where agreements were reached on assignment of the mandates, with only partial consideration of local Arab desires. Syria went as promised to France, while Britain got its territories in Palestine and Iraq. The mandates were to be only temporary and were to provide the natives with training that would enable them ultimately to achieve full independence. The Balfour Declaration was incorporated into Britain's mandate for Palestine, thus satisfying the Zionist aspirations. France's share in the Mosul oil operations was confirmed, and it was given the right to construct a pipeline across Iraq and Syria to Alexandretta so that it could ship its oil to Europe. Thus was laid the basis for the violence and disturbances that plagued the Arab world until it achieved full independence after World War II. The final treaty with the Ottoman Empire was, however, delayed due to the disputes among the Allies and the seemingly irreconcilable differences among the minority groups. It finally was to be signed only in August 1920 at Sèvres, but in the meantime events in Anatolia deprived it of any practical value.

The Turkish Reaction

The events of the Allied occupation and of the settlement developed in Paris evoked a wide range of reactions within Ottoman government and society. Many Ottomans felt that the only solution was to cooperate with the Allies, especially the British, as the only hope for some kind of compromise to save something for the Turks. This group included Sultan Vahideddin and the Istanbul government, which was led principally by Grand Vezir Tevfik Paşa (November 11, 1918–March 3; 1919, October 21, 1920–November 4, 1922), the sultan's son-in-law Damat Ferit Paşa (March 4, 1919–October 1, 1919, April 5–October 17, 1920), Ali Rıza Paşa (October 2, 1919–March 3, 1920), and Sâlih Hulûsi Paşa (March 8–April 2, 1920), who cooperated fully with the occupation authorities, imprisoning all those cited for crimes, justly or unjustly, by the high commissioners and their subordinates. Talat, Cemal, and Enver fled on a German freighter (November 2), the CUP was disbanded, and its property confiscated. In its place the Liberal Union Party (*Hürriyet ve Itilâf Fırkası*) was revived under Damat Ferit's leadership, and its politicians were happy to gain revenge against the CUP at long last. Declaring that it had been the CUP that had been defeated, not the Turkish nation, it concluded that it was the only party with a wide enough base to rebuild the nation and to govern. But soon its prewar divisions between conservatives and moderates surfaced once again. When the former managed to gain control, the latter, including most of the nationalists, began to look toward the new national movement which, as we shall see, was just beginning to build in Anatolia.[186]

In the meantime, the surviving members of the CUP joined several new political groups. Its parliamentary members formed the Regeneration Party (*Teceddüt*

Fırkası), which espoused a secularist and national policy. This group included several men who later were to rise as leading nationalist figures, the journalist Yunus Nadi, Tevfik Rüştü Aras, later foreign minister, and the historian Şemsettin Günaltay, prime minister in 1949–1950. Though it disavowed any direct connection with the CUP, it attempted to take over many of the latter's local branches as it expanded into Anatolia, in the process putting its leaders in a position to pursue the nationalist cause as soon as their movement in Istanbul was suppressed.[187] Another CUP offshoot was the Ottoman Freedom-Loving People's Party (*Osmanlı Hürriyetperver Avam Fırkası*), which developed its own liberal social and economic policies while emphasizing both popular sovereignty and continuation of the sultanate, more or less the kind of constitutional sultanate that had been attempted before the war. It tried to unite all the Ottoman political groups in the face of the foreign occupation, but the demand of many that all active CUP members be purged from its ranks and lack of cooperation among the different elements led to its collapse.[188]

Another attempt to secure political unification came from the National Congress (*Milli Kongre*), organized by a group led by Abdurrahman Şeref Bey, last court historian, and Dr. Esat, an Istanbul optometrist who had been chairman of the National Education Society (*Milli Talim ve Terbiye Cemiyeti*), which had tried to spread the ideals of Turkish nationalism to the masses during the later Young Turk period. Not a party as such, the National Congress held a series of meetings of delegates from all the major political groups in the capital, trying to reconcile their views, act as a spokesman for the defeated Turks, and mobilize popular opposition to the impending peace settlement. Though the movement failed, it did perform an important function by focusing Turkish public opinion on the immediate problem of enemy occupation and built support for the nationalist movement that eventually rose in Anatolia.[189]

In the face of the CUP revival and the proliferation of political groups opposing the peace settlement and Allied occupation, the sultan finally dissolved the Parliament (December 21, 1918) to deprive them of a forum and enable the government to rule by decree without the need of popular consultation.[190]

It should be recalled that while the CUP had become enmeshed in the military and nationalist aspirations of Enver and his associates, it had risen as a liberal party and had pushed through a number of basic economic and social reforms during the war. These now were systematically disbanded, as the government's alliance with the occupiers became a cover for reaction. Taxes bearing most heavily on the poor were doubled, trebled, and then doubled again to provide the government with needed funds while the rich remained largely untouched. Strict censorship was imposed to curb reactions to government policies as well as those of the occupiers.[191] The army and navy patriotic organizations were dissolved and their assets transferred to the Ministry of War.[192] The new Family Law was abolished,[193] and the ulema restored to power. Control of the religious schools and courts was transferred back to the *şeyhulislam*.[194] The Istanbul University was reorganized to curb student "troublemakers."[195] The religious courts were given their original functions and procedures and the secular courts curbed.[196] The Societies Law was strengthened to control all those who opposed the regime.[197] The Financial Reform Commission was abolished,[198] and the Allied desire to punish Young Turks for the so-called crimes of the former regime was satisfied with the arrest not only of people like former Grand Vezir Sait Halim but also the cream of Ottoman intellectual life, men such as Ziya Gökalp, Fuat Köprülü, and Hüseyin Cahit, who were declared to be implicated in the "massacres" and sent off to detention in Malta early in 1920.

The government was supported by a number of political groups united mainly by their opposition to the CUP and desire to do the best they could under the occupation, of which the most important were the Ottoman Peace and Welfare Party (*Sulh ve Selâmet-i Osmaniye Fırkası*), established in 1919 by the former Amasya deputy Ibrahim Hakkı Paşa and many ulema, and the Friends of England Association (*İngiliz Muhibler Cemiyeti*).[199] There were others who felt that cooperation with the Allies was a necessary evil only and that the Ottomans had to rely on enforcement of the Wilsonian principles to survive. Loyal to the old CUP social and economic programs, they formed several groups, including the General Welfare Committee (*Selamet-i Amme Heyeti*), the Wilsonian Principles Society, which included a number of liberal Ottoman writers among whom was Halide Edip, who through some previous work at Robert College was closer to the British than most of her colleagues and who therefore escaped deportation; also Refik Halit (Koray), Celal Nuri, Hüseyin Avni, Yunus Nadi, and Ahmet Emin Yalman; and the National Unity Party (*Vahdet-i Milliye Heyeti*), founded and led by the old Young Turk leader Ahmet Rıza. Members of these groups approached the Allied officers, explained the Turkish case, and generally tried to secure the same rights of self-determination that were being granted to the non-Turkish peoples of the former empire. But faced with the hostility of the government to their liberal political ideas and of the occupiers to their Muslim heritage, they soon had to join the more radical groups demanding action to save the Turks from their oppressors.[200]

Notes to Chapter 4

1 Edib, *Memoirs,* p. 258.

2 Edib, *Memoirs,* p. 260.

3 *Düstur*[2], I, 9–14.

4 Ahmad, pp. 19–20; Şeyhulislam Cemaleddin Efendi, *Hatırat-ı Siyasiye,* Istanbul, 1336/1917–1918, pp. 10–12.

5 *Sabah,* August 16, 1908; Ahmad, pp. 21–23; Kâmil Paşa, pp. 241–253.

6 *Düstur*[2], I, 1–105.

7 Tunaya, pp. 171–181, 206–210, 239–254.

8 E. F. Knight, *The Awakening of Turkey,* London, 1909, pp. 228–293.

9 Danişmend, IV, 368–369; Ahmad, pp. 24–28; Tunaya, p. 165 n. 4; Bayur, *Kâmil Paşa,* p. 296.

10 TV, December 18, 1908; tr. Ahmad, p. 29.

11 *Düstur*[2], I, 105–108.

12 Bayar, I, 167–171; Farhi, pp. 275–316; Celal Nuri, *İttihad-ı İslam,* Istanbul, 1918.

13 Tunaya, pp. 254–261.

14 Bayar, II, 344, 388, 391, 399, 402, 407, 631, 632.

15 Tunaya, pp. 261–275; Bayar, I, 167–171.

16 Tunaya, pp. 271–72; Farhi, p. 283.

17 Bayar, I, 291–293, 297–298.

18 Farhi, pp. 286–288.

19 Bayar, I, 141–166, 184–214.

20 Bayar, I, 267–288, 297–299.

21 TV, April 28, 1909; *Düstur*[2], I, 166–167.

22 The events of the counterrevolution are found in Sina Akşin, *31 Mart Olayı,* Istanbul, 1972; Ahmet Refik, *İnkilab-ı Azim,* Istanbul, 1324/1908–1909; Ali Cevat-Faik Reşit Unat, *İkinci Meşrutiyetin İlânı ve Otuzbir Mart Hâdisesi,* Ankara, 1960; Tarık

The Young Turk Period, 1908–1918   335

Tunaya, *Hürriyetin İlânı*, Istanbul, 1959.
23 Tunaya, pp. 206–212.
24 Tunaya, pp. 294–302.
25 Tunaya, pp. 275–276.
26 Tunaya, pp. 277–285.
27 Bayar, II, 449–454; Tunaya, pp. 315–344.
28 Tunaya, pp. 285–294.
29 Ahmed, p. 69n.
30 *Düstur²*, I, 638–644; A. Şeref Gözübüyük and Suna Kili, *Türk Anayasa Metinleri*, Ankara, 1957, pp. 70–73; Aristarchi, 7–18; Ahmad, pp. 59–61.
31 *Düstur²*, vols. I, II, III.
32 *Düstur²*, I, 357–363.
33 *Düstur²*, I, 383–385.
34 *Düstur²*, I, 624–629.
35 *Düstur²*, I, 749–751.
36 *Düstur²*, I, 752.
37 *Düstur²*, II, 300–311.
38 *Düstur²*, I, 169–174; Bayar, I, 306; Lewis, p. 213.
39 *Düstur²*, I, 327–329.
40 *Düstur²*, I, 604–608.
41 *Düstur²*, I, 395.
42 *Düstur²*, I, 404–406.
43 *Düstur²*, III, 410–416.
44 *Düstur²*, III, 467–479.
45 *Düstur²*, II, 33–37.
46 *Düstur²*, I, 665–666.
47 *Düstur²*, I, 658–663.
48 *Düstur²*, II, 189–190.
49 *Düstur²*, II, 89, III, 643.
50 *Düstur²*, I, 240, 637.
51 *Düstur²*, III, 30.
52 *Düstur²*, II, 22.
53 *Düstur²*, I, 790, II, 77, III, 395.
54 *Düstur²*, I, 268.
55 *Düstur²*, I, 281.
56 *Düstur²*, I, 322.
57 *Düstur²*, III, 73.
58 *Düstur²*, I, 634, 666.
59 *Düstur²*, I, 742.
60 *Düstur²*, II, 171.
61 Bayur, *Türk İnkilabı Tarihi*, II/4, pp. 400–404.
62 Bayar, II, 439–449; Lewis, p. 214.
63 Bayar, II, 487–496, 644–648.
64 Bayar, II, 488–496, 654–659.
65 Bayar, II, 486–502.
66 Tunaya, pp. 186–188.
67 Tunaya, p. 187; Lewis, p. 216.
68 Bayar, II, 508–515.
69 Bayar, II, 457–474.
70 Bayar, II, 474–482.
71 Ahmad, p. 106; Bayar, II, 482–483; Lewis, pp. 217–218.
72 Tunaya, pp. 345–358.
73 Bayar, II, 517–550.
74 Ahmad, pp. 107–108; Inal, pp. 1812–1815; Halit Ziya Uşaklıgil, *Saray ve Ötesi*, 3 vols., Istanbul, 1940–1941, III, 47–48.

75 Bayar, II, 558–569.

76 *Düstur*[2], VII, 4–7; TV 119, 23 Şaban 1330.

77 Stavrianos, pp. 532–533; Miller, pp. 500–501; *Mufassal Osmanlı Tarihi*, VI, 3485–3487.

78 Skendi, pp. 434–438; Bayar, III, 781–784.

79 *Düstur*[2], VII, 8–14; Bayar, II, 648–653.

80 Bayar, III, 796–802.

81 Bayar, III, 846–879; Miller, pp. 501–504; *Mufassal Osmanlı Tarihi*, VI, 3492–3497.

82 Bayar, III, 802–814, 846–847, 881–886.

83 Bayar, III, 986–993.

84 Bayar, III, 914–932; Ahmad, pp. 114–115.

85 January 17, 1913; Bayar, III, 954–970.

86 Ahmad, pp. 116–119.

87 Ali Fuat Türkgeldi, *Görüp Işittiklerim*, pp. 87–88; Bayar, IV, 1069–1103.

88 Bayar, IV, 1107–1112.

89 Bayar, IV, 1115–1117.

90 Bayar, IV, 1200–1202; Ahmad, pp. 123–124.

91 Ahmad, pp. 126–129.

92 Ahmad, pp. 130–131; Bayar, IV, 1202–1222; Stavrianos, p. 537.

93 Bayar, IV, 1238–1250; Ahmad, pp. 129–130; Türkgeldi, pp. 103–105; Cemal Paşa, *Hâtırat*, pp. 47–53.

94 Bayar, IV, 1250–1251.

95 Bayar, IV, 1312; *Düstur*[2], VII, 15–74.

96 Faik Reşit Unat, "Talat Paşa," *Aylık Ansiklopedi*, II, 442–444.

97 D. Rustow, "Djemal Pasha," EI[2], II, 531–532; Cemal Paşa, *Hâtırat;* Djemal Pasha, *Memories of a Turkish Statesman, 1913–1919*, London, n.d.

98 D. Rustow, "Enver Pasha," EI[2], II, 698–702.

99 Lewis, p. 222.

100 Bayar, II, 421–439; Tunaya, pp. 206–218.

101 The best recent study of Gökalp's life and career is found in Uriel Heyd, *Foundations of Turkish Nationalism*, London, 1950; see also Niyazi Berkes, "Gökalp, Ziya," EI[2], II, 1117–1118; Kâzım Nami Duru, *Ziya Gökalp*, Istanbul, 1949; Ziyaeddin Fahri, *Ziya Gökalp, sa vie et sa sociologie*, Paris, 1935; Ali Nüzhet Göksel, *Ziya Gökalp: hayatı ve eserleri*, Istanbul, 1949; Osman Tolga, *Ziya Gökalp ve iktisadi fikirleri*, Istanbul, 1949; and Cavit Tütengil, *Ziya Gökalp hakkında bir bibliografya denemesi*, Istanbul, 1949.

102 Tunaya, pp. 261–275.

103 Berkes, pp. 340–341.

104 Berkes, pp. 341–343.

105 Lewis, pp. 230–232; Berkes, pp. 338–340.

106 *Düstur*[2], V, 370, 514, 830, 843; VI, 73, 130, 167, 173, 220, 238, 513, 601, 820, 858, 1036, 1342, 1369, 1409.

107 *Düstur*[2], V, 665; VI, 578, 961.

108 *Düstur*[2], VI, 304.

109 *Düstur*[2], VI, 660.

110 *Düstur*[2], VI, 1369.

111 *Düstur*[2], V, 186–217.

112 *Düstur*[2], V, 217, 232, 660.

113 *Düstur*[2], V, 309, 385.

114 *Düstur*[2], V, 244; Lewis, p. 224.

115 *Düstur*[2], VI, 50–58.

116 Ergin, *Belediye*, I, 849–1338; *Düstur*[2], V, 377; Lewis, pp. 223–234.

117 *Düstur*[2], V, 352.

118 *Düstur*[2], VI, 146.

119 *Düstur*[2], VI, 207, 1027.

120 *Düstur*[2], VI, 207.

121 *Düstur²*, VI, 1335.
122 *Düstur²*, IX, 270–271.
123 *Düstur²*, IX, 272–274.
124 *Düstur²*, IX, 692–694.
125 *Düstur²*, IX, 745–753.
126 *Düstur²*, X, 505–508.
127 *Düstur²*, X, 554–557.
128 *Düstur²*, IX, 762–781; X, 52–57.
129 Berkes, pp. 390–391.
130 *Düstur²*, VIII, 853–857.
131 Berkes, pp. 385–388; Lewis, pp. 224–225.
132 *Düstur²*, IX, 99–104.
133 *Düstur²*, IX, 185–186.
134 Berkes, pp. 421–426.
135 Liman von Sanders, *Five Years in Turkey,* Annapolis, Md., 1927; Carl Muhlmann, *Deutschland und die Turkei, 1913–4,* Berlin, 1929; Ulrich Trumpener, *Germany and the Ottoman Empire, 1914–1918,* Princeton, N.J., 1968.
136 Cemal Paşa, *Hâtırat,* pp. 94–106.
137 Cemal Paşa, *Hâtırat,* pp. 109–124.
138 E. Jackh, *The Rising Crescent,* New York, 1944, pp. 10–21; Mühlmann, pp. 15–16; Trumpener, pp. 15–20; Mahmut Muhtar Paşa, *Maziye bir Nazar,* Istanbul, 1341, p. 233.
139 Cemal Paşa, *Hâtırat,* pp. 124–129; Bayur, III/1, pp. 194–274.
140 August 2, 1914; *Düstur²*, VI, 1412.
141 *Düstur²*, VI, 1022, 1023, 1025, 1026, 1030, 1036 and passim.
142 Irfan and Margarite Orga, *Atatürk,* London, 1962, p. 57.
143 Trumpener, pp. 23–25.
144 Trumpener, pp. 29–31.
145 Trumpener, pp. 23–40.
146 *Düstur²*, VI, 554.
147 Trumpener, p. 39.
148 *Düstur²*, VI, 558.
149 Trumpener, pp. 46–47.
150 Trumpener, pp. 49–51.
151 Trumpener, pp. 55–57.
152 *Düstur²*, VII, 125–127; Bayur, III/1, pp. 317–348.
153 Mühlmann, p. 326; Trumpener, p. 373.
154 Richard Hovannisian, *Armenia on the Road to Independence,* Berkeley and Los Angeles, 1967, pp. 41–42; Bayur, III/3, pp. 1–35; FO 2488/58350, 127233.
155 *Horizon,* Tiflis, November 30, 1914, quoted by Hovannisian, *Road to Independence,* p. 45; FO 2485, 2484/46942, 22083.
156 Hovannisian, *Road to Independence,* pp. 45–47; Bayur, III/1, pp. 349–380; W. E. D. Allen and P. Muratoff, *Caucasian Battlefields,* Cambridge, 1953, pp. 251–277; Ali Ihsan Sabis, *Harb Hatıralarım,* 2 vols., Ankara, 1951, II, 41–160; FO 2146 no. 70404; FO 2485; FO 2484, nos. 46942 and 22083.
157 Hovannisian, *Road to Independence,* pp. 47–48; FO 2146/70404, 2130/31341.
158 BVA, Meclis-i Vükela Mazbataları, decisions of May 14/27 and May 17/30, 1331/1915, quoted partly in Bayur, III/3, Ankara, 1957, pp. 35–40; *Düstur²*, VI, p. 609; May 27, 1915; FO 371/9158, 4376/P.I.O. 206.
159 *Düstur²*, VII, 737–740, 788; FO 371, File 4241, No. 170751.
160 The Ottoman population figures are documented on pp. 239–245; the best account of the Armenian movements and claims can be found in Richard Hovannisian, "The Ebb and Flow of the Armenian Minority in the Arab Middle East," *Middle East Journal,* 28 (1974), 20, and *Republic of Armenia,* I, 126; figures on the immigration from the Ottoman Empire to the United States are given in U.S. Department of Justice, *1975 Annual Report,* Immigration and Naturalization Service, Washington, D.C., 1975, pp. 63–64.

161 The best general account of the deportations and the general situation among the Armenians in Anatolia is Bayur, III/2, pp. 18–100, III/3, pp. 35–59, reproducing many secret documents from the Ottoman cabinet meetings held during the war. Close examination of the same documents has revealed no major omissions or exaggerations on the part of Bayur and no evidence to support the charges of official complicity. See also BVA, Bab-ı Âli Evrak Odası, dossiers no, 176908, 189354, 196578, 203987, and 148765, and FO 2130/11985, FO 2488/108070. The most reliable presentation of the Armenian case is in Hovannisian, *Road to Independence,* pp. 48–55.

162 Hovannisian, *Road to Independence,* p. 56; FO 2488, nos. 127223 and 58350.

163 BVA, Meclis-i Vükela mazbataları, debates of August 15–17, 1915; Bab-ı Âli Evrak Odası, no. 175, 321, "Van Ihtilali ve Katl-i Amı," 1 Zilkade 1333/10 September 1915.

164 Hovannisian, *Road to Independence,* p. 56.

165 Bayur, III/3, pp. 30–34; Ali Ihsan Sabis, *Harb Hatıralarım,* II, 185–196; Hovannisian, *Road to Independence,* pp. 53–58; Trumpener, pp. 204–233.

166 M. Gilbert, *Winston S. Churchill,* III, *1914–1916,* London, 1971, pp. 219–223.

167 *Mufassal Osmanlı Tarihi,* VI, 3531–3549; M. Larcher, *La guerre turque dans la guerre mondiale,* Paris, 1926; C. F. Aspinall-Oglander, *Military Operations, Gallipoli,* London, 1929; Alan Moorehead, *Gallipoli,* London, 1956; Gilbert, *Churchill,* III, 248–275, 317–417.

168 *Times,* January 6, 1918.

169 *Pravda,* January 13, 1918.

170 BVA, Bab-ı Âli Evrak Odası, no. 256103; Cevat Dursunoğlu, *Milli Mücadelede Erzurum,* Ankara, 1945, p. 25.

171 BVA, Bab-ı Âli Evrak Odası no. 316745, 363467; Hovannisian, *Road to Independence,* pp. 163–168.

172 *Türk Istiklal Harbi,* I. *Mondros Mütarekesi ve Tatbikatı,* Ankara, 1962, pp. 27–41.

173 *Mondros Mütarekesi,* pp. 57–74.

174 January, 1919; *Mondros Mütarekesi,* pp. 77–106.

175 *Mondros Mütarekesi,* pp. 107–167.

176 *Mondros Mütarekesi,* pp. 173–174.

177 *Mondros Mütarekesi,* pp. 128–149.

178 *Mondros Mütarekesi,* pp. 107–128.

179 Bayar, V, 1421–1423.

180 Calthorpe to Curzon, June 6, 1919, FO 406/41, pp. 131–133, No. 58, reproduced in Şimşir, I, 6–10.

181 Edib, *Turkish Ordeal,* pp. 7–11, 16–18; BVA, Bab-ı Ali Evrak Odası, no. 116235, 314567, 103465.

182 HTVD, no. 4 (June 3, 1953), nos. 64, 65, 68, 69, 71, 77, 83; Ali Fuat Türkgeldi, *Görüp İşittiklerim,* I, Ankara, 1949, p. 188.

183 Gilbert, *Churchill,* IV, *1916–1922,* London, 1975, pp. 472–489; Hovannisian, *Republic of Armenia,* I, 276–283.

184 Hovannisian, *Republic of Armenia,* I, 283–291.

185 A full exposition of the American involvement is found in Harry N. Howard, *Turkey, the Straits, and U.S. Policy,* Baltimore and London, 1974, pp. 51–129.

186 Weiker, p. 43.

187 Tunaya, pp. 412–414; Weiker, p. 42.

188 Tunaya, pp. 406–407; Weiker, pp. 41–42.

189 Tunaya, pp. 417–420; Weiker, p. 43.

190 *Düstur²,* XI, 72; Bayar, V, 1435–1458, 1544–1545.

191 *Düstur²,* XI, 117–119.

192 *Düstur²,* XI, 124, 183.

193 *Düstur²,* XI, 299–300.

194 *Düstur²,* XI, 351–352; XII, 69–70.

195 *Düstur²,* XI, 401–409.

196 *Düstur*², XII, 128–132.
197 *Düstur*², XII, 280.
198 *Düstur*², XII, 435.
199 Bayar, VII, 2179–2217, 2384–2390.
200 Bayar, V, 1440–1443; VI, 1865–1890.

5

The Turkish War for Independence, 1918–1923

The Turks were the only one of the Central Powers able to overturn immediately the vindictive settlements imposed by the Allies following World War I. Because Turkish resistance ultimately was led to success by Mustafa Kemal, it long has been assumed that he created it as well. He did, indeed, do more than anyone else to create the Turkish Republic on the ruins of the Ottoman Empire, but he accomplished this by bringing together elements of resistance that had already emerged. He coordinated their efforts, expressed their goals, personified their ambitions, and led them to victory.

The National Resistance Forces

Resistance appeared from the first days of the occupation while Mustafa Kemal still was in Cilicia. It came initially from within the Istanbul government itself, where many of the officials organized the secret Outpost Society (*Karakol Cemiyeti*) shortly after the armistice and used their positions to thwart the Allied demands as well as to send arms and ammunition to Anatolia. Small boats were loaded in the capital in the cover of darkness and sent out into the Aegean and the Black Sea to deliver their valuable cargoes.[1] There is considerable evidence that Talat Paşa himself stimulated the first resistance movements in Thrace before fleeing the country and that resistance in Istanbul was organized within the Ministry of Foreign Affairs.[2] When Mustafa Kemal, Kâzım Karabekir, and other leading officers returned to Istanbul to protest the demobilization orders, they were warmly received by the sultan and others and appointed to important positions in the areas remaining under direct Ottoman authority, where they could lead opposition almost under the noses of the Allies. As the movement spread through the countryside, many Istanbul officials also did all they could to conceal it from the occupying authorities until it was too late.[3]

Sympathetic members of the central government could have done nothing, however, without the active participation of the mass of the Turkish people. The old Middle Eastern tradition of self-help, of society organizing to govern and defend itself in the absence of effective government, again came to the fore. Organized resistance came first in the areas most seriously threatened by foreign or minority occupation, where Societies for the Defense of the Rights of Turks sprang up to defend local interests. At first they attempted to persuade the occupying authorities that their areas were in fact Turkish and that the imposition of foreign rule would violate their human rights. When such claims were ignored, they assumed local authority and organized their own resistance forces, which have come to be

340

known in Turkish history as the National Forces (*Kuvayi Milliye*). Ranging from roving guerrilla bands to regular volunteer militias attached to local political committees, the National Forces were highly heterogeneous, including not only soldiers but also civil servants, landowners, businessmen, artisans, religious leaders, peasants, nomads, bandits, members of the CUP as well as the other old political parties, women, and children – all united in reaction to the occupation and determined to be free.[4]

Strongly supporting the resistance movement in these early days was the Turkish Communist Party, organized first among Ottoman prisoners in Russian hands, some of whom came to the All-Russian Congress of International Prisoners of War held by the Bolsheviks in Moscow in April 1919, and later formed their own Congress of Turkish Radical Socialists in the same city on July 25 despite the protests of the Ottoman ambassador there at the time. Leader of the Turkish Communists was Mustafa Suphi, a Turkish intellectual who had fled to czarist Russia from the Young Turk police shortly before the war.[5] Their activity in Turkey after the war was predicated principally in reaction to the Allied use of Istanbul and the Straits to send ships, men, and arms into southern Russia to support those opposing the Bolsheviks, though this was supplemented, of course, by a desire to use the chaos in Turkey to establish a Communist regime there. Late in 1919 the Bolsheviks established the Central Bureau of the Communist Organizations of the Peoples of the East under the authority of the Communist International, with Mustafa Suphi publishing propaganda material in Turkish in a daily newspaper called *Yeni Dünya* (New World), printed for a time in the Crimea after it was evacuated by the French and then in Baku after May 1920. The Russians later claimed that thousands of Ottoman Communists joined the national struggle, but this does not seem to accord with the evidence, which indicates that, at best, there was in Anatolia a "small group of underground workers, former Turkish prisoners in Russia, which was not particularly large, but which worked very intensively."[6] By the end of 1920, Suphi's Communist Party had only 200 members in Turkey, mainly in Istanbul, the coal-mining port of Zonguldak (on the Black Sea), Trabzon, and the Caucasus. The Bolsheviks, however, gave general propaganda support to the Turkish resistance movement in the hope that it would relieve them of at least some of the Allied pressure in the south.

Beginnings of the War for Independence

The resistance movement began to develop into a full War for Independence when one of Mustafa Kemal's closest associates in the army, Ali Fuat Cebesoy, was sent to command the Twentieth Army corps in Ankara in March 1919 and began to send out agents to coordinate the national defense forces in the vicinity. On April 13 Kâzım Karabekir, hero of the previous conquests in the Caucasus, left Istanbul by boat to assume command of the Fifteenth Army corps at Erzurum, in charge also of the provinces of Van and Trabzon, with the full intention of inspiring resistance among the soldiers and populace of the area under his command.[7] Soon after his arrival he announced that he would work to free Anatolia from enemy rule and also regain Kars, Ardahan, Batum, and the Turkish portions of the Caucasus.[8] He took over a force that still had some 18,000 men, his first job being to secure the war matériel that the British were preparing to ship back to Istanbul.[9] When he heard that the British had turned Kars over to the new Armenian Republic and that it was preparing a new force to invade Anatolia, he joined the Society for the Defense of the Rights of the Eastern Provinces and vowed a struggle to the end to keep Anatolia Turkish.[10]

The next move came on May 5, 1919, when Mustafa Kemal, the greatest Ottoman military hero to emerge from the war, was appointed inspector general of the Ninth Army, encompassing much of eastern and north-central Anatolia from its center at Samsun, on the Black Sea.[11] His instructions were to restore order and security, gather the arms and ammunition laid down by the Ottoman forces, and prevent organized resistance against the government, exactly what the Allies had been pressing the Istanbul government to do. To undertake this, however, he was given command not only over the army but also over all the civil servants in the area.[12] With such extensive authority it appears fairly clear that he was intended to do much more than just gather arms. It has been suggested that the appointment simply was an accident; that the Allies and the government were anxious to get him out of Istanbul because of his vociferous opposition to the armistice and that this assignment was chosen because it was vacant at the time. Others suggest that his opponents arranged the assignment on the assumption that he would fail and his reputation would be ruined. In fact, however, it seems clear that he was sent because his superiors in the Ministry of War, and possibly the grand vezir and sultan, fully expected him to organize resistance.[13] Whatever the reason, he was urged to leave Istanbul at once before the Allies knew either of his appointment or his instructions, and he did so.

The Greek Invasion

Mustafa Kemal's assignment to Anatolia was followed almost immediately by the event that, more than any other, stimulated the Turkish War for Independence: the Greek invasion of Anatolia. With the United States and Italy opposing the British and French efforts at the peace conference to secure territory for Greece around Izmir, Venizelos sent an expeditionary force to take what he wanted, obtaining advance approval from Lloyd George and Clemenceau and also, at the last minute, from Wilson, who hoped that Italy's imperial ambitions would thus be frustrated and that "self-determination" would result. Legal justification for the landings was found in article 7 of the Mondros Armistice, which allowed the Allies "to occupy any strategic points in the event of any situation arising which threatens the security of the Allies." The National Resistance provided the pretext, and Venizelos needed little persuasion to use it. On May 14, 1919, an armada of British, American, and French warships brought an entire Greek division into the harbor of Izmir. The next day they landed amid a wild reception from the local Greek population, with church bells ringing, priests kissing the soldiers, and men and women falling to their knees before their "liberators." The landing was followed by a general slaughter of the Turkish population. Greek mobs roamed the streets, looting and killing, with those Turks who escaped being arrested by the Allied authorities. In Paris the powers went on to agree on a Greek mandate for Izmir and its vicinity, and the Italian zone was pushed to the south. The Istanbul government protested, but to no avail. The Greek army began moving into Anatolia, ravaging and raping as it went, with the local Greek population taking the opportunity to join in the massacre. By the end of July the Greeks had overcome the local Turkish defense forces and gained control of the greater and lesser Menderes valleys, a far more extensive advance than the Allies originally had intended. At this point the offensive was halted, partly at the insistence of the Allies but also because of the need to consolidate the unexpected conquests before a new offensive was launched.[14]

First Phase of the War for Independence, May 1919–March 1920

The War for Turkish Independence went through several distinct phases. The first began with Kemal's arrival at Samsun on May 19, 1919, and went on for about a year. During this period, his primary concern was to use his position as inspector general as well as his own prestige to secure general acceptance of his leadership. Soon after his arrival he was told stories of terrible Greek atrocities, not only in the southwest but also around Trabzon, where advocates of a Pontus Greek state had anticipated the arrival of the Greek army by instituting massacres of their own to remove the Turkish population.[15] Kemal, however, still was only an inspector. The national groups in the area had their own commanders, and they certainly did not recognize his authority. If anyone, it was to Kâzım Karabekir in Erzurum or to Ali Fuat Cebesoy in Ankara that they looked for leadership. But with the self-assurance that had made him such a great commander at Gallipoli and in Syria and such a difficult subordinate for both the Young Turks and the Germans, he soon began to act as if he was, indeed, the leader who would bring the Turks out of their darkest hour. By the end of May he was already writing to the local resistance forces and governors to suggest ways they might resist the Greeks,[16] and criticizing the grand vezir for not doing more toward this end.[17] He warned the British officers in Samsun that the Turks would never tolerate foreign occupation and sent a confidential letter to the corps commanders under his own authority emphasizing the need to raise a popular guerrilla force until a regular army could be organized for defense. Soon he left Samsun, where he had been under close British supervision, and moved into the interior where he was less likely to be arrested. Though it does not seem that Kemal concerted directly with Karabekir while they were in Istanbul, he now got the latter's agreement on joint action as well as the good news that he had not yet surrendered his own forces' weapons to the British.[18] Thus encouraged, Kemal traveled through the east spreading his message among commanders, governors, mayors, and local resistance forces, with the Greek advance to the Menderes strengthening both his resolve and the response.[19] When the British finally learned what he was doing, they got the Istanbul government to dismiss him and order all officials in Anatolia to refrain from accepting his direction (June 23); but to save the grand vezir further embarrassment Mustafa Kemal simply resigned his commission, thus making him officially a full-fledged rebel though in fact close cooperation with some Istanbul officials continued.

The Amasya Protocol

Mustafa Kemal had already been building a new base of support to replace the authority derived from his official position. On June 19, 1919, he met in Amasya with some of the men who were to join him in leading the national movement: Rauf Orbay, former minister of the navy and Ottoman delegate to Mondros; Ali Fuat Cebesoy, commander at Ankara; and Refet Bele, who commanded several corps near Samsun. On June 21 the three signed the Amasya Protocol, soon afterward accepted also by Kâzım Karabekir, which became more or less the first call for a national movement against the occupation. The message was a simple one:

1. The unity of the Fatherland and national independence are in danger.

2. The Istanbul government is unable to carry out its responsibilities.

3. It is only through the nation's effort and determination that national independence will be won.

4. It is necessary to establish a national committee, free from all external influences and control, that will review the national situation and make known to the world the people's desire for justice.

5. It has been decided to hold immediately a National Congress in Sivas, the most secure place in Anatolia.

6. Three representatives from each province should be sent immediately to the Sivas Congress.

7. To be prepared for every eventuality, this subject should be kept a national secret.[20]

Kemal also wrote a number of leading figures in Istanbul inviting them to join the national struggle, adding that "From now on Istanbul no longer rules Anatolia but will have to follow it," thus providing the rallying cry for the events that were to follow.[21]

While Kemal thus moved to secure national support, he also acted to get what help he could from outside. Just before the Amasya meeting, while in Havza, he met a Bolshevik delegation headed by Colonel Semen Budenny, who offered arms and ammunition in the hope of stemming Armenian expansionism in the Caucasus as well as to close Allied access to southern Russia through the Black Sea. Budenny also urged Kemal to accept Communist ideology for the new Turkey, but the latter said that such questions had to be postponed until Turkish independence was achieved. Thus were laid the bases for the assistance that was to be of utmost importance once the national movement was organized.

The Erzurum Congress, July 23–August 7, 1919

Even before the Sivas Congress was called, the Society for the Defense of the Rights of Eastern Anatolia had arranged a regional meeting to be held in July in Erzurum in response to the threat of further Armenian aggression in the east. Kemal attended it as well, using it to secure support from Kâzım Karabekir and other local nationalist leaders. The Istanbul government ordered Kâzım to arrest Kemal. But Kâzım refused, thus declaring his own revolt as well as his acceptance of Kemal's leadership.[22] The declaration drawn up at the Erzurum Congress, though the protection of the eastern provinces was its original concern, in fact became the basis for the national pact that followed. Its ten-point resolution set forth the principles for which the war for independence was to be fought and won:

1. The province of Trabzon, the district of Samsun, and the provinces of Erzurum, Sivas, Diyarbekir, Elazığ, Van, and Bitlis, sometimes called the "six provinces," are an integral whole which cannot be separated from each other or from Ottoman territory for any reason.

2. To preserve the integrity of the Ottoman Empire and our national independence and to protect the sultanate and the caliphate, it is essential that the national forces be put in charge and the national will be recognized as sovereign.

3. As all occupation and interference will be considered undertaken in be-

half of establishing Greek and Armenian states, the principle of united defense and resistance is resolved. The bestowing of new privileges to Christians in a manner to alter political control and social balance will not be allowed.

4. In case the central government, under foreign pressure, is forced to abandon any part of the territory, we are taking measures and making decisions to defend our national rights as well as the sultanate and the caliphate.

5. We reaffirm the legal rights, as indicated in the laws of the Ottoman state, of non-Muslims with whom we share our Fatherland. The protection of their property, life, and honor being among the basic tenets of our religious practices, national traditions, and legal principles, this policy is confirmed by the consensus of our Congress.

6. We are calling for a decision based on right and justice, one that respects our historic, cultural, and religious rights, and that rejects totally the theory of dividing lands and separating peoples who are within the boundaries established by the armistice signed by the Allies on October 30, 1918 and in eastern Anatolia, as well as in other regions, inhabited by a majority of Muslims and dominated by Muslims culturally and economically.

7. Our people honor and respect humanitarian and progressive developments and are appreciative of our own scientific, industrial, and economic conditions and needs. Therefore, on condition that the internal and external independence of our people and our state, and the territorial integrity of our country shall be conserved intact, we will accept with pleasure the scientific, industrial, and economic assistance of every state which will not nurture imperialistic tendencies towards our country and which will respect the principles of nationality as indicated under Article 6. We await, for the sake of preserving humanity and peace, the urgent signature of a peace based on these equitable and humanitarian conditions, which we consider to be our great national objective.

8. In this historical age when nations determine their own destinies, it is essential that our central government submit itself to the national will. As made clear by past events and their results, government decisions not based on the national will have no validity for the people and are not respected by foreign nations. In consequence, before the nation is forced into taking matters into its own hands to look for a remedy to its anguish, our central government should proceed without delay to convoke the national assembly and submit to it all the decisions to be taken relating to the fate of the nation and the country.

9. "The Society to Defend the Rights of Eastern Anatolia" (*Şarki Anadolu Müdafaa-i Hukuk Cemiyeti*) is the union of societies born out of the sufferings and calamities experienced by our land. This assembly is totally free of party interests. All Muslim compatriots are the natural members of this assembly.

10. A Representative Committee (*Heyet-i Temsiliye*) chosen by the Congress will work in its name to establish national unity on all levels from the village to the province.[23]

Thus Kemal and his colleagues at this point still were declaring that they were working to preserve the Ottoman nation; that all subjects, Muslim and non-Muslim, would have equal rights; that since the government in Istanbul was controlled by the occupiers, the national movement in Anatolia was assuming the burden of protecting the nation's rights; but that all of this still was done in support of the sultan-caliph, to rescue him and to protect in particular the eastern provinces.

Soon afterward a local congress was held at Alaşehir (August 16–25, 1919) so that the local defense organizations also could declare their support for the national movement: "The aim of the congress composed of brothers uniting against the danger to the nation is to unify the national movement and completely drive away the enemy."[24] This set the pattern for other local congresses that followed and manifested general support for the movement, which now was clearly led by Mustafa Kemal.

The Sivas Congress, September 4–11, 1919

Just as the Harbord Commission arrived in Istanbul (see pp. 331–332), Mustafa Kemal opened the National Congress at Sivas. Delegates came not only from the east but from all over the nation, including far-off Thrace. The resolutions adopted at Erzurum now were transformed into a national appeal, and the name of the organization changed to the Society to Defend the Rights and Interests of the Provinces of Anatolia and Rumeli. The resolutions adopted in Erzurum were reaffirmed with minor additions, such as a clause added to article 3 stating that the formation of an independent Greece on the Aydın, Manisa, and Balıkesir fronts was unacceptable. In content and spirit the Sivas Congress basically reinforced the stance taken at the Erzurum Congress.[25]

After the Sivas Congress the nationalists entered a strange in-between period, not yet severing ties with Istanbul but pulling their political and military forces together into a movement that inevitably presaged such a split. On September 22–23 an American investigating committee led by General Harbord came to Sivas and met with Kemal, receiving full assurance that Anatolia was, indeed, Turkish and that no mandate would be allowed or accepted. Additional Defense of the Rights of Turks committees were set up to center the movement's activities, particularly in Konya, Bursa, and other places in the west. In the face of the increasing national resistance, Damat Ferit resigned as grand vezir and was replaced by Ali Rıza Paşa (October 2, 1919), but the latter seems to have cooperated with Kemal and his associates even more than the previous leaders. In October 1919 he sent his minister of the navy, Salih Paşa, to negotiate with Kemal to secure some kind of agreement on national objectives, with the Istanbul government promising cooperation with the nationalists in return. Negotiations took place in Amasya on October 20–22, 1919, resulting in the Second Amasya Protocol. The government was asked to accept essentially all the resolutions of the Erzurum and Sivas congresses and to recognize the legality of the Society for the Defense of the Rights of Anatolia and Rumeli, promising also that the forthcoming session of the Chamber of Deputies would not be held in Istanbul so that it would be free of foreign domination. Provinces inhabited by Turks would not be ceded to enemies. No mandate would be accepted, and the integrity and independence of the Turkish fatherland would be safeguarded. Non-Muslims would be given no privileges that might undermine the national sovereignty and social balance. Only delegates approved of by the Nationalist Representative Committee would be sent to any peace conference with the Entente powers.[26] But Salih Paşa ultimately was unable to get the cabinet in Istanbul to ratify the agreement. Ali Rıza later announced that elections would, indeed, be held for a new Chamber of Deputies, but that it would meet in Istanbul the following January, a clear violation of the Amasya Protocol.

Elections followed. But since most of Anatolia and Thrace were in fact under the control of the nationalists, it was inevitable that their members would be and were elected, with Mustafa Kemal himself being chosen deputy from Erzurum. The Istanbul government thus, in a certain sense, was absorbing the national movement into the Parliament right under the noses of the Allies. It even went so far as to declare that Kemal had not really been dismissed from the army but only had resigned, restoring all his decorations as well as his rank (December 29).

As the elections went forward, the nationalists were immensely encouraged by the Harbord Commission report, which reached them in late November 1919. While recommending an American mandate, it went on to propose that all revenues be controlled by Turks and that foreign control over Turkey's financial machinery cease, including that of the Public Debt Commission. All countries formed out of former Ottoman possessions would have to take their reasonable share of the paper currency, foreign obligations, and reparation obligations of the empire. There would have to be a complete abrogation of all existing commercial agreements, especially the hated Capitulations. All foreign governments and troops should vacate the country. It was, indeed, a partial victory for the nationalists, with only the recommendation on the establishment of a mandate left to be overcome.[27]

The Last Ottoman Parliament

Kemal really did not expect the Allies either to accept the Harbord report or to respect his parliamentary immunity if he went to Istanbul. Hence he stayed in Anatolia, moving the Representative Committee's capital from Erzurum to Ankara so that he could meet with as many deputies as possible as they traveled to Istanbul to attend the Parliament and to keep in touch with them while they met. He also started a newspaper, the *Hakimiyet-i Milliye* (National Sovereignty), to speak for the movement both in Turkey and the outside world (January 10, 1920).

The last Ottoman Chamber of Deputies met in Istanbul starting on January 12, 1920. After the sultan's speech was presented, a welcoming telegram from Mustafa Kemal was read in the name of the Representative Committee, thus manifesting its claim to be the rightful government of Turkey. The British began to sense that something had been put over on them and that, in fact, the Istanbul government was not doing what it could to suppress the nationalists; so they secured the dismissal of both the minister of war and the chief of the general staff. The latter post went to Fevzi Çakmak (1876–1950), an able and relatively conservative officer who was known as one of the army's ablest field leaders and who soon was himself to become one of the principal military leaders of the national movement. On January 28 the deputies met secretly. Proposals were made to elect Mustafa Kemal president of the Chamber, but this was deferred in the certain knowledge that the British would prorogue the Chamber before it could do what had been planned all along, namely, accept the declaration of the Sivas Congress. This was done on February 17 as the National Pact (*Misak-ı Millî*), thus putting the Parliament itself on record as expressing the will of the Turkish people to regain full national integrity and independence:

> The members of the Ottoman Chamber of Deputies recognize and affirm that the independence of the State and future of the Nation can be assured only by complete respect for the following principles, which represent the maximum of sacrifice which must be undertaken to achieve a just and lasting peace, and that the continued existence of a stable Ottoman sultanate and society is impossible outside these principles:

1. The destiny of the portions of Ottoman territory under foreign occupation and peopled by an Arab majority at the time of the signing of the armistice on October 30, 1918 should be determined by a plebiscite of all inhabitants. All such territories inhabited by an Ottoman Muslim majority, united in religion, in race, and in aspirations, are imbued with feelings of mutual respect, concern, and devotion, and form an indivisible whole.

2. We accept a new plebiscite in the case of the three sancaks [Kars, Ardahan, and Batum] which had by general vote decided to join the mother country when they were first freed [from Russian occupation].

3. The juridical status of western Thrace, which has been made dependent on the peace treaty to be signed with Turkey, must also be determined in accordance with a free vote of the inhabitants.

4. The city of Istanbul, which is the seat of the Islamic caliphate and of the Ottoman sultanate and government, as well as the Sea of Marmara must be protected from every danger. So long as this principle is observed, whatever decision arrived at jointly by us and other states concerning the use for trade and communication of the Straits of the Black Sea and the Mediterranean shall be honored.

5. The rights of minorities as agreed on in the treaties concluded between the Allied powers and their enemies and certain of their associates shall be confirmed and assured by us on condition that Muslim minorities in neighbouring countries will benefit from the same rights.

6. Like every country, in order to secure a more effective and well-ordered administration that will enable us to develop our political, judicial, and financial affairs, we also need complete independence and sovereignty as a fundamental condition of our life and continued existence. Therefore we oppose restrictions that are harmful to our political, judicial, and financial development. The conditions of the settlement of our [foreign] debts shall be determined likewise, in a manner not contrary to these principles.[28]

The British authorities were, of course, enraged. The elections and Parliament had been presented to them as means to manifest national support for the Istanbul government, but instead the popularly elected Parliament had supported the man whom they considered to be the principal villain of the time, Mustafa Kemal.

The reply was quick in coming. Ali Rıza officially condemned the national resistance and began sending funds to Anatolia to encourage the organization of bands to oppose it.[29] Soon afterward a major revolt led by the Circassian bandit Ahmet Anzavur (see pp. 353–354) and supported by the British with arms and money rose to capture the area north of Balıkesir.[30] The Allies pressured Ali Rıza to arrest the leading nationalist sympathizers in Istanbul and to condemn Kemal and his associates, and when he refused they forced him to resign (March 3, 1920), with the far more malleable Salih Hulusi Paşa replacing him. The full weight of the government now was turned against the nationalists for the first time. On March 15, 1920, 150 leading civil servants and army officers in Istanbul were arrested and turned over to the Allies for internment in Malta. Included among them were most of the members of the *Karakol* organization, which now was broken up.[31] The next day Istanbul was put under martial law, and Allied troops replaced the Ottoman police in control of the city. Police entered the Parliament and arrested some of its leading members, after which it was dissolved on March 18.[32] The Salih Paşa cabinet was replaced with one headed once again by Damat Ferit Paşa (April 5), who was now determined to carry out the Allied desire to suppress the nationalists. Even the *şeyhulislam,* Dürrizade Abdullah Efendi, declared Kemal and all his associates to be infidels, to be shot on the spot.[33] Soon afterward they were also condemned to death *in absentia* by a special Martial Law Council (*Divan-ı Harb-i Örfi*) set up in Istanbul, setting the stage for a full civil war.

Second Phase of the War for Independence, March 1920–March 1922

The strong measures taken against the nationalists by the Istanbul government inaugurated a distinct new phase in the Turkish War for Independence. For the first time the nationalists claimed the sole right to rule the Turkish people. Mustafa Kemal declared the Representative Committee in Ankara the only lawful government of Turkey and ordered all civilian and military officials to obey it rather than the Istanbul government, since the latter was now fully under Allied control.[34] To make sure that everyone knew he was still fighting in the name of the sultan to rescue him from the Allies, Kemal appealed to the entire Islamic world asking for help against the infidel (March 17).[35] Plans were made to organize a new government and Parliament in Ankara, and the sultan was asked to accept its authority.[36] A flood of supporters moved from Istanbul to Ankara just ahead of the Allied dragnets. Included among them were Halide Edip, her husband, Adnan Adıvar, Ismet Inönü, Kemal's most important friend in the Ministry of War, and the last president of the Chamber of Deputies, Celaleddin Ârif. The latter's desertion of the capital was of great significance. As legally elected president of the last representative Ottoman Parliament, his claim that it had been dissolved illegally, in violation of the Constitution, enabled Kemal to assume full governmental powers for the Ankara regime. On March 19, 1920, he announced that the Turkish nation was establishing its own Parliament in Ankara under the name Grand National Assembly (*Büyük Millet Meclisi*).[37] Some 100 members of the Istanbul Parliament able to escape the Allied roundup joined 190 deputies elected around the country by the national resistance groups. On April 23, 1920, the new Assembly gathered for the first time, making Mustafa Kemal its first president and Ismet Inönü, now deputy from Edirne, chief of the General Staff. The new regime's determination to revolt against the Istanbul government and not the sultan was quickly made evident. It was resolved that:

1. The founding of a government is absolutely necessary.

2. It is not permissible to recognize a provisional chief of state nor to establish a regency.

3. It is fundamental to recognize that the real authority in the country is the national will as represented by the Assembly. There is no power superior to the Grand National Assembly.

4. The Grand National Assembly of Turkey embraces both the executive and legislative functions. A Council of State, chosen from the membership of the assembly and responsible to it, conducts the affairs of state. The President of the Assembly is ex-officio President of the Council. The Sultan-Caliph, as soon as he is free from the coercion to which he submits, shall take his place within the constitutional system in the manner to be determined by the Assembly.[38]

The Assembly thus was the real government, with the Council of State carrying on the daily affairs of government. The time for deciding the fate of the sultanate was postponed to a more propitious occasion, presumably after full independence was achieved. A parliamentary commission was established to draw up a constitution.

The Grand National Assembly as the Ankara Government: The Constitution of 1921

A new system was incorporated into the first constitution of the Turkish nation, passed by the Assembly on January 20, 1921, as the Law of Fundamental Organization (*Teşkilât-ı Esasiye Kanunu*). Both executive and legislative authority were "manifested and concentrated in the Grand National Assembly, which is the sole and rightful representative of the nation." The state of Turkey was to be run by the Assembly itself through the government of the Grand National Assembly. As a legislative body it would promulgate or abrogate all laws, conclude treaties, proclaim war, and the like. As an executive, it would administer "the departments into which its government is divided through the ministers it elects" and "give direction to the ministers, if necessary changing them." The president of the Assembly, Mustafa Kemal, was ex-officio president of the Council of Ministers, but he and the ministers were subject to Assembly direction on all matters. The 1876 Constitution's division of the state into provinces (vilayet), districts (*kaza*), and counties (*nahiye*) was retained. The provinces were made quite powerful and autonomous, with their administrative councils having the right to "organize and administer, in accordance with laws promulgated by the Grand National Assembly, matters relating to religious foundations, religious schools, public schools, health, economics, agriculture, public works, and social aid," while "external and internal political affairs, matters concerning the religious law, justice and the military, international economic relations, general government taxation, and matters concerning more than one province" remained to the Grand National Assembly. The administrators of the districts were to be appointed by the Grand National Assembly but were under the orders of the governors. The counties were defined as "corporative entities with autonomy in local life," and were to be ruled by administrative councils elected by their inhabitants, acting mainly in local judicial, economic and financial affairs. The provinces also were grouped "according to their economic and social relationships" into general inspectorships (*umumî müfettişlik*), whose holders were "charged with the maintenance of public security in general and with controlling the operations of all the departments in the general inspection zones, and with regulating harmoniously the mutual affairs of the provinces," thus in fact controlling the governors and provincial councils under the authority of the Grand National Assembly. All the nationalist forces were incorporated into a united army with a central command. The ministers were to be appointed by and responsible to the Assembly. Elections for the national and provincial assemblies were to be held every two years, for two-year terms, with the sessions being extensible for one additional year in emergencies. The Constitution of 1876, as amended in 1909, remained in force in all areas not covered by the new regulation.[39]

Soon afterward the National Pact was accepted as the Assembly's basic aim. It declared null and void all treaties, contracts, or other obligations signed by the Istanbul government after March 16, 1920, reserving thus for itself the sole right to make agreements and laws in the name of the Turkish people. The Assembly also assumed the right to confirm the appointment of diplomats and other representatives sent abroad, not because this was specifically provided in the Constitution, but since the shortages of trained diplomatic personnel in Ankara made it necessary for such persons to be chosen from among the deputies. One of the first laws passed by the new body was the National Treason Law, which essentially condemned to death anyone who betrayed the nation. Among the first to be affected were Damat Ferit and his associates.[40] Thus was the Ankara government firmly established and institutionalized, and its authority was accepted by most of the country.

The reasons for concentrating so much power in the Assembly varied from member to member. Kemal insisted on the Assembly's supremacy to remove the need for an executive position whose occupant would be like a substitute for the sultan: "The first goal of our struggle is to show our enemies, who intend to separate the sultanate from the caliphate, that the national will shall not allow this. . . . Accordingly there can be no question of designating a head of government, even a provisional one, or a regent-sultan in Anatolia. Therefore we are compelled to form a government without a head of government."[41] On the other hand Kemal's opponents in the Assembly also favored its supremacy, but to limit or obstruct his power and to enable them eventually to supplant him as leader of the national movement. Whatever the reasons, the relative freedom in which the Assembly members were elected provided a representation of different interests never before seen in Ottoman legislative bodies as well as an opportunity for those interests to express and assert themselves. Its members were current and former government officials, both civilian and military (40 percent), professionals (20 percent), local landowners and wealthy businessmen (20 percent), and Muslim religious leaders (17 percent).[42] The members also represented a wide spectrum of political and social beliefs:

There was the conflict of laicism with religious feeling, radicalism with reactionaryism, republicanism with monarchism, Turkism with Ottomanism. There was the ideal of racial interest and unity versus that of the religious community of Islam . . . each of which could survive in its own environment without contacting or harming the others, now come together in the Assembly, to be set against one another daily, with now one now the other emerging victorious.[43]

During most of the War for Independence, these differences crystallized around two interrelated issues involving the future of the Turkish nation – how it should be organized and what its relationship should be with the Russian Bolsheviks, who were offering more help in return for a move toward the left. The two major ideas around which opinions coalesced were called the "Eastern ideal" and "Western ideal." For supporters of the former, the East signified opposition to the Western imperialism that had engulfed the empire and all other Islamic countries, with Bolshevik Russia being the model because it had fought Western imperialism and replaced the czarist regime with a new revolutionary order. The Eastern ideal implied the replacement of the sultan-caliph with a new republican regime based on popular sovereignty and rule.[44] The supporters of the Western ideal, on the other hand, retained a strong attachment to the Young Turk idea of a constitutional regime based on essentially Western foundations. Beyond this, however, and partly in reaction to the Easternists, they supported the old Ottoman order based on the sultanate-caliphate, as limited and controlled by a constitution. They opposed any radical political, social, or economic reforms as well as close relations with the Soviets. Radical proposals from the Easternists, therefore, such as elections on a corporative basis or women's suffrage, were opposed on the grounds that they were no more than Bolshevism.[45] The attitudes of the two groups for or against the Bolsheviks should not be overemphasized, however. Most of the East-ernists were Turkish patriots and reformers in the Young Turk tradition, not just Communist sympathizers as claimed by their opponents. The Constitution of 1921 was mainly their work and reflected the ideals of Rousseau and the French Revolution more than it did the Soviet system.[46] On the other hand what the West-ernists wanted ignored the West's own reaction to the old regime and its growing commitment to the ideals of popular sovereignty. Instead, they emphasized its monarchical traditions and older social and economic systems. The Westernists were concerned with preserving the political and structural aspects of Islam, while the Easternists were attempting to prove that their ideas were compatible with its basic social tenets. The Islamic clergy was on both sides, sometimes holding the balance between them. The ideals of the Turkish Republic in the end were pro-duced by a dynamic interaction between them, not by the triumph of one over the other.[47] Kemal used the war to achieve almost dictatorial powers, and in formulat-ing the programs for the new Turkey came to adopt the radical programs of the Easternists without their Bolshevik overtones, and the constitutional liberalism of the Westernists without the sultanate. The synthesis was achieved in a populist program introduced on September 13, 1920.

The Civil War

With the Istanbul government still operating and also claiming jurisdiction over the entire country, the stage was set for a full civil war. The situation was quite similar to that in Anatolia in the early fifteenth century after Bayezit I's defeat by Tamerlane at the Battle of Ankara. In both cases rule over the Turks was contested by governments ruling in Anatolia and Europe, the empire was threat-ened by foreign invasion, and the land was infested by local rebellions and robber bands. And in both cases it was the heartland of Turkish life and traditions, Anatolia, that produced the victor.

In response to the declarations of the Grand National Assembly, the Istanbul government appointed its own extraordinary Anatolian general inspector (*Anadolu fevkalâde müfettiş-i umumî*) and a new Security Army (*Kuvayı Intizamiye*) to enforce its rights and battle the nationalists, with help from the British, with the latter forming in essence what came to be called the Caliphal Army starting in 1920.[48] Other bands rose to seek wealth and power for themselves in alliance with one or another of the governments, sometimes at the instigation of the Greeks, the British, or even the Communists, sometimes representing the large landowners and old *derebeys* who were seeking to regain their power. Most became little more than bandit forces, manned by a motley assortment of dispossessed peasants, Tatars from the Crimea and Central Asia, and Turkish and Kurdish nomads, always ready for a good fight against whoever was in power. These armies became so powerful that on April 29, 1920, the Grand National Assembly passed a law that prohibited "crimes against the nation" and set up Independence Courts (*Istiklâl Mahkemeleri*) to try and execute on the spot. These courts became a major instrument of the Ankara government to suppress opposition long after independence itself was achieved.[49]

Most famous of the private armies operating in Anatolia during the civil war was the Green Army (*Yeşil Ordu*), which posed a major threat to all sides. Orig-inally it was organized during the winter of 1920 "to evict from Asia the pene-tration and occupation of European imperialism." Its members were former

Unionists, known to and respected by Mustafa Kemal, including their secretary general, Hakkı Behiç Bey, and Yunus Nadi, an influential Istanbul journalist, whose journal *Yeni Gün* (New Day) had just been closed by the British and who in 1924 was to found the leading newspaper of republican Turkey, *Cumhuriyet* (The Republic). Its original objective was to counter the reactionary propaganda spread in Anatolia by agents of the Istanbul government and the Allies by popularizing the national movement and mobilizing the Turkish peasants in support of the national forces. As such it was supported and even encouraged by Kemal.[50] In fact, however, many of its members had a more radical purpose: They wished to combine Unionism, Pan-Islam, and socialism "to establish a socialist union in the world of Islam by modifying the Russian Revolution."[51] As such it soon attracted a number of groups opposing the Ankara government, including not only supporters of the Istanbul government but also anti-Kemalist Unionists and Communists connected with the Third International. This led Mustafa Kemal to get Hakkı Behiç to disband the organization late in 1921, though its various anti-Kemalist elements continued to act on their own during the next two years.[52]

Two other independent armies, both led by Circassians and gaining most of their supporters from the Tatar and Circassian refugees driven into Anatolia by the Russians, were also active. A left-inclined guerrilla movement led by Çerkes Ethem was at first quite successful against the Greeks near Izmir in 1919, and for some time it supported the national movement against the reactionary, right-oriented Caliphal Army and the anti-Ankara movements that the latter stimulated in the eastern Marmara region in 1920. Ultimately, however, Çerkes Ethem became increasingly rapacious toward the civilian population, Muslim and non-Muslim alike. He allied with the Green Army, occasionally supported various Communist manifestos being circulated, and showed no interest in submitting to the central control that was essential for the success of the new nationalist army being built by Ankara. Finally, Kemal sent a major force, which destroyed Çerkes Ethem's army in January 1921, forcing him to flee into the hands of the Greeks and, eventually, to exile in Italy.[53]

A more conservative movement was the force led by another Circassian, Ahmet Anzavur, who with money and arms from the Istanbul government and the British led two major revolts against the nationalists in the areas of Balıkesir and Gönen in October–December 1919 and again from February to June 1920. For a time leading the Caliphal Army as well, Anzavur's bands began to ravage the countryside, leading Mustafa Kemal to oppose him. He was finally beaten and sent on the run by Çerkes Ethem in April 1920, when the latter still was helping the Ankara government. Anzavur raised a new army, but he was defeated and killed and his army dispersed by the nationalists on May 15, 1920.[54]

The strongest local rebellions were in the areas of Bolu, Yozgat, and Düzce, the latter led by the Çapanoğlu *derebey* family, which tried to restore its old power until its army was hunted down and dispersed by the nationalists and its leading members hanged in Amasya in August 1920.[55] Such movements, however, continued to be troublesome in Anatolia well into the republican period, as it took time to reduce the old family forces that were revived by the civil war.

Then there were the Communists, who Mustafa Kemal opposed but felt unable to disperse because he needed help from the Russians. Mustafa Suphi remained in Russia sending propaganda literature into Anatolia. In response to his pleas, Kemal tolerated a number of Communist activities during 1920 including a new joint Communist-Unionist organization in Ankara called the People's Communist

Party (*Türk Halk İştirakiyûn Fırkası*), which had some connection with the Green Army.[56] This organization enabled the Communists to emerge to public view in Turkey for the first time. In addition, on October 18, 1920, Kemal allowed the formation of a separate Turkish Communist Party (*Türk Komünist Fırkası*), but it was operated mainly by some of his close associates in the Assembly.[57] Far less active or radical than the first-named group, it was a government tool to divide and confuse the Communists and their supporters. Soon the former was active enough to cause its suppression. The last straw came when it issued a joint declaration with the Green Army and Çerkes Ethem that they had "approved the Bolshevik party program passed by the Third International . . . and joined to unite all the social revolutionary movements in the country," and adopted the name Turkish People's Collectivist Bolshevik Party.[58] Communist agents became active around Ankara and Eskişehir and cooperated with Unionist groups in Erzurum and Trabzon, which were centers of Enver's supporters throughout the War for Independence.[59] This stimulated Kemal to criticize the Communists for working outside the organ of the people, the Grand National Assembly. After Çerkes Ethem was crushed and the Green Army broken up, he suppressed the Communists and brought their leaders to trial, though the final judgments were suspended until after the Treaty with Moscow was signed in March 1921, and the sentences were relatively light compared to some. The only violent action against the Turkish Communists came when Mustafa Suphi and a few friends entered Anatolia via Kars on December 28, 1920. Though they met with Ali Fuat Cebesoy and Kâzım Karabekir at Kars early in January 1921, they were arrested soon after. As they were being sent by boat to Erzurum for trial, they were assassinated by a group of pro-Enver supporters from Trabzon, apparently because of their fear that Suphi might bring discredit to Enver's efforts.[60]

What, indeed, had happened to Enver and his supporters? Enver, Cemal, Talat, and a few friends had fled from Istanbul the night of November 2, 1918, on a German freighter going to Odessa. From there they had gone on to Berlin, where they lived under assumed names, since the Entente victors were demanding their extradition for the "crimes" of their regime. Soon they were invited by Karl Radek to continue their work in Moscow, with full Bolshevik support for the "Turkish national struggle." Talat remained in Germany, where he was killed by an Armenian assassin on March 15, 1921. Cemal and Enver went to Moscow, and later to Central Asia, where they undertook a series of political activities with the ultimate intention of using the Bolsheviks to regain power in Turkey once the nationalists were defeated. With Bolshevik encouragement Enver proclaimed the organization of the Union of Islamic Revolutionary Societies (*Islam Ihtilâl Cemiyetleri Ittihadı*) and an affiliated Party of People's Councils (*Halk Şuralar Fırkası*), the former as the international Muslim revolutionary organization, the latter as its Turkish branch. On September 1–9, 1920, he attended the Congress of the Peoples of the East at Baku, meeting a Kemalist delegate who was present. But while Kemal generally encouraged Enver's work in the hope of using him to get Bolshevik aid, he never actually committed himself to anything. Enver had a small group of supporters in Anatolia, mainly at Trabzon, and about 40 secret Unionists in the Grand National Assembly were working to install Enver in place of Kemal at the right time. Enver moved from Moscow to Batum in the summer of 1921 just as the Greek offensive began, so that he could enter Anatolia quickly if Kemal was defeated. But following Kemal's victory over the Greeks at the Sakarya (September 1921), Enver abandoned his plans for Turkey and went into

Central Asia in the hope of leading its Muslims against both the British and the Russians. It was while leading a band in pursuance of this aim that he was killed in a battle with Russian forces near Çeken.[61] Cemal Paşa in the meantime had also worked to facilitate Kemal's contacts with the Bolsheviks, and then he spent time training the Afghan army. While passing Tiflis on his way to Moscow he was killed by two Armenian assassins (July 21, 1922).[62]

The Role of the Sultan

In the midst of all these conflicts and difficulties, the question arises whether the sultan was willing or able to provide effective leadership. As related by Sir Horace Rumbold, British ambassador in Istanbul, the ruler's interpretation of the activities and backgrounds of the nationalists indicated a disdain for the movement:

A handful of brigands had established complete ascendancy. They were few in number, but they had got a stranglehold on the people as a whole, profiting by their submissiveness, their timidity or their penury. Their strength lay in the backing of 16,000 military officers who were concerned for their own interests. . . . The Ankara leaders were men without any real stake in the country, with which they had no connection of blood or anything else. Moustafa Kemal was a Macedonian revolutionary of unknown origin. His blood might be anything, Bulgarian, Greek or Serbian for instance. He looked rather like a Serbian! Bekir Sami was a Circassian. They were all the same, Albanians, Circassians, anything but Turks. There was not a real Turk among them. He and his government were nevertheless powerless before them. The hold was such that there was no means of access to the real Turks, even by way of propaganda. The real Turks were loyal to the core, but they were intimidated or they were hoodwinked by fantastic misrepresentations like the story of his own captivity. These brigands were the men who sought his submission. They looked for external support and had found it in the Bolsheviks. The Angora leaders were still playing with them. They might discover and regret too late that they had brought on Turkey the fate of Azerbaijan. Muslim Turks would have no truck with Bolshevism, for it was incompatible with their religion, but if it were imposed on them by force, then what? [63]

Such was the leadership that the last sultan was giving his people in their hour of distress. Though it might be said that the remarks were intended to soothe Allied irritation at the nationalist movement, they contained no redeeming spark of sympathy for those who were trying to save the country.

Ankara's Preparations for War

In the meantime, Kemal was trying to organize his army for the ordeal to follow. The national forces were called back to Ankara to be trained, disciplined, and armed, and a new officers' school was established. An ambassador was sent to Moscow, and Russian arms and ammunition began to flow across the Black Sea in increasing amounts. After the *Karakol* association in Istanbul was broken up by the Allied suppression, a new and wider-based group was founded among the remaining civil servants and officers and called the National Defense Organization (*Müdafaa-i Milliye Teşkilâtı*). Its members again began sending arms and equipment to the nationalists while the telegraphers and postal officials used their positions to confuse the enemy regarding the strength of the nationalist movement.

The Treaty of Sèvres, August 10, 1920

The final break between Ankara and Istanbul came when the latter officially accepted the Treaty of Sèvres, which incorporated the will of the Allies as to how the Turks should be treated. It was, indeed, a vindictive document. The Arab provinces were detached from the empire, as decided already at San Remo. Greece, in addition to western Thrace (which it had just acquired from Bulgaria), received eastern Thrace, including Edirne, right up to the Çatalca line, only 40 kilometers from the Ottoman capital. The city of Izmir and its environs were put under Greek administration for a period of five years, after which what was left of the population would be allowed to request permanent incorporation into the Greek state if it wished. The Aegean Islands were given to Greece outright, while the Dodecanese, including Rhodes, went to Italy. Armenia was recognized as an independent state, with its boundaries to be determined by arbitration of President Wilson. The territory called Kurdistan, east of the Euphrates, was to gain autonomy with the right to opt for independence within a year if the Kurds wished. There would be international control of the Straits with demilitarization of the adjacent lands, but Istanbul would remain under nominal Ottoman control.

What of the Ottoman state that was left? Additional provisions made it certain that Turkish sovereignty would be very limited. The Ottoman army could have no more than 50,000 men, and they would be subject to the advice of foreign officers. Its armaments as well as the navy would be restricted. The Capitulations were restored and a new Allied commission was established to supervise and regulate not only the public debt but also the Ottoman state budget, taxes, customs duties, currency, and public loans, leaving the government with little control over its own policies. Finally, the Ottomans were required to make extensive concessions to the remaining non-Muslim minorities. The Turkish state that survived, thus, would be under the financial and military control of the powers, whose subjects would continue to exploit it. To the Turks, it projected a bleak future.[64] The Istanbul government's acceptance of the treaty was, however, a new weapon in the hands of the Turkish nationalists. The Grand National Assembly immediately declared all those who signed it, including the grand vezir, to be traitors.[65]

The Turko-Armenian War

In addition to facing the various bandit forces, the Ankara regime also had to fight wars in all parts of Anatolia. In the southeast were the French, sometimes in alliance with Armenian bands, pushing out from Cilicia and stimulating a guerrilla war. It was mainly a slow war of attrition, devastating the countryside, but with no substantial advances or retreats on either side. Much more important was the war carried on with the newly established Armenian Republic in the Caucasus. If the latter had been content with the boundaries gained in 1919, most likely there would have been no war and Armenia would probably have been able to put up a far better resistance than it did to the subsequent Bolshevik conquest. But the Armenians were determined to conquer eastern Anatolia, leaving the Turkish nationalists with little choice but to move against them despite the more pressing Greek danger. Armenian raids on Turkish border villages began in May 1920. Soon after, Karabekir was made commander of the eastern front (June 15, 1920). He organized an army to repel them and urged the Grand National Assembly to authorize an advance.[66] Despite the sufferings of Turkish peasants, the Assembly hesitated because of the Greek threat and limited its action to diplomatic protests.[67] In the end, the postponement proved propitious, for as we shall see the new Greek offensive began on June 22, 1920, and if part of the Turkish forces had been busy in the east they might never have been able to hold back the Greeks at the crucial time.

It was only after the Greek danger was contained in the fall of the same year that Karabekir finally was authorized to advance against the Armenians, but only to Kars (October 7). Right from the start, however, he was determined to go considerably further.[68] On October 30 Kars was taken. Karabekir then pushed beyond the old 1877 territory, forcing the Erivan government to ask for an armistice and agree to a peace treaty, signed at Alexandropol (Leninakan/Gümrü) on the night of December 2–3. The treaty never in fact was ratified, since the Armenian Republic soon after was taken over by the Bolsheviks, and it was superseded by the Turkish-Russian Treaty of Moscow of March 1921. But it was significant in establishing the boundaries of eastern Turkey, incorporated without change into the subsequent agreements that remain unaltered to the present day. The Armenians repudiated all claims on Turkish territory, agreed to reduce their armed forces, and promised to allow Turkish use of the railroads passing through their lands to the north. The Turks were allowed to occupy Alexandropol, thus giving them a good strategic position for the subsequent negotiations with the Russians. The arms left by the defeated Armenian forces were sent to the west to be used in the resistance then being mounted against the Greeks.[69] It should be noted that the Turkish offensive against the Armenian Republic was not, as has been alleged, accomplished in coordination with the Red Army. The Bolsheviks conquered Azerbaijan while the Armenians were fighting the Turks. It was only after the peace agreement was reached that they moved into Erivan and Sovietized its government, thus laying the basis for the Turko-Soviet Friendship Treaty that followed.

The First Greek Offensive to the First Battle of İnönü, June 1920–January 1921

At the center of the Turkish War for Independence was, above all else, the Greek invasion. It was the Greeks who were trying to conquer Anatolia, and it was the Greeks who had to be beaten if the other invaders were to be pushed out. The initial Greek occupation, as defined by the British as the Milne Line, encompassed Izmir and the surrounding area, starting from Ayvalık on the Aegean to the north, extending inland to Akmaz, south to Aydın, and then west to the Aegean near Selçuk, incorporating the valleys of the Bakır, the Gediz and the greater and lesser Menderes.[70] While the Greeks spent the winter of 1919–1920 consolidating their position and killing or driving out as many Turkish cultivators as possible, the Kemalists had withdrawn most of their forces to Ankara for training. The small force remaining was commanded by Mehmet Efe, and most of the active resistance was undertaken by bands such as that of Çerkes Ethem.[71]

In addition to arranging the mandate system, the San Remo Conference (April 19–26, 1920) also authorized Greek occupation of the entire province of Aydın as well as eastern Thrace and thus stimulated the resumption of the Greek offensive in southeastern Anatolia in late June 1920. Ali Fuat Cebesoy became commander of all the nationalist forces facing the Greeks, but with limited numbers of men and weapons there was little he could do. The initial Greek drive went on until mid-July, with Alaşehir, Balıkesir, Bandırma, and the old capital of Bursa falling in rapid succession while the British moved in to take Gemlik and Izmir (July 6). The Greek offensive into eastern Thrace was completed in a week (July 20–27), and only Allied pressure kept them from taking Istanbul. In August the Greek advance in Anatolia captured Gallipoli (August 4), and Uşak (August 29) and cut the Aydın–Izmir–Eğridir railroad, the main transportation line in the southwest (August 26). It was at this point that Karabekir undertook the offensive against the Armenians under the assumption that the Allies would keep the Greeks from going beyond the territories granted them at San Remo.

But the Greeks wanted more. A third offensive began in late October. The Grand National Assembly panicked and began to think of moving to Sivas. Ali Fuat was removed as commander of the western front and sent as ambassador to Moscow, and the front was divided into two. Chief of the General Staff Ismet (who later was to take the surname of Inönü) was put in charge of the western part, while Albay Refet Bele was appointed to defend the south. Ismet now worked to consolidate all the forces that had worked independently against the Greeks.[72] Even as Ismet's forces were hunting down those of Çerkes Ethem, the Greeks resumed their offensive along a front stretching from Eskişehir through Bursa to Uşak (January 6, 1921). This time, however, Ismet's forces made their first stand, at the Inönü River just north of Kütahya. After a pitched battle, the First Battle of the Inönü, the Greeks began to retreat toward Bursa (January 10), marking the first major Turkish victory in the war. Though some efforts were made to mount a pursuit, the Turks were unable to follow up the victory not only because of exhaustion and lack of supplies but also because of the need to suppress Çerkes Ethem as well as the Green Army.[73]

The London Conference

The Entente for the first time began to see the need to make some kind of arrangement with the Turkish nationalists; thus a conference was called at London (February 21–March 12, 1921) to salvage the Sèvres Treaty by getting the nationalists to agree with the Istanbul government, which also was invited to send representatives. But nothing was accomplished, since the Ankara representative, Bekir Sami, insisted that the delegate from Istanbul leave before the negotiations even started and refused the Allied demand to make Sèvres the basis for the discussions. The only positive result of the conference came from contacts made by the Turks with the French foreign minister, Franklin-Bouillon, which ultimately led France to be the first of the Allies to break the solid front and recognize the Ankara government.[74]

The Turkish-Soviet Treaty

It was at this time also that the Turkish-Soviet Treaty of Friendship finally was signed in Moscow (March 16, 1921). This enabled the Ankara government to begin the process of breaking out of the diplomatic isolation imposed on it by the Entente powers as well as by the circumstances of its birth. It now was being recognized by a major power as the sole representative of Turkey. The Turkish national claims, moreover, defined as "the territory which the National Pact declares to be Turkey," were recognized, including the eastern boundaries set by the Alexandropol Treaty, with only three exceptions: Batum was left to the Soviet

Republic of Georgia, though Turkey was to have free use of it; Nahcivan, with a largely Turkish population, was to become an autonomous Soviet Republic under the protection of Azerbaijan; and while Turkish sovereignty over the Straits was recognized, their final status was to be determined subsequently by agreement among the Black Sea littoral states, of which three out of six were parts of the Soviet Union: Russia, the Ukraine, and Georgia. The parties agreed not to recognize any international agreement not accepted by the other, with the Soviet Union specifically promising not to accept the Treaty of Sèvres. Both states agreed to regard as null all treaties concluded between the Ottoman Empire and czarist Russia, including the Capitulations. New treaties would be concluded to regulate all relations between the two. Both parties promised to refrain from supporting "seditious groups and activities on the other's territory," thus giving Kemal the legal justification he wanted to suppress the Turkish Communists.[75]

From the Second Greek Offensive to the Battle of the Sakarya, March–July 1921

Following the First Battle of the Inönü, the Greeks fell back to their previous positions between Bursa and Uşak. After waiting to see the outcome of the London Conference, they began a new offensive (March 23, 1921). Adapazarı and Afyon Karahisar fell in rapid succession. Again Ismet Bey marshaled his forces along the Inönü. This time the Greeks pressed their attack, so that the Second Battle of the Inönü went on from March 27 to April 1. Even after they were pushed back from the river, the Greeks continued to press until finally on the night of April 6–7 they fell back, thus providing the second major Turkish victory. Again the Turks failed to follow it up because of lack of adequate manpower and supplies.[76]

The summer of 1921 was in many ways the most crucial period of the entire Turkish War for Independence. In Greece Venizelos had fallen in the elections of November 1920, and policy was now being made by King Constantine and the Royalists, who held even more romantic and reactionary views. In preparation for a new offensive the king and his government went to Izmir (June 13, 1921), embarking significantly not at the port but at the spot where the Crusaders had set foot centuries before. Up to this point Soviet military aid to Turkey had been limited, and the Turkish nationalists were critically short of money as well as arms. Half the Assembly's budget was devoted to defense, and when money was not available the salaries of soldiers and civil servants had to be suspended for months on end.[77] But now as a result of the new agreement the Soviets began to send major shipments of arms and money.[78] Still, however, the Turkish forces remained inferior to those of the Greeks in both numbers and equipment.[79]

Kemal also had political difficulties at home. Though all the members of the Grand National Assembly had affirmed their allegiance to the Society for the Defense of the Rights of Anatolia and Rumelia, as time went on they formed different parliamentary groups, because of political differences that had existed in the national movement all along. The groups on the right were composed of religious and economic conservatives as well as Unionist supporters of Enver and included members of the ulema and a few civil servants and businessmen. The majority, moderately leftist and including both Easternists and Westernists, clustered around Kemal, while there was a small radical group of Communists on the extreme left.[80] Most of the conservatives also opposed any move to end the sultanate and considered the Ankara government as a temporary group that would go out of existence once victory was won, while Kemal and his followers considered the war not only as a period of military campaigns but also as a situation to be used to prepare the way for a new state as envisioned in the 1921 Constitution. In response to the opposition, Kemal formed his own political association in the Assembly (May 1921), the Group for the Defense of the Rights of Anatolia and Rumeli (*Anadolu ve Rumeli Müdafaa-i Hukuk Grubu*). Policy now was made in it under his leadership before it was presented to the full Assembly for its approval.[81] In reaction, the different opposing groups coalesced into the Society for the Protection of Sacred Institutions (*Muhafaza-i Mukaddesat Cemiyeti*), declaring their allegiance to the sultan and the Constitution of 1876 and their insistence that the theocratic basis of the Ottoman state would have to be continued under the leadership of the sultan-caliph.[82] Kemal had a clear majority in the Assembly, and his position was further strengthened when he made an agreement with Italy by which it abandoned its positions in the south and allowed the nationalists to take over (May 1921). He also was helped soon afterward when nationalist detachments retook Izmit from the Greeks, though only after the latter had burned the city and massacred many of its inhabitants (June 28, 1921).[83]

The Battle of the Sakarya

After six months of preparation the remanned and rearmed Greek army began a new offensive on July 13, 1921, advancing between Kütahya and Eskişehir and hitting especially hard at the Turkish left flank to cut its communications with Ankara if possible. Threatened with envelopment Ismet ordered a retreat, leaving Afyon Karahisar, Kütahya, and Eskişehir to the enemy while basing his entire defense plans on the last natural boundary before Ankara, the Sakarya River (July 23–25, 1921). The Assembly panicked. Karabekir, just returned from his victory over the Armenians and long resentful at Kemal's prominence in the nationalist movement, now led the opposition. He claimed that the Greeks could no longer be stopped and demanded that Kemal's powers be reduced so that a new policy could be developed. Kemal's opponents advocated that Kemal be made commander in chief of the armed forces with full powers so that he could bear the blame when the army suffered what seemed to be an inevitable defeat. Kemal agreed (August 4, 1921) on condition only that he be authorized to exercise all the powers normally given the Assembly for the next three months. Both proposals were approved, and he took full charge of the preparations to meet the Greek assault.[84]

Despite the Soviet help, supplies were short as the Turkish army prepared to meet the Greeks. Every household was required to provide a pair of underclothing, socks, and sandals. All men's clothing in stores was turned over to the army, with payment to be made later. Forty percent of all food and gasoline supplies were requisitioned. Owners of transport vehicles had to provide free transportation for the army. Twenty percent of all farm animals and carts were to be given up. And owners of rifles, guns, and ammunition had to surrender them to the army, a major sacrifice for the hardy men of Anatolia.[85] All the reserves were sent to the Sakarya. With Kemal as commander in chief, Fevzi Çakmak became chief of the General Staff in Ankara and Ismet Bey commanded the troops on the battle lines. The Greek advance toward the Sakarya began on August 13, with Ankara their objective. Halide Edip volunteered for military service and was made a sergeant on the western front, a major step forward for Turkish women.[86] The battle began when the Greeks approached the Sakarya and continued for over three weeks. The thunder of cannon was plainly heard in Ankara. Most of the politicians and the people who had gathered there to fight for the Turkish nation were poised to leave if the Greeks broke through – not to surrender, but to retreat further into Anatolia in order to continue the fight. The crucial moment came when the Greek army tried to take Haymana, 40 kilometers south of Ankara. For 11 days (August 21–September 2) they pushed against the town, leveling its buildings, but the Turks held out. It was now a sustained war of attrition, and it seemed that the Greeks would prevail. But they also had their problems. The advance through Anatolia had lengthened their lines of supply and communication. Their ravaging of the countryside and slaughter of Turkish peasants had left little food. They were running out of ammunition. It seemed only a question of time, then, before one side or the other would break. The break came suddenly on September 8. A small Turkish counterattack on the enemy's left flank was so successful that Kemal decided that this was the Greeks' weak point, and he exploited it. By September 13 the Greeks were in flight. The battle had been won. The Turkish nation had been saved.[87] Mustafa Kemal returned in triumph to Ankara, where a grateful assembly awarded him the rank of marshal of the army (*müşir*) as well as the title gazi, "fighter for the faith against the infidel."[88]

Again the Turks were unable to follow up the victory, and they continued to refrain for another year. In the meantime, the Turkish army was reorganized and rearmed. The outside world began to accept the inevitability of a Turkish victory and to make the necessary adjustments. The first foreign diplomat to arrive was Franklin-Bouillon, who signed the treaty that came to bear his name (October 20, 1921) by which France agreed to withdraw from Cilicia, and it did so soon afterward. French recognition of the Ankara government allowed the nationalists to demobilize the army in the south and transfer its soldiers and weapons to the west in preparation for the final advance against the Greeks. France also agreed to accept the National Pact instead of the Treaty of Sèvres, moving the boundary between Turkey and its Syrian mandate to its present line except for Hatay (Alexandretta), whose fate was determined later, the city joining the Turkish Republic as a result of a plebiscite held in 1938. The first revision of the Sèvres provisions gave the Turks a precedent they used in all subsequent negotiations with the other powers. France in turn was able to move its forces back into Syria to face the uprisings of the Arab nationalists who also were protesting the peace settlement.[89] Britain protested the unilateral French move, but itself agreed on an exchange of prisoners with the Ankara government and released the detainees on Malta. On March 22 the foreign ministers of Britain, France, and Italy offered a truce to the governments of Istanbul, Ankara and Greece, but Kemal stated that he would agree only after all foreign armies were evacuated from Turkey. The Greeks still were in Anatolia, however, and it appeared that the Turkish army still was not ready to drive them out.

Politics in Ankara

Delay in driving the Greeks out again stimulated opposition to Kemal in Ankara. Important army leaders such as Kâzım Karabekir, Rauf Orbay, and Refet Bele resigned and gained election to the Assembly as deputies, and they were highly critical of Kemal's military policies. The parliamentary opposition was reorganized into the Second Defense of Rights Group, which included Unionists, Westernists, supporters of the caliphate, and others who opposed Kemal for personal reasons. Its declared aim was to prevent autocracy, establish the rule of law in place of Kemal's personal rule, and to establish rule by the Assembly as a whole rather than by any group. It advocated an end to the special Independence Courts set up to try those who had committed crimes against the nation; repeal of laws giving coercive powers to the government; liberalization of the election laws; and rules to forbid the president of the Assembly and the ministers from belonging to any political group.[90] The new group did not have a majority, only 118 members out of 437 in all. But with many of Kemal's supporters out of Ankara on official missions, at times it was able to secure majorities on the floor of the Assembly and to stymie or criticize the policies of the Council of Ministers. On July 8, 1922, it used one such occasion to pass a law ending Kemal's right to nominate ministers for the Assembly's approval, returning to the original system by which members elected ministers from among themselves by secret ballot. In addition, the chairmanship of the Council of Ministers was separated from that of president of the Assembly, with Kemal retaining only the latter post while finally supporting the election of his old comrade Rauf Orbay to the former (July 12, 1922). Kemal's powers, though limited for the first time, were still considerable, and he assured the Assembly that the army would indeed drive the Greeks out as soon as it was ready.[91] In the end Kemal was able to retain most of his power despite the changes, because his rivals supported the opposition only behind the scenes, fearing that to do so publicly might endanger the national movement against the Greeks.[92]

New Peace Proposals

Considering the extent of Turkish successes it is remarkable to see what the Allies still hoped to impose as a peace settlement. Meeting in London early in March, the Entente foreign ministers again proposed an armistice that would include establishing an Armenian state in eastern Anatolia, removing Turkish troops from the Straits area, Turkish abandonment to the Greeks of Izmir and eastern Thrace, including Edirne, raising the Sèvres limits on the Turkish army to 85,000 men, eliminating the European financial controls over the Turkish government provided at Sèvres but retaining the Capitulations and Public Debt Commission, and so forth. These proposals were so widely at variance with the National Pact that it was easy for all groups in the Assembly to agree on their rejection as well as on a renewal of Kemal's demand for complete evacuation before negotiations began.[93]

The Great Offensive

All through the summer of 1922 the Turkish military preparations continued while criticism of Kemal's military leadership increased in Ankara. Finally, on August 26 the Turkish army began to move forward in what has come to be known to the Turks as the Great Offensive (*Büyük Taarruz*). A force stretching 100 kilometers from Iznik to Afyon Karahisar advanced against the enemy. The major Greek defense positions were overrun on August 26, and Izmit also fell the same day. On August 30, the Greek army was defeated at Dumlupınar, with half of its soldiers captured or slain and its equipment entirely lost. As thousands of Greek soldiers fled toward Izmir, on September 1 Mustafa Kemal issued his most famous order to the Turkish army: "Armies, your first goal is the Mediterranean – Forward!"[94] Prayers for the success of the nationalist efforts were said at the Fatih and Aya

Sofya mosques in Istanbul. On September 2 Eskişehir was captured, and the Greek government asked Britain to arrange a truce that would preserve its rule in Izmir at least.[95] Kemal would have none of this. Balıkesir was taken on September 6, and Aydın and Manisa the next day, the latter burned by the Greeks before their departure. The government in Athens resigned. Two days later the Turkish cavalry raced into Izmir to the cheers of thousands. Bursa was taken on September 10. The next day Kemal's forces headed for the Bosporus, the Sea of Marmara, and the Dardanelles, where the Allied garrisons were reinforced by British, French, and Italian soldiers from Istanbul. Gemlik and Mudanya fell on September 11, with an entire Greek division surrendering. Thousands of Greek soldiers and peasants flooded into Izmir from all over Anatolia and were loaded on Allied transport ships for shipment back to Greece. Civil government in Izmir was now back in Turkish hands, and desperate efforts were made to keep order and prevent looting. On September 13 a fire broke out in the Armenian quarter of the city. It spread rapidly through gasoline-soaked buildings while the Turkish army's efforts to extinguish it were stymied by the discovery that all the city's fire hoses had been cut and the fire cisterns emptied. In a single day as many as 25,000 buildings were burned and half the great city destroyed. Perhaps the last atrocity of the war was the suggestion, quickly taken up by the Western press, that the victorious Turkish army was responsible for burning the conquered second city of the old empire. Actual culpability has never been proved.[96]

In the meantime, the advance continued. On September 14, 1922, Bergama and Kuşadası fell into Turkish hands and the French government proposed the return of eastern Thrace. The Istanbul government sent a telegram of congratulations to Kemal, praising what it called "one of the greatest victories in Ottoman [!] history."[97] On September 18 he was able to announce that the Greek army in Anatolia was completely destroyed.[98] The same day the Allied commanders asked the Turkish forces to move back from the Straits and to observe their neutrality as well as that of Istanbul. The British army prepared for war, sending out a call to London for reinforcements. At home, however, the General Staff reported that the time of year would be "most unpropitious for field operations, and the hardships to which the troops will be subjected will be much more trying to the British than the Turks, who are more or less inured to them."[99] The British cabinet decided to resist the Turks if necessary at the Dardanelles and to ask for French and Italian help to enable the Greeks to remain in eastern Thrace.[100] On September 19, however, the former abandoned their positions at the Straits, leaving the British alone to face the Turks if they wished to do so. On September 24 Kemal's troops moved into the Straits zones and refused British requests to leave; conflict seemed near. The British cabinet was divided on the matter. In the end the situation was resolved by the British General Harrington, now Allied commander in Istanbul, who kept his own men from firing on the Turks, warned the cabinet against any rash adventure, and convinced Kemal that he could get what he wanted at a peace conference if he abstained from forcing a conflict. On September 27 at his persuasion the Greek fleet left Istanbul. The same day King Constantine was overthrown and a new regime established in Athens. The British cabinet decided to force the Greeks to withdraw behind the Maritsa in Thrace, and the withdrawal began. This convinced Kemal to accept a truce with the British and the opening of armistice talks (September 29), and so the crisis was averted. The achievement of the National Pact was almost a reality. Only a major intervention would enable the Greeks to triumph, and this was something that Britain no longer was willing to undertake. The Turkish War for Independence had achieved its goals. Anatolia was clear of the enemy. Eastern Thrace was being evacuated. On October 2 Kemal returned to a wild reception in Ankara. The war was over. The Turks had won.

The Armistice of Mudanya

The conference to arrange the armistice began on October 3, 1922, at the Marmara sea resort town of Mudanya. Unlike Mondros, now it was the Turkish representative, Ismet Inönü, commander of the victorious western armies, who took the chair, while it was the British and the Greeks who were the vanquished. The British still expected Kemal to make concessions, however, and were startled when he continued to demand fulfillment of the National Pact – so the conference dragged on far beyond the original expectations. While the British troops in Istanbul prepared for a Kemalist attack, the Turkish troops bypassed the city and began mopping up in Thrace. The only concession that Ismet made to the British was an agreement that his troops would not advance any farther toward the Dardanelles. In the end it was the British who had to yield. The Armistice of Mudanya was signed on October 11. By its terms the Greek army would move west of the Maritsa, turning over its positions in Thrace to the Allies, who would in turn surrender them to the Turks. The Allies would occupy the right bank of the Maritsa, and Allied forces would stay in Thrace for a month to assure law and order. In return Kemal's army would recognize continued British occupation of the Straits zones until the final treaty was signed. This arrangement included also Istanbul, which thus would have to wait a little while longer for liberation.[101]

Refet Bele now was sent as special representative of the Grand National Assembly to arrange the recovery of Thrace. On October 19 he arrived in Istanbul, the first nationalist representative to reach the old capital since the victory, and he was greeted by a massive reception. The British did not allow the hundred Turkish gendarmes who came with him to land until the next day, however, so that it was only then that the victory parade took place from the Sirkeci boat station up the Divan Yolu to the Aya Sofya mosque, where prayers were offered in gratitude for the Turkish success. The ancient city now witnessed a scene of mass emotion such as never had taken place before in its long history, while the gendarmes marched along.[102]

End of the Ottoman Empire

Events now came thick and fast as all sides prepared for the peace conference, which the Allies proposed to be held at Lausanne. In England the Conservatives, never too happy with Lloyd George, forced his replacement with Bonar Law, though Lord Curzon, long a friend of the Greeks, remained as foreign minister. In Istanbul the change in regimes was even more dramatic and unusual. The Allies had signed the Mudanya Armistice with the victorious Ankara government, but there still was an Ottoman government in Istanbul, led by the sultan, with Tevfik Paşa as grand vezir – a government, indeed, that had condemned Kemal and the other nationalist leaders to death. Kemal had postponed confronting the problem of what to do with the sultanate until independence was achieved. It still was a problem, since many of Kemal's strongest supporters retained a strong reverence for the sultan. What, then, was to be done?

The problem was, in a way, solved by the British, who sent invitations for the Lausanne Conference to both the Istanbul and the Ankara governments (October 27, 1922). Right after the latter accepted, Tevfik Paşa said he would be happy to join in representing Turkey at the peace conference. Was the Istanbul government going to resume its power now that the war was over? This was not likely. Aside from all other considerations, such a move would have cost hundreds of nationalist politicians and administrators the positions and power that they had earned during the years of suffering in Ankara. Kemal, therefore, judged that he had sufficient support to push through what he could not have done during the dark days in Ankara. In a cabinet meeting on October 31 he declared that the only solution was to abolish the sultanate and, thus, the Istanbul regime. No one disagreed. On November 1, 1922, the Grand National Assembly enacted new legislation separating the sultanate and the caliphate and abolishing the former. The caliph was left as no more than the leading Muslim religious dignitary, to be chosen by the National Assembly at its convenience.[103] By this act the Istanbul government lost its legal foundation. The entire Ottoman Ruling Class, given its position by the sultan, was thus dispossessed of its rank and functions. Refet Bele informed the Allies that Istanbul thereafter would be under the administration of the Grand National Assembly. On November 4 the Tevfik Paşa cabinet resigned, and the official Ottoman newspaper, *Takvim-i Vekayi,* published its last issue. The next day Refet ordered the Istanbul ministries to stop their activities. The Istanbul government simply ceased to exist.[104] The Grand National Assembly promulgated laws providing severance pay or pensions for bureaucrats still serving in Istanbul. Many, of course, already had or would soon join the Ankara government, which desperately needed manpower. Others retired in order to remain in Istanbul.

The last scene in the drama of Ottoman history approached. Sultan Vahideddin fled the city aboard a British destroyer along with his son, his chamberlain, and a few servants and eunuchs, claiming that his life was in danger (November 16), going first to Malta and then to permanent exile in San Remo.[105] The next day the Assembly deposed Vahideddin as caliph. After Kemal declared "the Turkish people possess all sovereignty without any condition. It does not accept the Caliph's participation in rule in any meaning, any form, any way, by any means,"[106] the choice went to Abdulmecit II (1868–1944), son of Abdulaziz.[107] The new caliph issued a declaration to the Muslims of the world asking them to accept his leadership. The same day the traditional ceremony of homage was performed in the Topkapı Palace. It seemed possible at least that the new arrangement might work, with the caliph's continued existence mollifying those who might otherwise have opposed the Ankara government.

The Conference and Treaty of Lausanne

In the meantime the Lausanne Conference began on November 21, 1922. The Ankara government was represented by Ismet Inönü, who had a very difficult task. He was representing the nation that had overturned the Sèvres peace settlement, but the Allies still tried to treat him as representative of a defeated nation. Ismet had been chosen because of his firmness at Mudanya, but just to make sure that he made no concessions Minister of Health Rıza Nur was set beside him. He was hardly needed, however. Whenever offensive proposals were made by the Allies, Ismet, long hard of hearing, simply pretended not to hear. Ismet maintained the basic position of the Ankara government, that it had to be treated as an independent and sovereign state, equal with all others at the conference. In discussing matters regarding control of Turkish finances and justice, protection for the minorities, the Capitulations, the Straits, and the like, he absolutely refused to budge on any proposal that in any way would compromise Turkish sovereignty. Lord Curzon, the British delegate, "often assumed the role of a weary schoolmaster admonishing a stupid pupil. Ismet refused to learn. When the American observer brought the two men together to discuss the judicial capitulations in Turkey, Curzon shouted and beat the wall with his cane. Ismet held out for complete sovereignty and said that the adjustment of such matters took time."[108] One of the British representatives, reported that "Ismet Pasha, who was well-attended by a phalanx of forbidding-looking Turks seemed impervious to all argument on the subject, and his obtuseness and obstinacy put the patience of the Allied delegates to a severe test."[109] Ismet used his deafness to gain time and think out his replies, exasperating some of the other delegates but gaining his points. He used the rivalries of the Allies and their fear of the Bolsheviks to Turkish advantage. As the conference went on, Kemal further strengthened the Turkish position by occupying the last towns in eastern Thrace. He improved his political position at home by organizing his own political party, the People's Party (*Halk Fırkası*) on December 6.[110] He also sent a huge volume to Lausanne chronicling the Greek atrocities in Thrace and Anatolia. An economic congress was held at Izmir to stress the need for Turkish economic and financial independence. After long months of stalemate the Lausanne Conference recessed (February 4, 1923). When Ismet returned to Ankara, he was severely criticized for the few concessions he had made. The Grand National Assembly then drew up its own peace proposals (March 8, 1923),[111] which Ismet brought back to Lausanne, stimulating new arguments when the conference reconvened on April 23. Three more months of haggling followed, with Ismet making only the most essential concessions while wearing down the opposition, whose press and public became more and more anxious for peace.[112]

Finally, on July 24, 1923, the articles of the Treaty of Lausanne were signed. The territorial integrity of the Turkish nation, as specified by the National Pact, was confirmed with the sole exception of Mosul. Turkey retained eastern Thrace to the Maritsa River along with the railroad town of Karaağaç, on the western bank, added in return for Turkish withdrawal of all reparation claims from Greece. Greece got the Aegean Islands themselves because of their Greek populations, but excluded were the surrounding waters and the islands of Imbros and Tenedos because of their strategic importance at the entrance to the Dardanelles. The boundary with Syria followed the provisions of the Franklin-Bouillon agreement, thus excluding both Hatay (Alexandretta) and Antioch for the moment. Despite the largely Kurdish and Turkish nature of its inhabitants, Britain retained control of the Mosul area in its capacity as mandatory for Iraq because of the oil deposits of the area. Though its final disposition was left to the direct negotiation of the parties, in the end the League of Nations awarded it permanently to Iraq. Armenia and Kurdistan were not mentioned, and the regions in question were given to Turkey in accordance with the principle of self-determination. In return Turkey renounced "all rights and title whatsoever over or respecting the territories situated outside the frontiers laid down in the present Treaty and the islands other than those over which her sovereignty is recognized by the said Treaty," thus establishing an anti-irredentist policy that has remained a basic element of the Turkish Republic's foreign policy ever since.

Though the treaty provided for Turkey to gain full sovereignty within its own boundaries, its terms were vague and implementation took time. For instance, it was stated that "each of the High Contracting Parties hereby accepts, insofar as it is concerned, the complete abolition of the Capitulations in Turkey in every respect." Yet Turkey also was forced to accept the continued application of all concessionary contracts entered into force before October 20, 1914, and it was only in 1929 that it was able to gain full control over its own customs policies. Other privileges and concessions previously granted to foreigners were eliminated later only as a result of the firm policy of the Turkish government. Insofar as the public debt was concerned, the treaty only determined its size and allocated its obligations among Turkey and the other successor states of the Ottoman Empire. Important questions such as the status of the Public Debt Commission and the monetary value of the debt were so hotly disputed during the conference that they were finally left out of the treaty. The Public Debt Commission had not actually been abolished during the war, but all the enemy representatives and staff had left and the debt payments had been suspended except to the bondholders in the Central Power states. When the Allies took over in Istanbul, they resuscitated the commission with their own representatives, while those of the Central Powers went home, thus reversing the situation. In the end, after long negotiation, the debt of the former empire as a whole was evaluated at 129.4 million Turkish liras (100 kuruş equal 1 lira) and the annual payments at 8.66 million liras, with the Turkish Republic's share being 84.6 and 5.8 million liras respectively. However, the Turkish Republic refused to accept Abdulhamit's Decree of Muharrem, which allocated revenues to the Public Debt Commission to make these payments, and no provisions were inserted at Lausanne for its restoration. In fact, it never was restored. Turkey continued to protest the amount of its obligation as set by the treaty, and no further payments were made until 1929. In the end, through the mediation of the League of Nations, a settlement was reached whereby the Turkish debt was reduced to 8 million gold liras (80 million paper liras) and the annual payments to 700,000 gold liras (7 million paper liras), starting in 1933. These payments continued until the last bonds were liquidated in 1944.[113]

The noneconomic provisions of Lausanne were more definite and final. The foreign and mixed courts were abolished and foreign subjects forced to accept the jurisdiction of Turkish courts. Foreign observers were allowed to watch over the latter, but they could only report and complain if necessary. All foreign postal systems in Turkey were ended. The Turks were allowed to build their military forces without any limitation of size or armament. They were, however, required to leave a demilitarized zone along the Greek border in Thrace to prevent any incidents. The problem of reparation claims was solved when Greece recognized "her obligation to pay for the damage caused in Anatolia by the acts of the Greek army or administration which were contrary to the laws of war," and Turkey renounced its claims "in consideration of the financial situation of Greece resulting from the prolongation of the war and its consequences." The Turks and the Allies mutually renounced reparation claims against each other for all wartime damage. All foreign rights to supervise Turkish handling of its minorities were ended. Turkey simply declared that it would protect the life and liberty of all inhabitants, regardless of birth, nationality, language. Turkish nationals of non-Turkish speech would be allowed to use their own language in public and private intercourse and even before the courts. Finally, non-Muslim Turks would be allowed to establish and operate whatever charitable, religious, social, and educational institutions they wished.

These provisions were accepted by the Turkish government, and have been observed in full to the present day.

All properties of Allied nationals confiscated during the war were restored, with a mixed arbitration tribunal set up to settle disputes on the subject. The only real limitation placed on Turkish sovereignty outside the financial field came in regard to the Straits, which were internationalized under the control of a mixed commission whose chairman always was to be Turkish. The lands on both sides of the Straits were demilitarized, but Turkey was allowed to send its troops through the neutral zones as needed as well as to station as many as 12,000 men in Istanbul. Turkey finally regained full control over the Straits by the Agreement of Montreux in 1936.

Finally, a separate agreement between Greece and Turkey arranged for a compulsory exchange of population, involving about 1.3 million Greeks and a half-million Turks in all. It included all Greeks living in Anatolia and Thrace with the exception of those who had lived in Istanbul before 1918, and all Turks in Greece except those in western Thrace. The exchange had in fact begun during the latter days of the War for Independence when thousands of Greeks were transported from Izmir to Greece. It left both sides far more homogeneous than before.

The Treaty of Lausanne thus certified and legalized the victory won by the Turkish War for Independence. The National boundaries were secured almost completely. There were no more foreign rights and privileges in the new Turkey. Some deputies in Ankara criticized the abandonment of Mosul and Hatay, but the Assembly approved the accord on August 23 by a vote of 227 to 14.[114]

The achievement at Lausanne gave Kemal the prestige and authority needed to finish the job of creating a new state. But first the Allied troops had to leave. The final evacuation of the British troops in Istanbul was scheduled for October 2, 1923. The square in front of the Dolmabahçe Palace was prepared for the final ceremony. Guards of honor representing the different Allied armies marched by. As the British soldiers saluted the Turkish flag, the Turkish crowd broke through the lines of the guards and swarmed into the midst of the ceremony in a happy boisterous spirit of celebration. When the British Coldstream Guards marched to their boats, the Turks began to clap and whistle in tune with the cadence. The Coldstream band played "Mustafa Kemal Is Our Commander," and the Turks applauded. The soldiers embarked onto their launches and sailed into the middle of the Bosporus while the British band played "Auld Lang Syne." The first – and last – foreign occupation of Muslim Istanbul had come to an end.[115] On October 6 a full division of the Turkish national army marched into Istanbul amid the cheers of thousands of Turks.[116] The same day, Damat Ferit Paşa, who had fled to Yugoslavia, died of natural causes in Niş. On October 13 the Grand National Assembly passed a new law making Ankara the official capital of the Turkish state.[117] On October 29 it accepted a new constitution that declared the state to be a republic with sovereignty coming from the people. Kemal was elected first president and Ismet Inönü first prime minister of the Turkish Republic.[118]

There was only one step left, elimination of the caliphate. Abdulmecit had held the office in a reasonably inoffensive way. But as the thrill of Lausanne wore out, he became the center for the opponents of the new regime, who began to intrigue to restore the sultanate and the sultan. When the caliph wrote Kemal asking for increased privileges, the president reacted: "Let the caliph and the whole world know that the caliph and the caliphate which have been preserved have no real meaning and no real existence. We cannot expose the Turkish Republic to any sort of danger to its independence by its continued existence. The position of Caliphate in the end has for us no more importance than a historic memory."[119] On February 29 Abdulmecit attended his last Friday *Selamlık,* the last such ceremony ever attended officially by a member of the Ottoman dynasty. Four days later, on March 3, 1924, the Grand National Assembly abolished the caliphate, thus ending the Ottoman dynasty and empire.[120] The next day Abdulmecit left Istanbul. The Ottoman Empire was finally extinguished, almost 640 years from the time that Osman had founded the dynasty. A new era in Turkish history had begun.

Notes to Chapter 5

1 Samih Nafiz Kansu, *İki Devrin Perde Arkası,* Istanbul, 1957, pp. 217–221; Tunaya, pp. 520–533.

2 Selek, I, 82; T. Bıyıklıoğlu, *Trakyada Milli Mücadele,* 2 vols., Ankara, I, 124; Rifat Mevlanazade, *Türk İnkilâbının İçyüzü,* Aleppo, 1929.

3 Bayar, V, 1572–1582.

4 Midilli Ahmet. *Türk İstiklâl Harbinin Başında Milli Mücadele,* Ankara, 1928; Bayar, VII, 2368–2383.

5 Tunaya, pp. 358–361; Ahmed Bedevi Kuran, *Osmanlı İmparatorluğunda İnkilâp Hareketleri ve Milli Mücadele,* Istanbul, 1956, pp. 548–550. Kuran was another Turkish exile in Moscow at the time. Ilhan E. Darendelioğlu, *Türkiye'de Komünist Hareketleri, 1910–1973,* Ankara, 1973.

6 E. H. Carr, *The Bolshevik Revolution, 1917–1923,* vol. III, London, 1952, p. 299.

7 Karabekir, pp. 2–9, 16–17.

8 Karabekir, pp. 19–23.

9 Rawlinson, *Adventures in the Near East 1918–1922,* London and New York, 1923; Karabekir, pp. 161–162.

10 May 30, 1919; Karabekir, pp. 31, 48, 65, 78; Hovannisian, *Republic of Armenia,* I, 426–428.

11 Bıyıklıoğlu, *Atatürk Anadoluda,* pp. 47–48; HTVD no. 1; *Tar. Ves.,* II/12, p. 402.

12 HTVD, Sept. 1952, nos. 3–6; Bıyıklıoğlu, *Atatürk Anadoluda,* pp. 42–46; Selek, I, 172–180.

13 Bıyıklıoğlu, *Atatürk Anadoluda,* p. 43; Lord Kinross, *Atatürk,* New York, 1965, pp. 149–153, 156–157; HTVD, Sept. 1952, n. 6.

14 *Türk İstiklâl Harbı,* II/2, pp. 120–124; Bayar, VI, 1768–1818, 1903–2046, VII, 2253–2263, VIII, 2474–2567.

15 Bayar, V, 1457–1465, VIII, 2581–2589, 2752–2755.

16 HTVD no. 4, June 1953, doc. 64–65, 69, 71, 77; no. 5, Sept. 1955, no. 92.

17 *Atatürk TTB,* pp. 23–24.

18 Karabekir, pp. 35–36, 43; F. Kandemir, *Milli Mücadele başlangıcında Mustafa Kemal arkadaşları ve karşısındakiler,* Istanbul, 1964, pp. 35–36.

19 *Speech,* pp. 28–30.

20 Kili, *Kemalism; Speech,* pp. 30–34; *Nutuk,* I, 30–34.

21 Bayar, VIII, 2595–2602; *Nutuk,* I, 35, III, 916–917.

22 Bayar, VIII, 2632–2656, 2760–2763.

23 Goloğlu, *Erzurum Kongresi,* pp. 201–203; Bayar, VIII, 2670–2681, 2764–2778.

24 Şerafettin Turan, *Balıkesir ve Alaşehir Kongreleri ve Hacim Muhittin Çarıklı'nın Kuvayı Milliye Hatıraları,* Istanbul, 1967, pp. 44, 161, 212; *Türk İstiklâl Harbı,* II/1, p. 21; Bayar, VIII, 2718–2736.

25 Goloğlu, *Sivas Kongresi,* pp. 232–234; an English tr. can be found in E. G. Mears, *Modern Turkey,* New York, 1924, pp. 624–627; *Tar. Ves.* I/1, June 1941.

26 Kili, *Kemalism,* pp. 15–16; *Nutuk,* I, 243; *Türk İstiklâl Harbı,* II/2, p. 62; Selek, I, 310.

27 Mears, pp. 631–633; *New York Times,* October 18, 1919.

28 Meclis-i Mebusan, *Zabıt Ceridesi*, 4 devre 11 inikad, 17 Şubat 1336/17 February 1920, p. 114; Goloğlu, *Üçüncü Meşrutiyet, 1920*, pp. 80–1; an English tr. in Mears, pp. 629–631; *New York Times*, October 1, 1922; see also Bıyıklıoğlu, *Trakyada Milli Mücadele*, I, 195; *Türk İstiklâl Harbı*, II/2, pp. 95, 100, II/6, kp. IV, 15; Ahmed Emin (Yalman), *Turkey in the World War*, New Haven, 1930, pp. 276–277; Kili, *Kemalism*, pp. 224–225.

29 *Documents on British Foreign Policy*, First Series, XVII, 59–60.

30 *Nutuk*, II, 443; *Türk İstiklâl Harbı*, II/2, 41, VI, 27.

31 *Türk İstiklâl Harbı*, II/6 kp. IV, p. 16; Türkgeldi, *Görüp Işittiklerim*, p. 259.

32 *Türk İstiklâl Harbı*, II/2, pp. 97, 101, II/6, kp. IV, 16; Söylemezoğlu, p. 197; Kansu, I, 553; Mears, p. 631.

33 Söylemezoğlu, p. 216; Ahmet Hilmi Kalaç, *Kendi Kitabım*, Istanbul, 1960, p. 169.

34 *Nutuk*, I, 417–419; Kansu, p. 556; *Türk İstiklâl Harbı*, II/2, p. 101; Yalman, *Yakın Tarihte*, II, 54.

35 *Atatürk TTB*, IV, 258.

36 *Documents on British Foreign Policy*, First Series, XVII, 49–50, February 7, 1921.

37 HTVD, no. 13, September 1955, doc. 337; *Nutuk*, I, 421; *Türk İstiklâl Harbı*, II/2, p. 158; Nurettin Peker, *İstiklâl Savaşının Vesika ve Resimleri*, 1955, pp. 159–160.

38 TBMM, *Zabıt Ceridesi*, 70–79; Webster, p. 86.

39 Kili, *Constitutional Developments*, pp. 160–162; Şeref Gözübüyük and S. Kili, ed., *Türk Anayasa Metinleri*, Ankara, 1947, pp. 86–87; *Atatürk Söylev*, I, 206–210.

40 TBMM, *Zabıt Ceridesi*, I/1, p. 145; *Türk İstiklâl Harbı*, II/2, p. 340.

41 *Atatürk Söylev*, I, 58–59.

42 F. W. Frey, *The Turkish Political Elite*, Cambridge, Mass., 1965, p. 181; T. Bıyıklıoğlu, "Birinci Türkiye Büyük Millet Meclis'inin Hukuki Statüsü ve İhtilâlcı Karakteri," *Belleten*, 24 (1960), 658n; Goloğlu, *Üçüncü Meşrutiyet*, pp. 295–303.

43 Samet Ağaoğlu, *Kuvayı Milliye Ruhu*, Istanbul, 1944, pp. 31–32.

44 TBMM, *Zabıt Ceridesi*, I, May 11, 1920, V, November 18, 1920, pp. 364–365; Berkes, pp. 438–440.

45 TBMM, *Zabıt Ceridesi*, V, 368–369, XIV, 22.

46 *Atatürk Söylev*, I, 209.

47 Edib, *Turkish Ordeal*, pp. 170–173; Halil Ibrahim Karal, "Turkish Relations with Soviet Russia During the National Liberation War of Turkey, 1918–1922," unpublished Ph.D. dissertation, University of California, Los Angeles, 1967, pp. 160–166.

48 HTVD, no. 11 (March 1955), doc. 271; *Türk İstiklâl Harbı*, II/2, 83; VI, 76; Bıyıklıoğlu, *Atatürk Anadoluda*, I, 58, 85; Goloğlu, *Üçüncü Meşrutiyet*, p. 143.

49 Kılıç Ali, *İstiklâl Mahkemesi Hatıraları*, Istanbul, 1955.

50 *Speech*, pp. 401–402; Edib, *Turkish Ordeal*, pp. 172–174; Kılıç Ali, *İstiklâl Mahkemesi*, pp. 1–52.

51 Yunus Nadi, *Çerkes Ethem Kuvvetlerinin Ihaneti*, Istanbul, 1955, p. 11.

52 *Speech*, p. 404; Cebesoy, *Hatıraları*, p. 466.

53 Selek, I, 317–319; *Speech*, pp. 423–466; Cemal Kutay, *Çerkez Ethem Dosyası*, 2 vols., Istanbul, 1973; Edib, *Turkish Ordeal*, pp. 231–237; Özalp, I, 166–170.

54 *Türk İstiklâl Harbı* II/2, p. 84, VI, 71; Özalp, I, 65–71, 108–116.

55 Halis Asarkaya, *Ulusal Savaşta Tokat*, Ankara, 1936, p. 121.

56 Tevetoğlu, *Türkiye'de Sosyalist* pp. 184–190; Tunaya, p. 532.

57 Cebesoy, *Hatıraları*, pp. 507, 509; Tunaya, p. 531, *Atatürk TTB*, II, 358; Tevetoğlu, *Türkiyede Sosyalist*, pp. 184, 303; Hikmet Bayur, "Mustafa Subhi ve Milli Mücadeleye El Koymaya Çalışan Başı Dışarda Akımlar," *Belleten*, 35 (1971), 587–654.

58 *Yakın Tarihte*, I, 297.

59 Karabekir, pp. 929–930; *Speech*, pp. 412–414.

60 Fethi Tevetoğlu, *Açıklıyorum*, Ankara, 1965, p. 195; Karabekir, p. 114; Sami Sabit Karaman, *İstiklal Mücadelesi ve Enver Paşa*, Izmit, 1949.

61 D. Rustow, "Enver Pasha," EI², II. 700–702.

62 D. Rustow, "Djemal Pasha," EI², II, 531.

63 *Documents on British Foreign Policy,* First Series, XVII, pp. 89–90.

64 Mears, pp. 634–642. Reşat Ekrem Koçu, *Osmanlı Muahedeleri ve Kapitulasiyonlar, 1300–1920* . . . , Istanbul, 1934, pp. 274–281.

65 TBMM, *Zabıt Ceridesi,* I Devre III, 299; *Türk İstiklâl Harbı,* II/6, kp. IV, 17.

66 *Türk İstiklâl Harbı;* III, 92, 273. FO 5042/E692, FO 5211/E15253, FO 5045/E2809, FO 5045/E2736, FO 4963/E14103, FO5041/E357.

67 Cebesoy, *Moskova Hatıraları,* Istanbul, 1955, pp. 33–35, 91–92; *Atatürk* TTB, pp. 337–340.

68 Karabekir, p. 840.

69 Karabekir, pp. 950–952.

70 *Türk İstiklâl Harbı,* II/2, pp. 120–124 and map no. 6.

71 Bayar, VII, 2075–2105, 2137–2179.

72 *Nutuk,* II, 544; Yunus Nadi, *Çerkes Edhem,* p. 97.

73 *Türk İstiklâl Harbı,* II/2, pp. 194–343.

74 *Türk İstiklâl Harbı,* II/3, p. 260; Şimşir, p. 15; Selek, II, 203.

75 Webster, p. 93; *Nutuk,* II, 460; Karabekir, pp. 884; *Türk İstiklâl Harbı,* II, 225, 255.

76 *Türk İstiklâl Harbı,* II/3, pp. 249–585.

77 Selek, I, 106–115, II, 151–158.

78 Karabekir, pp. 882, 1165; Cebesoy, *Moskova Hatıraları,* p. 82.

79 Selek, II, 189, 232–236, 283.

80 Kili, *Kemalism,* p. 27; Webster, p. 97.

81 Tunaya, pp. 553–559; *Tar. Ves.,* III/13 (1949), 12–15.

82 Selek, I, 592; Kili, *Kemalism,* p. 29.

83 Rahmi Apak, *İstiklâl Savaşında Garp Cephesi Nasıl Kuruldu,* Ankara, 1942, p. 143; *Türk İstiklâl Harbı,* V, 33, 35; Özalp, I, 179.

84 TBMM, *Zabıt Ceridesi,* XII, 19–21; *Nutuk,* II, 612, *Speech,* pp. 515–517; *Türk İstiklâl Harbı,* II/6, kp. 1., p. 194, IV, 229.

85 *Nutuk,* II, 616; *Atatürk TTB,* IV, 394–400.

86 *Atatürk Söylev,* 135.

87 Özalp, I, 213; TV, II/8, 92; *Nutuk,* II, 618, Selek, I, 287.

88 TBMM, *Zabıt Ceridesi,* I/12, 264; *Nutuk,* II, 620; *Türk İstiklâl Harbı,* II/2, 584; *Tar. Ves.,* II/8, 96; *Düstur³,* II, 143.

89 *Düstur³,* II, 98–107; Hurewitz, *Diplomacy¹,* II, 98–100; *Nutuk,* II, 624; Selek, I, 667; *Türk İstiklâl Harbı,* II/6, kp. 1, p. 10, IV, 249, 252.

90 Tunaya, pp. 533–539; Weiker, p. 45; TV, III/13 (1949), pp. 12–15.

91 *Nutuk,* II, 633; Goloğlu, *Cumhuriyete doğru,* p. 255; Karabekir, pp. 440–443; TBMM, *Zabıt Ceridesi,* I/21, p. 359.

92 Weiker, p. 46.

93 *Türk İstiklâl Harbı,* II/6, ktb. 1, p. 325, II/6, ktb. 4, p. 37; Şimşir, p. 377.

94 *Türk İstiklâl Harbı,* II/6, kp. 2, p. 277, *Atatürk TTB,* IV, 450.

95 Şimşir, p. 479.

96 *Türk İstiklâl Harbı,* II/6, kp. 3, p. 156; Edib, *Türkün Ateşle İmtihanı,* p. 292.

97 M. Sertoğlu, "Atatürkle İlgili Üç Belge," *Belgelerle Türk Tarihi Dergisi,* I/1 (1967), 3–7.

98 *Türk İstiklâl Harbı,* II/6, kp. 3, p. 226.

99 David Walder, *The Chanak Affair,* London, 1969, p. 281.

100 Walder, p. 281.

101 *Nutuk,* II, 679; *Türk İstiklâl Harbı,* II/6, kp. 4, pp. 36, 83; Bıyıklıoğlu, *Trakyada Milli Mücadele,* I, 450–454; Reşat Ekrem (Koçu), *Osmanlı Muahedeleri,* pp. 312–317.

102 Fethi Tevetoğlu, *Atatürkle Samsuna Çıkanlar,* pp. 77–81.

103 *Nutuk,* II, 683, 689, 691; TBMM, *Zabıt Ceridesi,* I/24, pp. 314–315; *Türk İstiklâl Harbı,* II/6, kp. 4, pp. 111–112; *Düstur³,* III, 152.

104 *Türk İstiklâl Harbı,* II/6, kp. 4, pp. 112–113; Tevetoğlu, *Atatürkle Samsuna Çıkanlar,* p. 86.

105 Bıyıklıoğlu, *Atatürk Anadoluda,* pp. 49–59; Walder, pp. 333–334; *Nutuk,* II, 692; TBMM, *Zabıt Ceridesi,* I/24, p. 562; *Türk İstiklâl Harbı,* II/6, kp. 4, p. 112.

106 *Nutuk,* II, 699–700.

107 TBMM, *Zabıt Ceridesi,* I/24, pp. 564–565; *Türk İstiklâl Harbı,* II/6, kp. 4, p. 113.

108 Davison, "Lausanne," pp. 201–202.

109 *Documents on British Foreign Policy, 1919–1939,* First Series, XVIII, London, 1972, no. 478, p. 690.

110 *Nutuk,* II, 718.

111 *Türk İstiklâl Harbı,* II/6, kp. 4, p. 213; Sabis, V, 362; Goloğlu, *Türkiye Cumhuriyeti,* Ankara, 1971, p. 139.

112 *Documents on British Foreign Policy,* First Series, XVIII, 688–1064; Seha L. Meray, *Lozan Barış Konferansı. Tutanaklar-Belgeler,* Ankara, 1969; Roderic Davison, "Turkish Diplomacy from Mudros to Lausanne," G. A. Craig and F. Gilbert, eds., *The Diplomats, 1919–1939,* Princeton, N.J., 1967, pp. 172–209; Ali Naci Karacan, *Lozan,* İstanbul, 1971; M. Cemil Bilsel, *Lozan,* 2 vols., Ankara, 1933.

113 Hershlag¹, pp. 27–30; I. Hakkı Yeniay, *Yeni Osmanlı Borçları Tarihi,* Istanbul, 1964, pp. 113–358.

114 TBMM, *Zabıt Ceridesi,* II/1, pp. 264–284; Davison, "Lausanne," p. 208.

115 Walder, pp. 349–352; Yalman, *Yakın Tarihte,* III, 79–80; Ali Fuat Erden, *Atatürk,* Ankara, 1952, p. 91.

116 Yalman, *Yakın Tarihte,* III, 86–87.

117 TBMM, *Zabıt Ceridesi,* II/2, pp. 665, 670; *Nutuk,* II, 796.

118 TBMM, *Zabıt Ceridesi,* II/3, pp. 99, 103.

119 *Nutuk,* II, 846–848.

120 TBMM, *Zabıt Ceridesi,* II/7, pp. 7, 24, 27, 69; *Nutuk,* II, 849.

6

The Turkish Republic, 1923–1975

The Turks had won their independence, but a decade of war and revolution, massacre and countermassacre, banditry, blockade, and foreign occupation had decimated the population and shattered the economy of the lands that composed the new Turkey.

The Turkish Society and Economy in 1923

The disruption was massive. Most non-Muslims were gone, with the Greek community reduced from 1.8 million to 120,000 the Armenians from 1.3 million to 100,000. No less than 2.5 million Turks had died during the war, leaving a population of 13,269,606 in Anatolia and eastern Thrace.[1] Foreign trade had fallen drastically, exports from 2.5 to 0.8 billion kuruş, imports from 4.5 to 1.4 billion kuruş between 1911 and 1923. State revenues declined from 2.87 to 1.8 billion kuruş, with the only consolation being that the dismantlement of the vast bureaucracy of Istanbul had left expenditures at 1.72 billion kuruş, providing a surplus for the first time in many years.[2] The retail price index had skyrocketed from 100 in 1914 to 1279 in 1923, and prices were to continue rising during the remainder of the 1920s.[3]

The years of sustained war effort followed by disastrous economic prospects might have led the nationalists of the young Republic to espouse an aggressive militaristic policy like that of the Young Turk leaders of the previous decade. Or they might have resorted to a highly nationalistic, revanchist, dictatorial regime, as in Nazi Germany, by harping on the misfortunes that had beset the nation. Instead, the Turkish Republic adopted a constructive policy based on a positive self-image and optimistic assessment of its future as a nation. Crucial to the success of this attitude were the psychological impact of having won the War for Independence and the quality and nature of the leadership provided in the formative years of the new nation-state. It was Mustafa Kemal, later to be given the surname Atatürk ("Father of the Turks") by a grateful nation, who used his reputation as victor on the battlefield to secure the respect of the people and inspire and guide them in the years of peace and reconstruction that followed.

The Age of Mustafa Kemal Atatürk, 1923–1938

Equipped with hindsight provided by history, the circumstances of Atatürk's life and career, from his humble origins to his education and war service, seem to have had a specific purpose and direction: achievement of the rebirth of the Turkish nation out of the ashes of the Ottoman Empire. Born in Salonica in 1881, his father was a bureaucrat on the lowest levels of the Ottoman civil service, thus making him a member of the Ruling Class, but without the kind of loyalty and respect for tradition that other nationalists higher in the social order retained throughout their lives. Mustafa Kemal had a feeling for the needs and thoughts of the common man almost unique among his colleagues. During his school years, in the military preparatory school in Salonica where he first showed the brilliance that earned him the pseudonym Kemal (meaning excellent, mature) from his teacher, in the Istanbul military academy which he entered in 1899, and in his subsequent military career in Damascus and Istanbul, he demonstrated a number of personal qualities that made him a difficult colleague and subordinate but later on an effective national leader. He was very difficult to get along with: When he knew his friends or superiors were wrong, he told them so; when he was proved right, he made sure that they knew. He was extremely impatient with stupidity as well as with those who refused to accept his brilliance. He was highly authoritarian with his subordinates, but he refused to respect the authority of his superiors. In both the Young Turk movement and the army, therefore, he did not receive the positions and ranks that his talent and experience entitled him to, probably saving his political career from an untimely end by removing him from the Young Turk coterie that had brought the nation to disaster. After the Young Turks came to power, they sent him first to Libya (1911–1912), then as military attaché to Bulgaria and Berlin. During World War I, they assigned him first to Gallipoli (1915), then to the Caucasus (1916), and finally to Syria (1917), mainly to relieve themselves of his constant criticism when in Istanbul. Though Kemal admired German military efficiency, he resented what he considered to be the arrogance of the German advisers, and in reaction gained a similar reputation among the Germans and Austrians who served with him. But wherever he was sent, his basic military knowledge and unusual ability to understand, inspire, and lead his men achieved victory in the face of adversity and so brought him the military reputation that was to propel him to the top in the period of chaos that followed the war. During the War for Independence, the same qualities enabled him to lead the Turks to victory. When the local leaders and generals refused to accept his authority, he appealed directly to the people and got them to force their leaders to join him. His authoritarian nature, his belief that only he was right, his inability to accept opposition, his ability to appeal to the common people – all those qualities that had made him a bad colleague and a good soldier now achieved the union of forces necessary for Turkish victory. He also demonstrated a quality not evidenced before, an ability to put first things first, to subordinate long-term principles to the solution of short-range problems, to analyze and use political forces, and to postpone radical changes until the way was prepared for them. Thus it was that during the War for Independence he declared that he was fighting to restore the sultan, thus gaining for the national movement the support of all those who revered the sultanate. Even after the Grand National Assembly had been established in the name of the people, he still maintained that this was being done because the sultan was in the hands of the Allies and that he could therefore not take the lead in saving the Turkish nation. The mass following he gained after driving the Greeks into the sea enabled him to proceed to abolish the sultanate. And it was only after he assured the final triumph of the National Pact at Lausanne that he eliminated the caliphate and created the Turkish Republic. These same qualities of patience and sense of timing were to serve him well during the years of the Republic.

What did Mustafa Kemal envisage for the Turkish nation? His basic ideas and policies, developed in hundreds of speeches, programs, and laws from the early days of the War for Independence to his death in 1938, have come to be known as Kemalism. Developed originally out of the struggles and debates among the Easternists and Westernists during the early days of the Grand National Assembly and partly included in the new Constitution enacted in 1924 to replace that promulgated during the war, they later were made part of the political programs of the Republican People's Party (*Cumhuriyet Halk Partisi*), which he created as his principal instrument to secure them. In February 1937 they were brought together in six ideologies written into article 2 of the Constitution: Republicanism, Nationalism, Populism, Revolutionism, Secularism, and Statism. These became the bases for most of the programs developed by Kemal and his successors from 1923 to the present day. The first four principles reflected the ideological basis of the new political structuring, and the last two expressed the policies that were to provide a philosophical framework for reforms.

Republicanism (Cumhuriyetçilik)

Republicanism involved not only replacement of the sultanate by the Republic but also elimination of the whole Ottoman social system through which a small Ruling Class governed and the mass of subjects existed to support it. Kemal's moves to abolish the sultanate and caliphate culminated the process by which the old Ottoman idea of reform had evolved from restoration of old institutions to their destruction and replacement by new ones. The Men of the Tanzimat and Abdulhamit II had applied this new concept mainly to the empire's physical apparatus but had not really extended it to its social bases. Now the sultanate, the caliphate, and the Ruling Class gave way to a republic, manifesting and organizing the sovereignty of the people and their right to rule themselves for their own benefit. The new slogan was "Sovereignty Belongs to the Nation" (*Hâkimiyet Milletindir*). The Republic was to be by and for the people. The people learned that their interests were identical with those of the Republic and that its continued existence and prosperity were essential for theirs.

Nationalism (Milliyetçilik)

Nationalism, and particularly Turkish nationalism (*Türkçülük*), was the essential rallying cry for the War for Independence and the Republic. The territorial losses and the refusal of the minorities to renounce their national aspirations in favor of a multinational Ottoman state turned Ottomanism to Turkish nationalism. The flight of the minorities during the wars left the Turkish Muslims with 97.3 percent of the total population in 1927, thus making the Republic ethnically and culturally homogeneous and leaving it in a position to fulfill the aims and goals of Turkish nationalism.

The doctrines of nationalism were expounded by the state through the press, the schools and various branches of government, through the Republican People's Party, and through the Turkish Hearth organization inherited from the Young Turks. The main obstacle that had to be overcome was the feeling of scorn heaped on "the Turk" by Ottomans and foreigners alike over the centuries. In reaction, the Kemalist tenets asserted that the Turks were the direct descendants of the world's greatest conquering race, that they had played a leading role in the origins and development of world civilization, and that it was the Turks who had contributed most to what had been great in the Ottoman Empire. The Turkish Historical Society (*Türk Tarih Kurumu*) was founded in 1925 to show the Turks what they had done in history. Nationalist theories of language and history were expounded, such as the Sun-Language theory, which maintained that Turkish was the first language on earth and that all other languages developed from it; that the Turks were the first people and that all human achievement had essentially Turkish origins; that there was an unbroken thread of Turkish history in Anatolia from the beginning of mankind, not merely from the eleventh century; and that they first appeared in history as Sumerians and Hittites.

A very important element of Turkish nationalism was the increased Turkification of the language under the leadership of the Turkish Language Society (*Türk Dil Kurumu*) founded in 1926. Arabic and Persian were eliminated from the school curriculums. Words of foreign origin were replaced by those of purely Turkish origin, as used by the people, found in old texts, or simply invented according to the rules of Turkish morphology. The Latin script was introduced in place of the Arabic script as the vehicle of the new Turkish. Linguistic nationalism was followed both to make it easier for people to learn to read and also to cut young Turks off from their Ottoman heritage and to replace the conservative mentality of the past with a modern and liberal one. Kemal wanted thus to create a generation of Turks that would not only be proud of its race but would also regard reform and change according to the needs of the time as natural, rather than always looking back to the way things had been done in the "good old days" as had so many Ottoman reformers in the past.

The theories of Turkish nationalism expounded in the 1920s and 1930s were extreme, but they were not created as part of a search for truth as such. Rather, they were weapons to achieve the Republic's aims, and as soon as they had accomplished their purpose, they were mostly abandoned. Turkish nationalism replaced regionalism and unified the Turkish people around common goals. It prevented the class struggles and ideological divisiveness that might have resulted in a period of rapid change. It created a feeling of national solidarity in place of the discredited ideologies of Ottomanism and Pan-Islam. Turkish nationalism encouraged the Turks to build their own land, without fostering aggressive irredentist aspirations. Turkish nationalism was not imperialistic; it did not seek to achieve greatness by regaining lands once ruled by the Ottomans, even in the case of areas still inhabited by considerable Turkish minorities. The Pan-Turkish emphasis of the Young Turks also was ignored and suppressed. The emphasis now was on building a modern state for the Turks within the boundaries of the Republic created by the Treaty of Lausanne. The Republic's only aim regarding the lost territories was to make sure that the Turks living in them were treated fairly and justly.

Thus it was that on June 5, 1926, Turkey signed a treaty with Great Britain surrendering all rights to Mosul in return for 10 percent of the oil produced in the area and British agreement to refrain from further agitation on behalf of the Kurds or Armenians, thus restoring the old friendship between the two and leading to British participation in the Turkish economy. Turkish nationalism was not hostile to its neighbors, even those that it had fought recently. The main objective now was cooperation for mutual benefit. On December 30, 1930, Greece and Turkey concluded a treaty of friendship settling the boundary and population exchange problems, agreeing to naval equality in the eastern Mediterranean, and reaffirming the status quo, partly in fear of Bulgarian desires to regain access to the Aegean through western Thrace.[4] Trade and friendship treaties signed in 1930 with Britain,

Hungary, Germany, Bulgaria, and others also marked Turkey's reentry into the concert of nations, culminating with its entry into the League of Nations on July 18, 1932.[5] In the face of Italian aggression in Ethiopia and the fear of similar moves in the Middle East, Turkey supported the League of Nations as well as its Balkan neighbors and moved closer to Britain and France. On February 9, 1934, Turkey joined the Balkan Entente Treaty signed in Athens, with Greece, Yugoslavia, and Rumania guaranteeing each other's territorial integrity and independence and establishing machinery to settle disputes among the signatories.[6] The Balkan non-signatory was Bulgaria, which continued to nourish ambitions in Macedonia, western Thrace, and the Dobruca despite improving relations with Turkey. Only two major problems prevented a full rapprochement with the world, the Straits, and the province of Alexandretta. On April 11, 1936, Turkey asked the signatories of the Lausanne Treaty for permission to fortify the Straits and resume full sovereignty. The result was the Agreement of Montreux (July 20, 1936), by which the Turkish proposals were accepted by all the Lausanne signatories excepting Italy, which finally acquiesced in a separate agreement (May 2, 1938).[7]

The matter of Alexandretta (Hatay) was harder to solve, since its population was equally divided between Turks and Arabs and another nation, Syria (under French mandate), was involved. The Franklin-Bouillon agreement (1921) had established an autonomous regime there under the French. This satisfied the Turks until September 1936 when France promised Syria its full independence, including Alexandretta. Atatürk responded with a demand that the latter be given its own independence (October 9, 1936). He also formed the Hatay Independence Society (*Hatay Erginlik Cemiyeti*) in Istanbul to centralize the activities of its residents living outside the province and wishing to make their protests known.[8] Turkey then brought the matter to the League of Nations, resulting in an agreement for a special arrangement that would give Alexandretta independence, demilitarize it, and guarantee the rights of its Turkish inhabitants.[9] Turkey was so satisfied by this that it joined the Sa'adabad Pact with Iran, Iraq, and Afghanistan, which provided the signatories with the same kind of territorial guarantees and mutual assistance that the Balkan Pact had done in the west (July 8, 1937).[10] But when the new Alexandretta regime went into effect and elections were held (November 29, 1937), France responded to Syrian pressure with a decision to give the Turks only a minority representation in the provincial government and Parliament. This so angered Turkey that it denounced its 1926 friendship treaty with Syria and protested to the League (December 15, 1937). Finally, an agreement was reached with France (July 3, 1938) by which the province was made into a joint Franco-Turkish protectorate, with troops from both sides to guarantee order pending a general election to determine its fate.[11] After a summer of campaigning, the elections (July 21) provided a Turkish majority of 22 to 18 in the National Assembly. The new state, now called Hatay, began using Turkish flags, and petitioned Ankara for union. This was impossible as long as the French remained there, but France finally agreed to annexation in return for Turkish entry into a nonaggression pact (July 23, 1939), followed by a similar agreement with Britain. In return for Turkey's support in the conflict then unfolding with Nazi Germany, then, France and Britain acquiesced in the establishment of Turkish rule in a province that according to its population make-up probably could have justly gone to either of its neighbors.

If there was a harmful aspect to the nationalism of the Turkish Republic, it involved a self-imposed isolation of individuals from the world and an overly self-centered view of Turkey. Though Western institutions, practices, and ideas were accepted, instruction in foreign languages and non-Turkish history was reduced in the schools, partly in reaction to overemphasis of foreign languages and history before World War I, partly also so that the official language and history theories would remain unquestioned. While the foreign and minority schools were allowed to continue operating, they could not expand, and their social science instruction in particular was subject to the guidelines of the Ministry of Education. Turkish newspapers concentrated almost entirely on internal affairs. This created a whole generation of educated people who knew little of the world, could not read Western publications, and viewed the world largely in terms of its relationship to Turkey. We shall see later how this isolation and self-centeredness broke down during and after World War II.

Populism (Halkçılık)

Closely connected with Turkish nationalism was the Kemalist doctrine of Populism, a corollary to Republicanism, that government was of the people, not the Ruling Class. This idea had various manifestations. One was that all citizens of the Republic were equal regardless of class, rank, religion, or occupation. So it was that the 1924 Constitution specified that "The People of Turkey, regardless of religion and race, are Turks as regards citizenship" (article 88). "All Turks are equal before the law and are expected to conscientiously abide by it. Every kind of group, class, family, and individual special privilege is abolished and prohibited" (article 69). Every Turk, regardless of origin, was given the same right to practice "the philosophical creed, religion, or doctrine to which he may adhere" (article 75). Citizens therefore could no longer be given different rights and positions according to their *millets*. While Lausanne essentially confirmed the autonomy of the latter, the promise of equality under the Republic was sufficient to convince the Jews to renounce their separate legal status and rights (October 8, 1925), the Armenians following three weeks later and the Greeks, after much more debate, on January 7, 1926. The *millets* continued to provide religious and social leadership for their coreligionists and separate schools, hospitals, and other social institutions for those wishing to use them, with the government insisting only that all *millet* children receive their elementary education in the state schools or according to curriculums established by the Ministry of Education, in order to provide the common bonds needed for them to participate fully in Turkish life (March 23, 1931).[12] A further step toward equality came in 1928 when the articles of the 1924 Constitution specifying Islam as the state religion, including reference to Allah in the official oath and requiring the National Assembly to enforce the *Şeriat*, were replaced by articles separating religion and state and declaring the Turkish Republic a secular state.[13] Since then members of the non-Muslim religions have had full legal equality in the Turkish Republic.

The second basic premise of Populism involved government by and for the people. Institutions had to be developed to enable the Republic's citizens to share in the process of rule. This was formally accomplished through the Grand National Assembly. Since its foundation, the Assembly had been given both legislative and executive powers, the latter carried out through the president of the Republic, elected by it, and the former through the Council of Ministers, chosen by and responsible to the president. Judicial functions were carried out in the name of the Assembly, in accordance with the law, by courts that were independent of it. At first the vote was given only to every male Turk aged 18 or over, but in 1934 women also were given the right to vote and serve as deputies. Representatives were elected for four-year terms by the people, but through an indirect voting system until 1946, when direct elections were substituted. The deputies' immunities were guaranteed by provisions that only the Grand National Assembly could surrender one of its members to the authorities for trial and that if he was found guilty, execution of the sentence had to wait until the expiration of his term. The Assembly was to convene annually on November 1 without being convoked by any other authority; only it had the right to decide on its dissolution and the holding of new elections. Legislation could be initiated either by its members or by the cabinet collectively. It could not recess for more than six months during the year, but if it was in recess, the president of the Republic or president of the Council of Ministers could recall it in case of emergency. The Assembly also had to reconvene if requested by one-fifth of its members. Debates were to be public, with reports fully published, but the Assembly could also meet in secret session and decide on the propriety of publishing such discussions. The president's term was set at four years, but he could be reelected by the Assembly and, of course, Kemal continued in that position through the remainder of his life. The president's powers seemed limited, at least on paper. Though he was a member of the Assembly, he could not participate in debates or vote. He could veto a law within ten days of its passage, but the deputies could pass it over his veto by majority vote. All decrees promulgated by the president also were signed by the prime minister and the relevant minister, while the latter two alone were responsible for their enforcement. The president did have power, however, and this came mainly from his right to designate the prime minister from among the members of the Assembly, with the other ministers being chosen by the latter but approved by the president before being presented collectively for the approval of the Assembly. Once approved and in office, however, they were responsible to the Assembly rather than to the president for the government's policies and programs.

The powers of the Assembly were enforced by the constitutional provisions regarding the budget. The government had to present it annually to the Assembly for its approval at the opening of each session, and it also had to present a statement of fiscal accounting to the Assembly no later than the beginning of the second year following the fiscal year. Budgets were approved only for one year; the government could not spend money beyond the budgetary provisions without additional Assembly approval; and the latter also could establish its own Accounting Office "to control the revenues and expenditures of State on behalf of the Grand National Assembly" (articles 95–101).

One of the few Tanzimat relics left in the republican period was the Council of State (*Şurayı Devlet,* later called *Danıştay*), whose members were elected by the Assembly "from among those who have held important posts, who possess great experience, who are specialists or who are otherwise qualified." Its duties involved deciding administrative controversies, advising on the contents and propriety of legislative proposals and government contracts and concessions, sanctioning cabinet regulations, providing for execution of the laws passed by the Assembly, acting as a court of appeal in matters of administrative justice, and deciding on conflicts among organs of government (articles 51–52). In many ways, thus, the Council of State evolved into a Supreme Court, and in its participation in both the legislative and executive processes it gained a far more active role than similar bodies in other countries.

The Constitution provided that "judges are independent in the conduct of trials and in the rendering of their judgments. They shall be protected from any sort of intervention and are subject only to the law. Neither the Grand National Assembly of Turkey nor the Cabinet may modify, alter, delay or influence the execution of their judgments" (article 54). Every person could use all legal means needed to defend his rights before the courts. And a High Court (*Divan-ı Âli*) of 21 members, of whom 11 were chosen from among members of the Court of Appeals (*Temyiz Mahkemesi*) and 10 from the Council of State, was established to try members of the cabinet, the Council of State, and the Court of Appeals "in all questions pertaining to the performance of their duties" (article 61).

The old districts and communes were retained, but the old large vilayets established by the Tanzimat were now broken into 62 new provinces. Their governors were nominally given much more autonomy than their nineteenth-century Ottoman predecessors, but this meant little in practice, since the Constitution also established general inspectorship (*müfettişlik*) districts, each including from 10 to 14 provinces, which dealt with all military and health matters as well as most questions of education and finance. In addition, each province had military, financial, and educational officials appointed by and responsible to the Ankara ministries, leaving the governors to do no more than coordinate their activities and represent the prime minister's office in the process of administration.

There was no prohibition of a multitude of parties in the Constitution. But Kemalism came to dictate that the people's interests could best be served by focusing its energies into the party that Kemal had evolved out of the Committee to Defend the Rights of Anatolia and Rumeli, called first simply the People's Party (*Halk Fırkası*) and after the establishment of the Republic, the Republican People's Party (*Cumhuriyet Halk Partisi*) (hereafter abbreviated as the RPP). There were several opposition groups during the War for Independence, as we have seen. Only the Second Group (*İkinci Gurup*) was important, however, since it included a number of Kemal's close associates. But since it basically represented the Westernists in the Assembly and included some who opposed the basic tenets of Kemalism, especially Secularism, Kemal made very certain that in the elections held in August 1923 for delegates to the second Grand National Assembly its members were defeated, thus leaving full control to his own party.[14] It was mainly subsequent challenges to secularism and modernism that led Kemal to exclude rival parties in later years. Soon after the caliphate was abolished, a number of leading military figures of the revolution, including Kâzım Karabekir, Ali Fuat Cebesoy, Refet Bele, and Rauf Orbay, attacked the government's secularist and modernist policies. Kemal reacted by demanding that they give up either their military positions or their assembly seats. They resigned from the former and also from the RPP (October 26–November 9, 1924), joining many members of the Second Group to form the Progressive Republican Party (*Terakkiperver Cumhuriyet Fırkası*), which included also many respected civilian nationalists like Adnan Adıvar and his wife, Halide Edip. The new party carried on the spirit of the Westernists and the Second Group. It opposed abolition of the caliphate and the secularizing policies of the government. But it was reformist in its own way. It encouraged free enterprise and foreign capital investment more than the government's current economic policies and declared its full support for Republicanism, Democracy, and Liberalism. Imitating the RPP, it began to build its own national organization to secure a mass following. Criticizing Kemal's merging of the government and the RPP, it demanded that he be above party. Kemal at first tried to reconcile the existence of the new group with the people's need for practice in the exercise of democracy, going as far as to replace

Prime Minister Ismet Inönü, a particular object of their criticism, with Ali Fethi Okyar to meet some of their criticism. Kemal apparently allowed the party to grow because he felt that by this time opposition to the Republic was so weak that it could no longer gain mass support. But the new party's existence unleashed such a torrent of willing supporters from all sides of the political spectrum that the president and his associates soon were forced to recognize their error. It was the party's very success that doomed it, since it stimulated the rise of a number of violent opposition groups whose existence finally convinced the government to suppress all of them.[15]

Early in 1925 a serious revolt began in southeastern Anatolia led by the Kurds. It was stimulated by the Russian Communists, who no longer could use the Armenians as weapons of disruption, and by the Turkish conservatives to express their own opposition to the government's religious and secularist policies. Ravaging widely in the area of Diyarbekir under the leadership of Şeyh Sait, the rebels burned and looted Elazığ and a number of smaller towns. As the movement attracted sympathy among conservative groups in Istanbul and elsewhere, Kemal acted decisively to curb it before it became a rallying point for a general reaction against the Republic. On March 3 Ismet replaced Ali Fethi as prime minister. He got the Assembly to issue the Restoration-of-Order Law (March 4, 1925), by which the government was given virtual dictatorial powers for a period of two years, with Independence Tribunals (*Istiklâl Mahkemesi*) again being established in Ankara and the eastern provinces to convict, imprison, and/or execute rebels according to the gravity of their crimes.[16] The rebels soon were disbanded. Şeyh Sait and his chief assistants were captured (April 15), convicted by the Eastern Independence Tribunal (May 25), and executed (June 29), thus putting the cap for the moment on both the Kurdish and the conservative reactions.[17]

The experience, however, convinced Kemal that continued existence of opposition parties would only focus and deepen these and other sources of discontent. On June 3, 1925, therefore, the Council of Ministers decreed that the Progressive Republican Party be dissolved after its founders had been pressured to do so and refused.[18] On August 12 the Istanbul newspaper *Vatan* was closed and its founder and editor, Ahmet Emin Yalman, arrested, both orders eventually, however, being rescinded.[19] The same day the Ankara Independence Tribunal convicted the well-known Communist poet Nazım Hikmet and several of his colleagues of spreading Communist propaganda. This indicated that there were limits on the extent Kemal would allow the Russians to take advantage of their Turkish friendship.[20] Since these measures came just before the government's introduction of new clothing regulations and decrees closing the dervish lodges (*tekkes*) (see pp. 385-386), their object was clear; a minority of conservative agitators would not be allowed to use the new democracy to stir popular opposition to secularism. In the process the kind of political opposition represented by the Progressive Republican Party also had to be sacrificed.

The Restoration-of-Order Law and the Independence Tribunals were abolished soon afterward (March 2 and 7, 1927), but renewed Kurdish uprisings in the summers of 1927 and 1928, supported by coalitions of Communist and reactionary groups around the country, made the government reluctant to sanction any new political opposition despite European criticisms in this regard. The Restoration-of-Order law was revived late in 1927, and it was only after the last Kurdish movement had been suppressed on March 4, 1929 that Kemal felt secure enough to tell the Assembly that he did not feel it had to be renewed.

Kemal now felt he had achieved the basic aim of his initial reforms, general acceptance of the Republic and of Secularism, so that the time had come for a new opposition party to give the Assembly, the government, the people, and even the RPP the kind of stimulus needed for them to work more efficiently and rapidly for the common good. As depression and economic crisis were stirring the kind of internal criticism that might have gained revolutionary content unless given some means of expression, Kemal sought to create a limited opposition, channeling the discontent into a harmless movement that he could control. To lead the opposition Kemal chose his former prime minister, Ali Fethi Okyar, who since his dismissal in 1925 had been ambassador to Paris. Emerging from a long meeting with Kemal, Ali Fethi announced the formation of the Free Republican Party (*Serbest Cumhuriyet Fırkası*), with a program that differed from that of the government mainly on questions of financial and economic policy while accepting its other basic principles. Ali Fethi soon began to build a national organization, touring the country to enlist mass support, advocating an end to state monopolies and the encouragement of free enterprise and foreign investment, lower taxes, closer ties with Turkey's Balkan neighbors and the League of Nations, and a freer political climate.[21] Kemal wavered between allowing the party enough parliamentary strength to exercise significant opposition and limiting its role in fear of weakening the government. In the end, only 15 RPP deputies went over, including the journalist Ahmet Ağaoğlu, who became its principal spokesman, Nuri Conker, its first secretary general, Mehmet Emin Yurdakul, the "Poet of the Revolution," and, surprising to many, Kemal's sister Makbule, his "gift" to the movement.[22]

In the end the Free Republicans, like their predecessors, were doomed by their success in stimulating the opposition not only of those republican supporters who wanted to criticize the rigors and mistakes of the RPP regime but also of the reactionaries and Communists, who sought to use the movement despite Ali Fethi's rigorous efforts to avoid their embrace. As he traveled around western Anatolia, his public gatherings were accompanied by numerous incidents, as radical mobs used the occasion to attack RPP buildings. The extent of popular support for the new party again began to alarm the government.[23] In addition, ministers and other political leaders who bore the brunt of the new party's quite justified criticisms of inefficiency, dishonesty, or failure began to resent its existence and used their access to the president to convince him it should be ended. When conservatives in other parts of the country began to form their own illegal parties, Kemal began to feel that the situation was getting out of hand.[24] The final blow came in the Assembly debate of November 15, 1930, when Ali Fethi complained of large-scale irregularities that he felt had cost his party many seats in the recent elections. Most RPP members replied by attributing the Free Republican Party's failure to its own inadequacies, in the usual political manner, but one went so far as to accuse Ali Fethi himself of treason during the War for Independence. Ali Fethi replied with attacks on the RPP, and the debate degenerated, leading Kemal, who was an interested observer, to conclude that Turkey was not yet ready for a responsible opposition and to order the party to disband as rapidly as possible (November 17, 1930).[25] The president's will was carried out immediately by the party leaders, and it was officially dissolved by cabinet decree (December 21, 1930), thus ending Kemal's second effort to establish an opposition. A number of Free Republican Party deputies, however, continued to cooperate in the Assembly on an unofficial basis for some time afterward.[26]

It was, then, through the instrument of a single party, the RPP, that the Kemalist programs were formulated and carried through, with Kemal controlling the Assembly, and thus the government, through the party. It was declared to be a "republican, populist, nationalist political organization," with Kemal as its permanent chairman. Membership was limited to the elite of Turkish society, who were admitted through a complicated system of introductions and examinations and were required to accept strict party discipline, regularly attend party meetings, and work as the party directed. Party branches were organized throughout the country to include representatives of all the major political, economic, and social groups that supported the Republic's aims. The party, therefore, became the means of reconciling and mediating what differences existed in approach and method so that its decisions, as carried out in the Assembly, did represent the merging views of the nation, at least those in the nation who approved the ideals of Kemalism.

In order to remedy the deficiencies exposed by the Free Republican Party episode, the RPP also became the government's principal agent for mass political education and indoctrination in the ideals of the Republic. This kind of adult-education program had begun with the Turkish Hearth movement, which had played an important role in initially organizing Turkish national feeling against the peace settlement and the Allied occupation. But its energies had been absorbed by the nationalist movement and it did not recover its early vigor during the early years of the Republic. In 1932, therefore, it was abolished and its branches were absorbed into a new organization set up by the RPP, the People's Houses (*Halk Evleri*), established in the cities and larger towns, and, later, the People's Rooms (*Halk Odaları*), opened in the small towns and villages.[27] The main objective of the new organization was to educate people in the Kemalist ideals and to create ideological unity between the educated elite running the party and the Assembly, and the masses. Thus the opponents of the Republic would be deprived of possible mass support for their subversive ideas. The People's Houses and the People's Rooms functioned on several levels. They became adult-education centers as well as schools for political education for Turks of all ages. They became community centers, with programs of sports, movies, and cultural activities. They developed their own educational courses, research, and publication in areas needed to support the Kemalist doctrines, especially in Turkish history, language, and folklore. Their fine-arts sections presented performances and encouraged mass participation in the presentation of modern music and art. Their sports sections emphasized team sports to develop a feeling of cooperation for the common effort. Their social divisions cared for those in need. The adult-education sections offered courses on reading, handicrafts, fine arts, health and hygiene, and the like. Village affairs sections were established in some areas to improve the physical and social condition of the villagers and to encourage a feeling of unity between them and the city dwellers by arranging visits. The principal organ of the movement was *Ülkü* (Ideal), published by the Ankara People's House starting in 1932 under the editorship of RPP General Secretary Recep Peker for four years and then of the distinguished historian Fuat Köprülü until 1941. Many local People's Houses published their own journals and books, which included useful material on local history, folklore, and society. There also was the *Halk Bilgisi Haberleri* (News of Folk Culture), edited after 1927 by the folklorist Pertev Naili Boratov, who made it into a major instrument of research into social and religious groups, nomadic tribes, agricultural methods, and other matters of interest to the villages. At its peak in 1940 the People's House movement had some 130,000 members, and it had a major impact on developing public opinion in town and country.[28]

The dictatorship of president and party, made possible by the principle of Populism and its claim that all interests in the state are embodied in the party and represented by its president, has been criticized as having denied the Turkish people their right to govern themselves. Such criticism would be more just if Kemal's totalitarianism had been used to misrule the people, regain lost territories, or persecute minorities. But in fact the policies of the government were directed toward modernizing the nation and improving its people's lives. The forms of democracy were provided so that people and politicians could gain experience in their use. While the opposition parties were suppressed during most of the era of Atatürk he encouraged public discussion of the major issues, himself answering his critics in speeches to the Assembly, in the press, and while traveling around the country to speak with the people. That the system did in fact work as intended is demonstrated by the success of Turkish democracy in the years following his death, when the institutions that he left produced a nation that is modern, vibrant, and democratic.

Revolutionism (Inkılâpçılık)

Another Kemalist doctrine reflecting the philosophical basis of change was Revolutionism. It involved a readiness, even zeal, to transform the traditional Ottoman society into a modern one by radical, forced measures aimed at achieving success within the span of a single generation. This method was dictated by the need to protect the nation against its enemies and also to justify the radical measures taken to establish the Republic. Revolutionism basically involved the use of whatever was needed to make sure that the revolution begun in 1919 would achieve its aims. So it was that the RPP declared in 1935 that it did not consider itself and the conduct of the state to be limited to gradual, evolutionary steps of development. It committed itself to defending the principles that had been developed as part of revolutionism.[29]

The modernism that was to be achieved through the institutions developed out of Republicanism and Populism – for the objectives of Nationalism, and through the techniques of Revolutionism – was supplemented by two more Kemalist doctrines, which directed and defined the outlook and policies of the state: Secularism and Statism.

Secularism (Layiklik)

Secularism involved not just separation of the state from the institutions of Islam but also liberation of the individual mind from the restraints imposed by the traditional Islamic concepts and practices, and modernization of all aspects of state and society that had been molded by Islamic traditions and ways. Liberation of the state had to come first. Abolition of the caliphate was followed by a series of reforms to end the union of state and religion that had characterized the Ottoman Empire, thus in turn ending the ability of the religious class to limit and control the state. The position and office of *şeyhulislam* and the Ministry of Religious Foundations were abolished and replaced by small departments for Religious Affairs (*Diyanet İşleri Müdürlüğü*) and Religious Foundations (*Evkaf Müdürlüğü*), placed directly under the prime minister's office. The foundation properties were retained and administered separately. But their revenues went to the treasury, which used most of them for general state purposes while allotting only as much as was needed to finance the maintenance of the mosques and other religious buildings and to pay the salaries of a bare minimum of religious officials. Most members of the ulema were pensioned off (March 3, 1924).[30] The entire system of religious schools also was eliminated, with the *mekteps* and *medreses* being incorporated into a unified system of national education under the direction of the Ministry of Education.[31]

The periodic revolts and disturbances of Muslim conservatives often were direct responses to these and other measures that eliminated the remaining bases of their former power. On April 8, 1924, a National Law Court Organization Regulation (*Mahkeme Teşkilatı Kanunu*) abolished the *Şeriat* courts, retired their judges, and transferred their jurisdiction to the secular courts.[32] Soon after, the *Mecelle* and the *Şeriat* were replaced by new secular codes of civil law (*Türk Medeni Kanunu*, October 4, 1926),[33] criminal law (*Türk Ceza Kanunu*, July 1, 1926),[34] and commercial law (*Türk Ticaret Kanunu*), based respectively on the corresponding Swiss, Italian, and German codes. On November 30, 1925, the Assembly closed the dervish lodges (*tekke*) and cells (*zaviye*) as well as all religious tombs (*türbe*), abolished religious titles and their use, and prohibited the wearing of clerical garb in public except under special circumstances such as funerals.[35] The 1928 changes in the Constitution ending the stipulations that Islam was the state religion and that the government had to support the *Şeriat*, thus were only confirmations of what had already been done to undermine the religious institutions and leaders, though the latter's influence over the masses, particularly in the countryside, continued for some time.

Other changes were directed more toward undermining the religious classes indirectly by encouraging a spirit of modernism in the minds and hearts of everyone in the republic. Polygamy was abolished and divorce by court action introduced, with women being given extensive grounds to divorce their husbands. The wearing of turbans and fezzes in public was prohibited, and the hat was made the official headgear, thus ending the traditional indications of distinctions in rank, class, and religion (November 25, 1925).[36] The use of the veil was discouraged, particularly in the cities, but it never actually was made illegal. Civil marriages were made compulsory for all, though those wishing to do so still could have religious marriages as well (September 1, 1926). Muslim women now begun to expose themselves in beauty contests, and in 1929 the first Turkish beauty queen was chosen.[37] Women were allowed to vote and be elected, first in the municipalities (April 3, 1930, then the village councils of elders (October 26, 1933), and finally in national elections for the Grand National Assembly (December 1934).[38] Women were admitted to the public schools, the civil service, and the professions on an increasingly equal basis with men.

A series of further shocks assaulted the conservatives and emboldened the modernists. In 1925 the international time and calendar systems replaced the traditional Islamic ones, which already had been reduced to limited usage by the end of the nineteenth century (December 26, 1925).[39] Six years later the metric system definitively replaced the old measures of weight and capacity (March 26, 1931).[40] Buildings and houses had to be numbered and all streets named, in the European fashion, supplementing but never quite replacing the Middle Eastern system of locating houses in relation to the major squares and places in their vicinities (April 10, 1927).[41] Spirits and alcohol were made legal for Muslims, and their production and sale were continued in a government monopoly so that the treasury would receive all the profits (March 22, 1926).[42] Statues and paintings of Kemal began to appear in public places in October 1926, flouting the old Muslim tradition against the representation of living things. Government decrees required that *tuğras* and religious phrases be removed from the exteriors of public buildings, and their use on private buildings was discouraged as well (May 5, 1927).[43]

An indirect but most effective step toward breaking old religious traditions came in the area of language and its use. On November 1, 1928, the Grand National Assembly required all Turks to learn and use Latin letters in place of the traditional Arabic ones by the beginning of the new year, either by passing an examination or by attending a system of special national schools (*millet mektepleri*) established to teach their use. By the middle of 1929 all publications were being printed in the new script, while the use of Arabic and Persian even for religious books was strictly prohibited.[44] Instruction in these languages was also, of course, ended in the schools (September 1929). Turkish translations of the Koran, anathema to orthodox Muslims, were written with government encouragement and recited publicly on January 22, 1932, creating a sensation among many. A public Friday service was recited in Turkish for the first time at the Süleymaniye mosque only a few days later,[45] and just a year after Turkish was required in both calls to prayer and in prayer in the mosques around the country.[46] The use of Turkish in place of the foreign geographic names commonly in use – thus Istanbul in place of Constantinople and Edirne instead of Adrianople – also was urged on all foreign companies and embassies, with an encouraging response. Citizens were required to adopt family names (June 21, 1934), with the Assembly subsequently giving Kemal the name Atatürk and forbidding that name to anyone else, while he in turn suggested names to many of his associates, including that of Inönü, site of the famous battles, to his old friend the prime minister, who now became Ismet Inönü.[47] The use of official titles like Paşa, Bey, and Efendi was prohibited, and all positions and ranks connected with these titles were abolished.[48] The final steps came with the adoption of Western clothing and with making Sunday, instead of the Muslim Friday holiday, the official day of rest.[49]

An important element of secularism was the development of a modern system of education throughout the Republic. Here direction was left to the Ministry of Education, helped by an Education Council (*Maarif Şurası*), which included ministry officials and representatives of the various levels of education, both teachers and administrators, who met periodically to develop policy on matters of curriculum and school regulations. At first the nation was divided into 12 education districts, each controlled by a superintendent of education (*maarif emini*) appointed by and responsible to the ministry rather than the provincial officials. But subsequently control over education was decentralized, with the districts abolished and each province given its own Education Director (*maarif müdürü*), appointed by the governor and responsible not only for carrying out the ministry's directives but also for modifying them to meet local problems and needs.

Public education now was completely divorced from religion, and religious lessons were forbidden, leaving them to the family or, where they existed, to *hocas* maintained privately, mainly in the smaller villages. Elementary education was made compulsory and free for all children, regardless of religion, to assure a common training. The basic structure of elementary, intermediate, and lycée education inherited from the nineteenth century was retained, and changes in curriculum and length of terms of study were introduced to strengthen the lower levels and make them more than just preparatory stages for secondary education. As time went on, foreign experts, including John Dewey, were brought to Turkey to recommend further changes. Large-scale programs training new teachers and building new schools soon made the ideal of compulsory elementary education a reality all over the nation. The old problems of securing sufficient teachers for the more distant rural areas continued, however, to limit the extension of the higher levels as rapidly as they were needed. Though emphasis was on technical and career training, the schools continued to provide a kind of literary and classical education not suited to the needs of many, especially in the rural areas. The teachers also, while usually well trained, soon became parts of an educational bureaucracy that tended to discourage innovation and interest, a problem certainly not unique to Turkey. As the result of the government efforts, however, the number of schools in the country doubled between 1923 and 1940, from 5,062 to 11,040; the number of teachers increased by 133 percent, from 12,458 to 28,298; and the number of students increased by slightly less than 300 percent, from 352,668 to 1,050,159. Literacy improved slowly but steadily. In 1927 only 10.6 percent of the population (17.4 percent of the men and 4.7 percent of the women) could read. By 1940 this had improved to only 22.4 percent (33.9 percent of the men and 11.2 percent of the women), with Istanbul much above the national average, though still no more than half the population there could read.[50] Disparities in literacy between urban and rural dwellers and between men and women continued to be marked, with only a very few village children going beyond the elementary levels due to family opposition and the lack of economic incentives.

At the higher levels also the educational plant begun by the Tanzimat was retained but modernized, often with the help of foreign experts and teachers. The Ottoman University (*Dar ül-Fünun*) was reorganized as the University of Istanbul in 1933. In the process, however, the Ministry of Education gained much more control than before, and many members of the old staff were replaced by German refugees, improving the quality of education but setting a precedent for further government intervention in later years. In January 1936 the Faculty of Language and History-Geography (*Dil ve Tarih-Coğrafya Fakültesi*) was opened as the nucleus of the new University of Ankara. The old Civil Service School (*Mekteb-i Mülkiye*) of Istanbul, only recently reorganized into the School of Political Sciences (*Siyasal Bilgiler Okulu*), was moved to Ankara. The numbers of vocational, technical, and teacher-training schools were increased, technical academies enlarged, and the War Academy (*Harbiye*) transferred to Ankara. Between 1923 and 1940 the number of higher faculties and technical schools increased from 9 to 20, teachers from 328 to 1,013, and students from 2,914 to 12,147, a sizable though not substantial improvement.[51]

Though the secularism of the Republic was aimed at lessening the influence of the clergy and creating an environment in which the individual could follow his religious beliefs without having to embrace predetermined dogma and conform to strict rules, it did not intend to abandon Islam as some of its opponents have claimed. The secularist program never opposed religion as such. There were no atheistic institutes on the Soviet model. The state was not anticlerical as long as the ulema made no overt attempt to interfere with the reforms. Worship at mosques was not forbidden. Religious leaders never were prevented from performing their religious functions. But the education centered in the secular schools and People's Houses did attack the obscurantism of the Muslim clergy and mysticism of the dervishes. Young people questioned the value of traditional rites and were indifferent to the teachings of the clergy. Attendance at mosque services in Kemal's time was limited largely to the older generation except in the villages, where the influence of the ulema remained strong. On the whole, however, by World War II the secularist policies of the Republic had achieved their main goals. The leaders of religion had little influence on the masses in the cities, and their hold in the villages decreased as communications were improved and the villagers benefited from education and economic development and an increased movement of population to the cities. People now accepted the ideas that civil affairs could be carried out better by government officials than by the clergy and that the doctrines of traditional Islam as propounded by the ulema were not always sufficient to cope with the demands of modern life. But as in the case of other programs of the Republic, this victory was achieved at a price. An entire generation of Muslim Turks was deprived of any education in the values of their religion except that provided sporadically by parents and a few *hocas*. Nationalism commanded the spiritual commitment once reserved to religion but was unable to provide the spiritual solace and philosophical comprehensiveness provided by Islam. The reconciliation of nationalism and spiritual needs was to come about gradually, as the tension created by rapid secularization diminished and a balance emerged.

Statism (Etatism) and the Economic Development of the Turkish Republic

The Republic's economic policies in Atatürk's time followed a confusing and only partly successful mixture of private enterprise and governmental supervision and participation in a program which came to be known as Statism.

In the area of agriculture, which remained by far the largest segment of the Turkish economy, the Republic took over the policies of the Young Turk period, adding assistance and some incentives to encourage the cultivator. In 1924 the Conscription Law required the army to train conscripts from the villages in the use of machines and new cultivation techniques in the course of their military service.[52] The Village Law encouraged local initiative and the use of modern methods and provided means to instruct cultivators on how to improve their standards of living and develop useful home industries (March 18, 1924).[53] The Ministry of Agriculture was reorganized to function effectively and provide agricultural training and advice about new crops, methods, and machines (March 3, 1924).[54] The Agricultural Bank (*Ziraat Bankası*) was transformed into a major instrument of agricultural development. It was required to accept the advice of Local Needs Commissions (*Mahallî Ihtiyaç Komisyonları*) so that its loans would be given to small as well as large landowners (February 24, 1924).[55] Its capital was increased, dividends to shareholders suspended, and credit facilities raised to 100 percent of capital. In addition to granting loans it also was ordered to use its funds to buy agricultural produce to maintain prices, sell equipment to peasants at minimum cost, buy and improve land to increase the cultivable areas, and to invest and participate in private companies dealing with agriculture in some way. As a result, its loans to peasants increased spectacularly, from only 4.8 million kuruş in 1923 to 25.9 million kuruş in 1929, still not equal to demand but much better than before.[56] To meet the demands for credit, a new Agricultural Credit Cooperative (*Ziraî Kredi Kooperatifleri*) system was established in June 1929 under the control of the Agricultural Bank. Some 572 cooperatives around the nation rescued many more peasants from the moneylenders, though in the end this program also suffered from lack of sufficient capital.[57]

Other approaches also were tried to help the cultivators. The tithe (*öşür*), long a symbol of the peasant's exploitation, finally was replaced with a new tax on produce set at only 6 kuruş per thousand, including the old shares set aside for education and public works.[58] This in turn was replaced by a tax on agricultural income, which subjected the cultivators to even less taxation (March 1926). But the new system left almost the entire support of the government to the city dwellers through increasingly heavy excise, income, and customs taxes, which made the development of urban trade and industry just that much more difficult. By such means, however, the Republic assured the support, or at least the acquiescence, of most peasants for its secularist reforms in succeeding years.

Important reforms also were introduced in landownership. As a first step, the extensive landholdings of religious foundations were subjected to direct state control, and the lot of peasants on them was improved at least to the level of the other cultivators. The Civil Law Code of 1926 unified the old Ottoman landholding categories set up in 1858 and ended on paper the last traces of feudal ownership, though many landowners in fact continued to maintain their hold on large estates and to exercise control over the peasants, particularly in the southwest and northeast. Various laws were passed in the 1920s to distribute state-owned lands or those recently restored to cultivation to peasants, particularly to those who had been dispossessed and their homes and fields burned by the Greeks and Armenians before and during the War for Independence as well as refugees from the Balkans and Central Asia.[59] But no where near the amount of land needed was available or distributed in this way, and landless peasants remained a serious problem to modern times.[60]

To train peasants in the use of new equipment and in new methods of cultivation the Ministry of Agriculture drew on the experts and provincial agricultural stations inherited from the Young Turks and began a program that was extended by the Rural Instruction Reform Law of 1927. Agricultural and veterinary institutions were established at Ankara and around the country.[61] The Agricultural Societies (*Ziraat Odaları*) established during the Tanzimat had been reorganized and expanded just before World War I,[62] and their activities in demonstrating new equipment and distributing seed were now encouraged by ministry grants and exemptions from customs duties for imported equipment.[63] The ministry also secured the passage of laws that encouraged the cultivation of new crops such as hazelnuts, lemons, tea, vegetables, and potatoes, also providing irrigation systems and helping eradicate malaria and other diseases that affected the cultivators' ability to work.[64] Experimental stations were established around the country, and the ministry developed its own agencies in the regions and districts to improve seeds and help the cultivators to obtain and use them. Agricultural experts were sent to Europe and America to learn the new methods. New forest conservation techniques were introduced to rescue what had survived the severe exploitation of the nineteenth century. And the rural road network was expanded from almost 14,000 kilometers of paved road and 14,450 kilometers of dirt roads in 1923 to 18,378 kilometers and 23,112 kilometers respectively in 1941, helping the cultivators to get their crops to market and secure the supplies that they needed.[65] As a result, agricultural production increased by 58 percent overall between 1923 and 1932, with grains up by 100 percent, tobacco by 57 percent, and cotton by 67 percent over their wartime lows.[66] From 1934 to 1941 the land devoted to grain increased from 6.55 to 8.2 million hectares; vegetables from 408,694 to 428,755 hectares; cotton from 248,961 to 327,785 hectares; and potatoes from 55,075 to 72,899 hectares, with production improving accordingly.[67]

Industrial development in the first decade of the Republic was even slower than that of agriculture. For one thing, Turkish industry started from a much less developed level. The Young Turks had encouraged industrial expansion by tax concessions and customs exemptions for imported machinery, but what little developed as a result had been destroyed during the wars that followed.[68] In addition, after long years of exploitation by foreign capitalists and the minorities, Turkish entrepreneurs were cowed and uncertain, inexperienced, and without accumulated capital. Kemal and those around him first concentrated on buying up what foreign enterprises remained, particularly in the public utilities and the exploitation of natural resources. The government also worked to mobilize what capital and enterprise the Turks had. In August 1924 the *İş Bankası* (Business Bank) was established by directive of the president as a publicly controlled but privately owned and financed savings bank to provide capital for Turks wishing to develop factories and businesses.[69] It invested in a number of small enterprises, but its main efforts in the 1920s and 1930s were devoted to the development of coal mines at Zonguldak, on the Black Sea, a necessary preliminary for heavy industry in the country.[70] Imported machinery intended for export industries and agriculture was exempted from customs duties.[71] On April 19, 1925, the Assembly established the Turkish Industrial and Mining Bank (*Türk Sanayi ve Maadin Bankası*) to provide government capital to develop state industries.[72] Industry also was encouraged by regulations giving a new legal status to the Chambers of Trade and Commerce (*Ticaret ve Sanayi Odaları*) started under Abdulhamit. They were made agents of the government to develop the crafts and trades, providing funds to train apprentices and upgrade artisans, settling disputes among workers in different guilds, setting standards of quality and conditions of employment, and providing facilities for savings, insurance, pensions, and social security, formerly provided by the craft guilds themselves.[73]

The most important industrial law of the 1920s was the Law for the Encouragement of Industry (*Teşvik-i Sanayi Kanunu*), promulgated on May 28, 1927.[74] Factories and mines were granted free land as well as exemptions from property, land, and profit taxes, and even from telephone and telegraph charges, to help set them on their way under private control. Government departments were required to purchase native products even when the price was higher and quality lower than that of foreign competition, and the government was authorized to provide each factory with subsidies equal to as much as 10 percent of its output. In return, employment had to be limited mainly to Turkish citizens, with foreign workers admitted only under certain severe restrictions. Those who built new factories under this law were allowed monopolies in their fields for 25 years, without any government intervention aside from that required to enforce the law itself.[75]

Though there was some improvement in industry in the 1920s, the government was dissatisfied with the rate of growth achieved through private enterprise. Starting in 1930, therefore, it turned to statism, or increased state supervision, control, and direction of industrial production. The then current international economic crisis as well as criticisms of the Free Republican Party seemed to necessitate firm measures that would enable the Turkish economy to survive. Statism, as expressed in the RPP program of 1931, was direct and to the point. It stated that when the nation's interests called for it, particularly in industry, the instrumentality of the state would be used to bring prosperity. Nevertheless, the state would continue to allow private enterprise: "The determination of which specific areas the state will enter is dependent on the needs of the situation. If it is determined that such intervention is needed, and there are private enterprises operating in the area, the taking-over of the latter will be governed by a special law in each case. . . ."[76]

The first step in the Statist program came in 1929 as soon as the Lausanne Treaty was no longer in force, when a series of protective customs duties was set up to protect nascent Turkish industry.[77] On June 11, 1930, the Central Bank of the

Turkish Republic was set up (*Türkiye Cümhuriyeti Merkez Bankası*) with the sole right to issue and control currency, a function that had previously been handled by the private Ottoman Bank in conjunction with the state treasury.[78] This gave the government full control of national monetary policy for the first time. The new bank was authorized to "contribute to the economic development of the country" by regulating the money supply and interest rates and adopting other fiscal devices to assure the stability of Turkish currency, then beginning to get caught up in the international monetary and economic crisis.[79]

Statist economic policy in Turkey was developed mainly in two Five-Year Plans adapted from the Soviet model in the 1930s. The plans emphasized industrial over agricultural development and involved the use of government capital, enterprise, and control in developing the new industries. Because of the country's low standard of living, the government did not follow the Soviet model of allocating all its resources to develop both capital and producer goods. Instead, it emphasized industries that would provide consumer goods and only to a lesser extent machinery for heavy industry. It aimed to reduce imports to establish a favorable trade balance and to meet local demand by developing native industries. Industrialization would also create an internal market for the country's raw materials, for which demands and prices had fallen because of the international crisis.

The first Five-Year Plan involved the development of chemical, earthenware, iron, paper, sulfur, sponge, cotton textile, worsted, and hemp industries in particular. The already established sugar industry was included later because of its importance to the economy. There was an attempt to locate industrial plants near areas that produced needed raw materials in order to facilitate transportation, diversify regional economies, and provide alternative employment for farmers. The textile industry was particularly emphasized, since, as we have seen, the adverse Ottoman trade balances had come from the need to import almost all textiles. Large state banks were developed as the main agencies for fulfilling the plan under the general supervision of the government. The Turkish Industrial and Mining Bank was divided into the State Industry Office (*Devlet Sanayi Ofisi*), charged with establishing and supervising the operations of state factories, and the Industrial Credit Bank (*Sanayi Kredi Bankası*), which provided capital to private industrial enterprises.[80] Later they were brought back together as the *Sümerbank* (Sumerian Bank), which took the lead in both light and heavy industrial development (June 3, 1933), operating state factories, planning and establishing new factories and industries according to the plan, with state capital, and participating in other enterprises in cooperation with private capital, thus also acting as a regular credit bank for businessmen.[81] As time went on, it invested in all areas of industry, taking over large shares of the production of cotton and wool goods, coke, cement, and leather and securing a virtual monopoly of the synthetics, of paper, iron, phosphate, steel, and lubricating-oil industries. It also opened vocational schools in connection with its major industries, providing scholarships to promising students for advanced study in Turkey and abroad.[82] In more recent times the *Sümerbank* also has developed its own chain of department stores to sell the products of its factories, becoming one of the leading mercantile operations in the country and serving also to keep commercial prices down by competing with private industries and merchants.

Other state banks also performed significant roles in developing Turkey's economy during and after the Atatürk years. The *Etibank* (Hittite Bank) was established in June 1935 to develop the Republic's natural wealth. It invested in enterprises in mineral and petroleum exploration and exploitation, electric-power facilities, coal mining and distribution, and the selling of these products in and out of the country.[83] The *Denizcilik Bankası* (Maritime Bank) was established on December 27, 1938, to operate the nationalized fleet of the Republic, including long-distance and commuter passenger and freight services, port facilities, and the like.[84] The *Ziraat Bankası* (Agricultural Bank) continued to invest widely, not only in enterprises that processed and distributed agricultural products and equipment but also in diverse activities such as insurance, cotton weaving, electric, textile, jute, and lumber industries and in private banks and savings associations in the provinces. The *Emlâk Kredi Bankası* (Real Estate Credit Bank), formed with state capital in 1927 but with 45 percent of its stock held privately, functioned to provide credit for both private and public construction, and later also participated in various commercial and industrial enterprises. The *İller Bankası* (Bank of the Provinces), formed in 1933 with capital from payments of 5 percent of the tax revenues of the provincial, municipal, and village governments, financed projects implementing the developmental plans of these administrations. Later also the Department of Religious Foundations formed its own *Vakıflar Bankası* (Foundations Bank), using income from foundations and private accounts to invest in a wide range of enterprises in and out of the country.

In addition, though not organized as banks, two other major state companies were established: (1) the Land Products Office (*Toprak Mahsulleri Ofisi*), to maintain agricultural price levels by buying and selling certain crops (June 24, 1938),[85] and (2) the Monopolies Company (*İnhisarlar*) to control the French-owned *Régie* tobacco company and later also to administer state monopolies established over alcoholic beverages and spirits, matches, tea, and salt and, for a time, also oil and gasoline.[86] Among the private banks the most important was and is the *İş Bankası* (Business Bank), founded in 1924 at the initiative of Kemal to encourage savings and economic development. It played a major role in developing Turkish railways, lumber, coal, sugar, textile, glass, sugar, cement, electric, and insurance enterprises, cooperating with the *Sümerbank* in several developments. It also supplied credit to Turkish merchants interested in participating in foreign trade, establishing several export companies and branches abroad. The *Türk Ticaret Bankası* (Turkish Commercial Bank), established in 1924 with private capital, invested mainly in department stores, insurance, electric, and cotton thread and textile industries. These and other public and private banks have remained the major forces in Turkish economic development to the present day, though private capital on one side and direct state planning on the other have assumed important roles in recent times.

Foreign investors were reluctant to enter the Turkish loan market for some time because of the long stalemate over the final payment of the old public debt. But the Turkish government did solicit and secure some foreign loans starting, in June 1930, with an American loan, followed by one from the Soviet government in 1934 to carry out the first Five-Year Plan, and loans from Britain, France, and Germany later to help pay for the nationalized railway and utility companies.[87] These loans were not of major significance in the total picture of Turkish finances, but they did enable the government to eliminate foreign control of the major public works and services by the end of the 1930s.

The second Five-Year Plan, accepted by the cabinet on September 18, 1936, aimed much more than the first at developing capital industries, and emphasized mining, electricity, ports, and heavy factory machinery. Whereas Russia contributed most advice and financial help to the first plan, Britain also participated in developing the second. Heavy industry was to be based on local raw materials, with a complex of coal and steel mills in the Black Sea coastal area around Zonguldak and Karabük, electric plants to power them, and railways to carry the product where it was needed. Eastern Turkey was to be industrialized by the construction of yarn, cement, sugar, and meat-processing factories and by building a new port at Trabzon. Factories also were to be built to make agricultural equipment, jute, aluminum, and textiles, again to lessen Turkish dependence on foreign imports in these areas. The tremendous housing shortage left from the war years was to be relieved by new housing developments, and efforts were to be made to increase agricultural exports.[88] The plan had only begun to be implemented, however, when it was disrupted by the outbreak of World War II.

Statism and the Five-Year Plans did not outlaw private enterprise, but the manner in which they were carried out certainly discouraged investment in the areas taken over by the government. Although the state enterprises made major contributions toward industrial development, they were not too efficient. In time, this led the government to encourage competition from private enterprise in order to stimulate increased efficiency in the state enterprises and secure the participation of private capital when needed. The first step came on June 17, 1938, when the Law on the Organization, Management, and Supervision of Economic Associations divided the enterprises of each state bank and other state bodies into separate establishments (*müesseseler*), which provided supervision, and these in turn into institutions (*teşekküller*), organized as corporate institutions, with financial and administrative autonomy and limited liability in relation to capital. The latter were now subjected to private law and expected to make profits, but their stock and overall supervision remained in the hands of the banks. At times also provisions were made for their transformation into joint-stock companies, with the entry of private capital and even management as circumstances warranted.[89] Under the new law the *Sümerbank,* for example, created the Yarn and Fabric Association, the Leather and Shoe Industry Association, the Turkish Steel and Iron Factories Association, and the Cement Industries Association.

Business activity was regulated by the Commercial Code of May 29, 1926.[90] Anyone with the legal ability to make contracts could engage in trade, including women (with the permission of their husbands), and foreign nationals, but excluding all government employees and judges. Firms had to register with the Commercial Court of their area and affiliate with the local chamber of commerce and/or industry, which was directed by an executive appointed by the Ministry of Commerce and which enforced state policies regarding businesses, including price and quality controls as well as settling all disputes among members, with no right of appeal.

One conspicuous deficiency in the Statist program was its failure to modernize the Turkish tax system, which remained essentially as it had been in the late nineteenth century, with the sole exception of the replacement of the tithe with a land tax. Even though the latter partly compensated the treasury for the lost revenues, and animal taxes also were increased, it was the city dwellers who now paid most of the cost of government, exactly the opposite of the Ottoman system, whereby the taxes on produce were the major source of government revenue. Even among the taxes imposed in the cities the old profits and excise taxes provided the bulk of the revenue, while a regular income tax was imposed only after World War II.

Turkey's industrial development in the 1930s created a growing working class that required the introduction and enforcement of various labor and social regulations. The Republic's programs in this respect reflected the idea of populism that society was composed of functional groups, with the government's main task being that of merging the interests of all, thus achieving social unity and order and avoiding class distinctions and conflicts. Labor, thus, had to achieve its aims through state action. But the state was very slow in acting because of the overriding need to encourage industrial development. Meanwhile, the workers suffered the consequences and could do little to change their poor conditions of labor and compensation. The first major labor law came in January 1924 when all employers were required to allow their workers a holiday of at least one day a week, Friday, but subsequent proposals to limit the duration of weekly labor to 60 hours were defeated by the Assembly on numerous occasions. Legislation favoring labor actually came first from the Ministry of Health, established in 1915.[91] It secured passage of the Public Health Law in 1930, providing for health councils on the provincial and municipal levels to care for general health and set standards of sanitation for both public and private institutions. The working hours of pregnant women and minor children were somewhat restricted and industrial health and safety standards established but not actually enforced.[92] Craftsmen and small merchants also were allowed to organize their own craft guilds (*esnaf odası*), but these were left under the control of the chambers of commerce, which were mainly concerned with the interests of the employers, while workers were not allowed to form unions "based on class lines." In the Penal Code they were denied the right to strike, though employers also were prohibited from locking out employees in the case of disputes.[93]

Foreign workers were subject to the same regulations and were also affected by a 1932 law that limited to Turkish citizens the right to engage in certain professions, such as medicine, dentistry, veterinary medicine, and law, with special permission being required to hire foreign experts in these fields. Turks also were given a monopoly in trades and occupations such as hairdressing, photography, printing, making clothing and shoes, peddling, selling goods produced by the state monopoly, working in public transportation; this also applied to musicians, laborers in building, iron, and wood factories, guards, doorkeepers, janitors, waiters and servants in public establishments, and nightclub singers and dancers.[94] While these restrictions may seem harsh, they should be interpreted in the light of the situation in the Ottoman Empire, where many subjects took foreign citizenship to escape Ottoman laws and many enterprises owned or operated by foreigners or members of the minorities actively discriminated against Muslims and Turks. Foreigners, however, were still allowed to own, transfer, bequeath, or sell personal property and real estate as long as Turkish citizens were allowed the same rights in the foreigners' home countries, and they were allowed to work in certain specialized occupations where there were not yet enough Turks, such as aircraft mechanics and pilots.

The first comprehensive Turkish labor code was enacted only in 1936. Its coverage was very limited, extending only to establishments employing ten workers or more (only 15 percent of the total at that time) and excluding all agricultural and government workers.[95] Stressing the need for balance between capital and labor, it prohibited strikes and lockouts, authorized "worker delegates" to represent dissatisfied workers, and in the event of disputes required all sides to negotiate and, if necessary, to accept arbitration. Much of the law attempted to establish a kind of worker welfare that would make strikes unnecessary. The basic workweek was set at 48 hours for the first time, normally 8 hours daily for six days, with the official weekend holiday from Saturday afternoon to Monday morning. Overtime labor was allowed for no more than 3 hours daily and 90 hours annually, and then only with the worker's consent, with supplementary pay of from 25 to 50 percent. Those leaving their jobs were entitled to receive from their employers a certificate indicating the extent, nature, and quality of their work. Pregnant women were to be excused from work before and after confinement and with half-pay as long as they had already worked for the same employer for at least six months.[96] Since enforcement of the labor code was sporadic and workers were not given the right to organize and strike, their overall condition remained poor.

The results of Atatürk's economic policies were less than the government claimed but certainly far better than his critics maintained. Coal production increased by only slightly less than 100 percent in a decade, from 1.59 million tons in 1930 to 3.019 million tons in 1940. During the same period, chrome production increased by almost 600 percent, from 28,000 to 170,000 tons; iron production at Karabük from nothing to 130,000 tons in 1940; and overall mineral production from a base index of 100 in 1930 to 157 in 1935, and 232 in 1940.[97] The textile industry developed sufficiently for it to meet about 80 percent of the country's textile needs, reducing fabric imports from a value of about 51.1 million Turkish liras in 1927 to 11.9 million liras in 1939.[98] Between 1924 and 1929 production of cotton products increased from 70 to 3,773 tons, wool from 400 to 763 tons, and silk from 2 to 31 tons.[99] Sugar production, which started only in 1926, rose from 5,162 to 95,192 tons between 1927 and 1930.[100] The number of kilometers of railroads almost doubled between 1927 and 1940, from 4,637 to 7,381, while roads also increased from 22,053 to 41,582 kilometers. The net national income increased from a base index of 100 in 1927 to 125.8 thirteen years later, while foreign trade went from an overall deficit in the 1920s to a clear surplus during most of the 1930s.[101] The normal state budget was balanced during most of the Atatürk years. A rapidly increasing tax revenue matched most of the statist expenditures, helped considerably by drastic reductions in military costs, which now took no more than 30 percent of the budget. Turkish financial reserves increased almost sixfold while controls on the movement of currency outside the country enabled the government to increase the value of the Turkish lira on the world market from 2.12 liras per dollar in 1930 to 1.28 in 1939.[102]

Atatürk's Final Years and Death

As time went on and his presidency was confirmed for life, Atatürk became increasingly autocratic, treating even minor instances of opposition as rebellion and sending into exile some of his oldest associates, including Rauf Orbay, Halide Edip, and Adnan Adıvar, for criticizing some of his policies. Thus it was that after over 20 years of collaboration with Atatürk, Ismet Inönü himself was forced to resign as prime minister (October 25, 1937) in favor of his long-time minister of finance, Celal Bayar, ostensibly because of minor disagreements with the president, though there are some suggestions that the incident was arranged so that whatever reaction there might be against Atatürk following his death, Inönü would not be deprived of the succession.

Atatürk followed a heavy schedule of work, traveling regularly around the country by train to spread the ideals of the Republic among the masses through a personal image that only he could supply. Isolation and heavy work, however, drove him to an increasingly dissolute private life, which finally caught up with him in 1938. On March 11 the public first was made aware of the fact that the president was ill, as it turned out with cirrhosis of the liver. On March 24 the Turkish government purchased the yacht *Savarona* in England for his personal use, and thereafter he spent most of his time resting on it, even holding cabinet meetings next to his bed. On September 5 Atatürk was transferred to the Dolmabahçe Palace as his condition became worse. He wrote his final will and left his entire fortune to the nation. On October 17 he fell into a deep coma from which he emerged only with difficulty two days later. The seriousness of his illness became apparent to the public for the first time. A literal "death watch" now began, with medical bulletins being issued twice a day. On October 29, the 15th anniversary of the Republic, the students of the Kuleli Army Lycée sailed past the palace on the Bosporus, serenading the president with the strains of the national anthem. Two days later Celal Bayar read the president's speech to the new session of the Grand National Assembly, the first time Kemal was unable to do so himself. On November 8, 1938, he fell into his final coma, and two days later he succumbed to his illness at the relatively young age of 57. His death precipitated a wave of mass sorrow unequaled in Turkish history, with mourning crowds silently observing the funeral train as it brought the president back to Ankara and as he was interred at the Ethnographic Museum (November 30, 1938). The body remained there until it was transferred to the *Anıt Kabir* (The Mausoleum-Monument), the permanent tomb especially built for him, on November 10, 1953. The "Father of the Turkish nation" had found his final resting place.

The Inönü Years, 1938–1950

There was no dispute at all about Atatürk's successor. He was the man who had done more than anyone else to help him save and modernize the nation, his loyal lieutenant Ismet Inönü, who was unanimously elected president of the Republic by the Grand National Assembly on November 11, 1938, and life president of the RPP two weeks later. Inönü's years as president were dominated by two major crises, World War II, which broke out less than a year after he assumed power, and the increasing demand for liberal reforms that followed the war.

Turkish Neutrality During World War II

Inönü and most of his associates and countrymen remembered all too well how the Ottoman Empire had been dragged to its destruction and the Turkish nation threatened with extinction by involvement in World War I. Nevertheless, circumstances had dictated Turkey's involvement in a number of international alliances. In the face of the Italian threat, relations with Britain had been improved in the mid-1930s, culminating with the visit of King Edward VIII to Istanbul while cruising the Mediterranean in his yacht (September 4–5, 1936) and by Inönü's visit to London to attend the coronation of George VI (May 9–10, 1937). New credit agreements followed (May 27), providing in particular for British participation in the industrial development of the second Five-Year Plan and leading to a treaty of mutual guarantee between the two (May 12, 1939), which soon was followed by the Franco-Turkish Agreement (June 23, 1939), which accompanied the Hatay settlement. The Turks entered these agreements mainly because of fear of Germany and Italy and also on the assumption that there would be no difficulty with the Soviet Union because of its strong opposition to nazism and fascism. But with the Nazi-Soviet alliance (August 23, 1939) and joint invasion of Poland, it seemed very possible that they might go on to overrun Turkey as well. Turkey attempted to secure a Russian guarantee for its territorial integrity so that its previous agreements with Britain and France could be transformed into open alliances. But Germany, facing encirclement from the south as the result of British-French agreements with Rumania and Greece (April 1939), worked to prevent this and also to secure Turkish friendship or at least neutrality so that Britain could not send help to Rumania through Turkish territory. Russia supported the German policy, and continued to threaten Turkey to keep the Allies out of the Balkans. It demanded Turkish agreement to close the Straits to foreign warships and to garrison them with Russian troops through a mutual-assistance pact (October 2, 1939). The Turks could not accept this proposal, if for no other reason than it would violate their obligations under the Montreux Convention and might well lead to war with the Allies.

On October 19, 1939, Turkey entered a mutual-assistance agreement with Britain and France. But it was arranged to prevent Turkish participation in a war unless the Republic's interests were directly involved, such as aggression by a European power in a war in the Mediterranean, in which case the Allies would help Turkey. Turkey's obligations to help Greece and Rumania by the terms of the pre-war Balkan Pact would thus also be honored. Turkey was allowed to exclude any action against the Soviet Union regardless of other obligations. France and Britain promised to give loans to help Turkey rearm and settle its commercial debt. The Russians were highly critical of the agreement despite the fact that they were excluded, but their own subsequent involvement in Poland and then with Germany prevented them from expressing their hostility by an open attack.

As World War II went on, its shifts and starts prevented Turkey from joining the Allies. It also avoided any entanglement with Germany, thus staying neutral. As Italy invaded and conquered Greece (October 1940) and Albania, and Germany in turn conquered Yugoslavia, Greece, Rumania, and Bulgaria, taking Crete and moving into North Africa in early 1941, Turkey was increasingly isolated from its nominal allies and exposed to the German threat without much hope of assistance except from Russia, whose position still was not very clear. Germany now was represented in Ankara by Franz von Papen, who had come to the Ottoman Empire during World War I as an assistant to von Falkenhayn. As long as the Allies seemed to be winning, his main effort was directed to keep Turkey from joining them. But once Germany began to win in Europe, he attempted to tighten relations with Turkey in various ways. His first victory came early in 1941 when he got the Turks to close the Straits to the ships of all nations, preventing the Allies from helping Russia, which was by then at war against Germany. He then attempted to get permission for German troops to pass through Turkey to attack the British and French in Iraq, Syria, and Iran, promising in return territories in Thrace and a guarantee of Turkish security. Turkey, however, realized that agreement to such terms would mean essentially a declaration of war on the Allies; thus it ultimately agreed only to a treaty of nonaggression with Germany (June 18, 1941), which specifically excluded commitments previously made by the parties. Germany, following its invasion of Russia (June 22, 1940), increased its demands on Turkey to include the supply of raw materials, particularly manganese and chrome, but the Turks were able to avoid a commitment on the grounds that they already had agreed to send these metals to Britain. In the end, Turkey was able to sell these metals to both sides at very high prices while avoiding a break with either. A trade agreement with Germany (October 9, 1941) provided some chrome in exchange for war equipment, but little more. In 1942 von Papen pressed the Turks once again for transit rights to the east, disclosing new Russian claims to the Straits made to Germany while they were allies, and also encouraging the surviving Pan-Turanians in Turkey to undermine the Soviet Union by stirring its Turkish minorities to revolt. Turkey avoided a final commitment on the pretext that such actions, if openly supported by its government, might cause the Russians to massacre their entire Turkish population, particularly since Armenians had become very strong in the Communist party. As a result, all Germany was able to get was new trade agreements, but Turkey was able to avoid any commitments that might cause an open break with the Western Allies. The Allies, in the meantime, encouraged Turkish neutrality, since they no longer were in any position to help Turkey in case it entered the war openly on their behalf.[103]

While Turkey thus managed to maintain itself in uneasy neutrality, its internal economic situation deteriorated rapidly as a result of the war. Because of the imminent threats of invasion, first by Russia and then by Germany, İnönü had to mobilize the Turkish army, putting over 1 million men under arms and doubling the military's share of the budget. The mobilization was a tremendous burden on an economy that had not been very strong to begin with. Withdrawal of thousands of men from the work force reduced agricultural and industrial production markedly, while the war actions and blockades in the Mediterranean halted the flow of most imports and exports, causing serious shortages of most goods and spare parts and depriving Turkey of many of its foreign markets. The armed forces provided a new source of competition on the market, taking goods needed by civilians. There were severe shortages of goods and a wild inflation, with the overall price index in Istanbul increasing from 101.4 in 1939 to 232.5 in 1942 and 354.4 in 1945, while the food price index increased from 100 in 1938 to 1113 in 1944 before falling to 568.8 in 1945 due to the reopening of the Mediterranean in the late years of the war.[104] The total national product fell during the war from 7690.3 to 5941.6 million Turkish liras, while per capita income dropped from 431.53 to 316.22 liras during the same years, a reduction of almost one quarter.[105]

The government tried various solutions to its financial problems. The National Defense Law of 1940 enabled it to require compulsory labor from citizens in the mines and factories, causing discontent but at least enabling it to meet the needs of the army.[106] Production, foreign trade, and government revenues fell while military expenditures increased. Increasingly, the war budgets of the government were in deficit.[107] Attempts to meet the crisis by printing money and by internal borrowing only fueled the inflation. A 10 percent tax on agricultural production imposed in 1942 helped somewhat but was not enough in itself. Efforts to ration goods were unsuccessful, since both retailers and buyers were able to circumvent the controls and create a flourishing black market. Shopkeepers and wholesalers reaped extremely high profits at the expense of an exasperated public, and in particular the civil servants, whose salaries had to be reduced so that the government could make ends meet.

All these difficulties and frustrations culminated in the Capital Levy (*Varlık Vergisi*) passed by the Assembly on November 11, 1942. It was designed to tax the previously untaxed commercial wealth in the Republic and to curb the inflationary spiral. The method was quite similar to tax measures introduced elsewhere in Europe at the time – a single tax on the capital of all property owners, business-men, farmers, corporations, and others liable to pay the annual profits tax. Because of the difficulty of securing honest estimates from the capital holders themselves, the assessments were made by special local committees of government financial experts and local property owners appointed by and responsible to the municipali-ties. Their decisions could not be appealed, and defaulters were subject to interest penalties and, if prolonged, to property confiscation, arrest, and deportation to work camps. Most Muslim Turks considered the tax a patriotic obligation and paid. Many non-Muslim citizens and foreigners resident in Turkey, however, never con-sidered the country their home and did all they could to conceal their wealth and avoid the tax. This in turn stimulated the assessment committees to increase the estimates of non-Muslims' capital wealth over what was apparent, on the assump-tion of concealment. While many non-Muslims in fact paid their just tax at the same rate as Muslims, others whose concealed wealth was not in fact sufficient or who did not wish to produce it under any circumstances were forced to sell all or part of their businesses or properties to pay the tax. In the end, since the minori-ties continued to form the bulk of the commercial community in Istanbul, they paid most of the tax, about 53 percent of the total collections of 315 million Turk-ish liras, with Muslims paying 36.5 percent and foreign subjects 10.5 percent. The latter, who assumed falsely that Muslims were paying nothing, or a reduced rate, accused the government of prejudice, an argument that the outside world readily accepted. The long-range result of the tax was to encourage non-Muslims to trans-fer their investment and commercial activities to other countries as soon as they were able to do so after the war, leaving Muslims in charge of most commercial activity in the years that followed.[108]

The only positive economic result of the war came in the latter two years (1943–1945) when Turkey, as it came closer to the Western Allies, began to receive lend-lease help to increase production and exports, and accumulated a sufficient amount of foreign credit to finance much of its postwar economic recovery. In December 1942 the British began to pressure Turkey to enter the war on the Allied side, but Churchill agreed that Turkey would have to be fully armed first. Allied weapons and air advisers began to come to Turkey in 1943, but İnönü still held back be-cause of quite justified fears that Germany still could bomb Istanbul without fear of Allied retaliation. The Allies appreciated Turkey's hesitations, but at the Mos-cow and Teheran conferences (October–November 1943) they decided to pres-sure the Turks to enter the war as soon as possible. İnönü continued to put them off until the spring of 1944, when the rapidly developing German collapse led him to break the economic and political ties that von Papen had built and, finally, to declare war on Germany on February 23, 1945, just in time to become a charter member of the United Nations.

The Postwar Crisis

The end of the war in Europe did not mean the end of the war for Turkey. After World War II the Republic had to defend itself against commissars who were very interested in achieving the imperialistic plans of the czars. Even before the declaration of war on Germany, Turkey had opened the Straits for Allied sup-plies to Russia (January 12, 1945), but the Russians were far less willing to for-get the previous closure than were Turkey's friends. On March 21 the Russians abrogated the treaty of friendship and nonaggression signed with Turkey in 1925.

At the same time, just as they were extending their rule over the states of Eastern Europe, they demanded the restoration of Kars and Ardahan in the east and of parts of Thrace to Bulgaria, now under Communist control. The Soviets also demanded revision of the Montreux Convention to assure them of access to the Straits in war as well as peace and also to allow them to establish military bases along both the Bosporus and the Dardanelles. In 1946 the Soviet government continued to pressure the Turks for an agreement and also emulated its actions after World War I by publishing selected documents to demonstrate Turkish sympathy for the Nazis. The Turkish government refused the Russian demands, and when Communist groups in the country began to agitate for concessions, they were suppressed. Russian pressure mounted. The Russians also began to support Communist guerrillas in Greece, and in the face of their previous tactics in the Balkans and Iran, it appeared very likely that some kind of attack on Turkey might follow.

Turkey Joins the West

It was at this juncture, on March 12, 1947, that President Harry S Truman proposed to Congress a program to provide both Turkey and Greece with military and economic assistance to help protect them from the Russians, part of the Truman Doctrine developed to resist further Soviet imperialism as an essential element of American security. Congress's decision to grant the requested assistance was the start of a growing American involvement in Turkish security and economic development, which was to become a basic element in the policies of both countries during the next three decades. American military experts came to Ankara for discussions that led to the Turkish-American agreement on military aid and cooperation, ratified in Ankara on September 1, 1947. Beginning in 1948 Turkey began to receive military equipment and help in building up its transportation systems, which soon transformed its army into a major military force. The Marshall Plan, announced on June 5, 1947, and Turkey's subsequent admission into the Organization for European Economic Cooperation further strengthened its economic ties with the United States (April 16. 1948), leading to a direct economic agreement between the two nations (July 8, 1948), which became a second pillar of their relations. Turkey's military contribution to the U.N. effort in Korea, starting in June 1950, and its subsequent entry into the North Atlantic Treaty Organization (February 18, 1952), after overcoming initial British and French objections to extension of their strategic commitments, made it an integral part of the joint efforts of the Western nations to defend themselves from Russian expansion and confirmed Turkey as a full member of the Western alliance. This ended the isolation that had begun during World War II. Economic and military cooperation with the West has remained the basis of Turkey's foreign policy and an essential pillar of Western defenses ever since.

The New Liberalism

Turkey's entry into the Western world following the war was paralleled by new and more liberal political, economic, and social attitudes and policies in the country. The war had so developed and manifested the different classes and groups among the Turkish population that it was no longer possible to satisfy them all within the confines of a single party or under the kind of authoritarian rule Atatürk had maintained. The old Statist policies and the need to maintain tight controls during the war had greatly increased the number of civil servants and made them into a significant political force. In addition, by the end of the war overall literacy had increased to 30 percent, and twice that amount in the cities. By now Turkey had a significant intellectual class, based mainly in the universities, which was able to influence public opinion and government policy. A new middle class of industrialists and businessmen also emerged out of the economic development of the 1930s, with common interests focused by the government's wartime financial policies, which had, indeed, affected Muslims in proportion to their wealth as much as non-Muslims. The rural landowners continued to form their own middle class, partly allied with that in the cities in the hope of removing government controls that limited their ability to gain profits from their properties. The number of factory workers had increased from 25,000 in 1923 to almost 300,000 in 1946, and at least twice that number were employed in agriculture and small industry. All these groups emerged from the war with a clear idea of their distinct existence and interests and a determination to improve their lot through political action.[109]

The resulting pressures affected the government as well as the RPP. Their response was a series of liberal measures intended to show that the existing regime could continue to focus and meet the needs of all interests as it had since the Republic was established. To appease the urban workers the prohibitions against trade unions were lifted and their existence and legal position codified in the 1947 Trade Union Law,[110] which allowed worker and employer unions but did not repeal the old provisions prohibiting both strikes and lockouts. That the workers were, indeed, interested in joint industrial action is shown by the rise of several hundred such organizations within a very short time. As many as 75,000 workers were involved in unions by the end of 1949, still only a small proportion of the total but a fairly substantial beginning.[111] In addition a Ministry of Labor (*Çalışma Bakanlığı*) was now established to look after their interests.[112] It secured passage of a number of welfare laws providing for accident insurance, maternity benefits, labor exchanges, and even the eight-hour day and paid holidays.[113] Perhaps even more revolutionary was the personal income tax system (June 3, 1949), which replaced the old profits tax at long last,[114] with a proportional tax of from 15 to 45 percent levied on wages, salaries, and income from trade and commerce, real estate, and from private investments. Exemptions, however, were granted to all income from agriculture, domestic labor, royalties from books and music, and the like, thus throwing the burden on the urban population even more than before. Soon afterward, the Corporation Tax Law (June 7, 1949) imposed a 35 percent tax on the net profits of corporations, lowering it to 10 percent for cooperative societies and capital associations.[115] Petroleum companies were charged a tax of 50 percent of their profits, while customs, inheritance, and excise taxes were increased to redistribute the burden among the various groups of Turkish society.[116] Finally, the Land Distribution Law (June 11, 1945) provided for the distribution to landless peasants of state and foundation lands as well as privately owned estates above 200 *dönüms* in extent. Peasants were also provided with machinery and sufficient seed to cultivate the land. These measures weakened the rural middle class and large landowners, who were allowed to receive compensation only after going through long and complicated procedures.[117]

Liberalization also was felt in many other areas. Government controls over the sale and pricing of goods sold by private shopkeepers were relaxed. Products of state industries could be sold in privately owned shops. The Press Law was amended so that newspapers no longer had to post bond for good behavior and the government could no longer close them by its own decision instead of going through judicial channels.[118] The Societies Law was amended to allow the establishment of associations "on a class basis," with the courts and not the government being allowed to suppress them if they violated the law.[119] Workers, professionals, and, significantly, newspeople, thus could form their own professional or craft organizations instead of being forced to remain in the government-controlled chambers and syndicates that had dominated them in the past.[120] The universities were given autonomy in internal administration and in educational and disciplinary matters. They were allowed to elect their own rectors, govern through elected university senates, and form their own disciplinary committees to judge faculty and students for violating university regulations. But their finances remained under government control. In 1948 when the government wanted to discharge four Ankara University sociology professors for their Marxist views, it had to do so by indirect means, abolishing the budgetary provisions for their salaries and courses, since the established university councils refused to comply. This of course established a precedent for attacks on university freedom in later years, but at the moment it was the exception and was conceded in order to protect the Turkish universities from the kind of Communist penetration that had helped end the independence of Turkey's neighbors in the Balkans.[121]

The Rise of Political Opposition: The Democratic Party

All these measures helped Turkey's workers and intellectuals, but they increased expectations beyond the government's readiness to satisfy them. Urban workers were happy with their new unions and benefits but wanted greatly increased wages and the right to strike, while their employers opposed the concessions that had been made already. In the countryside landlord opposition limited the actual distribution of land as authorized by law. The intellectuals, particularly those in the universities, demanded far more political and cultural freedom than they had, while the civil servants opposed any measures that threatened to limit their traditional privileged position. The result was an increase of political activity, at first in the RPP and then outside. Also the concurrent rise of a popular and independent press made it possible for the different discontented groups to express their views and to gain wide support throughout the country.

Opposition to the RPP's autocratic rule had risen even within the party soon after Atatürk's death, but it had been subordinated to the more pressing national needs during the war. Once peace was achieved, however, the party was split between the conservatives wishing to retain its privileged position as the instrument of modernization and a more liberal group, which felt that further democratization and liberalization were essential if Turkey was to take its place among the other advanced nations. Despite all the liberal measures that followed, there were others who wanted to go even further. Led by four distinguished party members – Celal Bayar, former prime minister and minister of finance, Fuat Köprülü, the distinguished historian, and two deputies, Adnan Menderes and Refik Koraltan – they left the RPP altogether late in 1945, building support through the efforts of the newspaper *Vatan*, edited by Ahmet Emin Yalman; on January 7, 1946, they formed the Democratic Party (*Demokrat Parti*) to advocate their ideas. The Democrats set out to build their own national organization, but they hardly were able to match that of the RPP, which had an organic connection with the government and reached the people directly through its control of the People's Houses. Some RPP members wanted to suppress the new party from the start, but Inönü strongly defended its right to organize and in fact pushed through amendments to the election laws to assure secrecy of the ballot. The Democrats feared that this would not be sufficient, since the government still controlled the election apparatus and ballot counting but decided to participate in the 1946 elections anyway because of the tremendous groundswell of support that rose in response to their call.

The National Election of 1946

Turkey now experienced its first real election campaign, and there was a great deal of popular enthusiasm and participation. The Democrats quickly attracted the support of all the discontented groups in the country, though many of these were unable to agree with each other. Complaining particularly about the continued inflation and the innumerable cases of bureaucratic tyranny and blundering that had taken place during the long years of RPP rule, the Democrats lacked time to develop a systematic program of their own beyond simply promising to do better. They were helped by the support of Marshal Fevzi Çakmak, one of the last living heroes of the War for Independence, who joined because of anger over the government's decision to retire him in 1944 after 23 years of service, to give the army younger and more energetic command.

Despite the excitement, in the elections themselves (July 21, 1946) the RPP won a landslide victory, gaining 395 seats in the Grand National Assembly compared with only 64 for the Democrats and 6 for independent candidates. The Democrats did gain a majority of the seats from Istanbul, 18 out of 27, but the RPP reaped the result of years of propaganda in the countryside as well as the long-standing tax concessions given to the rural population. There also were accusations of government fraud, probably with some justification. The RPP was more than just a political organization; for many of its members, it was a religion. It was their lives, it was the nation – and many of them used their positions to alter the election results despite Inönü's orders to the contrary. In addition, the elections took place before the Democrats really had a chance to build a national following and make their candidates known, and it is very likely that they would have lost by a considerable majority even if the elections had been conducted with complete honesty.[122]

The Democrats' Struggle to Survive

The Democrats now settled down to build their program and organization to compete more successfully in the next elections, scheduled for 1950. It was a difficult four years, with the very existence of the opposition being under constant threat of suppression by the more radical groups in the RPP. The new prime minister, Recep Peker (1946–1947), led those who strongly disliked the opposition's existence, also introducing many of the liberal measures mentioned previously to steal the latter's thunder and prove that it was not needed. In addition, to stabilize the economy and bring lower prices the wartime import restrictions were mostly lifted and much of the hard currency amassed during the war by sales of chrome and manganese was used to import capital and civilian goods. The Turkish lira also was devalued to a rate of 2.80 to the dollar to fulfill the arrangements of the

Bretton Woods international conference, which stabilized and regularized the world's currency exchanges in the postwar world. This resulted in a general price rise that, on top of what had happened during the war, greatly distressed the public. Once again the merchants were making fortunes, and most of the imports were luxury goods, which the nation could ill afford in view of the need to develop its economy.[123] This gave the Democrat members in the Assembly, led by Menderes, an opportunity to develop their reputations with attacks on the government. Without a tradition of responsible opposition, debates were not always constructive. The Democrats sometimes attacked to seek political advantage regardless of the actual issues. Peker replied with repressive measures, extending martial law, suppressing the Socialists and Communists, and coming close to suppressing the Democrats as well, but he was held back by Inönü, who used the new connection with the United States to support the liberal regime regardless of the consequences to his party. He finally gained enough support in the party to force Peker's resignation (September 1, 1947), substituting the more liberal and tolerant regime of Hasan Saka (1947–1949), who worked to establish a true democratic system with equal treatment for all parties in return for respect of the basic institutions and ideals of the government.[124]

The RPP now also was liberalized. More and more, the People's Houses were emphasized as cultural centers for general public use rather than party centers. While Inönü remained RPP party chairman, actual direction was turned over to the vice chairman to begin the process of separating party and government. The RPP council, formerly restricted to the close associates of the president and prime minister, now was elected by and from among all members, and it in turn elected the secretary general as well as the Central Executive Committee. Delegates to the RPP conventions now were chosen by the local organizations instead of the central secretariat. Divisions between the conservatives and liberals in the party continued, but as public opinion became more important, the popular representatives' influence grew. For the first time the RPP began to act as if it had to win popular approval to retain its ruling position rather than being the autocratic agent of an autocratic president. Once the threat of government action was removed, the disparate elements in the Democratic Party also began to fight, leading to a series of resignations and dismissals. The majority, led by the party founders, applied party discipline to remove their opponents and then worked to build a strong party organization throughout the country. Those ousted formed their own Nation Party (*Millet Partisi*), led by Osman Bölükbaşı and including Fevzi Çakmak, which attracted the more conservative and religious elements of both major parties by declaring its support for an end to state capitalism, reduced taxes, emphasis on individual initiative and work and an uplift of moral standards through a nationalistic and religious program of education and emphasis on the home and family.[125]

The existence of the Nation Party and liberalization of the RPP finally forced the Democratic Party to define its program. It pressed the government to turn the election machinery over to the judiciary, demanded increased political and economic freedom, and called for the use of American assistance to help raise living standards rather than build up the armed forces.[126] In reaction to this the RPP installed the new Şemsettin Günaltay government in 1949, which promised not only free elections but also many of the same things advocated by the opposition, including optional classes on religion in elementary schools, encouragement of private enterprise, tax reforms, and economic projects to help the masses.

The Elections of 1950

New election laws curbed the government's ability to suppress the opposition, enabling all parties to campaign on the issues. The RPP promised to modify the rigors of Statism, stimulate private enterprise, increase agricultural credit, encourage foreign capital, provide tax reforms, and limit inflation. It also offered to create a Senate to curb the majority in the Assembly and to eliminate the six principles of Kemalism from the Constitution, though they were to remain part of the party's own objectives. Now a competing political party, the RPP offered what the masses wanted: more schools, credit, farm equipment, seed and water in the countryside, houses, roads, telephones, and electricity in the towns. The Democrats continued to concentrate on criticizing the RPP. In addition, they demanded an end to the government monopolies, encouragement of private enterprise, and balancing the budget and reducing taxes to solve the nation's economic problems. They also promised to end the monopoly of power granted the Assembly and to make the executive and judiciary equal with it on the American model to establish a more equitable democracy. The Nation Party continued to stress a more conservative and religious approach though its campaign for free enterprise had been largely taken over by the Democrats.[127]

The campaign of 1950 was far more orderly and secure than in 1946. There was no interference with the opposition, enabling the Democrats in particular to organize in the villages for the first time and receive support from all those who had built up grievances during the long years of RPP rule. Peasants wanted more land, landowners hoped for fewer restrictions, workers advocated more welfare laws and higher wages, employers wanted more freedom from government control, intellectuals demanded full freedom – all saw what they wanted to see in the Democratic platform.

The results of the elections (May 14, 1950) astonished even the Democrats. With 90 percent of the voters going to the polls, Democratic candidates received 53.3 percent of the vote, the RPP only 39.9 percent, the Nation Party 3 percent, and various independents 3.8 percent (see Table 6.1). Because of the district system then in use, the majority party received all the seats in each; out of a total of 487 Grand National Assembly seats, the Democrats won 86.2 percent to only 12.9 percent for the RPP, and the Nation Party gained only 1 seat.[128] The Democratic victory has been attributed to many factors, including American influence, better organization, and even a bad harvest in 1949, but the real reason seems to have been simply the accumulated frustrations and hostilities of 25 years of RPP rule. Perhaps the people of Turkey simply decided that it was time for a change. Whatever the cause, it was a political revolution. The party that had won the nation's independence and guided its destinies without opposition for a quarter-century had been voted out of office, and it turned over its power without protest. As a matter of fact, a few of its diehard members still hoped to retain office, perhaps through army intervention, but İnönü used his great prestige to make certain that this did not happen. He insisted on accepting the will of the people and thus establishing the basis for the kind of democratic regime that he and Atatürk had long hoped for.

The Democratic Years, 1950–1960

On May 29, 1950, the new Assembly elected Celal Bayar as president, Adnan Menderes, deputy from Istanbul, as prime minister, and Fuat Köprülü as foreign

Table 6.1 *Turkish Assembly election results, 1950–1973: the major parties*

Party	1950	1954	1957	1961	1965	1969	1973
Justice Party							
Votes				3,527,435	4,921,235	4,229,712	3,197,897
% of vote				34.8	52.9	46.5	29.8
Assembly seats				158	240	256	149
Republican People's Party							
Votes	3,176,561	3,161,696	3,753,136	3,724,752	2,675,785	2,487,006	3,570,583
% of votes	39.9	34.8	40.6	36.7	28.7	27.4	33.3
Assembly seats	63	31	178	173	134	143	185
Democratic Party							
Votes	4,241,393	5,151,550	4,372,621				1,275,502
% of votes	53.3	56.6	47.3				11.9
Assembly seats	420	505	424				45
Reliance Party							
Votes						597,818	564,343
% of vote						6.6	5.3
Assembly seats						15	13
National Salvation Party							
Votes							1,265,771
% of vote							11.8
Assembly seats							48

New Turkey Party							
Votes				1,391,934	346,514	197,929	250,414
% of vote				13.7	3.7	2.2	3.1
Assembly seats				65	19	6	1
Turkish Workers' Party							
Votes					276,101	243,631	
% of vote					3.0	2.7	
Assembly seats					14	2	
Nation Party							
Votes			582,704			292,961	62,377
% of votes			6.3			3.2	0.6
Assembly seats			31			6	—
Peasant's Party/Republican Peasant's National Party							
Votes		434,085		1,415,390	208,959		
% of votes		4.8		14.0	2.2		
Assembly seats		—		54	11		
Registered voters	8,905,743	10,262,063	12,078,623	12,924,395	3,679,753	14,788,552	16,798,164
Number voting	7,953,055	9,095,617	9,250,949	10,522,716	9,748,678	9,516,035	11,223,843
Percent voting	89.3	88.6	76.6	81.0	71.3	64.3	66.8

Source: Türkiye İstatistik Yıllığı 1973, Ankara, 1974, p. 145.

minister. The three leaders represented respectively the old guard civil servants, the new middle class, and the intellectuals. There was a sufficient majority in the Assembly to achieve all the Democrats' promises, and, with strong American economic and military support, the new government seemed to have a promising future. Real power and leadership went to Prime Minister Menderes instead of the president, thus presaging a regime in which the government would, indeed, be responsible to the people through their representatives. The achievement of real democracy was not quite that simple, however. Three major problems rose to bedevil the government, create tremendous hostility between it and the RPP, now in opposition, and eventually lead it into the same kind of autocracy that it had so strongly criticized in the past. The first problem was economic. The Democrats promised rapid economic growth accompanied and mainly achieved by a relaxation of the stringent controls of the statist policies of the past and by encouragement of private enterprise. At first they were quite successful. Once barriers were removed, investment from public and private sources soared, and the economy grew rapidly. Bank credits, for example, increased from 1.275 billion Turkish liras in 1950 to 7.787 billion Turkish liras in 1957 and 9.522 billion Turkish liras in 1960, with investment flowing into all sectors of the economy.[129] Production also rose fantastically. In agriculture, land under cultivation, which had remained at about 14.5 billion hectares between 1940 and 1950, rose to 23.264 billion hectares by 1960.[130] The number of tractors in use increased from 1,756 in 1949 to 42,136 in 1960![131] Total agricultural output almost doubled, from an index of 70 in 1950 to 130 in 1960–1961.[132] Industrial production rose from an index of 100 in 1948 to 256 in 1960, with the manufacturing portion up to 279, the food industry to 311, and electrical power to 390![133] Coal output doubled. The number of factories, homes, and other buildings increased tremendously, particularly in the smaller towns and cities. All-weather roads extended from 9,093 kilometers in 1948 to 23,826 kilometers in 1961, commercial vehicles in use from 14,100 to 68,400, private cars from 8,000 to 45,800.[134] Even the rate of population growth doubled, from an average of 23 per 1,000 between 1945 and 1950 to 57 per 1,000 in the years to 1955 and 50 per 1,000 the next five years. From a total population of 13.64 million in 1927 and 20.947 million in 1950, thus, it shot up to 24.065 million in 1955 and 27.755 in 1960, reflecting an increased birth rate and massive improvements in health and medical facilities.[135] The number of schools increased from 18,282 to 25,922 and students from 1.785 million to 2.932 million during the decade.[136] Literacy increased from 33.5 to 43.7 percent.[137] The gross national product at market prices increased from 496 Turkish liras to 1,836 Turkish liras during the decade, and the net national product, figured at constant money value, which had just doubled between 1927 and 1950, increased by 50 percent in the Democratic decade, from 434 to 601 Turkish liras. Per capita income increased from 96 Turkish liras (in 1938) to 428 (in 1950) and 1,598 Turkish liras (in 1960) if figured at current prices, and from 432 to 434 to 601 Turkish liras respectively, figured at constant prices.[138] Villages, towns, and the great city of Istanbul experienced physical changes as roads were widened, new arteries penetrated isolated regions, and buildings mushroomed.

The statistics are impressive, and the mass of Turks certainly benefited. But the tremendous economic expansion was achieved at a price that eventually undermined the regime and seriously threatened democracy itself. The government budget, which had been more or less balanced in the later 1940s, now fell into chronic debt, averaging 296.5 million Turkish liras of arrears annually, almost 20 percent of the average revenues.[139] The public debt more than tripled, from 2.565 to 9.342 million Turkish liras between 1950 and 1960.[140] The money supply increased by 408 percent, from 1.594 to 9.256 billion Turkish liras, while national income grew in constant prices by only 200 percent, from 8.815 to 16.312 Turkish liras.[141] While per capita income at constant prices thus rose, this affected only certain elements of the population, while most were exposed to the ravages of a massive inflation. The general index of wholesale prices increased from 46 to 126 and the cost of living in Istanbul from 54 to 133 during the decade.[142] And the balance of foreign trade, which had been in surplus continuously between 1930 and 1946, and which already had turned to deficit during the last four RPP years as the government tried to satisfy consumer demands, now fell into increasing deficit, with exports increasing, to be sure, from a value of $263.4 million to $320.7 million, but imports increasing far more, from $278.4 million to $468.2 million. It should be pointed out, however, that most of these imports were machinery and fuels needed to continue the nation's economic development and that following the Democrats' fall from power in 1960 the deficit became even more severe, increasing from 498 million to 2,903 million Turkish liras in 1963.[143] In sum, the Democrats achieved a remarkable growth rate, as much as 5 percent a year, but it was accomplished in such a hectic way that it undermined the total economy before the nation was able to really reap the results. The long-term prospects were in fact bright, and if the government could have controlled the side effects until the results could show, it might have remained in power for a much longer time. But two other major areas where disputes rose as well as reaction to its economic policies clouded its undeniable achievements.

The second major area of difficulty was that of religion, where the government was accused of trying to reverse the Kemalist secular policies. Actually, it was the RPP that in 1949, as part of its liberalization efforts, had allowed religious instruction to be provided to those students in the public schools whose parents requested it. But the Democratic Party's following included many conservatives who were kept out of the hands of the Nation Party by promises of increased religious instruction, and these promises had to be honored. The Menderes regime soon extended religious instruction to all schools and required all Muslim children to receive it unless their parents specifically requested exemption. The RPP had restored the old Faculty of Divinity, originally at the University of Istanbul but then transferred to Ankara, to train religious leaders. The Democrats greatly expanded its budget, providing more teachers and fellowships. They also established the *imam-hatip* schools in 1951 to train lesser religious functionaries, ended the use of the Turkish call to prayer and translation of the Koran, using Arabic again, and encouraged public celebrations of the major holidays. Much of this in fact reflected a general popular feeling that the RPP had gone too far in undermining the national faith without providing a true substitute. Much of it, however, also reflected the desire of the religious leaders to regain some of the influence that the reforms of Atatürk had taken from them. Religious books and pamphlets again appeared, with certain bookshops specializing in their sale and becoming centers of religion-oriented activities. Religious leaders began to appear in public and once again preach opposition to Secularism. There was renewed interest in the dervish orders. The government began to invest large amounts of money in repairing old mosques and building new ones.

It is doubtful that these measures really had any significant effect. A whole new generation had grown up without paying much attention to the *hocas*, and however much the latter sought to regain influence, they succeeded only among the ever-lessening group of religious conservatives who had been there all along. At best the "religious revival" gave Turkish youth an idea of their faith, providing them historical perspective as well as spiritual guidance in a period of rapid changes. But government support of religion soon became a political issue for the opposition, provided it with an emotional appeal, and brought accusations of abandonment of the secularist principle.

The third major problem, and the one that in the end destroyed the Democratic regime and threatened to disrupt the entire progression of Turkey toward democracy, involved political freedom. Neither the Democrats nor the Republicans really understood how to oppose responsibly or to accept opposition fairly. The result was often harsh RPP criticism of the government's economic and religious policies, to which the Democrats became excessively sensitive and responded by suppressing the opposition. Much of the initial problem came from the universities, many of whose leaders sought to use the autonomy given them in 1946 to make them into bases for political action. The University Law of 1946 had organized the universities according to the German system, with a small number of institutes and professorial chairs and many assistants forced to serve the latter at low pay for many years until vacancies arose. Since there were no retirement laws and pensions were poor in comparison with salaries, few left their chairs until they died, even further limiting opportunities for promotion and causing severe struggles for the vacancies when they did become available. With unhappy and poorly paid junior faculty members forming factions in consequence, it is not surprising that many of them turned to politics, hoping to achieve their ambitions by association with one or another of the parties and sometimes rising quite high in politics as a result of their undoubted abilities to express themselves. One of the results of the situation was a tendency to bring politics into the classroom. Faculty members went beyond their right to participate in politics as citizens and used their university positions to inflict their views on their students, particularly in the faculties of law and political science, which became hotbeds of opposition politics. Since it was the Democrats who were in power, and since most faculty members favored Statist approaches to economic problems, most of them joined the RPP and led the growing chorus of criticism of the party in power.[144]

The Democrats certainly had a sufficient majority in the Assembly to overcome all opposition. But when the criticism started in mid-1953, the next national elections were only a year away. The government leaders, many themselves university people, knew how much the articulateness of the intellectuals and their access to mass media might sway public opinion. Thus the repression effort began, against not only the universities but also the press, the RPP, and the other opposition parties. On July 12, 1953, the Nation Party was banned on the grounds that it was trying to use religion to subvert the Republic. Charges were brought against the leaders of several branches that they were harboring reactionary elements hostile to the reforms of Atatürk.[145] On July 21 the Assembly amended the University Law to restrict further the universities' control of their own budgets and, thereby, of their educational and personnel policies.[146] On December 14 a new law directed that "all moveable and immoveable properties, moneys, titles and claims and other valuables held in the possession of the Republican People's Party . . . shall be invested in the Treasury . . . provided only, however, that such of the moveables existing in buildings used exclusively as party premises . . . shall be left to the Republican People's Party."[147] Ostensibly this was done to compensate the nation for "past misappropriation of public funds" by the RPP, but since it allegedly owed far more than the value of its assets, everything was confiscated, and the party newspaper, *Ulus*, was forced to suspend publication. The People's Houses also were confiscated and closed, and despite a government effort to replace them with a revived Turkish Hearths Society (*Türk Ocakları*), the entire organization disappeared, but was later revived and was active as late as 1975. On February 2, 1954, the Peasant's Party (*Köylü Partisi*), later to develop into the Republican Peasant's Nationalist Party (*Cumhuriyetçi Köylü Millet Partisi*), was founded as successor to the Nation Party. Its program demanded constitutional guarantees for religious and civil rights and the creation of a constitutional court to pass on the legality of laws passed by the Assembly. It soon began to cooperate with the RPP, leading the government to respond with laws prohibiting such cooperation and imposing prison sentences and fines on newspapermen whose writing "could be harmful to the political or financial prestige of the state" or was "an invasion of private life," even when the allegedly injured parties failed to complain.[148]

The new laws were not extensively applied before the election campaigns of 1954. But as it turned out, the Democrats had underestimated their strength. The worsening situation had not really harmed the popularity they had gained among the many people who had benefited from the new regime. Therefore, the Democratic Party won the 1954 national elections (May 2, 1954) with increased majorities of the popular vote (56.6 percent, as against 34.8 for the RPP and 4.8 for the Peasant's Party) and also of the Assembly seats (505 of the 541 seats) (see Table 6.1). As soon as the new Assembly was organized, however, the opposition became more vitriolic than ever and the government responded in kind. All government officials and employees, including university professors and judges, were made subject to retirement as soon as they completed 25 years of government service or became 60 years of age, compared with the previous regulations, which had provided for retirement after 30 years of service or at the age of 65 and enabled university people at least to remain beyond these limits (June 21, 1954).[149] The same government employees also now could be dismissed or retired by the authorities who employed them, without statement of reason or appeal, and on pensions ranging from one-half to one-fourth of their salaries according to length of service (July 4, 1954).[150] In addition, university teachers were ordered to limit their activities "to scientific, educational writing" and to avoid using their positions for "active partisan politics." Menderes defended the restrictions on the grounds that they were remedies "against the terrible disease of bureaucracy aggravated by inefficient employees who remain in the ranks of the civil service."[151]

Within a short time the laws were being applied, particularly to the universities and the courts. On July 13, 1954, 4 judges and 17 professors at the University of Ankara were retired. Before the year was finished three newspapermen had been jailed and four others dismissed for similar reasons.[152] In 1955 the RPP general secretary, Kasım Gülek, was jailed for insulting the government in a political speech. When difficulties arose over Cyprus (see pp. 430–431), five newspapers were suspended, including the RPP organ *Ulus* once again, for violating censorship regulations. In September 1955 a leading economics professor at the University of Istanbul, Osman Okyar, was suspended for writing an article that questioned the value and duration of American assistance. During the remaining years of the Democratic decade, this situation intensified. The universities became active centers of RPP political activity and propaganda, and the government replied with suspensions, restrictions, and imprisonments. In October 1955 a number of Democratic Party members were dismissed for refusal to accept party discipline, and others resigned in disagreement with the party leaders. On December 11 many of them joined to form the new Freedom Party (*Hürriyet Partisi*), which declared that it would not adhere to "outmoded doctrines" such as liberalism or Statism but would, rather, support a rational program of economic planning combined with a democratic regime and constitutionally secured legislative process,[153] essentially what has happened in Turkey since 1960. Soon after, the government used the increased multiplicity of opposition parties for its own advantage by passing a new Election Law that not only prohibited party coalitions, thus preventing a united front against it, but also gave the party winning a plurality of votes in each district all of its deputies even when it did not secure a majority.[154]

Through all the political turmoil, while the Democratic Party and the intellectual community grew further apart, the government's economic achievements continued to gain it the support of the mass of the people. This was especially true in the countryside, which had most of the votes, where the government moved to satisfy the cultivators with new roads, irrigation, electricity, buildings, schools, and hospitals in the smaller towns and villages while the big cities struggled vainly to keep up with their rapidly rising populations. The amount of government land distributed to cultivators increased enormously during the Menderes years, from 389,212 decares given to 8,359 families in 1949 to an average of 2 million decares distributed to 45,000 families yearly until 1956, and then about 1.3 million decares yearly until 1960.[155] Farmers also benefited from some 50,000 tractors distributed annually, a tremendous expansion of credit cooperatives, and a vast rural electrification program. Most city workers, shopkeepers, small factory owners, providers of services, and other residents of the growing towns also were enjoying much higher standards of living than before, and they appreciated it. In sum, then, while the intellectuals and civil servants with relatively fixed incomes were antagonized by the inflation and the shortages, the masses "never had it so good" and the government prospered. In the October 1957 national elections, then, the Democratic Party again emerged victorious, though with only a plurality of the votes, 47.2 percent to 40.6 for the RPP, 7 percent for the Republican Nation Party, and 3.8 for the Freedom Party; the Democrats got a higher percentage of the seats than their popular vote warranted because of the district representation rule, 70 percent (424 seats), while the RPP increased to 29 percent (178 seats) and the Nation Party to six (see Table 6.1). The Freedom Party failed to win a single seat and soon merged with the RPP.[156]

The election results only contributed to further political tumult. The RPP, thirsty for victory and with an increased representation in the Assembly, stepped up the violence and frequency of its attacks on Menderes and his associates, and the government retaliated by continued acts of repression. Violence mounted in and out of the Assembly, with all sides acting primarily for political advantage and with very little responsibility. In May 1959 the old warrior Ismet Inönü was attacked by a pro-Democratic mob while traveling in the countryside and again on his return to Istanbul. More incidents followed, with the government forbidding the press from publishing news of them. The economic situation also worsened. The government's insistence on continued industrialization and rapid capital improvement added to the inflation and brought the nation to the brink of international bankruptcy.

Finally, in 1960 in return for loans from an international consortium, the government was forced to accept an economic-stabilization program to reduce inflation and restore monetary order. With the help of the International Monetary Fund a new program was worked out. It involved severe restrictions on deficit financing and credit expansion, devaluation of the Turkish lira, consolidation of the public debt, an end to price controls, and a more rational program of internal investment.[157] The inflation was reduced, the budget and foreign trade again were in surplus, and the crisis seemed to be over. But neither the government nor the opposition was satisfied. The Democrats' basic philosophy remained strongly expansionist, and they soon attempted to evade the program that had been forced on them, particularly since the reduced capital expenditures were causing discontent among their supporters both in the countryside and the towns. The RPP also was unhappy with a situation that threatened to deprive it of the victory for which it had aimed for so long, and it sought out new ways of opposing the government. The press, the universities, and the RPP criticized the government both for its previous economic blunders and for the results of the new stabilization policies. In February 1960 they accused a number of high officials of corruption and profiteering. The army and police were used to block the activities of Inönü and his colleagues, but this only increased the vehemence of the opposition. On April 18 two Democratic deputies introduced a bill in the Assembly to investigate the RPP and the press. Inönü replied with a violent condemnation of both the proposal and the government, and the debate soon degenerated into the worst kind of personal accusations. After the RPP members finally walked out, the Democrats who remained used their temporary majority to prohibit all political activity and to appoint an Investigation Committee composed of the most partisan Democratic representatives (April 18, 1960).

The Revolution of May 27, 1960

The RPP walkout and the creation of the Investigation Committee touched off violent demonstrations in the cities, but the government was able to keep order both because it controlled the police and the army and retained majority support outside Istanbul and Ankara. In the end, however, the government's determination to press ahead against the opposition led to open revolt. On April 27 the Investigation Committee was given the right to imprison any citizens, close any newspapers, or suspend any law that interfered with its work. In response, the politically active students and faculty of Istanbul University demonstrated openly against the government (April 28), followed by those in Ankara a day later. While the majority of the university community probably sympathized with the demonstrators, they remained out of the fray, hoping only to complete their studies and avoid bloodshed. As usual, however, the radicals had their way. Police and soldiers moved in and bloody clashes followed, with many injured and a few students killed. Thus was set off the sequence of events that was to topple the government, though news of these clashes was kept out of the press by government order. The government immediately closed the universities (April 29), thus making all suffer for the actions of the militant few and causing many to join the demonstrators. Since the Investigation Committee continued its work, stories soon spread of secret arrests and inquisitions, further increasing the tension. Most newspapers by now were suspended, and foreign periodicals reporting on the situation were refused entry into the country.[158]

When the Revolution of 1960 finally came, it was a product not so much of street action, however, as of many of the same social forces that had achieved the

Young Turk Revolution a half-century earlier, stimulated and led by the modernized bureaucracy and the army. It was organized and planned by students and faculty at the War College and the Faculty of Political Science, both of which had been moved to Ankara but remained principal channels through which the nation's modernizing elite was recruited and trained. Considering themselves the defenders of the reforms against the new middle classes brought to power through the instrument of the Democratic party, they moved to take over. Leadership of the rebels was assumed at least as early as May 3, 1960, by General Cemal Gürsel, commander of the army, who first wrote to the prime minister demanding reforms and then went on leave to assume more active direction of the plotting. On May 27, as the agitation in the streets reached a new peak, a group of officers led by Gürsel, commanding the key military units in Istanbul and Ankara and using the students of the war academies, arrested Menderes, Bayar, and most other members of the cabinet along with many Democratic deputies. The remaining elements of the armed forces immediately declared their support. Martial law was imposed and the coup accepted throughout the country with very little opposition, even by those who continued to support the Menderes regime.

Thus ended the Democratic Party era that had begun so optimistically just a decade before. The government, which gained power because the autocratic RPP allowed free elections and accepted their result, now had lost its ability to govern. Its efforts to suppress the opposition had led the army to intervene in Turkish politics for the first time since the Young Turk period. In the end, the attempt to combine rapid economic development with political liberalization had created too many problems. The intellectuals had arrogated for themselves the role of voice of a nation whose citizens were mostly happy with the government's policies despite the difficulties involved. The government in turn had forgotten the circumstances by which it assumed power and had become needlessly sensitive to criticism, which, if only left alone, might never have stimulated the kind of opposition that finally toppled it. The evolution of Turkish democracy had received a staggering blow. The question now was whether the army would assume power, as armies had done under similar circumstances in other modernizing countries, or whether somehow the orderly progression of Turkish democracy would resume.

The National Unity Committee, 1960–1961

That the actual revolution was carried out by the military without the direct participation of the intellectuals in the universities is indicated by what happened during the next few days. General Gürsel and 38 officers representing all branches of the armed forces organized themselves into the National Unity Committee (*Milli Birlik Komitesi,* hereafter referred to as NUC), to operate the country, assuming legal powers under a provisional law (June 12, 1960) that it promulgated soon afterward, though executive power remained in the hands of the civilian Council of Ministers, which it appointed and controlled.

The NUC declared that the revolution "was not against any individual or any group. . . . Every citizen regardless of his identity and party affiliation shall be treated in accordance with the law and principles of justice." The civilian intellectuals called in to write the new constitution soon attempted to use it to achieve their longstanding hopes for social reforms through an autocracy. The NUC replied, however, that it had no intention of ruling beyond the time needed to try and punish those responsible for betraying Turkish democracy and to draw up a new constitution better able to protect the nation from abuses in the future.[159] That there were several NUC officers who agreed with the intellectuals and opposed the committee's decision to limit its term and relinquish power as soon as possible was indicated soon afterward when 14 member officers were ousted and sent out of the country, mostly as military attachés to Turkish embassies around the world (November 13, 1960).

The NUC remained in power for little more than a year. It concentrated mainly on its basic objectives of trying the Democratic leaders and writing a new consituation, but it also inaugurated major policy changes in the areas of economics and finance in order to set the subsequent regime on a new course. First it acted to stem the inflation that had undermined national unity in previous years. Most of the large construction and city rebuilding projects were stopped. The banks were closed, personal accounts of leading politicians and businessmen frozen, and loans suspended. Partial banking activity resumed only after the interest rate on borrowing was raised to 12 percent to reduce the expansion of credit. The purchase of government bonds was made compulsory to wage earners to soak up demand. Price controls were introduced, causing food prices in particular to drop, to the despair of the farmers and pleasure of the townspeople. The chambers of commerce and industry as well as the artisan guilds were forced to elect new administrative boards to remove those who had cooperated with the Democrats. Land taxes were increased tenfold, building taxes two to six times, and the income tax was doubled, while all those subject to the latter were required to declare their total assets, causing many to fear a new capital tax. As time went on, some of these measures were modified to facilitate the restoration of normal business activity, but much of their impact remained.[160]

The NUC also carried out its own brand of social reforms, though hardly the kind envisaged by the intellectuals. The salaries of military officers and men were greatly increased. Special army stores were opened, selling scarce goods at subsidized low prices, and other fringe benefits were added, making the total military pay at least 60 percent higher than that of their civilian counterparts in the bureaucracy. Democratic Party supporters and sympathizers were purged from the army and the government, though the former at least were given high pensions. And 147 members of the university faculties were dismissed on the accusation that they had been spending most of their time in outside occupations (as doctors, engineers, and so on); but the list included many who had been meeting their obligations but whose names had been reported by political, personal, and academic rivals.[161] A new University Law was introduced, not only to restore and strengthen university autonomy, but also to introduce internal reforms that the faculties had been unwilling to accept themselves. The younger faculty members were given more of a voice in university affairs, providing them with more opportunities for promotion through merit, at least partly through provisions for the normal retirement of the professors. Also, faculty members were required to be present at the universities during the working hours from Monday through Friday, a radical innovation indeed.[162] Other laws also were introduced during the NUC year to wrap up the destruction of the Democratic Party regime and hasten achievement of social progress. A State Planning Organization was established and Turkish Cultural Societies were formed to take the place of the People's Houses. Both institutions were later written into the Constitution. The High Court of Justice was reorganized so that it could try the accused Democrats.[163] The military went ahead with energy and enthusiasm, but many of the measures were so drastic that the economy almost came to a halt and not only businessmen but also workers and peasants began to show increasing unrest and a desire for restoration of a civilian regime that would provide for representation and protect their interests.

The Democratic Party itself was abolished and its property confiscated on September 29, 1960. Soon afterward, 592 of its leading members were brought to trial at Yassıada, in the Sea of Marmara opposite Istanbul (October 14, 1960–September 15, 1961), by the High Court now composed of civilian and military judges. The charges included cases of corruption by individual members of the governments, accusations of incitement of riots against the Greeks in Istanbul during the Cyprus crisis in 1955 (see pp. 429–430), using the state radio for partisan purposes, inciting the attacks against the RPP leaders, illegally entering university grounds, illegal expropriation of private property, imposing the rule of one class on another, and subversion of the Constitution by violating its guarantees. In the end, 15 of the defendants were sentenced to death, with Adnan Menderes, Foreign Minister Fatin Rüştü Zorlu, and Finance Minister Hasan Polatkan being hanged (September 16, 1961), while Celal Bayar and the other 11 had their sentences commuted to life imprisonment by the NUC. Also 31 other defendants were sentenced to life imprisonment, including 4 former cabinet ministers, 8 members of the Investigation Committee, the former governor of Istanbul, and a number of Democratic deputies. Four hundred other Democrats were given lesser sentences, and 123 were entirely acquitted, including Fuat Köprülü, who had soured on the regime and resigned somewhat before its final collapse.[164]

The Constitution of 1961

The new Constitution was drawn up by a Constituent Assembly that included 272 members and acted as the Parliament during the NUC period. Among its members were 10 appointed by the president and 18 by the NUC. All members of the cabinet were included along with 75 elected from the provinces, 49 by the RPP, 25 by the Republican Peasant's National Party (the only other party to survive from the previous regime), and the rest from various professional, craft, and business groups.[165] Most had been associated previously with the RPP, since the Democrats were excluded. Despite this, there were sharp differences between liberals and social-reform-minded autocratic groups, the former representing the propertied class, the latter emerging more from the intellectual elitists who wanted to restore some kind of autocratic regime to achieve their aims. In the end, the Constitution that emerged represented a compromise between the two groups, emphasizing not only human and property rights and freedoms as part of a liberal, constitutional regime but also more radical economic and social programs. On July 9, 1961, the new Constitution, in force to the present day, was ratified by a popular vote of 61 percent (6,348,191) in favor; 39 percent (3,934,370) were opposed, and 19 percent (2,412,840) abstained, the latter more as an expression of discontent with the continued NUC rule than with the Constitution itself.

The new government organization based on the 1961 Constitution is widely different from that established during the War for Independence and incorporated into the 1924 Constitution. It involves a system of division of powers and checks and balances to prevent autocracy. The Grand National Assembly is composed of two bodies instead of one, and its duties are specifically legislative as well as including the ratification of treaties and the power to authorize the use of the armed forces (articles 63–66). The lower house, or National Assembly, is composed of 450 deputies elected for four-year terms by direct general ballot (article 67). The number of deputies for each province is relative to the size of its population, and each party receives the same proportion of the provincial seats as its popular vote in that province. The upper house, or Senate of the Republic, is composed of 150 members elected for six-year terms at two-year intervals, with 15 additional members appointed by the president of the Republic "from among people distinguished for their services in various fields, at least ten of whom cannot belong to any party" (articles 70, 72). The chairman and members of the NUC also were made ex-officio members of the Senate as long as they remained outside the parties. The elective Senate seats are distributed by province, from one to six according to population, with the party receiving a majority of votes in each province receiving all its seats except in Istanbul and Ankara. Elections are under control of the courts, with a Supreme Election Board and local election boards established to carry out the election process independent of government control (article 75).

The Grand National Assembly is required to convene on November 1 each year without any convocation and to remain in session at least seven months (article 83). The chairmen and vice chairmen of the two houses are elected by their own members and are forbidden from participating in party activities or debates while serving in these positions (article 84). The two houses develop their own rules of organization, with the stipulation, however, that all parties must be represented on committees in proportion to their total representation in each house (articles 84, 85). Both houses can debate and make parliamentary investigations, but only the lower house can interpellate ministers (article 89). Laws can be initiated either by members of both houses or by the Council of Ministers (article 91), but the lower house has final authority in legislation. It debates bills first and submits those it approves to the Senate. If the latter approves of a submitted bill, it becomes a law. If the Senate approves with amendments, the result becomes law if the Assembly concurs. If the Senate rejects the National Assembly's proposal, however, the latter can pass it anyway by an absolute majority if the rejection was by that much and by two-thirds vote if the Senate rejection was by two-thirds or more (article 92). The president of the Republic also can veto legislation, but the Grand National Assembly can override it simply by reenacting the law, after which the president is required to promulgate it (article 93). Budgetary procedures are somewhat different. The cabinet budget goes first to a joint committee of the two houses and then is debated and approved by the Senate before it goes on to the National Assembly (article 94).

The president of the Republic is elected for a seven-year term by and from among the members of the Grand National Assembly aged at least 40 and with a higher education, by a two-thirds majority on a secret ballot or by a simple majority if no one is elected on the first two ballots. Once elected, the president must disassociate from his party; his Assembly membership is ended, and he is not eligible for reelection (article 95). He can preside over the Council of Ministers when necessary, act as head of state, issue decrees, which must be signed by the prime minister, and he can be impeached for high treason only by a two-thirds vote of both branches of the Grand National Assembly (articles 98, 99). The president appoints the prime minister from among members of the Assembly. The other ministers are nominated by the latter and appointed by the former, either from among Assembly members or "those qualified for election as deputies," that is, suitable persons from outside (article 105). If the Council of Ministers is defeated three times by a vote of no confidence by the National Assembly (articles 89, 104), elections can be called by the president (article 108). A Provisional Council of Ministers composed of party members in proportion to their Assembly membership then acts as the government until the new Assembly is elected, except for the posts of ministers of justice, interior, and communications, which are turned over to nonparty administrators during the interregnum (article 109). The Council of Ministers is now the real executive body, with the prime minister's duties being to promote the cooperation of the ministries and supervise implementation of the government policies. With his longer term of office, ineligibility for reelection, political neutrality, and ability to preside over the Council of Ministers, the president is intended to be a person above party, a mediator among political forces, far different from the position assumed by both Atatürk and İnönü.

Also included is the old Council of State, the only Ottoman institution to survive all the twists and turmoils of republican Turkey. Its prestige was seriously threatened during the later Democratic years when the government prevented it from acting effectively against illegal acts or unwarranted dismissals of public officials, but the new Constitution has attempted to restore its ability to curb the government by ensuring its independence from both the legislature and government. Article 114 declares that no act of administration can be excluded from the control of the courts, including the Council of State, thus ending the practice of nullifying such authority by government decree. Article 140 assures its independence by having its members elected by an independent committee composed of members of the Constitutional Court, named both by the Council of Ministers and the General Council of the Council of State. The Council of State acts mainly as an administrative court of first instance in cases not referred first to other courts, and of final appeal in all cases. It is supposed to hear and settle administrative disputes, advise the government on draft laws, treaties, and contracts, and also hear appeals from the decisions of the tax courts.

Strong efforts also were made to assure the autonomy of the courts: ". . . judges shall be independent in the discharge of their duties"; and "no organ, office, agency or individual may give orders or instructions to courts or judges in connection with the discharge of their judicial duty . . ." (article 132). The appointment, promotion, transfer, disciplining, and retirement of judges are now made by a Supreme Council of Judges chosen by the judges themselves. Military courts can try civilians only for military offenses prescribed by special laws (article 138), even in periods of martial law. The basic court structure remains the same as before, with a Court of Cassation acting as the final appeals court. The most important change was the provision of a Constitutional Court to review the constitutionality of laws and to try the president, prime minister, other ministers, and the chief judicial and executive officers for offenses connected with their duties (articles 145–147).

The basic rights and duties of Turkish citizens are clearly defined in the first sections of the Constitution. As in the 1924 Constitution all citizens of the Republic are defined as Turks regardless of religion (article 54). Every person has the right of personal freedom (article 14), privacy (article 15), immunity of domicile (article 16), freedom of communication (article 17), freedom to travel and reside where he or she likes (article 18), freedom of religious faith and worship and freedom from abuse of one's religion by others (article 19). The press is assured of freedom from censorship (article 22), and it can be "restricted by law only to safeguard national security or public morality, prevent attacks on the dignity, honor and rights of individuals, prevent instigations to commit crimes and assure proper implementation of judicial functions" (article 22). Publications cannot be subjected to requirements of prior permission or deposit of a guarantee fund (articles 23, 24), and "all persons are free to congregate or march in demonstrations without prior permission so long as they are unarmed and have no intent to assault," with this right being restricted "only for the purposes of maintaining public order or morality" (article 29). Individuals can be arrested by the police "if there is a strong case for indictment," but they must be informed of the charges at once and cannot be held for more than 24 hours without court sanction (article 30).

All citizens are entitled to vote and be elected in free, open, and secret elections on the basis of equality, direct suffrage, and public counting (articles 54, 55). Political parties can be formed without prior permission, and whether in power or opposition are declared to be "indispensable entities of democratic political life" (article 56). They are, however, expected to "conform to the principles of a democratic and secular republic, based on human rights and liberties, and to the fundamental principle of the State's territorial and national integrity," or they can be dissolved (article 57). They are accountable for their income and expenditures and for their internal affairs and activities to the Constitutional Court (article 57). All Turkish citizens are entitled to attend public schools and to enter public service or the army regardless of religion or sex (articles 58, 59, 60).

Perhaps the most interesting part of the Constitution of 1961 is its inclusion of many of the social and economic rights desired by the more radical members of the Constituent Assembly. The family is declared to be "the fundamental unit of Turkish Society" (article 35), and the state is required to do whatever is necessary to protect it as well as "the mother and the child." Everyone can own and inherit property (article 36), but the exercise of property rights cannot conflict with public welfare, and the state can legislate to achieve efficient ultilization of land and to provide land for those cultivators lacking it by measures such as defining and limiting the size of landholdings and helping farmers acquire agricultural implements (article 37). The state is authorized to expropriate any private immoveable property in return for just compensation (articles 38, 39). Private enterprise is free, but it can be restricted in the public interest, nationalized for compensation when necessary (articles 39–40), and regulated to assure its functioning "in an atmosphere of security and stability consistent with the requirements of the national economy and the objectives of the society" (article 40). The state is bound to regulate economic and social life "in a manner consistent with justice and the principle of full employment, with the objective of assuring for everyone a standard of living befitting human dignity" (article 41). Every person has not only the right but the duty to "be engaged in some occupation, trade, or business." The state must "protect workers and promote employment by adopting social, economic, and financial measures" to give them "a decent human existence so that stable employment" may be secured and unemployment avoided. Workers' rights are specified. No one "can be employed at a job that does not suit his age, capacity, and sex," and special permission is needed to employ children, young people, and women (article 43). Every worker "has the right to rest," but the exact requirements for paid annual vacations and payment for work on holidays and weekends when required are left to special legislation (article 44). The state can pass laws to assure workers a decent and livable wage (article 45). Both employers and employees can establish their own unions and federations without prior permission and can resign from such associations freely, with the state acting only to assure that their operation "shall not conflict with democratic principles" (article 46). Workers can bargain collectively and strike (article 47) but only in accordance with legal regulations, and the state is required to provide or help provide social security, insurance, and welfare organizations (article 48). The state must ensure that everyone is provided with health and educational facilities, with primary education being free and compulsory for both males and females and scholarships provided to help able students to achieve the "highest level of learning consistent with their abilities" (article 50). The state also must promote agricultural and urban cooperatives (article 51) and "take the necessary measures to provide the people with adequate nourishment, to assure an increase in agricultural production . . . enhance the value of agricultural products and the toil of those engaged in agriculture" (article 52).

The State Planning Organization is entitled to develop plans for economic, social, and cultural development (article 129), though its structure and the implementation of its plans were left to special regulation by law. All natural wealth and resources are under state control, and private exploitation can be carried out only with state permission and supervision (article 130).

The provincial, district, and local governmental bodies are retained as before with the exception that "provincial administration is based on the principle of self-government" and regional self-government organizations also are allowed to carry out "specific public services" (article 115). Civil servants are entitled to protection by law in disciplinary cases (article 118), and they cannot join political parties (article 119) or discriminate among citizens because of their political views. Universities can be established and operated only by the state and are declared to be "public corporate bodies enjoying academic and administrative autonomy" (article 120), with self-government through "organs consisting of qualified members of the teaching staff." Teachers and assistants can be removed from their positions only by the universities and through university procedures. They are free to engage in research and publication, are exempted from the restrictions forbidding civil servants from joining political parties, but are forbidden from assuming executive positions except in case of "the central organizations of political parties" (article 120), thus enabling them to function as political leaders and in other capacities. Radio and television broadcasting is placed under "autonomous public corporate bodies," with the obligation to broadcast "along the principles of impartiality" (article 121). Finally, civil servants receiving illegal orders from superiors are ordered to execute them only after protesting their illegality and receiving written orders to proceed, except where such orders and their fulfillment themselves constitute crimes, in which case both the superior and the civil servant are criminally liable (article 125). All articles of the Constitution can be amended by a two-thirds vote of each chamber of the Grand National Assembly except article 1, which declares the Turkish state to be a republic (article 155).[166]

The Constitution of 1961 thus provides significant changes from its predecessors, but since much of its implementation is subject to the directives of the individual ministries and body of legal precedent built up over the entire republican period, in many cases the effect of the changes has been slight, particularly since some civil servants preserve old mentalities and traditions of action that do not always conform with the spirit or laws of the new Republic.

The Politics of the Second Republic Since 1961

The division of Turkish society along class lines, manifested and accentuated by the Democratic Party's rise and decade of power, was further encouraged by the events that caused its collapse and the establishment of the Second Republic. In more than a decade since the Constitution of 1961 was introduced, moreover, these divisions have become more vivid than ever. The bureaucracies of the government and army, which dominated the state during the Atatürk period, remain wedded to policies mainly reflecting and supporting their own well-being, but with their monopoly of power gone they have had to ally with one or another of the new political interests and groups to achieve their ends. The intellectuals, whose hopes that the 1961 Constitution would achieve all their liberal economic and social ambitions have dimmed, have tended to move away from the existing constitutional structure and toward the more radical Socialist movement that would accomplish their objectives by revolutionary change. The new middle class, interested mainly in preserving and extending its prosperity both in the towns and countryside, has come to associate with groups wishing to limit social reforms and promote free enterprise. The religious nationalists and conservatives have splintered into their own radical groups with limited, but potentially dangerous, influence among the masses. The armed forces, divided internally among liberals and conservatives, have sought generally to keep the civilian regimes progressive, with their extreme elements also splitting away to join the more liberal and conservative groups in society as a whole (see Table 6.2).

Under the 1961 structure of government, however, all these interest groups still have had to work through political parties. With the Democratic Party seemingly put out of existence, the RPP initially emerged as the most important remaining political force, apparently assured of resuming the power lost in 1950. It never was able to accomplish this promise in the decade of the 1960s, however, because many in the country associated it with the 1960 coup and the trials that followed, while the new mercantile classes and peasants who prospered so much under the Democrats feared that an RPP triumph would restore the old Statism that had seemingly suppressed them in the past. Still including both conservative and liberal elements, the RPP program in 1961 expressed general proposals that could satisfy everyone. Private as well as public enterprise was to be encouraged, a more equitable system of taxation developed, land given to the peasants, and social security and social services provided for all workers. Foreign capital was to be attracted, but under strong government supervision, and the alliance with the West would be preserved.

Table 6.2. *The Senate results, 1961–1968*

Party	1961 Votes	Seats won	1964 Votes	Seats won	1966 Votes	Seats won	1968 Votes	Seats won
Justice Party	3,560,675	71	1,385,655	31	1,688,316	35	1,656,802	38
Republican People's Party	3,734,285	36	1,125,783	19	877,066	13	899,444	13
Reliance Party							284,234	1
New Turkey Party	1,401,637	27	96,427	—	70,043	1		
Turkish Workers' Party					116,375	1	157,062	—
Nation Party					157,115	1	200,737	1
Republican Peasant's National Party	1,350,892	16	83,400	—	57,367	1	66,232	—
Registered voters	12,926,837		4,668,865		5,466,284		5,420,255	
Number voting	10,519,659		2,808,592		3,072,393		3,595,976	
Percent cast	81.4		60.2		56.2		66.3	

Source: Türkiye İstatistik Yıllığı, 1973, p. 147.

The RPP thus emerged as a progressive but basically middle-class liberal party, somewhat more socialistic than before but still moderate.

Such an approach was hardly acceptable to the many groups that had coalesced in and around the Democratic Party and that now sought out a new vehicle to express their interests and political ambitions. Several parties emerged to secure the Democratic vote. The New Turkey Party (*Yeni Türkiye Partisi*) was founded in February 1961, at least partly by members of the Freedom Party group that had split from the Democrats in 1957. Accepting private enterprise and rapid industrialization as basic necessities for economic development, it advocated government action to achieve this end, but with more of a balance between the nation's financial capacities and efficiency of production than had been the case in the past. Religious education would be encouraged to give Turkish youth an idea of their heritage, but secularism was accepted as a basic principle and freedom for all religions encouraged. Foreign capital would be accepted but controlled. Land would be divided among the peasants, but only as long as the proliferation of small holdings did not hurt production. State planning would be used not to control all aspects of the economy but merely to coordinate and harmonize its different elements.

The Republican Peasant's National Party (*Cumhuriyetçi Köylü Millet Partisi*) emerged as somewhat more conservative than the New Turkey Party but took on its more definitive position on the right only after June 1962, when its founder and leader, Osman Bölükbaşı left to form the new Nation Party, and March 1965, when it was joined and partly taken over by a nationalist group led by one of the members of the NUC, Alparslan Türkeş. The new RPNP, now basically a secular and nationalist group, emphasizes also social and religious aims more or less in the pattern of the National Socialist movements of prewar Germany and Italy. It accepts the democratic regime established in 1961 but does not really emphasize it, advocating instead strong state action to achieve its aims. Workers are to be given social security and even allowed to participate in industrial management, to organize, and to strike. On the other hand, party and government are to reconcile class differences. Private enterprise is encouraged, but capitalistic exploitation and excessive profits are to be discouraged. Planning is needed so that society can be organized and controlled for its own good. People should be educated and directed through their entire lives. Land should be distributed but large units retained to encourage production, while private property is to be recognized and encouraged. Turkish nationalism and Islam are to be emphasized as basic pillars of the society of the Republic.

In the meantime, the Nation Party restored in 1962 by Osman Bölükbaşı also emphasizes private enterprise and economic planning, but unlike the RPNP it strongly defends political democracy and rejects the extremes of political and social organization advocated both by the right and the left. Religion is emphasized and all forms of socialism and communism rejected because of their basically godless approaches. Turkish nationalism should influence foreign policy. Turkey's actions should reflect less what its Western allies want and more what its own interests are in relation to the Arab countries and Cyprus. It also should avoid any kind of cooperation with the Soviet Union. Religion and morality should be emphasized to guide Turkish society.

In the end, however, most of the old Democratic vote has been captured by the more moderate conservatism espoused by the Justice Party (*Adalet Partisi*), founded in February 1961 by one of the military officers retired by the NUC, Ragıp Gümüşpala, and led after his sudden death in 1964 by a career engineer, Süleyman

Demirel. With the NUC still in control during the 1961 elections, the Justice Party had to develop an independent program, and could not openly pose as the direct heir of the Democratic Party. It did so though in fact, however, and took over much of the latter's electoral apparatus around the country. Its basic position is only slightly right of center, with its conservative position stemming not so much from the more authoritarian approaches of the other groups on the right but, rather, from old-fashioned liberalism, very much like that of the Democrats, advocacy of the maximum amount of freedom for the individual whether he be a worker, a peasant, a merchant, or a factory owner. Private enterprise is to be encouraged, though state enterprise can be accepted when necessary. The party's concern for rural support is expressed through its declarations against any kind of rural income or animal taxes and its support of reductions of taxes on small merchants and traders. Land reform is emphasized, but landowners would be allowed to retain at least small estates, and small plots would be discouraged so as not to lessen productivity. Workers would be allowed to strike, and the government would give them social security, socialized health care, and the like. Education would be reformed to end elitism among the intellectuals; villages and towns would be given more autonomy to control their destinies according to their own needs. Planning would be a voluntary effort to coordinate the different elements of the economy, with worker representatives helping develop goals. Foreign capital would be encouraged, and with little control as long as the overall national objectives are achieved. Unemployment would be remedied by money payments and also by finding work for those able and willing to do so. Universities would be reformed so that they could better meet the students' needs and interests, and academic advice would be heeded by the government as much as possible. The party itself has been divided into liberal and conservative wings, but Demirel has favored the former, while the latter have tended to go off into the more conservative groups, particularly at times when the party actually has achieved power.

During the 1960s, the strongest left-wing group was the Turkish Workers' Party (*Türkiye İşçi Partisi*), formed in 1961 by a number of Istanbul union leaders and a year later made into a full-fledged Socialist party after leadership was assumed by Mehmet Ali Aybar, a noted Ankara Socialist. Calling all the other parties reactionary, the Workers' Party followed the Marxist line of criticizing American "imperialism" and claiming that Turkish interests were sacrificed in return for American help. While he went on to advocate an independent foreign policy, Aybar also maintained that it would be in Atatürk's tradition for Turkey to cooperate with its more immediate neighbors, particularly the Soviet Union. Including both workers and intellectuals in its candidate lists, the Workers' Party emphasized restoration of state control over heavy industry and all the basic units of production, with private enterprise being allowed to continue though slowly disappearing as a result of its uselessness in a Socialist state. The banks, insurance companies, foreign trade, and the use of foreign capital would be nationalized along with the exploitation of mineral resources. Landholdings would be restricted to 500 *dönüms* (about 125 acres) per person; large landholdings would be expropriated, and locally elected peasant groups would execute the land laws. While all the parties accept social reforms for the workers, the Workers' Party alone demanded a 5-day, 40-hour week, with prohibitions against employer lockouts of workers. The People's Houses would be reorganized and developed to provide for adult education and control, and youth would be organized and educated so that it would recognize and preserve the ideals of the Socialist state. In a strongly property-oriented state, however, the Workers' Party was not able to expound more radical ideas while in opposition; thus it stated that property rights would be preserved as long as the owners did not use them for exploitation. The democratic regime would be retained, with minority rights respected. Democracy would be extended to include not only voting but also popular participation in the affairs of local and provincial government as well as the factories and businesses, but with strong party guidance to suppress whoever would use this freedom to preserve the "exploitation" of the past.[167]

Turkish politics since 1961 have very much reflected the new democracy created by the Constitution. The different social classes and political groups, which were united under the RPP by Atatürk and Inönü and which began to split apart during the Democratic decade, have now risen to reflect their individual interests. Since the major parties in turn have tried to gain the support of different groups by widening their appeal as much as possible, very much in the American manner, they have come to emulate the old RPP much more than they might care to admit. The major parties have become almost evenly balanced, securing the majorities needed to govern by coalition arrangements with the small parties. The old NUC, largely retired into the background, has chosen to exercise a moderate influence from behind the scenes, acting mainly through the presidents of the Republic, all of whom have been former military officers, to push the squabbling parties to overcome their differences in order to enact the reforms envisaged in the Constitution while retaining the essentially civilian democracy that is the basis of its program.[168]

The national elections held on October 15, 1961, were carried out in complete freedom and without government or army interference despite the continued rule of the NUC. Though the latter gave the RPP its moral support and the other parties had only just been organized, the RPP gained only 36.7 percent of the popular vote and 38 percent of the Assembly seats. The Justice Party gained 34.8 percent of the vote and 35 percent of the seats, while the balance of power was left to the New Turkey Party, which received 13 percent of the vote and 14.5 percent of the seats, and the Republican Peasant's National Party, with 14.0 percent of the vote and 12 percent of the seats (see Table 6.1). In the Senate, on the other hand, since the old electoral system prevailed, with the majority or plurality party in each district receiving all the seats, the Justice Party, with about the same vote as in the Assembly elections, received 47 percent of the seats, while the RPP received only 24 percent, the New Turkey Party 14 percent, and the Republican Peasant's National Party 13.6 percent. Under the circumstances a coalition government seemed necessary, and the NUC thought of annulling the elections because of the fear that no one could govern effectively. It finally agreed to accept the situation and retire from the scene, however, when the RPP and the Justice Party agreed to a coalition with the trusted elder statesman Ismet Inönü as prime minister, while the NUC leader, Cemal Gürsel, was unanimously elected president to watch over the situation.

During the four years of Inönü's prime ministry (1961-1964), much of the deadlock that the NUC had feared in fact ensued, and Inönü was forced to rule through three successive coalitions. The first was not destined to last too long, since it brought together political leaders who differed in personality and ambition as well as policy. In the end the Justice Party's insistence on more liberal economic policies and the pardon of the imprisoned Democratic Party leaders conflicted with the more Statist views of the RPP as well as with the military's insistence that nothing be done that might be interpreted as criticizing or undoing the results of the revolution. It was at this time that many intellectuals turned to the Workers' Party in frustration over the Parliament's inability to act, while several rightist groups banded together under the leadership of Colonel Türkeş and his associates. Democracy, however, continued to prevail. In June 1962 the first coalition broke up, and İnönü formed his second coalition among the RPP and the small parties, remaining with the Peasant Party after the New Turkey Party, startled by the loss of half of its votes in the municipal elections of November 17, 1963, withdrew in a vain effort to regain its following. A third coalition, formed in January 1964, continued to govern for another year, but by then the Justice Party was making such gains in popular esteem that it seemed certain to prevail in the next elections. Without an overall majority İnönü was unable to take decisive action to snap the nation out of the economic stagnation that had set in with the revolution, or to enact any of the major reforms. The most important problem that faced the regime was the privileged position of the rural sector, which paid only a small portion of the taxes while benefiting from the huge subsidies provided in the past by the Democrats to gain its support. This not only burdened the treasury but also deprived the peasants of the incentive needed to improve their efficiency. In the end, İnönü was unable to secure more than a very small new agricultural income tax (1964), while other reform efforts, such as that to distribute land, were defeated. İnönü at least did secure the release of 283 imprisoned Democrats in October 1962 and the remainder in 1964, returning the 147 dismissed university teachers to their jobs and the dispossessed large landowners to their lands to restore political normalcy and end the tremendous divisions in society that these acts had caused. In these efforts he again displayed political acumen and courage, securing the support of the army and of his own party for measures that were quite unpopular to many of their members and supporters.

Meanwhile, Süleyman Demirel had assumed leadership of the Justice Party and was rebuilding it in a new image, moving it away from the old Democratic ties and ideology. Since he was an engineer, he projected the image of the new kind of technocrat able and willing to steer the nation according to the needs of the time rather than in fulfillment of outmoded political philosophies. This image was strengthened by his moves to give control of the party machinery to professional and technical experts in place of the more conservative politicians who came over from the Democrats. He also was able to develop a sufficiently modernist policy to satisfy the demands of the army as well as his own professional supporters for reform while he retained enough of a rural and religious approach so as not to alienate his peasant followers, who still provided most of the votes. With party affiliations in the Assembly increasingly fluid, he finally forced the third İnönü coalition to resign by a no-confidence vote on the budget in February 1965, so that, in accordance with the constitution, an all-party government ruled until the new elections were held.

During the election campaign, the Justice Party presented an image of a vigorous, dynamic group with a positive policy to move the nation ahead. The RPP, on the other hand, still led by the aging İnönü, though now with the help of an energetic young secretary general named Kasım Gülek, gave the appearance of merely holding together a number of disparate groups to keep power, mainly to keep the Justice Party out. Many of its most vigorous intellectual supporters by now had gone to the Workers' Party, while those who remained fought strongly with the party leaders over the future direction of both party and country. The December 1964 Electoral Law established the principle of the "national remainder" in distributing parliamentary seats, setting aside a certain number of seats to be distributed to the parties according to their overall proportion of the vote in addition to those elected locally. The purpose of the law was to help the smaller parties, but many saw in it a government effort to deny the Justice Party the triumph that its popularity seemed to presage, further adding to its support. In the elections held on October 10, 1965, the Justice Party did, indeed, gain a victory, with 52.9 percent of the popular vote providing it with a bare majority of Assembly seats, 53 percent, while the RPP gained 28.7 percent of the votes and 29.7 percent of the seats and Bölükbaşı's new Nation Party received 6.3 and 6.8 percent respectively. The Senate elections held the same year gave the Justice Party 59.4 percent of the vote and 35 out of the 52 seats up for the election, while the RPP won only 13 seats and 29 percent of the vote (see Table 6.1).[169]

With an overall parliamentary majority, between 1965 and 1970 the Demirel government was able to push ahead to fulfill its programs in a way that Inönü, now in opposition, never had been able to do with coalition regimes. Its policy was determined by its desire to promote economic development and social justice, not only in reaction to the Constitution and the insistence of the army, but also to the increasingly strident demands of the more radical left-wing groups, composed mainly of trade unionists and militant students, who began to manifest their opposition by street demonstrations and even more violent activities. Economic policy followed the mixed approach dictated in the Constitution. The Demirel government used both private and state control to stimulate growth and prosperity through plans provided by the State Planning Organization. The leftist organizations, which now came to include most university teachers and students and many professionals, became more and more adamant in criticizing the government for not going much faster despite the fact that most people were satisfied by policies that increased their prosperity without the hectic excesses of the Menderes years. Relations of the government with the army were better than anticipated, mainly as a result of Demirel's decision to get his party to elect another general, Cevdet Sunay, as President after Gürsel's death in 1966. Demirel also continued the effort to modernize the army, improving the conditions of its officers and men and avoiding direct interference in its affairs, while Sunay in turn kept the officers from mixing too much in politics. The main problem that continued to cause friction between government and army involved the question of amnesty for the Democratic politicians, including Celal Bayar, who had been released from jail by Inönü but still were deprived of political rights because of their prior convictions. A law to this effect was pushed through the Assembly, but it was defeated in the Senate in 1969 just before the new elections. Following the elections, however, the amnesty was passed without significant reaction from the army. Bayar retired to write his memoirs, while the other Democrats found that the Justice Party and the smaller groups by now had evolved new leadership structures that they could not really influence by their mere presence.

Government relations with the RPP became increasingly bitter, however. The clashes came initially over RPP criticism of the government tendency to favor its religious supporters by following the Democratic policy of building mosques, allowing religious lessons in the schools, and even encouraging the use of loudspeakers in the cities to amplify the call to prayer. By this time, however, secularism was such an accepted policy of the Republic that people lost interest in the subject; hence this issue could not be exploited. On the other hand, the RPP came under the leadership of a dynamic new secretary general, Bülent Ecevit, who developed a much more leftist program than before, transforming the party into a democratic socialist group to absorb many of the intellectuals and others who had been going off to the more extreme parties. The government, however, continued to carry the day for some time because of the success of its economic programs. There were the old problems of deficit spending and a deficit trade balance once again, but despite this the 5 percent growth rate achieved under the Democrats actually was increased to 6.6 percent during the new Five-Year Plan (1962-1967), although the population was increasing at a rate of from 2.5 to 3 percent annually. Industrial production was rising by as much as 9 percent annually. Private enterprise contributed significantly, and though the agricultural sector of the economy did not quite achieve some of its goals, its growth and general prosperity still were significant. Between 1962, the first year that the new government's policies really had an impact, and 1970, while population increased from 28.9 to 35.2 million, per capita income stated in constant terms increased 35.3 percent (from 2,546 to 3,445 Turkish liras), while in the current prices understood by the people the increase was 109 percent (from 1,905 to 3,982 Turkish liras). Overall agricultural production, stated in Turkish liras in absolute terms, rose from 25.143 billion to 32.65 billion, or 29.82 percent; industrial production from 13.01 billion to 28.25 billion, or 117 percent; construction from 4.58 billion to 8.3 billion, or 81 percent; trade from 6.275 billion to 12.048 billion, or 92 percent; government services from 7.35 billion to 12.257 billion, or 66.7 percent; income from Turkish workers and sales abroad from a deficit of 275 million to a surplus to 1.47 billion, or 634 percent; and the total national product from 73.65 billion to 121.376 billion, or 64.8 percent.[170] During the same decade the number of schools increased from 25,922 to 41,667, or 60.7 percent, and the number of students from 2.984 to 6.492 million, or 117 percent![171] Industrial workers were happy both because of their increased incomes and buying power and also because of the development of trade unionism and permission to strike (1963), which was freely used in subsequent years. Agricultural cultivators were receiving more income than ever, particularly with their limited tax burden and continued government subsidies. Even the nonpolitical elements in the universities were pleased by the autonomy and liberalization provided by the NUC reforms, and also by the tremendous expansion of the bureaucracy to meet the increasing duties of government, which provided good jobs for graduates.

The only drawback, as in many aspects of the Democratic regime, was financial. There now was plenty of investment capital, coming not only from the United States but also from a consortium forced by the European Economic Community, the World Bank, and even the Soviet Union. The migration of close to a million Turkish workers to fill the needs of the booming industries of West Germany and other nations of Western Europe also provided Turkey with an additional significant source of foreign income as well as an opportunity to train its workers in more modern methods and disciplines of work. But with a tremendously increasing internal demand and rapid investment, the result was a new inflation, with the overall consumer price index in Istanbul increasing from 100 in 1958 to 148 in 1970, and in Ankara from 100 to 155.[172] As the vast majority of the population enjoyed the new prosperity, the inflation had little effect on the government's political position except to provide new fuel for the ideologically oriented opposition of the extreme leftists and rightists and the politically oriented position of the RPP. The latter sometimes cooperated with the extremists for the sake of opposition, attempting to block the government's programs simply to secure power for itself. But the more conservative elements in the party criticized the leaders for this, while its leftists continued to oppose the party as an inadequate vehicle for securing their aims. The Justice Party, on the other hand, reacted to the RPP tactics by condemning ideologically formulated social ideas, but in the process alienated many of its own intellectuals and technical experts and came to rely more and more on its rural and urban proletarian supporters. The end result was a restoration of the RPP as the party of the intellectual and technical elite while leaving the Justice Party to an ever-more uneasy balance between the modernist elements led by Demirel and the more conservative religious and rural groups seeking his ouster. In addition, there was a proliferation of new minor parties, particularly on the right, including the Reliance Party (*Güven Partisi*). In the national elections of October 12, 1969, both major parties lost votes. The Justice Party declined from 52.9 to 46.5 percent of the total vote, though it increased its Assembly seats to 56.8 percent, and the RPP retained 27 percent of the vote and got 3.7 percent of the seats. The old small parties largely faded, while the Reliance Party gained 6.6 percent of the vote and a small number of seats (see Table 6.1). In a sense, therefore, Turkey was evolving a two-party system, with the lesser parties largely falling aside.[173]

The polarization of Turkish politics evidenced in the 1969 elections led Bülent Ecevit to carry out a major reorganization of the RPP during 1970, driving out most of the older elements, including Ismet İnönü (who subsequently was made a lifetime senator, acting as an elder-statesman above politics until his death in 1974 after a half-century of service to his nation), and recasting the party in a more liberal and progressive image. The Justice Party, still led by Demirel, continued to direct the country's economic development, but since its conservative elements had gained somewhat increased power, it was reluctant to push through any further social or economic reforms. In the meantime, the left-wing radicals took more and more to the streets, demanding fundamental changes in the structure of Turkish society and also using the American military presence and Turkish attachment to NATO as a focus for their attacks, pushing the government and both major parties toward an increasingly independent kind of foreign policy. With the radicals now using the tactics developed so long before by the minority terrorists, the RPP seized on the government's inability to suppress them as another issue of criticism. In reaction to the emerging left the main conservative parties, the Reliance, Nation, and New Turkey parties, formed a coalition (October 17, 1970), only to see their more religious elements form the conservative National Salvation Party (*Milli Selâmet Partisi*), while some of the old Democrats left the existing parties to organize the new Democratic Party.[174] The government's inability to control the violence of the extreme left eroded its support despite the continued development and prosperity. Inflation added to the furor. Members gradually left its group in the National Assembly so that by January 1971 it had lost its absolute majority. And with the RPP's continued refusal to cooperate in any kind of coalition, it also lost its ability to govern effectively insofar as major decisions and policies were concerned. As a result, the military finally forced the Demirel government to resign (March 12, 1971), leaving the nation to be governed by a series of nonparty coalitions, led by Nihat Erim (March 26–May 21, 1971), Ferit Melen (May 22, 1972–April 10, 1973), and Naim Talu (April 15–October 1973), until the next elections were held.

Under pressure from the army, at first both major parties cooperated with the new regime, but as Ecevit continued his effort to reconstitute the RPP as a left-of-center progressive force, he finally got it to withdraw its members on the grounds that the government was in fact a right-wing coalition (November 4, 1972). With the Justice Party still divided between its own conservatives and liberals and the nonparty governments seemingly unable to handle the terrorists or to develop major new reform programs, the public gradually swung back to the RPP as well as toward the more radical parties, making it more difficult than ever for any single party to secure a majority let alone organize a harmonious government and follow a rational policy. In the national elections held on October 14, 1973, the RPP secured only 33.3 percent of the vote, the Justice Party 29.8, the Democratic Party 11.9, the National Salvation Party 11.8, and the Reliance Party 5.3 percent. The RPP ended up with 185 seats in the Assembly and the Justice Party with 149, forcing both to seek the coalition support of the minority parties to form a government (see Table 6.1). Though the RPP had the largest vote, since all the other smaller parties were more radical it avoided a coalition at first. The most likely coalition seemed to be one between the Justice and Nation parties, whose policies were similar, but they were unable to get together for some time because of the personal politics and rivalries that have bedeviled recent Turkish political life. Under military pressure, therefore, it was left for the RPP to join forces with the National Salvation Party, an uneasy union that lasted for only six months (February–September 1974) and broke up over the widely diverging views of its members on both domestic and foreign policy. After a long period of nonparty government, Demirel was able to form a new coalition with the minority conservative parties (March 31, 1975). Since the new government held only a plurality in the Assembly and the RPP continued to amass popular support, it seemed possible that the latter might regain power in the next elections unless the Justice Party itself moved leftward to match the changing popular mood.

Foreign Policy, 1950–1975

Perhaps one of the brightest aspects of the new Turkey has been the general agreement of all the major parties on the basic lines of foreign policy. The Soviet efforts to take over significant portions of the country in 1946 led the nation into a strong postwar alliance with the West that has remained basically unaltered. The RPP took steps to join NATO soon after the Marshall Plan had been introduced, and, although its efforts were frustrated for a time by NATO politics, when the opportunity arose to demonstrate Turkish support for the United Nations' effort in Korea, the Democrats accepted the invitation to help so willingly that Turkey's subsequent entrance into NATO (18 February 1952) was assured. This was supplemented by moves to strengthen the nation's ties with both Europe and the Balkans. It soon joined the Organization for European Economic Cooperation (the Common Market), with an associate status taking cognizance of its relatively undeveloped economy, but with hopes of gaining full membership by 1995. The regional alliances of the 1930s also were revived by defense agreements with Greece and Yugoslavia and a mutual defense agreement with Pakistan (1954). The latter soon developed into the Baghdad Pact, later called the Central Treaty Organization, which included also Great Britain and Iran and, for a time, Iraq. The United States was not formally included in the latter but provided strong support and encouragement, supplemented by a bilateral defense agreement with Turkey signed in March 1959. The Arab countries attempted to secure closer relations with Turkey on the basis of religious unity, but all the postwar Turkish governments, regardless of their policy toward religion within the country, continued to base their response on overall national and secular considerations. Turkey, therefore, remained friendly with the Arabs except at times with Syria because of its claims on Hatay. There have been continued good diplomatic and economic relations between Turkey and Israel, suspended only briefly during the Arab-Israeli War of 1967. Since 1964 also the Muslim members of CENTO, Turkey, Iran, and Pakistan, have joined in the Regional Cooperation for Development (RCD) Organization, which has carried forth a number of joint economic and cultural projects with the hope of political cooperation as well. Turkish relations with Iraq, on the other hand, were made more difficult by the latter's orientation toward Russia as well as its long preoccupation with the Kurdish revolt in the north, brought to an end only in 1975. While the Iraqis at times accused Turkey of encouraging the Kurds, Turkey was not at all anxious to stimulate a similar movement within its own borders and therefore refrained from any overt action, with Iran providing the Kurds with most of their support. Although Armenian and Greek exiles and their supporters tried to instill anti-Muslim sentiments and national aspirations into the political life of the countries where they settled – particularly in the United States, France, and Britain – Turkey effectively countered their claims by pointing out that what massacres had occurred in the past were the result of minority terrorism and not of government policy and that in any case the Republic could no more be held responsible for the actions of the sultans than could the commissars of the Soviet Union for the repressive policies of the czars. Turkey's key strategic position in NATO also led its partners to place realistic national interests above the pleadings of the minorities.

The most difficult question of foreign policy to trouble Turkey after 1950 was that of Cyprus, caused not by any Turkish desire to annex the island, but rather by the tendency of the island's ruling Greek majority to exclude the Turkish minority from significant participation in its political and economic life and by the efforts of a militant Greek minority to achieve *enosis* (union) with Greece. Agitation toward this end began while the British controlled the island. Greek attacks on the Turkish minority periodically caused strained relations between Greece and Turkey starting in 1955. In February 1959 the problem was solved temporarily by an agreement among Turkey, Greece, and Britain, concluded in Zurich and London, by which Cyprus became an independent republic (August 16, 1960), with protection for the Turkish minority under the guarantee of the three signatories, which were allowed to station small garrisons on the island for that purpose. Turkey's position toward Cyprus after 1959 was to secure full implementation of that settlement. But most of the key governmental positions on the island were controlled by Greeks, who also managed to dominate trade and the economy and left only the worst lands and positions to the Turks. In addition, renewed demand for union with Greece led to a civil war during 1964. Agitated by stories and pictures of massacres in the press, Turkish public opinion strongly supported the idea of military intervention to protect the Turks on the island, particularly in view of the longstanding Greek persecution of the Turkish minority in western Thrace, and in August Turkish airplanes attacked coastal fortifications. But Turkey's NATO allies, led by the United States, applied severe pressure to prevent a clash between it and fellow member Greece, causing the government to call off its invasion force at the last minute and leave the settlement to the United Nations. Greek subjects living in Turkey were, however, expelled because of their strong support for *enosis,* and impetus was given to the anti-American agitation of the Turkish radicals, who took advantage of the popular belief that the United States should have supported Turkey under the terms of their bilateral agreements.

Relations between Turkey and the United States deteriorated subsequently. Radical agitation forced the government to restrict American bases, prevent the U.S. Mediterranean fleet from retaining its home base at Izmir and visiting Istanbul, and gradually phase out other American military operations in the country. Peace finally returned to Cyprus in 1965, but there was no final agreement, and the Turkish minority remained as oppressed as it had been before. The Cyprus Greek government, led by Archbishop President Makarios, did manage to suppress the more radical *enosis* elements led by General Grivas, but its tendency to join the third world nations in world affairs and to use its position to enhance the position and status of the Greek Orthodox church on the island seriously disturbed the Turks, who were in any case increasingly unhappy at rule by a religious figure. During the summer of 1967, new attacks on the Turkish minority led Demirel to attempt an agreement to safeguard their interests, but American pressure again prevented the kind of Turkish intervention that might have secured a solution, leaving a stalemate that allowed conditions to deteriorate further. The United States got Greece to withdraw its regular troops, but it substituted Greek officers sent as "volunteers" to command the National Guard of Cyprus. In addition, with the Greek military dictatorship in control in Athens, General Grivas returned to Cyprus to organize support for a new move toward *enosis*. The continued stalemate increased internal pressure on the Turkish government to lessen its American connections and improve those with the Soviet Union, leading to economic and cultural agreements with the latter in 1970. Turkey, however, continued to recognize the possibility of Soviet military attack. Along with a strong connection with NATO, then, it has maintained its substantial military forces in readiness and continued to accept American military assistance and advice.

A new chapter in the Cyprus quarrel came in the summer of 1974 when the National Guard, under the leadership of its Greek army officers, carried out a coup that forced Makarios to flee and installed a regime led by the radical Greek nationalist Nikos Sampson, who declared his intention of bringing the island into union with Greece. The United Nations and United States attempted to resolve the situation peacefully once again, but their apparent intention of accepting the coup and, possibly, *enosis,* as a *fait accompli* and large-scale Greek massacres of the Turkish minority finally led Turkey to intervene with an expeditionary force that overwhelmed the National Guard and took control of the northern part of the island. Greece's blatant effort to intervene in Cyprus and, even more important, its failure led the junta in control of Greece to install a civilian government led by Constantine Karamanlis. It was hoped that the restoration of civilian rule and the semblance of democracy would satisfy its Greek critics and also enable the government to use the old Western religious prejudices against Turkey so that foreign pressure would force the Turkish army out of the island and restore the previous situation. Turkey, however, used its presence to enforce a division of the island's population, taking over the north for a new Turkish Federated State of Cyprus and declaring its willingness to withdraw as soon as the new arrangement was recognized, possibly in conjunction with a Cypriote Federal Republic. Turkey's position remained one of supporting continued Cypriote independence under international guarantee, but with full autonomy for the Turkish areas so that the minority would no longer be exposed to the kind of political and economic subjection that had existed previously under the Makarios regime, and would have security of life and property.

The only other major question that arose in the mid-1970s to trouble Turkey's relations with its Western friends concerned its substantial crop of opium poppies, which, as processed illegally in western Europe and the United States, came to form a part of the supply of illicit drugs circulated through the world. In 1971 Turkey agreed to phase out the crop entirely so as to reduce the international supply. But this policy was the subject of intense internal criticism that came to a climax in the 1973 elections. The U.S. government gave Turkey funds to compensate the peasants affected, but very little actually reached them. In addition, Turkish resentment against the American failure to help in Cyprus contributed to a reaction against dictation in what seemed to be a purely internal matter. Many Turks could not understand why they were forced to bear the brunt of solving the American drug problem while the United States did nothing to curb the health-endangering tobacco crop in its own country and allowed American drug companies to manufacture and export far more drugs than could be used in legitimate medical activities. Since there was, in any case, no drug problem in Turkey, a majority of the population favored restoration of the poppy crop, and thus all parties in the 1973 elections joined in condemning the old agreement. One of the first acts of the Ecevit coalition government was to distribute seed and prepare the way for a resumption of poppy production, though under strict government controls to prevent illicit drug traffic. Subsequent investigation by the International Narcotics Control Board and the U.N. Secretariat completed on July 13, 1976, indicated that these controls were fully effective and that there had "not been any diversion or leakage to the illicit market."[175]

The issues of Cyprus and poppies in themselves were not serious or fundamental enough to strain Turkey's relations with the West. But they were escalated especially by foreign and minority political activity, particularly in the United States, where in the absence of a substantial number of Turkish–American constituents, the Congress easily succumbed to the political pressure applied not only by its Greek–American constituents but also by the smaller Armenian–American minority, which sought to gain American support for the fulfillment of its national aspirations. A consequence of this kind of pressure was that all United States military assistance to Turkey was suspended early in 1975. Ostensibly this was done to force Turkish evacuation of Cyprus and to restore Greek rule there. But without corresponding American pressure to force compromises in the Greek position (American military assistance to Greece was continued), Greece was encouraged to make new demands. In particular it brought forth a longstanding dream to gain control of the Aegean by claiming that the continental shelves of the islands that it controlled along the western and southern shores of Turkey, by virtue of the Treaty of Lausanne, placed that sea entirely within the national boundaries of Greece, and sent out exploratory ships that seemed to offer the possibility of the discovery of substantial oil deposits in what had previously been considered international or Turkish waters. Inevitably, the Turkish government stiffened its resolve to maintain its position in Cyprus as well as its insistence on full possession of the territorial waters off its Aegean coasts; and while not ceasing to fulfill its NATO commitments, it suspended American control of its substantial air bases and observation posts in the country, entered into closer economic and political relations with the Soviet Union, and began to explore the possibility of joining some kind of grouping with the Islamic countries of the world. This raised the specter of a major change in Turkey's foreign policy, including, perhaps, withdrawal from NATO and alignment with the third world block of noncommitted nations in international affairs.

Within Turkey itself the crisis seemed to strengthen the political extremes. The conservatives and reactionaries, now seemingly represented by the National Salvation Party, emphasized Islam in both internal and foreign relations. The more radical left-wing groups sought to use the situation to secure a significant turn toward socialism internally as well as closer relations with the Soviet bloc. Though foreign politics thus threatened to force major changes in Turkey's foreign and domestic policies, as the last quarter of the twentieth century began and Turkey celebrated the one-hundredth anniversary of its first Constitution, with its basically homogeneous population and commitment to modernism and democracy, it could still look forward to a continuation of the changes begun with the establishment of the Republic just a half-century before.

Notes to Chapter 6

1 Başvekâlet Istatistik Umum Müdürlüğü, *Istatistik Yıllığı,* hereafter abbreviated as IY, V (1931–1932), 35–99; République Turque, Office Central de Statistique, *Population de la Turquie par vilayets et cazas par villes et villages d'après le recensement du 28 Octobre 1927,* Angora, 1928.

2 The figures for 1911 are from *Ihsaiyat-ı Maliye,* III; those for 1923 and 1926 are from IY, V, 237–272, 337.

3 IY, V, 302–333.

4 *Düstur³,* XV, 124.

5 TBMM, *Zabıt Ceridesi,* IV/9, pp. 537, 543.

6 *Düstur³,* XX, 119.

7 *Cumhuriyet,* July 22, 1936; *Düstur³,* XVII, 665; RG, 3374.

8 *Cumhuriyet,* December 28, 1936.

9 *Düstur³,* XX, 893; RG 4255; *Cumhuriyet,* May 29, 30, 1937.

10 *Düstur³,* XIX, 151; RG 3819.

11 *Cumhuriyet,* July 4, 1938.

12 T. C. Maarif Vekâleti, *Maarif Ilgili Kanunlar,* Ankara, 1947, p. 144.

13 TBMM, *Zabıt Ceridesi,* III/3, 104, 112, 125.

14 Selek, I, 601; Kili, *Kemalism,* 118.

15 Yalman, *Yakın Tarihte,* III, 152; Fethi Tevetoğlu, *Atatürkle Samsuna Çıkanlar,* pp. 99–100; Goloğlu, *Devrimler ve Tepkiler,* p. 81; Cebesoy, *Siyasi Hatıralar,* II, 111; Weiker, pp. 47–50; Tunaya, pp. 606–672.

16 Behçet Cemal, *Şeyh Sait Isyanı,* Istanbul, 1955, pp. 25–29, 55–56, 60; Yalman, *Yakın Tarihte,* III, 162–163; Cebesoy, *Siyasi Hâtıralar,* II, 145–146; TBMM, *Zabıt Ceridesi,* II/15, pp. 156, 166; Neşet Çağatay, *Türkiyede Gerici Eylemler,* Ankara, 1972, p. 30.

17 Cemal, pp. 112–114; Cemal, *Şeyh Sait Isyanı,* pp. 112–114; Yalman, *Yakın Tarihte,* III, 166; Cebesoy, *Siyasi Hâtıraları,* II, 171–172.

18 Cebesoy, *Siyasi Hâtıraları,* II, 161; Yalman, *Yakın Tarihte,* III, 162; Tevetoğlu, *Atatürkle,* pp. 104–105.

19 Yalman, *Yakın Tarihte,* III, 171.

20 Tevetoğlu, *Türkiyede Sosyalist,* pp. 392–394.

21 Weiker, pp. 70–71.

22 Weiker, pp. 76–80; Ahmet Ağaoğlu, *Serbest Fırka Hatıraları,* Ankara, 1969; Goloğlu, *Devrimler ve Tepkiler,* pp. 279–280.

23 Weiker, pp. 107–127.

24 Tunaya, pp. 622–635; Goloğlu, *Devrimler ve Tepkiler,* pp. 297–280.

25 TBMM, *Zabıt Ceridesi,* II/22, pp. 16–73.

26 Weiker, pp. 128–140; Kili, *Kemalism,* pp. 120–122; Goloğlu, *Devrimler ve Tepkiler,* p. 298.

27 Tunaya, p. 597; Weiker, p. 171.

28 Weiker, pp. 168–183; Kemal Karpat, "The People's Houses in Turkey, Establishment and Growth," *Middle East Journal*, 17 (1963), 55–67; Karpat, "The Impact of the People's Houses on the Development of Communication in Turkey, 1931–1951," *Welt des Islams*, 15 (1974), 69–84; Hasan Taner, *Halkevleri Bibliyografyası*, Ankara, 1944; *XV Yıldönümünde Halkevleri ve Halkodaları*, Ankara, 1947.

29 Webster, pp. 307–309; Kili, *Kemalism*, p. 79.

30 TBMM, *Zabıt Ceridesi*, II/7, p. 24.

31 TBMM, *Zabıt Ceredesi*, II/7, p. 27; *Nutuk*, II, 849.

32 TBMM, *Zabıt Ceridesi*, II/8, p. 49.

33 TBMM, *Zabıt Ceridesi*, II/22, p. 334.

34 TBMM, *Zabıt Ceridesi*, II/23, p. 4.

35 TBMM, *Zabıt Ceridesi*, II/19, pp. 311–312.

36 TBMM, *Zabıt Ceridesi*, II/19, p. 247.

37 *Cumhuriyet*, September 3, 1929.

38 TBMM, *Zabıt Ceridesi*, IV/25; *Hakimiyet-i Milliye*, October 24, 1933.

39 TBMM, *Zabıt Ceridesi*, II/19, pp. 115, 133.

40 TBMM, *Zabıt Ceridesi*, III/26, p. 106.

41 TBMM, *Zabıt Ceridesi*, II/31, pp. 54–55.

42 TBMM, *Zabıt Ceridesi*, II/23, p. 356.

43 TBMM, *Zabıt Ceridesi*, II/32, p. 336.

44 TBMM, *Zabıt Ceridesi*, III/5, p. 12.

45 *Cumhuriyet*, February 7, 1932.

46 *Cumhuriyet*, February 8, 1933.

47 TBMM, *Zabıt Ceridesi*, IV/23, p. 259.

48 TBMM, *Zabıt Ceridesi*, IV/25, pp. 50–52.

49 TBMM, *Zabıt Ceridesi*, V/3, pp. 115, 304.

50 IY, 1959, pp. 79, 145; Türkiye Cumhuriyeti, Devlet Istatistik Enstitüsü, *Milli Eğitim Hareketleri, 1942–1972*, Ankara, 1973, p. 11.

51 IY, 1959, p. 163; A. Kazamias, *Education and the Quest for Modernity in Turkey*, London, 1966; Webster, pp. 210–239.

52 *Düstur³*, V, 292.

53 *Düstur³*, V, 336.

54 *Düstur³*, V, 324.

55 *Düstur³*, V, 302.

56 Hershlag¹, pp. 56–57.

57 TBMM, *Zabıt Ceridesi*, III/12, p. 131; *Düstur³*, X, 691; RG 1208; Hershlag¹, p. 146.

58 *Düstur³*, VI, 57; RG 84; February 17, 1925.

59 *Düstur³*, V, 336 (1924), VI, 191 (1925).

60 Ömer Lütfi Barkan, "La Loi sur la distribution des terreaux agricultures, etc.," *Revue de la Faculté des Sciences Economiques*, Université d'Istanbul, Octobre, 1944–Janvier, 1945; Reşat Aktan, "Problems of Land Reform in Turkey," *Middle East Journal*, 20, 317–344.

61 *Düstur³*, V, 292; Hershlag¹, p. 54.

62 *Düstur³*, IV, 541–544.

63 *Düstur³*, III, law no. 1457.

64 *Düstur³*, VII, 116, XI, 540, XXIII, 116.

65 IY, XIII (1941–1942), 359.

66 Hershlag¹, p. 57.

67 IY, XIII (1941–1942), 157.

68 Richard Robinson, *The First Turkish Republic*, Cambridge, Mass., 1963, p. 102, Hershlag¹, p. 61.

69 *Düstur³*, VII, 1145, VIII, 1734, VIII, 2062; Hüsamettin Toros, *Türkiye Sanayii*, 2 vols., Ankara, 1954, I, 263.

70 Robinson, *Republic*, p. 105.

71 *Düstur³*, IV, 86.
72 *Düstur³*, VI, 212.
73 *Düstur³*, VI, 274–276; Hershlag¹, pp. 61–62; April 22, 1925.
74 *Düstur³*, VIII, 655; Hershlag¹, pp. 62–64.
75 Robinson, *Republic*, pp. 105–106.
76 Weiker, pp. 250–251.
77 *Düstur³*, VI, 9, VII, 1440, 1466, VIII, 654, 953, X, 724, XI, 9, 79, 185, 455, 684, 694, XII, 197.
78 *Düstur³*, XI, 671; RG 1533.
79 Hershlag¹, pp. 111–112.
80 *Düstur³*, XIII, 920–925, July 3, 1932, XIII, 936–943, July 7, 1932.
81 *Düstur³*, XIV, 433, June 3, 1933; Hershlag¹, pp. 118–119.
82 Hershlag¹, p. 120.
83 *Düstur³*, XVI, 704; RG 3035, TBMM, V/4, p. 274; Hershlag¹, pp. 119–121.
84 *Düstur³*, XIX, 116; RG 3796; TBMM, V/21, p. 129.
85 *Düstur³*, XIX, 661; RG 3958; TBMM, V/26, p. 318.
86 Hershlag¹, p. 68; *Düstur³*, VI, 442, VIII, 993, XI, 449, XIV, 4654; RG 645, 1509, and 2425.
87 Hershlag¹, pp. 121–124; Robinson, *Republic*, p. 107.
88 Türkiye Cumhuriyeti Iktisat Vekâleti, Sanayi Tetkik Heyeti, *2inci Beş Yıllık Sanayi Planı*, Ankara, 1936; Hershlag¹, pp. 106–108.
89 RG 3950; Hershlag¹, p. 178.
90 *Düstur³*, VII, 1217; RG 406.
91 *Düstur³*, VIII, 666.
92 *Düstur³*, XI, 143–178; RG 1489; TBMM, *Zabıt Ceridesi*, III/18, pp. 121, 123; April 24, 1930.
93 *Düstur³*, VII, 519; RG 320.
94 R. Robinson, *Investment in Turkey*, Washington, 1956, pp. 44–45; *Düstur³*, XIII, 519–520.
95 *Düstur³*, XVII, 448; RG 3330; TBMM, *Zabıt Ceridesi*, V/12, p. 114; June 8, 1936.
96 Webster, pp. 255–257.
97 IY, 1942–1945, pp. 292–293; Hershlag¹, pp. 125–131.
98 IY, XIII, 220; Hershlag¹, p. 133.
99 Weiker, p. 27.
100 IY, 1941–1942, p. 205; IY, 1959, p. 296; Hershlag¹, p. 135.
101 IY, XIII, 210.
102 IY, XIII, 259–280; Webster, p. 117; Hershlag¹, pp. 109–117.
103 *Documents on German Foreign Policy, 1918–1945*, Series D, vols. V–X, Washington, D.C., 1953–1964.
104 IY, XVII (1949), pp. 220, 228.
105 IY, 1963, p. 42.
106 *Düstur³*, XXI, 443; RG 2892.
107 IY, XVII, 249; Hershlag¹, p. 201.
108 The only Turkish discussion of the tax, Faik Ökte, *Varlık Vergisi Faciası*, Istanbul, 1951, is highly critical of the government. See also E. C. Clark, "The Turkish Varlik Vergisi Reconsidered," *Middle Eastern Studies*, 7 (1972), 205–206; L. V. Thomas and R. N. Frye, *The United States and Turkey and Iran*, Cambridge, Mass., 1952, pp. 94–95.
109 This process is described best by Kemal Karpat. *Turkey's Politics*, pp. 98–133.
110 *Düstur³*, XXVIII, 929; RG 6542.
111 Hershlag¹, p. 294; Karpat, *Turkey's Politics*, p. 110.
112 *Düstur³*, XXVI, 1228, XXVII, 860; RG 6042, 6219.
113 *Düstur³*, XX, 218, XXII, 3, 200, XXVI, 1262, XXXII, 5837; RG 4658, 7885, 4165, 4736, 6051.
114 *Düstur³*, XXX, 1125; RG 7228.
115 RG 7229.

116 Hershlag[1], pp. 199–200.

117 Düstur[3], XXVI, 1169; RG 6032.

118 Düstur[3], XXVII, 1322; RG 6336.

119 Düstur[3], XXVII, 1253; RG 6329.

120 Düstur[3], XXVII, 1320.

121 Included among the four were Pertev Naili Boratav and Niyazi Berkes, both distinguished scholars; see Walter Weiker, *Revolution,* p. 50; Karpat, *Turkey's Politics,* pp. 372–373.

122 Karpat, *Turkey's Politics,* pp. 160–164.

123 Karpat, *Turkey's Politics,* pp. 172–173.

124 Karpat, *Turkey's Politics,* pp. 188–203.

125 Tunaya, pp. 712–715; Karpat, *Turkey's Politics,* pp. 219–220.

126 Karpat, *Turkey's Politics,* pp. 220–228.

127 Karpat, *Turkey's Politics,* pp. 220–241.

128 IY, 1971, p. 143; the figures in Karpat, *Turkey's Politics,* p. 241, are slightly different.

129 Türkiye İş Bankası, *Review of Economic Conditions,* March–April, 1966; Hershlag, *Challenge,* p. 333.

130 IY, 1971, p. 180.

131 IY, 1963, p. 197.

132 Hershlag, *Challenge,* pp. 350–352.

133 Hershlag, *Challenge,* p. 361.

134 Hershlag, *Challenge,* p. 366.

135 IY, 1963, p. 42.

136 IY, 1971, p. 113.

137 *Milli Eğitim Hareketleri, 1927–1966,* Ankara, 1967; *Milli Eğitim Hareketleri, 1942–1972,* Ankara, 1973.

138 *Türkiye Milli Geliri. Toplam Harcamaları ve Yatırımları, 1938, 1948–1970,* Ankara, Başbakanlık Devlet İstatistik Enstitüsü, 1972, p. 20.

139 IY, 1963, p. 315; Hershlag, *Challenge,* pp. 336–337.

140 Hershlag, *Challenge,* p. 338.

141 Hershlag, *Challenge,* p. 285.

142 IY, 1963, pp. 295–312; Hershlag, *Challenge,* p. 334.

143 IY, 1963, p. 237; Hershlag, *Challenge,* pp. 369–370.

144 Weiker, *Revolution,* p. 50.

145 *Cumhuriyet,* July 13, 1953.

146 Düstur[3], XXXIV, 1963; RG 8469.

147 Düstur[3], XXV, 78.

148 Düstur[3], XXV, 144–145; RG 8660.

149 Düstur[3], XXV, 1939; RG 8738.

150 Düstur[3], XXXV, 1995–1956; RG 8649.

151 Richard Robinson, *Developments Respecting Turkey, July 1953–October 1954,* New York, 1954, p. 15.

152 Weiker, p. 10; Robinson, *Developments,* pp. 16–19.

153 Robinson, *Developments,* III, 15.

154 Weiker, *Revolution,* p. 11.

155 Robinson, *Developments,* IV, 224; Hershlag, *Challenge,* p. 359.

156 IY, 1971, p. 143.

157 Weiker, *Revolution,* p. 13; E. J. Cohn, *Turkish Economic, Social, and Political Change,* New York, 1970, p. 24.

158 Ali Fuad Başgil, *La révolution militaire de 1960 en Turquie,* Geneva, 1963; G. S. Harris, "The Causes of the 1960 Revolution in Turkey," *Middle East Journal,* 24 (1970), 438–454.

159 Weiker, *Revolution,* pp. 20–21; Sabahat Erdemir, ed., *Milli Birliğe Doğru,* Ankara, 1960, p. 293.

160 K. Karpat, *Social Change and Politics in Turkey,* Leiden, 1973, pp. 235–237.

161 Weiker, *Revolution,* pp. 53–55.

162 Weiker, *Revolution,* pp. 52–55.

163 *İnkilap Kanunları,* 2 vols., Istanbul, 1961; *Düstur: Dördüncü Tertib,* 2 vols., Ankara, 1961; K. Karpat, "Political Developments in Turkey, 1950–1970," *Middle Eastern Studies,* 8 (1972), 359–360.

164 Weiker, *Revolution,* pp. 25–44.

165 Server Feridun, *Anayasalar ve Siyasi Belgeler,* Istanbul, 1962, pp. 91–107; Karpat, *Social Change,* p. 238.

166 RG 10859, July 20, 1961; official translation, prepared by S. Balkan, Kemal H. Karpat, and Ahmet Uysal, was published in Ankara in 1961 and is reprinted in S. Kili, *Turkish Constitutional Developments,* pp. 172–204. See also Walter Weiker, *Revolution,* pp. 72–81; C. H. Dodd, *Politics and Government in Turkey,* Berkeley and Los Angeles, 1969, pp. 107–127; and Rona Aybay, *Karşılaştırmalı 1961 Anayasası Metin Kitabı,* Istanbul, 1963, which compares the relevant articles with those of the 1876, 1909, and 1924 constitutions.

167 Dodd, pp. 135–162; Karpat, *Social Change,* p. 243; see also Weiker, *Revolution,* pp. 84–105; J. Landau, *Radical Politics in Modern Turkey,* Leiden, 1974.

168 Kemal Karpat, "Ideology in Turkey After the Revolution of 1960: Nationalism and Socialism," TYIR, 6 (1965), 68–118.

169 Landau, pp. 247–264.

170 IY, 1971, p. 41.

171 IY, 1971, p. 113.

172 IY, 1971, p. 438.

173 IY, 1971, p. 142; M. Hyland, "Crisis at the Polls: Turkey's 1969 Elections," *Middle East Journal,* 24 (1970), 1–16; Landau, pp. 276–286.

174 J. M. Landau, "The National Salvation Party in Turkey," *Asian and African Studies,* 3 (1976), 1–57.

175 U.N. Press Section, Office of Public Information, Press Release SOC/NAR/199, July 21, 1976; *Washington Post,* July 5, 1976.

Appendix

The Ottoman Grand Vezirs and Prime Ministers, 1839–1922

Name	Term	Dates of Service
1. Koca Husrev Mehmet Paşa	1	July 2, 1839–June 8, 1840
2. Mehmet Emin Rauf Paşa	3	June 8, 1840–December 4, 1841
3. Topal Izzet Mehmet Paşa	2	December 4, 1841–August 30, 1842
4. Mehmet Emin Rauf Paşa	4	August 30,1842–September 28, 1846
5. Koca Mustafa Reşit Paşa	1	September 28, 1846–April 28, 1848
6. Ibrahim Sarım Paşa	1	April 29, 1848–August 12, 1848
7. Koca Mustafa Reşit Paşa	2	August 12, 1848–January 26, 1852
8. Mehmet Emin Rauf Paşa	5	January 26, 1852–March 5, 1852
9. Koca Mustafa Reşit Paşa	3	March 5, 1852–August 5, 1852
10. Mehmet Emin Âli Paşa	1	August 6, 1852–October 3, 1852
11. Damat Mehmet Ali Paşa	1	October 3, 1852–May 13, 1853
12. Mustafa Nâili Paşa	1	May 14, 1853–July 8, 1853
13. Mustafa Nâili Paşa	2	July 10, 1853–May 29, 1854
14. Kıbrıslı Mehmet Emin Paşa	1	May 29, 1854–November 23, 1854
15. Koca Mustafa Reşit Paşa	4	November 23, 1854–May 2, 1855
16. Mehmet Emin Âli Paşa	2	May 2, 1855–November 1, 1856
17. Koca Mustafa Reşit Paşa	5	November 1, 1856–August 6, 1857
18. Mustafa Nâili Paşa	3	August 6, 1857–October 22, 1857
19. Koca Mustafa Reşit Paşa	6	October 22, 1857–January 7, 1858
20. Mehmet Emin Âli Paşa	3	January 11, 1858–October 18, 1859
21. Kıbrıslı Mehmet Emin Paşa	2	October 18, 1859–December 23, 1859
22. Mehmet Rüştü Paşa	1	December 24, 1859–May 27, 1860
23. Kıbrıslı Mehmet Emin Paşa	3	May 28, 1860–August 6, 1861
24. Mehmet Emin Âli Paşa	4	August 6, 1861–November 22, 1861
25. Mehmet Fuat Paşa	1	November 22, 1861–January 2, 1863
26. Yusuf Kâmil Paşa	1	January 5, 1863–June 1, 1863
27. Mehmet Fuat Paşa	2	June 1, 1863–June 5, 1866
28. Mehmet Rüştü Paşa	2	June 5, 1866–February 11, 1867
29. Mehmet Emin Âli Paşa	5	February 11, 1867–September 7, 1871

Source: Ismail Hami Danişmend, *Osmanlı Devlet Erkânı,* Istanbul, 1971, pp. 75–108; see also Maria Todorova, "Composition of the Ruling Elite of the Ottoman Empire in the Period of Reforms (1826–1878)", *Etudes balkaniques,* 12 (1976), 103–113; and Ezel Kural Shaw, "Midhat Pasha, Reformer or Revolutionary? His Administrative Career and Contribution to the Constitution of 1876," unpublished Ph.D. dissertation, Harvard University, 1975, p. 390.

Name	Term	Dates of Service
30. Mahmut Nedim Paşa	1	September 8, 1871–July 31, 1872
31. Midhat Paşa	1	July 31, 1872–October 19, 1872
32. Mehmet Rüştü Paşa	3	October 19, 1872–February 15, 1873
33. Ahmet Esat Paşa	1	February 15, 1873–April 15, 1873
34. Mehmet Rüştü Paşa, Şirvanizade	1	April 15, 1873–February 13, 1874
35. Hüseyin Avni Paşa	1	February 15, 1874–April 25, 1875
36. Ahmet Esat Paşa	2	April 26, 1875–August 26, 1875
37. Mahmut Nedim Paşa	2	August 26, 1875–May 11, 1876
38. Mehmet Rüştü Paşa	4	May 12, 1876–December 19, 1876
39. Midhat Paşa	2	December 19, 1876–February 5, 1877
40. Ibrahim Ethem Paşa	1	February 5, 1877–January 11, 1878
41. Ahmet Hamdi Paşa	1	January 11, 1878–February 4, 1878
42. Ahmet Vefik Paşa	1	February 4, 1878–April 18, 1878
43. Mehmet Sâdık Paşa	1	April 18, 1878–May 28, 1878
44. Mehmet Rüştü Paşa	5	May 28,1878–June 4, 1878
45. Mehmet Esat Saffet Paşa	1	June 4, 1878–December 4, 1878
46. Hayreddin Paşa	1	December 4, 1878–July 29, 1879
47. Ahmet Ârifi Paşa	1	July 29, 1879–October 18, 1879
48. Mehmet Sait Paşa	1	October 18, 1879–June 9, 1880
49. Mehmet Kadri Paşa	1	June 9, 1880–September 12, 1880
50. Mehmet Sait Paşa	2	September 12, 1880–May 2, 1882
51. Abdurrahman Nureddin Paşa	1	May 2, 1882–July 11, 1882
52. Mehmet Sait Paşa	3	July 12, 1882–November 30, 1882
53. Ahmet Vefik Paşa	2	November 30, 1882–December 3, 1882
54. Mehmet Sait Paşa	4	December 3, 1882–September 25, 1885
55. Mehmet Kâmil Paşa	1	September 25, 1885–September 4, 1891
56. Ahmet Cevat Paşa	1	September 4, 1891–June 8, 1895
57. Mehmet Sait Paşa	5	June 8, 1895–October 1, 1895
58. Mehmet Kâmil Paşa	2	October 2, 1895–November 7, 1895
59. Halil Rifat Paşa	1	November 7, 1895–November 9, 1901
60. Mehmet Sait Paşa	6	November 18, 1901–January 14, 1903
61. Mehmet Ferit Paşa	1	January 14, 1903–July 22, 1908
62. Mehmet Sait Paşa	7	July 22, 1908–August 4, 1908
63. Mehmet Kâmil Paşa	3	August 5, 1908–February 14, 1909
64. Hüseyin Hilmi Paşa	1	February 14, 1909–April 13, 1909
65. Ahmet Tevfik Paşa	1	April 14, 1909–May 5, 1909
66. Hüseyin Hilmi Paşa	2	May 5, 1909–December 28, 1909
67. Ibrahim Hakkı Paşa	1	January 12, 1910–September 29, 1911
68. Mehmet Sait Paşa	8	September 30, 1911–December 30, 1911
69. Mehmet Sait Paşa	9	December 31, 1911–July 16, 1912
70. Ahmet Muhtar Paşa	1	July 22, 1912–October 29, 1912
71. Mehmet Kâmil Paşa	4	October 29, 1912–January 23, 1913
72. Mahmut Şevket Paşa	1	January 23, 1913–June 11, 1913
73. Sait Halim Paşa	1	June 12, 1913–February 3, 1917
74. Mehmet Talat Paşa	1	February 4, 1917–October 8, 1918
75. Ahmet Izzet Paşa	1	October 14, 1918–November 8, 1918
76. Ahmet Tevfik Paşa	2	November 11, 1918–January 12, 1919
77. Ahmet Tevfik Paşa	3	January 13, 1919–March 3, 1919
78. Damat Ferit Paşa	1	March 4, 1919–May 16, 1919

Name	Term	Dates of Service
79. Damat Ferit Paşa	2	May 19, 1919–July 20, 1919
80. Damat Ferit Paşa	3	July 21, 1919–October 1, 1919
81. Ali Rıza Paşa	1	October 2, 1919–March 3, 1920
82. Sâlih Hulûsi Paşa	1	March 8, 1920–April 2, 1920
83. Damat Ferit Paşa	4	April 5, 1920–July 30, 1920
84. Damat Ferit Paşa	5	July 31, 1920–October 17, 1920
85. Ahmet Tevfik Paşa	4	October 21, 1920–November 4, 1922

Presidents of the Turkish Republic

Name	Dates of Service
1. Mustafa Kemal Atatürk	October 29, 1923–November 10, 1938
2. Ismet Inönü	November 11, 1938–May 14, 1950
3. Celal Bayar	May 22, 1950–May 27, 1960
4. Cemal Gürsel	May 27, 1960–March 28, 1966
5. Cevdet Sunay	March 28, 1966–March 28, 1973
6. Fahri Korutürk	April 6, 1973–

Prime Ministers of the Grand National Assembly and the Turkish Republic

Names	Dates of Service
1. Mustafa Kemal Atatürk	May 3, 1920–January 24,1921
2. Fevzi Çakmak	January 24,1921–July 9, 1922
3. Rauf Orbay	July 12, 1922–August 13, 1923
4. Fethi Okyar	August 14, 1923–October 27, 1923
5. Ismet Inönü	November 30, 1923–November 21, 1924
6. Fethi Okyar	November 21, 1924–March 2, 1925
7. Ismet Inönü	March 4, 1925–October 25, 1937
8. Celal Bayar	October 25, 1937–January 25, 1939
9. Refik Saydam	January 25, 1939–July 8, 1942
10. Şükrü Saraçoğlu	July 8, 1942–August 5, 1946
11. Recep Peker	August 5, 1946–September 9, 1947
12. Hasan Saka	September 9, 1947–January 14, 1949
13. Şemsettin Günaltay	January 15,1949–May 22, 1950
14. Adnan Menderes	May 22, 1950–May 27, 1960
15. Cemal Gürsel	May 28, 1960–November 20, 1961
16. Ismet Inönü	November 20, 1961–February 21, 1965
17. Suat Hayri Ürgüplü	February 21, 1965–October 22, 1965
18. Süleyman Demirel	October 27, 1965–March 19, 1971
19. Nihat Erim	March 19, 1971–April 17, 1972
Ferit Melen (acting P.M.)	April 17, 1972–April 29, 1972
20. Suat Hayri Ürgüplü	April 29, 1972–May 13, 1972
21. Ferit Melen	May 15, 1972–April 7, 1973
22. Naim Talu	April 12, 1973–January 25, 1974
23. Bülent Ecevit	January 25, 1974–November 17, 1974
24. Sâdi Irmak	November 17,1974–March 31, 1975
25. Süleyman Demirel	March 31, 1975–

Bibliography: History of the Ottoman Empire and Modern Turkey, 1808–1975

I. General Histories

The most useful work is that of Bernard Lewis, *The Emergence of Modern Turkey*, London and New York, 1961, 2nd. ed., 1968. Niyazi Berkes, *The Development of Secularism in Turkey*, Montreal, 1964, is an extremely perceptive analysis of intellectual and political developments concerned with secularism. M. S. Anderson, *The Eastern Question, 1774–1923: A Study in International Relations*, London and New York, 1966, is the best study of European diplomacy as it affected the Ottoman Empire. The most authoritative Turkish survey of the period to 1922 is [Midhat Sertoğlu] *Resimli-Haritalı Mufassal Osmanlı Tarihi* (Detailed Ottoman History, with Illustrations and Maps), vol. V, Istanbul, 1962, and vol. VI, Istanbul, 1963.

II. Bibliographies

Hans-Jürgen Kornrumpf, *Osmanische Bibliographie mit Besonderer Berücksichtigung der Türkei in Europa*, Leiden/Köln, 1973. Enver Koray, *Türkiye Tarih Yayınları Bibliyografyası* (Bibliography of Turkish History Publications), 2 vols., Istanbul, 1959, 1971. Fehmi Edhem Karatay, *Istanbul Üniversitesi Kütüphanesi. Türkçe Basmalar* (Istanbul University Library. Turkish Printed Works), 2 vols., Istanbul, 1956, cites most historical works printed in Turkey from 1729 to the adoption of the new letters in 1928. J. D. Pearson, *Index Islamicus, 1906–1955*, Cambridge, 1958, and supplements. Muzaffer Gökman, *Atatürk ve Devrimleri Tarihi Bibliyografyası: Bibliography of the History of Atatürk and His Reforms*, Istanbul, 1968. F. Başbuğoğlu et al., *Cumhuriyet Döneminde Bibliyografyaların Bibliyografyası* (Bibliography of Bibliographies in the Republican Period), Ankara, 1973.

III. Reference Works

I. A. Gövsa, *Türk Meşhurları Ansiklopedisi* (Encyclopedia of Famous Turks), Istanbul, 1946. Şemsettin Sami, *Kamus el-Âlâm. Tarih ve coğrafya lugatı* (Dictionary of Names. Dictionary of History and Geography), 6 vols., Istanbul, 1306–16/1888–98. Ahmet Rifat, *Lugat-ı Tarihiye ve Coğrafiye* (Historical and Geographical Dictionary), 7 vols., Istanbul, 1299–1300/1882–3. Osman Nebioğlu, *Türkiye'de Kim Kimdir* (Who's Who in Turkey), Istanbul, 1961–1962. Mehmet Süreyya, *Sicil-i Osmani* (The Ottoman Register), 4 vols., Istanbul, 1890–1893; continued by G. Oransay, *Osmanlı Devletinde Kim Kimdi?* I. Osmanoğulları (Who Was Who in the Ottoman State? Vol. I, The Ottoman Dynasty), Ankara, 1969. Bursalı Mehmet Tahir, *Osmanlı Müellifleri* (Ottoman Authors), 3 vols., Istanbul, 1915–1928, with index by Ahmet Ramzi, *Miftah el-Kutup ve Esami-i Müellifin Fihristi* (Key to Books and Index to the Names of Authors), Istanbul, 1928, both republished in modern letters by A. F. Yavuz and I. Özen, *Osmanlı Müellifleri* (Ottoman Authors), Istanbul, 2 vols., 1972. The most extensive dictionary of Ottoman administrative and technical terms is M. Z. Pakalın, *Osmanlı Tarih Deyimleri ve Terimleri Sözlüğü* (Dictionary of Ottoman Historical Terms and Expressions), 3 vols., Istanbul, 1946–1956. See also M. Sertoğlu, *Resimli Osmanlı Tarihi Ansiklopedisi* (Illustrated Ottoman History Encyclopedia), Istanbul, 1952.

IV.   Official Laws and Documents

All the Ottoman laws and documents cited in this study are in the Prime Minister's Archives (*Başvekâlet Arşivi* abbreviated as BVA, also called *Başbakanlık Arşivi*) in Istanbul. See M. Sertoğlu, *Muhteva Bakımından Başvekâlet Arşivi* (Contents of the Prime Minister's Archives), Ankara, 1955, and S. J. Shaw, "Archival Sources for Ottoman History: The Archives of Turkey," JAOS, 80 (1962), 1–12, "The Yıldız Palace Archives of Abdülhamid II," *Archivium Ottomanicum,* 3 (1971), 211–237, "Turkish Source Materials for Egyptian History,"*Political and Social Change in Modern Egypt,* ed. P. Holt, London and New York, 1968, pp. 28–48, and "Ottoman Archival Materials for the Nineteenth and Early Twentieth Centuries: The Archives of Istanbul," IJMES, 6 (1975), 94–114. Many of the laws themselves were published in the official Ottoman newspaper, *Takvim-i Vekayi* (Chronicle of Events, abbreviated as TV), which appeared in three series between 1831 and 1923. After 1921 all laws and regulations issued by the Ankara government have been published in the *Resmi Gazete* (Official Newspaper), abbreviated as RG. In addition, those currently in force were gathered in the *Düstur*[1] (Code of Laws), of which the first volume was published originally in 1863 and then reprinted, with additions, in 1865 and 1872. Volumes II, III, and IV were published respectively in 1873, 1876, and 1879. Four supplements (*Zeyil*) were issued between 1879 and 1884, adding new laws and changes in old ones, and a volume entitled *Mütemmim* (Completion), containing laws added between 1872 and 1907, appeared in 1919. This series was concluded with an additional four volumes entitled *Düstur: Birinci Tertib* (Code of Laws: First Series), covering the years from 1883 through 1908, published in modern letters in Ankara between 1937 and 1943. The laws and regulations of the Young Turk period were published in 11 volumes in the *Düstur: Tertib-i Sani* (Code of Laws: Second Series), Ankara, 1911–1928, abbreviated as *Düstur*[2], containing laws published in Istanbul through October 30, 1922. The laws issued by the Grand National Assembly in Ankara from April 23, 1920, to October 31, 1970, were published in 41 volumes as *Düstur: Tertib-i Salis* (Code of Laws: Third Series), abbreviated as *Düstur*[3], in Ankara from 1921 to 1971. There is a full index to this series to vol. 38 (1957), *Üçüncü Tertip Düsturun 1–38 inci ciltlerinde münderiç Kanun, Tefsir, Nizamname, Talimatname ve Kararlara ait Umumi Tahlili Fihristi* (General Analytic Index to the Laws, Commentaries, Regulations, Instructions, and Decisions published in volumes 1–38 of the Third Series of the Code of Laws), Ankara, 1958. Those issued by the National Unity Committee from May 27, 1960, to November 1, 1961, were published as the *Düstur: Dördüncü Tertib* (Code of Laws: Fourth Series), abbreviated as *Düstur*[4], in 3 vols., Ankara, 1961; and those issued under the 1961 Constitution are being published as *Düstur: Beşinci Tertib* (Code of Laws: Fifth Series), abbreviated as *Düstur*[5], November 1961 to date. Volumes 39–41 of the third *Düstur,* all those of the fourth, and volumes 1–9 of the fifth were indexed in *Üçüncü Tertip Düsturun 39–41 inci, Dördüncü Tertip Düsturun 1 inci, Beşinci Tertip Düsturun 1–9 uncu ciltlerinde münderiç mevzuata ait Genel Tahlili Fihrist* (General Analytic Index to the subjects published in volumes 39–41 of the Third Series Code of Laws, the first volume of the Fourth Series Code of Laws (consisting of three parts), and volumes 1–9 of the Fifth Series Code of Laws, Ankara, 1972.

Laws, regulations and other administrative decrees issued since 1908 also have been published in the Debates (*Zabıtname*) of the Ottoman Parliament and the Debate Registers (*Zabıt Ceridesi*) of the Grand National Assembly; also in the Decisions (*Kararname*) of the Grand National Assembly, the Senate (since 1961), and the Council of Ministers, and in the administrative regulations published by the individual ministries and departments.

Some of the nineteenth-century laws were published in translation in G. Aristarchi Bey, *Législation ottomane, ou recueil des lois, règlements, ordonnances, traités, capitulations, et autres documents officiels de l'Empire Ottoman,* 7 vols., Constantinople, 1873–1888; G. Young, *Corps de droit ottoman; recueil des codes, lois, règlements, ordonnances et actes les plus importants du droit intérieur, et d'études sur le droit coutumier de l'Empire ottoman,* 7 vols., Oxford, 1905–1906; Gabriel Noradounghian, *Recueil d'actes internationaux de l'Empire Ottoman,* 4 vols., Paris, 1897–1903; W. E. Grigsby, *The Medjelle or Ottoman Civil Law,* London, 1895; C. R. Tyler, *The Mejelle,* Nicosia, 1901; C. G. Walpole, *The Ottoman Penal Code,* London, 1888. Unfortunately, however, many of the law translations are incomplete and the historical discussions often are inaccurate. Most of the Ottoman financial regulations were published separately by the Ministry of Finance, *Kavanin ve Nizamat ve Muharrerat-ı Maliye Mecmuası* (Journal of Financial Laws, Regulations, and Decrees), 6 vols., Istanbul, 1326/1910, and 3 vols., Istanbul, 1338/1922. They were summarized, with relevant financial statistics, in the same ministry's *Ihsaiyat-ı Maliye* (Financial Statistics), 3 vols., Istanbul, 1327–30/1911–14. Ottoman treaty texts are given in *Muahedat Mecmuası,* 5 vols., Istanbul, 1294–1298/1877–1881, and I. de Testa, *Recueil des traités de la Porte Ottomane avec les puissances etrangères depuis 1536,* 11 vols. Paris, 1864–1911.

Many laws and regulations, and other important information, were printed in the yearbooks (*Salname*) published both for the empire as a whole (*Salname-i Devlet-i Aliye-i Osmaniye*) annually starting in 1263/1846–7, and less regularly for individual provinces, ministries, and other government institutions. For a complete list of all yearbooks published see H. R. Ertuğ, "Osmanlı Devrinde Salnameler" (Yearbooks in the Ottoman Period), *Hayat Tarih Mecmuası,* IX (7), no. 103 (1973), 15–22, IX (8), no. 104 (1973), 10–16. Provincial yearbooks (*Il Yıllığı*), containing similar information, have been published occasionally for most provinces during the republican period.

V. The Reign of Mahmut II, 1808–1839

The period of Bayraktar Mustafa Paşa is described in Ismail Hakkı Uzunçarşılı, *Meşhur Rumeli Âyanından Tirsinikli Ismail, Yılık Oğlu Süleyman Ağalar ve Alemdar Mustafa Paşa* (The Famous Rumelia Notables; Tirsinikli Ismail and Yılık oğlu Süleyman Ağas and Alemdar Mustafa Paşa), Istanbul, 1942; A. F. Miller, *Mustafa Pasha Bayrakdar,* Moscow, 1947; Juchereau de St. Denys, *Histoire de l'Empire Ottoman depuis 1792 jusqu'en 1844,* 4 vols., Paris, 1844, and the same author's *Les Révolutions de Constantinople en 1807 et 1808,* 2 vols., Paris, 1819; Ottokar von Schlechta-Wssehrd, *Die Revolutionen in Constantinopel in den Jahren 1807 und 1808,* Vienna, 1882; Ahmet Asım Efendi, *Tarih-i Asım* (Asım's History), 2 vols., Istanbul, n.d. This period and the subsequent years of Mahmut's reign are described in Ahmet Cevdet, *Tarih-i Cevdet* (Cevdet's History), 1st ed., abbreviated as Cevdet[1], 12 vols., Istanbul, 1854–1883, 2nd ed., abbreviated as Cevdet[2], 12 vols., Istanbul, 1884–1891; Mehmet Ataullah Şanizade, *Şanizade Tarihi* (Şanizade's History), 4 vols., Istanbul, 1290–1/1873–4; Ahmet Ata, *Tarih-i Ata* (Ata's History), 5 vols., Istanbul, 1292–3/1875–6. The destruction of the Janissary corps and its results are described in Avigdor Levy, "The Military Policy of Sultan Mahmud II, 1808–1839," unpublished Ph.D. dissertation, Harvard University, 1968; H. A. Reed, "The Destruction of the Janissaries by Mahmud II in June 1826," unpublished Ph.D. dissertation, Princeton University, 1951; Ahmet Cevat, *Tarih-i Askeri-i Osmani. I. Yeniçeriler* (History of the Ottoman Army, Vol. I, The Janissaries), Istanbul, 1297/1880, tr. G. Macridès, *Etat Militaire Ottoman depuis La Fondation de l'Empire jusqu'en nos jours, Tome I. Libre I: Le Corps des Janissaires,* Constantinople, 1882; Mehmet Esat Efendi, *Tarih-i Esat Efendi* (Esat Efendi's History), 2 vols., Istanbul University Library, MS TY 6002–6005, and *Üss-ü Zafer* (The Bases of the Victory), Istanbul 1243/1877, 2nd. ed., 1293/1876, tr. Caussin de Perceval, *Précis historique de la destruction du corps des janissaires par le Sultan Mahmoud en 1826,* Paris, 1833.

On Ali Paşa of Janina and the origins of the Greek Revolution as well as the war with

Russia, see Dennis N. Skiotis, "The Lion and the Phoenix: Ali Pasha and the Greek Revolution, 1819-1822," unpublished Ph.D. dissertation, Harvard University, 1974, and "From Bandit to Pasha: First Steps in the Rise of Power of Ali of Tepelen, 1750–1784," IJMES, 2 (1971), 219–244; also G. Remérand, *Ali de Tébélen: Pacha de Janina, 1744–1822*, Paris, 1928; W. Plomer, *Ali the Lion*, London, 1936; J. W. Baggally, *Ali Pasha and Great Britain*, Oxford, 1938; A. Boppe, *L'Albanie et Napoléon*, Paris, 1914; N. G. Svoronos, *Histoire de la Grèce Moderne*, Paris, 1953; C. W. Crawley, *The Question of Greek Independence*, London, 1931; L. S. Stavrianos, *Balkan Federation: A History of the Movement Toward Balkan Unity in Modern Times*, Northampton, Mass., 1944; C. K. Webster, *The Foreign Policy of Castlereagh, 1815–1822*, London, 1925; H. Temperley, *The Foreign Policy of Canning, 1822–1827*, London, 1925; C. K. Webster, *The Foreign Policy of Palmerston, 1830–1840*, 2 vols., London, 1951; N. Botzaris, *Visions Balkaniques dans la préparation de la Révolution grecque, 1789–1821*, Geneva, 1962; E. M. Edmonds, *The Greek War of Independence, 1821–1833*, Chicago, 1968; C. A. Frazee, *The Orthodox Church and Independent Greece, 1821–1852*, London, 1969; Fahrettin ve Seyfi, *1820—1827 Mora Isyanı* (The Morea Revolt of 1820–1827), Istanbul, 1934; Col. F. R. Chesney, *The Russo-Turkish Campaign of 1828 and 1829*, New York, 1854; W. E. D. Allen and P. Muratoff, *Caucasian Battlefields: A History of the Wars on the Turco-Caucasian Border, 1828–1921*, Cambridge, 1953; Ahmet Muhtar Paşa, *1244 (1828) Türkiye Rusya Seferi ve Edirne Muahedesi* (The War of 1828 Between Turkey and Russia and the Peace of Edirne), 2 vols., Ankara, 1928; Celal Erkin, *Türk-Rus Harbi, 1828 (Kafkas Cephesi)* (The Turko-Russian War, 1828 [The Caucasus Front]), Istanbul, 1940; H. von Moltke, *The Russians in Bulgaria and Rumelia in 1828 and 1829*, London, 1854.

The reforms of Mohammad Ali/Mehmet Ali are discussed in H. A. B. Rivlin, *The Agricultural Policy of Muhammad 'Ali in Egypt*, Cambridge, Mass., 1961; P. M. Holt, *Egypt and the Fertile Crescent, 1516–1922*, Ithaca, N.Y., 1966, pp. 176–192; G. Baer, *A History of Landownership in Modern Egypt, 1800–1950*, London and New York, 1962; Abdurrahman al-Rafi'i, *Asr Mohammad 'Ali* (The Age of Mohammad Ali), Cairo, 1954; H. Dodwell, *The Founder of Modern Egypt: A Study of Muhammad Ali*, Cambridge, England, 1931. On the Egyptian Crises of 1831–1833 and 1838–1841 see M. Sabry, *l'Empire Egyptien sous Mohamed Ali et la question d'Orient, 1811–1849*, Paris, 1930; Şinasi Altındağ, *Kavalalı Mehmet Ali Paşa isyanı: Mısır Meselesi, 1831–1841* (The Revolt of Mehmet Ali Paşa of Kavala: The Egyptian Question), I, Ankara, 1945; F. Rodkey, *The Turco-Egyptian Question in the Relations of England, France and Russia*, Urbana, 1921; C. K. Webster, *The Foreign Policy of Palmerston, 1830–1841*, 2 vols., London, 1951; and P. E. Mosely, *Russian Diplomacy and the Opening of the Eastern Question, 1838–1839*, Cambridge, Mass., 1934.

Mahmut II's reforms are studied in Avigdor Levy, "The Officer Corps in Sultan Mahmud II's New Ottoman Army, 1826–1839," IJMES, 2 (1971), 21–39; C. V. Findley, "From Reis Efendi to Foreign Minister, Ottoman Bureaucratic Reform and the Creation of the Foreign Ministry," unpublished Ph.D. dissertation, Harvard University, 1969, partly published as "The Legacy of Tradition to Reform: Origins of the Ottoman Foreign Ministry," IJMES, 1 (1970), 334–357, and "The Foundation of the Ottoman Foreign Ministry: The Beginnings of Bureaucratic Reform Under Selim III and Mahmud II," IJMES, 3 (1972), 388–416; E. Z. Karal, *Osmanlı Tarihi, V. Cilt. Nizam-ı Cedit ve Tanzimat Devirleri, 1789–1856* (Ottoman History, vol. V, The Periods of the Nizam-ı Cedit and the Tanzimat, 1789–1856), Ankara, 1947; Lewis, *Emergence*, pp. 75–103; Berkes, *Development*, pp. 89–135; F. E. Bailey, *British Policy and the Turkish Reform Movement: A Study in Anglo-Turkish Relations, 1826–1853*, Cambridge, Mass., 1942; J. Bastelberger, *Die Militärischen Reformen, unter Mahmud II*, Gotha, 1874; Ahmet Cevad Eren, *Mahmud II Zamanında Bosna-Hersek* (Bosnia and Herzegovina in the period of Mahmut II), Istanbul, 1965; Georg Rosen, *Geschichte der Türkei von dem Siege der Reform in Jahre 1826 bis zum Pariser Tractat vom 1856*, 2 vols., Leipzig, 1866–1867; and Reşat Kaynar, *Mustafa Reşid Paşa ve Tanzimat* (Mustafa Reşit Paşa and the Tanzimat), Ankara, 1954, pp. 63–98, 120–160, 317–502. The most important chronicles of the period, in addition to those mentioned previously, are those of the official historian Ahmet Lütfi, *Tarih-i Lütfi* (Lütfi's History), 8 vols., Istanbul, 1290–1328/1873–90, and Hızır Ilyas Efendi, *Vekayi Letaif-i Enderun* (Events of the Inner Service), Istanbul, 1276/1859. Useful contemporary descriptions by westerners in the Empire are General Comte Antoine François Andreossy, *Constantinople et le Bosphore de Thrace*, 3rd ed., Paris, 1841; Ami Boué, *La Turquie d'Europe* . . . , 4 vols., Paris, 1840; Sir Adolphus Slade, *Records of Travels in Turkey, Greece, Etc., in the Years 1829, 1830 and 1831*, 2 vols., Philadelphia, Pa., 1833; Rev. Robert Walsh, *A Residence at Constantinople*, 2 vols., London, 1836; and Charles White, *Three Years in Constantinople*, 3 vols., London, 1846.

The politics of Mahmut's reign are described in M. C. Şehabeddin Tekindağ, "Halet Efendi," IA, V, 123–125; Orhan Köprülü, "Gâlib Paşa," IA, IV, 710–714; Uriel Heyd, "The Ottoman Ulemâ and Westernization in the Time of Selim III and Mahmud II," *Scripta Hierosolymitana*, IX (Jerusalem, 1961), 63–96; Fevziye Abdullah, "Izzet Molla," IA, V, 1264–1267; M. Münir Aktepe, "Esad Efendi," IA, IV, 363–365; Halil Inalcık, "Husrev Paşa, Mehmed," IA, V, 609–616; Reşat Kaynar, *Mustafa Reşit Paşa ve Tanzimat* (Mustafa Reşit Paşa and the Tanzimat), Ankara, 1954; Orhan Köprülü, "Hüseyin Paşa, Amcazade," IA, V, 646–650; Ercüment Kuran, "Reşid Paşa, Mustafa," IA, IX, 701–705; Ercüment Kuran, "Halet Efendi," EI², III, pp. 90–91; Faik Reşit Unat, "Başhoca Ishak Efendi," *Belleten*, 28 (1964), 89–116.

VI. *The Tanzimat Reform Era, 1839–1876*

General descriptions of the Tanzimat reform period can be found in A. Cevad Eren, "Tanzimat," IA, XI, 709–765; E. K. Karal, *Osmanlı Tarihi, V. Cilt, Nizam-ı Cedit ve Tanzimat Devirleri, 1789–1856* (Ottoman History, Vol. V., The Nizam-ı Cedit and Tanzimat periods, 1789–1856), Ankara, 1956; the excellent work of R. H. Davison, *Reform in the Ottoman Empire, 1856–1876*, Princeton, N.J., 1963; Berkes, *Secularism*, pp. 137–223; Lewis, *Emergence*, pp. 104–125; and T. C. Maarif Vekâleti, *Tanzimat*, I, Istanbul, 1940; E. Engelhardt, *La Turquie et le Tanzimat, ou histoire des réformes dans l'Empire ottoman depuis 1826 jusqu'à nos jours*, 2 vols., Paris, 1882–1884 is outdated but still useful. The official chronicle of the period is Ahmet Lütfi, *Tarih-i Lütfi* (Lütfi's history), vols. IX–XIII, covering the years 1846–1876, found in manuscript form only at the libraries of the Turkish Historical Society, Ankara (Türk Tarih Kurumu), MS 531/1–7, 5032–4, 4812, and the Istanbul Archeological Museum, MS 1340–5, 1349.

Important information about the Tanzimat also is found in autobiographical and biographical works concerning its leading figures: Ibnülemin Mahmud Kemal Inal, *Osmanlı Devrinde son Sadrıâzamlar* (The Last Grand Vezirs in the Ottoman Period), 14 parts in 6 vols., Istanbul, 1940–1953; Mehmed Zeki Pakalın, *Son Sadrâzamlar ve Başvekiller* (The Last Grand Vezirs and Prime Ministers), 5 vols., Istanbul, 1940–1948; Mehmed Zeki Pakalın, *Tanzimat Maliye Nazırları* (Tanzimat Finance ministers), 2 vols., Istanbul, 1939–1940; Haluk Y. Şehsuvaroğlu, *Sultan Aziz, Hayatı, Hal'i, Ölümü* (Sultan Abdulaziz, His Life, His Deposition, His Death), Istanbul, n.d.; Reşat Kaynar, *Mustafa Reşit Paşa ve Tanzimat*, Ankara, 1954; Ercümend Kuran, "Reşid Paşa," IA, IX, 701–705; Ali Fuat, *Rical-i Mühimme-i siyasiye* (Important Political Men), Istanbul, 1928; M. Cavid Baysun, "Mustafa Reşid Paşa'nın Siyasî Yazıları" (The Political Writings of Mustafa Reşit Paşa), *Tarih Dergisi*, 6 (1954), 39–52, 10 (1959), 59–70, 11 (1960), 121–142, 12 (1961), 43–62; Mehmet Salâhettin, *Bir Türk diplomatının evrak-ı siyasiyesi* (The political papers of a Turkish diplomat), Istanbul, 1306/1888–1889; Şerafeddin Turan, "Pertev Paşa," IA, 554–556; A. H. Ongunsu, "Âli Paşa," IA, I, 335–340; O. F. Köprülü, "Fuad Paşa," IA, IV, 672–681; Abdürrahman Şeref, *Tarih Musahebeleri* (Historical Conversations), Istanbul, 1339; Ahmet Cevdet Paşa, *Tezâkir* (Memoirs), ed. Cavid Baysun, 4 vols., Ankara, 1953–1967; Âli Ölmezoğlu, "Cevdet Paşa," IA, III, 114–123; R. L. Chambers, "The Education of a Nineteenth Century Ottoman *Âlim*, Ahmed Cevdet Paşa," IJMES, 3 (1973), 440–464; Fatma Aliye, *Ahmet Cevdet Paşa ve Zamanı* (Cevdet Paşa and His Time), Istanbul, 1332/1914; Ebül'ula Mardin, *Medeni Hukuk Cephesinden Ahmet Cevdet Paşa* (Ahmet Cevdet Pasha from the View of Civil Law), Istanbul, 1946; M. Cavid Baysun, "Cevdet Paşa, Şahsiyetine ve ilim sahasındaki faaliyetine dair" (Cevdet Paşa, concerning his personality and activities in the cultural field), *Türkiyat Mecmuası*, 11 (1954), 213–230; Ezel Kural Shaw, "Midhat Pasha, Reformer or Revolutionary? His Administrative Career and Contributions to the Constitution of 1876," unpublished Ph.D. dissertation, Harvard University, 1975; Ali Haydar Midhat, ed., *Midhat Paşa, Hayat-ı Siyasiyesi, Hidamatı, Menfa Hayatı* (Midhat Paşa, His Political Life, His Services, and His Life in Exile), 2 vols., Istanbul, 1325, partly tr. in Ali Haydar Midhat, *The Life of Midhat Pasha . . .*, London, 1903; I. H. Uzunçarşılı, *Midhat Paşa ve Yıldız Mahkemesi* (Midhat Paşa and the Yıldız Trial), Ankara, 1967; Kâmil Paşa, *Tarih-i Siyasi-i Devlet-i Aliye-i Osmaniye* (The Political History of the Ottoman State), 3 vols., Istanbul, 1325–1327/1907–1909.

Studies of particular aspects of the Tanzimat include Z. F. Fındıkoğlu, "Tanzimatta içtimai hayat" (Social life in the Tanzimat), *Tanzimat*, I, 619–659; T. Gökbilgin, "Tanzimat Hareketinin Osmanlı Müesseselerine ve Teşkilâtına Etkileri (Influences of the Tanzimat Movement on Ottoman Institutions and Organization), *Belleten*, 31 (1967), 93–111; H. N. Howard, "President Lincoln's Minister Resident to the Sublime Porte: Edward Joy Morris," *Balkan Studies*, 3 (1962), 1–28; Halil Inalcık, "Tanzimat'ın uygulanması ve sosyal tepkileri" (The execution and social results of the Tanzimat), *Belleten*, 28 (1964), 623–690, *Tanzimat ve Bulgar Meselesi* (The Tanzimat and the Bulgarian Problem), Ankara, 1943, "Bosnada Tanzimatın tatbikine ait vesikalar" (Documents on the execution of the Tanzimat in Bosnia), *Tar. Ves.*, I/5 (1942), 374–389; G. L. Iseminger, "The Old Turkish Hands: The British Levantine Consuls, 1856–1876," *MEJ*, 22 (1968), 297–316; David Finnie, *Pioneers East*, Cambridge, Mass., 1965; E. Z. Karal, "Tanzimat devri vesikaları. Rüşvetin kaldırılması için yapılan teşebbüsler" (Efforts to eliminate bribery. Documents of the Tanzimat period," *Tar. Ves.*, I/1 (1941), 45–65, and "Zarif Paşa'nın hatıratı, 1816–1862" (The Memoires of Zarif Paşa, 1816–1862), *Belleten*, 4 (1940), 443–494; E. Kırşehirlioğlu, *Türkiyede Misyoner faaliyetleri* (Missionary activities in Turkey), Istanbul, 1963; E. de Leone, *L'impèro ottomano nel primo periodo delle riforme (Tanzimat) secondo fonti italiani*, Milano, 1967; Moshe Maoz, *Ottoman Reform in Syria and Palestine*, Oxford, 1968; W. Miller, *The Ottoman Empire and Its Successors, 1801–1927*, London, 1966; S. J. Shaw, "Some Aspects of the Aims and Achievements of the Nineteenth Century Ottoman Reformers," and A. Hourani, "Ottoman Reform and the Politics of Notables," in *Beginnings of Modernization in the Middle East: The Nineteenth Century*, ed. W. Polk and R. Chambers, Chicago, 1968, pp. 29–39, 41–68.

Financial and administrative reforms are studied in Maliye Nezareti, *Ihsaiyat-ı Maliye. Varidat ve Masarif-i Umumiyeyi Muhtevidir* (Financial Statistics, Including General Revenues and Expenditures), vol. I (1325/1909–1910), Istanbul, 1327/1911–1912; S. J. Shaw, "The Central Legislative Councils in the Nineteenth Century Ottoman Reform Movement Before 1876," IJMES, 1 (1970), 51–84, and "The Origins of Representative Government in the Ottoman Empire: The Provincial Representative Councils, 1839–1876," *Near Eastern Round Table, 1967–1968*, ed. R. Winder, New York, 1969, pp. 53–142; R. H. Davison, "The Advent of the Principle of Representation in the Government of the Ottoman Empire," *Beginnings of Modernization*, pp. 93–108; and Halil Inalcık, "Sened-i Ittifak ve Gülhane Hatt-ı Hümayunu" (The Document of Agreement and the Imperial Rescript of Gülhane), *Belleten*, 28 (1964), 603–622. Ottoman finances and financial reforms have been studied in S. J. Shaw, "The Nineteenth Century Ottoman Tax Reforms and Revenue System," IJMES, 6 (1975), 421–459; also in Abdurrahman Vefik Bey, *Tekalif Kavaidi* (Tax Principles), 2 vols., Istanbul, 1330/1914–1915; Süleyman Sudi, *Defter-i Muktesit* (The Economic Register), 3 vols., Istanbul, 1307/1891–1892; A. du Velay, *Essai sur l'Histoire Financière de la Turquie*, Paris, 1903; C. Morawitz, *Les Finances de la Turquie*, Paris, 1902; D. C. Blaisdell, *European Financial Control in the Ottoman Empire*, New York, 1929; I. Hakkı Yeniay, *Yeni Osmanlı Borçları Tarihi* (A New History of the Ottoman Public Debts), Istanbul, 1944; C. Işıksal, "Türkiyede ilk bankacılık hareketi ve

Osmanlı Bankasının kurulması" (The first bank movements in Turkey and the foundation of the Ottoman Bank), *Belgelerle Türk Tarih Dergisi,* 10 (1968), 72–79; H. Mutluçağ, "Düyun-u umumiye ve reji soygunu" (The plunder of the public debt and the tobacco Règie), *Belgelerle Türk Tarih Dergisi,* 2 (1967), 33–39; R. Ş. Suvla, "Tanzimat Devrinde istikrazlar" (Loans in the Tanzimat Period), *Tanzimat,* 263–288.

Municipal reforms are described in Osman Ergin, *Mecelle-i Umur-u Belediye* (Journal of Municipal Affairs), 5 vols., Istanbul, 1914–1922; B. Lewis, "Baladiyya; (1) Turkey," EI², I, 972–975; C. Orhonlu, "Mesleki bir teşekkül olarak kaldırımcılık ve Osmanlı Şehir yolları hakkında bazı düşünceler" (Some thoughts on the paving profession as a professional organization, and on Ottoman city streets), *Güney-Doğu Avrupa Araştırmaları Dergisi,* 1, 93–138; and "Osmanlı Türkleri devrinde Istanbulda kayıkçılık ve kayık işletmeciliği" (Small boats and their operation in Istanbul in the age of Ottoman Turks), *Tarih Dergisi,* 16 (1966), 109–134; Ş. Turan, "Osmanlı teşkilatında hassa mimarlar" (The Imperial Architects in Ottoman Organization), *Tarih Araştıramaları Dergisi,* I (1963), 157–202.

Useful contemporary accounts of the Tanzimat period include Ahmet Midhat Efendi, *Üss-ü İnkılap* (The Basis of the Revolution), 2 vols., Istanbul, 1294–5/1877–8, which describes events from 1856 to 1876; B. C. Collas, *La Turquie en 1861,* Paris, 1861, and *La Turquie en 1864,* Paris, 1864; F. Eichmann, *Die Reformen des osmanischen Reiches . . . ,* Berlin, 1858; J. L. Farley, *Modern Turkey,* London, 1872, *Turkey,* London, 1866, and *The Decline of Turkey, Financially and Politically,* London, 1875; Cyrus Hamlin, *My Life and Times,* Boston, 1893, and *Among the Turks,* New York, 1878; Mahmut Celaleddin, *Mirat-i Hakikat* (Mirror of the Truth), 3 vols., Istanbul, 1326–1327/1908–1909; Osman Seify Bey (F. Millingen), *La Turquie sous le règne d'Abdul Aziz, 1862–1867,* Paris, 1868; A. D. Mordtmann, *Anatolien, Skizzen und Reisebriefe, 1850–1859,* ed. F. Babinger, Hannover, 1925, and *Stambul und das moderne Türkenthum: politische, sociale und biographische bilder, von einem Osmanen,* 2 vols., Leipzig, 1877–1878; G. Rosen, *Geschichte der Türkei von dem Siege der Reform in jahre 1826 bis zum Pariser Tractat vom Jahre 1856,* 2 vols., Leipzig, 1866–1867; J. H. Ubicini, *La Turquie actuelle,* Paris, 1855 and *Letters on Turkey,* 2 vols., London, 1856; J. H. Ubicini and Pavet de Courteille, *Etat Présent de l'Empire ottoman . . . ,* Paris, 1876.

Educational modernization is discussed in Osman Ergin, *Türkiye Maarif Tarihi* (History of Turkey's Education), 5 vols., Istanbul, 1939–1943; Faik Reşit Unat, *Türkiye Eğitim Sisteminin Gelişmesine Tarihi Bir Bakış* (A Historical Survey of the Modernization of Turkey's System of Education), Ankara, 1964; Mahmut Cevat, *Maarif-i Umumiye Nezareti Tarihçe-i Teşkilat ve İcraatı* (History of the Organization and Activities of the Ministry of Public Education), Istanbul, 1338/1919–1920; *Salname-i Nezaret-i Maarif-i Umumiyesi* (Yearbook of the Ministry of Public Education), vols. I (1316/1898–9), II (1317/1899–1900), III (1318/1900–1), IV (1319/1901–2); A. M. Kazamias, *Education and the Quest for Modernity in Turkey,* London, 1966; F. Isfendiyaroğlu, *Galatasaray Tarihi* (History of Galatasaray), I (Istanbul, 1952); Ali Çankaya, *Mülkiye Tarihi ve Mülkiyeliler* (The Civil Service School and the Civil Servants), 2 vols., Ankara, 1954; Mehmet Esat, *Mirat-ı Mektep-i Harbiye* (Mirror of the War Academy), Istanbul, 1310/1892; Dr. Galip Ata (Ataç), *Tıp Fakültesi* (The Medical Faculty), Istanbul, 1341/1925; Osman Nuri Ergin, *Istanbul Tıp Mektepleri* (Medical Schools in Istanbul), Istanbul, 1940 and Rıza Tahsin (Gencer), *Mirat-ı Mekteb-i Tıbbiye* (Mirror of the Medical School), Istanbul, 1328/1910. On elementary school modernization, see Aziz Berker, *Türkiyede İlk Öğretim* (Elementary Education in Turkey), I, *1839–1908,* Ankara, 1945; Vedat Günyol, "Mektep," IA, VII, 655–659. The *medreses* in the Tanzimat period are studied in M. Şerafettin Yaltkaya, "Tanzimattan evvel ve sonra Medreseler," *Tanzimat,* I (Istanbul, 1940), 463–467; On middle education see S. Celâl Antel, "Tanzimat Maarifi" (Tanzimat Education), *Tanzimat,* I, 441–462; M. Lütfü, "Tanzimattan sonra Türkiyede Maarif Teşkilatı (Educational Organization in Turkey after the Tanzimat), TTEM, no. 17 (94), 302–317; Ihsan Sungu, "Mekteb-i Maarif-i Adliye'nin tesisi" (The Foundation of the Education

School of Mahmut II), *Tar Ves.*, I/3, 212–225; and Hasan Ali Yücel, *Türkiyede Orta Öğretim* (Middle Education in Turkey), Istanbul, 1938. On higher education see Mehmet Ali Ayni, *Darülfünun Tarihi* (History of the University), Istanbul, 1937; and Cemil Bilsel, *Istanbul Üniversitesi Tarihi* (History of Istanbul University), Istanbul, 1943. The engineering and technical schools are studied in Mehmet Esat, *Mirat-ı Mühendishane-i Berri-i Hümayun* (Mirror of the Imperial Army Engineering School), Istanbul, 1312/ 1894, and Çağatay Uluçay and Enver Kartekin, *Yüksek Mühendis Okulu* (The Higher Engineering School), Istanbul, 1958.

Judicial and legal reforms are described by Hıfzı Veldet, "Kanunlaştırma hareketleri ve Tanzimat" (Law-making movements and the Tanzimat), *Tanzimat*, I, 139–209; Mustafa Reşit Belgesay, "Tanzimat ve Adliye Teşkilatı" (The Tanzimat and Judicial Organization), *Tanzimat*, I, 211–230; Tahir Taner, "Tanzimat devrinde ceza hukuku" (Criminal Law in the Tanzimat period) *Tanzimat*, I, 221–232; Ebül'ulâ Mardin, "The Development of the Shari'a under the Ottoman Empire," S. S. Onar, "The Majalla," and H. Liebesny, "The Development of Western Judicial Privileges," in *Law in the Middle East*, ed. M. Khadduri and H. Liebesny, I, *Origin and Development of Islamic Law*, Washington, D.C., 1955, pp. 279–333. O. Öztürk, *Osmanlı Hukuk Tarihinde Mecelle*, Istanbul, 1973.

The influx of refugees into the empire is studied by Ahmet Refik (Altınay), "Mülteciler meselesine dair" (On the problem of refugees), *TTEM*, sene 12/89, 13/90; Ahmet C. Eren, *Türkiyede Göç ve Göçmen Meseleleri* (The Problems of Migration and Refugees in Turkey), Istanbul, 1966; M. Pinson, "Ottoman Colonization of the Circassians in Rumeli after the Crimean War," *Etudes Balkaniques*, 3 (1975), 71–85, and "Demographic Warfare: An Aspect of Ottoman and Russian Policy, 1854–1866," unpublished Ph.D. dissertation, Harvard University, 1970; T. Gökbilgin, *Rumeli'de Yörükler, Tatarlar ve Evlad-ı Fatihan* (The Yörüks, The Tatars, and the Evlad-ı Fatihan in Rumeli), Istanbul, 1957; Bilal Şimşir, *Rumeli'den Türk Göçleri: Emigrations Turques des Balkans. Belgeler-Documents*, 2 vols., Ankara, 1968–1970, and *Contribution à l'Histoire des Populations Turques en Bulgarie 1876–1880*, Ankara, 1966; Adam Lewak, *Szieje emigracje polskiej w Turcji, 1831–1878*, Warsaw, 1935; Mehmet Eroz, "Türkiyede Islav Muhacirleri ve Kazaklar etrafında bazı kaynaklar" (Some sources on the Slavic refugees and the Kazaks in Turkey), *Sosyoloji Konferansları*, 1964, pp. 121–136; F. Z. Fındıkoğlu, "Türkiyede Slav Muhacirleri" (Slavic Immigrants in Turkey), *Sosyoloji Konferansları*, 1964, pp. 1–30; and "Türkiyede Islav Muhacirlerine dair" (On the slavic refugees in Turkey), *Iktisat Dergisi*, 1 (1966), 39–55; Feyzi Gözaydın, *Kırım Türklerinin Yerleşme ve Göçmeleri* (The Settlement and Immigration of the Crimean Turks), Istanbul, 1948; A. Cebeci, "Bulgaristan Türkleri'nin Göçü hakkında" (On the emigration of the Bulgarian Turks), *Türk Kültürü*, 6 (1968), 189–199; B. Cvetkova, "Changements intervenus dans la condition de la population des terres bulgares," *Etudes Historiques* (Sofia), 5, 291–318; A. Deliorman, "Birinci Cihan savaşı'nın sonuna kadar Makedonyada Türk nüfusu meselesi" (The Turkish population problem in Macedonia to the end of World War I), *Türk Kültürü*, 3 (1965), 589–593, 4 (1966), 246–253, and "Die Frage des Anteils der türkischen Bevölkerung in Mazedonien," *Cultura Turcica*, 2 (1965), 199–212; S. Hodzic, "Migracije muslimanskog stanovnistva iz Srbije u sjeveroistocnu Bosne izmedu 1788–1863," *Clanci i gradja za kulturnu istoriju Istocne Bosne*, 2 (1958), 65–143; C. Orhonlu, "Balkan Türklerinin durumu" (The condition of the Balkan Turks), *Türk Kültürü*, II/21 (1964), 49–60; D. Pantazopoulos, *The Balkan Exchange of Minorities and Its Impact on Greece*, The Hague, 1962; and Andrew Gould, "Pashas and Brigands: Ottoman Provincial Reform and Its Impact on the Nomadic Tribes of Southern Anatolia, 1840–1885," unpublished Ph.D. dissertation, University of California, Los Angeles, 1973.

Ottoman economic development during the nineteenth century has not been fully studied. The most useful information is found in Z. Y. Hershlag, *Introduction to the Modern Economic History of the Middle East*, Leiden, 1964; Charles Issawi, ed., *The Economic History of the Middle East, 1800–1914*, Chicago and London, 1966; Afet Inan, *Aperçu général sur l'histoire économique de l'Empire turc-ottoman*, Istanbul, 1941; M. A. Cook, ed., *Studies in the Economic History of the Middle East from the Rise of Islam to the Present*

Day, London, 1970. On agriculture see Donald Quataert, "Ottoman Reform and Agriculture in Anatolia, 1876–1908," unpublished Ph.D. dissertation, University of California, Los Angeles, 1973; Ziraat Bakanlığı, *Türk ziraat tarihine bir bakış* (A look at Turkish agricultural history), Istanbul, 1938; Reşat Aktan, "Agricultural Policy of Turkey," unpublished Ph.D. dissertation, University of California, Berkeley, 1950; Y. S. Atasağun, *Türkiye Cumhuriyeti Ziraat Bankası, 1888–1939* (The Agricultural Bank of the Turkish Republic), Istanbul, 1939; V. Cuinet, *La Turquie d'Asie. . .*, 4 vols., Paris, 1891–1894; Vedat Eldem, *Osmanlı İmparatorluğunun iktisadi şartları hakkında bir tetkik*, Ankara, 1970; E. F. Nickoley, "Agriculture," *Modern Turkey*, ed. E. Mears, New York, 1924, pp. 280–302; Mustafa Rasim, *Çiftçilik* (Farming), 2 vols., Istanbul, 1302. Very little has been done on industry aside from Ömer Celal Sarç, "Tanzimat ve Sanayimiz" (The Tanzimat and Our Industry), *Tanzimat*, I (1940), 423–440; F. Dalsar, *Türk sanayi ve ticaret tarihinde Bursada ipekçilik* (The silk industry of Bursa in the History of Turkish industry and trade), Istanbul, 1960; N. V. Mihov (Michoff), *Contribution à l'histoire du commerce de la Turquie et de la Bulgarie. III. Rapports consulaires français, Documents officiels et autres documents*, Svichtov, 1950; O. Sençer, *Türkiyede işçi sınıfı* (The Working Class in Turkey), Istanbul, 1969; Y. K. Tengirsenk, "Tanzimat devrinde Osmanlı devletinin harici ticaret siyaseti" (The foreign trade policy of the Ottoman state in the period of the Tanzimat), *Tanzimat*, I, 289–320; Hakkı Nezihi, *50 Yıllık Oda Hayatı, 1882–1932* (The Fifty-Years of the Chamber of Commerce), Istanbul, 1932; Celal Aybar, *Osmanlı İmparatorluğunun ticaret muvazenesi, 1878–1913* (The trade balance of the Ottoman Empire, 1878–1913), Ankara, 1939; L. Gordon, *American Relations with Turkey, 1830–1930*, Philadelphia, 1932; R. Hoffman, *Great Britain and the German Trade Rivalry, 1875–1914*, repr., New York, 1964; E. G. Mears, "Levantine Concession Hunting," *Modern Turkey*, ed. E. Mears, New York, 1924, pp. 354–383; D. Platt, *Finance, Trade and Politics in British Foreign Policy, 1815–1914*, Oxford, 1968; V. J. Puryear, *International Economics and Diplomacy in the Near East*, Stanford, Calif., 1935.

The development of Ottoman communications has not been adequately considered. On the postal and telegraph systems see Aziz Akıncan, *Türkiyede Posta ve Telgrafçılık* (The Post and Telegraph in Turkey), Edirne, n.d.; Şekip Eskin, *Posta, Telgraf ve Telefon Tarihi* (History of the Post, the Telegraph, and the Telephone), Ankara, 1942; and Ali Nusret Pulhan, *Türk Pulları Kataloğu* (Catalog of Turkish Stamps), XII, Istanbul, 1973. On the railroads see E. M. Earle, *Turkey, the Great Powers and the Bagdad Railway*, New York, 1923; H. Hecker, "Die Eisenbahnen der asiatischen Türkei," *Archiv für Eisenbahnwesen*, 1914, pp. 744–800, 1057–1087, 1283–1321, 1539–1584; J. M. Landau, *The Hejaz Railway and the Muslim Pilgrimage: A Case of Ottoman Political Propaganda*, Detroit, 1971; Ahmet Onar, *Türkiye Demiryolları Tarihi, 1860–1953* (History of the Turkish Railroads, 1860–1953), Istanbul, 1953; V. Pressel, *Les Chemins de Fer en Turquie d'Asie*, Zurich, 1902; and E. G. Mears, "Transportation and Communication," *Modern Turkey*, ed. E. Mears, New York, 1924, pp. 201–237.

The situation of the minority *millet*s and the effect of the reforms on them are discussed in R. Davison, *Reform in the Ottoman Empire*, pp. 52–80, 114–135; Leon Arpée, *The Armenian Awakening: A History of the Armenian Church, 1820–1860*, Chicago, 1909; A. Sarkissian, *History of the Armenian Question to 1885*, Urbana, Ill., 1938; Esat Uras, *Tarihte Ermeniler ve Ermeni Meselesi* (The Armenians in History and the Armenian Problem), Ankara, 1950; C. A. Frazee, *The Orthodox Church and Independent Greece, 1921–1951*, London, 1969; L. Hadrovacs, *Le peuple serbe et son église sous la domination turque*, Paris, 1947; D. Hopwood, *The Russian Presence in Syria and Palestine, 1843–1914*, Oxford, 1969; G. Jäschke, "Die Türkische-Orthodoxe Kirche," *Der Islam*, 39 (1964), 95–124; B. R. Özoran, "Turks and the Greek Orthodox Church," *Cultura Turcica*, 2 (1965), 28–41; S. Runciman, *The Great Church in Captivity*, Cambridge, 1968; Stavro Skendi, "Religion in Albania During the Ottoman Rule," *Südost Forschungen*, 15 (1956), 311–327; and Crypto-Christianity in the Balkan Area Under the Ottomans," *Slavic Studies*, 26 (1967), 227–246; M. Ş. Tekindağ, "Osmanlı idaresinde patrik ve patrikhane" (The patriarch and the patriarchate under Ottoman administration), *Belgelerle Türk*

Tarihi Dergisi, 1 (1967), 52–55, 2 (1967), 91–104; B. Uşaklığıl, "La Turquie et la Patriarcat d'Istanbul," *Cultura Turcica*, I/2 (1964), 286–304; Avram Galanté, *Histoire des Juifs d'Istanbul*, 1942, *Histoire des Juifs d'Anatolie*, Istanbul, 1939, *Documents officiels turcs concernant les Juifs* de *Turquie*, Istanbul, 1941, *Recueil de nouveaux documents concernant les juifs de Turquie*, Istanbul, 1949, and *Appendice à l'histoire des Juifs d'Anatolie*, Istanbul, 1948; M. Franco, *Essai sur l'histoire des israélites de 'Empire ottoman depuis les originés jusqu'à nos jours*, Paris, 1897.

Nineteenth-century Ottoman cultural development and the Young Ottoman movement are described in Ahmet Hamdi Tanpınar, *XIX Asır Türk Edebiyatı Tarihi* (History of 19th-Century Turkish Literature), Istanbul, 2nd ed., 1956; Nihat Sami Banarlı, *Türk Edebiyatı Tarihi* (History of Turkish Literature), Istanbul, n.d.; Şerif Mardin, *The Genesis of Young Ottoman Thought: A Study in the Modernization of Turkish Political Ideas*, Princeton, N.J., 1962; Kenan Akyüz, "La Littérature Moderne de la Turquie," *Philologiae Turcicae Fundamenta*, ed. L. Bazin et al., II, ed. Pertev Naili Boratov, Wiesbaden, 1964, pp. 465–634; Ismail Habib (Sevük), *Türk Teceddüt Edebiyatı Tarihi* (History of Turkish Reform Literature), Istanbul, 1924, and *Edebî yeniliğimiz, Tanzimattan beri* (Our Literary modernization, since the Tanzimat), 2 vols., Istanbul, 1940; Ihsan Sungu, "Tanzimat ve Yeni Osmanlılar" (The Tanzimat and the Young Ottomans), *Tanzimat I*, 777–857; Cevdet Perin, *Tanzimat Edebiyatında Fransız Tesiri* (French influence in Tanzimat Literature), Istanbul, 1942; Kamuran Birand, *Aydınlanma devri devlet felsefesinin Tanzimata tesiri* (The influence of the Enlightenment period political philosophy on the Tanzimat), Ankara, 1955; Selim Nüzhet Gerçek, *Türk gazeteciliği, 1831–1881* (Turkish Journalism), 1931; Refik Ahmet Sevengil, *Türk Tiyatrosu Tarihi, III, Tanzimat Tiyatrosu* (History of Turkish Theater, Vol. III, The Tanzimat Theater), Istanbul, 1961, and *Türk Tiyatrosu Tarihi, IV, Saray Tiyatrosu* (History of Turkish Theater, vol. IV, The Palace Theater), Istanbul, 1962; Metin And, *A History of Theater and Popular Entertainment in Turkey*, Ankara, 1963–1964; N. Martinovitch, *The Turkish Theater*, New York, 1933.

On the Lebanese crisis see Col. Churchill, *The Druzes and the Maronites Under the Turkish Rule from 1840 to 1860*, London, 1862; M. Tayyip Gökbilgin, "1840tan 1861'a kadar Cebel-i Lübnan meselesi ve Dürziler" (The Mount Lebanon problem and the Druzes from 1840 to 1861), *Belleten*, 10 (1946), 641–703; A. L. Tibawi, *A Modern History of Syria Including Lebanon and Palestine*, Oxford, 1966; Y. al-Hakim, *Beyrut wa Lübnan fi ahd Âl Osman* (Beirut and Lebanon in the Age of the Ottomans), Beirut, 1964; M. Ş. Tekindağ, "XVIII. ve XIX. asırlarda Cebel Lübnan Şihab Oğulları" (The Şihabi family of Mount Lebanon in the 18th and 19th centuries) *Tarih Dergisi*, 9 (1958), 31–44; L. Hatir, *Ahd al-mutasarrifin fi Lübnan, 1861–1918* (The Age of the Mutasarrifs in the Lebanon, 1861–1918), Beirut, 1967; and A. Tarabain, *Lübnan mund 'ahd al-mutasarrifin ilâ bidâyat al-intidab* (Lebanon in the time of the Mutasarrifs until the beginning of the mandate), Cairo, 1968.

Syria and Palestine in the nineteenth century are discussed in H. L. Bodman, *Political Factions in Aleppo, 1760–1826*, Chapel Hill, N.C., 1963; Y. al-Hakim, *Suriya wal-ahd al-Usmani* (Syria and Ottoman rule), Beirut, 1966; D. Hopwood, *The Russian Presence in Syria and Palestine, 1843–1914*, Oxford, 1969; Moshe Maoz, *Ottoman Reform in Syria and Palestine, 1840–1861*, Oxford, 1968; T. Stavrou, *Russian Interests in Palestine, 1882–1914*, Thessaloniki, 1963; A. L. Tibawi, *American Interests in Syria, 1800–1901*, Oxford, 1966. On Iraq see A. al-'Allâf, *Bağdad al-kadima, 1286/1869–1335/1917* (Old Baghdad, 1869–1917), Baghdad, 1960; Abbas al-'Azzawi, *Tarih al-Irak bayn al-Ihtilalayn* (History of Iraq between the Occupations), 7 vols., Baghdad, 1955; Ş. Dumlugi, *Midhat Başa*, Baghdad, 1952; A. Jwaideh, "Municipal Government in Baghdad and Basra from 1869 to 1914," unpublished B. Litt. thesis, Oxford University, 1953; S. Longrigg, *Four Centuries of Modern Irak*, Oxford, 1925, repr., 1968. The Arabian Peninsula is ably studied in R. B. Winder, *Saudi Arabia in the 19th Century*, New York, 1965; also T. Marston, *Britain's Imperial Role in the Red Sea Area, 1800–1878*, Hamden, Conn., 1961; J. Plass and U. Gehride, *Die Aden-Grenze in der Südarabienfrage, 1900–1967*, Opladen, 1967; H. St. John Philby, *Saudi Arabia*, London, 1955. There are a number of excellent studies of the Principalities, though mainly from European and not Ottoman sources. The best are: R. W. Seton-Watson, *A History of the Roumanians from Roman Times to the Completion of Unity*, Cambridge, 1934, reprinted 1963; N. Iorga, *Geschichte des rumänischen Volkes*, 2 vols., Gotha, 1905; A. D. Xenopol, *Histoire des Roumains de la Dacie Trajane depuis les origines jusqu'à l'union des principautés en 1859*, 2 vols., Paris, 1896; M. M. Alexandrescu-Dersca, "Sur le régime des ressortissants ottomans en Moldavie, 1711–1829," *Studia et Acta Orientalia*, 5–6 (1967), 143–182; D. Berindei, *L'union des principautés Roumains*, Bucharest, 1967; G. G. Florescu and M. E. Florescu, "L'Agence des Principautés Unies à Constantinople, 1859–1866," *Studia et Acta Orientalia*, 5–6 (1967), 221–243; R. N. Florescu, "The Rumanian Principalities and the Origins of the Crimean War," *Slavonic and East European Review*, 65 (1967), 324–342; J. C. Campbell, "The Transylvanian Question in 1849," *Journal of Central European Affairs*, 2 (1942), 20–34; T. W. Riker, *The Making of Roumania: A Study of an International Problem, 1856–1866*, Oxford, 1931; R. N. Florescu, "The Uniate Church: Catalyst of Rumanian National Consciousness," *Slavonic and East European Review*, 45 (1967), 324–342; B. Jelavich, *Russia and the Rumanian National Cause, 1858–1859*, Bloomington, Ind., 1959; I. Matei, "Sur les relations d'Ahmed Vefik Pacha avec les Roumains," *Studia et Acta Orientalia*, 7 (1968), 95–131.

On the Crimean War and the Peace of Paris, H. Temperley, *England and the Near East: The Crimea*, London, 1936; V. J. Puryear, *England, Russia and the Straits Question, 1844–1856*, Berkeley, Calif., 1931; C. Rousset, *Histoire de la guerre de Crimée*, 2 vols., Paris, 1877; G. B. Henderson, *Crimean War Diplomacy and Other Historical Essays*, Glasgow, 1947; G. H. Bolsover, "Nicholas I and the Partition of Turkey," *Slavonic and East European Review*, 27 (1948), 115–145; B. Jelavich, *A Century of Russian Foreign Policy, 1814–1914*, New York, 1964; Bekir Sıdkı Baykal, "Makamat-ı Mübareke Meselesi ve Babıâli" (The Problem of the Holy Places and the Sublime Porte), *Belleten*, 23 (1959), 241–266; W. E. Mosse, *The Rise and Fall of the Crimean System*, London, 1963. The best available works on Egypt in the nineteenth century until the British occupation are P. M. Holt, *Political and Social Change in Modern Egypt: Historical Studies from the Ottoman Conquest to the United Arab Republic*, London, 1968, and *Egypt and the Fertile Crescent, 1516–1922*, Ithaca, N.Y., 1966; Abdurrahman al-Rafi'i, *Asr Ismail* (The Age of Ismail), 2 vols., Cairo, 1948.

Serbia's rise to independence is described in E. Gaumant, *La Formation de la Yougoslavie, XVᵉ–XXᵉ siècles*, Paris, 1930; H. W. V. Temperley, *History of Serbia*, London, 1917; G. Yakschitch, *L'Europe et la résurrection de la Serbie, 1804–1834*, Paris, 1907; C. Jirecek, *Geschichte der Serben*, 2 vols., Gotha, 1911–1918, repr., Amsterdam, 1967; C. Jelavich, *Tsarist Russia and Balkan Nationalism*, Berkeley, Calif., 1959; H. Kaleshi and H. J. Kornrumpf, "Das Wilajet Prizren," *Südost Forschungen*, 26 (1967), 176–238; D. MacKenzie, *The Serbs and Russian Pan-Slavism, 1875–1878*, Ithaca, N.Y., 1967; S. K. Pavlowitch, *Anglo Russian Rivalry in Serbia, 1837–1839*, Paris/The Hague, 1961; D. Slijepcević, *The Macedonian Question: The Struggle for Southern Serbia*, Chicago, 1968.

Bosnia and Herzegovina are studied in A. C. Eren, *Mahmud II zamanında Bosna-Hersek* (Bosnia and Herzegovina in the time of Mahmut II), Istanbul, 1965; B. Djurdjev, "Bosnia," *EI²*, I, 1261–1275; J. V. A. Fine, "The Bosnian Church: Its Place in Medieval Bosnia from the Twelfth to the Fifteenth Century," unpublished Ph.D. dissertation, Harvard University, 1969; Halil Inalcık, "Bosnada Tanzimatın tatbikine ait vesikalar" (Documents on the application of the Tanzimat in Bosnia), *Tar. Ves.*, 1 (1942), 374–389; G. Jaksić, *Bosna i Hercegovina na Berlinskom kongresu* (Bosnia and Herzegovina at the Congress of Berlin), Belgrade, 1955; A. Sućeska, "Die Rechtstellung der Bevölkerung in den Städten Bosniens und der Herzegowina unter den Osmanen (1463–1878)," *Südost-Europa Jahrbuch*, 8 (1968), 84–99.

Ottoman rule in Crete is described in Cemal Tukin, "Girit" (Crete), IA, IV, 791–804; *Salname-i Vilayet-i Girit* (Yearbook of the Province of Crete), Hanya, 1310/1892–1893; Hüseyin Kâmi Hanyevi, *Girit Tarihi* (History of Crete), Istanbul, 1288/1871. The revolt in Crete and resulting Ottoman-Greek War are analyzed in Süleyman Tevfik and

A. Zühdi, *Devlet-i Aliye-i Osmaniye-Yunan Muharebesi* (The Battle Between the Otto-
man Empire and Greece), Istanbul, 1315; A. Turot, *L'Insurrection crétoise et la guerre
Gréco-Turque*, Paris, 1898; W. Stillman, *The Cretan Insurrection of 1866–1867–1868*,
New York, 1874; Münir Aktepe, *Mehmed Salâhî: Girid Meslesi, 1866–1889* (Mehmet
Salahi and the Crete Problem, 1866–89), Istanbul, 1967; T. C. Gnkur. Bşk., Harb Tarihi
Dairesi, *1897 Osmanlı Yunan Harbi* (The Ottoman-Greek War of 1897), Ankara, 1965;
K. Bourne, "Great Britain and the Cretan Revolt, 1866–1869," *Slavonic and East Euro-
pean Review*, 25 (1956), 74–94; R. E. Kasperson, *The Dodecanese: Diversity and Unity
in Island Politics*, Chicago, 1966; G. Markopoulos, "King George I and the Expansion of
Greece, 1875–1881," *Balkan Studies*, 9 (1968), 21–40, and "The Selection of Prince George
of Greece as High Commissioner in Crete," *Balkan Studies*, 10 (1969), 335–350; A. A.
Pallis, ed., *The Cretan Drama. The Life and Memoires of Prince George of Greece, High
Commissioner in Crete (1898–1906)*, New York, 1963; L. Sigalos, *The Greek Claims on
Northern Epirus*, Chicago, 1967; B. Sutter, "Die Grossmächte und die Erhaltung des
europäischen Friedens zu beginn der Kreta-Krise von 1897," *Südost Forschungen*, 21
(1962), 214–269; C. Tukin, "Osmanlı Imparatorluğunda Girit isyanları" (The Cretan
revolts in the Ottoman Empire), *Belleten*, 9 (1945), 163–206; D. Xanalatos, "The Greeks
and the Turks on the Eve of the Balkan Wars," *Balkan Studies*, 3 (1963), 277–296. Âli
Paşa's reforms in Crete are described in some detail in A. H. Ongonsu, "Âli Paşa," IA,
I, 335–339.

The most authoritative summary of the Balkan Crisis of 1875–1878 is W. Langer, *Euro-
pean Alliances and Alignments, 1871–1890*, 2nd ed., New York, 1950; also D. Harris,
A Diplomatic History of the Balkan Crisis of 1875–1878: The First Year, Stanford, Calif.,
1939/1968; M. D. Stojanović, *The Great Powers and the Balkans, 1875–1878*, Cambridge,
England, 1938; B. H. Sumner, *Russia and the Balkans, 1870–1880*, Oxford, 1937;
S. Goriainov, *La question d'Orient à la veille du traité de Berlin, 1870–1878*, Paris, 1948;
W. Medlicott, *The Congress of Berlin and After*, London, 1938, and *Bismarck, Gladstone,
and the Concert of Europe*, London, 1956.

Ottoman rule in Bulgaria and the Bulgarian revolt are discussed in Ezel Kural Shaw,
"Midhat Pasha, Reformer or Revolutionary?" unpublished Ph.D. dissertation, Harvard
University, 1975, pp. 77–172; M. Macdermott, *A History of Bulgaria, 1393–1885*, London,
1962; Halil Inalcık, *Tanzimat ve Bulgar Meselesi* (The Tanzimat and the Bulgarian
Problem), Ankara, 1943; D. Kosev, "Les rapports agraires et le mouvement paysan en
Bulgarie de la fin du XVIIIe siècle à nos jours," *Etudes Historiques*, 5 (1970), 57–99;
M. Leo, *La Bulgarie et son peuple sous la domination ottomane*, Sofia, 1948; Bilal Şimşir,
Rumeliden Türk göçleri (The migrations of Turks from Rumeli), 2 vols., Ankara, 1968;
G. D. Todorov and N. Zecev, "Documents ayant trait aux luttes des Bulgares pour une
église et des écoles nationales en Macédoine vers le milieu du XIXe siecle," *Etudes His-
toriques*, 3 (1966), 173–239; R. Shannon, *Gladstone and the Bulgarian Agitation, 1876*,
London, 1963; David Harris, *Britain and the Bulgarian Horrors of 1876*, Chicago, 1939.

On the deposition of Abdulaziz, the short reign of Murat V, the Çerkes Hasan incident,
the death of Abdulaziz, and the enthronement of Abdulhamit II see Davison, pp. 317–346,
for an excellent summary; *Mufassal Osmanlı Tarihi*, VI, 3253–3263; H. Şehsuvaroğlu,
Sultan Aziz, Hayatı, Hal'i, Ölümü (Sultan Aziz, His Life, His Deposition, His Death),
Istanbul, 1949, pp. 86–205; I. H. Uzunçarşılı, *Midhat Paşa ve Yıldız Mahkemesi* (Midhat
Paşa and the Yıldız Trial), Ankara, 1967; Mahmut Celaleddin, *Mirat-ı Hakikat* (Mirror
of Truth), 3 vols., Istanbul, 1326–1327/1908–1909; Ahmet Midhat Efendi, *Üss-ü Inkilap*
(The Base of the Revolt), Istanbul, 1294/1877; Ahmet Saip Bey, *Vaka-yı Abdul-Aziz*
(The Event of Abdulaziz), Cairo, 1326/1910, Süleyman Paşa, *Hiss-i Inkilap* (The Feel-
ing of Revolution), Istanbul, 1326/1910; I. H. Uzunçarşılı, "Murad V," IA, VIII, 647–
651, "Beşinci Murad'ı Avrupa'ya kaçırma teşebbüsü" (The effort to abduct Murat V to
Europe), *Belleten*, 10 (1946), 195–209, "Beşinci Sultan Murad'ın tedâvisine ve ölümüne
ait rapor ve mektuplar, 1876–1905" (Reports and letters on the treatment and death of
Murat V, 1876–1905), *Belleten*, 10 (1945), 317–367, "Çerkes Hasan vak'ası" (The Çerkes
Hasan Affair), *Belleten*, 9 (1945), 89–133, *Midhat Paşa ve Taif Mahkumları* (Midhat

Paşa and the Prisoners of Taif), Ankara, 1950, *Midhat ve Rüştü Paşaların tevkiflerine dair vesikalar* (Documents concerning the imprisonment of Midhat Paşa and Rüştü Paşa), Ankara, 1946; and "Sultan Abdülaziz vak'asına dair vak'anüvis Lütfi Efendinin bir risalesi" (A memoire by court historian Lütfi Efendi on the deposition of Sultan Abdulaziz), *Belleten*, 7 (1943), 349–373.

VII. The Reign of Abdulhamit II, 1876–1909

There is no adequate biography of Abdulhamit or account of his reign. The only work on the subject with some comprehensiveness, Osman Nuri, *Abd ul-Hamid-i Sani ve Devr-i Saltanatı: Hayat-ı Hususiye ve siyasiyesi* (Abdulhamit II and the Period of His Sultanate: His Private and Political Life), 1 vol. in 3, Istanbul, 1327/1911, was written shortly after his deposition, emphasizes mainly political and diplomatic matters, and is badly out of date. The same comments apply to Ahmet Saip, *Abdülhamidin evail-i saltanatı* (The beginnings of Abdulhamit's sultanate), Cairo, 1326/1910, which is also very hostile toward the subject. All the European-language books on Abdulhamit are biased, inaccurate, and mostly useless, including E. Pears, *Life of Abd ul-Hamid*, London, 1917; Joan Haslip, *The Sultan: The Life of Abdul Hamid II*, London, 1958; V. Berard, *La Politique du Sultan*, Paris, 1897; A. Wittlin, *Abdul Hamid, Shadow of God*, London, 1940; G. Dorys, *Abdul Hamid Intime*, Paris, 1902; G. Roy, *Abdul Hamid le Sultan Rouge*, Paris, 1936; Mourad Bey, *Le Palais de Yildiz et la Sublime Porte*, Paris, 1897; and Paul Regla, *Les Secrets de Yildiz*, Paris, 1897.

The most comprehensive work available on the empire during Abdulhamit's reign is E. Z. Karal, *Osmanlı Tarihi, VIII. Cilt. Birinci Meşrutiyet ve Istibdat Devirleri, 1876–1907* (Ottoman History, Vol. VIII, The First Constitutional and Absolutist Periods, 1876–1907), Ankara, 1962. It can be supplemented with memoirs from the period, including Selek Yayınevi, *Ikinci Abdülhamid'ın Hatıra Defteri* (The Memoirs of Abdulhamit), Istanbul, 1960; Ismet Bozdağ, *Ikinci Abdülhamid'ın Hatıra Defteri* (Abdulhamit II's Memoir Book), Bursa, 1946; Vedat Urfi, *Hatırat-ı Sultan Abdülhamit Han-ı Sani* (Memoirs of Sultan Abdulhamit II), Istanbul, 1340/1921; and Ali Vehbi Bey, *Pensées et Souvenirs de l'Ex Sultan Abdul-Hamid*, Paris, 1910, works that at least purport to be the recollections of the sultan himself; also those of members of his family and others close to him; Tahsin Paşa, *Abdülhamit ve Yıldız Hatıraları* (Memories of Abdulhamit and of Yıldız), Istanbul, 1931; and Ayşe Osmanoğlu, *Babam Abdülhamid* (My Father Abdulhamit), Istanbul, 1960. A number of leading political figures of the time also have left substantial memoirs: Kâmil Paşa, *Hâtırat-ı Sadr-ı Esbak Kâmil Paşa* (Memoirs of the Former Grand Vezir Kâmil Paşa), Istanbul, 1329/1913; Sait Paşa, *Hatırat-ı Sait Paşa* (The Memoirs of Sait Paşa), 3 vols., Istanbul, 1328/1912; *Kâmil Paşanın Ayan Reisi Sait Paşa'ya Cevapları* (The Answers of Kâmil Paşa to the President of the Council of Notables Sait Paşa), 2nd ed., Istanbul, 1328/1912; *Sait Paşanın Kâmil Paşa hâtıratına cevapları. Şarki Rumeli, Mısır ve Ermeni meseleleri* (The answers of Sait Paşa to the Memoirs of Kâmil Paşa. The problems of East Rumeli, Egypt, and Armenia), Istanbul, 1327/1911; Ismail Müştak Mayakon, *Yıldızda Neler Gördüm* (What I Saw at Yıldız), Istanbul, 1940; Ali Haydar Midhat, *Hâtıralarım, 1872–1946* (My Memoirs, 1872–1946), Istanbul, 1946; Rıza Nur, *Hayat ve Hatıratım* (My Life and Memoirs), 2 vols., Istanbul, 1968; Ali Fuat Türkgeldi, *Görüp Işittiklerim* (What I Saw and Heard), Ank., 1951, and *Mesâil-i Mühimme-i Siyasiyye* (Important Political Issues), 2 vols., Ankara, 1957–1960; Ziya Şakir, *Sultan Hamid'ın Son Günleri* (The Last Days of Sultan Hamit), Istanbul, 1943; Ismail Kemal, *The Memoires of Ismail Kemal Bey*, ed. Sommerville Story, London, 1920.

Information can also be secured from biographies of the leading figures of the reign: Ibnülemin Mahmud Kemal Inal, *Osmanlı Devrinde Son Sadrâzamlar* (The Last Grand Vezirs in the Ottoman Period), 14 parts in 6 vols., Istanbul, 1940–1953; M. Z. Pakalın, *Son Sadrâzamlar ve Başvekiller* (The Last Grand Vezirs and Prime Ministers), 5 vols.,

Istanbul, 1940–1949; Djemaleddin Bey, *Sultan Murad V. The Turkish Dynastic Mystery, 1876–1895,* London, 1895; Ibrahim Alaeddin Gövsa, *Türk Meşhurları Ansiklopedisi* (Encyclopedia of Famous Turks) Istanbul, 1946; Comte E. de Kératy, *Mourad V: Prince Sultan Prisonnier d'Etat, 1840–1878,* 2nd ed., Paris, 1878; Midhat Cemal Kuntay, *Namık Kemal devrinin insanları ve olayları arasında* (Namık Kemal Among the men and events of his time), 3 vols., Istanbul, 1944–1949; Ahmet Saip, *Tarih-i Sultan Murad-ı Hamis* (History of Sultan Murad V), Cairo, n.d.; Ercümend Kuran, "Said Paşa," IA, X, 82–86; Hilmi Kâmil Bayur, *Sadrazam Kâmil Paşa – Siyasî Hayatı* (Grand Vezir Kâmil Paşa – His Political Life), Ankara, 1954; Ercümend Kuran, "Ibrahim Edhem Paşa," EI², III, 993; Ahmed Hamdi Tanpınar, "Ahmed Vefik," IA, I, 207–210; Murat Uraz, *Ahmed Vefik Paşa,* Istanbul, 1944; and Ercümend Kuran, "Küçük Said Paşa (1840–1914) as a Turkish Modernist," IJMES, 1 (1970), 124–132.

Most of the reports of foreign diplomats and travelers in the empire during Abdulhamit's reign display religious and racial prejudice as well as gross inaccuracy. But one can cull useful information from some of them, such as Paul Fesch, *Constantinople aux derniers jours d'Abdul-Hamid,* Paris, 1907; A. Vambéry, *La Turquie d'aujourd'hui et d'avant quarante ans,* tr. G. Tirard, Paris, 1898; F. von der Goltz and W. Foerster, *General-feldmarschall Colmar Freiherr von der Goltz Denkwürdigkeiten,* Berlin, 1929; E. Lindow, *Freiherr Marshall von Bieberstein als Botschafter in Konstantinopel, 1897–1912,* Danzig, 1934; C. Smith, *The Embassy of Sir William White at Constantinople, 1886–1891,* London, 1957; C. Kuentzer, *AbdulHamid II und die Reformen in der Türkei,* Leipzig, 1897; Paul de Regla, *La Turquie officielle: Constantinople, son gouvernement, ses habitants, son présent et avenir,* Geneva, 1891; H. O. Dwight, *Turkish Life in War Time,* New York, 1881; Cyrus Hamlin, *My Life and Times,* Boston, 1893; Sir Edwin Pears, *Forty Years in Constantinople,* London, 1916; R. Davey, *The Sultan and His Subjects,* 2 vols., New York, 1897; C. Hecquard, *La Turquie sous Abdul-Hamid II . . . ,* Brussels, 1901; A. D. Mordtmann, *Stambul und das Moderne Türkenthum,* 2 vols., Leipzig, 1877.

For an English text of the Constitution of 1876 and its evolution see Ezel Kural Shaw, "Midhat Paşa, Reformer or Revolutionary," unpublished Ph.D. dissertation, Harvard University, 1975, pp. 287–364; useful summaries are provided by R. Davison, pp. 358–408, and B. Lewis, "Düstur," EI², II, 640–644; R. Devereux, *The First Ottoman Constitutional Period: A Study of the Midhat Constitution and Parliament,* Baltimore, 1963, is based on limited use of the Ottoman sources. The works of Azimzade Hakkı, *Türkiyede Meclis-i Mebusan* (The Council of Deputies in Turkey), Cairo, 1907, and Hakkı Tarık Us, *Meclis-i Mebusan, 1293:1877 Zabıt Ceridesi* (The Council of Deputies, 1293/1877 debate minutes), 2 vols., Istanbul, 1940–1954, reconstruct the parliamentary debates on the basis of the contemporary newspaper reports, since the actual records were destroyed by fire. See also Bekir Sıdkı Baykal, "Birinci Meşrutiyete dair belgeler" (Documents concerning the First Constitution), *Belleten,* 21 (1960), 601–636, and "93 Meşrutiyeti" (The Constitution of 1293/1876), *Belleten,* 6 (1942), 45–83; A. Soydan, *La Constitution Turque de 1293 (1876) et les modifications apportées par celle de 1329 (1909),* Paris, 1955; and A. Ubicini, *La Constitution ottomane du 7 zilhidjé 1293,* Constantinople, 1877. The text of the Constitution can be found in *Düstur¹,* IV, 2–20, with amendments in *Düstur²,* I, 11, 638, VI, 749, VII, 224. The official French translation is in Aristarchi, V, 1–25. An unofficial English text is reprinted in Kili, *Constitutional Developments.* The papers of the commission that drew up the Constitution are found in the Yıldız Palace Archives, Istanbul (see S. J. Shaw, "Yıldız Palace Archives," *Archivum Ottomanicum,* 3 (1971), 214–216, 224).

The Constantinople Conference (called the Naval Arsenal Conference/*Tersane Konferansı* by the Turks) is discussed in Langer, *European Alliances and Alignments,* pp. 89–120; Y. T. Kurat, *Henry Layard'ın Istanbul Elçiliği* (The Istanbul Embassy of Henry Layard), Ankara, 1968; and I. H. Uzunçarşılı, "Tersane Konferansının mukarreratı hakkında Şura mazbatası" (The report of the Council of State on the Naval Arsenal Conference), *Tarih Dergisi,* 6 (1954), 123–140. The Russo-Turkish War of 1877–1878 is described in Y. T. Kurat, "1877–78 Osmanlı-Rus harbinin sebepleri" (The Causes of the Russo-Turkish war of 1877–78), *Belleten,* 26 (1962), 567–592; T. Y. Öztuna, *Resimlerle 93 Harbi. 1877–78 Türk-Rus Savaşı* (The War of 1293 illustrated. The Turkish-Russian Struggle of 1877–78), Istanbul, 1969; P. Fortunatow, *Der Krieg 1877–78 und die Befreiung Bulgariens,* Berlin, 1953. Armenian assistance to the Russians is documented in W. E. D. Allen and P. Muratoff, *Caucasian Battlefields,* Cambridge, 1953, and C. B. Norman, *Armenia and the Campaign of 1877,* London, 1878.

On the French occupation of North Africa see Abdurrahman Çaycı, *Büyük Sahra'da Türk-Fransız Rekabeti, 1858–1911* (Turkish-French Rivalry in the Great Sahara, 1858–1911), Erzurum, 1970, "L'Entente italo-turque de 1863," *Les Cahiers de Tunisie,* 53–56 (1966), 41–52, "Italya'daki Tunus konsoloslukları meselesi ve 1863 Osmanlı-Italyan anlaşması" (The problem of the consuls of Tunis in Italy and the Ottoman-Italian agreement of 1863), *Belleten,* 30 (1966), 603–611, "Italya'nın Tunus'ta üstünlük teşebbüsü" (Italy's effort to gain supremacy in Tunis), *VI. Türk Tarih Kongresi,* Ankara, 1967, pp. 497–519; *La question tunisienne et la politiqueottomane 1881–1913,* Erzurum, 1963; G. Esquer, *Histoire de l'Algérie, 1830–1960,* Paris, 1960; E. Kuran, *Cezayir'in Fransızlar tarafından işgalı karşısında Osmanlı siyaseti, 1827–1847* (Ottoman policy against the French occupation of Algeria), Istanbul, 1957; and J. Ganiage, *Les origines du protectorat français en Tunisie, 1861–1881,* Paris, 1959. On the British occupation of Egypt see F. Charles Roux, *Les origines de l'expédition d'Egypte,* Paris, 1910; David Landes, *Bankers and Pashas in Egypt,* Cambridge, Mass., 1965; M. Kleine, *Deutschland und die ägyptische Frage, 1875–1890,* Griefswald, 1927; L. Ragats, *The Question of Egypt in Anglo-French relations, 1875–1904,* Edinburgh, 1922; Lord Cromer, *Modern Egypt,* London, 1908; J. Marlowe, *Anglo-Egyptian Relations, 1800–1953,* London, 1954; Bab-ı Âli, Hariciye Nezareti, *Mısır Meselesi* (The Egyptian Problem), Istanbul, 1334; and Langer, *European Alliances and Alignments,* pp. 251–280.

Bulgaria after the Congress of Berlin, Ottoman reforms in East Rumelia, and the ultimate occupation by Bulgaria are discussed by K. Kratchounov, *La Politique extérieure de la Bulgarie, 1880–1920,* Sofia, 1932; Hilmi Kâmil Bayur, "Şarki Rumeli meselesine dair" (On the Problem of East Rumelia), *Belleten,* 20 (1946), 527–530; J. V. Königslöw, *Ferdinand von Bulgarien,* Munich, 1970; K. K. Sarova, "L'union de la Bulgarie du Nord et de la Bulgarie du Sud (1885)," *Etudes Balkaniques,* 6 (1967), 97–121; and J. Mitev, "L'attitude de la Russie et de l'Angleterre à l'égard de l'union de la Bulgarie en 1885," *Etudes Historiques,* 1 (1960), 347–377. Albanian nationalism is described in Stavro Skendi, *The Albanian National Awakening, 1878–1912,* Princeton, N.J., 1967; S. Story, ed., *The Memoirs of Ismail Kemal Bey,* New York, 1920; H. Inalcık, "Arnawutluk," EI², I, 650–658; P. Bartl, *Die albanischen Muslime zur Zeit der nationalen Unabhändigkeitsbewegung, 1878–1912,* Wiesbaden, 1968; Kâzım Nami Duru, *Arnavutluk ve Makedonya hatıralarım* (My memories of Albania and Macedonia), Istanbul, 1959; and P. Pipinellis, *Europe and the Albanian Question,* Chicago, 1963.

The most objective study of the Armenian Question is W. L. Langer, *The Diplomacy of Imperialism,* New York, 1956, pp. 145–166, 321–350. An excellent account of Armenian terrorist activities, based on documents captured from the Armenian terror societies, is Nazım Paşa, *Ermeni Tarih-i Vukuatı* (History of the Armenian Event), manuscript in the Yıldız Palace Archives, BVA, Istanbul, K36/Z131/no. 139 (80). See also E. Z. Karal, *Osmanlı Tarihi,* VIII, 126–145. The role of the Armenians in the Ottoman Empire is discussed in Esat Uras, *Türk Devleti Hizmetinde Ermeniler, 1453–1953* (Armenians in the Service of the Turkish State, 1453–1953), Istanbul, 1953. The Armenian point of view is best presented in L. Nalbandian, *The Armenian Revolutionary Movement,* Berkeley and Los Angeles, 1963; and A. O. Sarkissian, *History of the Armenian Question to 1885,* Urbana, Ill., 1938. The Macedonian Question is discussed in H. R. Wilkinson, *Maps and Politics: A Review of the Ethnographic Cartography of Macedonia,* Liverpool, 1951; Huey Kostanick, "Macedonia: A Study in Political Geography," unpublished Ph.D. dissertation, Clark University, 1948; Langer, *Diplomacy of Imperialism,* pp. 303–354; D. Dakin, *The Greek Struggle in Macedonia, 1897–1913,* Salonica, 1966; E. Barker,

Macedonia: Its Place in Balkan Power Politics, London, 1950; C. Anastasoff, *The Tragic Peninsula: A History of the Macedonian Movement for Independence Since 1878,* St. Louis, 1938; K. Kyriakidis, *The Northern Ethnological Boundaries of Hellenism,* Salonica, 1955; Münir Aktepe, "Mehmed Salâhî Bey ve II. Abdülhamid'e Selânik hakkında sunduğu rapor" (Mehmet Selahi Bey and a report submitted to Abdulhamid II on Salonica), *Tarih Dergisi,* 17 (1967), 79–96; S. S. Papadopoulos, "Ecoles et associations grecques dans la Macédoine du nord durant le dernier siècle de la domination turque," *Balkan Studies,* 3 (1962), 397–442; and D. Slijepceviç, *The Macedonian Question: The Struggle for Southern Serbia,* Chicago, 1958.

Abdulhamit's reform plans were indicated in a series of memoirs now found in the Yıldız Palace Archives, of which the most comprehensive was published by S. J. Shaw, "A Promise of Reform: Two Complimentary Documents," IJMES, 4 (1973), 359–365. Accounts of his financial, economic and social reforms and of cultural development during his reign are cited in part VI of this bibliography, "The Tanzimat Reform Era, 1839–1876." His military reforms are studied in M. A. Griffeths, "The Reorganization of the Ottoman Army Under Abdülhamid II, 1880–1897," unpublished Ph.D. dissertation, University of California, Los Angeles, 1966; also see von der Goltz, *Generalfeld-marschall Colman Freiherr von der Goltz – Das Leben eines grossen Soldaten,* Göttingen, 1960; Pertev Demirhan, *Goltz Paşanın Hatırası ve Hal Tercümesi* (The Memoirs and Biography of Goltz Paşa), Istanbul, 1949; Izzet Pasha, *Denkwürdigkeiten des Marshalls Izzet Pasha,* Leipzig, 1927; I. Felgerhaurer, *Die Militär Bildungsanstalt der Türkei und ihre jünsten Reformen,* Berlin, 1887, Hajo Holborn, *Deutschland und die Türkei, 1878–1890,* Berlin, 1926; L. Lamouche, *L'Organisation militaire de l'Empire Ottoman,* Paris, 1895; L. von Schlözer, *Das Türkische Heer,* Leipzig, 1901. The Ottoman navy is discussed in O. Öndeş, "Abdülhamid devrinde donanma" (The fleet in the period of Abdulhamit II), *Belgelerle Türk Tarih Dergisi,* no. 19 (1969), 68–78; no. 20 (1969), 71–75; no. 21 (1969), 70–73; no. 22 (1969), 78–80; no. 24 (1969), 64–88.

The Young Turk movement has been ably studied by E. E. Ramsaur, *The Young Turks: Prelude to the Revolution of 1908,* Princeton, N.J., 1957; Şerif Mardin, *Jön Türklerin Siyasi Fikirleri, 1895–1908* (The Political Thoughts of the Young Turks, 1895–1908), Ankara, 1964; Y. H. Bayur, *Türk Inkılabı Tarihi, Cilt II, Kısım IV, Fikir cereyanları, inkılâp hareketleri, iç didişmeler. Birinci genel savaşın patlaması* (History of the Turkish Revolution, Vol. II, Part 4, Movements of thought, revolutionary movements, internal disorders, the outbreak of the first general war), Ankara, 1952; P. Fesch, *Constantinople aux dernier jours d'Abdul Hamid,* Paris, 1907; Ahmed Bedevi Kuran, *Inkilap Tarihimiz ve Jön Türkler* (History of Our Revolution and the Young Turks), Istanbul, 1945, *Inkilâp Tarihimiz ve Ittihad ve Terakki* (History of Our Revolution and Union and Progress), Istanbul, 1948, and *Osmanlı Imparatorluğunda Inkilap Hareketleri ve Milli Mücadele* (Revolutionary Movements in the Ottoman Empire and the National Struggle), Istanbul, 1956; Ibrahim Temo, *Ittihat ve Terakki Cemiyetinin Teşekkülü* (The formation of the Union and Progress Society), Mecidiye, Rumania, 1939; Tarık Z. Tunaya, *Türkiyede Siyasî Partiler, 1859–1952* (Political Parties in Turkey, 1859–1952), Istanbul, 1952.

The development of secularism, Pan-Islam, and Turkish nationalism is described by Berkes, pp. 253–333; David Kushner, *The Origins of Turkish Nationalism,* London, 1977; H. N. Orkun, *Türkçülüğün Tarihi* (History of Turkism), Ankara, 1944; Uriel Heyd, *Foundations of Turkish Nationalism,* London, 1950; C. W. Hostler, *Turkism and the Soviets,* London, 1957; Niyāzi Berkes, ed., *Turkish Nationalism and Western Civilization: Selected Essays of Ziya Gökalp,* New York, 1959; Kâzım Nami Duru, *Ziya Gökalp,* Istanbul, 1948; Ziyaeddin Fahri, *Ziya Gökalp, sa vie et sa sociologie,* Paris, 1935; Ali Nüzhet Göksel, *Ziya Gökalp, Hayatı ve Eserleri* (Ziya Gökalp, His life and Works), Istanbul, 1948; D. E. Lee, "The Origins of Pan-Islamism," *American Historical Review,* 38 (1942), 278–287; and G. Arnakis, "Turanism, an Aspect of Turkish Nationalism," *Balkan Studies,* 1 (1960), 19–32.

VIII. The Young Turk Period, 1908–1918

The most comprehensive study of the Young Turk period is Yusuf Hikmet Bayur, *Türk Inkilabı Tarihi* (History of the Turkish Revolution), 3 vols. in 10 parts, Ankara, 1940–1967. Feroz Ahmad, *The Young Turks: The Committee of Union and Progress in Turkish Politics, 1908–1914,* Oxford, 1969, is a history of the politics of the period and should be supplemented by Lewis, *Emergence,* pp. 206–233 and Berkes, *Secularism,* pp. 325–428. Sertoğlu, *Mufassal Osmanlı Tarihi,* VI (1963), 3414–3525 is excellent.

As with the period of Abdulhamit II, the Young Turk period also is illuminated by numerous memoirs and biographies: H. K. Bayur, *Sadrazam Kâmil Paşa Siyasî Hayatı* (The Political Life of Grand Vezir Kâmil Paşa), Ankara, 1954; Cemal Paşa, *Hâtırat, 1913–1922* (Memoirs, 1913–1922), Istanbul, 1922, published also in English as Djemal Pasha, *Memoires of a Turkish Statesman, 1913–1919,* New York, 1922, and in modern letters as Cemal Paşa, *Hatıralar,* ed. B. Cemal, Istanbul, 1959; Ali Haydar Midhat, *Hatıralarım, 1872–1946* (My Memoirs, 1872–1946), Istanbul, 1946; Ahmet Niyazi, *Hatırat-ı Niyazi* (The Memoirs of Niyazi), Istanbul, 1326/1910; Cemaleddin Efendi, *Hatırat-ı Siyasiye* (Political Memoirs), Istanbul, 1336/1920; Kâzım Nami Duru, *Ittihat ve Terakki Hatıralarım* (My Memoirs of Union and Progress) Istanbul, 1957; Ahmet Bedevi Kuran, *Harbiye Mektebinde Hürriyet Mücadelesi* (The Struggle for Liberty in the Army School), Istanbul, n.d.; Enver Bolayır, *Talat Paşa'nın Hatıraları* (The Memoirs of Talat Paşa), Istanbul, 1946, 1958; D. A. Rustow, "Enwer Pasha," EI², II, 698–702; Ş. S. Aydemir, *Makedonya'dan Ortaasya'ya Enver Paşa* (Enver Paşa from Macedonia to Central Asia), 3 vols., Istanbul, 1970–1972. Samih Nafız Tansu, *2 Devrin Perde Arkası* (Behind the Curtain of 2 Periods), Istanbul, 1957; Halit Ziya Uşaklıgil, *Saray ve Ötesi* (The Palace and Beyond), 2 vols., Istanbul, 1940–1941; Celal Bayar, *Ben de Yazdım: Milli Mücadeleye Giriş* (I Also Have Written: Entering the National Struggle), 8 vols., Istanbul, 1972–1976; Sir Andrew Ryan, *The Last of the Dragomans,* London, 1951; Liman von Sanders, *Five Years in Turkey,* Annapolis, 1927; E. F. Tugay, *Three Centuries: Family Chronicles of Turkey and Egypt,* Oxford, 1963; Fahri Bey, *Ibretnüma. Mabeynci Fahri Bey'in Hatıraları ve ilgili bazı belgeler* (The Letter of Admonition. The Memoirs of Chamberlain Fahri Bey and some related documents), Ankara, 1968; Dr. Rıza Nur, *Hayat ve hâtıratım* (My life and memoirs), Istanbul, 1967; Şadiye Osmanoğlu, *Hayatım, Acı ve Tatlı Günleri* (The bitter and sweet days of my life), Istanbul, 1966

On the proclamation of the 1908 Constitution see I. H. Uzunçarşılı, "1908 yılında Ikinci Meşrutiyetin ne suretle ilân edildiğine dair vesikalar" (Documents on how the second constitution was proclaimed in the year 1908), *Belleten,* 20 (1956), 103–174. The reaction of March 31/April 13, 1909, is studied by David Farhi, "The Şeriat as a Political Slogan – or the 'Incident of the 31st Mart,'" *Middle Eastern Studies,* 7 (1971), 275–316; Sina Akşin, *31 Mart Olayı* (The Event of March 31), Istanbul, 1972; Faik Reşit Unat, ed., "Ikinci Meşrutiyet devri üzerine bazı düşünceler" (Some thoughts on the period of the Second Constitution), *Belleten,* 23 (1959), 267–285; I. Ilgar, "31 Mart ve Hareket Ordusu" (The 31st of March and the Operation Army), *Belgelerle Türk Tarihi Dergisi,* 6 (1968), 23–31; Bedi Şehsuvaroğlu, "Ikinci Meşrutiyet ve Atıf Bey" (The Second Constitution and Atıf Bey), *Belleten,* 23 (1959), 307–334; and Faik Reşit Unat, "Atatürk'ün II. Meşrutiyet inkılâbının hazırlanmasındaki rolüne ait bir belge" (A Document on the role of Atatürk in the Second Constitutional revolution), *Belleten,* 26 (1962), 601–624.

The Austrian annexation of Bosnia and Herzegovina is studied by B. E. Schmitt, *The Annexation of Bosnia, 1908–1909,* Cambridge, Mass., 1937; W. D. David, *European Diplomacy in the Near Eastern Question, 1906–1909,* Urbana, Ill., 1940; and G. Wittrock, *Österrike-Ungern i Bosniska krisen 1908–09,* Uppsala, 1939. On the Albanian revolt see S. Skendi, *The Albanian National Awakening, 1878–1912,* Princeton, N.J., 1967. The Tripolitanian War is studied by W. C. Askew, *Europe and Italy's Acquisition of Libya,* Durham, N.C., 1942; A. J. Cachia, *Libya Under the Second Ottoman Occupation, 1835–*

458   *Bibliography*

1911, Tripoli, 1945; and Emir Ali Haydar, *1327–1328 Türkiye-Italya Harbi Tarih-i Bahrisi* (The Naval History of the 1911–1912 Turkish-Italian War), Istanbul, 1329/1913, The Balkan Wars are described in Bayur, *Türk Inkilabı Tarihi*, II/1–3, Ankara, 1943–1951; E. C. Helmreich, *The Diplomacy of the Balkan Wars, 1912–1913*, Cambridge, Mass., 1938; T. C. Gnkur. Bşk. Harb Tarihi Dairesi, *Balkan Harbi Tarihi* (History of the Balkan War), 7 vols., Istanbul/Ankara, 1938–1965. Ottoman military reorganization before World War I is presented from the German point of view in Ulrich Trumpener, *Germany and the Ottoman Empire, 1914–1918*, Princeton, N.J., 1968; C. Mühlmann, *Deutschland und die Türkei, 1913–1914*, Berlin, 1929; and Liman von Sanders, *My Five Years in Turkey*, Annapolis, Md., 1927.

IX. World War I, 1914–1918

Turkey's entry into the war is discussed by Bayur, *Türk Inkilabı Tarihi*, III/1, pp. 194–274; E. Jackh, *The Rising Crescent*, New York and Toronto, 1944, pp. 10–21; Trumpener, *Germany and the Ottoman Empire*, pp. 15–20, and "Turkey's Entry into World War I: An Assessment of Responsibilities," *Journal of Modern History*, 34 (1962), 369–380; Midhat Sertoğlu, "Birinci Cihan Savaşına girişimizin gerçek sebebleri" (The real reasons for our entry into the First World War), *Belgelerle Türk Tarihi Dergisi*, 15 (1968), 3–13; E. R. Vere Hodge, *Turkish Foreign Policy, 1914–1918*, Geneva, 1950; B. W. Tuchman, *The Guns of August*, New York, 1962, pp. 137–162; H. N. Howard, *The Partition of Turkey: A Diplomatic History, 1913–1923*, Norman, Okla., 1931; and F. G. Weber, *Eagles on the Crescent: Germany, Austria and the Diplomacy of the Turkish Alliance, 1914–1918*, Ithaca, N.Y., 1970.

The Ottoman war effort is described in great detail in the official Turkish General Staff war history, General Fahri Belen, *Birinci Cihan Harbinde Türk Harbi* (The Turkish War During the First World War), 5 vols., Ankara, 1963–1967; also Bayur, *Türk Inkilabı Tarihi*, III/1–4, Ankara, 1953–1967; M. Larcher, *La guerre turque dans la guerre mondiale*, Paris, 1926; and the works of Trumpener, Howard, and Weber, cited previously. Internal conditions in the empire during the war have not been adequately studied. The best account is Ahmed Emin (Yalman), *Turkey in the World War*, New Haven, Conn., and London, 1930. Halide Edib, *The Memoires of Halidé Edib*, London, 1926, and Irfan Orga, *Portrait of a Turkish Family*, London, 1950, recall personal experiences. See also K. T. Helfferich, *Die deutsche Türkenpolitik*, Berlin, 1921; and Lewis Einstein, *Inside Constantinople*, London, 1917.

The war on the Balkan front is described by C. Theodoulou, *Greece and the Entente, August 1, 1914–September 25, 1916*, Salonica, 1971; F. Feyler, *La Campagne de Macédoine, 1916–1918*, 2 vols., Geneva, 1920–1921, and *Les Campagnes de Serbie, 1914 et 1915*, Geneva and Paris, 1926; A. J. Toynbee, *The Western Question in Greece and Turkey*, 2nd ed., London, 1923; A. Palmer, *The Gardeners of Salonica: The Macedonian Campaign, 1915–1918*, London, 1965; M. B. Petrovich, *Russian Diplomacy and Eastern Europe, 1914–1917*, New York, 1963; and C. Falls and A. F. Becke, *Military Operations in Macedonia*, 2 vols., London, 1933.

The campaigns in eastern Anatolia and the Caucasus are discussed in the war histories of Belen and Bayur, cited previously, and W. E. D. Allen and P. Muratoff, *Caucasian Battlefields*, Cambridge, 1953; Ali Ihsan Sabis, *Harb Hatıralarım* (My War Memories), 2 vols., Istanbul, 1943–1951; and Arif Baytin, *Ilk Dünya Harbinde Kafkas Cephesi* (The Caucasus Front in the First World War), Istanbul, 1946. The Armenian interpretation is given in R. G. Hovanissian, *Armenia on the Road to Independence, 1918*, Berkeley and Los Angeles, 1967; and Trumpener, *Germany and the Ottoman Empire*, pp. 204–233. An excellent collection of Turkish documents is presented in Salahi R. Sonyel, "Yeni Belgelerin Işığı altında Ermeni Tehcirleri – Armenian Deportations: A Re-Appraisal in the Light of New Documents," *Belleten*, 36 (1972), 31–69.

See also F. Kazemzadeh, *The Struggle for Transcaucasia, 1914–1921*, New York, 1951; F. Gusee, *Die Kaukasusfront im Weltkrieg*, Leipzig, 1940. On the Armenian Question as such see also R. H. Davison, "The Armenian Crisis, 1912–1914," *American Historical Review*, 43 (1948) ; J. B. Gidney, *A Mandate for Armenia*, Kent, Ohio, 1967 ; S. E. Kerr, *The Lions of Marash: Personal Experiences with American Near East Relief, 1919–1922*, Albany, N.Y., 1973; Milli Kongre, *The Turco-Armenian Question: The Turkish Point of View*, London, 1919; C. Korganoff, *La participation des Arméniens à la guerre mondiale sur le front du Caucase, 1914–1918*, Paris, 1927; Johannes Lepsius, *Deutschland und Armenien, 1914–1918*, Potsdam, 1918, *Der Todesgang des armenischen Volkes*, Potsdam, 1930, and "The Armenian Question," *Muslim World*, 10 (1920), 341–355; A. Poidebard, *Le rôle militaire des Arméniens sur le front du Caucase*, Paris, 1920; and Gwynne Dyer, "Turkish 'Falsifiers' and Armenian 'Deceivers': Historiography and the Armenian Massacres," *Middle Eastern Studies*, 12 (1976), 99–107.

The Gallipoli campaign has been studied extensively. For the most recent research see R. James, *Gallipoli: The History of a Noble Blunder*, New York, 1965; Alan Moorehead, *Gallipoli*, New York, 1956; T. Higgens, *Winston Churchill and the Dardanelles*, New York, 1963; M. Gilbert, *Winston S. Churchill, III, 1914–1916, The Challenge of War*, Boston, 1971, pp. 188–223, 351–447; Celal Erikan, *Çanakkalede Türk zaferi* (The Turkish Victory at Çanakkale), Ankara, 1954; Cemil Conk, *Çanakkale Conkbayırı savaşları* (The Conkbayırı battles at Çanakkale), Ankara, 1959; Kadri Ener, *Çanakkale'den hatıralar* (Memories of Çanakkale), Istanbul, 1954; and Mustafa Kemal, *Anafartalar Muharebatına ait Tarihçe* (A Short History of the Anafartalar Battles), Ankara, 1962. The German view is presented in H. Kannegiesser, *The Campaign in Gallipoli*, London, 1928; Liman von Sanders, *My Five Years in Turkey*, Annapolis, Md., 1927; H. Lorey, *Der Krieg in den türkischen Gewässern*, I, Berlin, 1928; and C. Mühlmann, *Der Kampf um die Dardanellen*, Oldenburg, 1927.

The campaign in Mesopotamia/Iraq is described in A. J. Barker, *The Bastard War*, New York, 1967; A. T. Wilson, *Loyalties: Mesopotamia, 1914–1917*, London, 1930, and *Mesopotamia, 1917–1920: A Clash of Loyalties*, London, 1931; C. V. Townshend, *My Campaign in Mesopotamia*, London, 1920; A. Kearsey, *A Study of the Strategy and Tactics of the Mesopotamian Campaign, 1914–1917*, London, 1934; H. von Kiesling, *Mit Feldmarshall V. d. Goltz Pacha in Mesopotamia und Persien*, Leipzig, 1922; and F. J. Moberly, *The Campaign in Mesopotamia, 1914–1918*, 4 vols., London, 1923–1927. The Yıldırım Army is discussed in Ahmed Sedat Paşa (Doğruer), *Yıldırım Akıbeti* (The Fate of Yıldırım), Istanbul, 1927; Hüseyin Hüsnü Emir, *Yıldırım*, Istanbul, 1337/1919; and Dr. Steuber, *'Yıldırım,' Deutsche Streiter auf heiligem Boden*, Berlin, 1922, tr. as *Yıldırım* by Nihat, Istanbul, 1932.

The Egyptian and Syrian campaigns and the Arab Revolt are discussed in Elie Kedourie, *England and the Middle East. The Vital Years, 1914–1921*, London, 1956; H. M. Sacher, *The Emergence of the Middle East, 1914–1924*, New York, 1959; G. Antonius, *The Arab Awakening*, London, 1938; Zeine N. Zeine, *Arab-Turkish Relations and the Emergence of Arab Nationalism*, Beirut, 1959; Kress von Kressenstein, *Mit den Türken zum Suezkanal*, Berlin, 1938; A. Wavell, *Allenby: Soldier and Statesman*, London, 1940; M. G. E. Bowman-Manifold, *An Outline of the Egyptian and Palestine Campaigns 1914 to 1918*, Chatham, 1922; Richard Aldington, *Lawrence of Arabia*, London, 1955; Brian Gardner, *Allenby of Arabia*, New York, 1966; T. E. Lawrence, *Seven Pillars of Wisdom*, London, 1935, and *Revolt in the Desert*, London, 1927; Suleiman Mousa, *T. E. Lawrence: An Arab View*, London, 1966; Sir Ronald Storrs, *Orientations*, London, 1937; and J. Nevakivi, *Britain, France and the Arab Middle East, 1914–1920*, London, 1969. The Ottoman side of the campaign is inadequately given in Vecihi, *Filistin ricatı* (Retreat from Palestine), Istanbul, 1337/1921; Djemal Pasha, *Memoires of a Turkish Statesman, 1913–1919*, New York, 1922; and Halide Edib, *Memoires of Halide Edib*, London, 1926. See also N. Z. Ajay, Jr., "Political Intrigue and Suppression in Lebanon During World War I," *IJMES*, 5 (1947), 140–160; and A. Yammime, *Quatre Ans de Misère: Le Liban et la Syrie Pendant la Guerre*, Cairo, 1922.

The wartime secret agreements dividing the Ottoman Empire are described in H. N. Howard, *The Partition of Turkey*, Norman, Okla., 1931 and *Turkey, the Straits and U.S.*

Policy, Baltimore, 1974; L. Evans, *United States Policy and the Partition of Turkey, 1914–1924*, Baltimore, 1965; R. Bullard, *Britain and the Middle East*, London, 1951; W. W. Gottlieb, *Studies in Secret Diplomacy During the First World War*, London, 1957; L. Stein, *The Balfour Declaration*, London, 1961; A. Pingaud, *Histoire Diplomatique de la France pendant la grande guerre*, 2 vols., Paris, 1938–1940; Hüseyin Rahmi, *Cihan Harbi esnasında Avrupa hükümetleriyle Türkiye. Anadolu'nun taksimi* (The European governments and Turkey during the World War. The division of Anatolia), Istanbul, 1927, repr. as *Sovyet Devleti Arşivi Gizli Belgelerinde Anadolunun Taksimi Planı* (The Plan to Divide Anatolia, in the secret documents of the Soviet State Archives), Istanbul, 1972; and R. Albrecht-Carré, *Italy at the Paris Peace Conference. The Paris Peace, History and Documents*, New York, 1938.

X. The Postwar Occupation of Turkey and the Turkish War for Independence, 1919–1923

The postwar efforts to occupy various parts of the defeated Ottoman Empire are studied in detail in Tevfik Bıyıklıoğlu, *Türk Istiklâl Harbi, I. Mondros Mütarekesi ve Tatbikatı* (The Turkish War for Independence. I. The Truce of Mondros and Its Application), Ankara, 1962, and "Birinci Dünya Harbinde (1914–1918) ve Mondros Mütarekesi sıralarında (30 Ekim 1918–11 Ekim 1922) Boğazlar problemi" (The Straits problem between the First World War (1914–1918) and the Truce of Mondros (October 30, 1918–October 11, 1922), *Belleten*, 24 (1960), 79–93; Halide Edib (Adıvar), *The Turkish Ordeal*, London, 1928, and *The Daughter of Smyrna*, Lahore, 1940; A. A. Pallis, *Greece's Anatolian Venture – and After*, London, 1937; Prince Andrew of Greece, *Towards Disaster: The Greek Army in Asia Minor in 1921*, London, 1930, and *War Memoires*, London, 1928; R. Albrecht-Carré, *Italy at the Peace Conference*, New York, 1938; H. H. Cummings, *Franco-British Rivalry in the Post-War Near East*, New York, 1938; Harry N. Howard, *The Partition of Turkey*, Norman, Okla., 1931, and *The King-Crane Commission*, Beirut, 1963; R. Hovannisian, *Armenia on the Road to Independence, 1918*, Berkeley and Los Angeles, 1967, and *The Republic of Armenia*, vol. I, *The First Year, 1918–1919*, Berkeley and Los Angeles, 1971; and Firuz Kazemzadeh, *The Struggle for Trans-Caucasia, 1917–1921*, New York, 1951.

The Turkish War for Independence that followed has been the subject of numerous studies. Excellent chronologies and bibliographies of the period are provided by G. Jäschke, *Die Türkei seit dem Weltkriege: Geschichteskalender, 1918–1928*, Berlin, 1929 (published also in *Welt des Islams*, 10, 1927–1929), revised and partly published (to 1923) in Turkish translation as *Türk Kurtuluş Savaşı Kronolojisi: Mondros'tan Mudanya'ya kadar 30 Ekim 1918–11 Ekim 1922* (Chronology of the Turkish Struggle for Liberation, from Mondros to Modanya, October 30, 1918–October 11, 1922), Ankara, 1970, and *Türk Kurtuluş Savaşı Kronolojisi, Mudanya Mütarekesinden 1923 sonuna kadar* (Chronology of the Turkish Struggle for Liberation, from the Truce of Mudanya to the end of 1923), Ankara, 1974. Also see Utkan Kocatürk, *Atatürk ve Türk Devrimi Kronolijisi, 1918–1938* (Chronology of Atatürk and the Turkish Revolution), Ankara, 1973; and Muzaffer Gökman, *Atatürk ve Devrimleri Tarihi Bibliyografyası. Bibliography of the History of Atatürk and His Reforms*, Istanbul, 1968.

The most authoritative and detailed history of the War for Independence is that published by the History Department of the Turkish General Staff, Genelkurmay Başkanlığı Harp Tarihi Dairesi, *Türk Istiklâl Harbi* (The Turkish War for Independence) 6 vols., Ankara, 1962–1968. See also Tevfik Bıyıklıoğlu, *Trakyada Milli Mücadele* (The National Struggle in Thrace), 2 vols., Ankara, 1955–1956, and *Atatürk Anadoluda, 1919–1921* (Atatürk in Anatolia, 1919–1921), Ankara, 1959; G. Jaeschke, *Kurtuluş Savaşı ile ilgili İngiliz Belgeleri* (English documents related to the War for Liberation), Ankara, 1971; Kâzım Özalp, *Milli Mücadele, 1919–1922* (The National Struggle, 1919–1922), 2 vols., Ankara, 1971–1972; Mahmut Goloğlu, *Milli Mücadele Tarihi* (History of the National Struggle), 5 vols.: (I) *Erzurum Kongresi* (The Congress of Erzurum), Ankara, 1968; (II) *Sivas Kongresi* (The Congress of Sivas), Ankara, 1969; (III) *Üçüncü Meşrutiyet*,

1920 (The Third Constitution, 1920), Ankara, 1970; (IV) *Cumhuriyete Doğru, 1921–1922* (Toward the Republic, 1921–1922) Ankara, 1971; (V) *Türkiye Cumhuriyeti, 1923* (The Turkish Republic, 1923), Ankara, 1971; Mustafa Kemal, *Nutuk, Gazi Mustafa Kemal tarafından* (The Speech, by Gazi Mustafa Kemal), 2 vols., Ankara, 1927; many reprints, of which *Nutuk,* 3 vols., Ankara, 1960–1961, was used in this study. Its official English translation was *A Speech Delivered by Ghazi Mustapha Kemal, President of the Turkish Republic, October 1927,* Leipzig, 1929; see also T. Gökbilgin, *Milli Mücadele Başlarken* (Starting the National Struggle), 2 vols., Ankara, 1959–1965; Sabahattin Selek, *Milli Mücadele. Anadolu Ihtilâlı* (The National Struggle. Revolt in Anatolia), 2 vols., Ankara, 1963–1965.

Among the hundreds of memoirs and other histories of the war are Celal Bayar, *Ben de Yazdım: Milli Mücadeleye Giriş* (I Also Have Written: Entering the National Struggle), 8 vols., Istanbul, 1965–1972; Kemal Arıburnu, *Milli Mücadelede Istanbul Mitingleri* (Meetings in Istanbul During the National Struggle), Ankara, 1955; Falih Rıfkı Atay, *Atatürk'ün Bana Anlattıkları* (What Atatürk Explained to Me), Istanbul, 1955, and *Atatürk'ün Hatıraları, 1914–1919* (Atatürk's Memoirs), Ankara, 1965; Ş. Turan, *Balıkesir ve Alaşehir Kongreleri ve Hacım Muhittin Çarıklı'nın Kuvayı Milliye Hatıraları, 1919–1920* (The Congresses of Balıkesir and Alaşehir and Hacım Muhittin Çarıklı's Memoirs of the National Forces, 1919–1920), Ankara, 1967; Ali Fuat Cebesoy, *Milli Mücadele Hatıraları* (Memoirs of the National Struggle), I, Istanbul, 1953, *Moskova Hâtıraları* (Memoirs of Moscow), Istanbul, 1955, and *General Ali Fuat Cebesoy'un siyasi hâtıraları* (General Ali Fuat Cebesoy's political memoires), 2 vols., Istanbul, 1957–1960; Mazhar Müfit Kansu, *Erzurumdan Ölümüne kadar Atatürkle beraber* (With Atatürk from Erzurum until his death), 2 vols., Ankara, 1966–1968; Sami Sabit Karaman, *Istiklâl Mücadelesi ve Enver Paşa* (Enver Paşa and the National Struggle), Izmit, 1949; Kâzım Karabekir, *Istiklâl Harbimiz* (Our War for Independence), Istanbul, 1960, and *Istiklâl Harbinde Enver Paşa* (Enver Paşa in the War for Independence), Istanbul, 1967; Süleyman Külçe, *Mareşal Fevzi Çakmak,* Istanbul, 1953; Alfred Rawlinson, *Adventures in the Near East,* London, 1923; Ali Ihsan Sabis, *Harb Hâtıralarım. Istiklâl Harbi* (My War Memories. The War for Independence), Istanbul, 1951; Fethi Tevetoğlu, *Türkiye'de Sosyalist ve Kömünist Faaliyetler* (Socialist and Communist Activities in Turkey), Ankara, 1967; Ilhan E. Darendelioğlu, *Türkiye'de Komünist Hareketleri, 1910–1973* (The Communist Movements in Turkey, 1910–1973), Ankara, 1973. Ali Fuat Türkgeldi, *Mondros ve Mudanya Mütarekelerinin Tarihi* (History of the Mondros and Mudanya Truces), Ankara, 1948; Yunus Nadi, *Mustafa Kemal Samsunda* (Mustafa Kemal in Samsun), Istanbul, 1955, *Ankara'nın Ilk günleri* (The First days of Ankara), Istanbul, 1955, and *Çerkes Ethem kuvvetlerinin ihaneti* (Betrayal by the forces of Çerkes Ethem), Istanbul, 1955; *Anadoluda Yunan zulüm ve vahşeti* (Greek misdeeds and atrocities in Anatolia), 3 vols., Ankara, 1922; *Atrocités Greques. Documents et rapports officiels,* Constantinople, 1922; Cemal Bardakçı, *Anadolu isyanları* (Anatolian revolts), Istanbul, 1940; A. Cerrahoğlu, *Türkiyede sosyalizm, 1848–1925* (Socialism in Turkey), Istanbul, 1968; Ömer Sami Coşar, *Milli Mücadelede Basın* (The Press during the National Struggle), Istanbul, 1964; A. Gökoğlu, *Inkilâbımızda posta ve telgrafçılar* (Postal and telegraph men during our revolution), Istanbul, 1938; Zühdü Güven, *Anzavur isyanı* (The Anzavur revolt), Istanbul, 1948, and *Istiklâl Savaşı hatıralarından acı bir safha* (A bitter page of the War for Independence memories), Ankara, 1965; Mithat Işın, *Istiklâl harbi deniz cephesi* (The naval front of the War for Independence), Istanbul, 1946; Sami Sabit Karaman, *Trabzon ve Kars Hâtıraları, 1921–2. Istiklâl Mücadelesi ve Enver Paşa* (Memories of Trabzon and Kars, 1921–2. The War for Independence and Enver Paşa), Izmir, 1949; Yakup Kadri Karaosmanoğlu, *Vatan yolunda: Milli Mücadele hâtıraları* (On the Fatherland Road. Memories of the National Struggle), Istanbul, 1958; Cemal Kutay, *Çerkes Ethem hâdisesi* (The Çerkes Edhem Affair), Istanbul, 1955; Çerkes Ethem, *Hâtırat* (Memoires), Istanbul, 1962; Kadir Mısırlıoğlu, *Kadir: Türkün siyah kitabı. Anadoluda Yunan mezalimi* (The Black Book of the Turks. Greek atrocities in Anatolia), Istanbul, 1966; Nurettin Peker, *1918–1923 Istiklâl Savaşının vesika ve resimleri* (Documents and pictures of the

1918–1923 War for Independence), Istanbul, 1955; Elaine D. Smith, *Turkey: Origins of the Kemalist Movement and the Government of the Grand National Assembly, 1910–1923,* Washington, 1959; Cemal Kutay, *Çerkez Ethem Dosyası* (The Dossier of Çerkes Ethem), 2 vols., Istanbul, 1973; Rahmi Apak, *İstiklâl Savaşında Garp Cephesi Nasıl Kuruldu* (How the Western Front was Established During the War for Independence), Ankara, 1942; Ahmed Emin Yalman, *Turkey in My Time,* Norman, Okla., 1956, and *Yakın Tarihte Gördüklerim ve Geçirdiklerim* (What I Have Seen and Experienced in Recent Times), 4 vols., Istanbul, n.d., S. R. Sonyel, *Türk Kurtuluş Savaşı ve Dış Politika* (The Turkish War for Independence and Foreign Policy), I, Ankara, 1974; Salahi (Sonyel) Ramadan, "The Foreign Policy of the Turkish Nationalists, 1919–1923," unpublished Ph.D. dissertation, University of London, 1971; and A. E. Montgomery, "Allied Policies in Turkey from the Armistice of Mudros, 30th October 1918 to the Treaty of Lausanne, 24th July 1923," unpublished Ph.D. dissertation, University of London, 1969.

Letters and documents issued during the War for Independence have been published in the following principal collections: T. C. Genelkurmay Başkanlığı Harp Tarihi Dairesi, *Harb Tarihi Vesikaları Dergisi* (Journal of War History Documents), Ankara, 18 vols., 68 issues, 1951–1969; with 1510 documents; Mustafa Kemal Atatürk, *Atatürk'ün Söylev ve Demeçleri* (Atatürk's speeches and statements), 4 vols., Ankara, 1945–1964, with vol. IV having the title *Atatürk'ün Tamim, Telgraf ve Beyannameleri* (Atatürk's Circulars, Telegrams, and Manifestos), Ankara, 1964; and Kâzım Karabekir, *İstikâl Harbimiz* (Our War for Independence), Istanbul, 1960. British documents concerning the war period are found in Bilâl N. Şimşir, *İngiliz Belgelerinde Atatürk (1919–1938), Cilt I, Nisan 1919–Mart 1920. British Documents on Atatürk (1919–1938) Vol. I, April 1919– March 1920,* Ankara, 1973; W. N. Medlicott, D. Dakin, and M. E. Lambert, *Documents on British Foreign Policy, 1919–1939,* First Series, vol. XVII, *Greece and Turkey, January 1, 1921–September 2, 1922,* London, 1970, and vol. XVIII, *Greece and Turkey, September 3, 1922–July 24, 1923,* London, 1972.

The Lausanne Conference is dealt with in Medlicott et al., *Documents on British Foreign Policy,* XVIII, 990–1064; Ali Naci Karacan, *Lozan,* Istanbul, 1971; M. Cemil Bilsel, *Lozan,* 2 vols., Ankara, 1933; Seha L. Meray, *Lozan Barış Konferansı. Tutanaklar-Belgeler* (The Lausanne Peace Conference, Minutes-Documents), Ankara, 1969; Great Britain, Cmd. 1814, Turkey No. 1 (1923), *Lausanne Conference on Near Eastern Affairs, 1922–1923. Records of Proceedings and Draft Terms of Peace,* London, 1923; Jane Degras, ed., *Soviet Documents on Foreign Policy,* 3 vols., London, 1951–1952; France, Ministère des Affaires Etrangères, *Documents diplomatiques. Conférence de Lausanne sur les affaires du proche-orient (1922–3) Recueil des Actes de la Conférence. Première série, I–IV, Deuxième série, I–II,* Paris, 1923; T. C. Hariciye Vekâleti, *Lozan Konferansı, 1922–1923,* 2 vols., in 7, Istanbul, 1340–1924. An excellent account of the conference is given by R. Davison, "Turkish Diplomacy from Mudros to Lausanne," *The Diplomats, 1919–1939,* G. A. Craig and F. Gilbert, eds., Princeton, N.J., 1953, and "Middle East Nationalism; Lausanne Thirty Years After," *Middle East Journal,* 7 (1953), 324–348. See also Harry J. Psomiades, *The Eastern Question: The Last Phase: A Study in Greek-Turkish Diplomacy,* Thessaloniki, 1968; H. Howard, *Turkey, The Straits and U.S. Policy,* Baltimore, 1974, pp. 113–126, and *The Partition of Turkey,* Norman, Okla., 1931; Ali Naci Karacan, *Lozan Konferansı ve İsmet Paşa* (The Lausanne Conference and İsmet Paşa), Istanbul, 1943; Ahmet Kayıhan, *Lozan ve Batı Trakya: 1913 de İlk Türk Cumhuriyeti* (Lausanne and Western Thrace: The First Turkish Republic in 1913), Istanbul, 1967; Harold Nicolson, *Curzon: The Last Phase, 1919–1925. A Study in Post War Diplomacy,* London, 1934. The exchanges of population and other agreements between Turkey and Greece that followed Lausanne are studied in Dimitri Pantzopoulos, *The Balkan Exchange of Minorities and Its Impact upon Greece,* The Hague, 1962; K. G. Andreades, *The Moslem Minority in Western Thrace,* Thessaloniki, 1956; and H. J. Psomiades, *The Eastern Question: The Last Phase. A Study in Greek-Turkish Diplomacy,* Thessaloniki, 1968; Paul Helmreich, *From Paris to Sèvres: The Partition of the Ottoman Empire at the Peace Conference of 1919–1920,* Columbus, Ohio, 1974.

XI. *The Turkish Republic, 1923–1975*

Though there is no adequate overall account of the Republic, there are some excellent monographs on particular subjects. The most useful general works are Geoffrey Lewis, *Turkey*, London, 1955, and *Modern Turkey*, London, 1974; M. P. Price, *A History of Turkey, from Empire to Republic*, London, 1956; Andrew Mango, *Turkey*, London, 1968; and L. V. Thomas and R. N. Frye, *The United States and Turkey and Iran*, Cambridge, Mass., 1951 (repr. New York, 1971), which provide only short historical surveys. The only adequate history of the Republic in Turkish is Enver Ziya Karal, *Türkiye Cumhuriyeti Tarihi* (History of the Turkish Republic), 1st ed., Istanbul, 1945 (2nd ed., Istanbul, 1954; 3rd ed., Istanbul, 1960).

The Atatürk years are covered extensively. D. E. Webster, *The Turkey of Atatürk: Social Process in the Turkish Reformation*, Philadelphia, Pa., 1939, is a classic study that remains unsurpassed in many areas. Eleanor Bisbee, *The New Turks: Pioneers of the Republic, 1920–1950*, Philadelphia, Pa., 1951, is very perceptive, particularly on social development. The most detailed and objective biography of Atatürk is Lord Kinross, *Atatürk: A Biography of Mustafa Kemal, Father of Modern Turkey*, New York and London, 1965. Other useful biographical treatments are Irfan Orga, *Phoenix Ascendant: The Rise of Modern Turkey*, London, 1958; Irfan and Margarete Orga, *Atatürk*, London, 1962; H. C. Armstrong, *Grey Wolf, Mustafa Kemal. An Intimate Study of a Dictator*, London, 1935, tr. into Turkish by Peyami Safa, *Bozkurt* (Grey Wolf), Istanbul, 1955, and answered by Sadi Borak, *Armstrong'tan Bozkurt: Mustafa Kemal ve iftiralara cevap* (The Grey Wolf by Armstrong; Mustafa Kemal and answers to slanders), Istanbul, 1955; Şevket Süreyya Aydemir, *Tek Adam* (The Only Man), 3 vols., Istanbul, 1963–1965. His political philosophy is studied by Suna Kili, *Kemalism*, Robert College, Bebek, Istanbul, 1969; and F. P. Latimer, "The Political Philosophy of Mustapha Kemal Atatürk," unpublished Ph.D. dissertation, Princeton University, 1960. The most useful chronologies of his era are Utkan Kocatürk, *Atatürk ve Türk Devrimi Kronolojisi, 1918–1938* (Chronology of Atatürk and the Turkish Revolution, 1918–1938), Ankara, 1973; H. Jäschke, *Die Türkei seit dem Weltkriege*, II, *Türkischer Geschichtskalender 1918–1928*, Berlin, 1929 (also published in *Welt des Islams*, 10, 1927–1929), *Die Türkei seit dem Weltkriege*, II, *Türkischer Geschichtskalender für 1929 mit neuem Nachtrag zu 1918–1928*, Berlin, 1930 (also in *Welt des Islams*, 12, 1930), *Die Türkei seit dem Weltkriege*, III. *Geschichtskalender für 1930*, Berlin, 1931 (also in *Welt des Islams*, 13, 1930–1931), *Die Türkei seit dem Weltkriege*, IV. *Türkischer Geschichtskalendar für 1931–1932*, Berlin, 1933 (also in *Welt des Islams*, 15, 1933), *Die Türkei in den Jahren 1933 und 1934* (offprint from *Mitteilungen des Seminars für Orientalische Sprachen zu Berlin*, 38/2, 1935), *Die Türkei seit dem Weltkriege: Personen und Sachregister, 1918–1934*, Berlin, 1939, and *Die Türkei in den Jahren 1935–1941: Geschichtskalender mit Personen und Sachregister*, Leipzig, 1943. See also Dahiliye Vekâleti Matbuat Umum Müdürlüğü, *Ayın Tarihi* (History of the Month), Ankara, 1339/1923–1940.

Constitutional and political developments are discussed in Suna Kili, *Turkish Constitutional Developments and Assembly Debates on the Constitutions of 1924 and 1961*, Bebek, Istanbul, 1971; Ş. Gözübüyük and Z. Sezgin, *1924 Anayasası hakkındaki Meclis görüşmeleri* (Assembly discussions on the 1924 Constitution), Ankara, 1957; S. Kili and Ş. Gözübüyük, *Türk Anayasa Metinleri: Tanzimattan Bugüne kadar* (Turkish Constitutional Texts: From the Tanzimat to the Present Day), Ankara, 1957; Kâzım Öztürk, *Türkiye Cumhuriyeti Anayasası* (The Constitution of the Turkish Republic), 3 vols. Ankara, 1966; Rona Aybay, *Karşılaştırmalı 1961 Anayasası* (A Comparative Study of the 1961 Constitution), Istanbul, 1963; Abid A. Al-Maryati, *Middle Eastern Constitutions and Electoral Laws*, New York, 1968, pp. 333–412; H. M. Davis, *Constitutions, Electoral Laws, Treaties of States in the Near and Middle East*, Durham, N.C., 1947.

Politics in the Atatürk era are studied by Kemal H. Karpat, *Turkey's Politics: The Transition to a Multi-Party System*, Princeton, N.J., 1959; Tarık Z. Tunaya, *Türkiyede Siyasi Partiler, 1859–1952* (Political Parties in Turkey, 1859–1952), Istanbul, 1952;

Walter F. Weiker, *Political Tutelage and Democracy in Turkey: The Free Party and Its Aftermath,* Leiden, 1963; Dankwart A. Rustow, "The Army and the Founding of the Turkish Republic," *World Politics,* XI/4 (July 1959), and "Politics and Islam in Turkey, 1920–1935," *Islam and the West,* ed. R. N. Frye, The Hague, 1957. On Turkish politics since Atatürk see C. H. Dodd, *Politics and Government in Turkey,* Berkeley and Los Angeles, 1969; K. H. Karpat, ed., *Social Change and Politics in Turkey: A Structural-Historical Analysis,* Leiden, 1973; Jacob M. Landau, *Radical Politics in Modern Turkey,* Leiden, 1974; Ismet Giritli, *Fifty Years of Turkish Political Development, 1919–1969,* Istanbul, 1969; George S. Harris, *The Origins of Communism in Turkey,* Stanford, Calif., 1967; W. F. Weiker, *The Turkish Revolution, 1960–1961, Aspects of Military Politics,* Washington, D.C., 1963; G. Jäschke, *Die Türkei in den Jahren 1942–1951,* Wiesbaden, 1955; Richard D. Robinson, *Developments Respecting Turkey, 1953–1957,* 4 vols., New York, 1954–1957. On the Turkish bureaucracy see Frederick W. Frey, *The Turkish Political Elite,* Cambridge, Mass., 1965; R. D. Robinson, *High Level Manpower in Economic Development: The Turkish Case,* Cambridge, Mass., 1967; L. L. and N. P. Roos, *Managers of Modernization: Organizations and Elites in Turkey, 1950–1969* Cambridge, Mass., 1971; A. T. J. Matthews, *Emergent Turkish Administrators,* Ankara, 1955; and J. B. Kingsbury and Tahir Aktan, *The Public Service in Turkey: Organization, Recruitment and Training,* Brussels, 1955. On government organization and operation see Ernest Kurnow, *The Turkish Budgetary Process,* Ankara, 1956; A. L. Strum and C. Mıhçıoğlu, *Bibliography on Public Administration in Turkey, 1928–57,* Ankara, 1958; A. Gorvine and L. L. Barber, *Organization and Functions of Turkish Ministries,* Ankara, 1957; Fehmi Yavuz, *Problems of Turkish Local Administration,* Ankara, 1965; Doğan Dolmiz, *Turkish Government Organization Manual,* Ankara, 1959; and Institute of Public Administration for Turkey and the Middle East, *Turkish Government Organization Manual,* 2nd ed., Ankara, 1966.

Society and religion in Turkey are discussed in Halide Edib (Adıvar), *Turkey Faces West,* London, 1930, and *Conflict of East and West in Turkey,* Lahore, 1935; H. E. Allen, *The Turkish Transformation: A Study in Social and Religious Development,* Chicago, Ill., 1935; E. Bisbee, *The New Turks, Pioneers of the Republic, 1920–1950,* Philadelphia, Pa., 1951, 2nd. ed., 1956; Nermin Erdentung, *A Study on the Social Structure of a Turkish Village,* Ankara, 1959; Irfan Orga, *Portrait of a Turkish Family,* New York, 1950; J. E. Pierce, *Life in a Turkish Village,* New York, 1964; Firouz Bahrampour, *Turkey: Political and Social Transformation,* Brooklyn, N.Y., 1967; Selma Ekrem, *Turkey Old and New,* New York, 1963; Kaare Grønbech, *The Turkish System of Kinship,* Copenhagen, 1953; Mahmud Makal, *A Village in Anatolia,* London, 1954; Kemal Karpat, *Social Change and Politics in Turkey: A Structural-Historical Analysis,* Leiden, 1973, *Political and Social Thought in the Contemporary Middle East,* London, 1968, and "Social themes in Contemporary Turkish literature," *Middle East Journal,* 14 (1960), 29–44, 153–168; G. Jaeschke, *Der Islam in der neuen Türkei,* Leiden, 1951; H. Reed, "The Religious Life of Modern Turkish Muslims," *Islam and the West,* ed. R. N. Frye, The Hague, 1957, pp. 108–148, "The Revival of Islam in Secular Turkey," *Middle East Journal,* 8 (1954), 267–282, and "Turkey's New Imam-Hatip Schools," *Die Welt des Islams,* n.s. 4 (1955), 150–163; Paul Stirling, "Religious Change in Republican Turkey," *Middle East Journal,* 12 (1958), 395–408; L. V. Thomas, "Recent Developments in Turkish Islam," *Middle East Journal,* 6 (1952), 22–40; Neda Armaner, *İslâm dininden ayrılan cereyanlar: nurculuk* (Movements separating from the religion of Islam: Nurcu'ism), Ankara, 1964; Bekir Berk and N. Polat, *İslami hareket ve Türkeş* (The Islamist movement and Türkeş), Istanbul, 1969; F. Güventürk, *Din ışığı altında nurculuğun içyüzü* (The inner side of nurcu'ism in the light of religion), Istanbul, 1964; Osman Turan, *Türkiyede mânevi buhran: din ve lâiklik* (The spiritual crisis in Turkey: Religion and Laicism) Ankara, 1964; and Tarık Tunaya, *İslâmcılık cereyanı* (The Islamist movement), Istanbul, 1962. The People's Houses are described in Kemal Parpat, "The People's Houses in Turkey, Establishment and Growth," *Middle East Journal,* 17 (1963), 55–67, "The Impact of the

People's Houses on the Development of Communications in Turkey, 1931–1951," *Welt des Islams*, 15 (1974), 69–84; *XV Yıldönümünde Halkevleri ve Halkodaları* (The 15th Anniversary of the People's Houses and People's Rooms), Ankara, 1947; and Hasan Taner, *Halkevleri Bibliyografyası* (Bibliography of People's Houses), Ankara, 1944. On educational development see Andreas Kazamias, *Education and the Quest for Modernity in Turkey*, London, 1966; Ilhan Başgöz and H. Wilson, *Educational Problems in Turkey, 1920–1940*, Bloomington, Ind., and the Hague, 1968; Nevzat Ayas, *Türkiye Cumhuriyeti Millî Eğitim* (National education in the Turkish Republic), Ankara, 1948.

Turkish economic development is studied by Z. Y. Hershlag, *Turkey: An Economy in Transition*, The Hague, 1958, and *Turkey: The Challenge of Growth*, Leiden, 1968; E. J. Cohn, *Turkish Economic, Social and Political Change*, New York, 1970; Nermin Abadan, *Batı Almanyadaki Türk İşçileri ve Sorunları* (The Turkish Workers in West Germany and Their Problems), Ankara, 1954; R. Aktan, *Analysis and Assessment of the Economic Effects of Public Law 480 Title I Program: Turkey*, Ankara, 1966; H. B. Chenery, G. E. Brandow, and E. J. Cohn, *Turkish Investment and Economic Development*, Ankara, 1953; B. and G. Helling, *Rural Turkey: A New Socio-Statistical Appraisal*, Istanbul, 1958; M. D. Rivkin, *Area Development for National Growth: The Turkish Precedent*, New York, 1965; F. Shorter, ed., *Four Studies of Economic Development in Turkey*, London, 1967; T. C. State Planning Organization, Republic of Turkey, *First Five Year Development Plan, 1963–1967*, Ankara, 1963, and *Second Five Year Development Plan, 1968–1972*, Ankara, 1967; R. D. Robinson, *The First Turkish Republic*, Cambridge, Mass., 1965; R. W. Kerwin, "Etatism and the Industrialization of Turkey," unpublished Ph.D. dissertation, School of Advanced International Studies, Johns Hopkins University, 1956; and OECD, *Economic Surveys, Turkey*, Paris, 1972.

On the foreign policy of the Republic see E. R. Vere-Hodge, *Turkish Foreign Policy, 1918–1948*, Ambilly-Annemasse, 1950; Altemir Kılıç, *Turkey and the World*, Washington, D.C., 1959; Ferenc Vali, *Bridge Across the Bosphorus: The Foreign Policy of Turkey*, Baltimore, 1971, and *The Turkish Straits and NATO*, Stanford, Calif., 1952; R. J. Kerner and H. N. Howard, *The Balkan Conferences and the Balkan Entente, 1930–5*, Berkeley, Calif., 1936; H. N. Howard, *Turkey, the Straits and U.S Policy*, Baltimore and London, 1974, and *The Problem of the Turkish Straits*, Washington, D.C., Department of State, 1947; E. and T. Aghjon, *Actes de Montreux*, Paris, 1937; S. R. Sonyel, *Türk Kurtuluş Savaşı ve Dış Politika* (The Turkish War of Independence and Foreign Policy), I, Ankara, 1973; A. E. Montgomery, "Allied Policies in Turkey from the Armistice of Mudros, 30th October, 1918 to the Treaty of Lausanne, 24th July 1923," unpublished Ph.D. dissertation, University of London, 1969; Salahi (Sonyel) Ramadan, "The Foreign Policy of the Turkish Nationalists, 1919–1923," unpublished Ph.D. dissertation, University of London, 1971; A. Akşin, *Atatürk'ün dış politika ilkeleri ve diplomasisi* (The principles and diplomacy of Atatürk's foreign policy), 2 parts, Istanbul, 1964–1966; Yusuf Hikmet Bayur, *Türkiye Devletinin dış siyasası* (The foreign policy of the Turkish state), Istanbul, 1938, 2nd ed., 1942; R. S. Burçak, *Türk-Rus-İngiliz münasebetleri 1791–1941* (Turkish-Russian-English relations, 1791–1941), Istanbul, 1946; L. J. Gordon, *American Relations with Turkey, 1830–1930: An Economic Interpretation*, Philadelphia, Pa., 1932; A. N. Kurat, *Türk-Amerikan münasbetlerine kısa bir bakış, 1800–1959* (A short look at Turkish-American relations, 1800–1959), Ankara, 1952; H. F. Gürsel, *Tarih boyunca Türk-Rus ilişkileri* (Turko-Russian relations in history), Istanbul, 1968; H. W. Hartman, *Die auswaertige Politik der Türkei, 1923–1940*, Zürich, 1941; Haluk Ülman, *Türk-Amerikan diplomatik münasebetleri, 1939–1947* (Turkish-American diplomatic relations, 1939–1947), Ankara, 1961; A. Gündüz Ökçün, *A Guide to Turkish Treaties, 1920–1964*, Ankara, 1966; R. L. Daniel, *American Philanthropy in the Near East, 1820–1960*, Athens, Ohio, 1970; J. A. DeNovo, *American Interests and Policies in the Middle East, 1900–1939*, Minneapolis, Minn., 1963; D. H. Finnie, *Pioneers East: The Early American Experience in the Middle East*, Cambridge, Mass., 1967; J. L. Grabill, *Protestant Diplomacy and the Near East: Missionary Influence on American Policy, 1810–1927*, Minneapolis, Minn.,

1971; G. S. Harris, *The Troubled Alliance: The United States and Turkey: Their Problems in Historical Perspective, 1945–1971*, Stanford, Calif., 1972; and R. R. Trask, *The United States Response to Turkish Nationalism and Reform, 1914–1939*, Leiden, 1971.

On Turkish politics and problems since 1960 see Jacob M. Landau, *Radical Politics in Modern Turkey*, Leiden, 1974; Suna Kili, *1960–1975 Döneminde Cumhuriyet Halk Partisinde Gelişmeler* (Developments in the Republican People's Party in the period 1960–1975), Istanbul, 1976. C. H. Dodd, *Politics and Government in Turkey*, Manchester, England, 1969; Ahmet Taner Kişali, *Forces politiques dans la Turquie moderne*, Ankara, 1968; L. L. and N. P. Roos, *Managers of Modernization: Organizations and Elites in Turkey (1950–1969)*, Cambridge, Mass., 1971. The most useful descriptions of Turkey are Richard N. Robinson, *Investment in Turkey: Basic Information for United States Businessmen*, Washington, D.C., Department of Commerce, 1956; T. D. Roberts et al., *Area Handbook for the Republic of Turkey*, U.S. Government Printing Office, April, 1970; *Nagel's Encyclopaedia Guide: Turkey*, New York, Geneva, Paris, and Munich, 1968; E. Fodor and Kanık Arıcanlı, *Fodor's Turkey*, New York, 1969, and later editions; Hachette World Guides, *Turkey*, Paris, 1960 and 1970; and Shell Company of Turkey, Ltd., *Motorist Guide to Turkey*, Istanbul, n.d. By far the best guide to Istanbul is Hilary Sumner-Boyd and John Freely, *Strolling Through Istanbul: A Guide to the City*, Redhouse Press, Istanbul, 1972. Among the older guides Ernest Mamboury, *Istanbul Touristique* (Istanbul, latest ed., 1951) and *Ankara Touristique* are particularly good. The only detailed maps of Istanbul can be found in Istanbul Belediyesi, *Istanbul, Şehir Rehberi, 1971* (City Guide to Istanbul, 1971), Istanbul, 1972. Out of date in some respects but still a classic treatment is Great Britain, Naval Intelligence Division, Geographical Handbook Series, *Turkey*, 2 vols., London, 1942.

Up-to-date statistical Information can be derived from the publications of the State Institute of Statistics/Devlet Istatistik Enstitüsü, Ankara, including its *Türkiye Istatistik Yıllığı* (Statistical Yearbook of Turkey), abbreviated in this work as IY, published most recently for 1963, 1964–1965, 1968, and 1971, its *Aylık Istatistik Bülteni* (Monthly Bulletin of Statistics), and a wide range of specialized monographs. The *Annual Report* of the Central Bank of Turkey and the *Review of Economic Conditions* of the Türkiye Iş Bankası (Turkish Business Bank), both published in English as well as Turkish, are extremely useful. Laws and governmental decrees are published daily in the T. C. *Resmi Gazete*, by the prime minister's office.

Index

This Index has been formulated to serve also as a glossary. Parentheses are used to indicate alternate names, exact translations, and dates; definitions and explanations follow colons. Muslim names are alphabetized by first name except for individuals who lived in the Turkish Republic and became well-known under the family names they adopted after 1934.

electoral laws, 90, 181, 185, 186, 276, 277, 282, 350, 379, 403, 405, 412, 416–417, 419, 425–426

electricity, electric power, 230, 306, 308, 392, 393, 408, 412

Eleşkirt river valley, 191

Elfi Bey, Mehmet : Egyptian Mamluk leader in early 19th century, 10

Elliot, Sir Henry, 179

Emine Sultan (1898–   ) : daughter of Prince Süleyman Efendi (son of Abdulmecit I), niece of Abdulhamit II, wife of Enver Paşa (1911–1922), 299

Eminönü : section of Istanbul, 230

Emlâk Kredi Bankası (Real Estate Credit Bank, founded June 14, 1945), 392

Emniyet-i Umumi Müdürlüğü (Department of Public Security), 286

employment restrictions, 390, 394

Emtia Gümrük İdaresi, see Commodity Customs Administration

Encümen-i Adliye (Supreme Judicial Council), 75

Encümen-i Daniş (Academy of Knowledge) : operated 1851–1862, 65, 109, 110, 263

Enderun-u Hümayun: inner section of Sultan's palace, Imperial Palace Service, *see* sultan, palace of

endowments, *see* religious foundations

engineering, engineering schools, 11, 23, 27, 29, 41, 48, 64, 75, 107–110, 249, 251

Enos (Enez), Enos-Midye line, 295, 296, 320

Enver Paşa (1881–1922) : one of founders of CUP, member of CUP triumvirate ruling Ottoman Empire after 1913, minister of war during World War I, 266–267, 276, 281, 290, 295, 297, 299, 300, 308, 310–311, 312–314, 323–326, 332, 457, 461

Epirus, 148, 151, 181, 184, 190, 196, 206, 294, 297

equality, 50, 59, 125, 127–128, 132, 157, 164, 177, 275, 276, 282, 378, 418, 419

Erbakan, Necmettin : conservative political leader in Justice Party, left in 1970 to form Party for National Order/*Milli Nizam Partisi* (1970–1971), leader of National Salvation Party/*Milli Selâmet Partisi* since 1972, 428–429, 433

Ereğli, 234

Erenköy, 254

Erfurt, Agreement of (1808), 13

Ergani, 234

Erim, Nihat (1912–   ) : lawyer, director

of newspaper *Ulus* (1950–   ), prime minister of Turkey (1971–1972), 428

Erivan : capital of Republic of Armenia, 16, 32, 316, 326, 331

Erkân-ı Harbiye, see General Staff

Ersoy, Mehmet Âkif (1870–1936) : poet, Islamist leader, 303, 304

Erzincan, 201, 323, 325

Erzurum, 16, 31, 32, 44, 86, 90, 98, 107, 138, 183, 186, 201–203, 246, 314, 315, 321–325, 341, 343, 354; congress of (1919), 344–346

Esat, Dr. (Işık), 333

Esat Efendi, Mehmet (1785–1847) : chronicler of destruction of Janissaries (1826), official chronicler (*vakanüvis*), editor of *Takvim-i Vekayi,* first minister of education (1846–1847), 443

esham (bonds), *esham-ı cedid* (new bonds), issued 1865, *see* bonds

Eskişehir, 234, 354, 358, 360, 363

esnaf odası, see guilds

Eşkinciyan corps, 19–20, 22

eşraf: name applied to 19th-century provincial notables, 114

Et Meydanı : public square in Istanbul, 20

Etatism (Statism) : program of state financing and control of key elements of Turkish economy, developed in 1930's under leadership of Celal Bayar, 390–395, 401, 405, 408, 412, 421

Ethnike Hetairia (Ethnic Band) : Greek national society established in 1894 to expand Greek territory, foment revolts, annexation of Crete, Macedonia, 206, 209

Eti Bank (The Hittite Bank) : established October 23, 1935, 391–392

eunuchs, 214

Euphrates (Fırat) river, 105, 319

European Economic Cooperation (EEC) Organization (the Common Market, founded 1957), entry of Turkey (December 1, 1964), 400, 427, 429

evkaf (sing. *vakıf,* Arabic *waqf*), *see* religious foundations

Evlad-ı Fatihân: Anatolian Turkish tribes settled in parts of Rumeli, with special salaries, tax exemptions; newly organized by Mahmut II (1828), abolished by Tanzimat (1845), 26

excise taxes (*rüsum-u sitte*/the six taxes, on document stamps, spirits, fishing, salt, tobacco and silk) : administered by *Rüsumat Nezareti*/Ministry of Excise Taxes, turned over to Public Debt Commission

kanun-u muvakkat (temporary law), 299, 311
kapı kethüdası: representative of province in Ministry of Interior, 72
kapıkulu: slaves of the Porte, 3, 9, 24–26
kapudan-ı derya, kapudan paşa, see grand admiral
Kapudan-ı Ticaret Mektebi, see Merchant Marine Academy
Kara George (Karageorgoviç, George Petrović) (1762–1817) : Serbian national leader, ruler of Serbia (ruled 1808–1813), 13, 14, 148
Karaağaç, 366
Karabekir, Kâzım (1882–1948) : career army officer, fought terrorists in Macedonia (1907), member of Operation Army (1909), fought in Albania and Balkan wars, at Dardanelles and in Iraq as aide to von der Goltz in World War I, commanded eastern front in War for Independence, political opponent of Atatürk (1924–1926), reentered RPP after Atatürk's death (1938) and became deputy to Grand National Assembly, 319, 325, 340–344, 354, 356–358, 360–361, 380, 461
Karabük, 393, 395
Karageorgević, Alexander : prince of Serbia (ruled 1842–1858), 148
Karakol Cemiyeti, see Outpost Society
Karaman, 2, 123
Karamanlis, Constantine (1907–   ) : prime minister of Greece (1955–1963, 1974–   ), 431
Karaosmanoğlu : Anatolian notable family ; ruled Aydın, Saruhan, 2, 3, 15
kararname: governmental administrative decision with force of law, 299
Karatodori (Karatheodori) Paşa, Alexander (1833–1906) : Abdulhamit II's advisor on foreign policy, Ottoman plenipotentiary at Congress of Berlin (1878), member of Council of State, chief translator of *mabeyin-i hümayun* (1880–1906), 190, 206, 214
kariye: village, 89
Karlowitz, Treaty of (1699), 17
Kars, 32, 86, 138, 139, 183, 184, 186, 189–191, 315, 322, 325, 328, 331, 341, 348, 354, 357, 400
Kartal, 123
Kasaba, 121
Kasımpaşa, 48, 75
Kastamonu, 123, 124, 235, 236
kâtib-i sani: assistant scribe, 213
Kavala, 297

kavas: messenger, doorkeeper, watchman, policeman, 46
kaymakam (substitute) : lieutenant, sub-governor, district chief, 24, 39, 84, 86–88, 109, 149–152
Kayseri, 201
kaza: judicial and/or administrative district, subdivision of a *sancak,* 84–86, 89, 90, 100, 119, 121, 152, 350
Kazan, 261
kazasker (*kadı asker*) : military judge, chief judge of Anatolia or Rumelia, 74
Kâzım Nami, *see* Duru
Keldani, 239
Kemal, Mustafa, *see* Atatürk
Kemalism, 375, 405
Kerkuk, 318, 327
Kermanşah, 314
kethüda (lieutenant, steward, deputy) : government representative in a city district, 81
kethüda-ı rikâb-ı hümayun: steward of the sultan's court, 8
khedive (*Hidiv*) : title applied to Ottoman governor of Egypt after 1867, 71, 111, 131, 145, 160, 214
Kilid-ı Bahr fort, 318
King-Crane Commission : report of (August 28, 1919), 331
Kisselev, Count Paul (1788–1872) : Russian general, chief administrator of Russian-occupied principalities of Wallachia and Moldavia (1829–1834), 135–136
Kırklareli, 294
knez (Serb : notable), 14, 15, 147
kocabaşı: millet administrative leader, 46, 126
Komanovo, 292, 294
komiser: city police commissioner, 215
Konya, 41, 44, 121, 123, 230, 321, 329, 346 ; Battle of (1839), 32
Koraltan, Refik (1891–   ) : one of founders of Democratic Party, member of Grand National Assembly since foundation, career police administrator, chief of Independence Tribunal No. 5 and member of Istanbul Independence Tribunal, 402
Koran, Koranic studies, 251, 304 ; translation of into Turkish, 386, 409
Koray, Refik Halit, 334
Korean War, 429
Korutürk, Fahri (1903–   ) : career soldier, president of Turkey (1973–   ), 440
Kosova (Kossovo), 195, 208, 209, 388, 294